Blaise Pascal, the force of whose intellect has never been in doubt, could have given us the most challenging apologia for the Christian faith that post-Renaissance man had known. He did devote several months to working on such a project, noting down his thoughts spontaneously and then classifying them, sorting out about half of his apologetic fragments into dossiers which represented embryonic chapters. He maintained that his principal claim to originality lay in this ordering of his thoughts. Yet he never revealed his plan, and unfortunately was interrupted in his work by illness and then death.

Anthony R. Pugh has carefully examined Pascal's process of classification in order to determine his rigorous but subtle argument. Pascal systematically reduces the hostility of the unbeliever by showing the logical consequences of his position and by presenting different facets of the Christian faith. He is always aware that Christianity is not a position that can be reasoned and proved correct, although he believes that reason, properly used, will be profoundly satisfied with the fullness, complexity, and coherence of the Christian account of man.

Professor Pugh discusses how Pascal's thinking gradually evolved during the years before he set down his ideas for a new kind of apology. It is possible to detect ways in which the plan itself grew in complexity. This shift in emphasis sheds unexpected light on the often disputed authenticity of Filleau de la Chaise's account of the apologia. Dr Pugh also discusses the theory that Pascal abandoned his apologia because he realized that he had set himself an impossible task, arguing that this theory is unsubstantiated by any known evidence, and that if Pascal did not complete his task, it was not because the problem had no solution but because he had resolved it to his own satisfaction once he had visualized the complete design.

Anthony R. Pugh is Professor of French at the University of New Brunswick and the author of a previous volume in the University of Toronto Romance Series, *Balzac's Recurring Characters*.

ANTHONY R. PUGH

The Composition of Pascal's Apologia

UNIVERSITY OF TORONTO PRESS

Toronto Buffalo London

© University of Toronto Press 1984
Toronto   Buffalo   London
Printed in Canada
ISBN 0-8020-5611-3

University of Toronto Romance Series 49

Canadian Cataloguing in Publication Data

Pugh, Anthony R., 1931-
The composition of Pascal's Apologia

(University of Toronto romance series,
ISSN 0082-5336 ; 49)
Bibliography: p.
Includes index.
ISBN 0-8020-5611-3

1. Pascal, Blaise, 1623-1662. Pensées.
2. Apologetics - 17th century. 3. Catholic Church
- Doctrinal and controversial works - Catholic
authors. I. Title. II. Series

B1901.P44P8   239   C83-098386-4

This book has been published with the help of a grant from
the Canadian Federation for the Humanities, using funds
provided by the Social Sciences and Humanities Research
Council of Canada, and grants from the University of New
Brunswick and the Publications Fund of the University of
Toronto Press.

For Annie, Dalton, Margaret

Contents

viii Contents

Acknowledgments

I cannot remember when I first read a *pensée* of Pascal,
but I can recall vividly a series of lectures given in
the University of Cambridge by May Wallas of Newnham
College, which I attended as a third-year undergraduate.
In her first lecture she gave out a basic reading list,
and it included the Brunschvicg minor edition of the
Pensées et Opuscules. At the beginning of her second lecture, she spoke of the revised Delmas edition, which she
had been studying (this was November 1952), and advised
us to use it rather than the Brunschvicg. Thus right from
the start I was made dramatically aware of the editorial
problem, and led in the direction of the Copy and the
latest research. It is a pleasure to begin this book with
a tribute to a fine scholar and a great teacher.

I recall too that the best essay I wrote that year was
on Pascal, and that he quickly became a 'maître à penser.'
Some years later, with a thesis on Proust completed, I
was asked by an interviewing board what further research
I had in mind, and I replied 'Pascal.' I was distracted
by Balzac, but having to offer a special subject to
Honours students of the Queen's University of Belfast, I
chose Pascal, and I lectured on him regularly in the sixties. A stimulating tutorial with one of these students,
Aileen McGarry, led me to consider seriously preparing
an edition for students based on Lafuma (whose Seuil
presentation was by that time enjoying wide currency).
For a graduate seminar at the University of New Brunswick
I was able to do most of the necessary sorting and selection.

It was not, however, until 1975, with Balzac behind me
and a sabbatical year ahead of me, that I was able to
devote myself properly to Pascal, and I then wished to
examine the problem of the classification of the *pensées*
in detail rather than to get involved with student editions.

The first part of this book was written that year. The
second part took much longer, and filled three summers
and a six-month sabbatical in 1980. I am grateful to the
University of New Brunswick for making the two leaves
possible, and to the Department of Romance Languages
(especially to the Chairman, Robert Whalen), for giving
me encouragement and secretarial assistance during the
time this book has been on the stocks. I received finan-
cial help from the Canada Council and its successor the
Social Sciences and Humanities Research Council of Canada
in the form of two six-month Leave Fellowships, with
travel grants,and generous research grants for the summers
of 1978 and 1979. The Research Fund of the University of
New Brunswick supported my research in the summer of 1977
and (in part) in the summer of 1980.

I wish to thank a long succession of secretaries in the
Department of Romance Languages at UNB for grappling with
a typescript which was rarely straightforward. In particu-
lar I would name Cristina Argaez, who handled most of the
more complicated material, and freed me from many anxieties
Thanks are due also the staff of six libraries – the
Bibliothèque Nationale in Paris, the British Library in
London, the Taylorian Institute in Oxford, and the
libraries of the Universities of Bristol, Harvard, and
New Brunswick for all, in their different ways, making
my task easier than it might have been – and to Ron
Schoeffel and Jean Wilson of the University of Toronto
Press for their strong support and constant good humour.

Many colleagues and friends have exchanged ideas with
me, or answered requests concerning specific questions:
Donald Charlton of the University of Warwick, Hugh Davidson
of the University of Virginia, Alan Gabbey of The Queen's
University, Belfast, Fred Krieger of the Atlantic School
of Theology, Nova Scotia, Moya Longstaffe of Belfast,
Sara Melzer of the University of California at Los Angeles,
Elizabeth Moles of the University of Glasgow, Roger Pierrot
of the Bibliothèque Nationale, Ulrich Simon of The University of London, King's College, Derek Watts of the University of Exeter, and David Wetsel, currently of the University of Texas. I am particularly grateful to Annie Barnes,
one-time Reader in French at the University of Oxford,
for her constant interest and encouragement, and to Dalton
London of the University of New Brunswick, who besides
substantially reducing the printing costs by removing
several hundred redundant commas from the typescript

Acknowledgments xi

which he read with care, has always been ready to listen
when I have wanted to talk. The third dedicatee is my
youngest daughter, who has been a deeper source of inspiration than she will ever realize.

Finally, I thank my wife Mary for taking more than her
fair share of domestic responsibility, thus allowing me
to pursue my research without distraction. Works of
scholarship are not produced by scholars alone.

Anthony R. Pugh
Fredericton, July 1980

Abbreviations

ELLF	*Etudes de langue et littérature françaises*
FF	*French Forum*
FR	*French Review*
FS	*French Studies*
IL	*Information littéraire*
MLN	*Modern Language Notes*
MLR	*Modern Language Review*
NFS	*Nottingham French Studies*
PFSL	*Papers in French Seventeenth-Century Literature*
RHLF	*Revue d'Histoire littéraire de la France*
RHPC	*Revue d'Histoire de la Philosophie et d'Histoire Générale de la Civilisation*
RLC	*Revue de Littérature Comparée*
RN	*Romance Notes*
RNP	*Revue neo-scolastique de philosophie*
RR	*Romanic Review*
RSH	*Revue des Sciences humaines*
RUO	*Revue de l'Université d'Ottawa*
SAPR	*Sociéte des Amis de Port-Royal*
SPT	*Les Sciences philosophiques et theologiques*
YFS	*Yale French Studies*

Other

BN	Bibliothèque Nationale, Paris

INTRODUCTION

Introduction

'Qu'on ne dise pas que je n'ai rien dit de nouveau, la
disposition des matières est nouvelle...'[1] Thus Pascal
asks us to judge his apologia[2] for the Christian faith
not by the originality of the single thoughts which compose it, but by the new way in which the thoughts are
ordered. It is a humble and yet a confident claim. Pascal
knows the extent of his debt to a long tradition of commentators on the human condition and on Scripture, but
he knows also that traditional apologetics have failed
to make an impact on the serenely sceptical *honnête homme*
of his own time, and he believes himself capable of presenting the Christian case in such a way that the *honnête
homme* will be disarmed. It would appear essential therefore, if we are to assess Pascal's originality, or to
judge his argument, or indeed if we are to be stirred
ourselves by his presentation, that we should first pay
due attention to the shape of the argument, to the 'disposition des matières.'

And yet, by a capricious series of events, that is the
one thing which we cannot be sure that we have grasped.
Pascal wrote his thoughts down as they came to him, postponing the task of arranging them in order until later,
and when he died in 1662 his executors found the thousand-
odd fragments to be, as his nephew Etienne Périer later
put it, 'enfilés en diverses liasses mais sans aucun ordre
et sans aucune suite.'[3] If the 'disposition des matières,'
on which all depends, strikes a reader as sympathetic as
Etienne Périer as only an 'amas confus, sans ordre, sans
suite, qui ne pouvait servir à rien,' all hope of sub-
mitting Pascal's argument to the kind of assessment he
asked for would seem doomed.

It might be, of course, that we could find more order
in the original 'confusion' than did Pascal's friends;
but we would first have to put ourselves in contact with

his papers in the state in which he left them. How could
that be done? The manuscripts have naturally not remained
in their original sequence, and for nearly three centuries
it looked as if we should never be able to put Périer's
statements to the test. Périer assured us that Pascal's
heirs had copied out the manuscripts exactly as they
found them, but once the first generation of editors had
passed away, it was not even known whether the original
copy had survived. Two seventeenth-century copies found
their way to the Bibliothèque Nationale, but they were
not subjected to any really close scrutiny; instead they
served merely to help decipher the manuscript,[4] once
Victor Cousin, in 1842, had enjoined upon editors the
necessity to be much more respectful of Pascal's text
than their predecessors had been.[5]

In the last thirty or forty years, however, the reliability of the BN Copies has been demonstrated, and it
is generally accepted that through the Copies we can
learn precisely how Pascal left his papers; consequently,
if there is any clue to what he meant by the 'disposition
des matières,' it must be found here. It is the purpose
of the present book to show in some detail how Pascal's
plan can be deduced from the evidence with greater precision than has generally been admitted, even by modern
scholars who are familiar with the Copies. I have tried
to reveal the 'disposition des matières' and thus pave
the way for a fuller understanding and assessment of this
exceptionally acute and imaginative thinker. In this introduction I shall briefly trace the disappearance and
re-emergence of the vital evidence, and discuss how the
evidence is to be interpreted and used. In order to
lighten the narrative, all detail has been relegated to
the notes, which are as a consequence copious and intricate.

(a) the disappearance of the evidence

After the material had been copied out, in the months
following Pascal's death in 1662, it was proposed to
edit and publish it, and the task was undertaken by a
group of people representing diverse interests, but all
connected in some degree with Port-Royal, and all ac-
quainted with Pascal. The 'committee,' as it is often
called, was chaired by Pascal's close friend, the Duc de
Roannez. It was plainly impossible to publish the fragment

as they stood. Even were it not politically tactless to
do so, many of them were incomprehensible without a gloss,
and even if they had been reformulated in a way contemporary readers could understand, there was still the
problem of the 'disposition des matières': a book which
gave the impression of confusion would not be to the
taste of readers in the 1660s. So the first editors
selected, rewrote, and rearranged the material in an
order which made some kind of acceptable sense.[6]
   In making these changes they were not trying to distort
Pascal's intentions, and something, certainly, of his
spirit survived the refurbishing of the texts.[7] They even
tried to reveal Pascal's overall strategy. They had not
forgotten what Pascal himself had said when he had presented his project to them, apparently in a lengthy lecture sometime in 1658, and they commissioned Filleau de
la Chaise, secretary to the Duc de Roannez, to write a
preface giving the outline of Pascal's argument. In the
event Filleau's garrulous account did not satisfy the
family, and Etienne Périer wrote a more succinct version,
which forms part of the preface to the Port-Royal edition,
which appeared in 1670.[8] From the same quarter came other
reports of Pascal's design.[9] But the 1670 edition itself
did not attempt to reconstruct the Apologia along the
lines indicated.
   Eighteenth-century editors, with one minor exception,
made no attempt to find an order which would have been
closer to Pascal's preoccupations than to their own.[10]
The nineteenth century, which returned to the manuscript
and gave the text itself a much-needed face-lift, saw
several well-meaning attempts to arrive at a less arbitrary solution, guided by Filleau's *Discours*, clues in
the *pensées* themselves, and the editors' own intuition.[11]
Some editors were more sanguine than others,[12] but the
results were very different from each other in all respects save the very general outline.[13]
   Brunschvicg, in his monumental edition of 1904, and in
the earlier, less comprehensive edition of 1897, was more
honest, and chose to present the fragments systematically,
with no claims to know Pascal's mind on the subject, and
with no time wasted on second-hand witnesses.[14] After
him many voices have repeated the statement that Pascal's
plan is unknown and unknowable.[15]
   Meanwhile, the *Discours* of Filleau and the other contemporary accounts continued to beckon.[16] Vinet, Frantin,

and Sainte-Beuve had drawn on them;[17] E. Jassens, in an
important study, scrutinized the 'objective' evidence,
concluded that it was incomplete and contradictory, but
argued that Filleau could be trusted as far as he goes,
and that the outline, at least, of Pascal's argument was
clear.[18] Many commentators have agreed, explicitly or
implicitly.[19] H.F. Stewart put his trust squarely in
Filleau, and arranged the apologetic fragments in the
light of Filleau's paragraphs.[20] Jacques Chevalier also
used Filleau as the basis of his editions.[21] This approach
naturally puts a great burden on Filleau, whose authority
could be called into question, and though it was a sensible solution, it was clearly a *pis-aller*; Filleau would
have less prestige if there were documented proof of
Pascal's own thinking on the subject. But could such
proof ever be produced?

(b) the reappearance of the evidence

The only possible way to recover Pascal's authentic plan
would be to study, without prejudice, the order in which
the fragments had been found at his death.[22] To do this,
two possibilities needed to be examined: the manuscript
which is located in the Bibliothèque Nationale ('Original
des *Pensées* de Pascal,' *manuscrits, fonds français*, 9202 -
generally known as the 'Recueil Original'), and the two
Copies also preserved in the *fonds français* of the
Bibliothèque Nationale under the numbers 9203 and 12449.
Both copies satisfy one criterion: in both the order in
which the fragments appear seems very confused.

The manuscript, obviously invaluable for discovering
what Pascal actually wrote, is of little help in our
search for a plan. In order to keep them from deteriorating
the fragmentary pieces of paper were pasted, early in the
eighteenth century, onto large sheets. The edges were
trimmed in the interests of economy, and the spaces filled
in by other papers of the right size; further, the sheets
themselves were bound in a random order.[23]

In 1896, Gustave Michaut, radically rejecting as vain
all attempts to impose significant order on the fragments,
published them in the order of the Recueil Original.[24]
This was, he admitted, merely to replace arbitrary order
by arbitrary disorder,[25] although until the Recueil
Original had been properly studied, we could not know
that, and clearly it was useful to researchers, if not

to readers, to have an edition which could be used in
conjunction with the manuscript. Brunschvicg also followed
the order of the Recueil Original when he published a
valuable photostat edition of the *Pensées* in 1905.[26] It
was not feasible to rearrange the fragments in the order
Brunschvicg had used in his editions of 1897 and 1904,
and such a rearrangement would have removed half the usefulness of the new edition, which was that it showed us
exactly how the manuscript looks. But useful though these
publications were, they had nothing to tell us of the
'disposition des matières' which Pascal himself had had
in mind.

The other possibility would have been to follow the
order of one or other of the two Copies. Michaut believed
that the Copies were made for the Port-Royal edition, the
order of the fragments in them hardly better than that of
the Recueil Original.[27] Brunschvicg came to the same conclusion,[28] for a very precise reason. He noted (and the
fact will be of crucial importance in later examinations
of the Copies) that Copy 9203 — like many critics, he
regarded Copy 12449 as a derivative, and ignored it —
divided into two parts, the first part relatively organized, and the second not. He opined that it was a copy
made as part of the preparations for the Port-Royal edition, dividing *pensées* retained from *pensées* rejected,
and such was Brunschvicg's authority that his explanation
was accepted uncritically, despite the fact that a rapid
comparison of Copy 9203 with the Port-Royal edition would
have shown that his explanation did not hold water for a
moment.[29]

It was forty years, in fact, before two editors, working independently, took a fresh look at Copy 9203. Joseph
Dédieu was struck by the relative coherence of the first
part, which he assumed to reflect the 'liasses' described
by Etienne Périer,[30] and he jumped immediately to the
conclusion that these sections, all of which have titles,
'révéleraient ainsi les principes de la réflexion de
Pascal ... Ce sont là des idées directrices, qui semblent
rappeler avec vraisemblance les principaux arguments dont
Pascal se proposait d'établir la valeur.'[31] He did not
think either the titles or the order were literally
Pascal's own — he attributed both to the copyists — but
as the copyists were probably respecting the order in
which they found the papers, the order should, he thought,
be taken seriously. The following year (1938), Zacharie

Tourneur went further, producing several good arguments in favour of the authenticity of the so-called 'first' copy.[32] It is clear, he said, that the copyists were scrupulously faithful to what they found. It is clear too that Pascal had set up a number of divisions, because in the fragments there are a handful of cross-references in Pascal's hand. Moreover, Tourneur noticed that some sheets of the manuscript show traces of pin-holes, and that in some instances Pascal had visibly added something after the pin had been put in place. He concluded that it was therefore extremely likely that the chapters with titles correspond to dossiers in which Pascal had himself carefully filed a number (nearly 400 in all) of his fragments.

After the war, Copy 9203 received new defenders. In 1947 Paul-Louis Couchoud, whose suspicions had been aroused back in 1900, gave an accurate description of it. It divided, he said, into 27 + 34 sections, the first group bearing titles, the second group being without, but both representing *liasses*, which he described very precisely, using the analogy of seventeenth-century banking methods. He drew attention to three tables which recorded the titles, which he believed to come from Pascal himself.[3]

Finally Louis Lafuma succeeded in identifying the Copy mentioned by Etienne Périer. He revealed more of the Copy's secrets, and managed, not without a struggle, to impose his views on the world.[34] His particular contributions (leaving to one side the most important of all: the preparation of an edition based on the order of the first Copy) were: to show that Pascal had worked on large sheets of paper, which he cut into fragments for the purpose of classifying the separate thoughts,[35] and to give an explanation for the two halves of the Copy, arguing that the first half represented the chapters of the Apologia, with a number of fragments already assigned to their appropriate chapters, while the second half represented papers Pascal had not sorted, either because they had nothing to do with the Apologia, or because he was prevented by illness from pursuing his task of classifying. In some respects - undervaluing the table, restricting the word *liasse* to the first half, and miscounting the number of sections in both halves - Lafuma is less correct than Couchoud,[36] but it was with Lafuma that sceptics picked th-eir quarrel, and the next stages of the research were conducted around his formulations.

We can distinguish three issues: the basic argument that
the twenty-seven sections of the first part of Copy 9203
represent twenty-seven dossiers constituted by Pascal
himself; the order of these twenty-seven dossiers; and
finally (a matter which has received attention only quite
recently) the status of the fragments which lie outside
the titled dossiers.

Lafuma's argument that Pascal was himself responsible
for cutting up and filing several fragments is virtually
irrefutable. Not only does the manuscript contain large
sheets and small scraps of paper of assorted sizes,
tailored to the length of what is written on them; some
of the large sheets contain more than one fragment,
separated by a line, and on some of the small pieces the
original dividing line can still be seen. When R.E.
Lacombe attempted to put forward an alternative hypothesis,
attributing the filing to the Duc de Roannez, Lafuma de-
molished his case with a battery of arguments which it
would be perverse not to accept.[37]

The disagreement was thus not with Lafuma's conclusion,
but with the importance to be attached to it. Even as an
exercise in sorting, it was said, the twenty-seven dossiers
are unimpressive. There are specific instances where
fragments are manifestly in the wrong bundle, and it would
be unwise to deduce anything about Pascal's plan from
evidence which bears trace of such carelessness.[38] Nobody
answered the precise charges, and it seems to have been
tacitly agreed that there are indeed a handful of misplaced fragments.[39] Nevertheless, it seems to have been
generally agreed also that these misplaced fragments are
not sufficiently numerous to invalidate the claim that
each bundle has its own character and meaning.

More important was the debate over the order in which
the bundles should be arranged. Were the bundles merely
a way of filing notes, or did they represent a plan?[40]
Many critics have been unwilling to concede the latter
possibility, and if we were reduced to hypotheses, it
would certainly be easy to say that there are apparent
incoherences which make it difficult to attribute the
order confidently to Pascal. However, the facts point
quite clearly to Pascal as the person responsible.[41]
The argument is bound up with the status of a table of
titles for which there is no manuscript, but which appears
twice on Copy 9203 and once on Copy 12449.[42] Did Pascal
compose the original table? There is no reasonable doubt

that the titles themselves are Pascal's; to say that the
titles are in some cases strange backfires, as unexpected
titles are more likely to be due to the author than to a
humble and generally scrupulous copyist.[43] More significant, several individual fragments have titles in Pascal's
hand,[44] similar or identical to the titles of the table,
and other fragments, as I have said, refer specifically
to other sections by title.[45] Only a very few chapter-
titles survive in the manuscript,[46] but every section is
titled in the Copies, the title often being longer than
the one in the table, but clearly related.[47] One must
simply assume that the titles disappeared before the
Recueil Original was prepared. This assumption is made
plausible by the fact that what titles we do have are on
small fragile flyers or *papillons*.[48]

But the fact that the titles on the table are authentic
does not necessarily mean that the table itself is
Pascal's too. It could conceivably be the work of a
copyist – Lafuma attributed it to Nicole and Arnauld –   [49]
who chose the titles from the flyers (abbreviating
several), and simply recorded the order in which the
liasses had been handed down. Anyone holding this view
has two awkward facts to explain. First, all three copies
of the table set out the titles in the same way, with ten
well spaced in a left-hand column, and the rest, more
crushed, in a right-hand column;[50] moreover, all the
copies record an alternative title, carefully scored out,
for the fifth *liasse*.[51] We are thus dealing with a
'figured copy,' which would be inconceivable if the
original were not regarded as particularly valuable. A
mere check-list, noted by a copyist, would not be treated
with such reverence. Second, there is one title – 'La
nature est corrompue' – which has no corresponding chapter among the twenty-seven titles *liasses*; no copyist
could have invented it.[52] That *liasse* has been located
recently among the unsorted papers,[53] which strengthens
the view that the table has nothing to do with a copyist's
record, but must have been made out by Pascal himself.
(We are thus obliged to talk now of twenty-eight, not
twenty-seven sections.) Even the fact that the table appears twice on Copy 9203 only served to increase confidence in the witness of the Copies. It was filed at the
head of a series of fragments prepared for sorting, but
not yet distributed; on Copy 12449 this group comes just
before the twenty-seven bundles. But in Copy 9203, each

section was recorded in a separate exercise book, and the
separate books were not kept together; consequently the
copyists made two copies of the table, one to stay in the
correct place, and the other to accompany the block of
titled sections, where it would be readily accessible to
anyone working on them.[54] Finally, the different ordering
of the two Copies furnishes yet another argument in favour
of the view that the order of the twenty-seven *liasses* is
genuine, because the group of twenty-seven sections is
identical in both copies, showing that it was regarded as
a single unbreakable unit, unlike the thirty-four series
of unclassed papers, which split into seven independent
groups, differently set out in the two Copies.

If we accept that the table records faithfully a list
drawn up by Pascal himself, we still need to ask whether
it is simply an inventory of the dossiers Pascal was
working on,[55] or whether it represents the sequence in
which he visualized his twenty-eight sections. There is
no objective proof that the list does reflect Pascal's
thoughts on the order of his bundles; the titles are not
numbered, and there are no arrows indicating a reshuffle.
We are thus obliged to ask whether the order here recorded
makes sense. Critics have not been lacking to express
scepticism. Henri Gouhier maintains that the first bundle
comprises working notes, not notes for an introduction,
that the title of 11°, 'A.P.R.,' shows that it cannot
belong to the same sequence as the rest, that the title
of 12°, 'Commencement,' is manifestly out of place, that
'Loi figurative' (19°)[56] cannot logically be separated
from 'Figures particulières' (25°), and that the 'Preuves
de Moïse (23°) would 'probably' have inaugurated the
section on proofs.[57] Marcel Guersant joins 'Divertissement' (8°) to the three sections on 'Misère' (2°-4°),
and inverts 5° and 6°, although he defines them both as
showing what is good in a man.[58] Annie Barnes finds
sections 11°-12° confusing: 'Ces deux commencements ne
s'excluent-ils pas l'un l'autre? Il est bien difficile
de combiner sinon de concilier toutes ces tentatives de
convertir l'incrédule.'[59] Louis Marin turned them into
an introduction.[60] Patricia Topliss is worried about
sections 11°-14°, which she says are 'placed at a point
where they appear to interrupt rather than to advance
the movement of the Apology.'[61] The matter is further
complicated by the long fragment no. 427, which is manifestly connected with section 12°, and which a long

tradition sees as an introduction to the Apologia.[62]
Patricia Topliss's solution is to place the contents of
liasses 12° (including nos 427 and 418), 14° (15°), and
13° in a general preface.[63] Similarly, Pol Ernst, whose
study of the classified fragments is predicated on total
trust in the evidence of the Copy, proposed nevertheless
in his appendix to insert the first ten chapters between
15° and 16° (17°), arguing that they are to be subsumed
under the title, otherwise inexplicable, of 'La nature
est corrompue' (the 'blank' title).[64]

None of these arguments is conclusive. One has the
impression that commentators assume they know what Pascal's
principles of classification and ordering must be, and
that disconcerting evidence simply discredits itself,
rather than obliging them to revalue their assumptions.
It could equally well be that the evidence is genuine,
and that after careful examination it can be justified
and its disconcerting features understood. Until we have
scrutinized all the evidence fairly, it would seem reasonable to assume that in the twenty-seven titled chapters
of the Copies we do have the rudiments of Pascal's plan.[65]

At this point, we encounter a third battalion ready to
attack. Even if it is agreed that Pascal himself set up
twenty-eight dossiers to store material for the twenty-
eight chapters of a carefully conceived apologia, we
cannot, we are reminded, talk of a definitive plan.[66]
There are discrepancies, which suggest that it was evolving, and nothing proves that Pascal would not have modified it further. There are more unsorted fragments than
sorted ones, and Pascal evidently abandoned the sorting
quite early. Would the later fragments even have fitted
the categories already set up? Maybe Pascal abandoned
the sorting not because he was ill (Lafuma's contention),
but because his plan no longer satisfied him? Gilberte,
his sister, apparently had no objection to the first
editors rearranging the order, and she would not have
been consciously unfaithful to Pascal's wishes.

There is some force in this argument, which cautions
us not to claim too much for Pascal's plan. There is,
however, no proof that Pascal was dissatisfied with his
plan and some clear indications that later fragments
were written with the twenty-eight titles in mind. The
last argument advanced above could be answered by saying
that the family would not have wished to present the lecture of 1658 as indicating the basic design, if they had
reason to believe that he no longer held those views.[67]

The most radical formulation of the view that no plan can be called definitive was made by Lucien Goldmann, who argued that any order would have betrayed the profound implications of the *Pensées* themselves, in other words, that even if Pascal had not been prevented by illness from continuing with his work, he would have had to abandon it for reasons of internal consistency.[68] One is not obliged to agree with Goldmann, whose views betray a philosopher's rather than an artist's understanding of form. He shelves rather too glibly a problem which exercised Pascal considerably, and I shall for my part resist such temptations until the Copies have been fully exploited.

(c) availability of the evidence

In order to exploit the order of the Copies, we needed to have an edition which presented the order of one or other Copy faithfully. However 'confusing' the Copy chosen might seem to the non-specialist, the scholar needs to come to grips with it directly if he is to escape from the dilemma which seemed inevitable for nearly 300 years - even if he arrives later at the conclusion that the hope offered by the Copies is illusory. Surprisingly there was initially considerable reluctance to provide such an edition. While editors made their claims for the authority of Copy 9203 in their respective introductions, they persisted in diverging from the order of the Copy, sometimes considerably, in their texts. Dedieu was the worst offender: although he claimed specifically to have preserved the twenty-six (sic) sections of the first part as exactly as possible, in fact he took the greatest liberties with the material, and it is impossible to learn anything from Dedieu's edition about the order of the fragments in the Copy. Tourneur was much more faithful, but even he was not above a few adjustments where he thought Pascal had nodded,[69] and in the second part of his edition he makes a distinction, unknown to either Copy, between material which is irrelevant to the Apologia, and material which in his view properly belongs there.[70]

Lafuma in his first edition (Delmas), made the same distinction, relegating the fragments deemed irrelevant to a supplementary volume.[71] The great advantage of Lafuma's work is that he presented the titled sections strictly according to the order of the Copy 9203.

However, his respect for the Copy did not extend to the second half of that document, and he felt no compunction about redistributing the relevant 'unsorted' fragments among the titled sections. Fortunately, he did keep the two kinds of fragment, classed and unclassed, separate; in each section, the classified fragments, in the order of the Copy, are followed by three asterisks and a selection of unclassed fragments.[72] If one assumes that the secret of the 'disposition des matières' is more likely to be found in the twenty-seven embryonic chapters than in the unsorted papers, then Lafuma's Delmas edition provides, at last, the vital evidence.

It would nevertheless have been more satisfactory if we could have had access to the complete evidence, that is, to all sixty-one sections mentioned by Couchoud. And so Louis Lafuma, while he continued to defend the Delmas arrangement, and to supervise a revised edition (1952), gave us the objective edition we urgently needed.[73] It appeared in 1951, put out by the Editions du Luxembourg, in three volumes. It was expensive, and could not easily supplant the Delmas or even the Brunschvicg texts, but the notes and documentation were superior to Delmas, and the lay-out extremely clear. In the 1960s, the Luxembourg numbering was used for the Seuil Intégrale edition, which has given it wide currency.[74] Until it is supplanted, it would be unthinkable to revert to any other system of reference for a scholarly work on the text of the *Pensées*.[75]

Since 1962 we have had the additional benefit of a photographic reproduction of the manuscript in the order of the Luxembourg edition. This does not wholly replace the Brunschvicg 1905 edition, as Lafuma, who was responsible, did not reproduce the shape of the papers themselves; but it is much more convenient than the unwieldy loose-leaf monster of Brunschvicg.[76]

One might mention here a criticism made of Lafuma's order by J. Mantoy and subsequently by J. Steinmann, who went as far as to produce an edition which corrected what he thought was an error of judgment on Lafuma's part.[77] Observing that the system of filing adopted by Pascal meant that the first paper filed stayed at the bottom of the pile, Steinmann proposed systematically to reverse the order of the papers in each of Lafuma's twenty-seven sections.[78] The point is well taken, and in chapter 31 I shall argue that the order of filing does give clues to the evolution of Pascal's plan. But the order in which

the papers were filed does not correspond to the order
in which they were written and has practically no importance for the intelligibility of Pascal's design. So,
while admitting that Lafuma ought perhaps logically to
have done what Steinmann suggested in the first place,
the matter does not seem significant enough to hold it
seriously against the Lafuma edition, which presents
both the classed and the unclassed fragments in the order
of Copy 9203.

It has always been obvious that Lafuma attached much
more importance to the twenty-seven titled bundles than
to what he called the unclassed papers. His willingness
to redistribute the latter among the former is one indication of this. And as I have said, his description of
the second half of Copy 9203 is less satisfactory than
Couchoud's. To Lafuma, the unclassed papers were not in
'liasses' like the twenty-seven titled sections - the
word would be inappropriate, he said, when some units
contained only one sheet, although it does fit some of
the other units. He described them (miscounting by one)
as 'trente-trois séries de textes que le copiste semble
avoir parfois délimités au hasard.'[79] They were made up,
he said, of 'papiers non classés, retrouvés dans sa
chambre après sa mort et mis en paquets par ceux qui les
ont recueillis.'[80] Raymond Francis rightly criticized
Lafuma on this score[81] - the role assigned to Pascal's
heirs is quite arbitrary - and Jean Mesnard has recently
submitted the whole matter to a careful scrutiny, concluding that there is no reason to regard the thirty-
four 'séries' as different, in their material constitution, from the twenty-seven 'liasses'; they do not, for
the most part, comprise separate small fragments like
the twenty-seven bundles with titles, but they are all
duly constituted units.[82] Their unity is, however, formal and chronological only and I shall continue to use
the word 'unclassed' to refer to them.

It is surprising that twenty-five years went by before
anyone criticized Lafuma's initial decision to base his
edition on Copy 9203, rather than on the other Copy
(12449).[83] It is difficult to understand why Lafuma made
this decision, when he himself wrote that it is Copy
12449, and not Copy 9203, which conforms most closely
to the original order of the papers.[84] The chief difference between the two versions is that the untitled series
are not in the same order. Now, Copy 12449 is written

consecutively through a number of exercise-books, whereas
in Copy 9203 each of the sixty-one sections starts in a
fresh book. The books of Copy 9203 were bound together,
as Lafuma saw, in the eighteenth century.[85] There is thus
no guarantee whatsoever that the order has any significance, whereas the order followed in Copy 12449, being
immutable (any dislocation in the order of books would
create a non sequitur and could quickly be set right),
must correspond to the state of the papers when the copy
was made, and hence has a good chance of preserving the
authentic, perhaps even a significant order.

Two critics have given Copy 12449 the long overdue
scrutiny which these facts invited. Philippe Sellier has
argued that the order of Copy 12449 enables us to establish the chronological sequence, and he has produced an
edition which follows this order.[86] Jean Mesnard, in his
full-length study of the *Pensées*, comes to conclusions
which differ slightly from Sellier's, but he too finds
in the so-called unsorted fragments many signs that
Pascal's intentions were not quite what Lafuma presumed.[87]
However, these recent developments, while they have a
bearing on several details of the present book, do not
affect its main purpose, which is to analyse the twenty-
eight titled sections in an attempt to discover what
Pascal had in mind when he bade us judge him by the 'disposition des matières.'

(d) interpretation of the evidence

It is clear that Lafuma's edition, supplemented by subsequent research which that edition itself inspired,
does enable us to come much closer than previous generations had dreamed to the order in which Pascal left his
papers. Arguments advanced to diminish the significance
of the Copies have not proved particularly damaging, and
it is legitimate to believe that in the material now
available to us there lie the clues which will reveal
the plan by which Pascal asked us to assess his Apologia.[88]
Even if the two Copies may still have surprises for us,
we should be able to agree now on the status to be accorded to them, and devote more energy to interpreting
the evidence which Lafuma made available.

Two lines of enquiry would seem to be open. First, if
the twenty-eight dossiers contain the bare bones of an
apologia in twenty-eight chapters, can we work out in

detail how Pascal conceived his original presentation of the Christian case? Second, what can the thirty-four or thirty-five series of unclassed papers, correctly dated and ordered in chronological sequence, tell us about the genesis and evolution of the Apologia, and do they oblige us to modify the results of the first enquiry?

As well as accepting the authenticity of the classification and the tables, anyone wishing to interpret the evidence has to make, at least provisionally, two further assumptions. The first of these concerns the importance of the classification. We have seen that some writers on Pascal resisted the claims made for the Copies because, they said, it was obvious that Pascal was rather careless in the way he tackled the task of sorting and ordering his material; it would therefore be foolish to try to find subtle explanations for odd details which are due solely to haste. However, that diagnosis itself rests on another premise, namely that we can tell in advance what principles guided Pascal's classification – thematic divisions, maybe, or straightforward logical discourse. It is just as reasonable to assume, in the face of disconcerting details, that we are put out because we have not understood the principles, and to begin by trusting Pascal, and hope that by taking the data we have quite seriously, we shall end by uncovering the principles. This hypothesis is at least worth trying; if it leads nowhere, we shall be obliged to fall back on the alternative theory of carelessness, but we should surely start by trying to find a more worthy explanation than that.

The other assumption has to do with the unclassed papers. There is clearly a danger in supplementing the evidence of the fragments which Pascal is known to have sorted, by fragments which he did not assimilate to the titled dossiers. We cannot be sure to which part of the Apologia any of the unsorted fragments would have been assigned, as is shown by the very divergent attempts which editors have made to allocate them to one or other of the twenty-eight chapters.[89] Indeed, none of the material outside the twenty-eight dossiers is necessarily part of the Apologia at all, and some quite definitely is not. Fragments written after the classifying had been completed – completed by inserting a title on each bundle, and tying it up – might have shown Pascal that there were inadequacies in his original scheme, which would explain why he did not reopen the dossiers and continue sorting.

The safest course would therefore be to ignore the unsorted papers as far as possible. Yet one is loath to act in that way. Several sheets had already been cut up by Pascal, with the evident intention of classifying the resulting fragments, and one could easily imagine contingent reasons – health, working conditions – why he did not continue in the same way as before. Many unsorted fragments have titles which link them explicitly to specific chapters, and many more have links of theme or idea which bring them into the same orbit as classified fragments. Frequently the unsorted *Pensées* complement the classified ones, by explaining allusions, amplifying the same thought, or by showing links where the classified fragments simply present two apparently unrelated notions. Even though we can never be sure just how Pascal would have assigned a given fragment, the evidence of the unclassed fragments is much too important to be systematically ignored.[90] Nor need divergent editorial choices discourage us. There are two main reasons for them. One is that there are many fragments which touch on the preoccupations of more than one chapter; Pascal did not always write with a particular chapter in mind. An editor cannot easily quote the same fragment more than once, and must therefore opt for one possibility and exclude the others. An interpreter can, indeed must, be more flexible. Second, and probably more important, the choice of chapter for a fragment not allocated by Pascal presupposes a careful study of the principles behind the original classification, principles which, I have said, are not at first obvious. Given some of the suggestions editors have made,[91] one can only conclude that not enough thought was given to this preparatory study. The present book is an attempt to fill this very gap.

It is surprising that the revelations of Lafuma were not seized upon immediately by scholars interested in discerning the plan. Sister Marie Louise Hubert, who published a book entitled *Pascal's Unfinished Apologia* in 1952,[92] failed to exploit the material made available by Lafuma. In her chapter on 'Internal evidence of Pascal's plan' (pp 98-118), she limited herself to *liasses* 1° and 11°, and she did not list the twenty-eight titles until her conclusion (pp 145-6).

The evidence, nevertheless, was available. As early as 1951, Jean Mesnard assessed the revelation of Copy 9203 with exquisite precision, and presented a sensitive

account of what he called the 'movement' of the Apologia.
His four introductory paragraphs should be read carefully.
One quotation must suffice here:

> D'une façon générale, les fragments que les éditeurs
> avaient tendance à grouper autour de quelques idées
> centrales ... se repartissent tout au long de l'ouvrage
> et appuient successivement des raisonnements très
> divers. Au lieu d'un classement rigide et systématique,
> nous trouvons un savant entrelacement de thèmes, une
> composition subtile, musicale, une argumentation souple
> et nuancée, quoique toujours rigoureuse.[93]

The scope of the book in which this most judicious assessment appears - a student guide, covering the whole
of Pascal in 200 octavo pages - precluded any detailed
justification, which may be why other writers have continued to look on the twenty-eight titles as so many
subject headings, implying a fairly rigid scheme. Thus
Edmond Morot-Sir in 1973 doubts the value of the dossiers
on the grounds that Pascal would surely have 'cherché des
effets démonstratifs convergents, et non suivi un plan
continu et systématique.'[94] But that is precisely, Mesnard
had said, the kind of effect Copy 9203 does show. His
description had evidently fallen on deaf ears, and would
need to be justified at length. It was clearly necessary
publicly to scrutinize each fragment, face all the difficult cases (which are actually more numerous than the
sceptics ever imagined), and try to understand the implications of their being put where the copy records
them, always assuming that Pascal knew exactly what he
was doing.[95]
    This detailed enquiry into the sense of each classified
bundle was undertaken by Pol Ernst, whose book, published
in 1970, runs to over 700 large pages.[96] In his introduction, he defines his task as bringing to light something
as real and as important as the 'confusion,' namely
'l'unité et la cohérence profonde de ces matériaux, leur
continuité logique, leur dynamisme foncier.' He rightly
saw that the meaning of each *liasse* would never be clear
if we always read the fragments in the order of the
Copies. Pascal never sorted the fragments within each
bundle into a coherent order, and even if editors feel
obliged never to interfere with the facts, however arbitrary, an interpreter is bound to seek for the pattern

which the facts can at times conceal.[97] Had Ernst tackled
the issues differently, the present book (the main lines
of which were already laid down) would have been left
unwritten. But Ernst's book suffered from a number of
methodological flaws. In order to discover the unity of
each section, Ernst limited himself strictly to the fragments classified by Pascal. Reasonable caution, one might
think.[98] Unfortunately this meant that Ernst had to supply his own links between fragments when judicious use
of the unclassed papers would often have provided a more
convincing, or a more suggestive link, in Pascal's own
words. Second, Ernst frequently fits fragments together
according to his own analysis of the content, and analysis, especially when done in terms of themes, can distort
the perspective in which the themes are seen. It follows
that his way of linking one chapter with another is also
not always very convincing. For these and other reasons,[99]
Ernst's conclusions were significantly different from
what I believed the evidence would yield, and so I did
not abandon the ambition to tackle the same questions
myself.

My aim has been to understand why Pascal arranged his
fragments in the way he did, and hence to give as accurate an account as possible, first of the significance
of each of the twenty-eight sections, and second of the
relation of each section to the overall apologetic argument. The results of a very long and detailed enquiry
seem to me fully to justify the initial hypotheses and
to confirm Mesnard's intuition that the composition of
the Apologia is subtle and supple, not rigid and systematic. One can find perfectly plausible explanations for
almost everything in the classified sections, without
any need at all to force the evidence.[100] And these explanations all point to the astonishing imaginative coherence of the Apologia. Once one is convinced of this,
the objections of detail raised by critics fade away.
One even finds an answer to the most corrosive criticism
of all: to the objection that once Pascal has begun to
knit it all together, it would have all been changed.
Everyone knows, it is said, how a plan gets modified in
the execution.[101] This supposes that the 'plan' consists
of logically organized headings and subheadings, and
that only the actual writing can supply those organic
relationships which make for a properly imaginative design. The content and sequence of the twenty-eight chapter

Pascal envisaged seem, however, to correspond, not to
the first rather simple outline, but to the subtle and
intricate design which emerges after much reflection.
Etienne Périer has told us that his uncle

> avait toujours accoutumé de songer beaucoup aux choses,
> et de les disposer dans son esprit avant que de les
> produire au-dehors, pour bien considérer et examiner
> avec soin celles qu'il fallait mettre les premières ou
> les dernières, et l'ordre qu'il leur devait donner à
> toutes ...[102]

All the evidence suggests that Pascal set up his dossiers
not in order to do some preliminary sorting, but as a
consequence of having seen in detail how his argument
should be conducted.[103] Or rather (to anticipate genetic
considerations), that while the plan may have been schematic at the time Pascal began to classify, it developed
almost immediately into the imaginative design revealed
by the twenty-eight titled *liasses*. Which is not to say,
of course, that it could not, or would not, have been
modified had Pascal lived longer.[104] But that is pure
speculation, and quite irrelevant to our subject. When
Pascal talked proudly of the 'disposition des matières,'
he was referring to something already worked out in his
mind.

The results of the investigation I have undertaken also
tend to confirm my assumption concerning the unclassified
papers, namely that it is legitimate to use them to eli-
cit Pascal's plan. Here I might be accused of arguing in
a circle: it is not surprising that the unclassed fragments should fit into a scheme if the scheme is in part
derived from them in the first place. I would hope not
to have fallen into so elementary a trap. I have certainly made liberal use of the unclassed fragments; as
the index shows, nearly all of them, except for those
which have virtually no relevance for the Apologia, have
been cited at what I consider the appropriate place. But
in every case, it is my analysis of the classified *Pensées*,
eked out by unsorted fragments which are plainly glosses
upon them, which has defined the basic problems; other
unclassified fragments have then been used if they shed
light on the problem, and the rest have only been introduced once the problem has been solved and the implication of the *liasses* known clearly enough for me to be

confident that they are not being forced into a mould to which they do not really belong. I would not pretend that each and every unclassed fragment has its niche in the twenty-eight chapters. But it is striking that *none of them introduces ideas which the twenty-eight chapters could not accommodate*. One can therefore conclude that while Pascal did not write each fragment with a specific chapter in mind, virtually all his apologetic fragments were written within the framework of the twenty-eight chapters. If he might conceivably have expanded the design we know, there is no evidence at all that the expansion was necessary when he laid down his pen.

The main body of this book is therefore a study of each of the twenty-eight sections in turn. Each section is treated in a separate chapter, and in each chapter I have adhered to the same plan. I begin with the problems posed by the section and the basic evidence. I then state my conclusions and list the unsorted fragments I have used in addition to the ones assigned to that section.[105] In these lists, I give the source of all the fragments and identify any which are known for certain to have been composed after the spring of 1660, so that readers can make the necessary adjustment if they wish to regard late fragments differently from fragments written before, or simultaneously with, the setting up of the titled *liasses*. I then argue my case in detail, mentioning all the relevant fragments. Where the material of the section warrants it, I have subdivided my chapter (using small letters), and these subdivisions appear also in the statement of my conclusions.[106]

There is just one modification to Pascal's written order which I have felt obliged to make: I have been constrained to reverse the order of the fourteenth and fifteenth *liasses*: 'Excellence de cette manière de prouver Dieu' and 'Transition de la connaissance de l'homme à Dieu.' I did so reluctantly, as this could seem like reintroducing an element of arbitrary subjectivism into an account which takes as its prime justification a conviction that the 'table des titres' of the BN Copies is genuine. However, I am persuaded that the placing of the dossier entitled 'Transition' constituted a special case. In my first draft, the suggestion was made tentatively at the end of the fifteenth chapter (as it then was). Once mooted, however, the hypothesis smoothed out so many other problems concerning the block which covers

sections 12° to 17° that it seemed more sensible to re-
cast this part of the study, boldly placing 'Excellence'
after 'Transition.' The reasons for doing so, which are
cumulative, are reviewed in a separate appendix. Because
of this switch, and also because I restore 'La nature est
corrumpue,' my numbering of the twenty-eight chapters
unavoidably differs from that of Lafuma.[107]
   In chapter 29 I reconstruct the outline of the Apologia
which my enquiry has led me to discern in the evidence at
our disposal.[108] Here I incorporate some of the modifications which I believe that material would have imposed on
Pascal if he had put it all in order, with no radical
alterations. Apart from reversing 14° and 15°, this involves fragments which look beyond the specific section
in which they are filed. Some sections form subdivisions
of a single stage in the argument rather than separate
stages, and in these cases matter pertaining to the block,
best placed at the beginning or the end, is sometimes
found in one of the intermediate sections.
   It should perhaps be emphasized that I do not claim to
have written Pascal's unwritten Apologia for him. Even
if my allocation of unsorted fragments is accepted as
being in the spirit of Pascal, it is still obvious that
there would have been a vast amount of rewriting to be
done, and rewriting can easily produce unforeseen new
developments. Nevertheless, I believe that we can say
that if Pascal had based an expository lecture on all
relevant fragments now extant, it would have a shape
very like the outline given in this twenty-ninth chapter,
a shape already coherent and satisfying.
   One further criticism has to be anticipated. By con-
ceiving the Apologia as a single argument, and assimi-
lating fragments known to have been written after the
twenty-eight bundles had been set up, one runs the risk
of underestimating the evolution in Pascal's thinking
which may have taken place during the last five or six
years of his life. I have already said that the plan to
which the twenty-eight chapters bear witness appears to
have taken later developments without strain. It is,
however, worth reviewing the evidence in more detail.
As well as the evolution of the Apologia, the genesis
needs to be considered, particularly as it looks from
internal evidence (mentioned on several occasions in my
opening chapters) that the plan itself developed from
something relatively simple to something much more complex.

I noted that critics have spotted discrepancies in the early sections; many of these can be explained on the simple hypothesis, which needs to be tested by external criteria, that the plan came into clearer focus as Pascal proceeded with his classification. Several of the earliest fragments undoubtedly antedate the plan. Ironically, these include some of the fragments about Order often quoted to prove that the plan failed to satisfy Pascal, whereas probably the plan helped him to resolve the frustrations recorded in those fragments.[109] The second part of my study is given over to this question. It is much more specialized in interest than the first part. In chapter 30 I look at those writings of Pascal before mid-1657 which had an obvious bearing on the Apologia. In chapter 31 I scrutinize the *liasses* in an attempt to see if traces of an earlier and simpler plan can be detected. I have included some discussion of the evidence of Filleau de la Chaise, Etienne Périer, and other acquaintances of Pascal. In chapter 32 I look at all the Units not relevant to chapter 30 to see what fragments possibly belong to Pascal's later years, after he had stopped sorting his fragments into bundles. My conclusion is that very little can be proved to have been written after 1658, and I believe that Pascal had accomplished more before his illness than is generally admitted. I do not pretend to have given a complete account of this delicate question, on which much more work needs to be done. Certainly I find nothing to justify believing that Pascal found the plan he had evolved inadequate.

The test of any piece of scholarly work is that it should prompt new questions. The text with which I began implies that an examination of the 'disposition des matières' is a necessary preliminary to an assessment of the value and originality of the Apologia. This assessment has been attempted many times, of course; but maybe it needs to be tackled afresh. In a short concluding chapter, I outline various ideas on Pascal as an apologist and as a writer, which my research has suggested.

There is finally another use to which this research, if it be accepted, could be put, and that is to guide an editor wishing to prepare a selection of *Pensées* for the general public. Scholars tend to shy away from such a task, understandably seeing their role as presenting the facts as objectively as possible. But when that has been done – and we must presume that the edition promised

by Jean Mesnard will come as close as possible to realizing the ideal[110] - Pascal has not been fully served until
his message has been made accessible to the kind of
reader he himself had in mind.[111] By the very nature of
the case - that Pascal left us with pieces of a jig-saw
puzzle, not with a complete Apologia - a scholarly edition will be more concerned with identifying the pieces
so that others can compose the puzzle, than with presuming
to do the puzzle for us. Strictly speaking, of course,
the puzzle cannot be done, and I have been careful to
insist that in clarifying Pascal's plan, I have not
claimed that I could construct the book Pascal might
one day have completed.

Nevertheless, there is something absurd about jealously
keeping the pieces of a puzzle in their box, and if my
reading of the evidence has produced an order which corresponds as closely as possible to the plan implied by
that evidence, it should be possible to say to a non-
specialist: 'You wish to read Pascal's *Pensées*? You know,
do you not, that most of them were intended for an
Apologia which he never finished? Well, we know now that
he did set up his chapters, and file a large number of
the relevant fragments, and scholars have studied the
classification and learned a lot about what Pascal must
have intended to do. So here we are giving you a large
selection of the fragments, arranged in a way that preserves Pascal's inferred design with the maximum fidelity.
You will have to contend with more notes and editorial
comment than perhaps you are used to; that is partly
because many of the fragments are difficult to understand
as they are, because they allude to passages in the
Bible, or in Montaigne's *Essays*, or to ideas which Pascal
explained in other places, but partly too because the
fragmentary state of the text often obscures the links
between ideas; in those cases a judicious commentary can
clarify the march of the argument.' I personally believe
that such an edition should give the source for each
fragment (classed or unclassed, possible date), but it
must not try to duplicate the work of a scholarly edition, which will be organized on quite different principles. We must hope that when the present era of eco-
nomic stringency is over, such an edition will be commissioned.[112]

PART ONE: THE DESIGN

1
Ordre

How would Pascal have begun his Apologia? The evidence
which would permit a confident answer to this question
is fragmentary, and even deceptive. Would he, for example,
have begun with a preface? There is only one fragment
with the title 'Préface,' no. 190, and it is classed by
Pascal in a bundle which lies in the centre of the twenty-
eight he envisaged.[1] In Unit XXVII there is a sheet containing a pair of fragments entitled respectively 'Préface
de la première partie' and 'Préface de la seconde partie'
(780-1), and fragment 190 is much closer to the second
than to the first. We are thus thrown back on no. 780,
seven or eight lines, comprising two paragraphs, and
explicitly meant as a sketch for a preface to part one
only.

Alternatively, would Pascal perhaps have led in with
a first chapter, corresponding to the first bundle of
classified fragments? This first bundle is entitled
'Ordre,' and one naturally assumes that it was to have
been the basis of an opening chapter. The content of the
bundle is puzzling however, as it touches on various
problems of ordering, referring to quite specific issues
which belong to later chapters of the Apologia. Very
understandably, some commentators have assumed that in
the first dossier we have rough notes of Pascal, which
would not have come into the finished work.[2] Taking a
diametrically opposed view, Pol Ernst assumes that the
first bundle was by definition a first chapter, and with
considerable, indeed excessive ingenuity, builds a hypothetical introduction out of these twelve fragments alone.[3]

Careful reading of other unclassified fragments, many
of them bearing the title 'Ordre' (and therefore destined
for the first bundle), suggest a more satisfactory solution to the problem.[4] The most significant facts would
seem to be that one of these supplementary fragments on

'Ordre' uses the phrase 'discours d'ordre,' and that
three of them echo or anticipate the first paragraph of
no. 780, the 'préface de la première partie.' The 'discours d'ordre' is therefore to be identified with a preface whose outline is in part revealed by fragments which
Pascal excluded from his classified *liasses*.

Discussion of this first section is divided into three:
(a) the first *liasse* collects a number of indications
concerning the way in which different ideas should be
related or extended; it shows Pascal hesitating between
different forms - letters, dialogue, discourses.
(b) the content of these notes places particular importance
on persuading the opponent that he should seek God, concentrating on the steps by which he could be brought to agree,
and the self-discipline which such a decision entails.
(c) clear evidence that these fragments were meant for
a preliminary discourse is given by a number of unclassed
fragments. Pascal would have justified and explained his
novel approach. However, the task of outlining the design
of his book in a fairly systematic way proved irksome,
and he abandoned the idea, while leaving (in the twelve
fragments of the first *liasse*) some indications of what
his preliminary discourse could contain.

Unclassed fragments cited in this chapter are: 387,
408 (I), 467 (XI), 527, 529, 532, 539, 584 (XXIII), 649,
652, 658, 669, 680, 683, 684, 689, 694, 696 (XXV), 737,
745 (XXVI), 780 (XXVII), 976 (from Port-Royal edition),
983 (from Ms Guerrier).[5]

(a) Et à cela lui répondre...   (5)

When the twelve fragments of section 1° are studied in
isolation, supplemented only by the few unclassed fragments which are cast in the same mould, one can envisage
two possible ways of grouping them. So many of them have
to do with arranging ideas in sequence, that one might
interpret this dossier as a collection of working notes
on ways to order the ideas of the Apologia, to which the
title 'Ordre' would be perfectly appropriate. Not all
the fragments fit this category, however, and a second
approach would be to analyse the content of the ideas
Pascal was arranging. They would then be seen to fall
into a discernible pattern; but their connection with
the theme of 'Ordre' would be elusive. In order to solve
the problem of this section, we shall be obliged to probe

more deeply. However, the two approaches just outlined
provide as good a way as any to define the nature of the
problem.

One motif which runs through section 1°, then, is that
of sequence. 'Et puis' (4), 'Et il répondra ... Et lui
répondre, etc.' (5), 'Après la lettre qu'on doit chercher
Dieu, faire la lettre d'ôter les obstacles' (11). Fragment no. 10 links the themes of *misère* and *divertissement*.
Among the unclassed papers, we find: 'Cette lettre avant
le divertissement' (408) and 'Après la corruption dire...'
(467, entitled 'Ordre'). Closely allied are the notes
which suggest new material for frames already set up, or
new frames for ideas Pascal would like to include. 'Dans
la lettre de l'injustice peut venir' (9); 'Une lettre de
la folie de la science humaine et de la philosophie,'
followed by three reminders of points made by Montaigne
(408).[6]

Interesting though they are, these indications of
groupings and sequences do not necessarily agree with
the plan subsequently elaborated. In no. 408, for instance, one of the three examples Pascal wished to use
in a letter which was to precede 'le divertissement' is
that of the '280 sortes de souverain bien dans Montaigne.'
Now, in no. 479 (XI), we find 'Pour les philosophes, deux
cent quatre-vingt souverains biens,' which links up with
sections 9° or 10°, that is, a section following 'Divertissement,' which is the title of section 8°. We should,
however, not be surprised to find inconsistencies of
this kind.

Much more surprising is the fact that no fewer than
five of these fragments (4, 5, 7, 9, and 11) talk of
letters whereas there are virtually no traces of letters
outside this section, except for no. 408, which is in the
same vein as the fragments assigned to this dossier. Four
hypotheses are available to account for this discrepancy.
One is to take the evidence literally, and noting that
all the references to letters except one come in the
first *liasse*, argue that the Apologia proper would have
been prefaced by an introduction taking the form of an
exchange of letters. That interpretation is open to the
obvious objection that an introduction encompassing so
many letters would have been inordinately long. No. 5
suggests that the correspondence would have been two-way
and very leisurely ('Une lettre d'exhortation à un ami
... Et il répondra ... Et lui répondre ... Et il

répondrait ... Et à cela lui répondre'). A second hypothesis is that the idea of a series of letters belongs
to an early stage in the elaboration of the Apologia,
and that Pascal abandoned it. Or else, more simply, we
say that the word 'letter' means no more than the words
'article' or 'chapter' which Pascal used elsewhere. In
fr. 76 Pascal talks of 'l'article suivant' and he is
probably referring to fr. 60, written on the same sheet.
These two fragments can be identified on other grounds
as the 'lettre de l'injustice' of no. 9 and the 'lettre
de la folie de la science humaine' of no. 408. Fragments
described elsewhere as letters were therefore not cast
in epistolary form. The same can be said of the other
'letters' Pascal refers to: the 'lettre pour porter à
rechercher Dieu' (4; a similar phrase comes in nos 5 and
11), the 'lettre d'ôter les obstacles qui est le discours
de la Machine' (11), the 'lettre qui marque l'utilité des
preuves' (7). All these letters are recognizable antec-
dents of sections, or of groups of *Pensées* within sections, of the published order. As fr. 60-76 is early, it
may be that the cluster of references to letters represents a decision taken and quickly rejected while Pascal
was elaborating his plan. That seems the only way to
salvage the second hypothesis. Otherwise we are left with
the third one, unless we opt for the hypothesis most opposed to the second one, and say that Pascal would have
cast his Apologia in letters with dialogues, like the
Provinciales. This is the view of A.J. Krailsheimer, who
says that Pascal would have characterized the interlocutor
as effectively as he characterized the 'good Father' in
the *Provinciales*[11]. Evidently this transposition would
have taken place late. If we hesitate to accept the idea
of a wholesale recasting at the stage of writing, then
we have to explain why Pascal should say 'letter' if he
did not mean it, and also why the references to letters
should all be concentrated in one dossier, unless that
section were to have been distinguished from the rest.
But would it have been distinguished by its form or its
function?

   The first section does not speak only of letters. Quite
apart from the reference to a 'discours de la Machine'
in no. 11 itself, there are hints that the Apologia might
have taken the form of dialogue (2, 3, and also 658).
Fragment no. 2 is entitled 'Ordre par dialogues,' and
comprises two pairs of sentences. No. 658, not explicitly

associated with this bundle, comprises two sentences,
each preceded by the word 'Conversation.' Fragment no. 3,
separated from No. 2 by a dividing line, but not touched
by Pascal's scissors, consists of two snatches of dialogue, the first incomplete and followed in the manuscript by a gap. As Pascal did not make his usual separation sign, it may be that the gap would have been filled
in by a short transition, linking the two remarks (both
are possible objections to the apologist's argument), and
justifying the inclusion of the whole fragment in the
bundle on Order.[12]

The Apologia we know is not conducted systematically
as a two-way argument, either as a formal exchange
between two correspondents, or as a freer, more rapid
exchange in dialogue. One can readily see why Pascal
abandoned these two possibilities. To have given the opponent the same amount of space would have created tension where Pascal did not want it, making it difficult
for him to explore freely the paradoxes and subtleties
in his own vision. There is in addition the danger that
if the author knows which side he is himself on, the opponent becomes an evident pretext. As a rhetorical device,
that can misfire, inviting the reader to accuse the writer
of loading the dice unfairly. If the part of the opponent
is reduced, this danger is all the greater. We cannot,
however, be sure that Pascal would not have reverted to
a one-way correspondence (on the lines of the *Provinciales*)
for the definitive version he never wrote.[13]

However, while there are no traces of letters in the
published text (other than the ones just mentioned),
there are several traces of embryonic dialogues. Often,
for dramatic reasons, possible objections to the apologist's argument are voiced briefly by the interlocutor.
These explosions merely bring to the surface the latent
presence of the opponent, whom Pascal never forgets. The
design eventually adopted for the Apologia implies a continuing debate and, as we shall see, Pascal's own tactics
grow out of a very precise appreciation of what the opponent can be expected to accept at each stage in the
argument.

Two fragments, nos 6 and 12, whose importance has been
seen by most commentators on Pascal, break free of this
concern with detail, and neither makes reference to letters or dialogues. Both are concerned with the order of
ideas, giving a bird's-eye view of the entire Apologia.

No. 6 indicates a work in two parts, and there are traces of this division elsewhere.[14] But fragment 6 supposes a simpler, less dynamic scheme than the design enshrined in the twenty-eight sections Pascal devised.

1 Partie, Misère de l'homme sans Dieu.
2 Partie, Félicité de l'homme avec Dieu
                autrement
1 Part[ie]. Que la nature est corrompue, par la nature
  même
2 Partie. Qu'il y a un Réparateur, par l'Ecriture.

Fragment 12 was originally entitled 'Division' or 'Divisions,' but the word was changed to 'Ordre' before Pascal had even finished writing it. Here the division appears to be threefold, with perhaps a preface. The description corresponds more closely to the plan we can discern in the twenty-eight dossiers, although it is still somewhat summary.[15]

Ordre.
Les hommes ont mépris pour la religion. Ils en ont haine et peur qu'elle soit vraie. Pour guérir cela il faut commencer par montrer que la religion n'est point contraire à la raison. Vénérable, en donner respect.
La rendre ensuite aimable, fair souhaiter aux bons qu'elle fût vraie et puis montrer qu'elle est vraie.

The last two sentences are then glossed:

Vénérable parce qu'elle a bien connu l'homme.
Aimable parce qu'elle promet le vrai bien.

Are all these fragments to be taken simply as working notes? That would seem provisionally at least to be the most natural interpretation of the first few we have considered, but nos 6 and 12 could more easily be seen as part of an introduction. No. 6 is more a note of the fundamental antitheses involved than a working plan. It does not tell us in what precise form the material was to have been cast. But it would serve very well for a general statement designed to prepare the way for the elaborate argument that will follow in subsequent sections. Similarly with no. 12. In its first version, beginning at 'Commencer par montrer,' we do have, in all probability, a note of the general lines Pascal wished

to follow. But by articulating the implicit attitude of
the unbeliever ('Les hommes ont mépris ... haine et peur
... Pour guérir cela il faut commencer, etc.'), the note
becomes much more like a preliminary explanation of the
approach he is going to take, so different from the traditional apologia.

After a first reading of the fragments Pascal placed
in his first dossier, then, we have noted references to
letters, to dialogues, and two fragments which give an
overall, objective view of the Apologia. Most of these
fragments seem to be working notes, suggestions about
ways to organize the material, which Pascal was to modify
further, if we may judge from the evidence of other
dossiers. Not much of this seems on the face of it suitable for an introduction, although the two 'objective'
fragments could well have that role. There are, moreover,
two fragments not yet discussed (1, 8), which seem even
more remote from any concern with an introduction, and
they do not even relate in any obvious way to the theme
of Order. Let us therefore examine the dossier afresh,
from a different angle.

(b) qu'on doit chercher Dieu (11)

If we move from questions of external form and arrangement to the subject-matter of these twelve fragments, we
find that they tend to fall into two groups, one relating
to the steps leading up to the 'lettre qu'on doit chercher
Dieu' (9, 10, 12), the other to the consequences of that
letter (4, 5, 7, 11, to which we may add 1, 2, 3, and 8).
Fragment 6 embraces both stages. The main preoccupation
of the first group is: why should the unbeliever seek
God in the first place? Pascal's answer to this question,
one of the crucial problems any apologist must face, is
found in no. 12, already quoted, which gives a basic premise of the whole Apologia: men reject religion, not because they know it to be false, but because they fear
the implications, for themselves, of accepting it. It
threatens their security, or their (selfish) pleasures,
and the apologist must show them that their fears and
suspicions are unfounded. In fact, religion does not
contradict reason, and it leads to a happiness far transcending secular pleasures.

A note which could conceivably have been adapted to
fit into the Apologia (983) makes an interesting gloss

on the psychology of no. 12: against the Duc de Roannez's
view that things sometimes please us for reasons which
we do not discover until later, Pascal argues that we
find the reasons precisely in order to justify a pleasure
which is not at all reasonable in origin.

The psychological mechanism at work here is further
explained in no. 539:

> La volonté est un des principaux organes de la créance,
> non qu'elle forme la créance, mais parce que les choses
> sont vraies ou fausses selon la face par où on les
> regarde. La volonté qui se plaît à l'une plus qu'à
> l'autre détourne l'esprit de considérer les qualités
> de celle qu'elle n'aime pas à voir, et ainsi l'esprit
> marchant d'une pièce avec la volonté s'arrête à
> regarder la face qu'elle aime et ainsi il en juge par
> ce qu'il y voit.

In this scheme, the demonstration of the truth of Christianity's claims ('montrer qu'elle est vraie') comes only
at the end of a long period of psychological preparation.
The first part of the enterprise, then, will show that
Christianity has understood man, and can offer him what
he most profoundly desires.

Fragment no. 6, already quoted, speaks of a binary design, and appears to cover, in a schematic way, the same
ground as no. 12, leaving much unsaid, but illuminating
very clearly the antithetical nature of some basic points,
viewed in two different ways. Fragments 9 and 10 fill in
certain details. The 'lettre de l'injustice' (9) will
necessarily contain evidence of what no. 6 calls the
'misère de l'homme sans Dieu,' and no. 10 notes nature's
antidote to *les misères de la vie humaine*: 'le divertissement.'

A second group is provided by the four fragments numbered 4, 5, 7, and 11. All of them imply that there is
to be a letter urging the agnostic to seek God. No. 4
suggests that the search might begin 'chez les philosophes, pyrrhoniens et dogmatistes' who will at least
get him worried. No. 11 simply links this letter on
seeking God to a second idea, the 'Machine.'

> Ordre. Après la lettre qu'on doit chercher Dieu, faire
> la lettre d'ôter les obstacles qui est le discours de
> la Machine, de préparer la Machine, de chercher par
> raison.

The sentence needs to be interpreted. I take it that 'qui
est' means 'in other words, what we have thought of as...'
and that 'le discours de la Machine,' previously conceived, now becomes a 'lettre d'ôter les obstacles.' I
take it also that 'préparer la Machine' is a new formulation of the same idea, and not a new idea. Finally,
'chercher par raison' seems to be an expansion of
'chercher Dieu,' not a stage which follows the 'discours
de la Machine.' It requires very little familiarity with
Pascal to recognize the idea here: that God can be sought
by reason, and that once reason is convinced, there are
obstacles to faith which are of the body, and which need
to be tackled consciously.

Fragment 5 traces in more detail the itinerary from the
'lettre qu'on doit chercher Dieu' to the 'Machine.' It is
not clear whether no. 5 represents an amplification of
no. 11, or whether no. 11 is a simplification of no. 5.
Psychological plausibility suggests the former, but it
is easier to read them in the order 5, 11:

Ordre.
Une lettre d'exhortation à un ami pour le porter à
chercher. Et il répondra: mais à quoi me servira de
chercher, rien ne paraît. Et lui répondre: ne désespérez
pas. Et il répondrait qu'il serait heureux de trouver
quelque lumière. Mais que selon cette religion même
quand il croirait ainsi cela ne lui servirait de rien.
Et qu'ainsi il aime autant ne point chercher. Et à
cela lui répondre: La Machine (5).

There are several ideas adumbrated here: that there is
no clear evidence for the existence of God, that even if
such evidence should be found, reason is not what counts,
that in view of that impasse, the unbeliever would rather
be left in peace. There are implications in that last
thought which are not touched on in section 1° as the
response 'La Machine' goes back to the previous sentence:
'cela ne lui servirait de rien.' One answer to this re-
fusal to enquire further is, however, given by an unclassed fragment, no. 387, entitled 'Ordre' and therefore
logically belonging to this section:

Ordre.
J'aurais bien plus peur de me tromper et de trouver que
la religion chrétienne soit vraie que non pas de me
tromper en la croyant vraie.

Like other fragments I have been discussing, this sentiment could be attributed to the half-converted opponent,
as part of the continuing dialogue,[16] but it could
equally well be Pascal's own position; it was for such
reasons that he was temperamentally incapable of understanding continued indifference.

The link which we find in no. 5, where the 'Machine'
is said to be the answer to doubts about the efficacity
of the proofs, is found again in no. 7, which also may
antedate no. 5: 'Lettre qui marque l'utilité des preuves.
Par la Machine.' The remainder of no. 7 reads like
Pascal's own formulation of the opponent's objection,
which he accepts as a valid one: 'La foi est différente
de la preuve. L'une est humaine et l'autre est un don de
Dieu.' Proof is at best the instrument of God-given faith,
faith being of the heart.

This rich cluster of ideas I shall be able to discuss
further, in connection with section 12°. One should note
that although the 'Discours de la Machine' can easily be
attached to section 12°, as we shall see, it does not
actually recur in any of the classified fragments.

I have said that there are fragments put into this
first bundle by Pascal whose connection with the theme
of Order is not immediately apparent. What I have just
written about the expansion of the sequel to the 'Lettre
pour porter à rechercher Dieu' will, however, help explain them. No. 2, for example ('Ordre par dialogues'),
gives two bewildered thoughts which could very approp-
riately strike one who was seeking 'chez les philosophes
... qui travailleront celui qui le recherche' (4), and
the two ideas mentioned in no. 3 belong to the stage of
the enquiry covered by the question: 'à quoi me servira
de chercher, rien ne paraît' (5). Ernst suggests plausibly
that the reply 'Vous vous trompez, il y a [...]' might
be voiced not by the apologist, sure of the immutability
of God, but by a dogmatist; Pascal would be playing one
philosophical school off against another.[17]

Two fragments remain: nos 1 and 8. No. 8, entitled
'Ordre,' cannot justifiably be separated from section 1°,
even if its content puts it more naturally with section
22°. And we should resist the temptation to ascribe the
inclusion of no. 1 (not titled, and closely allied to a
fragment placed by Pascal in section 17°, no. 204) to a
moment of carelessness. Both in fact grow out of the need
to give substance to the notion of 'light' and 'proof'

evoked in nos 5 and 7. For Pascal, the 'incontestable'
proofs - as opposed to the dubious proofs mentioned in
no. 3 - will be many and varied, and his argument will
draw heavily on the historical situation of the Jews,
and also on the Mahometans. Fragments 1 and 8 refer to
Mahometans and Jews respectively, no. 1 making an implied
comparison with the Jews. The ideas contained here expand
the notion that the evidence for God is to be sought in
the scriptures (6). Relevant also is the unclassified
no. 467:

Ordre.
Après la corruption dire: il est juste que tous ceux
qui sont en cet état le connaissent, et ceux qui s'y
plaisent, et ceux qui s'y déplaisent, mais il n'est
pas juste que tous voient la rédemption.

The idea will be developed in section 19°. Did Pascal
consider mentioning it in his first chapter, or is the
exclusion of no. 467 from the classified fragments a
sign that he did not think the preamble an appropriate
place for one of his subtlest reflections?
Our second enquiry has thus taken us a little further
than the first. Although the first impulse behind some
of the fragments was probably a wish to indicate how
gaps could be filled in and separate ideas related, the
broader canvas of no. 6 and (particularly) no. 12 put
things into new perspective, and Pascal kept for his
first bundle those fragments which would be relevant to
an elaboration of his basic intentions.[18] A reminder,
no more: one cannot believe that a first chapter would
have gone into as much detail as some of these fragments
suggest. That is the chief reason for not accepting Pol
Ernst's rather literal interpretation of this first
bundle as the nucleus of a preface in the form of an
exchange of letters. To certain objections (2 and 3),
Pascal would have countered, Ernst surmises, with the
first of two basic letters, urging the opponent to seek
God, before going on to urge him to change his way of
life. A second part would have given the plan of the
Apologia: the psychological tactics of no. 12 and the
two divisions of no. 6, which are amplified by 9 and
10 and by 8 and 1 respectively. Although one appreciates
Ernst's desire to make the first dossier a genuine opening section of the full Apologia, his rather complicated

solution does not satisfy us. It is difficult to see what would be gained by going over the ground – and such delicate ground – twice, the first time in a hurry and the second time with infinite care and subtlety. It would seem to me to be a gross error of tactics for Pascal to reveal so much so soon. Arguments of detail, developed before the opponent has been wooed into a responsive frame of mind by a portrayal of the problems posed by the human condition, and the philosophers' disputes about it, would lose all their effect, and undermine the Apologi itself.[19]

Fortunately the possibility exists of getting closer to Pascal's intentions. Among the unclassed fragments are some entitled 'Ordre,' and one headed 'Préface de la première partie.' They leave little doubt that the first bundle did have the function of a preface, and they suggest how most of the fragments, if not all (for problems do remain), could have been used in that context.

(c) Préface de la première partie (780)

Of the twelve fragments in Pascal's first dossier, only no. 12 specifically mentions first things. The plan Pascal intends to follow grows out of his understanding of why some men are hostile to religion. One can reasonably assume that an introduction would talk about the reasons for indifference. Pascal was always conscious of the adversary's independence, and would certainly have wanted to do all he could to ensure a sympathetic hearing of his case before he launched into the details of his argument. There are, however, no fragments one could confidently identify as belonging to a general preface.

Nor do the unclassed fragments mention a general preface. But one page contains both a 'Préface de la première partie' and a 'Préface de la seconde partie,' and the first paragraph of the first of these prefaces is very close in idea to three unclassed fragments entitled 'Ordre' and consequently destined for this first section. And one of these three fragments, no. 694, refers to a 'discours d'ordre.' On this evidence, it can be confidently stated that there would have been a section on 'Ordre' (the dossier, that is, does not just gather together a handful of working jottings), and that it would have had the function of a preface, if not to the whole Apologia, then at least to the first part.[20]

Fragment 780 ('Préface de la première partie') comprises
two paragraphs only. In the first Pascal announces that
he will 'parler de ceux qui ont traité de la connaissance
de soi-même, des divisions de Charron qui attristent et
ennuient.' He would therefore have used his preface to
criticize the way other writers have substituted neat
systems for true knowledge. Much more appropriate, he
says, is the 'confusion de Montaigne,' who leapt from
subject to subject.[21]
The three unclassed fragments entitled 'Ordre' echo
this first paragraph. Fragment 683 explains why Pascal
cannot rest satisfied with the traditional subdivisions
of *la morale*. The apparent advantage, of capturing a
complex issue in a quickly grasped formula, is in fact
no advantage, because if one idea is subsumed under another, it is concealed; to be itself seized it needs to
escape the categorization, and nothing is gained. It is
not in accordance with the laws of nature to tie one
thing up inside another. The final point is extended
slightly in no. 684.
In no. 694, he sees himself falling into the same trap,
setting out his thoughts on Vanity in a number of separate categories,

> mais l'ordre ne serait pas gardé. Je sais un peu ce
> que c'est, et combien peu de gens l'entendent. Nulle
> science humaine ne le peut garder. Saint Thomas ne
> l'a pas gardé. La mathématique le garde, mais elle
> est inutile en sa profondeur.[22]

In no. 532 (headed 'Pyrr[honisme],' implying that the
thoughts arose from reflecting on the sceptics, perhaps
meaning no more than that he had been reading Montaigne)
he puts in an uncompromising way his rejection of any
neat and over-simple order:

> Pyrr.
> J'écrirai ici mes pensées sans ordre et non pas peut-
> être dans une confusion sans dessein. C'est le véritable
> ordre et qui marquera toujours mon objet par le désordre
> même.
>   Je ferais trop d'honneur à mon sujet si je le traitais
> avec ordre puisque je veux montrer qu'il en est in-
> capable.[23]

Both these fragments (694 and 532) are, however, made in a very specific context, and I shall return to them.

After criticizing Charron and praising Montaigne for their contrasting approaches to handling their often similar material, fragment 780 goes on to qualify this praise for Montaigne. To write a self-portrait is, in Pascal's eyes, a mistaken ambition. Once again, other fragments amplify the ideas which no. 780 merely sketches. No. 649 puts the good and the bad in perspective, arguing that the absorption with the self in Montaigne's writings could have been corrected. (Montaigne's moral defects are more grave, and in no. 680 Pascal takes Montaigne to task for lasciviousness, credulity, and - particularly blame-worthy - a pagan attitude to dying, which is quoted in connection with section 12°.)

The self-portraiture of the *Essais* is not all loss, however, and Pascal allows that Montaigne's self-portrait does benefit the reader, who learns more about his own humanity through reading what Montaigne has written (689).[2] The notion is generalized and expanded in no. 652, where Pascal says we feel gratitude and sympathy for an author who opens our eyes. A preface could very easily accommodate this pair of *pensées* .

Would the thought they convey have carried Pascal to the topic of persuasion, very relevant to his problems as an apologist, having to cajole his opponent into accepting the religious position for himself? Very important in this connection is fragment 737 (XXVI), which follows on nicely from the remarks about self-knowledge through reading.

On se persuade mieux pour l'ordinaire par les raisons qu'on a soi-même trouvées que par celles qui sont venues dans l'esprit des autres.

But that is not Pascal's last word on the subject. Despite the fact that we are most deeply convinced by arguments of our own invention, Pascal knows that we can be influenced by the way a point is presented to us, and he wishes to avoid this kind of indirect influence on his opponent as much as possible, and leave all decisions to his opponent's judgment (his scepticism about human judgment notwithstanding) (529). Other fragments show Pascal's concern with coaxing the opponent and not offending him (669, cf. 584, 'éloquence qui persuade par

douceur'). Elsewhere Pascal the mathematician reflects
on the nature of proof, and the danger of simply amassing
examples which do not really constitute proof (527). In
addition to the fragments already cited, there are many
pensées on rhetoric, but here we begin to shade off into
an area which probably lies just outside the Apologia
proper.

The fragments I have been discussing have more the air
of personal memos - Pascal's attempts to define for his
own benefit the tone he should adopt in addressing the
interlocutor - than of statements intended for the public.[25] Probably all we need retain for a conjectural
preface is the belief that the apologist should hope
that his interlocutor will (with the apologist's discreet
help) arrive by his own reflections at the desired conclusions. It is logical to assume that by some such transition Pascal would have moved from Montaigne to define
his own purpose, and announce, briefly as befits an introduction, his general design.

This assumption is in fact supported by several fragments: not by the one entitled 'Préface,' which goes no
further than criticizing Montaigne for dwelling too long
on himself, but by those to which Pascal gave the title
'Ordre,' along with others, without title, which he put
in his first bundle. All we need do, to invent a transition, is to imagine the most natural movement away from
Montaigne: Pascal would surely have said that he wished
to lead his agnostic reader to make similar discoveries
about himself, and about man. And so, like Montaigne, he
has collected examples of human vanity (694), pinpointed
the problem, shown that the problem has not been solved,[26]
and that it will not be solved unless one takes religion
seriously, and undertakes a conscious search for God,
which will involve one in a regime of self-discipline.
This summary conflates no. 694 and various fragments in
1°: 4, 9, and 10 (which cover the same ground as 694);
12, 2, 5, 11, 387. Now fragment 694 ('Ordre') begins
with a significant phrase: 'J'aurais bien pris ce discours d'ordre comme celui-ci.' So we know there was to
have been a *discours d'ordre*, and that there is a natural
link between the preoccupations which were to have been
treated in it and some, if not all, of the material of
liasse 1°.[27]

In all probability, there would have been more to the
introduction than is contained in the sparse jottings of

Bundle 1° and in outlining this part of the Apologia in chapter 29, I discreetly amplify the data, drawing on the argument as it is actualized in the bundles Pascal constituted. One needs to add that by continuing beyond the letter in which the interlocutor is urged to seek God, and noting the kind of 'proofs' a rational and un-prejudiced enquirer may hope to find (8, 1), the first dossier seems to include more than just the material for an introductory chapter. It is perfectly possible that Pascal would have given a hint of the second part of his Apologia without arguing the point in detail, as in no. 6. In my summary (chapter 29) I place this broad view of the whole near the beginning, before Pascal embarks on the specific problems of organizing his material on the 'misère de l'homme.' This gives us a general statement of his approach (12) and overall design (6, amplified perhaps by 8 and 11), the thoughts on ordering the first part (780, 683-4, 694) and the sequel to this initial evocation of vanity: the need to search for God and the problems that entails (9, 10, 4, 2-3, 5, 11, 7), all admitted from the outset so that the reader will be pre-pared to trust him. Somewhere, no doubt, he would have remarked that although the individual observations he makes come from a common fund, the shape of his overall argument is new (696).

But we cannot tell exactly what might have happened, for, as fragment 694 shows, it was not long before Pascal ran into difficulties. The very first sequence would ap-pear, in résumé, to have all the faults of the 'divisions de Charron':

> J'aurais bien pris ce discours d'ordre comme celui-ci: pour montrer la vanité de toutes sortes de conditions, montrer la vanité des vies communes et puis la vanité des vies philosophiques, pyrrhoniennes, stoïques; mais l'ordre ne serait pas gardé.

Discouraged, Pascal abandoned, or postponed, the writing of a 'discours d'ordre.' 'La dernière chose qu'on trouve en faisant un ouvrage est de savoir celle qu'il faut mettre la première' (976). Fragments 683-4 and 696 were put to one side. So were the two paragraphs which record Pascal's decision to divide the introductory material between the two parts of his Apologia (780-1) - although one fragment entitled 'Préface' (190) did find its way into a dossier which occupies the place where the second preface would most conveniently fit.[28]

Nevertheless, not all was lost. Pascal did constitute a dossier 'Ordre,' initiated by a fragment which, in its revised form, gives a succinct overview of his strategy, and containing, as we have seen, many indications that he would have begun with a clear statement of his general approach. If in summarizing this statement we have had recourse to fragments which we know Pascal excluded from his classified papers, it is because by rejecting them, Pascal left a gap in his argument which he would have had to come to terms with one day. As he did not, we have no choice but to restore in spirit what he rejected in the letter.

Hasty conclusions have been drawn from the fragments discussed in this chapter. It is assumed by some that because Pascal will have no truck with the kind of systematic ordering favoured by Charron, the search for a plan is chimerical. But fragment 532, which would seem to lend substance to that argument ('J'écrirai ici mes pensées sans ordre...'), was plainly written at an early stage, when Pascal decided to amass a large number of disconnected fragments. Later, we know, he did undertake to classify them. Other fragments like 694 and 976[29] refer to the 'discours d'ordre,' and not to the whole enterprise, which Pascal nowhere disowned. Indeed he specifically asked that his originality be judged on the basis of 'la disposition des matières' (696). That classification does not entirely escape the charge of categorizing, à la Charron - particularly in the first chapters - but as we shall see, it develops a rhythm and a subtle counter-pointing, which may well be partly the cause of Pascal's impatience with a 'discours d'ordre' which, though necessary - one has to lead in somehow - could so easily have set the Apologia off on the wrong foot, by oversimplifying the complex and delicate argument.

2
Vanité

Having outlined his approach in the first 'discours,'
Pascal begins with the second section the exposition of
his intricate argument. It is not clear for some while
just where he is leading us. There are at least two reasons for this. Basically, Pascal's argument in this first
part is that if we limit ourselves to man's response to
the human condition outside the insights given by the
Christian religion, we shall find a series of unresolved
contradictions. As he is eventually to proceed by juxtaposing contradictory opinions, he has to begin by establishing at least one of the views which will later be
challenged. The first view chosen is the age-old belief
that 'all is vanity.' We shall find in chapter five, that
from one point of view, 'vain' beliefs can appear 'sane.'
Another fundamental tenet is that of the wretchedness of
the human condition. Is not the entire first part of the
Apologia designed to show the 'misère de l'homme sans
Dieu' (6)? Yet within the general picture of 'misère'
there are many nuances. The most important is that for
all his wretchedness, man is not devoid of greatness.
That will be the argument of section 6°, preparing for
the seventh section, which underlines the contradictory
nature of man. It is not surprising, then, that sections
2° and 3°, preparing the ground, are entitled, respectively, 'Vanité' and 'Misère.'

But there is another reason why the drift of these
early chapters is not immediately apparent. When we read
them carefully, we find that their function is not
clearly differentiated, that the main point emerges in
a rather devious way and is not the same as what the
titles 'Vanité' or 'Misère' imply; and we notice also
that there is a fourth bundle, headed 'Ennui et qualités
essentielles à l'homme,' which contains only three fragments (as compared with forty in 2° and twenty-four in

3°). In these first three sections there are clear signs
that some fragments were classified before the details
of the argument had settled in Pascal's mind, and in many
ways the sections overlap and repeat each other.[1] In my
summary of this part of the Apologia (chapter 29) I have
conflated 2°, 3°, and 4° to make a smoother flowing exposition. In chapter 31 (section a) I arrive at certain
conclusions about the way the plan must have come into
focus as Pascal diversified his chapter headings for
part one.

The themes of vanity and *misère* (the former, perhaps,
one specific manifestation of the latter) yield then,
in the course of the respective sections, to a different
preoccupation. The theme of the contradictory aspects of
the human condition is worked out in two principal fields:
man's search for the truth and man's search for happiness.
This point is made in section 2°. The first stage of the
demonstration will be to show that man is dependent on
too many factors to be able to pursue the truth with confidence and without deflecting. However, as stated above,
this theme emerges as the guiding idea only in retrospect; the evocation of the multiple aspects of our
weakness is more general.

The essence of sections 2° and 3° is contained in two
related fragments, one classified in 3° (75) and one
(403) not classified, but entitled (as an afterthought)
'Misère,' and referred to in section 3° (69):

Misère
Salomon et Job ont le mieux connu et le mieux parlé
de la misère de l'homme, l'un le plus heureux et
l'autre le plus malheureux. L'un connaissant la vanité
des plaisirs par expérience, l'autre la réalité des
maux (403).

L'Ecclésiaste montre que l'homme sans Dieu est dans
l'ignorance de tout et dans un malheur inévitable, car
c'est être malheureux que de vouloir et ne pouvoir. Or
il veut être heureux et assuré de quelque vérité. Et
cependant il ne peut ni savoir ni ne désirer point de
savoir. Il ne peut même douter (75).

Misère has a double aspect, corresponding to pleasure
and pain. To experience pain is to know our *misère*
directly, but experience of pleasure leads us to the

same awareness, because we come to see that it is 'vain.'
No. 75 explains *misère* in a more philosophical way, Without the aid of God we can have certain knowledge of nothing, and this too leads us to conclude that we are
wretched, as we have two basic needs, for happiness (the
word *heureux* here is strong, and implies deep satisfaction, experience of the sovereign good, etc.) and for
truth. Pascal does not expand on the first element of
the pair, but he is dogmatic about the second: we cannot
know if we have the truth, and we cannot silence our need
to know. Nor can we be content to doubt. All this is perhaps sufficient in itself to keep us from being 'heureux.'

As I have said, these two fragments are placed by Pascal
under the sign 'Misère.' A little later, he set up the
dossier 'Vanité,' which takes over all the themes just
analysed: not merely the vanity of pleasures, but also
the need for 'le vrai' and 'le bien,' and the impossibility of ever finding truth.

This second dossier turned out more substantial than
the third, and it sets the key to the rest, by its insistence on man's inability to reach truth unaided.

As in the previous chapter, I have first discussed the
fragments assigned to this dossier by Pascal (four sections), with the minimum assistance from the unclassified
fragments: 76; 197;[2] 413 (I); 634 (XXIV); 723 (XXV); 771
(XXVII); 890 (XXXIV); 1107. The very large amount of relevant unclassed material goes into a separate section (e).
The fragments used there are: 196; 412 (I); 505-8 (XX);
519, 531, 537, 542, 551-2, 558, 580-1, 583 (XXIII); 627-8,
630 (XXIV); 650, 656, 664, 671-3, 685, 697, 699, 709
(XXV); 742, 744, 750 (XXVI); 779 (XXVII); 802, 806, 814
(XXIX); 1104, 1106, 1107, 1108, and 1111.[3]

In the discussion of the second *liasse*, I shall develop
four points:

(a) the appearances of the word *vanité* give, as the basis
of the chapter, a simple collection of thoughts on the
preacher's text: 'All is vanity.' Pascal speaks of the
vanity of the world, of science, of respect for the so-
called great, of pleasure; and the same heading covers
the disproportion of cause and effect, and the prestige
of art, admired more than its own subject-matter.

(b) the section as a whole yields much more than this.
First, there is the distinction between two fields of endeavour (*le vrai*, *le bien*) and their relative importance.

(c) second, despite the claim that the search for *le bien*

is much more important than the search for truth, the
chapter concentrates on the inadequacy of reason, our instrument for discerning truth. Nos 44 and 45 give the main
thrust: the dominant role of the imagination, to which is
added a series of reflections on the elusiveness of justice,
the war between reason and the senses, and the influence
of amour-propre. Reason cannot solve its own problems.
(d) a final group, arising out of the theme of vanity by
a characteristically Pascalian explosion of ideas, brings
in the notion of 'le divertissement' and the wretchedness
of the human condition.
    A conclusion on these four sections relates the deve-
lopments to the starting-point, vanity.
(e) A large number of unclassified fragments can be attached to section 2° more readily than to any other section. In them we find echoes of the fragments on *le vrai*
and *le bien* and the impossibility of finding *le vrai*.
Imagination is treated in four fragments. The influence
of the senses of the body, the disproportionate effect
of small happenings, man's irrationality generally are
further illustrated. So are the theme of self-interest
and the allied themes of vanity and *gloire*.
    The conclusion must inevitably be that man is weak and
his weakness is spotlighted by the inadequacy of reason.
    It must be stressed that the order I have adopted in
this chapter is the order of presentation which I consider the best for my purpose. It would be foolish to claim
that Pascal would have adopted a similar order himself.
There was clearly a great deal of editorial work to be
done on this section before the material would be ready
to be written up.

(a) Qui ne voit pas la vanité du monde... (36)

The word *vanité*, which Pascal chooses as the title of
his second *liasse*, did not appear in the classified
pensees of section 1°, but an allied fragment (no. 694,
Ordre) suggests that the preface would have led off with
a demonstration of 'la vanité de toutes sortes de conditions.' Four fragments in the second section have the
title 'Vanité'; in three cases, the title was added after
the thought had been formulated. They are nos 16 ('Vanité.
Qu'une chose aussi visible qu'est la vanité du monde soit
si peu connue...'), 23 ('Vanité des sciences'), and 32
(Vanité. Les respects signifient: incommodez-vous'). This

last idea reappears in no. 80 (5°, untitled), where it
calls forth the comment: 'Cela est vain...' In the fourth
instance, no. 46, the title seems to have been written at
the same time as the fragment itself: 'Vanité. La cause
et les effets de l'amour. Cléopâtre.' This cryptic note
is plainly a reminder Pascal made, when he was working
on the second dossier, to include an idea we find formulated in two other fragments: nos 197 and 413.[4] In both
these fragments the disproportion between the cause and
effect of Antony's love for Cleopatra is cited as a perfect illustration of vanity. The word can be read in two
other fragments belonging to the second section: no. 36
('Qui ne voit pas la vanité du monde est bien vain lui-
même') and 40 ('Quelle vanité que la peinture...'), to
which we must add the 'durée vaine' of no. 31, referring
to the length of man's stay in a particular town, and
the quotation from Ecclesiastes, repeated in the Epistle
to the Romans, which is found in no. 14: 'Omnis creatura
subjecta est vanitati.'

If we extend our search to the other sections and to
the unclassified fragments, we can find many more instances of the word vanity. The clearest idea of what it
meant for Pascal comes in no. 93 (5°): 'Nous avons donc
montré que l'homme est vain par *l'estime qu'il fait des
choses qui ne sont point essentielles.*'[5] In these examples vanity has the Old Testament sense, all is vanity.
The modern meaning - desiring the esteem of others - is
also present as the theme of no. 31 and other fragments,
and the word is occasionally used elsewhere in that sense,
but such is not the implication of the title.[6]

We can therefore detect a simple idea at the basis of
this section, well summed up in no. 93. The things to
which we attach so much importance are 'vain,' although
we hide that fact from ourselves (36). Desire for honour
and prestige is one instance (16). Fragment 32 implies
the same thing. We respect and admire painting, not seeing that we are forced into inconsistency (40).[7] The
space and time we occupy on earth is so infinitesimal,
it is a sign of vanity that we attach the importance we
do to our existence (31). The observation about Cleopatra
illustrates 'vanity' by the wild disproportion between
cause and effect. Antony's love for Cleopatra was aroused
by a trivial detail, and that love had a far-reaching effect upon the destiny of the Roman empire. Akin to this
is the reminder of the bitter dispute within certain

religious orders over a matter as unimportant as the
length of a monk's cowl (18).
A basic layer of *liasse* 2°, then, has to do with the
false importance we attribute to things.

(b) incapables et de vrai et de bien (28)

In fact, this second bundle proves more ambitious in its
range than the fragments explicitly dealing with vanity
might suggest. One related theme (*le divertissement*,
which keeps young men from realizing the vanity of their
existence, 36) will be discussed in section (d) below.
Another can be traced to a fragment entitled 'Vanité des
sciences,' no. 23:

Vanité des sciences.
La science des choses extérieures ne me consolera pas
de l'ignorance de la morale au temps d'affliction,
mais la science des moeurs me consolera toujours de
l'ignorance des sciences extérieures.

The two sciences mentioned in no. 23 can be linked with
the twin motif of *le vrai* and *le bien* which is so important for the structure of the Apologia. It comes in other
fragments from this section (21, 28), and a sentence
struck from the manuscript of no. 44 read: '(L'imagination) juge souverainement du bien, du vrai, du juste.'
The intent of nos 21 and 28 is not to establish a hier-
archy between 'le vrai' and 'le bien' as in no. 23 but to
show that we are incapable of attaining either. In no. 21,
which I shall quote again in another context as it impinges also on the relation of reason and the senses,
Pascal observes that error comes if we cannot find the
juste milieu between two unbalanced positions. But whereas the science of perspective can teach us where is the
correct vantage-point for viewing a painting, who, he
asks, can tell us where the vantage point is 'dans la
vérité et dans la morale?'
Fragment 28, which expands an earlier (unclassed)
pensée, no. 890, is verbally more complex:

Faiblesse.
Toutes les occupations des hommes sont à avoir du bien
et ils ne sauraient avoir de titre pour montrer qu'ils
le possèdent par justice, car ils n'ont que la fantaisie

> des hommes, ni force pour le posséder sûrement.
>   Il en est de même de la science. Car la maladie l'ôte.
>   Nous sommes incapables et de vrai et de bien.

The complexity here comes from the play on words on the word 'bien.' The concreteness of the opening leads us to interpret 'du bien' as the equivalent of 'des biens.' Pol Ernst summarizes it by the phrase 'droit de propriéte.'[8] But by the end of the *pensée*, it is surely to be understood in the sense of that which gives the maximum satisfaction, which is the meaning it usually has in Pascal. Taken on the strictly concrete level, Pascal's thought is that neither justice nor force offers a foolproof guarantee of our right to possessions. Another very important fragment, no. 44, will introduce a similar idea.

No. 44, however, and the many fragments which it is convenient to relate to it, have more to do with truth and justice than with anything covered by the phrase 'la morale,' despite the fact that in no. 23 Pascal had implied that 'la morale' is a more important endeavour than the 'recherche du vrai.' Pascal will return to the 'recherche du bien,' in the usual sense of that term, in later sections (8°-10°). For the time being, he concentrates on the search for truth, the present section being dominated by the very long fragment entitled 'Imagination,' no. 44, which demolishes all man's claims for certainty in this sphere. Justice is an important subsidiary theme also, but it is not given as full a treatment as 'le vrai' and 'le bien.'

(c) *le chapitre des puissances trompeuses (45)*

For all its length, fragment 44 is not a complete essay. It is, rather, an essay of moderate length swollen by a long addition and a gigantic appendix. It begins as a reflection on 'cette partie dominante dans l'homme ... cette superbe puissance ennemie de la raison', and the first part deals with imagination, continually at war with reason and mocking our claim to be rational creatures. The basic argument is clear: imagination is no guide to truth or falsity, it has created a second nature, imaginative as opposed to reasonable. It brings a satisfaction reason cannot bring. If our imagination is not satisfied by something, we depreciate that thing.

From this point, Pascal proceeds by examples which bring
to light different aspects of the workings of the imagination. They include the law courts; 'l'affection ou la
haine changent la justice de face.' Several lines crossed
out on the manuscript show that Pascal was going to conclude his first part here and pass to the second but,
evidently struck by the appositeness of his reference to
justice, he added a paragraph on the measures taken by
magistrates to impress people's imagination, and this
suggested a new development (to which we shall return)
on the contrast between justice, obliged to have recourse
to an appeal to imagination, and force, which speaks its
own unambiguous language. Then Pascal returns to his conclusion:

> L'imagination dispose de tout; elle fait la beauté, la
> justice et le bonheur qui est le tout du monde.
> ...
> Voilà à peu près les effets de cette faculté trompeuse...

Here, recalling one of the sentences crossed out earlier
to make way for the passage on magistrates ('Voilà un des
principes d'erreur, mais ce n'est pas le seul'), Pascal
immediately added: 'Nous en avons bien d'autres principes,'
and so his essay on imagination receives an unexpected
extension, in which he lists three 'principes d'erreur'
to be added to the 'maîtresse d'erreur,' imagination.
New ideas carry no surer guarantee of their truth than
do established views, and the education which might correct error is itself unreliable. Second, illnesses 'nous
gâtent le jugement et le sens' (cf. no. 28, penultimate
sentence). And self-interest blinds us, as the laws of
the courts of justice recognize. 'La justice et la vérité
sont deux pointes si subtiles que nos instruments sont
trop mousses pour y toucher exactement.'
At this point the ideas are about to proliferate in
all directions, and drawing a line through the last sentences on the page, Pascal begins again with a paragraph
on what he had just called 'la guerre qui est entre les
sens et la raison' - a fourth additional principle -
noting 'Il faut commencer par là le chapitre des puissances trompeuses.'[9] Imagination, the starting-point of
no. 44, therefore becomes just one element in a 'chapter'
on 'les puissances trompeuses.'

The length and the sustained concentration of these pages force us to regard the ideas as the central themes of this second section. Other classified fragments comment on them, others give a new development to things merely hinted in no. 44, and we find that some fragments headed 'Vanité' fall into place nicely once no. 44 is accepted as the key.

One section of no. 44 has several echoes in other fragments placed in this second bundle: the added passage on magistrates and justice. In it Pascal explains that all the paraphernalia adopted by magistrates to impress people ('ces vains instruments qui frappent l'imagination') is fully justified, as our imagination dictates our attitude much more than cool reason does. The other way to impress people is by a show of force (less debatable than a claim to be just or reasonable), and rulers who do have this advantage display it. There is an echo of these thoughts in no. 28, already quoted, but there Pascal questioned whether force was strong enough to be a firm basis.

Further reflections on the idea of force can be found in fragments 25 and 26. We are so accustomed to seeing kings surrounded by visible signs of power that when we see them alone we immediately think of power, by association, and imagine kings to bear in their own persons the mark of authority. No. 26 begins: 'La puissance des rois est fondée sur la raison et sur la folie du peuple,' but we have to wait for section 5° for an explanation. Pascal's conclusion here is that there is no surer foundation than this 'folly,' weakness being much more certain to be found than reason.

The brief jotting numbered 19 also has to do with power: 'Il a quatre laquais' (and therefore should be treated with respect).

One sentence of no. 44 implies that men do not have 'la véritable justice.' 'Il demeure au-delà de l'eau' writes Pascal enigmatically (20); the note is expanded in no. 51, echoing no. 9 in the first bundle, where it was assigned to a 'lettre de l'injustice':

Pourquoi me tuez-vous à votre avantage? Je n'ai point d'armes.
- Et quoi, ne demeurez-vous pas de l'autre côté de l'eau? N
ami, si vous demeuriez de ce côte, je serais un assassin,
cela serait injuste de vous tuer de la sorte. Mais puisque
demeurez de l'autre côte, je suis un brave et cela est jus

'Plaisante justice qu'une rivière borne,' Pascal adds in
no. 60 (3°). Custom, rather than objective reason or
natural justice, governs laws of international relations.
  Perhaps we should fit in here the pair of fragments on
class structure, also dictated by differing customs
rather than by reason (30, 50).
  This is very little on which to build a political philosophy, and the matter will be properly explained only
in sections 3° and 5°. But section 2° does contain a kind
of conclusion, when Pascal writes that Christians accept
to be subjected to the established order (14). It is,
however, too early to understand the implications of this.
  Another main theme, outlined in no. 45 and in the last
sentence (deleted) of no. 44, is the war between reason
and the senses. No. 48 points out sarcastically how
easily 'rational' man is distracted by the slightest
noise, such as a fly's buzzing. No. 22 observes laconi-
cally that flies have other powers as well as that of
distracting us from thought.
  For our reason to function as it should, other conditions, having much more to do with the senses than with
reason, have to be fulfilled. This idea brings us back
to no. 21, which passed from the observation that reason
needed the co-operation of the senses in physical matters
(echoed in 38 and 41, the last-named doubling 723), to
the question: what could fulfil the conditions necessary
to decide abstract issues, in the fields of 'la vérité'
and 'la morale'? Thus the diverse topics belonging to
this section come back ultimately to the question of the
ground of our convictions and our actions, a motif which
recurs many times (26, 28, 33, 44). Senses and imagination combine to cause love. No. 46, on 'la cause et les
effets de l'amour,' would fit in here. But Pascal is as
much interested in the catastrophic effects as in the
trivial causes of Antony's love.
  One group bears on the general irrationality of human
behaviour. How do we account for the existence of a
ruler who combines with his power the life of an honest
worker (17, headed 'Inconstance et Bizarrerie')? Why
should a middle-aged man pursue fame and glory with the
appetite of a young man (49, on Caesar)? Why should we
laugh at the proximity of two faces, neither of which is
funny in itself (13)? Why should we admire the portrait
of a man whom we do not admire for his own qualities?
(40; we recall no. 44: 'l'imagination ... fait la
beauté').

Although self-interest is not discussed in the other
classified fragments (it is fully covered in several unclassed ones), the related theme of vanity in the modern
sense is mentioned several times. It is all part of 'cet
amour-propre' (44). Self-esteem is another motivation
which is not rational in origin. No. 31 points out that
our need for the esteem of others varies with the time
we are likely to spend in a given society; passers-by
do not require it. A reminder of our true perspective
is furnished by no. 42; 'Combien de royaumes nous ignorent!' 'La source de nos inclinations et du choix des
conditions' is often a word of admiration for someone
else which we overhear and which makes us envious (35).
The fullest gloss on this fragment is afforded by no. 634.

One particular manifestation of this need is 'la gloire,'
which makes a man prize good opinion higher than life itself. No. 37 is entitled 'Métiers,' thus linking it with
no. 35:

Métiers.
La douceur de la gloire est si grande qu'à quelque
objet qu'on l'attache, même à la mort, on l'aime.

No. 29 quotes Livy (via Montaigne) on the mass suicide
of the citizens of certain conquered Spanish cities;
Pascal concludes: 'Toute opinion peut être préférable à
la vie, dont l'amour paraît si fort et si naturel.' No.
15 cites the example of Paulus Aurelius's prisoner, the
King of Macedonia.

The last example recurs in section 6°, and the general
theme in 3°. Ernst associates with this group nos 16
('chercher les grandeurs') and 49 (Caesar), both of which
have to do with ambition as a driving force.

Cited in this section on reason is a fragment which is
found, crossed out, on the verso of fragment 60, filed
in section 3°: no. 76. The theme is the inadequacy of
reason in its own sphere. Pascal illustrates the contrary
identifications that have been made of *le souverain bien*,
the conflicting views held of the nature of the soul (cf.
1107) and of the body. It is true, Pascal adds in conclusion, that reason recognizes that it has not yet found
the truth, but it will not admit that it can never find
it. This claim must be destroyed.

These sentiments are echoed in no. 33. The astonishing
thing is, says Pascal, that in spite of all this over-

whelming evidence, men still exist who believe that we
can attain truth and justice. The existence of such
people serves only to strengthen the case of the pyrrhonians that man is 'capable des plus extravagantes opinions,'
a point cryptically made in no. 34.

Pyrrhonians are also mentioned in no. 52. There is no
logical reply to their position; their opponents can only
accuse them of bad faith. Man is indeed 'incapable du
vrai' (28).

(d) peu de chose nous console (43)

A final group of *pensées* touch on the notion of *le divertissement* and beyond that on the state of man generally.
le divertissement is the theme of section 8°, and it is
linked with the theme of *la misère* (3°), as we already
know from a fragment classed in the first bundle (10).
Fragment 36 shows why the theme is connected to this
second bundle also; this may well be the germ of the
later development. Just as the justice-force contrast
intruded into the essay on imagination, so here a simple
question on vanity receives an answer which raises a
totally new issue.

> Qui ne voit pas la vanité du monde est bien vain lui-
> même. Ainsi qui ne la voit, excepté de jeunes gens qui
> sont tous dans le bruit, dans le divertissement et dans
> la pensée de l'avenir.
> Mais ôtez leur divertissement vous les verrez se
> sécher d'ennui. Ils sentent alors leur néant sans le
> connaître, car c'est bien être malheureux que d'être
> dans une tristesse insupportable, aussitôt qu'on est
> réduit à se considérer, et à n'en être point diverti.

No. 47 is a particularly impressive and polished fragment on our inability to live fully each present moment,
preoccupied as we are with the past and (more frequently)
the future ('la pensée de l'avenir' of no. 36).

Fragment 39 also evokes the activities we invent to
distract us: chasing balls or hares ('le bruit' in the
same sentence of no. 36). This could be linked with
either the theme of vanity or the theme of irrationality,
but we do not know exactly what connection Pascal had in
mind when he classed this fragment with his second dossier.

What is the human condition, that man has to stop himself from thinking about? The question is fully answered only in section 8°, but section 2° does contain a couple of fragments on inconstancy, somewhat loosely connected with the main preoccupations of the rest of the section.
No. 24 notes three aspects of the human condition:

Condition de l'homme
Inconstance, ennui, inquiétude.

(Here Pascal comes perilously close to the 'divisions de Charron' criticized in his notes for a preface (780).) The jotting has more bearing on sections 3° and 4° than on 2°. No. 27, however, is about inconstancy, and no. 17 is entitled 'Inconstance et Bizarrerie.' When I quoted this last-named, I used the theme of *bizarrerie* rather than *inconstance* to connect it to the rest of the section. 'Inconstance' will recur as a title twice in section 3°. No. 27 detects in regular inconstancy a basic law of the universe and no. 771 expends further on this idea.
Finally, I follow Pol Ernst in associating no. 43 with the *pensées* on the human condition: 'Peu de chose nous console parce que peu de chose nous afflige.' Man lacks the true 'science des moeurs' which would offer genuine consolation (23).
It will be clear that two separate notions govern the organization of section 2°. The basic notion of vanity provides a first loose group of *pensées*. But the idea of imagination and man's fruitless attempts to find truth provokes a rich crop of new thoughts, and many fragments explore one or more of the countless aspects contained in this idea. In retrospect, the fragments entitled 'Vanité' can be made relevant to the new theme: not only no. 23, which I used to introduce it, but also no. 46 on the causes and effects of love, 16 on the desire for prestige, and 32 on respect. The last-named are not far removed from the twin concerns of justice and force, which grew out of the *pensées* on imagination.
My position then is that the section headed 'Vanité' absorbed elements of a 'chapitre sur les puissances trompeuses' which itself contained some elements of a 'lettre de l'injustice.' The section on vanity collected a large number of fragments, and so Pascal decided to open new dossiers to develop some of these ideas further, without removing the relevant fragments from the 'Vanité' file

itself. Consequently we shall be reminded of *pensées*
classified in 2° not only when 3° is discussed, but also
when we read later sections, notably 4°, 5°, 8°, and 14°.
Mention must be made of Ernst's distribution of the
forty fragments of section 2°. He proposes three subdivisions: 'Les puissances trompeuses dans l'ordre du vrai,
dans l'ordre du bien, dans l'ordre du bonheur,' to which
he gives the subtitles: 'La vanité de la vérité, la vanité
de la justice, la vanité de la béatitude.'[10] This is a
very satisfying scheme, but I belive that clarity has
been achieved at the expense of flexibility, and that
Ernst does not give enough consideration to the signs of
new directions, of new categories being discovered as
Pascal writes. I am not convinced that we should fit the
ideas into a scheme dictated largely by thematic considerations, and call it 'la structure dynamique de toute
la liasse.' I shall not commit myself to any opinion on
'dynamic structure' until we reach section 5°.

The links between the various centres of this chapter
become more intricate, and also more suggestive, when we
add the many unclassified fragments which have some relation to the themes we have discussed. So far I have
limited myself to a handful of indispensable reference-
points. But there are many more. In presenting them, I
shall follow the same general plan as in sections (b)
to (d).

(e) il faut ajouter (576)

In fragment no. 21 (see section b), Pascal had asked for
a criterion to help us find 'le vrai' and 'le bien,' akin
to the laws of perspective in painting. Four unclassed
fragments echo this fragment. The same parallel with
painting reappears in no. 558 where it is related also
to the infinite diversity of phenomena, and through that
to the disadvantages of rigid classification noted in
chapter 1 (section c). In nos 697 and 699 the analogue
has become a ship drifting away from land; the harbour
is a 'point fixe' which enables us to assert that it is
the ship and not the land which is moving. We need a
similar certainty in 'la morale.' No. 505 on the authority
for belief contains the argument that 'nier, croire et
douter' are as natural to men as running is to horses,
but whereas we can judge a horse's performance, we have
no rule we can apply to men's beliefs.

This last example brings the theme into a clear relation with one of the key notions of the chapter: the inadequacy of reason. We should not be content with hear-
say, or we would be forced to believe contradictory
things, nor with the authority of the ancients (what
authority did they have?), nor with universal agreement,
impossible to obtain, but only with 'le consentement de
vous à vous-même et la voix constante de votre raison.'
Yet once we examine the situation carefully, we see that
we have no option but to deny, accept, or doubt, and we
have no way of judging which of the three reactions is
the reasonable one.

Consequently, we do not know how to acquire thoughts;
they come by chance, and they disappear by chance (542).
Correct thinking could be trained by choosing carefully
those with whom we have dealings. But we cannot choose
well if we do not already think well, and thus we are
trapped in a vicious circle (814). What should our reaction be to the ignorance which we cannot dispel? One
fragment argues that 'common errors' have the good effect
of discouraging useless curiosity (744).

Pascal's second bundle was dominated by the fragment
on imagination, with its development listing other enemies of reason. Some of these ideas recur in the unclassed fragments.

Three mention the imagination. It is our imagination,
not our reason, which makes us attach great importance to
certain things in our lives, as 'un autre tour d'imagination' can at any time prove (531). Imagination magnifies
or reduces everything to our own size, he says in no. 551,
which relates this to our spiritual life. From the power
of the imagination, Pascal deduces not that we should
therefore follow it, as natural, but that we should resist it (196). There is a nice observation on the superior
strength of inclination compared to duty, and the corollary (1104).

The influence of the body is mentioned in two fragments,
nos 552 and 580. The first takes issue with Cicero, who
had remarked that we are dependent on the weather. Pascal
notes that his own moods are influenced more by forces
within than by things without. Even ill fortune can be
accompanied by a gay spirit, and good fortune by depres-
sion.[11] No. 580 is more neutral and offers the intriguing
thought that our notion of symmetry, which we look for
on a horizontal rather than a vertical plane, derives
from the position of our two eyes.

On the trivial causes of major events, and paralleling
the example of Cleopatra, is the recent instance of the
death of Cromwell, brought about by a tiny grain of sand,
and followed by the restoration of the monarchy (750).
More examples can be found to illustrate men's irrationality. Fragments 506, 507, and 508 consist almost
entirely of quotations from Roman authors, cited by
Montaigne, which could be used. No. 581 notes the absurdity portrayed by Scaramouche and by the doctor of farce.
    Pascal wrote in no. 44 that we dare not systematically
mistrust imagination, as it is sometimes beneficial.
Apparently self-interest is not an infallible guide either,
as people can act (tell lies, for example) with no such
motivation (742).
    Another aspect of amour-propre raised by no. 44 and
section 2° was man's need to be well thought of. 'Vanity'
in this sense is universal (627), found even in those who
denounce it ('moi qui écris ceci'). Pascal observes wryly
that 'On se retire et cache huit mois à la campagne, pour
en vivre quatre avec éclat à la Cour' (1108). Curiously,
we do not always do what we could to earn other people's
good opinion, simply citing referees (650), or talking
too much of our virtues (671). Our failure to reach *le
vrai* or *le bien* becomes a cause for pride (537).
    Fragment 628 ('Du désir d'être estimé de ceux avec qui
on est') reminds us that 'Nous perdons encore la vie avec
joie pourvu qu'on en parle.' The two themes are both present also in no. 806, where Pascal argues that we put an
imaginary, public self above our real self. Reputation
is more important to us than the reality. The supreme example is when a man's honour can only be saved if he
himself dies. The absurdity of *gloire* is further shown
in fragment 685, which points out that it is not found
in animals which compete with each other.
    All these diverse examples illustrate the weakness of
man and the vanity of his pretensions. Our nature is that
of an animal (630, 664). Anxiety (cf. no. 24) belongs not
to the mind alone, but to the self (583). We are always
subject to change (673, 802, also 519) - although we must
not forget a balancing truth; 'On a beau dire: il est crû,
il est changé, il est aussi le même' (779). This idea of
change is linked to the concern with reason, as when
Pascal writes that we never judge a thing twice in the
same way (672). For the idea of the inadequacy of our
reason is never far away. The cause of error is not
merely an individual failing, it is inevitable, given

human inadequacy (1111; the idea reappears at the end of
76). To wish to be totally reasonable is not reasonable
(412). Sleep is not an image of death, but of life (1106).
We cannot even know whether we are near to dying (709).
The thinker must be led to acknowledge the unpalatable
truth about the human condition. Whether I think my
thoughts through to their logical conclusion, or lose
track of them, the effect is the same: to strengthen my
conviction of 'mon néant' (656).

3
Misère

It is diffucult to avoid the impression that Pascal's
third dossier is simply an expansion of some of the
themes of the second. The parallels are so numerous that
it becomes a considerable test of one's ingenuity to draw
a clear dividing line between the two. Jean Mesnard makes
a broad distinction between 'le vrai' (2°) and 'le bien'
(3°), and defines 3° thus: 'Incapable d'atteindre la
vérité, l'homme trouvera-t-il le bien, sous ses trois
formes, vertu, justice, bonheur?'² This distinction certainly makes good sense of the result as we have it. But
it is by no means certain that Pascal was himself guided
by so clear a demarcation when he classified his fragments.
  Only one of the twenty-four fragments included by Pascal
in the dossier he entitled 'Misère' actually has *Misère*
as its own title, and that is ultracryptic:

Misère
Job et Salomon (69).

There are other fragments mentioning Job and Solomon
which I shall use both to elucidate no. 69 and also to
supply a framework for the discussion. One of these is
the *pensée* (403) which I also used to help define the
word Vanity in the previous chapter. We there saw the
twin themes of vanity and the inadequacy of reason as
aspects of man's wretchedness, and a fragment on Solomon
in the third section (75) strengthens this interpretation.
There are other aspects of *misère*, however, notably two
themes mentioned (but not explained) in another fragment
(74) which also couples the names of Job and Solomon:
conupiscence and injustice. There remain a handful of
isolated fragments which comment on various aspects of
misère mentioned in one or other of these two sections.

In greater detail, this discussion covers the following
matters:
(a) the 'vanité des plaisirs' and the 'realité des maux'
of 403, both treated in section 2°, here prompt thoughts
about man's fickleness and about 'le divertissement.'
(Most fragments on the latter are located in section 8°.)
References to Solomon lead us to consider *pensées* on the
inadequacy of reason and on concupiscence.
(b) the theme of concupiscence is not mentioned in any
of the other fragments in this section, but it is extensively treated outside the classified papers. Pascal in-
stitutes a dialogue with the *honnête homme* on this issue;
I have added a note citing other fragments on *honnêteté*,
less bellicose in tone.
(c) a main preoccupation of this section is injustice,
and the uncertain basis of laws. We have no way to recognize absolute justice, and have to rely on custom.
(d) certainty, stability, contentment, are all elusive.
We must try to understand ourselves, not because we can
discover truth, but because we will be doomed to *misère*
and injustice if we do nothing - however pleased with
ourselves we sometimes appear to be.
   It is clear that sections 2° and 3° explore different
facets of a single theme, that theme - the 'misère de
l'homme' - being most clearly adumbrated in section 3°.
Pascal is less interested in clear-cut thematic divisions
than in an argument based on the cut and thrust of dialectic. This method might conveivably be implied by no.
71, the fragment with which I conclude, but it does not
emerge clearly until a little later in the Apologia.
   I call upon the following unclassified *pensées*: 403
(I); 421 (II); 465 (XI); 597 (XXIV); 642, 657, 668 (XXV);
749 (XXXIV); 889 (XXXIII); 978.[3]

(a) Job et Salomon (69)

Only one of the fragments placed by Pascal in his third
bundle has the title 'Misère': no. 69, quoted at the
beginning of this chapter. It is clearly a reminder to
Pascal to include in his dossier a fragment mentioning
Job and Solomon. For this, there are two possible candidates. Of the classified fragments, only no. 74 qualifies,
but it is hardly less enigmatic, and if the pages are in
the order in which Pascal compiled them, no. 74 must already have been filed. The other, much more likely,
possibility is no. 403, which Pascal dictated.

Misère
Salomon et Job ont le mieux connu et le mieux parlé de
la misère de l'homme, l'un le plus heureux et l'autre
le plus malheureux. L'un connaissant la vanité des
plaisirs par expérience, l'autre la réalité des maux.

I shall take separately three motifs of this fragment
(the 'vanité des plaisirs,' the 'réalité des maux,' and
Solomon), and see how far they allow us to penetrate
into the third section.
As we have seen, the vanity of pleasures was a basic
layer of section 2°, although the precise phrase did not
appear in that section. It does, however, turn up in section 3°, no. 73, which links the experience of pleasure
with an observed characteristic of man, fickleness.

Le sentiment de la fausseté des plaisirs présents et
l'ignorance de la vanité des plaisirs absents cause
l'inconstance.

We have already met inconstancy as a theme in section 2°,
(17, 24, 27); it is the title of two fragments of section
3°: no. 55, which compares man to the pipes of an organ,
playable but 'bizarres, changeantes, variables' (no. 17
had allied *inconstance* and *bizarrerie* also), and no. 54
on the 'diversity' of the human soul.
As for *misère* in the sense of 'la réalité des maux,'
this is not an aspect pressed by Pascal, who is more
interested in the philosophical and psychological implications than in purely physical phenomena. The word
misère/misérable does not figure in other fragments of
section 3°, but the word *malheureux* is close in meaning,
and is found in no. 56, which recalls the search for the
mean in section 2°:

Nous sommes si malheureux que nous ne pouvons prendre
plaisir à une chose qu'à condition de nous fâcher si
elle réussit mal, ce que mille choses peuvent faire et
font à tout heure. Qui aurait trouvé le secret de se
réjouir du bien sans se fâcher du mal contraire aurait
trouvé le point. C'est le mouvement perpétuel.

Allied with this is no. 70: 'Si notre condition était
véritablement heureuse, il ne faudrait pas nous divertir
d'y penser.' This is a slightly shorter version of no.
889. We are perhaps surprised that there are no more

fragments on the theme of *le divertissement*, which was
linked with *misère* in no. 36, and no. 10 in section 1°.
The reason why the idea is not developed here is that
Pascal decided to consecrate an independent chapter to
it (8°). There are two indications that 'Divertissement'
started off as a division of 'Misère': two developments
of the theme, fragments 414 and 136, the latter being
the cornerstone of section 8°, are entitled 'Misère.'[4]
   The third motif in no. 403 was Solomon, and this too
takes us no further than ground already covered in the
previous section, making the section 'Misère' appear as
a conclusion to the reflections on Vanity. The reference
in no. 403 to Solomon, presumed author of the book
Ecclesiastes, is explained by no. 75, which also employs
the word 'malheureux':

   L'Ecclésiaste montre que l'homme sans Dieu est dans
   l'ignorance de tout et dans un malheur inévitable, car
   c'est être malheureux que de vouloir et ne pouvoir. Or
   il veut être heureux et assuré de quelque vérité. Et
   cependant il ne peut ni savoir ni ne désirer point de
   savoir. Il ne peut même douter.

This is clearly the best definition of the 'misère de
l'homme sans Dieu' and we quoted it at the outset of
chapter 2. It balances no. 28 ('Nous sommes incapables
et de vrai et de bien'). One difference between the two
fragments is that whereas no. 28 had rather more to say
about 'le bien' than 'le vrai,' with no. 75 it is the
other way round. This is curious, because section 2°,
where no. 28 was filed, tended to emphasize the inadequacy
of reason, whereas section 3°, where we find no. 75,
deals more with 'le bien' - happiness and justice. If
we exclude no. 76, which only belongs by accident to section 3° (it was discussed in chapter 2), we have only one
fragment which implies the weakness of reason as an instrument: no. 65, entitled 'Diversité.' (The title may
recall to mind no. 54, although the theme is different.)
No. 65 is very close to no. 558, which I included in my
discussion of section 2° because of its conclusion, which
joined up with no. 21. We have names and labels, Pascal
says in no. 65, but everything can be divided into sub-
categories 'à l'infini.'

*(b) pas moyen de satisfaire leur concupiscence sans faire
tort aux autres (74)*

Still using Job and Solomon as our Ariadne's thread, we
find two more important themes, and both relate more
easily to 'le bien' than to 'le vrai.' Job and Solomon
are mentioned again in fragment 74:

> Injustice.
>   Ils n'ont point trouvé d'autre moyen de satisfaire
> leur concupiscence sans faire tort aux autres.
>   Job et Salomon.

The word 'injustice' here applies to the self-assertion
of the individual, making unjust demands of others.[5] The
general theme of injustice will be discussed in section
(c) of this chapter.
   Fragment 74 is the only hint that section 3° would have
included thoughts on concupiscence. There are a large
number of unclassed fragments on the topic. Concupiscence
is not only unreasonable, it is an obstacle in the way
of happiness.
   The starting-point appears to be the so-called wager
manuscript ('Infini rien'), where Pascal writes that it
is unreasonable and unjust that we expect to be loved,
but it is born with us (421a).[6] He continues by saying
that order requires a movement from the particular to
the general, and that in reversing this movement, the
will is evidently 'depraved.' The manuscript containing
this fragment is a particularly rich one, and the idea
just quoted leads Pascal to remark that it is a strong
point in favour of Christianity that it alone teaches that
man is born in sin. Such an idea could not have come into
the Apologia at this stage, but it is interesting that
the same connection is made in another fragment (no. 617).
   Every man puts himself at the centre, above everyone
else; 'quel dérèglement de jugement!' (749). No. 668
explains why we do this:

> Chacun est un tout à soi-même, car lui mort le tout
> est mort pour soi. Et de là vient que chacun croit
> être tout à tous. Il ne faut pas juger de la nature
> selon nous mais selon elle.

Pascal wrote a sustained essay on *l'amour-propre*, no.
978. Starting from the same point about the *moi* wanting
to be loved and realizing that that is an unreasonable
desire, the essay develops the notion that the *moi* becomes as a result inescapably committed to combatting the
truth. Once again, therefore, we have Pascal defining
an obstacle in the way of our attainment of the truth.

Concupiscence also obstructs our efforts to attain happiness. Three fragments imagine a dialogue with the
honnête homme on the points just made (597, 642, 657).
It is a fact, says Pascal in no. 597, that 'le moi est
haïssable.' All the *honnête homme* can do is to make the
self less troublesome to others; he cannot take away the
basic injustice of the self's essential nature. No. 642
adds that the *honnête homme* sees that the ideas of those
who think like him go against the grain, but he cannot
explain why. Both these fragments explicitly mention
Miton. No. 657 answers another possible objection, that
pity for the suffering would seem to argue against concupiscence. Not at all, replies Pascal in his most La
Rochefoucauld vein, a show of pity can give a man a fine
reputation.[7]

The theme of concupiscence would probably have fitted
better in section 2°, as an extension of 'cet amour-
propre' which is evoked in no. 44. In my summary (chapter
29) I do make this change.

(c) injustice (74)

The title of no. 74 ('Injustice') had, I said, a limited
meaning. The word is elsewhere used with its usual application.

Even a cursory glance through section 3° shows that
Justice/Injustice is a main theme. The longest fragment,
no. 60, is a sustained development of the idea that
custom, not reason, is the only sure basis for law. In
addition, there are two fragments entitled 'Injustice,'
one entitled 'Justice,' one 'Tyrannie,' and two untitled
fragments on related subjects.

The first sentence of no. 60, subsequently crossed out,
linked it with the theme of section 2°, Vanity: 'en vérité
la vanité des lois il s'en déliverait, il est donc utile
de l'abuser.' We did indeed meet passages on justice in
section 2°. Pascal seemed above all concerned there with
showing that man can lay no claim to knowing where justice

lies (28, 33, 44). Justice and truth were parallel fields
of fruitless endeavour. What is permitted in time of war
shows that there are no universally binding laws (20, 51).
No. 60 starts from the question: what should be the
basis for ordering life on earth? Not the whims of individuals, as that would lead to confusion. Not justice
either, for we do not know justice, as the rest of the
long fragment makes plain. If we knew universal justice,
the problem would be solved once and for all. In its
place, we have to substitute custom, and we find laws
changing from country to country. This last thought in-
spires Pascal to sarcasm:

> On ne voit rien de juste ou d'injuste qui ne change de
> qualité en changeant de climat, trois degrés d'élévation
> du pôle renversent toute la jurisprudence, un méridien
> décide de la vérité. En peu d'années de possession les
> lois fondamentales changent, le droit a ses époques,
> l'entrée de Saturne au Lion nous marque l'origine d'un
> tel crime. Plaisante justice qu'une rivière borne.
> Vérité au-deçà des Pyrénées, erreur au-delà.

There are no known universal, natural laws, every crime
is somewhere regarded as a virtue. 'Se peut-il rien de
plus plaisant qu'un homme ait droit de me tuer parce
qu'il demeure au-delà de l'eau...?' Pascal asks, echoing
no. 51, (2°). Among the apposite Latin quotations noted
here is one found on fragment 507, which I mentioned in
connection with section 2°.
It follows that the safest basis for law - safer than
an appeal to reason, which is unreliable, safer than the
authority of a legislator or the convenience of a ruler -
is custom. The law should be obeyed because it is law,
not because it is just. On its claim to be just, there
will always be argument. Any attempt to make the current
laws more just will lead to anarchy.
An epigram (61) gives the gist of the argument, when
Pascal writes that fashion, which decides standards of
beauty, also decides standards of justice. The idea that
the law should be obeyed because it is the law is expressed very lucidly by fragment 66, entitled 'Injustice.'
The same idea, less clearly expressed, comes in no. 67,
which takes a sentence of Montaigne as its starting-point.
Another pair of fragments which we can relate to no.
60 deals with tyranny and usurpation (58, 64). It is true

that G. Chinard has warned against taking usurpation in
its modern sense, as in the seventeenth century it had
a neutral meaning of simply taking possession of an object.[8] Nevertheless in no. 60 (last paragraph), it does
have the unmistakeable implication of a political take-
over, 'introduite sans raison.' Pascal traces this back
to the universal trait, found in children (and beggars),
of saying 'this belongs to me' (64). The longer fragment
of tyranny (58) is of particular importance, because in
it Pascal defines tyranny by means of the concept of 'orders,' establishing a distinction which will recur in a
new guise at a crucial point in the Apologia (section
24°). Everything belongs to its appointed 'order,' and
tyranny begins when two orders are confused. A compressed
citation will show what Pascal has in mind:

> On rend différents devoirs aux différents mérites,
> devoir d'amour à l'agrément, devoir de crainte à la
> force, devoir de créance à la science...
>   (Le fort et le beau) ne s'entendent pas. Et leur
> faute est de vouloir régner partout. Rien ne le peut,
> non pas même la force: elle ne fait rien au royaume
> des savants...

When Pascal says that the law must be obeyed, he is not
advocating approval of the status quo in all cases.
    No. 59 can be linked to no. 60 by virtue of the theme
of international justice. The decision leading to the
monstrous situation mentioned in the third paragraph of
no. 60 and in no. 51 is made by one man, who is not im-
partial - an allusion, Mesnard believes, to Richelieu.[9]

(d) expansions of section 2°

The analysis of section 3° has left several fragments
unaccounted for. They are for the most part quite independent of each other, and some relate more easily to
what we have found in section 2° than to the main preoccupations of section 3°.
    The 'misère' of the human condition is evoked in two
fragments. No. 53 speaks of the 'bassesse de l'homme'
who submits to animals (an idea taken from Grotius); no.
57, like no. 56 and several in section 2°, reminds us
that excesses in either direction do not suit us:

Il n'est pas bon d'être trop libre.
Il n'est pas bon d'avoir toutes les nécessités.

No. 68 is very different, transposing the 'combien de
royaumes nous ignorent!' of no. 42 (2°) onto a metaphysical level. For the moment this fragment is isolated; its
note of personal anguish will be picked up in later sections (see chapter 14).

Fragment 62 can perhaps be linked with the theme of the
fall of the great; nothing can be relied upon. It must be
earlier in date than the similar reflection on the restoration of the English monarchy after the death of Cromwell
(750), which I connected with the Cleopatra fragments in
chapter 2.

Fragment 63 is closely related to the motif of admiration, condemned in section 2° (35); indeed, the title of
no. 35, 'Talon de soulier,' also appears, but crossed
out, on the manuscript of no. 63. Pascal has observed
how the children at Port-Royal are susceptible to the
imposed lack of compliments.

La gloire
    L'admiration gâte tout dès l'enfance. O que cela est
bien dit! ô qu'il a bien fait, qu'il est sage, etc.
    Les enfants de P.R. auxquels on ne donne point cet
aiguillon d'envie et de gloire tombent dans la non-
chalance.

Cf. no. 465: 'Ces enfants étonnés voient leurs camarades
respectés.'

Fragment 72 makes the same discrimination between *la
vérité* and *la morale* that we found in no. 23 (2°):

Il faut se connaître soi-même. Quand cela ne servirait
pas à trouver le vrai cela au moins sert à régler sa
vie, et il n'y a rien de plus juste.

It makes an appropriate conclusion to the two chapters,
although other conclusions are possible, including the
one fragment not yet mentioned, no. 71, which will act as
a springboard from which to jump into a new stage of the
argument.

It is clearly not very satisfying to connect so many
fragments from section 3° to the preoccupations of section

2°, rather than to relate them to the separate intention of the section to which they belong, but it seems to me that it would be forcing the evidence to do otherwise. Once again, my conclusions are thus radically different from those of Pol Ernst. Ernst's neat scheme starts from no. 75, 'l'homme sans Dieu est dans l'ignorance de tout et dans un malheur inévitable,' and the attempt at self-understanding (72). The key phrase to him is 'vouloir et ne pouvoir' (75) and this diagnosis, he proposes, binds together all the fragments, which illustrate things desired but shown to be unattainable - justice (74, 60, 64, 66, 61, 58, 59, 67), life (69, 82, 62), happiness (73, 70, 56), simplicity (65, 57), greatness (71, 63, 53), constancy (55, 54). Neither of the two slightly differing versions of this scheme put forward by Ernst is completely convincing.[10] He appears to me to be forcing Pascal's text into an antithetical mould for the sake of his own scheme, rather than disclosing the secret impulses behind Pascal's authentic patterns.

Jean Mesnard in his recent book on the *Pensées* also takes no. 75 as his starting-point, and distinguishes two main centres - the attraction of false objects (as we cannot know the true ones), and diversity, which includes inconstance and instability.[11] The analysis Mesnard gave in his earlier study, quoted at the beginning of this chapter, seems preferable. 'Incapable d'atteindre la vérité, l'homme trouvera-t-il le bien, sous ses trois formes, vertu, justice, bonheur?' Virtue and justice cannot be known, and we have to rely on custom; happiness is impossible because of our inconstancy, however ardently we desire it. Mesnard's divisions correspond quite closely to sections a, c, and d of the present chapter.

In general, however, sections 2° and 3° do make a rather different impression.

The truth is that Pascal was not very interested in purely thematic distinctions, his argument was to have a dynamic shape of its own. One last fragment gives a hint of this manner of proceeding, which will emerge clearly in section 5°. Fragment no. 71 reads:

Contradiction
Orgueil contrepesent toutes les misères, ou il cache ses misères, ou il les découvre; il se glorifie de les connaître.

This gives the reverse of the coin. We might have expected
the conclusion of this section to be the universality of
misère. But apparently there is a catch; we have our
pride, which can always have the last word, either concealing the truth from us (cf. no. 978) or making us
pleased with ourselves for realizing the truth, however
unpalatable. We have already come across this highly
characteristic pattern, whereby two travellers setting
out in opposite directions finish up in the same place,
in the unclassed fragment used to round off the previous
chapter (656).

On the inclusion of no. 71 in the third bundle, three
positions are possible. Pascal would perhaps have left
it there, giving an unexplained hint of what is to come.
If we do not accept that position, we have two alternatives. One is to say simply that it was a mistake, Pascal
in a moment of absent-mindedness placing in section 3° a
fragment clearly menat for section 7° (the title *Contradiction*, which reappears in no. 123, is barely distingui-
shable from *Contrariétés*, the title of section 7°). The
other alternative, which is the one we prefer, is to
hold that this fragment was placed in section 3° at a
time when the precise lay-out of the succeeding chapters
was not fully worked out.[12] Whatever the real facts of
the case, its presence in section 3° is a forceful reminder that we should not assume, when we are dealing
with Pascal, that we know exactly what conclusions he
would have drawn from the evidence he provides.

4
Ennui et qualités essentielles
à l'homme (77-9)

Pascal's fourth dossier contains only three short fragments, two of which are anecdotal in character, and the
third very general. It is not immediately clear how they
link together. The title does not solve the question as
it is not perfectly clear either: is Pascal thinking of
the relation of *ennui* to the qualities essential to man,
or is the meaning '*Ennui* and other qualities...'?
  The two elements of the title have already been touched
upon in earlier chapters. Various fragments had pointed
the way to an understanding of the essential aspects of
the human condition. In section 2°, fragment 24 read:
'Condition de l'homme. Inconstance, ennui, inquiétude.'
Inconstancy was illustrated in nos 17, 54, 55, and 73,
ennui in 36.[1] The theme of *ennui* receives its fullest
treatment in a long fragment which Pascal originally
entitled *Misère* but which was classed not in section 3°
but in section 8°, 'Divertissement.' Why did Pascal return to these notions, and what was his intention in allocating a separate dossier to them?
  Fragment 79, the first to be filed in this fourth
bundle, is the only one of three classified ones to mention *ennui*: 'L'ennui qu'on a de quitter les occupations
où l'on s'est attaché.' If one breaks with a routine with
which one is satisfied, one then finds it difficult to
return to the former routine without feeling 'misérable.'
There is on the face of it nothing which distinguishes
this fragment from several in section 3°. There is, however, another fragment, to which Pascal added the title
'Ennui,' implying that it was designated for section 4°,
and that is the unclassified no. 622:[2]

  Ennui
    Rien n'est si insupportable à l'homme que d'être dans
  un plein repos, sans passions, sans affaires, sans
  divertissement, sans application.

Il sent alors son néant, son abandon, son insuffisance, sa dépendance, son impuissance, son vide. Incontinent il sortira du fond de son âme l'ennui, la noirceur, la tristesse, le chagrin, le dépit, le désespoir.

(Our inability to tolerate *le repos* is noted also in no. 641, Unit XXV, which is more neutral in tone: 'Notre nature est dans le mouvement, le repos entier est la mort.') *Ennui*, then, used in its old sense of anguish, is the inevitable consequence of our condition. If we once stop to contemplate ourselves, we shall immediately be prey to feelings of black despair, as we realize our inadequacy. This explanation of *ennui* immediately illuminates no. 78, the most general of the three classified fragments:

Description de l'homme
Dépendance, désir d'indépendance, besoins.

The obvious interpretation of this, in the context to which Pascal has assigned it, is that we realize that we are dependent on factors over which we have no control (something which the previous chapters have illustrated many times), but this dependence irks us; we wish to be free. Naturally, this fragment is only a jotting, and it would be unwise to elaborate too liberally. It may possibly be theological in origin, and refer to our dependence on God, and our sinful desire to escape God's domination, with the consequent need to be released from the bondage of sin[3], but these implications would not be sensed by a reader at this stage in the Apologia.

In searching for the significance of this very short section, we are obliged to lean heavily on no. 622 and with it no. 78. Jean Mesnard puts it very well when he says that 'L'ennui fait atteindre le fond de la misère, le lieu où toute cause extérieure ou particulière du malheur s'efface devant la contradiction intime entre ce qu'est l'homme et ce qu'il voudrait être.'[4] But can this definition really be made to include the more anecdotal fragments, 77 and 79? Mesnard sees them as comments on 'divertissement,' which is a natural complement to 'ennui,' as no. 622 perhaps implies. Thus no. 77 gives an instance of distraction (travelling) and a benefit (of sorts) which accrues: boasting, while no. 79 illustrates a disadvantage which can follow distraction. Pol Ernst, on the other hand, links all three fragments to

the other element in the title, the 'qualités essentielles.' He draws attention to the fact that the man who
follows a passing fancy in no. 79 was perfectly happy
in his first state, and borrowing a phrase of Jean
Mesnard's he says that man is 'ballotté entre le repos
et l'agitation,'[5] and that this is an essential quality.
Another fundamental characteristic of man is that he
should be subject to dependence and necessity while longing for freedom (78) - a state which must lead to *ennui*.
No. 77, according to Ernst, contrasts curiosity with the
vice it seems to serve, vanity. He summarizes the chapter
thus: 'Notre désir de bonheur cache une misère essentielle
à l'homme, notre désir d'indépendance se heurte à une
dépendance essentielle à l'homme, notre désir de savoir
masque une vanité essentielle à l'homme.'[6] On the previous
page he had asked: 'la conscience des "qualités essentielles à l'homme" n'engendre-t-elle pas, nécessairement,
l'*ennui*?'

This is neat, though speculative, and it has the great
merit of making sense of the complete title: *ennui* is un-
avoidable, once we realize what are the qualities basic
to the human condition. Clearly Pascal would have had to
clarify his meaning considerably. There may be a very
specific reason why this dossier remained uncharacteris-
tically undeveloped. The theme of *ennui*, growing out of
the theme of *misère*, itself suggests a very important
new development: *le divertissement*. To begin with, all
these themes fitted into the general topic of *Misère*,
section 3°, with section 4° as an appendix and conclusion.
But the theme of *divertissement* was so rich in new possibilities that it needed to be put into a separate dossier;
moreover, the theme opened up new perspectives, which
required a much more complex pattern of chapters than
just the initial few, which showed aspects of 'la misère
de l'homme sans Dieu.' And so 'Divertissement' takes its
place as the eighth section in a complex progression.
This interpretation is supported by a careful reading of
no. 136, a long fragment which was originally entitled
'Misère.' but which became the corner-stone of section
8.   It absorbs the ideas of no. 622 ('Ennui'). So section 4° is really an abortive section, suggesting perhaps
a provisional conclusion to the first group of reflections,
but yielding to the imperious need to elaborate, in the
succeeding chapters, an argument of greater intricacy.

We shall have to wait until chapter 8 before we can
appreciate how *ennui* fits into this pattern; in the
intervening sections, Pascal returns to other motifs
of sections 2° and 3°, and through them presents a new
stage in his apologetic argument.

5
Raisons des effets

The list of titles prepared by Pascal shows that he had
intended to call his fifth bundle 'Opinions du peuple
saines,' but that he crossed that title out in favour of
'Raisons des effets.' The Copies reproduce the title-
page exactly,[1] and entitle the chapter itself simply
'Raisons des effets.' Eight fragments are actually entitled 'Raison(s) des effets,' and two more are headed
'Opinions du peuple saines,' while a third opens with
the sentence 'Le peuple a les opinions très saines.' An
almost identical phrase also appears in one of the fragments entitled 'Raison des effets' (no. 93), indicating
that the two titles cover the same ground.

This fifth section is in fact fairly homogeneous. If
we except two fragments which Pascal crossed out, and
which do not belong here at all (84 and 102),[2] we are
left with only two fragments (82 and 96) whose connection
is obscure.

I have included fourteen unclassed fragments in this
discussion: 510 (XXI); 520, 525, 533, 554, 577 (XXIII);
645, 665, 688, 711 (XXV); 767, 768 (XXVI); 797 (XXVIII);
828 (XXXI).[3]

The discussion is divided into four parts, with a conclusion.

(a) a first group of *pensées* sets out to show that the
situation already made clear to us - that many views
holding wide currency are vain - is not, after all, such
a bad thing, as the 'vain' opinions of the majority have
much to recommend them. The key fragment here is no. 101
('Le peuple a les opinions très saines').

(b) several people have correctly observed certain 'effects,' but have not understood the reasons for them.
They include Montaigne, Epictetus, and Saint Augustine
(577). The title 'Raisons des effets' is explained in this
last fragment, filed among the 'Miscellanea' of Unit XXIII.

(c) other fragments with the same title ('Raisons des effets') carry the argument about the opinion of the majority a stage further. Pascal is not concerned merely to reverse his previous stand and to praise the opinions he had shown to be vain. The opinions remain vain. His position is that the people, though right, are not right for the reasons they themselves give; and that those who dismiss them are not clever enough to see that those opinions are not so foolish after all. This progression Pascal describes as the 'renversement continuel du pour au contre' (93).

(d) one group of fragments stands out from the rest, as it revolves round one particular theme: the relation of justice and force. Force is, with concupiscence, a basic determinant of human society, unanswerable, while justice is a pretence.

Pascal's theory is that as force, not justice, presides over the institution of society, and as we do not know for sure what true justice is, we simply have had to designate the rulers 'just.'

The mythical notion of justice is one way in which society has been allowed to continue. Political theories on kingship, imagination bolstering a respect for the leading families, accepted laws, and the sway of the majority are all examples of other forces. Pascal has more to say about majority opinion, unwilling to accept new notions. Majority opinion, despite what he might once have thought to the contrary, is tyrannical.

Nevertheless, it is better to accept the status quo than to get involved in endless disputes, which is what would happen if people were educated to the truth without having the wisdom to see the advantages, for peace, of accepting the imperfections of the existing society. In this way Pascal rejoins his earlier argument about the wise man recognizing that the people are often right though for the wrong reason. And he hints that there is a Christian perspective transcending all these debates.

(e) the kind of argumentation found in this chapter is of fundamental importance for the shape of the sections which follow, and for what it tells us of Pascal's imagination. Any statement may be challenged; only when the topic has been explored from every point of view, and the resulting fragments pieced together in a significant pattern, shall we be able to attain a full understanding.

(a) opinions du peuple saines (94, 95)

Summing up his argument in one of the eight classified
fragments which have the title 'Raison(s) des effets'
(93), Pascal wrote:

> Nous avons donc montré que l'homme est vain par
> l'estime qu'il fait des choses qui ne sont point essen-
> tielles. Et toutes ces opinions sont détruites.
> Nous avons montré ensuite que toutes ces opinions
> sont très saines, et qu'ainsi toutes ces vanités étant
> très bien fondées, le peuple n'est pas si vain qu'on
> dit. Et ainsi nous avons détruit l'opinion qui détrui-
> sait celle du peuple...

The first layer of section 5° is constituted by this
destruction of points already apparently established.
The phrase 'opinions du peuple' covers all those shib-
boleths Pascal had exposed in the previous chapters, like
divertissement ('Les hommes s'occupent à suivre une balle
et un lièvre,' 39), *gloire* ('La douceur de la gloire est
si grande qu'à quelque objet qu'on l'attache, même à la
mort, on l'aime,' 37), travelling ('on ne voyagerait pas
sur la mer ... pour le seul plaisir de voir, sans espé-
rance d'en jamais communiquer,' 77), hereditary monarchy
('La puissance des rois est fondée sur la raison et sur
la folie du peuple,' 26); it includes the philosopher
whose imagination makes him fear walking across an abyss
on a plank, even if the plank is wide (44).
    All these examples are referred to in no. 101, together
with others we can guess, even if we cannot cite a precise text as illustration. It appears that those who
denigrate common opinion (among whom we had thought we
could count Pascal himself) are 'demi-savants'; another
fragment (90) calls them 'les demi-habiles':

> Les peuples a les opinions très saines. Par exemple
> 1. D'avoir choisi le divertissement, et la chasse
> plutôt que la prise. Les demi-savants s'en moquent et
> triomphent à montrer là-dessus la folie du monde, mais
> par une raison qu'ils ne pénètrent pas. On a raison:
> 2. D'avoir distingué les hommes par le dehors, comme
> par la noblesse ou le bien. Le monde triomphe encore à
> montrer combien cela est déraisonnable. Mais cela est
> très raisonnable. Cannibales se rient d'un enfant roi.

3. De s'offenser pour avoir reçu un soufflet ou de
tant désirer la gloire, mais cela est très souhaitable
à cause des autres biens essentiels qui y sont joints.
Et un homme qui a reçu un soufflet sans s'en ressentir
est accablé d'injures et de nécessités.
4. Travailler pour l'incertain, aller sur mer, passer
sur une planche (101).

(The phrase 'travailler pour l'incertain' is the subject
of an unclassified fragment, 577, which will be discussed
in section b.)
    The second paragraph of no. 101 is echoed in other
fragments of this fifth section. Both the fragments entitled 'Opinions du peuple saines' (94, 95) illustrate
the wisdom of respecting those who have nobility or
wealth. No. 94 is the counterpart to no. 30 ('On ne
choisit pas pour gouvener un vaisseau celui des voyageurs
qui est de la meilleur maison.') The system appears foolish, but the 'demi-habiles' do not see that the alternative is civil war:

    Opinions du peuple saines.
    Le plus grand des maux est les guerres civiles.
    Elles sont sûres si on veut récompenser les mérites,
    car tous diront qu'ils méritent. Le mal à craindre
    d'un sot qui succède par droit de naissance n'est si
    grand ni si sûr.[4]

Hereditary succession is also a way to resist the inevitable variability in human institutions, noted in no. 767.
    No. 95 commends the 'people' for respecting a man whose
dress shows that he is wealthy, able to command a bevy of
servants: 'Plus on a de bras, plus on est fort. Etre brave
c'est montrer sa force.' No. 89, which has the other
title, 'Raison des effets,' is close to no. 95, and
answers the implication of the cryptic fragment of section 2°, no. 19, 'Il a quatre laquais.' Here the repre-
sentative of the 'demi-habiles' is Montaigne himself:

    Raison des effets.
    Cela est admirable: on ne veut pas que j'honore un
    homme vêtu de brocatelle et suivi de sept ou huit
    laquais. Et quoi! il me fera donner des étrivières
    si je ne le salue. Cet habit c'est une force.

Another fragment, this time without title, shows the
same rejection of a position taken in section 2°. Fragment 32 had read simply 'Vanité. Les respects signifient:
incommodez-vous,' and the obvious implication was that
standing up to show respect to another person is really
absurd, a sign of the vanity of human behaviour. No. 80
answers it:

Le respect est: Incommodez-vous.
  Cela est vain en apparence mais très juste, car c'est
dire: je m'incommoderais bien si vous en aviez besoin,
puisque je le fais bien sans que cela vous serve, outre
que le respect est pour distinguer les grands. Or si le
respect était d'être en fauteuil on respecterait tout
le monde et ainsi on ne distinguerait pas. Mais étant
incommodé on distingue fort bien.

Two more untitled fragments (104, 87) require interpreting. No. 104 simply says that 'la noblesse est un
grand avantage' because it enables a young man of eighteen
to enjoy a respect which other men have to earn by thirty
years of endeavour. I take this to be the reply to another piece of pseudo-wisdom. From other fragments in
this section we glean that it is a commonly held opinion
that 'il faut honorer les gentilshommes ... parce que la
naissance est un avantage effectif' (92). The 'demi-
habiles' counter by saying that noblemen are not privileged beings at all ('la naissance n'est pas un avantage
de la personne mais du hasard,' 90). Pascal replies that
they are indeed privileged. It is, however, a much less
telling argument than others Pascal uses.
  In fragment 44, Pascal had made a distinction between
the magistrate who relies on an appeal to the imagination,
and the king who, having force on his side, does not need
to use trickery. 'Ils s'établissent par la force, les
autres par grimace.' No. 87 merely repeats this; its inclusion in section 5° implies the argument that the magistrate is quite right in trying to impress us, for he
has no other way to keep his necessary authority.
  Is it absurd to expect to be honoured for 'des charges
et des offices'? Not at all, replies fragment 688, for
we can only be loved for qualities which are not to be
identified with our real selves.
  It will be seen that nos 87, 89, and 95 all use the
word 'force.' Force is the clue to why popular wisdom

is right to honour certain accoutrements; they are the
sign of the owner's physical power, and imply a warning
of what might happen if the person is crossed. Important
though it is, however, there is no need to make force
into the principal theme of this first group. The three
fragments just alluded to imply that force has to be
treated with respect, but the essential argument they
propound, along with the other fragments discussed in
this section, is that views which are commonly held are
not so foolish as we may have been led to believe.

Fragment 89, I have said, has the title 'Raison des
effets.' Of the other seven fragments entitled 'raison(s)
des effets,' six will take us much further than those
discussed already. The seventh, no. 96, is rather enigmatic, but it can plausibly be interpreted as another
indication that there is a case to be made out for views
which appear 'vain.' The text itself probably needs to
be emended:

> Raison des effets.
> La faiblesse de l'homme est la cause de tant de beautés
> qu'on établit, comme de savoir bien jouer du luth n'est
> un mal qu'à cause de notre faiblesse.

The manuscript shows that Pascal originally wrote 'ne
point jouer,' but replaced it by the words 'savoir bien
jouer,' and it seems reasonable to act on a hint of
Brunschvicg's and assume that Pascal made the correction
hastily; that he should have kept his first version intact, and simply added the new phrase, thus:

> La faiblesse de l'homme est la cause de tant de
> beautés qu'on établit, comme de savoir bien jouer du
> luth. Ne point savoir bien jouer du luth n'est un mal
> qu'à cause de notre faiblesse.[5]

Even so, the text is not very clear, and not, perhaps,
very important. Probably the idea is that things we prize
as an experience of beauty have their roots in competi-
tiveness, but they should not on that account be despised.

(b) raisons des effets

The title Pascal came to prefer to 'opinions du peuple
saines' was 'raisons des effets,' and no fewer than eight

of the twenty-three fragments included in this bundle
have as title 'raisons (or raison) des effets.' Pascal
evidently wishes to stress, not that he has reversed his
stand on common opinion, but that he is looking at the
phenomena from a higher vantage-point. Of the eight fragments which have the revised title, two have already been
discussed (nos 89 and 96). In no. 89, which belongs in
spirit with no. 95, 'Opinions du peuple saines,' Pascal
took issue with Montaigne, seen as a 'demi-habile.'
Montaigne was not the only thinker of whom Pascal voiced
his disapproval for not seeing the merit on common belief. Epictetus is arraigned in no. 100 (with which we
must associate no. 98, which criticizes Montaigne as well,
and no. 99; both are untitled), and even Saint Augustine
is criticized in an important unclassed fragment, no. 577,
which gives the clearest statement we have of what exactly
Pascal meant by the title 'raisons des effets.'[6]

Fragment no. 100 is obscure, and the help we are given
by nos 98 and 99 and the unclassed no. 577 does not entirely dissipate the obscurity. Epictetus argued that if
we were pitied for having a headache which we did not
have, we could dismiss the unwelcome pity as an illusion,
concluding that we need not live in fear of the opinion
of others. Pascal puts his finger on the weak point in
Epictetus's argument; a headache is one thing, but where
it is a question of people believing us wrong or unjust,
we cannot be sure that we are right and they are wrong.
Epictetus's view that we are able to command our own
hearts is false. This idea will fall into place with
section 9°.

In no. 98 Pascal finds his own formulation, referring
to Epictetus only in the second paragraph. Montaigne had
asked, in his Essay *De l'Art de conférer*, why an 'esprit
mal rangé' irritates us whereas a 'corps mal bâti' does
not. Pascal makes the parallel more striking by coining
the phrase 'l'esprit boiteux,' and gives his answer: if
we have a sound body, this will be acknowledged by all,
including the man with a limp, whereas there will not be
universal consent, when I disagree with someone, that I
am the reasonable one. We have to distinguish, in Jean
Mesnard's phrase, between the contestable and the incontestable.[7]

The answer is continued in no. 99, which has a second
paragraph quite distinct from the first.[8] If a connection
is to be sought, it is in the word 'sot.' No. 99b begins:

'L'homme est ainsi fait qu'à force de lui dire qu'il est
un sot il le croit.' But it moves off in a new direction,
speaking of the necessity to reflect continually on God.
The indignity of feeling oneself a 'sot' is also noted
in 768.
The 'esprit boiteux' turns up again in no. 577, in
which Pascal says that Montaigne had observed the phenomenon, 'mais il n'a pas vu la raison de cet effet.' That
phrase shows why no. 100 has the title 'Raison des effets,'
and the conclusion to no. 577 (which also mentions Saint
Augustine, as nos 98 and 100 mention Montaigne and
Epictetus) gives us the general statement about the theme
which we need:

> Toutes ces personnes ont vu les effets mais ils n'ont
> pas vu les causes. Ils sont à l'égard de ceux qui ont
> découvert les causes comme ceux qui n'ont que les yeux
> à l'égard de ceux qui ont l'esprit. Car les effets
> sont comme sensibles et les causes sont visibles seule-
> ment à l'esprit. Et quoique ces effets-là se voient par
> l'esprit, cet esprit est à l'égard de l'esprit qui voit
> les causes comme les sens corporels à l'égard de l'esprit.

The allusion to Saint Augustine is this: 'Saint Augustin
a vu qu'on travaille pour l'incertain sur mer, en bataille
etc. - mais il n'a pas vu la règle des partis qui démontre
qu'il le doit.' This clearly links with the phrase
'travailler pour l'incertain, aller sur mer' in no. 101
(para. 4), but nothing so far enables us to explain the
'règle des partis' which is developed in section 12°.
Similarly the first part of no. 577 is a development on
the idea 'il ne faut rien faire que pour le certain,'
offered as an objection to the life of Christian commit-
ment Pascal is advocating, and it could not have been
introduced into the Apologia as early as section 5°
without weakening the impact such considerations will
have when the argument has reached the stage elaborated
in section 12°.

(c) toutes ces opinions sont détruites (93)

So far, we appear merely to have reversed the position
taken in earlier sections, in the light of an understanding denied to the 'demi-habiles.' In earlier sections,
opinions widely held were said to be 'vain,' but in

section 5°, they turn out to be 'sane' after all. Pascal
is not, however, allying himself uncritically with what
he calls 'le peuple.' Four of the fragments entitled
'Raison(s) des effets' (nos 90-3) make this clear. I have
already quoted two paragraphs of no. 93, finishing on the
phrase 'et ainsi nous avons détruit l'opinion qui détrui-
sait celle du peuple'; here now is the third paragraph:

> Mail il faut détruire maintenant cette dernière propo-
> sition et montrer qu'il demeure toujours vrai que le
> peuple est vain, quoique ses opinions soient saines,
> parce qu'il n'en sent pas la vérité où elle est et que
> la mettant où elle n'est pas, ses opinions sont tou-
> jours très fausses et très mal saines.

That fragment (93) has the subtitle 'renversement continuel du pour au contre,' a phrase which defines Pascal's
method admirably. In no. 90 the same method is called
'gradation.' The position Pascal adopts in relation to
'le peuple' is stated clearly in no. 92, with the same
familiar example of respect for the nobility:

> Raison des effets.
> Il est donc vrai de dire que tout le monde est dans
> l'illusion, car encore que les opinions du peuple soient
> saines, elles ne le sont pas dans sa tête, car il pense
> que la vérité est où elle n'est pas. La vérité est bien
> dans leurs opinions, mais non pas au point où ils se
> figurent. Il est vrai qu'il faut honorer les gentils-
> hommes, mais non pas parce que la naissance est un
> avantage effectif, etc.

No. 90 echoes this fragment, but it introduces two new
notions. One is that of the 'pensée de derrière,' announced in no. 91: 'Il faut avoir une pensée de derrière,
et juger de tout par là, en parlant cependant comme le
peuple.' (A fragment which belongs to the notes for the
Discours sur la condition des grands, no. 797, gives the
more explicit phrase, 'pensées de derrière la tête.')
The other notion is that the 'gradation' does not stop
with the 'habiles.' After the three stages 'peuple - demi-
habiles - habiles,' we progress to the 'dévots' (a kind of
'semi-christian') and the 'chrétiens parfaits,' and
Pascal concludes: 'Ainsi se vont les opinions se succé-
dant du pour au contre selon qu'on a de lumière.'

We know what the attitude of Christians is from no. 14,
in section 2°:

Les vrais chrétiens obéissent aux folies néanmoins,
non pas qu'ils respectent les folies, mais l'ordre
de Dieu qui pour la punition des hommes les a asservis
à ces folies.

This third group of *pensées*, therefore, proposes an
approach very different from the normal logical method,
by which irrefutable conclusions are accumulated in an
orderly sequence. Pascal seems rather to be saying that
many apparently firm conclusions are only half-truths,
and that there are equally firmly based complementary
half-truths. Moreover, he is implying that every stage
of the argument needs to be tested. Only the 'chrétiens
parfaits' have the full answer, and of course at this
stage of the Apologia, we are still with the 'demi-
habiles' and the 'habiles,' exploring the contradictions
in worldly wisdom before we venture into the realm of
revelation.
    Other fragments make the same kind of division as the
group just discussed. There is pure ignorance, says
Pascal in no. 83, there is wisdom which acknowledges its
ignorance, and between the two, the clever chaps who
think they know everything and who scorn the 'people'
and the 'savants.' Another fragment, unclassed, distinguishes clever people from 'les gens du commun,' but no
conclusion is drawn (510). Considerably more difficult
to explain is the brief fragment no. 82, quoting Christ's
injunction to 'become as little children.' Is it found
here because it goes against conventional 'smart' wisdom? Ernst links it to no. 83, which refers to the natural ignorance 'où se trouvent tous les hommes en nais-
sant,' but the link seems to me tenuous.[9]
    There is an extremely interesting fragment which has
been crossed out (520), that makes the 'renversement du
pour au contre' a personal experience to Pascal. The theme
is human justice, and again there is a reference to the
superior wisdom of Christians:

J'ai passé longtemps de ma vie en croyant qu'il y avait
une justice et en cela je ne me trompais pas, car il y
en a selon que Dieu nous l'a voulu révéler, mais je ne
le prenais pas ainsi et c'est en quoi je me trompais,

car je croyais que notre justice était essentiellement
juste, et que j'avais de quoi la connaître et en juger,
mais je me suis trouvé tant de fois en faute de jugement droit, qu'enfin je suis entré en défiance de moi
et puis des autres...

The continuation and conclusion, however, veer off on a
different tack, more on man's variability than on justice.

(d) justice force (103)

The last fragment with the title 'Raison des effets' is
no. 97:

Raison des effets.
La concupiscence et la force sont les sources de toutes
nos actions. La concupiscence fait les volontaires, la
force les involontaires.

I have discussed Pascal's treatment of concupiscence in
chapter 3, in connection with no. 74. Force comes into
focus in the present section. Pol Ernst simply divides
the subject-matter in two, the relation of force and
merit (which covers our sections a and c), and the relation of force and justice or truth (our sections b and
d). The division is certainly elegant, but it does seem
a little strained, and it rather underplays what is
surely the true dynamic centre here, the 'renversement
du pour au contre.' Only three of the fragments so far
discussed refer explicitly to force, nos 87, 89, and 95,
and for all their importance, noted in section (a), I
have preferred to regard them as examples of the 'opinions
du peuple saines' rather than as constituting a development of the theme of force. Ernst's analysis was sharply
criticized by T.W. Harrington, who rightly saw that the
dynamic impulse behind section 5° has more to do with
method than theme.[10] The scheme Harrington proposed to
replace that of Ernst has, however, not been followed
in this chapter.
    In earlier fragments (28, 44, 58), force has been kept
quite distinct from justice:

Toutes les occupations des hommes sont à avoir du bien
et ils ne sauraient avoir de titre pour montrer qu'ils
le possèdent par justice, car ils n'ont que la fantaisie
des hommes, ni force pour le posséder sûrement (28).

No. 44 made a contrast between the antics of magistrates
who do not have 'la véritable justice' and those who command directly by force, which is unanswerable. This distinction is picked up in no. 87, as we have seen. In the
notes for the *Discours sur les Grands* (797), Pascal observes, among other things, what happens if a 'simple
soldat' decides to attack a 'premier président': 'Quand
la force attaque la grimace...' The word had appeared
in no. 44 ('Les gens de guerre ... s'établissent par la
force, les autres par grimace'), but the difference
between these two quotations is important; in no. 797
Pascal is interested not in the distinction between force
and justice, but in the open conflict between the two.
    Fragment 86 reminds us of something we were told in
no. 60 (3°), that lacking true justice, we have taken
custom for our guide, and it goes on to sketch an explanation of the basis of our notions of justice, referring
us, by the word 'etc.', to other fragments which elaborate these ideas. No. 103, for example, entitled 'Justice
force,' puts the matter clearly, even schematically. Although we can never know justice, we like to believe that
we possess it. Our rulers originally became rulers not
because they were just, but because they were strong.
Justice and strength are rarely united in one person,
but we wish them to be united. Consequently we have two
alternatives. Either we say to a just man, 'You are
strong,' or we say to a strong man, 'You are just.' The
first alternative is plainly unpractical: we do not truly
know, in a manner beyond dispute, that he is just, and
it can be shown that he is not strong, whereas it cannot
be proved that the demonstrably strong man is not also
just. So we give the title of 'just' to the strong man.
    Nos 81 and 85 come to the same conclusion, and from
this basic position, several deductions are made concerning the way society has evolved.
    Society as we know it is not maintained by force; that
would be costly, inefficient, and unstable. So various
more flattering means are employed to preserve the status
quo, means which appeal to concupiscence and hence mould
our actions without our being aware of it. The myth of
justice is perhaps one of these means. A place must also
be found for political theories which are an attempt to
educate the rulers to their responsibilities (533).
    Another means is imagination, under which heading
Pascal includes the different forms of hereditary succession (*gentilshommes* in France, *roturiers* in

Switzerland, cf. no. 50). Our imagination is manipulated
to encourage respect for the great (828).

The opening words of no. 86 ('les moeurs de son pays')
and no. 81 ('les lois du pays') remind us of the force
of social custom. But no. 81 - and with it no. 85 -
stresses the view of the majority as a basis for stability. This too is an argument from strength (a truly
strong king, Pascal says, does not need to follow the
majority). Another fragment, no. 88, gives a non-political
example of the force of majority opinion. Pascal talks
of the cool reception given to inventors. This, he says,
is due not to custom (there are not enough inventors for
it to be possible to talk of custom), but of the strength
of the majority, who declare the new inventions 'impossible' without giving them a fair trial. Again, Pascal
is explaining an observed 'effect.'

It is possible to link this rather specific thought to
two unclassed fragments which generalize. In the conclusion to the first part of no. 44, on imagination, Pascal
had written that he would gladly subscribe to the views
of the author who wrote a book on 'l'opinone regina del
mondo.' In no. 665, he says that opinion and imagination
make a more acceptable ruler than force, and he compares
the two rulers to a queen and a tyrant. But no. 554 shows
that he has reflected further, and can no longer hold
such a comforting view of the matter:

> La force est la reine du monde et non pas l'opinion,
> mais l'opinion est celle qui use de la force.
> C'est la force qui fait l'opinion.

This scepticism about justice and the view of majority
opinion as tyrannical might seem to constitute a challenge
to the existing order, but such is not Pascal's intention.
The implication is rather that we should accept what is
so and not question it:

> La justice est ce qui est établi; et ainsi toutes nos
> lois établies seront nécessairement tenues pour justes
> sans être examinées, puisqu'elles sont établies (645).

If 'le plus grand des maux est les guerres civiles' (94),
anything which preserves us from strife is to be approved.

> Ne pouvant fortifier la justice on a justifié la force,
> afin que ... la paix fût, qui est le souverain bien (81)

Just as we follow the majority because it is strong, not because it is right, so we follow the received laws and opinions not because they are just or good, or 'saines,' but because they go unchallenged. 'Elles sont uniques et nous ôtent la racine de la diversité' (711). Admit the possibility of other opinions and one is faced with endless disputes and dissension. 'De là vient l'injustice de la Fronde, qui élève sa prétendue justice contre la force' (85). Justice is only a 'prétendue justice' (cf. 103) and to act on it leads only to injustice.

This idea is not entirely new to us; we met it in two *pensées* which Pascal put into section 2°: nos 66 and 67. Both had the title 'Injustice,' which recalls the 'lettre de l'injustice' mentioned in fragment 9.

We thus rejoin the argument of the third part of this chapter. Pascal's comments on justice should not be taken out of the specific context, that of the layers of understanding represented by 'le peuple, les demi-habiles, les habiles...' He is implying that ordinary people should not be given the wisdom which would make of them mere 'demi-savants,' arrogantly questioning everything and arriving at a state of chaos which would be worse than the present state, for all its imperfections. Even Montaigne did not attain the higher wisdom which acknowledges that the people are right, if for the wrong reason. In an important unclassed fragment (no. 525), he argues the point closely.

It would clearly be unjust to imprison Pascal in his first group, along with 'le peuple.' If he rejects the second group (Montaigne), it is from the superior vantage-point. The people may be right, but their reasons are weak. There is evidence enough that Pascal found the domination of true justice by force tyrannical, a confusion of 'orders' (cf. no. 58). We have seen that in fragment 90 he posits not three, but five layers, concluding with the 'chrétiens parfaits.' That superior vision is surely implied by the last sentence of no. 85: 'Il n'en est pas de même dans l'Eglise, car il y a une justice véritable et nulle violence.' The problem is to attain in certainty to that genuine justice.[11] We must not forget that, apart from occasional glimpses like the one just quoted, Pascal is not disclosing Christian perspectives in the first part of his Apologia. This is the 'misère de l'homme sans Dieu'; without revelation, Pascal is saying, justice escapes us, and in those circumstances, it is better to put up with what we

have, and live in peace, than to open an endless and
sterile debate.

(e) renversement continuel du pour au contre (93)

The fifth section has a significance which goes beyond
the interest of the topics Pascal analyses in it. In the
first sections ideas appeared to be grouped according to
certain general conclusions which Pascal deduced from the
evidence. If he had gone no further in his task of classifying than his fourth bundle, most readers, would, I believe, have assumed - as countless editors and commentators indeed did do - that his intention was simply to
paint as full a picture as possible of the 'misère de
l'homme sans Dieu,' stressing how unstable man is, how
uncertain his grasp of the things he expects and desires,
and interpreting many phenomena of experience in a way
which would strengthen this picture, and disturb the
reader. It would be clear that the divisions ('Vanité,'
'Misère,' 'Qualités essentielles') were not rigorously
maintained, and I have several times had recourse in my
analysis to the hypothesis that Pascal began with a
simple outline which revealed its potentialities only as
he worked with it. Although I shall have to introduce
that hypothesis again in treating the second part of the
Apologia,[12] the impression is very strong that from section 5° on, the argument advances with a clear purpose,
and in a manner we could not have foreseen. It becomes
truly Pascalian, not moving from single point to single
point, but building up a series of interlocking arguments.
   The key comes in the phrase 'renversement continuel du
pour au contre' (93). Pascal is a master of the half-
truth. Having convinced us that the 'opinions du peuple'
are 'vaines,' he goes on to show that, on the contrary,
the opinions in question are 'saines.' Obviously a serious thinker cannot leave it there, he must go on to
ask how these two irreconcilable views could be reconciled. The immediate answer is: by accepting only the
conclusions of the 'people,' not their reasoning. The
reasoning of the 'demi-habiles,' on the other hand, is
acceptable, but their conclusions are not, because they
have not considered enough of the evidence. Reversing
Pascal's title, we may say that they have good reasons,
but do not see the effects.

The implications of the position taken up here by Pascal
are multiple. The most important for us as readers, is
that we should reserve judgment on any statement Pascal
may choose to make. We must not assume that he believes
that statement unconditionally. It is likely to be one
part of a wider argument that sets one half-truth against
another. Nor can we be sure that the synthesis of two
half-truths leads to truth. Fragment no. 93 speaks of a
'renversement *continuel* du pour au contre,' and no. 90
very clearly sets forth five positions, not three. The
fifth position is that of the 'chrétiens parfaits,' and
we must not forget that Pascal is here only laying the
ground for his Apologia. No. 90 clearly invites us to
expect to find the provisional conclusions of this section revised later in the Apologia, and the last sentence
of no. 85 does likewise. We are not yet ready for an exposition of the Christian position.

Already, however, we can understand that Pascal intends
to proceed by contradictions, with the promise of subsequent reconciliation. This is more than an interesting
debating procedure. It reveals a profound characteristic
of Pascal's imagination, and we shall have countless
opportunities to see the different forms it takes. Its
impact on the design of the Apologia is immediately apparent from sections 6° and 7°. But we shall have to
wait until all the contradictory statements have been
made and reconciled before we can see the full beauty
and effectiveness of Pascal's highly original method.

6
Grandeur

In sections 2° to 5° Pascal has persistently challenged
man's pretensions to know truth and justice, finding
vanity and wretchedness to be the characteristic features
of the human condition. The title of his sixth bundle,
'Grandeur' (explained in no. 117 as 'la grandeur de
l'homme'), will therefore surprise. If so far Pascal has
won our adherence, we must realize now that we are like
the 'demi-habiles' of section 5°, seeing part of the
truth and taking it to be the last word. Pascal, evidently,
is continuing his tactic of a 'renversement continuel du
pour au contre.' Not that we should be completely surprised, for most men are privately persuaded of the greatness of man:

> leur nature, qui est plus forte que tout, les convain-
> quant de la grandeur de l'homme plus fortement que la
> raison ne les convainc de leur bassesse (470).

Pascal will do more, however, than merely appeal to an
instinct which may rest on illusion; he will present a
serious case for 'la grandeur.'
   Only five of the fourteen fragments included in the
bundle actually contain the word 'gradneur': 106 (the
only one to have the title 'Grandeur') with its double
118, 114, and 117 ('la grandeur de l'homme') with its
double 116. Four unclassified fragments can be added to
these: 411 ('Grandeur de l'homme'), 472 ('Grandeur'), 470
(already quoted), and 759. No. 759 is allied to no. 756,
although the latter used the word 'dignité' in place of
'grandeur.' There is no difficulty in discerning the
connection of the other nine classified fragments with
the main theme, and we can add to them nos 406, 437, 491,
620, 633, 738, 741, and 1109.[1]

Leaving aside no. 472 which, in spite of its title,
seems more in place in section 11° than here, we have
twenty-six fragments. Pascal rests his case on a five-
point argument, which takes into account several of the
objections which a reader of the previous sections might
be expected to raise:
(a) the order of society may not attain true justice,
but it is a remarkable achievement to have worked out
to order from self-love
(b) *misère* itself is a sign of greatness (potential if
not realized), as it implies that our true vocation is
not being fulfilled in our present state
(c) man is not solely material
(d) above all, man has the faculty of thought. This distinguishes him from animals, and makes him superior even
to the universe. Reason is not incompatible with *misère*;
the fact that man *knows* he is wretched shows his double
nature. Nor is the claim made for reason incompatible
with the attack on the dogmatists carried out in earlier
sections. Even if we are constantly beset by doubt, reason itself is admirable. Our nature, moreover, makes it
impossible for us to reject completely the opinions of
our fellows
(e) our nature also makes us incapable of rejecting the
claim of the dogmatist that we do have access to certain
basic truths, which are immune to doubt because known to
the heart, not to reason.

(a) un règlement admirable (118)

The previous section made two points particularly strongly.
One was the absurdity of claiming that our social order
is based on justice. Force and concupiscence are what
control human life. The other point was that every idea
should be tested by its opposite, in order to proceed by
a 'renversement continuel du pour au contre.' We shall
therefore not be surprised to find the ideas of section
5° subjected to the same scrutiny, and it may be significant that both the last fragment of the section (presumably the first to be placed in the dossier) and also the
only fragment which has as title the word 'Grandeur'
should challenge the ideas recently established.
Fragment 106 puts section 5° in a new light, by praising
the institution of the social order:

Grandeur.
Les raisons des effets marquent la grandeur de l'homme,
d'avoir tiré de la concupiscence un si bel ordre.

Its double, no. 118, reminds us also of no. 74 and its
satellites, the argument with the *honnête homme* about
concupiscence and virtue:

Grandeur de l'homme dans sa concupiscence même, d'en
avoir su tirer un règlement admirable et en avoir fait
un tableau de charité.

Though not ideal, the political and social systems we
have evolved are very much superior to what might be expected of a race dominated by concupiscence.

(b) misères d'un roi dépossédé (116)

These two fragments are, however, only a beginning. The
'raisons des effets' are only a portion of the evidence
considered so far, and on the face of it, it would seem
that man's essential *misère* is too firmly established to
allow us to talk now of his greatness.
But to say that is to forget that *misère* may be only
one side of the picture. Not all our impulses pull us
downwards.

Malgré la vue de toutes nos misères qui nous touchent,
qui nous tiennent à la gorge, nous avons un instinct
que nous ne pouvons réprimer qui nous élève (633).

Nor is it simply a matter of two opposing forces.
Pascal examines the implications of the word 'misère'
itself, and finds that paradoxically, it actually implies
at least the possibility of greatness. It is not, for
example, a word one would apply to a ruined house, which
has no feeling (437). Nor does one apply it to animals,
whose limitations are part of their nature and not felt
as *misères*. This notion is touched on in no. 117, which
elucidates and expands the brief fragment 116:

La grandeur de l'homme.
La grandeur de l'homme est si visible qu'elle se
tire même de sa misère, car ce qui est nature aux
animaux nous l'appelons misère en l'homme par ðu

nous reconnaissons que sa nature étant aujourd'hui
pareille à celle des animaux il est déchu d'une meil-
leure nature qui lui était propre autrefois.
    Car qui se trouve malheureux de n'être pas roi sinon
un roi dépossédé...

We are only truly 'malheureux' if we are deprived of
something we believe we have a right to, and our dissatisfaction with our lot suggests that we have a higher
nature, not fulfilled by human life as it is at present
experienced.

(c) quelque chose d'immatériel (108)

Another reason for claiming that man has the quality of
greatness is that his nature is not entirely material.
Two fragments in this bundle imply this argument, although they do not develop it. One (108) maintains that
pleasure is not felt locally by parts of the body, but
evidently by 'quelque chose d'immatériel.' The other
(115) argues that the Stoic injunction to control the
passions implies the existence within us of an immaterial
soul.

(d) roseau pensant (113)

But if Pascal does not expand on those two examples of
immateriality, he has much to say about a third manifestation: thought, or reason. Reason is a distinguishing
mark of the human species, and constitutes his fourth
claim to greatness. Fragment 759 states categorically:
'Pensée fait la grandeur de l'homme,' a sentiment echoed
in no. 756 ('Toute la dignité de l'homme est en la pensée'),
in no. 620 ('L'homme est visiblement fait pour penser.
C'est toute sa dignité et tout son mérite'), and in no.
491 ('la raison qui fait son être'). 'Le moi consiste
dans ma pensée' he will say in fragment 135 (in *liasse*
8°). A man might lack a limb or two, but, says Pascal,
'Je ne puis concevoir l'homme sans pensée. Ce serait une
pierre ou une brute' (111).
    In this, man is quite distinct from animals. Animals
are granted the faculty of will, unlike a calculating
machine, but 'la machine d'arithmétique fait des effets
qui approchent plus de la pensée que tout ce que font
les animaux' (741). Animals, that is, do their own

programming, but they do not reason. Three fragments, two of them placed in the sixth bundle, give examples of automatic behaviour in animals (107, 738, 105).[2]

By thought, man shows himself superior even to the universe itself, which the 'demi-habiles' would use to reduce man's importance (113):

> Roseau pensant.
> Ce n'est point de l'espace que je dois chercher ma dignité, mais c'est du règlement de ma pensée. Je n'aurai point d'avantage en possédant des terres. Par l'espace l'univers me comprend et m'engloutit comme un point: par la pensé je le comprends.

(This fragment is entitled 'Roseau pensant,' implying that it was written in the shadow of the celebrated fragment 200: 'L'homme n'est qu'un roseau, le plus faible de la nature, mais c'est un roseau pensant.' But although the ideas are similar, Pascal classed no. 200 in section 14° [Lafuma XV], and it cannot be considered here.)

This eloquent claim for reason is bound to raise certain questions in the reader's mind. Is it really consistent with the talk of *misère*? Is it consistent with the critique of reason given in earlier sections?

The first of these questions poses no problem for Pascal, who sees no contradiction, as we have already noted, in the co-existence of *misère* and *grandeur*. Of course man is wretched; but in *knowing* that he is wretched, he is also great. The fragment which expresses this idea (114) gives the impression that Pascal had not quite found the neat formula he was seeking; we find that formula in a fragment from section 7° which moves from this point to the next stage in the argument (no. 122): 'Il est donc misérable puisqu'il l'est, mais il est bien grand puisqu'il le connaît.'

This pattern of argument has been encountered before, in fragment 71, with which we concluded chapter 3: man was there said to be proud to know his wretchedness.

A more serious objection is that Pascal has already proved beyond any dispute that man's judgment is feeble. Pascal proposes three counters to meet this objection. The first is that we must distinguish between potential and achievement. Even if it has been wrongly used, and even if its deficiencies are manifest, in itself reason is good.

Pensée.
Toute la dignité de l'homme est en la pensée, mais
qu'est-ce que cette penséé? Qu'elle est sotte?[3] La
pensée est donc une chose admirable et incomparable
par sa nature. Il fallait qu'elle eût d'étranges
défauts pour être méprisable, mais elle en a de tels
que rien n'est plus ridicule. Qu'elle est grande par
sa nature, qu'elle est basse par ses défauts (756).

L'homme n'agit point par sa raison, qui fait son être
(491).[4]

The second counter is more ironic, an instance of
'renversement du pour au contre' which attempts to prove
that no sceptic is consistent in his doubt. One of the
symptoms of vanity was 'la gloire,' and our need for the
good report of our fellows. The 'sanity' of this had been
touched upon in section 5° (101). But it can be made to
yield to another conclusion. We have already read the
pensée on vanity which pointed out that even those who
are most vociferous in their condemnation of human judgment are not exempt from the need to feel themselves approved (627). Thus 'la recherche de la gloire,' which we
know to be 'la plus grande bassesse de l'homme' becomes,
by the same ironic turnabout that made 'la raison des
effets' a sign of greatness, 'la plus grande marque de
son excellence' (470). Vanity, too, is a sign of greatness. Needing to be thought well of by others as we do,
how can we deny that we have an elevated opinion of man
(411, 1109)?

(e) la clarté naturelle (109)

Amusing though that reversal is, it does not really
answer the objection that in the kind of debate which
separates dogmatists and sceptics, Pascal has sided unequivocally with the sceptics. He does, however, part
company with the sceptics on one important issue. In one
respect it is the dogmatists who have 'les opinions
saines.' For nobody can be a thoroughgoing sceptic. In
fragment 109, after strengthening the sceptics' case
still further, Pascal discloses the flaw in their position. Although in their debate with the dogmatists, the
victors' palm goes to them, the victory over rivals is
not total. They make the mistake of assuming that reason

has to do the whole job unaided. But there is something else, 'la clarté naturelle,' which is obscured, but not extinguished. This 'clarté naturelle,' unable to give a foolproof justification of itself, but proof all the same against scepticism, is the subject of the very important fragment 110:

> Quelque impuissance où nous soyons de le prouver par raison, cette impuissance ne conclut autre chose que la faiblesse de notre raison, mais non pas l'incertitude de toutes nos connaissances, comme ils le prétendent.

Certain basis things are known instinctively, by the heart, and they are known as surely as other things, accessible only to reason, are known. As Jean Mesnard says, the 'renversement continuel du pour au contre' is applied here to the sceptics who, having challenged our belief in reason, are challenged in their turn, from a superior vantage-point, that of the heart.[5] The position outlined here will be of capital importance in enabling Pascal to state the case for religion. Even here he concludes with a paragraph on faith, and the superiority of intuitive faith over a conviction due entirely to reasoning. The argument will be picked up in the next chapter, with another very important fragment, no. 131.

Fragment 112 ('Instinct et raison, marques de deux natures') is capable of different interpretations. It could refer to the elevated and the base in human nature, analogous to no. 633.[6] But fragment 406 invites us to link it to no. 110 and the incomplete victory of scepticism over dogmatism:

> Instinct, raison.
>   Nous avons une impuissance de prouver, invincible à tout le dogmatisme.
>   Nous avons une idée de la vérité invincible à tout le pyrrhonisme.

We are thus led back to the implication of no. 117 that there are two natures in man, one being his true state from which he has fallen. And reason has now become a sign of *misère*, because the instrument we are forced to rely upon is so inadequate.

Section 6° thus confirms the impression made by section 5°, that Pascal's method is a 'renversement continuel du

pour au contre'; at the same time, it witnesses to a
complexity which is not that of straightforward dialetic.
   The title, 'Grandeur,' suggests that facts are about
to be presented which will challenge what has preceded.
But no radical contradiction is implied. The new facts
do not dislodge the previous ones, they simply point to
different conclusions, or else the former facts are considered in a different light. What is really Pascalian
about the method is this use of ideas which are already
familiar. We are now able to recognize several recurring
motifs, and watch with interest as a new pattern emerges.
   In the overall design of the Apologia, section 6° is
very important, partly because it brings ideas into a
new focus, and also because in so doing it prepares for
further refinements to the pattern in later sections.

7
Contrariétés

If we have understood why sections on man's *bassesse*
were followed by one on *grandeur*, we will not be surprised
by the title of section 7°, 'Contrariétés.' Contradiction
is fundamental to the picture Pascal has been building
up - contradictions between one day's behaviour and the
next, contradictions between different aspects of the
same personality, contradictions between the two most
plausible views of what man's essential nature is. In
the seventh section, Pascal brings out these different
contradictions, argues that if we fail to understand that
both sides of each pair are to be taken seriously, we
can never comprehend our own nature, and he shows that
the key to the paradox will not be provided by natural
reason alone.

Of the thirteen fragments in the bundle, two are entitled 'Contrariétés.' One of them (124), along with one
entitled 'Contradiction' (123), does no more than note
some examples of man's contrariness. Most of the fragments, however, address themselves to the different
stages of the argument outlined above.

There is an unclassed fragment with the title 'Contrariétés' (458), but it fits best into the closing
phase of the Apologia.[1] On the other hand, sixteen unclassed fragments underline points made in the classified *pensées* of this section, nos 404 (I); 450 (V); 464
(XI); 521, 530, 576 (XXIII); 613, 619, 629 (XXIV); 646,
655, 691, 695 (XXV); 803 (XXIX); 886, 905 (XXXIV).

The presentation is divided into three:
(a) examples of observed contradictions are endless.
Faced by contradictions, we should pay attention to
both the contradictory elements. We have two natures,
corresponding to the titles 'Misère' and 'Grandeur.'
(b) failure to understand our double nature is very
dangerous. Self-knowledge will help each one of us to

make correct moral decisions and will lead us to realize
that we are 'incomprehensible monsters.' Either way, we
will be brought closer to Christianity.
(c) Pascal traces in detail how systematic reflection
upon the problem of the nature of man leads to a willingness to accept Christianity. Philosophers should not
stress *grandeur* above *misère*, or vice versa, but should
realize man's essential duality. In fragment 131, Pascal
examines the strengths and weaknesses of the sceptical
position, and several other fragments offer glosses. The
sceptics' basic position is strong; we cannot prove that
life is not a dream. What often passes for 'nature' is
not easily distinguished from custom. Yet we are bound
to act on certain ingrained assumptions. In all respects,
man faces in two directions. The only way out of the
dilemma is to turn to God for a revealed answer. The
Christian doctrine of the fall, though itself incomprehensible, has the great merit of taking all the evidence
into account.

(a) et grandeur et misère (122)

Fragment 124 ('Contrariétés') and 123 ('Contradiction')
are both brief jottings giving examples of everyday contradictions to be observed in man's attitudes. Another
very specific instance is furnished by no. 120, and no.
129 observes: 'Que de natures en celle de l'homme.' This
fragment is in all essential respects a double of no. 35,
from section 2°; the title ('Métier') is almost identical
with that of no. 37, also in section 2°. But the main
thrust of this section is more serious than just to mul-
tiply examples in the manner of section 2°. One of the
unclassified fragments (576) reads:

Les deux raisons contraires. Il faut commencer par là;
sans cela on n'entend rien, et tout est hérétique. Et
même à la fin de chaque vérité il faut ajouter qu'on
se souvient de la vérité opposée.

We have already realized, of course, that Pascal was
proceeding according to this method; in section 5° he
gave a totally different view of matters we thought already settled, and section 6° staked a claim for man's
greatness which we might have believed excluded by what
went before. More than that, he showed that 'misère' was

itself indissolubly linked with greatness, as without a
lost vocation for higher things, we would be content with
what we have (117, 6°).

Fragment 122 (which bears the initials A P.R., to be
explained in chapter 11), is entitled 'Grandeur et Misère,'
and it takes up this very point, that one cannot separate
the two concepts of *misère* and *grandeur*. If one person
makes out a strong case for *grandeur*, his listeners, provided they are so disposed, will simply be made more
conscious than ever of their *misère*, 'puisque c'est être
d'autant plus misérable qu'on est tombé de plus haut.'
If a person makes out a case for *misère*, this only points
to man's essential (lost) greatness. The truth is, man
is compounded of greatness and wretchedness. 'A mesure
que les hommes ont de lumière ils trouvent et grandeur
et misère dans l'homme.' Fragment 613, also headed
'Grandeur, misère,' quotes this phrase, and develops it
in exactly the same way as no. 90 in section 5°:

> Grandeur, misère.
>   A mesure qu'on a de lumière on découvre plus de
> grandeur et plus de bassesse dans l'homme.
>   Le commun des hommes.
>   Ceux qui sont plus élevés.
>   Les philosophes.
>   Ils étonnent le commun des hommes.
>   Les chrétiens, ils étonnent les philosophes.
>   Qui s'étonnera donc de voir que la religion ne fait
> que connaître à fond ce qu'on reconnaît d'autant plus
> qu'on a plus de lumière.

The point is, that we have two natures, corresponding to
misère and *grandeur*. If our experience teaches us of our
misère, the 'instinct ... qui nous élève' (633) teaches
us of our divine nature. This, I take it, is the sense
of no. 128: 'Deux choses instruisent l'homme de toute sa
nature: l'instinct et l'expérience.' And we neglect the
double lesson at our peril.

(b) que l'homme maintenant s'estime son prix (119)

It is as dangerous to allow a man to realize only one
side of his nature, as it is to keep him in ignorance
of both sides. He must be made to see that he is both
great and wretched, both angel and beast (121).

In no. 119 (entitled 'Contrariétés'), Pascal recapitu-
lates several of the main points of the elaborate demonstration of the previous sections: the *bassesse* (2°-4°),
the *grandeur* (6°), the capacity to know truth, together
with man's ineffectual attempts to use this capacity (cf.
no. 756, quoted in chapter 6):

Contrariétiés.
Après avoir montré la bassesse et la grandeur de
l'homme. Que l'homme maintenant s'estime son prix.
Qu'il s'aime, car il y a en lui une nature capable
de bien; mais qu'il n'aime pas cour cela les bassesses
qui y sont. Qu'il se méprise, parce que cette capacité
est vide; mais qu'il ne méprise pas pour cela cette
capacité naturelle. Qu'il se haïsse, qu'il s'aime: il
a en lui la capacité de connaître la vérité et d'être
heureux; mais il n'a point de vérité, ou constante ou
satisfaisante.

In the next paragraph, Pascal reveals clearly his missionary intention; self-knowledge will, he hopes, help
his reader to resist those parts of his lower nature
(passions, concupiscence), which are controlling him and
preventing him from making right decisions and keeping
to them:

Je voudrais donc porter l'homme à désirer d'en trouver,
à être prêt et dégagé des passions, pour la suivre où
il la trouvera, sachant combien sa connaissance s'est
obscurcie par les passions; je voudrais bien qu'il
haït en soi la concupiscence qui le détermine d'elle-
même, afin qu'elle ne l'aveuglât point pour faire son
choix, et qu'elle ne l'arrêtât point quand il aura choisi.

We are reminded that in no. 12 (1°) Pascal saw in the
passions the principal obstacle in the way of accepting
Christianity.
    In no. 130, a similar method - answering each valid
half-truth with the corresponding half-truth, *grandeur*
with *misère*, *misère* with *grandeur* - is said to be meant
to lead his opponent to see that he is a 'monstre incompréhensible.' A variant appears as no. 464: the opponent
must not be allowed to settle in either position (presumably because only if he is unsettled will he continue
his quest). Fragment 450 uses the same vocabulary as no.

119, saying that true religion will teach that man is
both great and wretched and teach us to love and loathe
ourselves. And so, awareness of our contradictions leads
us to, not away from, religion (404).

(c) l'homme passe infiniment l'homme (131)

If there are contradictions within man himself, there
are bound to be contradictory views of man. The fragments
discussed so far are all addressed to the individual, inviting him to recognize in his nature incomprehensible,
irreconcilable contradictions. The task of the individual,
sketched in no. 119, is to realize what are the obstacles
which keep him from seeking the truth, which he does not
know, but which he has the possibility of knowing. The
task of examining the contradictions in order to understand and resolve them belongs to the philosophers.

Philosophers have tended to close their eyes to the
aspect of man which is in contradiction with their own
view, finding him either 'grand et incomparable' or 'ab-
ject et vil,' according to whether they put more store
by man's destiny or by his observed behaviour:

> Car l'un nie la supposition de l'autre. L'un dit: il
> n'est point né à cette fin, car toutes ses actions y
> répugnent, l'autre dit: il s'éloigne de la fin quand
> il fait ces basses actions (127).

Could this be the implication also of the very enigmatic
no. 886: 'Pyrrhonien pour opiniâtre'?[2]

Instead of taking sides, a thinker should consider both
sides equally, and devote himself to seeing how they can
exist simultaneously. Faced with man's double nature,
some thinkers, remarks Pascal, following Montaigne, have
gone so far as to assume that he has two souls (629).

In this connection there is more to be said about the
sceptics and the dogmatists, whose dispute over the
powers and limitations of reason entered into the argument about man's greatness in section 6°.[3] In no. 110,
Pascal agreed with the dogmatists who say that certain
fundamentals are not subject to corrosive doubt. These
are 'les premiers principes,' known to the 'heart.'

The argument is continued in the long fragment no. 131,
which includes several sentences and paragraphs which
Pascal deleted, either in order to rewrite them, or

because he intended to develop the ideas elsewhere. He
allows that the sceptics are in a very strong position.
In one of the later paragraphs, he mentions some of their
criticisms of commonly held opinions in terms which show
how much he has himself drawn upon them; and he also remarks that it is not possible to be neutral, as that
simply plays into their hands. In the unclassed (and
scratched out) no. 521, he says that even the fact that
their case is not proven is merely one more instance of
the doubt which they claim to be all that reason can attain. In no. 33 (2°) Pascal said that the fact that not
everyone is sceptical is grist to the sceptics' mill.
Another unclassed fragment (905) speaks of our inability
to find a truth that cannot be contradicted, and the
heading he gives the fragment is 'Pyrrhonisme':

Chaque chose est ici vraie en partie, fausse en partie...
   Nous n'avons ni vrai, ni bien qu'en partie, et mêlé
de mal et de faux...
   Nous connaissons bien le mal et le faux. Mais que
dira-t-on qui soit bon?...

A sentence removed from no. 44 read: 'L'homme est donc
si heureusement fabriqué qu'il n'a aucun principe juste
du vrai, et plusieurs excellents du faux.'
   Pascal begins fragment 131 by allowing the sceptics to
reply to no. 110. They will concede that we might know
the truth of first principles by faith, revelation, or
inner certainty, but they challenge the status of this
so-called natural feeling.

Or ce sentiment naturel n'est pas une preuve convaincante de leur vérité, puisque n'y ayant point de certitude hors la foi, si l'homme est créé par un dieu
bon, par un démon méchant ou à l'aventure, il est en
doute si ces principes nous sont donnés ou véritables,
ou faux, ou incertains selon notre origine.

What we call 'sentiment' might be only fantasy,and reason cannot decide (530). One can also compare with this
the two fragments filed in the seventh bundle on nature
and custom (125 and 126), along with no. 646 on natural
feelings and reason, no. 616 ('La concupiscence nous est
devenue naturelle et a fait notre seconde nature') and
no. 630, which we allied to section 2°. Custom breeds

what we call second nature. Are we sure that what we call nature is not a first custom, bred in us by heredity and environment?

In fragment 131, where he seems to be thinking more of Descartes than Montaigne, Pascal gives the standard argument from our experience of dreaming (once again, an unclassed fragment should be brought in - no. 803, which gives an original development to the same idea). The dogmatists, he says, have no irrefutable answer.

But we all have to take sides on the issue, and Pascal remarks that in practice we are all dogmatists:

> Je m'arrête à l'unique fort des dogmatistes qui est qu'en parlant de bonne foi et sincèrement on ne peut douter des principes naturels...
>   Doutera-t-il de tout ... doutera-t-il s'il doute, doutera-t-il s'il est? On n'en peut venir là, et je mets en fait qu'il n'y a jamais eu de pyrrhonien effectif parfait. La nature soutient la raison impuissante et l'empêche d'extravaguer jusqu'à ce point.

'Nous savons que nous ne rêvons point,' he had written in no. 110. An unclassed fragment (655) noted similarly that 'peu parlent ... du pyrrhonisme en doutant.' (That remark was made as one of several examples of 'mensonge, duplicité, contrariété,' of contradictions between speech and spirit.) In no. 75 he had written, probably as an afterthought: 'il ne peut même douter.' And in no. 619, he writes:

> Tous leurs principes sont vrais, des pyrrhoniens, des stoïques, des athées etc. ... mais leurs conclusions sont fausses, parce que les principes opposés sont vrais aussi.

Yet it remains true that we can never prove that we possess truth with any certainty. The conclusion therefore must be that man is a fantastic mixture of extremes. The contradictions already noted are capped by this ultimate contradiction between conviction and doubt. Pascal makes his point in a series of powerful questions:

> Quelle chimère est-ce donc que l'homme? quelle nouveauté, quel monstre, quel chaos, quel sujet de contradictions, quel prodige? Juge de toutes choses, imbécile ver de

terre, dépositaire du vrai, cloaque d'incertitude et
d'erreur, gloire et rebut de l'univers.

How can we advance further? Neither pyrrhonist nor dogmatist can give the answer. Like the two types of thinker
evoked in no. 122 'ils se sont portés les uns sur les
autres par un cercle sans fin,' the first opposed by our
nature which refuses to be totally sceptical, the second
opposed by reason which is sceptical of any claim to have
attained truth.[4] Consequently, natural reason cannot
discern what is man's 'véritable condition.'

It follows, says Pascal, that as neither reason nor
nature can provide the answer, as 'l'homme passe infiniment l'homme,' he must turn to God for the answer. Before
the revelation of God's purpose in Christ, he says in no.
691, there was no possibility of understanding, and the
sceptics were right.[5] But now we have the Christian explanation of man. What is it?

The first sentence of the concluding section of fragment 131 is crossed out. It read: 'N'est-il donc pas
clair comme le jour que la condition de l'homme est
double?' Realization of this is an indispensable prerequisite of understanding. The Christian answer takes
into account man's double nature, by the doctrine of the
fall. Man is what he is, but not what he once was.

Si l'homme n'avait jamais été corrompu il jouirait dans
son innocence et de la vérité et de la félicité avec
assurance. Et si l'homme n'avait jamais été que corrompu
il n'aurait aucune idée ni de la vérité ni de la béatitude. Mais malheureux que nous sommes ... nous sentons
une image de la vérité et ne possédons que le mensonge.

The doctrine of the fall implies the transmission of sin
down the ages. Pascal finds another monstrous paradox
here: without this doctrine we cannot have any understanding of what man is, yet the doctrine itself is incomprehensible, even offensive. This notion is found also in
no. 695.

The last five paragraphs of no. 131 were all subsequently crossed out. In them, Pascal considered the
mystery of original sin further. He holds that God has
deliberately made the mystery incomprehensible, in order
to humiliate our reason. He defines the basic theological
truths of the two natures of man, one bringing him close

to God, the other bringing him close to the animals, and cites scriptural authority. This conclusion agrees with the unclassed no. 404:

> Toutes ces contrariétés qui semblaient le plus m'éloig-
> ner de la connaissance d'une religion est ce qui m'a
> le plus tôt conduit à la véritable.[6]

Pascal evidently decided that the time was not yet ripe for this development, that this seventh section should not go further than the bare statement of the Christian explanation of the paradox of man, admitting that it is itself difficult to comprehend. The argument will be continued in section 11°: meanwhile, Pascal, who has slipped into section 7° a number of references to 'le bien' as well as to 'le vrai,' will give more space to that aspect of the good life, neglected since it was first mentioned in section 2°.

8
Divertissement (132-9)

There is evidence to suggest that the theme of *divertis-sement*, which is the subject of the eighth section, was originally to have been treated in sections 2° and 3°.[1] The centrepiece, no. 136, was entitled 'Divertissement' only as an afterthought, the first title being 'Misère de l'homme.' Other fragments in sections 2° and 3° have announced the theme of *divertissement*. In section 2°, no. 39 is close to one of the ideas developed in no. 136: 'Les hommes s'occupent à suivre une balle et un lièvre: c'est le plaisir même des rois.' No. 36, taking a rather different viewpoint from the one developed in section 8°, said that everyone recognized the vanity of human exist-ence 'excepté de jeunes gens qui sont tous dans le bruit, dans le divertissement, et dans la pensée de l'avenir,' and it touched on one important function of *le divertis-sement*, that it is a bulwark against anguish:

Mais ôtez leur divertissement vous les verrez se sécher d'ennui. Ils sentent alors leur néant sans le connaître, car c'est bien être malheureux que d'être dans une tristesse insupportable, aussitot qu'on est réduit à se considérer, et à n'en être point diverti.

But it is more usual for Pascal to regard *le divertisse-ment* as a universal preoccupation. Even in the second section (no. 47), Pascal had said that we are all pre-occupied with the future, expecting a happiness which eludes us.

In section 3°, Pascal noted as evidence of our wretched-ness the fact that we need to be distracted from our own thoughts (70, repeating 889). A fragment in the very first bundle ('Ordre') read: 'Les misères de la vie humaine ont fondé tout cela. Comme ils ont vu cela, ils ont pris le divertissement' (10). In no. 414, entitled 'Misère,'

Pascal remarks that although *le divertissement* consoles us, by preventing us from facing the problem of the human condition squarely, it acts as 'la plus grande de nos misères.'

The very full development given to the subject in no. 136, together with the other seven fragments put with it in this eighth bundle, which can all be allied with no. 136, makes it understandable that Pascal should have wished to consider it as an independent theme. Possibly the first indication of this intention was section 4°, which was to have dealt with the 'qualités essentielles de l'homme,' singling out 'Ennui.' I cited in connection with section 4° an unclassed fragment, the only one actually to be entitled 'Ennui,' no. 622:

Ennui.
　　Rien n'est si insupportable à l'homme que d'être dans un plein repos, sans passions, sans affaires, sans divertissement, sans application.
　　Il sent alors son néant, son abandon, son insuffisance, sa dépendance, son impuissance, son vide.
　　Incontinent il sortira du fond de son âme l'ennui, la noirceur, la tristesse, le chagrin, le dépit, le désespoir.

In section 5° there is another reference to *le divertissement*, (no. 101):

Le peuple a les opinions très saines. Par exemple.
　　D'avoir choisi le divertissement, et la chasse plutôt que la prise. Les demi-savants s'en moquent et triomphent à montrer là-dessus la folie du monde, mais par une raison qu'ils ne pénètrent pas, on a raison.

In no. 620, which I included above along with section 6°, Pascal commented on the fact that we betray our vocation as thinkers, in terms which imply *le divertissement*, even if the word itself is not used:

Or à quoi pense le monde? ... à danser, à jouer du luth, à chanter, à faire des vers, à courir la bague etc. à se battre, à se faire roi, sans penser à ce que c'est qu'être roi et qu'être homme.

And no. 771, which I associated with no. 27 on change,

refers to the boredom experienced even by kings and princes.
Any of the fragments just quoted could conceivably have
been allocated or, in the case of the classified ones,
transferred to the bundle marked 'Divertissement,' had
Pascal ever got round to reconsidering fragments already
sorted. But with so many fragments still to classify, it
is understandable that he should postpone revision until
the first job was completed. With no. 136 he was more
lucky, as he was able to redirect it, from 'Misère' to
'Divertissement,' while he was still working on it. As
five of the seven fragments included with it in the
eighth dossier have the same title, 'Divertissement,'
we can assume that they were written at the same period,
and indeed they are all amplifications of aspects of no.
136. Other amplifications appear on the margins of no.
136, and could easily have been given separate numbers
and counted separately. Michel Le Guern, in an invaluable
article on the composition of no. 136, suggests that no.
39 was a marginal gloss also, which Pascal cut out and
put with his second bundle.[2]

I said earlier that the unclassified fragment 622 belonged, by its title, to section 4°. It too could well
have been a gloss on 136 (*ennui* being an obvious stimulus
to *divertissement*), and maybe we should not attach too
much importance to the title as a guide to its definitive
classification, particularly as section 4° was more or
less stillborn.

Not counting nos 620 and 622, there are nine unclassified fragments which it has seemed reasonable to include
in the discussion of section 8: nos 415 (I); 478 (XI);
522, 523 (XXIII); 638, 639, 687, 710 (XXV); 773 (XXVII).[3]
No. 414 is evoked as a possible conclusion to the section.

I begin the discussion with the two fragments which bear
no title (134, 135). They speak of our need to avoid
thinking about our condition, a point picked up in nos
133 and 138 as well as in no. 136. I then analyse the
long fragment in detail, incorporating en route nos 478
and 522. The remaining *pensées* amplify aspects of no. 136.

The general argument is as follows: we talk as if we
are looking forward to the day when we can rest from our
labours, our activities, but we are wrong. If we have
nothing to do, either we become bored, or else we start
to think about the human condition, and anything which
distracts us from thinking about the human condition is

welcome. It is the activity which is good for us, not
what the activity is geared to produce. Yet it is not
really good for us at all, as reflection leading to self-
knowledge is ultimately very salutary.

The nature of no. 136, in which Pascal discovers his
own thought in gradual stages, means that the argument
is nowhere set down as clearly as in the previous paragraph, but the main themes, and various possible connecting links, are unambiguous.

One final question remains to be mentioned: why did
Pascal delay this section on 'Divertissement' until now,
rather than substitute it for section 4° as being part
and parcel of 'Vanité' and 'Misère'? I shall discuss
this question in my final paragraph.

As we have a desire for truth, unquenchable for all our
misère, so we have a desire for happiness. Yet our higher
nature, cruelly dependent on our lower nature, merely
makes us aware of our failure. *Pensée* 135, which does
not specifically mention *le divertissement* or any of the
other motifs of the section, but which was nevertheless
placed in this bundle by Pascal, implies that despair
comes from an awareness of our own greatness. For although my essence is in my power to think - the cartesian
source is obvious - that power presupposes my bodily
existence, which is subject to various combinations of
chance events. There must be a being who is infinite,
eternal, necessary, but no individual mortal man is necessary to the universe.

No. 134 links this idea with the theme of *le divertissement*. At the same time it completes the sense of no.
75, which drew a parallel between the twin impulses for
happiness and truth, but then concentrated on truth:

> L'Ecclésiaste montre que l'homme sans Dieu est dans
> l'ignorance de tout et dans un malheur inévitable, car
> c'est être malheureux que de vouloir et ne pouvoir. Or
> il veut être heureux et assuré de quelque vérité. Et
> cependant il ne peut ni savoir ni ne désirer point de
> savoir. Il ne peut même douter (75).

Here is the text of no. 134:

> Nonobstant ces misères il veut être heureux et ne veut
> être qu'heureux, et ne peut ne vouloir pas l'être.

Mais comment s'y prendra-t-il? Il faudrait pour bien
faire qu'il se rendît immortel, mais ne le pouvant il
s'est avisé de s'empêcher d'y penser.

We cannot bear the thought of our own mortality; such
is the idea also of the cryptic no. 138, and of no. 133,
which adds 'la misère' and 'l'ignorance' to 'la mort' as
thoughts we wish to escape from.[4] In a personal note
(687), Pascal notes with surprise that though he expected
to find many more students of geometry, he was wrong, and
he explains this state of affairs by saying 'il lui est
meilleur de s'ignorer pour être heureux.'

'Le divertissement' is simply whatever stops us from
thinking about ourselves. The argument is given in full
in no. 136, a difficult fragment, as Pascal left it with
several loose ends untied - although others were pruned,
sometimes rashly. One has the impression that Pascal was
taken by surprise as he wrote; there are many passages
which read like conclusions, but the thought immediately
takes wing anew.[5]

Men give themselves over to feverish activity which
produces several harmful side-effects (danger, disputes,
etc.). So it would seem reasonable to dismiss *divertissement* as vanity, and come to the smug conclusion that
'tout le malheur des hommes vient d'une seule chose, qui
est de ne savoir pas demeurer en repos dans une chambre.'

But further reflection suggests that there is a good
reason for the universal practice of distraction. We
cannot bear to think about our wretched condition. Therefore, very sensibly, we distract ourselves. This is
equally true of a king, who will realize how precarious
his authority is. A kind of conclusion came in here,
which Pascal deleted:

L'unique bien des hommes consiste donc à être divertis
de penser à leur condition ou par une occupation qui
les en détourne, ou par quelque passion agréable et
nouvelle qui les occupe, ou par le jeu, la chasse,
quelque spectacle attachant, et enfin par ce qu'on
appelle divertissement.

(Fragment 478 notes that 'sans examiner toutes les occupations particulières, il suffit de les comprendre sous
le divertissement.')

Instead of concluding here, however, Pascal continued,

saying that the virtue in *le divertissement* lies in the
distracting activity, not in the goals we set ourselves
as the stimulus for activity. Solitude is therefore to
be shunned. A king (returning to the example of paragraph
three) is kept continually diverted. Consequently (another conclusion, balancing the opening), people who are
critical of *le divertissement* have not understood man's
nature. True, the hare we chase has no particular value,
but the chase itself has the very real advantage of keeping our minds off our parlous state.

As I read the evidence, Pascal added an example at this
point. The example is the advice given by Pyrrhus to take
rest (reported by Montaigne). It is bad advice, says
Pascal, as it assumes our condition to be happy, so that
we can be left alone with our thoughts. But that is to
misunderstand our nature. 'Aussi les hommes qui sentent
naturellement leur condition n'évitent rien tant que le
repos; il n'y a rien qu'ils ne fassent pour chercher le
trouble.' In the course of revising his text, this development was crossed out, except for the example which,
probably in error, was left intact.[6]

The next part of the fragment was rewritten many times.
The point comes over very clearly in the first draft:
those who seek distraction should not be criticized for
that; they should be criticized for not grasping the real
reason for desiring distraction, for believing the goals
set to be valuable in themselves:

> le mal est qu'ils recherchent [le tumulte] comme si la
> possession des choses qu'ils recherchent les devait
> rendre véritablement heureux, et c'est en quoi on a
> raison d'accuser leur recherche de vanité de sorte
> qu'en tout cela et ceux qui blâment et ceux qui sont
> blâmés n'entendent la véritable nature de l'homme.

It is another instance of the progression 'peuple - demi-
habiles - habiles.'

The revised version of this thought is less clear.
The second part of the new version was itself completely
rewritten. The expansion includes the word 'repos' as
being the goal we mistakenly believe we are after. It
has been anticipated by the reference to Pyrrhus, maintained above.

We rejoin the original text as the words 'Ils ont un
instinct secret.' It is a reflection on 'repos,' and it

has nothing to do with the 'renversement du pour au contre' of the first part. Pascal here uses the kind of argument we found in no. 117 about the 'roi dépossédé.' We have two instincts, he says, one pushing us towards distraction, to keep our minds off our *misère*, and the other which tells us that satisfaction is to be found in repose, not activity. This instinct, Pascal believes, is a vestige of 'la grandeur de notre première nature.' The result of having these two instincts is that we persuade ourselves that after our busy activity we shall find peace and satisfaction. But rest is unbearable, and we throw ourselves into more activity, always with the same illusory hope.

Concluding, Pascal mentions a new idea, that life without distraction engenders boredom (rather than anguish, implied hitherto). The rest of the paragraph (part of which was later removed) is another quasi-conclusion to the fragment. Pascal begins by saying that happiness can come only through 'le divertissement,' but it is a poor happiness which consists in being distracted from thinking about oneself. He appears to have started another new thought here, about the 'great' of this world, who can ensure that they are kept distracted.[7] (The idea is similar to what he had written about the kings earlier.) But he immediately returned to the theme of *ennui*. Even if one did not think about oneself, one would still be unhappy, because without *le divertissement*, one would be subjected to boredom. This seems to be independent of the idea of reflecting on the human condition. (If we look back to no. 36 [2°], we can see how Pascal conceived the relation between *ennui* and *divertissement*. Without *le divertissement*, Pascal says there, we find *l'ennui:* 'Ils sentent alors leur néant sans le connaître.' The next stage would be to become conscious of our *néant*, and experience despair.) Once again, we seem to have reached a conclusion, putting everything heard to date under the double heading of *misère* (man is naturally subject to *ennui*) and *vanité* (man is distracted by any trivial object).[8]

But once again, Pascal carries on further. Why should man find pleasure in such things? The motive force Pascal finds is vanity in the ordinary sense. Man acts in order to boast of what he has achieved. Most curious of all, some people spend most of their energies in denouncing vanity, and they are 'les plus sots de la bande' because they very literally should know better.

The following paragraph is intended to illustrate the contention, already mentioned, that the hunt is more important than what it produces. If you gave a man the object of his activity before he set out, he would not be pleased; yet if there were no object, he would have no motive. Hence, in order to act, he has to deceive himself, and believe that he really does want the object sought.

Idleness can threaten any happiness, and distraction can end any grief. Another conclusion, one would think. But no, Pascal is ready with one more example, to make his point vivid, after which he recopies his conclusion, with the two halves in the reverse order. (The example, of a bereaved father, comes from a longer fragment [522] where there was a conclusion not incorporated in the eighth section: that a man is equally foolish if he refuses distraction, as he is 'ni ange, ni bête, mais homme.' This idea will recur in the following section.)

Pascal's revisions are of two kinds. As well as changing the title from 'Misère' to 'Divertissement,' he added several unconnected thoughts in the margin, which editors have inserted, rather clumsily, into the text. He also made substantial changes to four passages, which have given his manuscript the aspect of a veritable labyrinth.

The first of these is a long suppression we have already mentioned, beginning with the sentence about Pyrrhus.

The second change comes one page later, where Pascal had given one of his quasi-conclusions (that happiness can come only through *le divertissement*). It concerns a manuscript page containing three paragraphs, which originally followed the sentence, now deleted, 'Nulle condition n'est heureuse sans bruit et sans divertissement, etc.'[9] It is not wholly clear what the sequence of events must have been, but it looks as if Pascal started to revise his second paragraph, then crossed it out, writing a much revised version of it in the margin at the bottom of the previous page; a cross-reference sign indicates that the third paragraph was to follow.[10] There is no indication, yet, what was to happen to the first paragraph. When I presented this part of the fragment, I implied that this first paragraph (about the distraction nobles offer themselves) was a kind of digression.

The third major change comes a few lines later. After the provisional conclusion of *misère* and *vanité*, I have said, Pascal had written a further development covering

two paragraphs, and he had displaced his conclusion when
he had the idea of adding an illustration at that point.[11]
When he revised his text, he decided to put the illustration in much earlier, and he recopied it, with a few im-
provements in wording, at the beginning of the passage.[12]
He evidently considered that it followed well from the
conclusion of the previous passage. One further advantage
of this is that the example of a distraction through hunt-
ing, given in the transferred passage, is mentioned also
at the beginning of the original development, and the
two texts fit together nicely. Pascal, however, had second
thoughts, probably because he could not see what could
replace the transferred passage at the end of the development, and he crossed out what he had just written, and
changed the subsequent reference to the hunt. Then he
had third thoughts, and did what he had done for the previous passage: he indicated, by moving the cross-reference
sign in the margin, that he would keep the link between
the end of the previous passage and the illustration he
had just considered moving, even if that meant cutting
out the whole of the two paragraphs that separated them.

Finally, Pascal found that yet again he was not ready
to call it a day. Employing his system of cross-references
once more, he indicated that the example of the nobility
employing people to divert them could be salvaged, and
could be inserted at the end of the piece.

Other fragments echo and expand parts of no. 136. Distraction is effective, because we cannot think of two
things simultaneously (523).[13] Another unclassed *pensée*
illustrates the thought that 'Rien ne nous plaît que le
combat, mais non pas la victoire' (773).[14] No. 137 is
quite a long development on the position of kings who
need distracting as much as anyone. The origin of this
is probably a marginal gloss on the fifth paragraph of
no. 136, which Pascal did not have room, on that manuscript, to develop fully.

One sentence of no. 136 which disappeared in the course
of revision, read: 'mais qu'on juge quel est ce bonheur
qui consiste à être diverti de penser à soi.' Other fragments question the idea that *le divertissement* can be
equated with happiness. No. 132 makes the point that *le
divertissement* makes man dependent on forces outside him.
Nor is it certain that distraction always brings undis-
turbed pleasure, because relaxation can tire if we have
too much of it (710). We never find happiness because

every state brings its own specific desires (638-9). It is thus not self-evident that all this activity necessarily makes a man happy. Nevertheless, counters Pascal (139), without it man would be more miserable. No. 415 makes the same point, more pungently, and is headed 'Agitation.'

None of these fragments suggests how Pascal would have concluded his chapter, but one can confidently assume that he would have wished to emphasize two ideas. One is stated clearly in the unclassed fragment which Pascal entitled 'Misère,' but which is specifically about *le divertissement*, no. 414. We would be better advised if we did contemplate our mortality, instead of running away from it, because deeper study might reveal a genuine answer to our need (an idea implied also by no. 36).

> Misère.
>   La seule chose qui nous console de nos misères est le divertissement. Et cependant c'est la plus grande de nos misères. Car c'est cela qui nous empêche principalement de songer à nous et qui nous fait perdre insensiblement. Sans cela nous serions dans l'ennui, et cet ennui nous pousserait à chercher un moyen plus solide d'en sortir, mais le divertissement nous amuse et nous fait arriver insensiblement à la mort.

And we have been given a clue as to the direction in which we might seek, when Pascal spoke in no. 136 of our double nature, a part of us desiring to rest, and then explained that desire as a vestige of our former nature. This argument is exactly parallel to the one found in section 7° (no. 131), which led from a similar realization to the Christian explanation of the fall. Here too we are on the threshold of a Christian account of the situation which has been expounded, but we do not actually cross that threshold before section 11°.

Pascal has been more concerned with why than what in this section, which is more indicative of his larger design than anything he put into section 3°. A brief retrospective glance at the earlier sections will show us why section 8° was left until after the sections 'Grandeur' and 'Contrariétés.' In section 2°, fragment 28 spoke of our fruitless search for three things: justice, truth, and 'le bien' (well-being, happiness, felicity):

Toutes les occupations des hommes sont à avoir du bien
et ils ne sauraient avoir de titre pour montrer qu'ils
le possèdent par justice, car ils n'ont que la fantaisie
des hommes, ni force pour le posséder sûrement.
    Il en est de même de la science...
    Nous sommes incapables et de vrai et de bien.

Justice and truth were touched on in fragment 44 in the
same chapter, justice and *le bien* in section 3°. Section
5°, which introduced the key figure 'renversement continuel du pour au contre,' concentrated on justice. Sections 6° and 7° applied the same method to man's search
for reason, coming to the conclusion that 'dépositaire
du vrai, cloaque d'incertitude et d'erreur,' man is an
incomprehensible mixture of contradictions, manifesting
a double nature for which only Christianity had any explanation.
    Sections 8° to 10° will look at man's search for the
sovereign good in the same way. Section 8°, we have seen,
begins with another example of the 'renversement,' picking
up the paragraph already quoted from no. 101, giving the
attitude of the 'habiles,' but implying that there is a
Christian perspective which changes things yet again.
The sections which follow will treat *le divertissement*
like pyrrhonism earlier, as one element in a diptych of
contradictions.

Philosophes

The seven fragments which Pascal placed in his ninth dossier all deal with the Stoic philosophers, who invited
man to unite himself with God, forgetting that such advice is totally unpractical. I have added to this group
six unclassed fragments: 626 (XXIV), 681 (XXV), 829
(XXXI), 933, 988 and 1112.[1] Taken as a separate group,
these thirteen *pensées* require very little in the way
of commentary.

They yield more once one attempts to fit them into the
evolving design of the Apologia. The basic pattern *misère-
grandeur-contrariétés* is easily discernible. In place of
the pyrrhonists and dogmatists and their opposed views
about man's ability to reach the truth, we now have
Epicureans and Stoics in disagreement about the nature
of the Sovereign Good, and once again Pascal believes
that both sides have failed completely to see the true
implications of their particular insights, as they rule
out the views of their opponents. The only way to advance
is to recognize the validity of both sides, to conclude
provisionally that man is incomprehensible and to examine
the explanations suggested by thinkers who have accepted
that the riddle of human nature is soluble. This development from this section 9°, leading to the explanation
advanced in section 11°, is not touched upon by any of
the classified fragments, but it seems that this is the
best place to insert a second group of unclassified
pensées which view the Stoics in this perspective: nos
398, 399, 400, 401, 407, 410 (I); 430 (III); 443 (V);
477 (XI); 621 (XXIV); 678 (XXV); 795 (XXVIII).[2]

(a) ce que les stoïques proposent (144)

In no. 136 Pascal had spoken of 'ceux qui font ... les
philosophes et qui croient que le monde est bien peu

raisonnable de passer tout le jour à courir après un
lièvre.' An unclassed fragment (no. 626) tells us more:

Recherche du vrai bien.
Le commun des hommes met le bien dans la fortune et dans
les biens du dehors ou au moins dans le divertissement.
Les philosophes ont montré la vanité de tout cela et
l'ont mis où ils ont pu.

The section 'Philosophes' deals with the Stoics who believe that 'Dieu est seul digne d'être aimé et d'être
admiré' (142). In this they have correctly located the
source of happiness. But it is not enough simply to issue
counsels of perfection, and Pascal criticizes the Stoics
for failing to understand the limitations of human nature.
It is firstly unreasonable to expect everyone to do
what a few can do (146, recalling no. 100), to expect
everyone to attain complete virtue (144), or to expect
to do regularly what one might accomplish once (829).
For man cannot reach God unaided, as is noted in a crisp
antithesis (141): a man who does not know his limitations
cannot hope to do so, and a man who does know his limitations will not presume to try. The only way to God is
Jesus Christ, says Pascal (140), revealing, but not
arguing for, the Christian resolution of the difficulty.
The philosophers talk of virtue, but they cannot recognize simple, unadorned virtue when they see it (1112).
One can perhaps attach to this thought Pascal's statement
in no. 681 that he could not admire a virtue which was
not accompanied by the corresponding counter-virtue.
Pascal believes that the Stoic philosophy ministers
to pride. ('Le lieu propre à la superbe est la sagesse,'
933.) The Stoics illustrate one of the three forms of
concupiscence (145), the *libido dominandi* mentioned in
no. 545 ('Tout ce qui est au monde est concupiscence de
la chair ou concupiscence des yeux ou orgueil de la
vie').[3] He accuses them of being inconsistent, of saying
that God alone deserves the love and admiration of men,
yet seeking the admiration and love of others for themselves (142; this balances the criticisms made of the
denouncers of vanity in nos 470 and 627).[4]
Fragment 694 (quoted in chapter 1) had named the Stoics
as an illustration of the 'vanité des vies philosophiques';
in no. 988 Pascal remarks that 'il est impossible que
Dieu soit jamais la fin s'il n'est le principe.'

Finally, no. 143 treats no. 626 (quoted above) to the characteristic Pascalian 'renversement.' The philosophers dismiss those who seek happiness outside themselves. But we have an instinct which obliges us to look outside. So we are unconvinced by the philosophers' injunction; 'on ne les croit pas et ceux qui les croient sont les plus vides et les plus sots.'

(b) ni ange ni bête (522, 678)

The logical continuation to this idea is provided by the unclassed no. 407:

> Les stoïques disent: rentrez au-dedans de vous-même, c'est là où vous trouverez votre repos. Et cela n'est pas vrai.
>   Les autres disent: sortez dehors et cherchez le bonheur en un divertissement. Et cela n'est pas vrai, les maladies viennent.
>   Le bonheur n'est ni hors de nous ni dans nous; il est en Dieu et hors et dans nous.

The Stoics are exclusive, they forget man's double nature, and hence they are both right and wrong.
    The fragment just quoted elevates the diversion-seekers to the status of a rival philosophical school, and although none of the classified fragments, in either section 8° or section 9° do that, there is a handful of unclassed *pensées* which view the Stoics as representing one of two contrasting attitudes to the Sovereign Good. This is very clear in no. 410 (which expands the jotting numbered 621):

> Cette guerre intérieure de la raison contre les passions a fait que ceux qui ont voulu avoir la paix se sont partagés en deux sectes. Les uns ont voulu renoncer aux passions et devenir dieux, les autres ont voulu renoncer à la raison et devenir bête brute ... Mais ils ne l'ont pu ni les uns ni les autres, et la raison demeure toujours qui accuse la bassesse et l'injustice des passions et qui trouble le repos de ceux qui s'y abandonnent. Et les passions sont toujours vivantes dans ceux qui y veulent renoncer.

('Peace' here is inner peace; when fragment 81 told us that 'La paix ... est le souverain bien,' it was referring

to civil peace.) The reason why the Epicureans are associated with beasts is explained in no. 795, where Pascal
argues that what disgraces a man is not yielding to the
flesh (as men, we are inevitably subject to the rule of
the flesh to some degree), but choosing carnal pleasure
where we do have a choice, that is, being dominated by
the flesh in circumstances where we could be master. The
Stoics make the opposite mistake, of forgetting that we
are flesh and treating us as gods or angels. The antithesis 'dieux/bêtes' of no. 410 reappears as 'ange/bête,'
as in the last sentence of no. 522, quoted in the previous
chapter ('Il n'est ni ange ni bête mais homme'; cf. also
no. 121: 'Il ne faut pas que l'homme croie qu'il est égal
aux bêtes, ni aux anges.'). In fragment 678 that opposition carries with it a stinging criticism of the Stoics:

> L'homme n'est ni ange ni bête, et le malheur veut que
> qui veut faire l'ange fait la bête.

No. 410, however, criticizes both factions equally,
and this is true of a number of fragments. Each is criticized for ignoring the other half of the picture, and
consequently the double nature of man. Neither group is
guilty of following error, but of ignoring a contrary
truth, which is dangerous (443). No. 399 indicates that
one cannot simply suppress contradictions:

> Si l'homme n'est fait pour Dieu, pourquoi n'est-il
> heureux qu'en Dieu?
> Si l'homme est fait pour Dieu, pourquoi est-il si
> contraire à Dieu?

The moral effect of these partial philosophies is pre-
dictably one-sided, neither 'des mouvements de grandeur
pure' nor 'des mouvements de bassesse pure' being appropriate to the human state (398). Humiliation should be
consciously cultivated in penitence, to be succeeded by
an elevation that is grounded in the grace of God.
Fragment 430 begins similarly: one group elevates man
unduly, the other humiliates him unduly. But it continues
differently, staying on the philosophical level and asking the question 'who, then is man?': 'sera-t-il egal à
Dieu ou aux bêtes? Quelle effroyable distance! Que serons-
nous donc?,' a phrase which echoes the question noted on
one of the fragments collected in the first dossier:
'Croirai-je que je ne suis rien? Croirai-je que je suis

Dieu?' (2). It goes on to explain the double nature of man by the fall, and notes that no philosopher can lead man back to the place from which he has fallen.

> Qui ne voit par tout cela que l'homme est égaré, qu'il est tombé de sa place, qu'il la cherche avec inquiétude, qu'il ne la peut plus retrouver. Et qui l'y adressera donc? Les plus grands hommes ne l'ont pu.[5]

We are reminded again of no. 140, 'J.-C. seul y mène.' Other unclassed fragments echo this paragraph of no. 430:

> L'homme ne sait à quel rang se mettre, il est visible-ment égaré et tombé de son vrai lieu sans le pouvoir retrouver. Il le cherche partout avec inquiétude et sans succès dans des ténèbres impénétrables (400).
>   Nous souhaitons la vérité et ne trouvons en nous qu'incertitude.
>   Nous recherchons le bonheur et ne trouvons que misère et mort.
>   Nous sommes incapables de ne pas souhaiter la vérité et le bonheur et sommes incapables ni de certitude ni de bonheur.
>   Ce désir nous est laissé tant pour nous punir que pour nous faire sentir d'où nous sommes tombés (401).

And this, no. 477, which picks up a note from section 3° ('Orgueil contrepesant toutes les misères,' 71):

> L'orgueil contrepèse et emporte toutes les misères. Voilà un étrange monstre, et un égarement bien visible. Le voilà tombé de sa place, il la cherche avec inquiétude C'est ce que tous les hommes font. Voyons qui l'aura trouvée.

The closeness of the parallel between the argument of section 9°, taken together with the amplification provided by the last group of fragments, and that of section 7° ('Contrariétés') will be clear. 'Grandeur et misère' (122) has become 'Grandeur et bassesse.' The opposition of Epicureans and Stoics mirrors the earlier opposition of sceptics and dogmatists. There are two ways of looking at man (127, 410). Everything is true in part, we are told (905), and heresy is to exclude the opposite truth (576). In both cases (sceptics-dogmatists, Epicureans-

Stoics), each school has a valid point to make, but makes
it in the wrong perspective (119, 398). In both sections
the irreconcilable claims of the two factions - each
challenged by one aspect of man's double nature - lead
the writer to wonder about the true nature of man (131,
430). In both cases, the aim is the same: to get the
opponent worried. 'Et puis le [Dieu] faire chercher
chez les philosophes, pyrrhoniens et dogmatistes qui
travailleront celui qui le recherche' (4). And in both
cases, the only resolution of the difficulty comes from
Christianity (131, 140).

10
Le Souverain Bien

At first glance, section 10° appears quite straightforward. It contains only two fragments. One (no. 147) is
a short note entitled 'Dispute du Souverain Bien' which
taxes the Stoics with inconsistency, while the other
(148) is a polished but incomplete fragment belonging
to a larger argument concerning the Sovereign Good and
our inability to find it without faith. It too mentions
the dispute, and commends the Platonists for having a
more sensible idea of 'le vrai bien' than most others.

In fact, no. 148 presents a number of problems, of
which its incompletion is only one. Its title ('Seconde
partie. Que l'homme sans la foi ne peut connaître le
vrai bien, ni la justice') suggests a framework not
wholly consistent with what we have deduced from the
dossiers themselves, and its content overlaps with the
two previous sections.

Examination of these problems leads to the following
conclusions:

(a) the theme of man's search for the Sovereign Good
parallels the theme of man's search for truth, treated
in section 6° and 7°.

(b) the heading of section 10° really includes the matter
of sections 8° and 9°, with no. 148 following logically
on the argument advanced in section 8°. Having presented
le divertissement as an elaborate but ultimately foolish
attempt to keep ourselves from thinking about our condition, Pascal now concludes that we should see that only
God can satisfy us.

(c) having lost contact with the real Good, man finds
false substitutes. The Stoics are mentioned in this connection, but not singled out. It is only the existence
of the ninth dossier which enables us to say that Pascal
would probably have found room to develop his ideas on
the Stoics.

(d) the last extant paragraph (interrupted) of no. 148 speaks of 'others,' presumably Platonists, who have argued that the Sovereign Good must be something freely accessible to all men, as all have the desire for a true satisfaction. From the title of no. 148, and from various unclassed fragments, we can assume that Pascal would have said that correct identification of the Sovereign Good is not enough, we must be given the means to attain it, and these are not possible outside Christianity. As with our longing for truth, our longing for the Sovereign Good which we cannot attain unaided suggests that our present condition is not appropriate to our fundamental nature, with which we are no longer in contact, except by the feeling of inadequacy.

(e) despite the title, there is no trace of any treatment of the theme of justice running parallel to the treatment of truth and the Sovereign Good.

The unclassified fragments included in our discussion are nos 396, 397, 408 (I), 479 (XI), 631 (XXIV), 661 (XXV), 805 (XXIX).[1]

(a) 'Seconde partie'

The words 'Seconde partie' which stand at the head of fragment 148 will certainly surprise. So far we have met the phrase only twice - in no. 6 (1°) where the second part of the Apologia was defined as 'Félicité de l'homme avec Dieu,' or 'qu'il y a un Réparateur, par l'Ecriture,' and in no. 781, 'Préface de la seconde partie,' mentioned as being the counterpart of no. 780 'Préface de la première partie,' discussed in chapter 1. In the preface to part two, Pascal proposed to treat writers who have begun their Apologia by talking with God, without preparing the sceptical listener in advance. Neither definition of the content of part two fits the content of no. 148.[2]

The rest of the heading given to no. 148 leads us to believe that the 'second part' constituted by this fragment was not the second part of the Apologia proper, but a second main division within the first part. Ignoring for the moment the phrase about justice, we have the indication 'Que l'homme sans la foi ne peut connaître la vérité.' The title, in other words, represents that moment in the genesis of the Apologia when Pascal decided to distinguish 'le vrai' and 'le bien' by treating them in separate compartments. In my discussion of the opening

sections I frequently noted a pairing of 'le vrai' and
'le bien,' or 'la vérité' and 'la morale' (21, 44, 72,
75) as if the two were to have been treated together.
Broadly speaking, section 2° concentrated on the weakness
of reason, and section 3° on the 'malheur' of the human
condition, although the division was not absolute. Sections 6° and 7° - 'Grandeur' (a counterblast to 'Misère'),
and 'Contrariétés' (the double nature of man) - insisted
very strongly on human reason and its multiple aspects,
although here again the key fragments (119, 131), and
also no. 905 ('Pyrrhonisme') make it clear that the
search for truth and the search for happiness go hand
in hand. Reason, Pascal argued, cannot attain certainty,
but we need certainty, and in fact God gives us, in
faith, a basis on which reason can legitimately build
(110, 131).

(b) notre impuissance d'arriver au bien (148)

If the title of no. 148 had been found at the beginning
of an eighth section, the design would have been clear.
But two sections have intervened, entitled respectively
'Divertissement' and 'Philosophes.' However, a very
slight adjustment to the text would be sufficient to
accommodate section 8° at the beginning of no. 148, following the title. The text of no. 148 begins: 'Tous les
hommes recherchent d'être heureux,' and it goes on to
say that this universal ambition is not realized, drawing
the conclusion that only God can satisfy us. Now, section
8° had contained the same opening sentence (no. 134: 'il
veut être heureux et ne veut être qu'heureux') and had
given the negative side of the question: we cannot be
happy once we start thinking about the human condition,
so we devise means to stop ourselves from thinking, which
Pascal calls 'distractions.' After subjecting the notion
of *le divertissement* to careful scrutiny in no. 136,
Pascal says that *le divertissement* is an illusion, it
cannot bring true happiness, and that we should be better
employed reflecting upon the human condition in general,
but specifically on 'notre impuissance d'arriver au bien
par nos efforts,' and this reflection leads rapidly to
the conclusion that man will be satisfied by God alone,
an argument which passes through the notion that we have
lost contact with our true nature.

Qu'est-ce donc que nous crie cette avidité et cette
impuissance sinon qu'il y a eu autrefois dans l'homme
un véritable bonheur, dont il ne lui reste maintenant
que la marque et la trace toute vide et qu'il essaye
inutilement de remplir de tout ce qui l'environne,
recherchant des choses absentes le secours qu'il
n'obtient pas des présentes, mais qui en sont toutes
incapables parce que ce gouffre infini ne peut être
rempli que par un objet infini et immuable, c'est à
dire que par Dieu même (148).

Although this position is not argued with any real rigour,
it is consistent with what Pascal had written in nos 131
and 136.

(c) Dispute du Souverain Bien (147)

Now the Stoics had identified the Sovereign Good with
God himself, as was implied by two fragments in the previous section: no. 142 ('Ils croient que Dieu est seul
digne d'être aimé et d'être admiré') and no. 140 ('Quand
Epictète aurait vu parfaitement bien le chemin...'). It
is rather surprising to find that the Stoics are not
singled out in no. 148. There are, however, two references
to them. Having established that '(Dieu) seul est son
véritable bien,' Pascal goes on to list eighteen diverse
objects that men have substituted for God, 'depuis qu'il
l'a quitté' (the last word replacing 'perdu'). (Normal
human love is excluded from the list, which includes
adultery and incest. But a personal note, no. 396, remarks that it is very wrong to encourage another person
to become attached to oneself.) He then adds a nineteenth,
more curious still:

Et depuis qu'il a perdu le vrai bien tout également
peut lui paraître tel jusqu'à sa destruction propre,
quoique si contraire à Dieu, à la raison et à la nature tout ensemble.

This statement is mirrored by the other fragment in the
tenth dossier, no. 147, with its twin theme of disagreement about the nature of the Sovereign Good, and self-
destruction counselled by some:

> Le Souverain Bien. Dispute du Souverain Bien.
> Ut sis contentus temet ipso et ex te nascentibus bonis.
> Il y a contradiction, car ils conseillent enfin de se
> tuer.
> Oh! quelle vie heureuse dont on se délivre comme de la
> peste!

It is striking that no. 148 omits the quotation from
Seneca, as well as the sarcasm of the last sentence.
The diversity of Sovereign Goods proposed by philosophers
is mentioned also in nos 408, 479, and 76.³ One could
cite also no. 805, which notes that 'chacun a ses fan-
taisies contraires à son propre bien dans l'idée même
qu'il a du bien.'
The Stoics are implicitly criticized in the following
paragraph also. Pascal categorizes three general areas
in which the Sovereign Good is sought:

> Les uns le cherchent dans l'autorité, les autres dans
> les curiosités et dans les sciences, les autres dans
> les voluptés.

From fragments 545 and 933, in which Pascal speaks of
the three concupiscences, it would appear that those who
seek the Sovereign Good in authority (Pascal had originally written 'les grandeurs') are to be identified with
'les sages' who 'ont pour objet la justice,' and who are
naturally prone to that form of concupiscence we call
pride (933), the *libido dominandi* (545). This point is
alloted to section 9° in fragment 145, and the accusation
of pride is frequent in that section. We can conclude
therefore, that just as section 8° would fit in at the
beginning of no. 148, so section 9° could be used to
amplify the remarks about the Stoics. Admittedly, no.
148 does not, as it stands, give any prominence to the
Stoics over other philosophers mentioned, but it is
likely that the sequel would have criticized the philosophers who are praised in the incomplete final paragraph
of the existing text; if so, a criticism of the Stoics
would not seem out of place.

(d) d'autres ont plus approché (148)

In the final paragraph Pascal allows that some thinkers
(evidently the Platonists) have seen that the Sovereign

Good cannot be identified with material objects and possessions:

> Ils ont compris que le vrai bien devait être tel que
> tous pussent le posséder à la fois sans diminution et
> sans envie, et que personne ne le pût perdre contre
> son gré, et leur raison est que ce désir étant naturel
> à l'homme puisqu'il est nécessairement dans tous et
> qu'il ne peut pas ne le pas avoir...

What their reasoning is, we do not know, as the manuscript
records only three more words, 'ils en concluent.'[4] But
we can assume that Pascal would have pointed out the flaw
in the philosophers' position, along the lines indicated
by the title 'Que l'homme sans la foi ne peut connaître
le vrai bien...' The positive conclusion will have to be,
that if the philosophers fail to provide us with the means
for finding God ('Les plus grands hommes ne l'ont pu'
430), Christianity does provide, in the person of Jesus,
the only certain Way, available to men of faith ('Epictète... n'y mène pas ... J.-C. seul y mène. Via veritas'
140). In that last example, the reference is once more
to the Stoics, and we hear no more of the Platonists.
The Stoics provide Pascal with more flexible material,
as they can be played off against the Epicureans, as we
saw in the second half of the previous chapter. There is
finally an unclassified fragment which fits in beautifully here, no. 631:

> Il est bon d'être lassé et fatigué par l'inutile re-
> cherche du vrai bien, afin de tendre les bras au
> Libérateur.

We shall find in section 14° a classified fragment (202)
which plays an exactly identical role in a parallel argument, about man's place in the physical universe.
    I drew attention at the end of the previous chapter to
the obvious similarities between Pascal's presentation
of the theme of Reason and his presentation of the theme
of the Sovereign Good. Two unclassed fragments which make
the parallel explicitly use examples found in this tenth
section: the ubiquity of false Goods, the need to find
substitutes if we are denied the authentic items, and
our inadequacy interpreted in the light of the fall:

> La vraie nature étant perdue, tout devient sa nature,
> comme le véritable bien étant perdu, tout devient son
> véritable bien (397).

> L'esprit croit naturellement et la volonté aime natu-
> rellement de sorte qu'à faute des vrais objets il faut
> qu'ils s'attachent aux faux (661).

We are again obliged to imagine a fusion of the ninth
and tenth dossiers if we are to grasp the movement of
Pascal's argument at this point.

(e) ni la justice

The last limb of the title of no. 148 implies that after
dealing with the Sovereign Good, Pascal would have something to say about Justice. Justice is, however, not mentioned in no. 148, and has indeed been covered already,
in earlier sections. Only two fragments have mentioned
justice along with 'le vrai' and 'le bien': the intricate
no. 28, doubled by no. 890, and a sentence on the manuscript of no. 44, which Pascal struck out: '[La raison]
juge souverainement du bien, du vrai, du juste.' In nos
33 and 617, justice is paired with reason. It emerges
more clearly as an independent theme in section 3°,
notably in nos 60 and 66. Pascal's point there was that
scepticism regarding justice can only lead to sedition.
He does not suggest how faith could teach man the true
nature of justice.

In section 5°, however, there is a hint of this, although it is approached obliquely. Section 5° is the
chapter on 'Raison des effets,' or the 'Opinions de peuple
saines,' and as a by-product, as it were, Pascal explains
how he sees the relation of justice (the appearance) and
force (the reality). Fragment 85 tells us that true justice is found in the Church. In fragment 90, where Pascal
explains the 'graduation' of opinions, he puts 'les chrétiens parfaits' at the peak of the scale. But although
one can imagine an argument running parallel to the way
that he treats truth and the Sovereign Good, there is no
trace of such an argument in the fragments we have. Evidently Pascal changed his mind on this detail of his plan.
The phrase - as well as the notation 'Seconde partie' -
may indeed go back to a project drafted before the present Apologia took shape.[5]

Summing up, we see no. 148 as a passage of exposition, covering a second subdivision of part one of the Apologia. It could easily have absorbed fragments which we assume to have been already written, classified in dossiers 8° and 9°. Together the three sections give a clear exposition of the theme 'Que l'homme sans la foi ne peut connaître le vrai bien,' to which we need only to add the corollary, that in faith man's true end, union with God, can be achieved.

11
A P[ort] R[oyal]

(149)

The eleventh dossier consists of a single text, covering
the recto and verso of three sheets of paper, and continued on a fourth sheet headed 'A.P.R. pour demain 2,'
which was filed in the nineteenth bundle. Page 1 is
headed 'A P.R.' and page 2 'A P.R. Pour demain Prosopopée.'
A separate fifth sheet, bearing the title 'A P R. Grandeur
et Misère' was put into the seventh bundle (no. 122).

The accepted interpretation of these initials is 'A
Port-Royal.' Many Pascal scholars have wondered if they
could conceal some other meaning, but Pol Ernst is the
only one to have proposed various alternatives, later
admitting that none of these interpretations is as satisfactory as the usual one.[1] Pascal is believed to have
given a lecture at Port-Royal some time in 1658; this
dossier would therefore contain notes made for that lecture.

The text as it stands needs a little editing. The verso
of page 2 begins with eight brief jottings whereas the
rest is written in sustained prose, and they appear to
precede the writing of page 1; a marginal note at the
bottom of page 2 (recto) is picked up and expanded towards
the bottom of page 3 (recto); and Pascal hesitates between
writing about God in the third person, and writing a
'prosopopoeia,' that is, a discourse purportedly pro-
nounced by God himself. These difficulties are, however,
more apparent than real, the thrust of the argument being
very clear: philosophers and humanist thinkers have given
us dilemmas, not solutions, and the only system which has
dodged none of the issues is Christianity. The Christian
doctrines themselves raise a number of questions, but
Christianity also provides ways of accepting these difficulties.

Summarized in that way, the relation of this section
to what has gone before - and to what will follow - seems

very straightforward, but more than one writer on Pascal
has considered the presence of the dossier as a serious
stumbling-block in the way of Lafuma's assumption that
the twenty-seven bundles form an orderly sequence. Henri
Gouhier would like it withdrawn from the classified
bundles altogether; Pol Ernst allows that it might be a
general introduction.[2] We shall simply take the text as
it stands - ignoring for the moment the marginal addition
at the top of page 1: 'Commencement, après avoir expliqué
l'incompréhensibilité.'

I see fragment 149 as passing through three stages:
(a) the first part sums up the position already reached:
the search for 'le vrai' and the search for 'le bien'
have not been rewarded by the various philosophers and
moralists; can we find the correct diagnosis and a cure
in the Christian religion?
(b) the Christian doctrine of the fall and redemption
both explains the truth about man and offers the possibility of genuine felicity. Objections that it is itself
'incomprehensible' and 'unbelievable' are dealt with.
(c) a more difficult objection to answer is that if
Christianity were true, its truth would be manifest to
all. Pascal sketches an answer to this criticism, which
will be fully developed, in stages, in subsequent sections:
such a simple way out of the difficulty absolves man too
easily from his crime of disobedience. God makes his
presence known in such a way that only genuine seekers
will find him.
(d) we conclude that fragment no. 149 follows logically
on the heels of section 10°, and leads smoothly to section 12° 'Commencement,' although some of the later ideas
expounded in the final section cannot be properly developed for some time yet.

Unclassed fragments introduced into this chapter are
limited to 431 (III), 472 (XI), 617 (XXIV), 788 (XXVII),
809 (XXIX), and 1113.[3]

(a) l'incompréhensibilité

The first part of the argument consists of an exceptionally clear statement of the dilemma posed by the previous
chapters. I have discerned a basic structure of antithesis and paradox; Pascal lays this basic structure bare,
ignoring all the refinements of paradox we have met on
the way. In my conclusion to the previous chapter, I

suggested that after a double conclusion on Epicureans and Stoics, one could expect another double conclusion on the twin search for 'le vrai' and 'le bien.' That is what we have here. The philosophers have failed to resolve the paradox, so they can no longer be considered. Is there a religion which will succeed where they have failed? We have been given the facts, the two antithetical elements existing side by side; it is the duty of religion to recognize both sides of the antithesis - as was said in no. 450, which I attached to section 7° - and explain them.

> Les grandeurs et les misères de l'homme sont tellement visibles qu'il faut nécessairement que la véritable regligion nous enseigne et qu'il y a quelque grand principe de grandeur en l'homme et qu'il y a un grand principe de misère.
> Il faut encore qu'elle nous rende raison de ces étonnantes contrariétés.

Similarly with the search for the Sovereign Good. A religion worthy of respect must teach that felicity is found in knowing and loving God, and that our concupiscence turns us away from God, making men 'pleins d'injustice'; it must explain this resistance, and provide us with a remedy. One of the unclassed fragments on concupiscence (617) led to the same conclusion about the duty of religion:

> C'est donc une manifeste injustice où nous sommes nés, dont nous ne pouvons nous défaire et dont il faut nous défaire.
> Cependant aucune religion n'a remarqué que ce fût un péché, ni que nous y fussions nés, ni que nous fussions obligés d'y résister, ni n'a pensé à nous en donner les remèdes.

Neither Stoics nor Epicureans have provided the remedies, says Pascal, echoing no. 398 (quoted in connection with section 9°). The Stoics have not cured us of presumption, as they have elevated man unduly; the Epicureans (with whom Pascal here allies the Mahometans) have not cured us of concupiscence. All these conflicting opinions, Pascal says in no. 404, led him to the religious quest. Is there a religion which will provide the diagnosis and the solution we still seek?

(b) la sagesse de Dieu

The answer is put into the first person, spoken by the
Eternal Wisdom.

Neither truth nor consolation will come from men, only
from God who created man. But man is no longer in the
state in and for which he was first created. 'Les ténèbres, la mortalité, les misères' came later, when man
had by his presumption claimed independence from God,
and suffered the consequences. He is at war with creation (no. 788 makes the same point) and with himself.
'Les sens indépendants de la raison et souvent maîtres
de la raison l'ont emporté à la recherche des plaisirs.'
He has retained some memory of his former state, but it
is a 'lumière confuse.' There is evidence of the Christian
explanation in the 'mouvements de grandeur ... que l'épreuve de tant de misères ne peut étouffer.' The Christian
account, positing the dual nature of man, explains the
contradictions in man which themselves have led to so
many conflicting, but partial, views of the human condition.

That development, which runs almost to the bottom of
the first sheet, gives the Christian explanation for the
'Contrariétés' of section 7°. The second page gives the
parallel answer, to the 'Dispute du Souverain Bien' of
section 10°, and at this point the writing begins to flow
less well.

The first version went over the ground quite rapidly.
The remedy to man's 'misères' will not come from men.
Human reason can go only to the point of recognizing that
man alone will never attain 'la vérité' or 'le bien.'
(Here we are still with section 7°, no. 131.) The philosophers do not have the answer, they have not understood
the nature of our 'véritable bien' or the truth about the
state of man. Only God can teach us 'quel est (notre)
véritable bien' and that 'la souveraine félicité consiste
à connaître Dieu, à s'unir à lui dans l'éternité.' (This
summary omits a few lines which will be discussed later,
in section c.)

Pascal crossed out several lines at this point (from
'votre véritable bien'), in order to go back to the philosophers and expand. Not knowing man's true nature,
philosophers have been unable to provide a remedy. One
sect has increased the power of pride, the other the power
of concupiscence, and that is no way to cure man of his
'injustices.' 'Je puis seule vous faire entendre qui vous

êtes, ce...' - clearly a double of the phrase crossed
out earlier, 'Je suis la seule qui puis vous apprendre
quel est votre véritable bien.' Maybe that passage would
have been copied out again here, we cannot tell, as the
sentence is left uncompleted, and a series of notes follow.

The doctrine of the fall expounded in this prosopopoeia
is not new to us. No. 136 spoke of 'un ... instinct
secret qui reste de la grandeur de notre première nature.'
In no. 117 Pascal deduced the fall from our use of the
word 'misère'

> par où nous reconnaissons que sa nature étant aujour-
> d'hui pareille à celle des animaux il est déchu d'une
> meilleure nature qui lui était propre autrefois

and in no. 131, from our sense of truth and felicity
coupled with our inability to attain them:

> Car enfin si l'homme n'avait jamais été corrompu il
> jouirait dans son innocence et de la vérité et de la
> félicité avec assurance. Et si l'homme n'avait jamais
> été que corrompu il n'aurait aucune idée ni de la
> vérité, ni de la béatitude

- a point taken up in no. 148:

> Qu'est-ce donc que nous crie cette avidité et cette
> impuissance sinon qu'il y a eu autrefois dans l'homme
> un véritable bonheur, dont il ne lui reste maintenant
> que la marque et la trace toute vide...

and in no. 401, which added a new notion, that of punishment:

> Nous sommes incapables de ne pas souhaiter la vérité
> et le bonheur ... Ce désir nous est laissé tant pour
> nous punir que pour nous faire sentir d'où nous sommes
> tombés.

In this way we are well prepared to hear the doctrine
- we have already been convinced of the bankruptcy of
the philosophers, and we are familiar with the outline
of the Christian teaching on the fall. The passage of
exposition proper is quite brief (two paragraphs only),

and clearly it does raise questions in our mind. But
Pascal is careful to insist that no other system has
fulfilled the conditions imposed, and that the doctrine
of man's two natures does fit the observed facts admirably.

Below this on page 2 are to be found a number of short
jottings, the last of which spills over onto a new page.
They must be notes taken in preparation for the lecture;
several of them are expanded in what we have read already
(on page 1),[4] others will be expanded later, and even
those not expanded could be incorporated into the argument with little difficulty.

Thus the fifth jotting ('Vous n'êtes pas dans l'état
de votre création') becomes the opening words of the
prosopopoeia ('Vous n'êtes plus maintenant en l'état où
je vous ai formés'), and the sixth becomes the last
sentence of the first part of the propopoeia. The jotting
contains the phrase 'Suivez vos movements. Observez-vous
vous-même et voyez si vous n'y trouverez pas les carac-
tères vivants de ces deux natures.' The full text did
have the word 'suivez,' but it was changed to 'observez':

> Observez maintenant tous les mouvements de grandeur
> et de gloire que l'épreuve de tant de misères ne peut
> étouffer et voyez s'il ne faut pas que la cause en
> soit en une autre nature.

The seventh jotting asks the question: 'Tant de contradictions se trouveraient-elles dans un sujet simple?'
The text of no. 149 does not make this precise point explicitly; it leaves the contradictions unexplained and
gives the Christian view that man's nature is double.
The question is, however, implicit in this very juxta-
position. I have already quoted (in chapter 7) fragment
629, in which Pascal reminded us that some thinkers have
rejected the idea of man as a unified being; we find the
idea again in section 14°.

The fourth jotting ('Ainsi cette double capacité') is
too brief to be interpreted precisely; clearly the
'double capacité' (for 'le vrai' and 'le bien') is part
of the case being argued. The word 'capacité' was used
in no. 119 ('Il a en lui la capacité de connaître la
vérité et d'être heureux'), and we can compare no. 401
above ('incapables de ne pas souhaiter la vérité et le
bonheur...')

The other notes belong to a later stage of the argument, to the exposition of the Christian doctrine itself. Thus the first ('Adam, J-C.') refers elliptically to the remedy which God does bring to concupiscence; a fragment filed in the nineteenth bundle explains it (226):

Toute la foi consiste en J-C. et en Adam et toute la morale en la concupiscence et en la grâce.

The three remaining remarks can be interpreted as answers to possible objections. The second and third (which belong together as two sides of a characteristic antithesis) meet the objection that Christianity talks of elevation and abasement, and is therefore no different from the Stoic and Epicurean philosophies:

Si on vous unit à Dieu c'est par grâce, non par nature.
Si on vous abaisse c'est par pénitence, non par nature.

The idea is expanded in the unclassed no. 398 which I quoted in chapter 9 because the expanded version is a precise criticism of the two philosophical schools.

Another objection is contained in the single word 'incompréhensible,' with which the opponent shrugs off the doctrine of the fall. But the fact that something is incomprehensible does not mean that it is false, says Pascal. Three unclassed fragments can be quoted here, nos 431, 809, and 1113.

Nous ne concevons ni l'état glorieux d'Adam, ni la nature de son péché, ni la transmission qui s'en est faite en nous. Ce sont choses qui se sont passées dans l'état d'une nature toute différente de la nôtre et qui passent l'état de notre capacité présente.

Tout cela nous est utile à savoir pour en sortir; et tout ce qu'il nous importe de connaître est que nous sommes misérables, corrompus, séparés de Dieu, mais rachetés par Jésus-Christ; et c'est de quoi nous avons des preuves admirables sur la terre.

Ainsi, les deux preuves de la corruption et de la rédemption se tirent des impies, qui vivent dans l'indifférence de la religion, et des Juifs, qui en sont les ennemis irréconciliables (431).

This moves from the matter of no. 149 (which echoes the

second paragraph as well as the first) to the preoccupations
of later sections: 12° (les impies) and 22 (les Juifs).

> Incompréhensible que Dieu soit et incompréhensible
> qu'il ne soit pas, que l'âme soit avec le corps, que
> nous n'ayons point d'âme, que le monde soit créé, qu'il
> ne soit pas, etc., que le péché originel soit et qu'il
> ne soit pas (809).

> Je ne trouve rien de si aisé que de traiter de roman
> tout cela (1113).[5]

It will be recalled that fragment 131 came to exactly
the same conclusion, echoed in no. 695 (quoted in chapter 7): 'Le péché originel est folie devant les hommes,
mais on le donne pour tel.'

Towards the bottom of the page Pascal noted another
objection: 'Incroyable que Dieu s'unisse à nous.' His
reply to this one, however, filled more than the space
which was left and continues on a new sheet (what I have
called the recto of page 2 evidently being full by the
time this was written). The basic point is clear. If we
say God would never join himself to us, it is because we
recognize our own unworthiness. But if we recognize our
unworthiness, we must admit that we can know nothing of
God's nature, and so we cannot dogmatically state that
God would not, in his mercy, come to meet us. God wants
us to know him and to love him, and even in our fallen
state we can dimly understand that God does exist, and
we do have the capacity to love. We thus arrive at the
same conclusion as the passage on page 2 (recto) which
was crossed out to allow for an expansion on the moral
ills of mankind: 'La souveraine félicité consiste à connaître Dieu, à s'unir à lui dans l'éternité. Votre devoir
est à l'aimer de tout votre coeur.'

(c) je n'ai pas voulu que cette connaissance fût si ouverte

The parts of the text discussed form a consistent and
comprehensible argument. All that is needed is for the
undeveloped sentences to be expanded in the same style
as the rest (if they have not been absorbed already),
and for a linking sentence to be supplied to effect the
transition to the final section, in which the speaker is
again man, not 'la Sagesse de Dieu.'

The sections still to be discussed present new ideas, and look forward to some of the later themes of the Apologia.

On page 2 (verso, before the jottings), Pascal had left an incomplete sentence: 'Je puis seule vous faire entendre qui vous êtes, ce'; he had also written in the margin 'Je ne demande pas de vous une créance aveugle,' but that phrase had later been crossed out. The incomplete sentence repeats a sentence found on the recto side of the same page: 'Je suis la seule qui puis vous apprendre ces choses et quel est votre véritable bien.' Several lines, beginning with this sentence, had been crossed out by Pascal, and I analysed them earlier. Perhaps they were to have been inserted after the sentence left incomplete. The passage which was crossed out is full of hesitations, and one of the ideas which Pascal seems to have temporarily abandoned was the following:

> Je les enseigne à ceux qui m'écoutent ... mais je n'ai pas voulu que cette connaissance fût si ouverte.

We shall meet this idea again very shortly.

The marginal note, which is perhaps the answer to another fancied objection – is the answer to all our problems obtained by simply listening uncritically to statements allegedly made by the Christian God? – is picked up in the space left towards the bottom of page 3: 'Je n'entends pas que vous soumettiez votre créance à moi sans raison, et ne prétends pas vous assujettir avec tyrannie.' God says that he will give enough proof to show that he exists and has authority over us, and that we are to trust him when other concepts are vouchsafed by revelation, which man alone can neither prove nor disprove. Plainly, if this argument is to carry any weight, it will need to be explained in detail.

A sketch of the explanation is in fact found overleaf. The first sentence packs a lot of new ideas into a short space:

> Dieu a voulu racheter les hommes et ouvrir le salut à ceux qui le chercheraient, mais les hommes s'en rendent si indignes qu'il est juste que Dieu refuse à quelques-uns, à cause de leur endurcissement, ce qu'il accorde aux autres par une miséricorde qui ne leur est pas due.

God's purpose includes the redemption of fallen man, by
offering salvation to those who seek him. It is just that
this salvation should not be automatic, and that those
who are 'hardened' should remain outside, while those
who are saved are saved by God's grace which they can
never hope to earn as of right by their own merit. The
sentence bristles with theological issues and difficulties which are worked over and over in subsequent chapters.
   Very little of what we have read has prepred us for
this explosion of ideas. The notion of redemption is,
however, implied by the cryptic 'Adam, J-C' of page 2,
and the infinity of God's mercy is hinted at in the answer to the objection beginning 'Incroyable que Dieu
s'unisse à nous.'
   The continuation likewise hustles us through new ideas.
God could have revealed himself in a way that admitted
no further dispute. But he did not wish to force those
who had turned away from him. On the other hand, he did
not wish to deprive those who were trying to find him of
all hope of ever finding him. The fragment ends therefore
with the distinction between those who wish to see God
and those who do not, between those who seek and those
who do not. God has respected this distinction, revealing
enough of himself to bring satisfaction to the first
category, but not making himself sufficiently manifest
to trouble those in the second category.
   A gloss on this is provided by no. 472:[6]

   La religion est une chose si grande qu'il est juste
   que ceux qui ne voudraient pas prendre la peine de la
   chercher, si elle est obscure, en soient privés. De
   quoi se plaint-on donc si elle est telle qu'on la
   puisse trouver en la cherchant?

(d) A Port-Royal?

The fragment 'A P.R.' has to be considered in two different roles: as notes for the lecture in which Pascal outlined his apologetic argument at Port Royal (if that is
the correct interpretation of the initials), and as the
documentation for a chapter of the Apologia he intended
to write for non-believers. The first of these roles does
not concern us immediately, unless it be felt that as a
result of having been conceived for the lecture, the text

does not adequately fulfil its second role, as material for the Apologia. That view has been taken by some. Indeed, the alleged difficulty of the eleventh section has been used as a reason for doubting that there is a coherent order in the sequence of bundles recorded by the copy. 'Que devient la chaîne si un maillon saute?' asks Henri Gouhier eloquently.

> On ne voit pas ce que signiferait la laisse A.P.R. sous le no. 11. Elle n'a de sens qu'en dehors de la série; elle ne correspond ni à un moment de l'exposé oral ni à un chapitre du livre projeté; elle représente le schéma de ce que Pascal comptait dire ou écrire avant de reprendre les preuves de l'apologétique traditionnelle.[7]

This seems altogether too wholesale, even too hasty a judgment. The first paragraphs of no. 149 sum up the argument about the human condition in a way no other fragment does, and there is no need to call this a scheme, that is an outline to be filled out elsewhere. They sum up the argument at the very point where a summing up is required.

Pol Ernst, who quotes Gouhier, does not go so far as to banish no. 149 from the Apologia altogether. He sees it as an introduction to the second part, but not as a conclusion to the first part, or as a transition between the two parts. His position is paradoxical, rather quixotic, but his only defence of it is by a rather empty rhetoric.

> Personne ne nous interdit d'y voir une 'Introduction générale'...
> Il nous faut en effet résister à la tentation qui consisterait à croire que cette liasse constitue une transition entre les dix premières liasses ... et les autres liasses...
> N'y aurait-il pas aussi quelque illusion à croire ... que la succession est *continue*...
> Ne concluons donc pas trop vite que la liasse A P.-R. constitue la charnière ideale, la transition nécessaire entre les dix premières liasses et les dix-sept autres. Rien n'est moins sûr. En tout cas, cela n'est pas démontré...[8]

In direct contrast to these views, my own is that the
proof of the pudding is in the eating, and that when so
many sections follow nicely on the conclusion of the
previous one, we should be ready to admit that there is
a *succession des liasses*; indeed, the succession is even
easier to detect in this instance than it sometimes is
in others.

Only in one particular matter does the content cause
any serious difficulty: in the richness of the theological ideas introduced into the final parts of the fragment.
We shall see that later sections deal with them one at a
time, section 12° concentrating on the distinction between
those who seek and those who remain indifferent. Only the
verso of page 3 and its sequel are seriously affected,
and one can imagine that they would have been rewritten
or adapted in some way. We have seen that the very last
sheet was put by Pascal into the nineteenth dossier
('Fondements'). Had this fragment been written on one
side only of each page, the previous page would in all
probability have gone there too (the break between the
two pages comes in the middle of a sentence). That would
have removed the difficulty. The reason why page 3 stayed
in section 11° is that the recto side is inseparable from
page 2. Putting the last few lines into the nineteenth
bundle would at least have reminded Pascal to bring the
rest over when it was free.

We are left, it seems, with only one problem: that of
the title and the marginal heading. 'A P.R.' is a heading
of quite a different kind from the other headings which
describe the theme of the section they announce. And the
note 'Commencement, après avoir expliqué l'incompréhensibilité' might at first glance invalidate the claim
that this is an eleventh section, in its right place as
the successor of ten sections already read.

Both Gouhier and Ernst interpret this note as meaning
that the idea found on page 2 ('Incompréhensible...')
was to have become the opening statement of the lecture.[9]
This seems to me to be indefensible. It makes a perfectly
coherent text unmanageable; no satisfactory order could
be imagined for the discourse if that was to become its
starting-point. There is a much simpler explanation. In
no. 130 Pascal had written:

(Je) le contredis toujours.

Jusqu'à ce qu'il comprenne
Qu'il est un monstre incompréhensible

His intention has been to show that man is 'incomprehensible' without some explanation like the one offered by
Christianity. Until the opponent has understood that,
there is no point in presenting the Christian doctrine.
Once he had, we can 'begin.' The word 'commencement'
would be more difficult to interpret if Pascal himself
had not given the clue. The twelfth dossier is in fact
entitled 'Commencement.' We shall see in the next chapter that in it Pascal begins his exposition of the positive case for Christianity. It does not imply the beginning of the enterprise, merely the beginning of the
'proofs,' after a long preparatory section leading the
opponent to a willingness to listen sympathetically.

This word 'commencement' gives us, finally, the answer
to the question: what is a dossier entitled 'A P.R.'
doing among the twenty-eight bundles? Let us assume that
Pascal had his first ten bundles constituted, as well as
a second set, beginning with one marked 'Commencement.'
Some material had been used for the lecture, in particular, a long text which effected the transition between
the two parts, of which the first page was headed 'A P.R.'
Sorting his papers after the lecture, the dossier which
had served for his talk found its rightful place after
the group which had shown man to be 'incomprehensible,'
just before the dossier entitled 'Commencement.' It was,
in a sense, a first part of that dossier.[10] So he wrote
at the top, in the margin: 'Commencement, après avoir
expliqué l'incompréhensibilité.' But he did not actually
thread it into the 'Commencement' dossier, and so when
he listed his bundles, it is recorded separately, with
the occasional title it in fact has on the manuscript:
'A P.R.'

12
Commencement (150-66)

The twelfth section, entitled 'Commencement,' presents
us with two related problems: that of the precise meaning of the title, and that of the real scope of the section, which contains seventeen classified fragments, all
short.

Faced with the strange fact that the twelfth title on
a list of twenty-eight is 'Commencement,' we can take
one of two positions. Either the table does not present
the titles in sequence (that is Henri Gouhier's view,[1]
but I have explained in my introduction why I cannot
share it), or else the title does not mean what it appears to mean. The matter is complicated by the existence
of a very important unclassed fragment, no. 427, which
plainly absorbs the material of *liasse* 12°,[2] as I shall
show in this chapter, and that fragment has often been
seen as part of a general preface.[3] Faced with a preface
which mirrors a dossier appearing in twelfth place, but
entitled 'Commencement,' it is natural to assume that
liasse 12° must be out of place.[4] Even the champions of
the table of titles have been tempted to wonder if the
table is as trustworthy as they had assumed,[5] but before
we abandon the table altogether, we should ask ourselves
if any serious difficulties are raised by assuming that
section 12° is in its rightful place, and that no. 427
does indeed form part of the argument at this point. For
my part, I see only one phrase in the whole fragment 427
which seems more appropriate to an introduction than to
an essay placed near the mid-point of the apologia: the
penultimate sentence, 'Qu'ils donnent à cette lecture
quelques-unes de ces heures qu'ils emploient si inutilement ailleurs,' and that is not an insuperable obstacle.
The positive gains, moreover, are tangible, and no. 427,
together with the fragments placed in section 12° and
many other related *pensées*, falls into place perfectly

as the logical sequel to the eleventh section. It can be
attached with no difficulty at all to no. 149 (11°), and
if we have been convinced of the logical ordering of the
first eleven bundles, we should be prepared to accept
section 12° as the next stage in the discussion. We have
already noted that no. 149, although it was placed in a
dossier entitled 'A P.R.,' had its own specific title of
'Commencement.'

Louis Lafuma and others read the title 'Commencement'
as implying 'Commencement de la seconde partie,'[6] and
while reserving my opinion on where exactly the second
part was to have begun, it does seem reasonable to regard the group of chapters which start with section 11°
as inaugurating a new phase in the Apologia. Sooner or
later, Pascal will consider his interlocutor ready to
hear the positive case for Christianity. He has already
shown how the humanist's view of life leads to a dilemma
which only Christianity can resolve. But he cannot leave
the opponent there. Some listeners may be already sympathetic, but indifference is not always easy to break. So
he envisages a transitional section which will put a
number of arguments concerning unbelief, unbelievers,
and the stages by which a man can pass from hostility
to sympathetic interest. That is the function of sections
12° and 14°.

In this chapter two broad groups of *pensées* are distinguished, plus an introduction which defines the category of man Pascal is addressing. The first group has
as its basic text no. 427, which is echoed in a number
of fragments in the twelfth bundle, including the only
one which has the title 'Commencement' (no. 164).[7] It
covers much ground; the essential point would seem to
be that death being our inevitable lot, indifference to
what awaits us is not a natural reaction. No. 427 can
be divided into three parts. No. 428 appears to be a revised and greatly abbreviated version of the first half
of the second part. Twenty-nine jottings which are expanded in parts two and three of no. 427 are set out as
no. 432.

The other group, which stresses the appeal to self-
interest, has as its centre the celebrated Wager fragment, or 'Infini rien' as it should more properly be
called (418). All commentators on this fragment remind
their readers that the two sheets containing it were not
classified, and that it is therefore uncertain whether

Pascal would have used it in his Apologia; a fortiori,
it is impossible to be sure where he would have placed
it. However, the argument, as it is emerging from the
present study, accommodates it without difficulty as an
appendix to section 12°, and indeed a couple of classified fragments in that section use similar vocabulary.
The theme of self-interest is present in no. 427, as well
as in nos 152 and 153, but the theme of 'les partis' mentioned in no. 153 and explained in no. 154 involves a
specific mathematical argument in favour of choosing
Christianity, and this is of course crucial in the Wager
fragment, which argues that even if we can know nothing
of the objective validity of Christianity, the principle
of self-interest, allied with the mathematics of gambling,
should dictate that we accept rather than reject Christianity.[8]

The 'Infini rien' fragment goes on to tell the non-
believer how he should proceed once the initial gamble
has been made. He must abjure self-love. These two notions – using mathematical analogies for our experience
of God, and living according to certain Christian disciplines – are echoed in many other fragments.

Several of those fragments use the word 'commencer';
this is how the non-believer should 'begin,' once the
initial choice is made. An alternative interpretation
of the title could therefore conceivably be: beginnings
of the Christian life. Or we might prefer 'commencement
de la recherche,' which makes the title a little more
general.[9] I would personally prefer a more general interpretation still. Pascal is dealing with three categories of non-believer, all of whom have heard the first
part of the Apologia. We are almost ready for the proofs,
but each category starts from a different point and must
accordingly be treated differently. Some are ready to
search, some are even ready to learn how to prepare for
faith, but for others the 'beginning' must be a brutal
confrontation with mortality and all it implies.[10]

The fragments which cover these topics unite them in
a variety of ways, and it will not be possible entirely
to avoid some overlapping and anticipation. But the following argument emerges quite clearly:
(a) of the various categories of unbeliever, only genuine
seekers can be approved; they should indeed be pitied.
Many men boast of their indifference. They serve to illustrate one element of the doctrine they attack: the

corruption of man. (The balancing doctrine, the redemption
of man, is the subject of no. 449, which opens with virtually the same formula as no. 427; see chapter 15.)
(b) the arguments they put against Christianity are invalid, and rest on inadequate knowledge of Christian
doctrine, which they confuse with deism. The questions
religion tackles are vital to each one of us, unlike
natural philosophy. To ignore them shows an unreasonable
and unnatural indifference to one's own well-being which
must be supernatural (divine) in origin.
(c) there is one final argument to put to the non-believer.
Given that God is unattainable without faith, and that
we have to either accept or reject Christianity, how can
we make a reasonable choice? It can be shown, Pascal argues, that we should accept out of sheer self-interest,
as there is no escape from *misère* save through the
Christian hope of eternal bliss. Yet the phrase 'accepting Christianity' is hollow unless it is accompanied by
a genuine conversion of the will, and that is a gift of
God. There are none the less acts of humility which make
the soul more receptive to Grace, and the seeker is en-
couraged to practise them.

As well as drawing on nos 427, 428 (III) and 432 (IV)[11]
for section (b), and no. 418 (II) for section (c), I
shall in this chapter use nos 383, 386, 387, 402, 405,
409 (I); 419-26 (II); 431 (III); 434 (IV); 441 (V); 482
(XI); 548, 577 (XXIII); 596, 612, 617, 632 (XXIV); 663,
682 (XXV); 748 (XXVI); 816 (XXIX); 821bis, 823 (XXX); 908
(XXXIV), and 924.[12] I shall also quote 326 from section 25ᶜ

(a) trois sortes de personnes (160)

We begin with an unclassified fragment which makes a
very simple link between the two parts of the presentation, no. 405. After reminding us that he has been
strongly critical of philosophers of both persuasions
and of pleasure-seekers, Pascal adds: 'Je ne puis ap-
prouver que ceux qui cherchent en gémissant.' This remark leads us to expect that from now on Pascal will
address himself to the seekers and produce the long-
awaited proofs. Elsewhere, however, and much more frequently, these anxious seekers are contrasted not with
philosophers, but with two different groups: those who
have already found God (to whom the Apologia is not
directed), and those who refuse to seek at all. The
immediate target will be the latter group.

Il n'y a que[13] trois sortes de personnes: les uns qui
servent Dieu l'ayant trouvé, les autres qui s'emploient
à le chercher ne l'ayant pas trouvé, les autres qui
vivent sans le chercher ni l'avoir trouvé. Les premiers
sont raisonnables et heureux, les derniers sont fous
et malheureux. Ceux du milieu sont malheureux et raisonnables (160).

The distinction between those who seek and those who do
not had been made in no. 149; after explaining that though
redemption is, by God's mercy, possible, it is not automatic, and that God would not force himself on the unwilling, Pascal said that God wishes to appear 'à dé-
couvert à ceux qui le cherchent de tout leur coeur, et
caché à ceux qui le fuient de tout leur coeur.'
  Two fragments classed in section 12° suggest that the
section would have begun with some remarks about the two
kinds of unbeliever, one viewed with sympathy, the other
with scorn (162, 156). Pascal's attitude to unbelievers
in the second category is actually more complex. Not
only is he trying to shake them out of their indifference
(especially those whose indifference is not deeply ingrained), he wishes to use them as a first proof of
Christianity. In the last chapter no. 431 was quoted as
an amplification of the irrelevance of the objection
that original sin was inconceivable. All we need know,
Pascal said there, is that we are corrupt yet redeemed.
'Ainsi, les deux preuves de la corruption et de la rédemption se tirent des impies, qui vivent dans l'indifférence de la religion, et des Juifs, qui en sont les
ennemis irréconciliables.' The theme of redemption and
the argument from the Jews will come later; meanwhile,
the impious will illustrate the corruption of man.

(b) ce que disent les impies (441)

One deduction made from listening to agnostics is negative: the objections they raise against Christianity
turn against themselves (441):

  Toutes les objections des uns et des autres ne vont
  que contre eux-mêmes, et point contre la religion.
  Tout ce que disent les impies.

(What lies behind the phrase 'les uns et les autres' is
obscure; it might be unbelievers and Jews, but it need

not be.) What in fact do 'les impies' say, which can be used as an argument against them?

Two fragments classified in section 12° illustrate Pascal's train of thought. Some things that they propose, such as that the soul is material, are no clearer than what Christians say (161), and observations advanced as contradictory to Christianity – that Christians die like animals and have ceremonies like Turks – are in fact not so (150). In no. 150, Pascal objects to the enemies of Christianity for attacking that faith without even finding out what its tenets are. He also finds it outrageous that they should treat so casually a matter of such importance: 'C'en serait assez pour une question de philosophie, mais ici où il va de tout...' This is clearly very like no. 164 on Copernicus:

> Commencement.
>   Cachot
>   Je trouve bon qu'on n'approfondisse pas l'opinion de Copernic. Mais ceci.
>   Il importe à toute la vie de savoir si l'âme est mortelle ou immortelle.

The reference 'Cachot' directs our attention to no. 163, which compares the human predicament to the situation of

> un homme dans un cachot, ne sachant pas si son arrêt est donné, n'ayant plus qu'une heure pour l'apprendre, cette heure suffisant s'il sait qu'il est donné pour le faire révoquer.

All these notions are gathered together in the long development, no. 427.

In no. 427 the false objection is that God does not manifest himself. The biblical doctrine of the 'Dieu caché,' mentioned, we have seen, at the end of no. 149, says no different. 'Qu'ils apprennent au moins quelle est la religion qu'ils combattent avant de la combattre.' A serious search of the evidence does produce results, but the examination conducted by these atheists is just not serious. And this indifference, says Pascal again, is outrageous.

Not only the arguments and questions of the indifferent person, but his indifference itself, is to Pascal a vindication of Christianity. He argues his case at some length in the second part of no. 427.

Toutes nos actions et nos pensées doivent prendre des
routes si différentes, selon qu'il y aura des biens
éternels à espèrer ou non, qu'il est impossible de
faire une démarche avec sens et jugement, qu'en les
réglant par la vue de ce point, qui doit être notre
dernier objet.

Having said that our behaviour in life depends on our
thinking about death, Pascal deduces that our duty should
be to find out all we can. No. 409 refers to the 'fausseté des philosophes qui ne discutaient pas l'immortalité de l'âme,' and no. 612 says much the same thing.

In spite of this, some people do not enquire at all
seriously about the claims made for Christianity, although 'il s'agit d'eux-mêmes, de leur éternité, de leur
tout.' They say glibly that the soul is material (161).
Now this attitude, says Pascal, is on purely human
grounds, demonstrably 'monstrous.' His argument is as
follows:
(1) 'Misère' and vanity characterize human life, as we
already know. (Fragment 153, in section 12°, says that
all the humanist can promise is 'amour-propre,' vain attempts to please others, and 'les peines certaines.')
(2) Death, which may be imminent, and is always inevitable, will lead either to annihilation (if they are
right) or to eternal *misère*. Annihilation is evoked in
a pair of vigorous *pensées*, nos 165 and 166.
(3) Happiness can come only from the hope of eternal
bliss. Otherwise we are like doomed men watching our
fellows die, waiting for our turn, without hope (434).[14]
(4) In these circumstances, to refuse to examine the
possible grounds for this hope is unjust. And actually
to boast about doubting is extravagant indeed.

In the revised version of this passage (no. 428),
Pascal omits several points, but he adds the explicit
statement that the attitude he is describing is unreasonable.

Pascal continues both 427 and 428 by caricaturing the
attitude he is attacking, rephrasing point (2) above. I
know nothing of the meaning of life, I know only that I
shall die.

Comme je ne sais d'où je viens, aussi je ne sais où je
vais; et je sais seulement qu'en sortant de ce monde
je tombe pour jamais dans le néant, ou dans les mains

d'un Dieu irrité, sans savoir à laquelle de ces deux
conditions je dois être éternellement en partage...

Therefore ('je conclus') I will not look, I will even
mock those who do, I will simply 'sans prévoyance et
sans crainte, tenter un si grand événement, et me laisser
mollement conduire à la mort.' ('Mollement' was the word
with which Pascal reproached Montaigne in no. 680.)[15]
One would never trust a man who can reason in that way,
Pascal says.

And now to Pascal's deduction, from this, in favour of
Christianity. His argument is that these unnatural feelings are totally the opposite of normal self-interest,
and so they illustrate the corruption of man. Usually
these men would use up a great amount of energy if they
thought their pleasure was at stake; yet when it is a
matter of eternal joy, they scoff. No. 823 gives a homely
analogy to drive the point home. Pascal observes this
'chose monstrueuse,' the co-existence of 'cette sensibi-
lité pour les moindres choses et cette étrange insensibi-
lité pour les plus grandes,' and finds in it evidence of
'un étrange renversement' (the note for this idea is 632;
cf. also no. 383), 'un assoupissement surnaturel, qui
marque une force toute-puissante qui le cause.' So these
people are blind, and behave in such an unnatural way
that we must assume their blindness has a supernatural
cause. This idea is sketched in no. 163, and also in no.
596: it is not just that God does not illuminate them,
God had evidently blinded them.

Un homme dans un cachot, ne sachant pas si son arrêt
est donné, n'ayant plus qu'une heure pour l'apprendre,
cette heure suffisant s'il sait qu'il est donné pour
le faire révoquer. Il est contre nature qu'il emploie
cette heure-là non à s'informer si l'arrêt est donné,
mais à jouer au piquet.

Ainsi il est surnaturel que l'homme etc. C'est un
appesantissement de la main de Dieu.

Ainsi non seulement le zèle de ceux qui le cherchent
prouve Dieu, mais l'aveuglement de ceux qui ne le
cherchent pas (163).

Like the notion of the hidden God, this idea was first
touched upon in no. 149.

One of the notes which form fragment 432 (821bis) suggests that this conclusion could be put into clearer
focus (paragraph 20, 'Nous en ferons le premier argument...').[16] And so, in no. 428 we find a different introduction, as well as a revised text for the first half
of part two, and the words 'folie' and 'aveuglement,'
emphasized in paragraph 20 of no. 432, are now spotlighted.
Having concluded that the irresponsible behaviour of
these people is supernatural, Pascal addresses his final
remarks to three groups of people, beginning with those
who make a show of being indifferent not out of any deep
conviction, but because it is the thing to do - an unworthy motive, especially in these circumstances, as no.
151 makes clear. It should be possible to convince them
that they will not be liked and trusted if they take as
their model people who speak so frivolously. Indeed, the
position of the agnostic is so unreasonable that he is
a better argument for Christianity than for agnosticism.
There is nothing to be ashamed of in not knowing the
answer to the riddle of the universe, whereas

Rien n'accuse davantage une extrême faiblesse d'esprit
que de ne pas connaître quel est le malheur d'un homme
sans Dieu.

(The phrase quoted, which appeared in the notes as simply
'Il ne faut pas dire de cela que c'est une marque de
raison,' 432/25, probably implies a play on the word
'esprit fort': cf. 'Athéisme marque de force d'esprit,
mais jusqu'à un certain degré seulement,' 157.) Such
people should recognize (going back to the distinction
made in no. 160) that there are only two kinds of reasonable people, those who have found God, and those who are
seeking him.
Pascal's penultimate word is for the wilfully indifferent themselves. He says it needs all the resources
of Christian charity to try to help them, and that he
hopes they will gain some benefit from reading his book,
even if they still resist. He seems a little more hope-
ful than when he noted in no. 432 'Cela montre qu'il n'y
a rien à leur dire non par mérpis, mais parce qu'ils n'ont
pas le sens commun. Il faut que Dieu les touche' (para.
4). And if they read it with a genuinely open mind - with
no resistance - then, he hopes, they will respond to the

various proofs he has collected, 'dans lesquelles j'ai
suivi à peu près cet ordre.' Two unclassed fragments
could be invoked to complete the unfinished sentence,
one giving five headings (402), the other twelve (482).
I shall discuss these two lists later.[17] The conclusion
is that the person willing to listen will find proofs
to satisfy him (482).

(c) Gageons donc qu'il est, sans hésiter (418)

Towards the end of 427, Pascal said that the only reasonable people are those who have found God and those who
are seeking him. The word 'raisonnable' cannot be allowed
to pass unchallenged. We might imagine the interlocutor
reminding Pascal of a point he made earlier, in fragment
110. There Pascal argued that reason has to build on a
base supplied by a kind of intuitive knowledge

> Car les connaissances des premiers principes, comme
> qu'il y a[18] espace, temps, mouvement, nombres, sont
> aussi fermes qu'aucune de celles que nos raisonnements
> nous donnent et c'est sur ces connaissances du coeur
> et de l'instinct qu'il faut que la raison s'appuie et
> qu'elle y fonde tout son discours.

Saving faith, said Pascal, is a truth known to the heart,
not to reason. (Cf. no. 155: 'Coeur Instinct Principes.')
If this is so, the argument might run, and if God has not
given me this faith, then what is the point of embarking
on a reasoned search for God? Pascal cannot give his full
answer at this stage, but he will not allow that his view
of faith should be used to justify agnosticism. This is
where we would wish to introduce the so-called Wager
fragment (Infini rien), which, like 427, is echoed in
part by some of the fragments classified in the twelfth
dossier. In the 'Infini rien' fragment, Pascal shows that
even if God is unattainable by reason, there are conceivably other grounds for faith, and by following the argument through, he reveals that we have a responsibility
in the dialogue with God which opens the door to true
faith.
   This is not the place to add to the mountain of commentaries on the most celebrated pensée of all. Our understanding has been immeasurably increased by the studies
of Brunet and Gouhier, who have clarified the text by

uncovering the different archeological layers which have
fused to make the version we read in our editions.[19]
Even though not all points have been settled, the essential argument is clear, even relatively simple.

The first part can be summed up in these words:

> Nous connaissons donc l'existence et la nature du fini
> parce que nous sommes finis et étendus comme lui.
>
>   Nous connaissons l'existence de l'infini et ignorons
> sa nature, parce qu'il a étendue comme nous, mais non
> pas des bornes comme nous.
>
>   Mais nous ne connaissons ni l'existence ni la nature
> de Dieu, parce qu'il n'a ni étendue, ni bornes.
>
>   Mais par la foi nous connaissons son existence, par
> la gloire nous connaîtrons sa nature.

Faith, however, cannot come into the discussion at this
point. By natural reason we cannot know for sure if God
exists, never mind what his nature is. We are accustomed
now to the distinction between 'le vrai' and 'le bien'
as the twin goals of human desire. If we cannot know the
truth, perhaps a rational scrutiny of the issue of 'le
bien,' here called beatitude, will help us to decide
whether we should, or should not, embrace Christianity.
We cannot remain neutral, we must wager either on the
truth of Christianity or the opposite. Now, if we bet
for, and are right, says Pascal, we take all the winnings;
if we wager for, and are wrong, we have lost nothing.
The objection that it is imprudent to risk all we are
sure of in the hope of something we cannot be sure of
is answered by recourse to the mathematical laws which
Pascal had recently evolved to decide on the distribution
of the stakes when gamblers interrupt their play before
it is complete.

It is not quite true, Pascal says, that we are left
in the dark, but he accepts that his interlocutor, obliged
to make the choice, is not yet ready for the proofs. If
he agrees (as Pascal assumes he will) that he should accept Christianity, how does he tackle his continuing unbelief? By recognizing that unbelief comes not from
rational conviction (reason, we agreed, cannot decide
either way), but from self-love. So he should try to
discipline his passions, and encourage attitudes of faith
by enrolling the powerful force of custom, which we know
to be an important ingredient in the formation of mental

attitudes. The paragraph on the manuscript immediately
following the last element incorporated into 418 (no.
419) makes the link very clear, mentioning faith, political authority (cf. no. 25, etc.), and mathematical
assumptions (cf. the first part of 418):

> La coutume est notre nature. Qui s'accoutume à la foi
> la croit et ne peut plus ne pas craindre l'enfer, et
> ne croit autre chose.
>   Qui s'accoutume à croire que le roi est terrible, etc.
>   Qui doute donc que notre âme étant accoutumée à voir
> nombre, espace, mouvement, croit cela et rien que cela
> (419).

The result, even on the simple level of self-interest,
will be gratifying, as the seeker will gain all the virtues admired by the *honnête homme* without the admixture
of selfishness which viciates *honnêteté* (cf. chapter 3),
and he will be increasingly convinced that he has made
the right choice.

A conclusion ('Si ce discours vous plaît...'), which
assumes victory for the speaker, neatly links the theme
of self-abasement with the description of God in the
first part as an 'être infini et sans parties,' for it
is a Christian mystery that in prayer a humble creature
can be united to the infinite and incomprehensible God,
and through that union a force can be unleashed which
opens the gates of faith to the unbeliever.

The position of this extremely interesting development
in the general design will be apparent. No. 427 concluded
with the urgent hope that the opponent would seek. But
there remains the obstacle that he 'cannot' believe, and
Pascal himself acknowledges that reason cannot force belief.

There is, however, always the appeal to self-interest,
and the argument that Christianity affords the only way
to appreciate 'le bien.' The strongest of all barriers
to Christianity are erected by self-love, not by reason.
Once the barriers of self-love are down, the opponent
will no longer resist the reasons which Christianity can
produce. We are close to the program spelled out in some
of the fragments entitled 'Ordre' (1°): 'La Machine' was
there given as the answer to the man who was willing to
look for evidence, but who had understood that such evidence could not provide faith (5); more simply, no. 11

referred to the 'discours de la Machine' which was to
follow the 'letter qu'on doit chercher Dieu.' And part
of the program outlined in no. 12 reads: 'La rendre ensuite aimable, faire souhaiter aux bons qu'elle fût
vraie et puis montrer qu'elle est vraie.'

Some of the ideas of no. 418 are glossed by other
fragments. The two sheets of the 'Infini rien' fragment
themselves – Unit II – contain eight other fragments
which editors number separately; all are suggested by
ideas contained in no. 418. For the most part they could
be fitted into the apologetic argument at this stage.[20]
One (no. 419) has been cited already in this section of
the present chapter.

On the mathematical argument about our understanding
infinity as an analogue of our understanding God, we
have no. 420, along with no. 682 and (more tenuously)
663.[21] Although faith is not defined in no. 418 itself,
a definition is forthcoming in no. 424 ('C'est le coeur
qui sent Dieu et non la raison. Voilà ce que c'est que
la foi. Dieu sensible au coeur, non à la raison'), and
this in turn suggests the famous formula of no. 423:
'Le coeur a ses raisons que la raison ne connaît point...'
The cryptic note of no. 155 is probably connected with
this new insight, as well as fragment 110 which we encountered in section 6°. The sequel to this sentence from
no. 423 strengthens the contention of no. 418 that the
real reason for rejecting God is self-love, which is not
rationally motivated. This suggests another development
on self-love, proving that we are born 'injustes et
dépravés,' and remarking that only Christianity is also
the only religion to provide remedies to self-love (421,
cf. 617). Christianity, unlike honnêteté, offers the
possibility of being both 'aimable' and 'heureux' (426).

Other fragments, not directly concerned with no. 418,
present some of the opponent's doubts about the line of
action recommended. No. 816 argues further that one has
to renounce pleasure as a prerequisite of faith, not wait
for faith and then reform. (Cf. 548: 'si on se convertis-
sait Dieu guérirait et pardonnerait'). No. 924 argues
that any suffering that ensues from turning to a new life
comes from the old Adam, not from the new man, and is
better than the 'fausse paix' of continued self-indulgence.[22]
No. 748 answers the objection that fear of hell counteracts the happiness born of Christian hope, Christian
fear being greatly preferable to the false security of

those who risk eternal damnation (cf. no. 387, quoted in chapter 1: 'J'aurais bien plus peur de me tromper et de trouver que la religion chrétienne soit vraie que non pas de me tromper en la croyant vraie'). Finally, no. 908, an early fragment going back to the quarrel with the Jesuits, contrasts this 'good fear' with the hopeless fear of someone who doubts God's evidence while fearing the consequences if it should turn out that he does exist.[23] Either way, Christian hope is the only antidote to *misère*.

The 'règle des partis,' used to give a strong mathematical argument in favour of wagering on the claims of Christianity (given that one has to wager one way or the other, and given that a purely rational proof has been ruled out), is evoked in other fragments, including three which Pascal classed in his twelfth dossier (nos 158, 154, and 153). No. 158 links the argument to the plea (made already, but not yet followed up) to search for signs of God's will:

Par les partis vous devez vous mettre en peine de re-chercher la vérité, car si vous mourrez sans adorer le vrai principe vous êtes perdu.
   Mais dites-vous, s'il avait voulu que je l'adorasse il m'aurait laissé des signes de sa volonté.
   Aussi a-t-il fait, mais vous les négligez. Cherchez-les donc; cela le vaut bien.

The other fragments, not always perfectly clear, appear to imply that if death is imminent, we are less blasé. The clearest formulation of the idea comes in no. 326, in section 25° (Lafuma XXIV). The prophecies, Pascal argues in that fragment, show that the Christian religion is not a matter of chance

Quiconque n'ayant plus que 8 jours à vivre ne trouvera pas que le parti est de croire que tout cela n'est pas un coup du hasard.
   Or si les passions ne nous tenaient point, 8 jours et cent ans sont une même chose (326).

Nos 386 and 159, combined, make a variant of the last sentence of that quotation. No. 154, headed 'Partis,' points out that our behaviour changes according to what we believe our expectation of life to be. (No. 155,

already quoted, is a marginal note to no. 154, and does
not seem to be related in theme.) The idea of 'les partis'
is further elaborated in no. 577, which includes a definition of the 'Raison des effets,' and so was quoted in
chapter 5. The same 'règle des partis' justifies our
working for things which are strictly speaking 'uncertain.' Religion is certainly no less possible than many
things we assume about our own futures. So the argument
that one should not work for an uncertain end is invalid
– not for the reason Saint Augustine gave but on mathematical grounds. No. 153 refers to 'le parti' with the
meaning of years to live, making the point that even if
one had ten years to live, one should ask what the non-
Christian has to offer that would make those ten years
satisfying and worthwhile. Life is uncertain, but on it
depends our destiny, in heaven or in hell (152).

Fragments 418 and 427 have thus both been concerned
with bringing the non-believer to a point where he will
be more sympathetic to the Christian case. The fear which,
Pascal told us in fragment 12, creates the chief obstacle
in the way of faith, has been diverted to the humanist
position itself, and Christianity has been described as
a 'religion aimable.' In the next two chapters, Pascal,
who in no. 418 had provisionally ruled the question 'is
Christianity true?' out of order, will reinstate the
claims of reason, in section 13° defining its role, and
in section 14° (Lafuma XV) showing how it can help the
person who is alarmed by Pascal's portrayal of a world
without God, to develop an attitude of humility, and to
understand some basic religious truths. These chapters
constitute, in our opinion, a transitional phase, preparing the way for the true second part, which will present the arguments in favour of Christianity.

13
Soumission et usage
de la raison (167-88)

If the reading of section 12° proposed above, with fragments 427 and 418 as the two cornerstones, is found acceptable, there can be no problem concerning the significance
of section 13°. God is known to the heart, not to reason,
we were told in no. 424, but reason can guide us, first
to making sensible choices and second to doing our part
in co-operating with God's grace. One can imagine that
there might be misgivings: is not reason being made the
servant of unreason? Fragment 418 gave a hostage to this
view, saying that Christians 'professent une religion
dont ils ne peuvent rendre raison; ils déclarent en
l'exposant au monde que c'est une sottise, *stultitiam*.'[1]
But in fragment 149 we could read a firm corrective,
words spoken by God himself: 'Je n'entends pas que vous
soumettiez votre créance à moi sans raison.' Section 13°
is intended to clarify the matter. In it Pascal argues
that the Christian has not abandoned reason, but that
reason itself recognizes its limitations and must be prepared to allow faith to take over at a certain point.
   In many ways it is a straightforward section. But there
are indications that its origins lie outside the Apologia
itself and that some of the fragments have changed function since they were first written. We read the twenty-
two *pensées* of this section as if they were all addressed
to the rationalist non-believer, but the original layer
probably defined the Christian position as against the
unreasonable elements within the Church.[2] Hence the full
title ('Soumission et usage de la raison: en quoi consiste le vrai christianisme,' 167) is echoed negatively
in no. 179 ('Il y a peu de vrai chrétiens. Je dis même
pour la foi.'). It is difficult to see no. 172 as being
aimed at the unbeliever, although it does define well
the positive role of reason, co-operating with grace:

La conduite de Dieu, qui dispose toutes choses avec
douceur, est de mettre la religion dans l'esprit par
les raisons et dans le coeur par la grâce, mais de la
vouloir mettre dans l'esprit et dans le coeur par la
force et par les menaces, ce n'est pas y mettre la
religion mais la terreur.[3]

One can readily appreciate the scheme Ernst adopts for
this chapter: the errors of superstitious Christians,
the errors of rationalists, and finally the true understanding of reason shown by authentic Christianity. However, as Ernst himself well says,[4] the primary objective
of this section within the Apologia is to persuade the
non-believer that he is not abdicating reason if he becomes a Christian, and it might seem better tactics to
tackle this issue directly at the outset. I am therefore
beginning with Pascal's general statement about the
'soumission et usage de la raison'; otherwise my arrangement, though independent of Ernst's, is not very dissimilar.

Pascal rules out any discussion of those unworthy
Christians whose belief is merely superstition. For reasonable people there are two positions: living entirely
by the light of reason, or acknowledging that reason has
to abdicate. Pascal believes that it is in fact only
reasonable to hold that reason is limited. His view is
perfectly consistent with the important no. 110, in section 6°. When reason allows that there are things it
cannot understand, supernatural elements like the miracles
of Jesus cease to be a stumbling-block. And once miracles
are admitted, as we shall see in later sections, significant consequences follow which it needs the full powers
of critical reason correctly to evaluate.

Unclassed fragments have little bearing on this section, and I mention only no. 820, from Unit XXIX.

True Christianity involves both the use of reason and
the submission of reason to other principles (167). Reason has three functions: to doubt, to assert, and to
submit, and one must be able to judge which function is
the appropriate one (170). The distinction between doubting and asserting had been dealt with in earlier sections
(6° and 7°); here, the essential distinction is between
exercising reason and exercising other functions which
transcend reason.

Certainly reason should not abdicate uncritically, and
sometimes what passes for belief is superstition or docil-
ity (187, 181). Fragment 178 refers to no. 286 in section
22° (Lafuma XXI): there are carnal and spiritual members
of all sects - Christians, Jews, and non-believers. 'Les
chrétiens grossiers croient que la Messie les a dispensés
d'aimer Dieu,' believing in the efficacy of ritual acts.
That is superstition, not at all the 'usage de la raison' to be found in true Christianity. God's way is
through reason and grace, not force (172, already quoted:
Pascal uses the same word as in the last paragraph of no.
149, *douceur*). Some members of the Church have abused
the trust of their people (186). As said above, this
polemical aside is of limited apologetic value, although
one can defend it by saying that Pascal does not want
Christianity to be judged by its most compromising repre-
sentatives.

Alternatively, one can say that Pascal is employing
his usual tactic of finding common ground with his opponent (the rationalist) in order to make it more difficult for his opponent to disagree with him. We can agree,
Pascal says, in finding superstition - that is, the ab-
dication of reason where reason has its proper role to
play - indefensible. But Pascal wants to convince us that
there are circumstances where reason should be prepared
to be overruled. So by way of preliminary, he draws a
parallel between what he calls the 'two excesses,' that
of excluding reason altogether, and that of relying
exclusively on reason (183). One fragment which admits
that there are many who believe through superstition
(179) points out that such people are like those sceptics
whose unbelief is based on 'libertinage' (and not reason).
Fragment 187 pairs superstition and incredulity as two
natural and pernicious vices. Fragments 176 and 177 note
that criteria like simple contradiction or rejection by
the majority afford no proof of the invalidity of a
religion's claims, any more than universal acceptance
proves those claims valid.

Reason therefore has a positive role, but is not complete master of all:

Si on soumet tout à la raison notre religion n'aura
rien de mystérieux et de surnaturel.
   Si on choque les principes de la raison notre religion sera absurde et ridicule (173).

Submission is itself reasonable, recognized by reason
as the correct reaction (174, 182). Reason knows that it
can be outflanked in purely natural domains (a point already made, and to be developed in section 14°), and so
the supernatural is likely to transcend it further (188).
Total rationalism is not reasonable, and rationalists
are condemned by reason itself (175).[5]

The leap into faith does not require a denial of what
ordinary experience teaches us (185). An interesting unclassed fragment (820) says that reason being 'flexible
à tout,' arguments for Christianity based on specific
reasons are weak. The arguments should be based on the
authority of the speaker, where the speaker is God, addressing us in Scripture. Pascal quotes the example of
the Jews of Berea (Acts 17:11), who 'searched the scriptures daily' for support for the claims Paul had made
(171). And in Scripture one finds the miracles.

Miracles above all else need to be explained to the
sceptic. Without them says Pascal, one would have no
overwhelming evidence for Christianity (169,[6] 184), as
it was by miracles that Jesus was able to establish
Christianity and therefore fulfil the prophecies, these
furnishing in turn another strong argument, making further miracles superfluous (180). This view is to be developed in later sections beginning with 17°. And once
the record of Scripture is accepted and the divinity of
Christ acknowledged, other objections fall into place,
such as not believing the doctrine of the Eucharist (168)
because the body of Christ is not visible to the eye (181).

14

Transition de la connaissance
de l'homme à Dieu (193-202)

After the title 'Soumission et usage de la raison' the
table des titres records the single word 'Excellence,'
followed in turn by the single word 'Transition.' Lafuma
allots the numbers XIV and XV respectively to these two
dossiers. However, as I explained brifely in my introduction, I have reason to believe that many difficulties
raised by this stage of the Apologia are resolved if we
reverse the order of these two sections. This is not the
most appropriate point at which to argue the matter in
detail, as the evidence is cumulative and will not all
be available until chapter 16. The issue is fully reviewed
in an appendix. For the time being, I shall use the idea
as a working hypothesis.

Both by its position and its constitution, the dossier
'Transition' is the most problematic of all. It comprises
only seven fragments, nos 195, 196, and 197 being the
numbers given to three fragments which can be read on
the verso side of the manuscript of no. 194; Pascal put
a line through all three of them. Most of the seven
fragments echo *pensées* in other dossiers, and they cover
a wide variety of topics.[1] Pol Ernst has shown that it
is possible to make a reasonably coherent argument out
of them, but it then becomes difficult to understand why
Pascal has given the argument independent existence, and
placed it where he has. My own analysis of the section,
however, differs sharply from Ernst's. I see the section
as basically a straightforward transition from no. 427
(in my view the key to section 12°) to the next phase of
the Apologia, with fragment 198 supplying the essential
framework. The argument is addressed now to the man who,
frightened by the mystery of the universe, is anxious to
seek further. Aspects of the mystery are expanded and it
is shown that reason, while not providing an answer, does
teach us what is man's true position in the universe. We

must trust God to help us in our search, which will start
by looking at the record of the world's religions.

The quite exceptional number of links between this section and earlier sections suggests that it was composed
of fragments originally intended for other parts of the
Apologia, and that in selecting material for dossier 14°
(my numbering), Pascal frequently left other expressions
of the same idea in the original places. It is therefore
a particular sequence of ideas which he wanted at this
point, and not an exhaustive treatment of any of the
separate ideas touched upon.

There are no unclassed fragments which would appear to
belong exclusively to this section; fragment 782, cited
in note 9, probably lies outside the Apologia altogether.
In the same note, I mention also 84, 553, and 887.

Section 12° allowed that people who had not found God
were of different kinds. In no. 427 Pascal concentrated
on the wilfully indifferent, trying to shake them out of
their complacency. At the end of the fragment, needing
to make a transition to that part of the Apologia which
will present the 'proofs' of Christianity, he fell back
on the device of assuming that they might read his book,
and that some of them would even bring 'une sincérité
parfaite' to the task. Psychologically, the transition
was not well motivated. So, in no. 418, he imagined the
argument continuing with an objection from the agnostic
which Pascal felt able to refute at some length. In that
fragment, and in the section following, Pascal answered
the point that, as reason cannot decide, there is no virtue in pursuing the matter, by showing that the decision
to turn one's back on a pagan way of life can be taken
rationally. Once the opponent had been led to see this,
he could be expected to approach the issue of proof –
evidently involving miracles and prophecies – with a
more sympathetic attitude than he had had previously.

But there is another route from the ignorance of God
assumed at the start of section 12° to the rational enquiry for which Pascal is preparing his opponent in these
transitional chapters. It could well be that with some
people the indifference would crumble at an earlier stage.
Pascal had indeed tried shock tactics in section 12°,
noting a series of painful images of the human condition
which were designed to produce a feeling of anguish which
would precipitate the search. That route is clearly
spelled out in fragment 198, filed in this fourteenth

bundle. The opening paragraph draws on the matter of no.
427 (with the exception of one detail), and the concluding
paragraph announces what the search for the true religion
would entail:

> En voyant l'aveuglement et la misère de l'homme, en
> regardant tout l'univers muet et l'homme sans lumière
> abandonné à lui-meme, et comme égaré dans ce recoin de
> l'univers sans savoir qui l'y a mis, ce qu'il y est
> venu faire, ce qu'il deviendra en mourant, incapable
> de toute connaissance, j'entre en effroi comme un homme
> qu'on aurait porté endormi dans une île déserte et
> effroyable, et qui s'éveillerait sans connaître où il
> est[2] et sans moyen d'en sortir. Et sur cela j'admire
> comment on n'entre point en désespoir d'un si misérable
> état. Je vois d'autres personnes auprès de moi d'une
> semblable nature. Je leur demande s'ils sont mieux
> instruits que moi. Ils me disent que non et sur cela
> ces miserables égarés, ayant regardé autour d'eux et
> ayant vu quelques objets plaisants s'y sont donnés et
> s'y sont attachés. Pour moi je n'ai pu y prendre d'at-
> tache et considérant combien il y a plus d'apparence
> qu'il y a autre chose que[3] ce que je vois j'ai recher-
> ché si ce Dieu n'aurait point laissé quelque marque de
> soi.
>   Je vois plusieurs religions contraires, et partant
> toutes fausses excepté une. Chacune veut être crue par
> sa propre autorité et menace les incrédules. Je ne les
> crois donc pas là-dessus. Chacun peut dire cela.
> Chacun peut se dire prophète mais je vois la chrétienne
> où[4] je trouve des prophéties, et c'est ce que chacun
> ne peut pas faire.

Fragment 198 thus gives, very clearly, the stages of
the reaction which leads from a realization of the enigma
of human destiny to the examination of Christianity, and
thereby explains the meaning of the full title of the
dossier: 'Transition de la connaissance de l'homme à
Dieu.' If one is not entrenched in hedonistic indifference, or if one is not content to be a sceptic (positions
answered in nos 427 and 418), then one's reaction, Pascal
assumes, will be what his own would be: one of stupefac-
tion at the indifference of others, and terror before
the enigmatic vastness of the world, engendering a des-
perate need to seek for some evidence for a solution to

the deep mystery of existence. The obvious place to expect such evidence would be in the world's religions.

The one detail in the first paragraph which does not
come from section 12° is the 'univers muet,' a motif
which is found in other fragments of this fourteenth
section, which has as guiding theme the examination of
the physical environment (nature, the universe).

Fragments 201 and 194 mirror the anguished questions
of the man evoked in the first part of no. 198. No. 201
('Le silence éternel de ces espaces infinis m'effraie')
is one of those cryptic utterances which have prompted
several mutually contradictory explanations.[5] The phrase
is, however, so close to the first sentence of no. 198
('en regardant tout l'univers muet ... j'entre en effroi')
that it would seem most reasonable to interpret it as the
reaction which Pascal believes to be the natural response
of a man without faith to the mystery of life. The man
without faith here is not Pascal, but certainly has the
reaction Pascal would expect himself to have, if he were
himself without faith. He represents Pascal's fictional
opponent at a new stage on his way to conversion.

No. 194 can be seen as the kind of perplexing question
about individual destiny which the man without faith might
be expected to formulate. As a finite creature, my existence is limited. But why should nature have chosen these
particular limitations for me? Justification for linking
nos 194 and 198 can be found in another fragment, no. 68,
which Pascal classed his third dossier.[6] This puts the
same kind of question as no. 194, but in a vocabulary
which resembles also that of no. 198:

Quand je considère *la petite durée de ma vie* absorbée
dans *l'éternité* précédente et suivante ... le petit
espace que je remplis et même que je vois abîme dans
l²infinie immensité des espaces que j'ignore et qui
m'ignorent, *je m'effraye* et m'étonne de me voir ici
plutôt que là, car il n'y a point de raison *pourquoi
ici plutôt que là*, pourquoi à présent plutôt que lors.
Qui m'y a mis? Par l'ordre et la conduite de qui ce
lieu et ce temps a-t-il été destiné à moi? (68)

In no. 198, Pascal has his speaker desire to see if
God 'n'aurait point laissé quelque marque de soi,' and
he finds clues in comparing the world's religions. We
have been warned already not to expect to find God in

nature. An examination of nature can nevertheless teach
us a useful lesson about ourselves. That emerges from
fragment 199, the most celebrated and the most memorable
unit in the fourteenth dossier and the longest single
pensée of the entire Apologia. For all its length it is
quite easy to summarize.[7] The title is 'Disproportion de
l'homme' and Pascal sets out to show man as 'un milieu
entre rien et tout.'[8] In the natural world we stand
between the infinitely small and the infinitely large.
All areas of human knowledge extend similarly from the
most lofty basic principles to minute details. Knowledge
itself is niether completely certain nor completely uncertain. If we understand our true position correctly,
we should not covet qualities which are relatively insig-
nificant. We cannot hope to understand either extreme,
and must be content with our position in the middle.[9] We
cannot even understand properly the area we occupy, partly
because elements cannot be separated from the whole, and
partly because of our dual nature, which effectively prevents us from intuitively understanding single natures,
while remaining opaque to our own understanding. Thus
reason's exploration of its own inadequacy provides insight into the true nature of the human condition, arriving at a just assessment of man's position, and of the
overwhelming and surpassing greatness of the creator.

Pensée 199 does more than repeat in a new way the point
made in the previous section about the limitations of
reason; it is itself a magnificent example of reason used
correctly. Like other fragments in this section, it takes
up ideas Pascal included in earlier stages of his argument. The paragraph about our inability to assimilate extremes is echoed very precisely in section 2° (see section
c of chapter 2). One fragment from that section, no. 41,
also exists in a version which bears the title: 'Deux
Infinis. Milieu' (723).[10]

Two of the three remaining fragments (200 and 193) also
have exact counterparts in earlier sections, and both
have to do with the right use of reason. No. 200 was evidently written before no. 113 (6°), because no. 113 refers
to it obliquely. The point is the same in both fragments:
man's dignity comes from his use of his mind, not from
his place in the physical universe. No. 200 adds the conclusion: 'Travaillons donc à bien penser: voilà le principe de la morale,' a most interesting sentence which
links the two aspects of man's endeavour which Pascal has
tended to separate, 'le vrai' and 'le bien.'

Reason, therefore, correctly used, can teach us something about our place in the world. With it we can deduce the existence of God the creator, and though we cannot hope to understand our own nature, we do have reason and can apply it to the field of conduct and ethics. Can we go further and use it to discern which of the world's religions is the true one? If we can do this, our moral understanding will be strengthened also, because that is something we know we can expect of a genuine religion.

No. 193 looks at this very question. Men give a lot of attention to secondary matters, but the fundamental choices in life are made for them, by fate. A man's religion, like his position in life, is often a matter of accepting uncritically the received opinions of society. How this affects a choice of trade is shown by no. 634, which elucidates the last part of no. 193. We are immediately put in mind of two other fragments, both classified by Pascal: no. 35 (section 2°) and no. 129 (7°). In the new context, the point to stress becomes the regret that religious affiliations should so often be chosen in the same casual way. There are religions which are often followed out of laziness; whereas religions should be examined carefully as they contain the evidence we are seeking. Believing this to be the correct interpretation, I have maintained the related no. 634 in chapter 2 as an adjunct to no. 35.

There is finally a conclusion, asking the bewildered seeker not to despair, as God will provide what is needed (202). In chapter 10 (section d), I suggested no. 631 as an exactly parallel conclusion to the section on 'le souverain bien.'

One can take these three fragments together. Contemplation of nature having concluded with an overwhelming sense of inadequacy, we ask how we can use our reason. The answer: to seek the good life, properly understood; and, with confidence in God, to examine the world's religions (we come back to the last paragraph of no. 198), to see if there are better reasons than custom for adhering to any one of them. These two invitations are taken up, successively, in the sections which follow.

15
Excellence de cette manière
de prouver Dieu (189-92)

As already explained, I am reversing Pascal's fourteenth
and fifteenth dossiers. Pascal has been concerned in the
last few chapters with the question: 'where do I start
looking?' In fragment 427, which was designed primarily
to provoke the unbeliever to start his search, Pascal
answered the objection that the non-believer might say
he had already looked for God, and failed to find him.
Do not expect, Pascal has replied, to find God clearly
and unambiguously manifest; he is a hidden God who has
'établi des marques sensibles dans l'Eglise pour se faire
reconnaître à ceux qui le chercheraient sincèrement.'
Part of section 12°, and section 13° also, explained the
role of reason in the acceptance of Christianity. Section
14° (fr. 199) showed just how far a rational examination
of the physical universe would take us: to a recognition
of the existence of a Creator. But reason was powerless
to see how man could make any kind of contact with such
a God. So that chapter led into an impasse. Fragment 198,
however, suggested that the examination should be conducted
in another direction, and centred on the world's religions.
This in effect repeats the hint given in no. 427. Of all
the different religions, Christianity, we are told, is
the only one which has 'prophecies,' but Pascal does not
explain at this stage why they are so important.

In section 15°, the prophecies are mentioned again. In
fragment 189, which is the most important of the classified *pensées* here, Pascal makes two points: that God can
be known only through Jesus, and that Jesus can be proved,
by the prophecies. We can leave the proof for a little
longer. The important thing to realize before we get into
that is that all other ways of looking for God are vain.
Why? Because, as earlier chapters have made clear, there
is a duality in man, which other schools perpetuate, by
having doctrines which are half true. Christianity alone
understands man's predicament, and furnishes the remedy.

The title of the fifteenth dossier, which might at
first sound strangely self-congratulatory,[1] is therefore
not a reference to Pascal's own apologetic method, but
to Christ who has provided the only sure means of access
to God, and the only sure evidence of God's existence,
nature, and purpose, as well as the only authoritative
understanding we can have of our significance as moral
beings. The key to Christian doctrine is in the twin notion of the fall of man and his redemption by God in
Christ, neither half of the doctrine being comprehensible
without the other. Deism, which acknowledges God the
creator, has an inadequate doctrine of man.

Although it is possible to grasp Pascal's point from
these four fragments alone, the real key to the chapter
is the long fragment no. 449. It is written in the same
vein as no. 427, and enables us to see quite clearly how
this section fits into this phase of the Apologia.[2] I
shall therefore build this chapter round a detailed analysis of no. 449, discussing the classified fragments at
the most appropriate point, half-way through. At the end
I shall call upon seven more of the unclassified fragments: 429, 442, 463, 466, 468, 623, and 781 ('Préface
de la seconde partie').[3] We are invited to look at no.
781 by the fact that one of the classified fragments,
no. 190, has the word 'Préface' added in the left margin.
We do not have to decide which is more appropriate for
this section, the sustained style of no. 449 or the more
obviously prefatory formulations of 190 and 781, but we
can note the implication that the section marks a new
departure within the Apologia. And this supports my hypothesis that sections 14° and 15° have been reversed. It
is my opinion that part two of the Apologia begins here,
sections 11° to 14° comprising, in the words of the title
of 14°, a 'transition de la connaissance de l'homme à Dieu.'

The text of no. 449 is a little confusing. In the absence of the manuscript, we are forced into conjectures
about how it was written. It looks as if the point with
which Pascal began (paragraph 1) expanded into an idea
which turned into a fuller introduction (paragraphs 2-4),
absorbing the first sentence of paragraph 1; the rest of
paragraph 1 is repeated, duly expanded, in paragraphs 5
and 6, by which time the argument is fully launched.

The introduction provided by this expansion reproaches
the enemies of Christianity with judging it as if it
taught simple deism. They see by the light of natural
reason that if there is a genuine religion it should be

at the centre of human life (Pascal picks up an idea first
stated in no. 148); Christianity manifestly is not at the
centre of all human life; therefore it is not genuine. But
it is deism which defines religion as the worship of an eter
nal, all-powerful God known naturally to man. The core of
the Christian religion on the other hand is the notion of
the fall and redemption of man. It is because man has faller
that religion has been banished from its rightful place.

Pascal wishes to insist on the significance of the Christian doctrine of the fall and redemption. The doctrine corresponds to a duality already established; reason could
grasp that man was both wretched and great and that it was
mistaken to stress one aspect at the expense of the other.
It is necessary to remind ourselves of no. 121 from section
7°:

> Il est dangereux de trop faire voir à l'homme combien
> il est égal aux bêtes, sans lui montrer sa grandeur.
> Et il est encore dangereux de lui trop faire voir sa
> grandeur sans sa bassesse. Il est encore plus dangereux
> de lui laisser ignorer l'un et l'autre, mais il est
> très avantageux de lui représenter l'un et l'autre.
> Il ne faut pas que l'homme croie qu'il est égal aux
> bêtes, ni aux anges, ni qu'il ignore l'un et l'autre,
> mais qu'il sache l'un et l'autre.

Man has to know the full picture if he is to evaluate himself properly. The philosophers who claimed that man could
attain communion with God were ministering to pride, those
who claimed that man could have no communion with God were
encouraging despair (section 9°). A true religion would
face this duality and provide a remedy (149, 11°).

No. 449 rejoins this argument:

> (La religion chrétienne) enseigne donc ensemble aux hom-
> mes ces deux vérités: et qu'il y a un Dieu, dont les hom-
> mes sont capables, et qu'il y a une corruption dans la
> nature, qui les en rend indignes. Il importe également
> aux hommes de connaître l'un et l'autre de ces points; et
> il est également dangereux à l'homme de connaître Dieu
> sans connaître sa misère, et de connaître sa misère sans
> connaître de Rédempteur qui l'en peut guérir. Une seule
> de ces connaissances fait ou la superbe des philosophes,
> qui ont connu Dieu et non leur misère, ou le désespoir
> des athées, qui connaissent leur misère sans Rédempteur.

God in his mercy has provided us with the means of understanding both the complementary truths about ourselves.

'On peut ... bien connaître Dieu sans sa misère, et sa
misère sans Dieu; mais on ne peut connaître Jésus-Christ
sans connaître tout ensemble et Dieu et sa misère.'

Before proceeding with the analysis of no. 449 I need to
underline this point, as it recurs in three of the four
classified fragments, and is implied in the fourth (191),
which says, referring to the Stoics, that it is useless
knowing God without knowing Jesus Christ. A marginal addition at the end of 189 tells us that as God is our redeemer
we cannot know him without realizing our iniquities from
which we need to be rescued. Those who know God without
knowing their wretchedness glorify themselves, not God.
The second part of no. 190 contrasts those who know God
without a mediator and who commune with him without a mediator, with those 'qui ont connu Dieu par médiateur,'
and who 'connaissent leur misère.' The dangers of exclusiveness and the sanity of Christianity are well summed
up in the characteristic fragment 192:

La connaissance de Dieu sans celle de sa misère fait
l'orgueil
    La connaissance de sa misère sans celle de Dieu fait
le désespoir.
    La connaissance de J-C. fait le milieu parce que nous
y trouvons et Dieu et notre misère.

Nos 189 and 190, which end with the ideas just cited,
both begin by contrasting the Christian evidence of God
with the deists' arguments. Metaphysical proofs are too
involved to have any lasting effect on us, Pascal says
in no. 190. And as we have seen, fragment 189 informs us
that proofs of God offered outside the Christian revelation are 'impuissantes' whereas the fulfilled prophecies,
historically documented, prove the claims of Jesus.[4] The
enormous superiority of Christianity as the way to religious truth is stated in terms which allow no argument:

Hors de là et sans l'écriture, sans le péché originel,
sans médiateur nécessaire, promis et arrivé, on ne
peut prouver absolument Dieu, ni enseigner ni bonne
doctrine, ni bonne morale. Mais par J-C. et en J-C. on
prouve Dieu et on enseigne la morale et la doctrine.
J-C. est donc le véritable Dieu des hommes.

In the continuation of no. 449, Pascal says he will not
attempt to prove the existence of God and other religious
truths by natural reason, as such proofs would not convince

a hardened unbeliever, and also because such philosophical
reasons are no use – they do not have any bearing upon man's
salvation. He describes the Christian God in lyrical terms
which are inspired by the experience enshrined in the
'Mémorial.'[5]

> Mais le Dieu d'Abraham, le Dieu d'Isaac, le Dieu de Jacob,
> le Dieu des chrétiens, est un Dieu d'amour et de consola-
> tion; c'est un Dieu qui remplit l'âme et le coeur de ceux
> qu'il possède; c'est un Dieu qui leur fait sentir intéri-
> eurement leur misère, et sa miséricorde infinie; qui
> s'unit au fond de leur âme; qui la remplit d'humilité,
> de joie, de confiance, d'amour; qui les rend incapables
> d'autre fin que de lui-même.

It is useless to look for God in any other way than through
the life and witness of Jesus. In nature we can find no
sure evidence, and that leads to atheism; in the philosophie
which give a notion of God attained without a mediator,
one can find only deism, not true religion. There may indeed
be no clear evidence of God in nature (whereas, if deism
were all, the evidence would surely be there), but there
is evidence for the corruption and redemption of man. (In
both 442 and 468 Pascal says that everything teaches either
one of these truths or the other. Compare also the last
sentence of 431, quoted in chapter 12.) And Pascal concludes
no. 449 with an explanation of the idea of the 'hidden
God' hinted at in no. 427 (quoted in the opening paragraph
of this chapter): God is not absent altogether, nor is his
presence completely obvious.

> Il ne faut pas qu'il ne voie rien du tout; il ne faut pas
> aussi qu'il en voie assez pour croire qu'il le possède,
> mais qu'il en voie assez pour connaître qu'il l'a perdu;
> car, pour connaître qu'on a perdu, il faut voir et ne
> voir pas; et c'est précisément l'état où est la nature.

The idea is probed further in a later section. As it is
worded here, we might imagine it as the answer to a cry
formulated in no. 429. Pascal there imagines his interlocutor, genuine in his search, examining nature and finding
tantalizingly little to satisfy his thirst, 'voyant trop
pour nier et trop peu pour m'assurer.' If only God would
speak unambiguously for once, so that he would know for
sure where he could find 'le vrai bien'! He adds that he
envies those who have the precious quality of faith, and
who seem by their behaviour not to appreciate their fortune.

(To that last point, no. 623 provides a reply neatly reminding us of a conclusion reached in no. 427: 'Si c'est
un aveuglement surnaturel de vivre sans chercher ce qu'on
est, c'en est un terrible de vivre mal en croyant Dieu.')

One of the fragments in the fifteenth dossier, no. 190
- already analysed above - is entitled 'Préface,' and we
know that two unclassed fragments have the same indication,
no. 780 ('Préface de la première partie') and no. 781
('Préface de la seconde partie'). No. 780 - the preface to
part one - was analysed in chapter 1; it was to have discussed Pascal's predecessors who dealt with the human condition. The preface to part two was to have been equally
critical of those who confidently prove God's existence
from nature. (Fragment 190 makes the same point.) This approach is quite useless, says Pascal, for those who are
genuinely seeking God, but have so far found only obscurity,
and it will only give Christianity a bad name. Scripture does
not teach such a naive doctrine. 'Elle dit au contraire que
Dieu est un Dieu caché et que depuis la corruption de la nature il les a laissés dans un aveuglement dont ils ne peuvent
sortir que par Jésus Christ.' We have been expecting Pascal
to make this point ever since reading section 1°, nos 2
and 3. That Christianity does not teach that God is to
be found in nature is asserted also by no. 466; rather,
Christianity teaches that man is contradictory. Nor does
the Old Testament teach such a doctrine (463).

The differences in the actual ordering of the ideas
which the fragments just discussed have in common show
that Pascal had not worked out the details of this stage
of his argument. But the main thrust is quite clear, and
the chapter could be reduced to these points: Christianity
teaches that there is a God, and that man can reach him;
it teaches also that man is corrupt, and cannot reach God
unaided. Through the person of Jesus, we learn both these
important truths. Abstract proofs of the existence of God
do not fully convince us, and leave our moral condition
unaffected. The examination of nature will not produce
clear evidence of God, but only of our corruption. The
person of Jesus, for whose claims there are historical
proofs, alone gives us a meaningful experience of the
reality of God and of our redemption. The two chapters
which follow are to develop in turn the themes of corruption and redemption, before Pascal tackles the big question of the authentication of Christianity.

16
La nature est corrompue

On the *table des titres* there are twenty-eight titles.
The friends and associates of Pascal who were the first
to work on his papers could find only twenty-seven dossiers, the missing one being the sixteenth, 'La nature
est corrompue.' Unless one shares Henri Gouhier's total
scepticism about the table of titles,[1] one would seem to
be faced with two alternatives. Either one ignores the
heading altogether, as Lafuma does in his Luxembourg
edition[2] (in the Seuil edition, he records the title,
giving it the number XVbis), or else one assumes that
the *pensées* which were to have filled it are still among
the unclassified ones. This was the approach adopted by
Robert Barrault in the Nouveux Classiques Larousse selection; he included nos 416, which has the title 'La nature
est corrompue,' and 491, headed 'Nature corrompue.'[3] This
solution harmonizes with the approach taken in this book.
More recently, however, Jean Mesnard has argued that the
dossier was constituted by Pascal, and comprised nos 416
and 417.[4] These are the last two fragments in the first
Unit of unclassed fragments, all of which had been prepared for filing, but not actually transferred to the
relevant dossiers. In the case of 416 and 417, the dossier was fabricated, and given a title, but it was not
put with the dossiers already constituted.
  I accept Mesnard's argument,[5] and am giving the dossier the number 16°, at the risk of confusing readers
by the discrepancy between my numbering of the remaining
sections and that of Lafuma.[6]
  Included in this chapter besides nos 416 and 417 are
nos 471 (XI), 491 (XVIII), 600 (XXIV), and 1110.[7]
  The two fragments which I am taking to the substance
of this section show that it is the sequel to section
15° - another reason for believing that sections 14° and
15° were put in the wrong order. In section 15° Pascal

said that only through Jesus can we know God, and through
Jesus we know our own wretchedness. No. 417 summarizes
these two related points, creating a new thought by fusing
them.

> Non seulement nous ne connaissons Dieu que par Jesus-
> Christ, mais nous ne nous connaissons nous-mêmes que
> par Jesus-Christ.

No. 417 is thus the natural end to the sequence which
passes from 449 through 189 and 192. Only by knowing Jesus
can we know God and truly know ourselves - two sides of
the same coin indeed, as the chief barrier between ourselves and God is our false assessment of ourselves and
out situation.

No. 416 speaks of the remedial act of God, something
implied in section 15° but not yet characterized:

> Sans J-C. il faut que l'homme soit dans le vice et dans
> la misère.
>   Avec J-C. l'homme est exempt de vice et de misère.
>   En lui est toute notre vertu et toute notre félicité.
>   Hors de lui il n'y a que vice, misère, erreur,
> ténèbres, mort, désespoir.

Four other unclassed fragments could be associated with
this section. In no. 471 Pascal tells us, a little surprisingly, that it is Christian teaching which has opened
his eyes to the corruption of man. Revelation thus
strengthens the argument of the first chapters. One might
gloss this by saying that in the first part of the Apologia
Pascal was playing a kind of game, confounding the sceptic
by his own evidence. But for him personally, the corruption
of man and the world is a theological truth.[8] No. 471 is
at the same time another answer to those who complain that
God is not manifest in the world. We can see, says Pascal,
that man has lost touch with God; what is manifest is the
balancing Christian truth, that nature is corrupt.

No. 1110 cites as evidence for corruption a precept of
the Book of Proverbs. No. 491, as mentioned, has the title
'Nature corrompue.' Failure to act according to reason
(6°) is evidence that nature is corrupt. It can be seen
as a conclusion to the thoughts on reason and motivation
which are scattered through sections 12°, 13°, and 14°,
at the same time reminding us of observations made earlier,

in sections 2° and 6°. It would then pair up with no.
600, which does not dissociate the corruption of reason
from the coming of the redeemer:

> La corruption de la raison paraît par tant de différen-
> tes et extravagantes moeurs. Il a fallu que la vérité
> soit venue, afin que l'homme ne véquît plus en soi-même.

It would be idle to pretend that section 16°, as represented by the two short fragments believed to have been
assigned to it by Pascal, is clearly distinct from the
sections which flank it. No. 417, we have seen, simply
clinches section 15°, and no. 416 would be perfectly at
home in section 17°, which contains many fragments on
the redemptive work of God. Nor does the handful of unclassed fragments containing the phrase 'nature corrompue'
justify a separate chapter on the topic. Nor is there
anything to indicate that Pascal wished to widen the
field, and follow the notion of the corruption of man
with the larger concept of the corruption of nature.
One could certainly suppose that Pascal intended the
following plan: Only through Jesus can we know God (15°).
Through him, we learn that man is corrupt (16°) and at
the same time redeemed (17°). But the fragments actually
filed in sections 15° and 16°, together with no. 449,
overlap and blur any such distinction.

17
Fausseté des autres religions

The negative-sounding title of the seventeenth section
(sixteenth in Lafmua's numbering) is misleading. There
are two themes treated in this section, and the title
applies only to one of them - arguably, the less important of the two. In fact, the 'falsity of other religions'
amounts to no more than a few observations on Mahometanism, designating weaknesses to which Christianity has
the corresponding strength. The larger part of the chapter
is taken up with a positive argument: Pascal links the
case for Christianity with points already made, by reminding us of what we require of an authentic religion,
and suggesting that Christianity meets those requirements.
This argument grows naturally out of the themes of the
preceding sections, which have unfolded the full Christian
doctrine of the fall and redemption of mankind, without,
so far, having explained the idea of redemption.

This chapter falls then naturally into two halves:
(a) Christianity recognizes man's duality, accounts for
it by the doctrine of the fall and redemption, explains
why man cannot fulfil his basic duty, to worship God,
and offers means to remedy his failure. It brings man to
a full and balanced assessment of himself, avoiding the
dangers of one-sidedness present in all rival and partial
systems.
(b) There are several specific ways in which Christianity
can be shown to be superior to Mahometanism and other
religions.

Included are eight unclassed fragments: 393 (I); 450
(V); 494, 495 (XVIII); 564-5 (XXIII); 595 (XXIV); and
833 (XXXIII).

*(a) il faut pour faire qu'une religion soit vraie qu'elle
ait connu notre nature (214)*

In order to fit this seventeenth section into the overall

argument of the Apologia, we should remind ourselves of what Pascal has said about man's duality and its relevance to the quest for the true religion. The duality of man was established by section 7°. In no. 119, Pascal drew the consequence that we must partly love and partly loathe ourselves. References to Christianity were limited, in the seventh section, to an allusion to the fall in no. 122 and a fuller explanation of that doctrine in no. 131. An unclassed fragment tells us however that 'Toutes ces contrariétés qui semblaient le plus m'éloigner de la connaissance d'une religion est (sic) ce qui m'a le plus tôt conduit à la véritable' (404).

How this could be so emerged very clearly in the opening paragraphs of no. 149 (11°, 'A P.R.'). If a religion is to be accepted by us as true, it must teach us that our nature is double, with elements of 'misère' and 'grandeur,' and it must be able to explain this duality:

> Les grandeurs et les misères de l'homme sont tellement visibles qu'il faut nécessairement que la véritable religion nous enseigne et qu'il y a quelque grand principe de grandeur en l'homme et qu'il y a un grand principe de misère.
> Il faut encore qu'elle nous rende raison des ces étonnantes contrariétés.

It must teach us that happiness lies in God, that it is our duty to love him, but that self-love turns us from him. It must explain these failings, and must provide the cure for them.

> Il faut que pour rendre l'homme heureux elle lui montre qu'il y a un Dieu, qu'on est obligé de l'aimer, que notre vraie félicité est d'être en lui et notre unique mal d'être séparé de lui, qu'elle reconnaisse que nous sommes pleins de ténèbres qui nous empêchent de le connaître et de l'aimer, et qu'ainsi nos devoirs nous obligeant d'aimer Dieu et nos concupiscences nous en détournant nous sommes pleins d'injustice. Il faut qu'elle nous rende raison de ces oppositions que nous avons à Dieu et à notre propre bien. Il faut qu'elle nous enseigne les remèdes à ces impuissances et les moyens d'obtenir ces remèdes.

Pascal argued that only Chritianity can do this. Mahomet

and various philosophical sects have stressed one side
of man's duality at the expense of the other, intensifying
thereby either pride or concupiscence. In no. 149 the
Christian doctrine of original sin was proposed as the
only satisfactory explanation, and the rest of the fragment discussed difficulties in the way of accepting that
doctrine.

Since section 11° there have been other attempts to
elaborate on the argument just analysed. The moral im-
balance created by one-sided philosophies and the com-
pleteness of the picture given by Christianity are the
main ideas in the fragments classifed in section 15°,
and the long fragment 449, which I interpreted as the
key to section 15°, also insisted on the double doctrine
of Christianity, mitigating the dangers of the other partial solutions offered.

This superiority of Christianity is in Pascal's eyes
a serious argument for its validity. No. 393 tells us that

La vraie nature de l'homme, son vrai bien et la vraie
religion sont choses dont la connaissance est inséparable.

One of the fragments in this seventeenth dossier (no.
215) states, more simply, that the true nature of man
(his duality) must be acknowledged by a religion claiming
to be true. This idea clearly echoes the first paragraph
of no. 149, and other ideas of that fragment are developed
in the present section. No. 205 covers the ground in a
fairly general way. Pascal repeats there that a true
religion will teach that we should worship and love God
alone, will show us why we fail to do so, and bring the
necessary cure. Pascal does not expand; as in no. 149 he
states the doctrine of the fall and redemption, through
Adam and Jesus, and remarks that if we were not sinful,
it would be unjust of God to expect from us a love which
we do not naturally offer him.

No. 206 is related: Pascal quotes Saint Augustine on
Cicero, about seeing the phenomenon, not the cause. The
phenomenon in question is 'misère,' and not, as Ernst
gratuitously assumes, concupiscence.[1]

Other fragments elaborate further. God as the first
principle, to be worshipped and loved, is the theme of
the early unclassified fragment no. 833: any true religion will insist on this. The 'impuissances' and the

'remèdes' are identified in no. 216, which shows that by
'la vraie religion,' Pascal is thinking quite specifically
of Christianity:

> La vraie religion enseigne nos devoirs, nos impuissances
> (orgueil et concupiscence) et les remèdes (humilité,
> mortification).²

A variant is provided by no. 214, which names prayer as
a Christian remedy. Another remedy is suggested perhaps
by no. 213, a quoation from Saint Bernard on the Johan-
nine theme that perfect love casteth out fear.

Other fragments touch on the moral implications of our
double nature, thus showing that Christianity fulfils
the requirements of no. 119, that men should both love
and loathe themselves. No. 450, which I linked with no.
149, stated this as another condition of the true religion:

> Il faudrait que la véritable religion enseignât la
> grandeur, la misère, portât à l'estime et au mépris
> de soi, à l'amour et à la haine.

Some fragments concentrate on the single aspect of self-
loathing: no. 220 says that Christianity will make an
immediate appeal to those who loathe themselves and seek
'un être véritablement aimable'; no. 564 states that virtue is to hate ourselves for our concupiscence, and to
seek 'un être véritablement aimable,' and goes on to make
the subtle point that as we cannot love what is outside
us, we must find a being who is inside us, but does not
coincide with us, a condition filled uniquely by God as
understood by Christianity.³ Nos 210 and 211 answer an
objection that on the human level we can take pride in
our achievement. Pascal had admitted as much in no. 118
(6°): 'Grandeur de l'homme dans sa concupiscence même,
d'en avoir su tirer un règlement admirable et en avoir
fait un tableau de charité,' but he had also reproached
the *honnête homme* with merely concealing, not destroying,
the selfish centre in man (597): 'Vous, Miton, le couv-
rez, vous ne l'ôtez point pour cela.' Put these two quotations together, and one has the essence of no. 211:

> On a fondé et tiré de la concupiscence des règles
> admirables de police, de morale et de justice.

Mais dans le fond, ce vilain fond de l'homme, ce *fig-
mentum malum* n'est que couvert. Il n'est pas ôté.

The longest fragment in the seventeenth dossier, no. 208,
again reminds us of the twin dangers of the various sects,
naming Stoics and Epicureans, and it goes on to show that
Christianity tempers both dangers with the balancing half-
truth. The notion is beautifully summed up in no. 212:

J-C. est un Dieu dont on s'approche sans orgueil et
sous lequel on s'abaisse sans désespoir.

Another application of Christianity's capacity to elevate
and humble is made in no. 219. Christianity is suited to
both intellectuals and to ordinary folk: 'Elle élève le
peuple à l'intérieur, et abaisse les superbes à l'extérieur.' Pascal concludes that our own experience will
lead us to accept Christianity, so perfectly is it in
tune with what we know of ourselves.

An excellent conclusion to this section, seen as the
culmination of a series of chapters, is afforded by fragment 595. Any observant man is aware of the wretchedness
of the human condition, and any reasonable man would wish
to escape it. One will therefore esteem a religion 'qui
connaît si bien les défauts de l'homme' and desire the
truth of a religion 'qui promet des remèdes si souhaitables.'

(b) différence entre J-C. et Mahomet (209)

The claims for religion analysed in the previous section
all imply as their shadow that other religions, being unable to fulfil the requirements as satisfactorily as does
Christianity, are ruled out as candidates for the position
of the true religion. Once again, the idea goes back to
no. 149:

Qu'on examine sur cela toutes les religions du monde
et qu'on voie s'il y en a une autre que la chrétienne
qui y satisfasse.

Pascal names the Mahometans 'qui nous ont donné les plaisirs de la terre pour tout bien, même dans l'éternité.'
In section 14°, no. 198 had indicated the necessity for
an examination of other religions:

Je vois plusieurs religions contraires, et partant
toutes fausses, excepté une. Chacune veut être crue
par sa propre autorité et manace les incrédules. Je ne
les crois donc pas là-dessus. Chacun peut dire cela.
Chacun peut se dire prophète mais je vois la chrétienne
où je trouve des prophéties, et c'est ce que chacun ne
peut pas faire.

This is the point taken up in the group of *pensées*
within section 17° which gives the section its title,
'Fausseté des autres religions.'

Mahomet sans autorité.
   Il faudrait donc que ses raisons fussent bien puis-
santes, n'ayant que leur propre force.
   Que dit-il donc? qu'il faut le croire. (203)

   Fausseté des autres religions.
   Ils n'ont point de témoins. Ceux-ci en ont.
   Dieu défie les autres religions de produire de telles
marques. Is. 43.9-44.8- (204)

The reference to Isaiah reads: 'Let them bring forth
their witnesses, that they may be justified ... Thus saith
the Lord ... ye are my witnesses.' The same biblical
reference is given in fragments 494-5, which define the
witnesses: 'Juifs témoins de Dieu.' 'C'est visiblement un
peuple fait exprès pour servir de témoin au messie.' It
is evidently relevant to quote again here fragment no. 1,
placed by Pascal in his first bundle, 'Ordre':

   Les psaumes chantés par toute le terre.

   Qui rend témoignage de Mahomet? lui-même.
   J-C. veut que son témoignage ne soit rien.

   La qualité de témoins fait qu'il faut qu'ils soient
toujours et partout et misérable(s);[4] il est seul.

The prophecies are mentioned again in no. 209, which
lists other differences between Jesus and Mahomet (the
killings ordered by Mahomet, the attitudes of the two
leaders to reading). So different are they, says Pascal,
that if Mahomet was to succeed on purely human terms,
then it follows that Jesus had to fail.

The remaining three fragments on Mahomet deal with his
teaching. Pascal sketches a theory he is to develop in
section 20°, that obscure passages in sacred writings
may be nonsense, or they may be genuine mysteries. If
those passages which are clear are puerile, the obscurities in the difficult parts are probably nonsense, but
if the clear passages are 'admirable,' we should be ready
to presume that the obscurities hide a profound meaning.
This thought is expressed in nos 217 and 218, more clearly
in the latter. Finally, no. 207 points out that the Koran
speaks sympathetically of Saint Matthew. This approval,
says Pascal, is inconsistent with its rejection of the
divinity of Jesus.

How these various arguments can be turned to the positive advantage of Christianity will be shown in later
sections. The section immediately following, however, on
'la religion aimable,' is a gloss on what I have called
the first part of section 17°.

18
Rendre la religion aimable

There are only two fragments in Pascal's eighteenth dossier (Lafuma XVII): nos 221 and 222. To these could be
added nos 910-12. The title reminds us of no. 12; 'La
rendre ensuite aimable, faire souhaiter aux bons qu'elle
fût vraie.' The word 'aimable' was explained thus: 'aimable parce qu'elle promet le vrai bien.' The search for
'le vrai bien' has been an abiding preoccupation of previous sections. The need has been established, and the
inadequacy of what various philosophical sects and religions have to offer has been made quite evident. Only God
can satisfy our thirst, and our desire is rendered ineffectual by our concupiscence. Christianity teaches
that man, having fallen, is redeemed. But Pascal had
to be careful here. The consequences of the fall are in-'
evitable. But Redemption is not automatic. If it were so,
the whole theological drama would be a charade. A fragment bearing the title 'Ordre' (no. 467) states:

> Après la corruption dire: il est juste que tous ceux
> qui sont en cet état le connaissent ... mais il n'est
> pas juste que tous voient la redemption.

A crucial distinction was made in the last paragraph of
no. 149, and developed in section 12°, between those who
seek and those who do not. Christianity brings man the
good news, but that is not the end of the story. If the
case presented up to and including section 17° is accepted,
we must next make a personal decision to accept Christianit
   That seems to be the thinking that lies behind section
18°. Christianity, says Pascal, is universal ('J-C. a
offert [le sacrifice] de la croix pour tous'), and not,
like the Jewish religion, the religion of a single people
merely: 'J-C. pour tous. Moïse pour un peuple' (221). In
no. 222 Pascal says that pagans do not hope for redemption,

Jews hope but in vain; 'Il n'y a de rédempteur que pour
les chrétiens.'

The inconsistency here is more apparent than real. In
order to be redeemed, it is necessary to have faith in
Jesus as redeemer; that possibility has been offered to
all men by God. If there is no redemption for the Jews,
that is because they must go further than the hope of
redemption taught by their faith, and accept that Jesus
was the promised Messiah. Pascal added to his manuscript
a cross-reference to the bundle entitled 'Perpétuité'
(22°), implying a distinction between spiritual Jews and
carnal Jews (cf. 289). That hardly affects the basic issue, however: that the sacrifice of Jesus was made for
all men, and we can accept that sacrifice by becoming
Christians, that is, by believing in Jesus.

Pascal develops the subject in three fragments which
succeed each other on the manuscript, and were indeed
not divided by Brunschvicg: 910-12.[1] The theological
position is clarified by the first paragraph of no. 911:

> J-C. rédempteur de tous. Oui, car il a offert comme un
> homme qui a racheté tous ceux qui voudront venir à lui.
> Ceux qui mourront en chemin, c'est leur malheur, mais
> quant à lui il leur offrait rédemption.

In no. 912 Pascal objects to the statement 'J-C. n'est
pas mort pour tous,' on the grounds that it is a belief
which provokes despair, and we know that Pascal has been
at pains to argue that Christianity avoids the excesses
of despair and pride.

19
Fondements de la religion et réponse aux objections (223-44)

The title of the nineteenth section (Lafuma XVIII) leads
us to expect that Pascal will inform us of the objective
basis for Christianity's claims, and answer objections
which the claims might suggest to his imagined hearer.
We have already been given several hints as to what the
basis might be in the preceding sections; but they have
not yet been pulled together into a single argument.

We do indeed find a number of fragments which fit into
this category, but the argument is still rather sketchy,
and most of the points made will be amplified and explained only in subsequent sections. The majority of fragments in the nineteenth dossier either have no apparent
connection with the theme of 'fondements,' or else they
relate it to a specific notion, variously described as
'Que Dieu s'est voulu cacher' or 'Aveugler, Eclaircir.'

In order to understand what Pascal intends by this combination of ideas, we need to return to no. 149 'A P.R.'
The first part of no. 149 had been expanded in section
17°, 'Fausseté des religions.' After showing that the
Christian doctrine of the fall and redemption of man explained the contradictions in the human condition, and
claiming that no other religion provided a cure, the manuscript of no. 149 had continued by answering objections
which might be made to the doctrine just expounded. These
ideas turn up again in section 19° - quite literally in
two instances, as one fragment (230) repeats verbatim a
sentence from no. 149, and the last page of no. 149 was
filed by Pascal not in the eleventh pile, but in this,
the nineteenth.

This stray page contains the last one-and-a-half sentences of no. 149. They conclude the longest of the answers to objections noted in no. 149, and set forth the
idea of God revealing himself in such a way that he remains hidden to all who neglect to seek him earnestly.

This notion, one of the keys to Pascal's thought, is
developed in section 19°, and it provides a way to explain several of the difficulties inherent in the fragments on the 'Fondements,' in which emphasis is placed
on the biblical record and the witness of the Jews:
  This chapter accordingly is divided into three:
(a) the objective claims of Christianity rest on the relation of Chritianity to the Jewish religion which, itself firmly based, predicted the Messiah. There is no
further need of prophecies and miracles, and we should
be prepared to accept the 'signs' delivered to former
generations.
(b) objections, not only to this argument but to Christian doctrine generally, were answered in no. 149 and
can be repeated here. Of particular importance is the
idea that God has given evidence for those who will seek,
but this evidence will not strike anyone who is not
searching seriously. This notion explains many difficulties and confirms the Christian in his position.
(c) moreover, the same principle resolves difficulties
in the record of the Jewish religion, and in the success
of Christ in establishing his Church. In all his manifestations God both conceals himself (from some) and reveals
himself (to others). With this key, we can see that
Christianity has a firm basis, and can accept it with
complete confidence.
  Pascal goes into great detail on the separate issues
raised here (the prophecies, the Old Testatment record,
the life of Jesus, etc.) in the sections which follow;
what distinguishes section 19° is the specific reference
to the theory which explains so many difficulties. The
distinction between a fragment on the prophecies which
mentions the 'hidden God,' and a fragment on the 'hidden
God' which mentions the prophecies, is a fine one, and
some fragments could clearly go equally well in this
chapter or in later ones. Pascal himself admits as much
in no. 223. In allocating unsorted fragments to this
section, I have limited myself to those which clarify
the basic doctrine. This gives twenty-one: nos 389, 394
(I), 438, 439, 440, 444, 445, 446, 448 (V); 461 (XI);
594 (XXIV); 734, 735, 758 (XXVI); 793 (XXVIII); 835
(XXXIII); 861, 882 (XXXIV); 921, 1114, 1115.[1]

(a) fondements de la religion

From what we have read already, we expect the 'fondements'
of Christianity to be of two sorts, subjective and objective. 'Les deux dondements: l'un intérieur, l'autre extérieur, la grâce, les miracles, tous deux surnaturels'
(861). No. 189 (15°) implied that Christ's claim was
based as much on his teaching as on the 'proof' he afforded of God's existence and nature:

> Mais par J-C. et en J-C. on prouve Dieu et on enseigne
> la morale et la doctrine. J-C. est donc le véritable
> Dieu des hommes.

No. 208 (17°) and a number of other fragments in the same
section argued that the manifest correctness of Christianity's diagnosis of the human situation and the superiority
of Christianity's moral doctrine was proof enough of its
claims:

> Qui peut donc refuser à ces célestes lumières de les
> croire et de les adorer?

On the other hand, another sentence in no. 189 told us
that

> pour prouver J-C. nous avons les prophéties qui sont
> des preuves solides et palpables.

No. 198 (14°) also said that where Christianity scores
is in its prophecies. In No. 180 (13°) Pascal argued
that the miracles of Jesus confirmed prophecies and
neither miracles nor prophecies are needed any more.

> J-C. a fait des miracles et les apôtres ensuite. Et
> les premiers saints en grand nombre, parce que les
> prophéties n'étant pas encore accomplies, et s'accom-
> plissant par eux, rien ne témoignait que les miracles.
> Il était prédit que le Messie convertirait les nations.
> Comment cette prophétie se fût-elle accomplie sans la
> conversion des nations, et comment les nations se
> fussent-elles converties au Messie, ne voyant pas ce
> dernier effet des prophéties qui le prouvent. Avant
> donc qu'il ait été mort, ressuscité et converti les
> nations, tout n'était pas accompli ... Maintenant il

n'en faut plus [de miracles] contre les Juifs, car les
prophéties accomplies sont un miracle subsistant.

The section on Islam (17°) hinted at other arguments.
The only fragment in section 19° to go further into
the matter is no. 243. It is the only fragment to have
included the word 'fondement' in its title. That title
was struck out, but is still relevant, as the first sentence reads: 'la religion païenne est sans fondement.'
The rest of the sentence (which was also subsequently
deleted) explains why. Pagan religion is based on oracles
unsubstantiated by any reliable written record. The
Mahometan religion does have a reliable written text as
its basis, but the case is weak: Mahomet was not predicted, he claimed no miracles, and his teaching on the subject of felicity and the sovereign good is absurd. Moreover, the faith of the individual Mahometan is not based
upon a careful reading of the book. (These criticisms
are familiar from nos 209 and 218, and part of 149.) The
Jewish religion, on the other hand, is based on a book
which is authentic, of real antiquity (a point developed
in section 22°, 'Perpétuite'), and used as the fountain-
head for all believers, and the Christian religion is
based on this firm foundation. Pascal distinguishes
between the genuine Jewish and Christian tradition, and
the distorted form given to the tradition by certain
practitioners.
We can isolate three topics here: teaching, miracles,
and prophecies. Teaching, or 'la morale,' has already
been discussed in section 17°. Two general objections
to miracles are answered in brief fragments in section
19°. Non-believers are quite ready, says Pascal, to believe miracles recorded by secular historians (224), and
it is only our familiarity with normal means of reproduction which make us think they are possible, and virgin
birth impossible (227). In no. 882, Pascal says that it
is habit rather than reason which causes us to find some
things impossible to believe, and others straightforward.
In itself, birth is more miraculous than resurrection.
We can add to this the argument of fragments 734 and 735
that the large number of false miracles does not mean
that all miracles are false, but that, on the contrary,
some must be true (or none would ever be believed). The
same argument applies to the false religions in the world.
I shall return to the question of miracles in chapter 24.

On the prophecies we have no. 240:

Preuve.
Prophétie avec accomplissement.
Ce qui a précédé et ce qui a suivi J-C.

The first sentence can be explained by reference to no. 180, already quoted. The second sentence ('ce qui a précédé et ce qui a suivi J-C.') recurs in two other fragments. On one occasion it is a marginal note to no. 608 which is about the tasks facing Jesus. It appears also in the course of a series of additions to no. 793, a complex fragment discussed at the end of the present chapter. The sense is: Jesus was predicted before his birth, and worshipped after his death, everything contributing to an interlocking set of proofs of the divine character of the Christian religion.

Two other unclassed fragments are relevant here, no. 594 and no. 1115. In both the argument is clear. No. 594 echoes no. 180:

L'événement ayant prouvé la divinité de ces prophéties le reste doit en être cru et par là nous voyons l'ordre du monde en cette sorte.

   Les miracles de la création et du déluge s'oubliant Dieu envoya la loi et les miracles de Moise, les prophètes qui prophétisent des choses particulières. Et pour préparer un miracle subsistant il prépare des prophéties et l'accomplissement. Mais les prophéties pouvant être suspectes il veut les rendre non suspectes etc.

1115 is similar:

Il y a toujours en des marques visibles de lui (Dieu) dans tous les temps. Les nôtres sont les prophéties. Les autres temps en ont eu d'autres. Toutes les preuves s'entretiennent toutes. Si l'une est vraie, l'autre l'est. Ainsi, chaque temps, ayant eu celles qui lui étaient propres, a connu par celles-là les autres. Ceux qui ont vu le Déluge ont cru la Création, et ont cru le Messie à venir. Ceux qui ont vu Moïse ont cru le Déluge et l'accomplissement des prophéties. Et nous qui voyons l'accomplissement des prophéties devons croire le Déluge et la Création.

In both those quotations I omitted the opening lines,
which were as follows:

> Conduite générale du monde envers l'Eglise. Dieu vou-
> lant aveugler et éclairer.

> Dieu est caché. Mais il se laisse trouver à ceux qui
> le cherchent.

In order to understand these formulae we must turn to
another group of *pensées* in this section, all of which
prolong the second half of no. 149.

(b) réponse aux objections

The first part of no. 149, expanded in section 17°, argued that of the world's religions, only Christianity
had an awareness of the contradictions in the human condition, explained them, and provided a remedy for them.
The explanation lay in the doctrine of the fall and redemption. The cure to the basic ills of pride and concupiscence was not defined in no. 149, which contented
itself with saying that the 'philosophers' had no cure.
For the balancing positive claim we had to wait for section 17°, especially no. 208.
   The fourth page of no. 149 began with a handful of
notes on the Christian doctrine as corresponding to the
two natures of man. The first read simply 'Adam, J-C,'
and the explanation actually comes in a fragment found
in section 19°, no. 226:

> Toute la foi consiste en J-C. et en Adam et toute la
> morale en la concupiscence et en la grâce.

Another note in the same dossier, subsequently expanded,
originally read:

> 2 natures en J-C. Deux avènements.
> 2 états de la nature de l'homme (241).

Pascal added the title: 'Source des contrariétés.'
   The manuscript of no. 149 continued by answering objections which might be made to the doctrine just expounded. The first objection was that the doctrine of
original sin is incomprehensible. But that is no argument

against the doctrine, said Pascal: 'Tout ce qui est incompréhensible ne laisse pas d'être.' He gave one example;
fragment 809 supplied more. Again, a fragment in the
nineteenth section corresponds to the note on no. 149,
namely no. 230, which repeats it without change.

The second objection was that God would never join himself to man. The objection is invalid, Pascal argued, because we cannot judge what God would or would not do. The
point is made again in section 19°, in no. 231 (crossed
out by Pascal) and no. 239.

The third objection was not formulated in no. 149, but
implicit in the last paragraph was a heading like no.
244: 'Objection des athées: Mais nous n'avons nulle
lumière.'² Pascal argued that, on the contrary, we are
not left without evidence of God. Two things need, however, to be known about the evidence: that it is only
partial (God is not going to make everything clear, but
will provide enough evidence to justify trust), and that
it will be found only by dint of searching seriously.
God has planted clues which will be spotted by the
seeker, but which will not be noticed by anyone who does
not take the necessary trouble.

This reply belongs equally to no. 149 and to section
19°; the last sheet containing the last one-and-a-half
sentences was placed in the nineteenth dossier, between
nos 241 and 242. We cannot tell how much of the last refutation was meant to go into section 19°: the last sentence only, or more than that – perhaps, even, the whole
passage. I shall give the final sentence the alternative
number 241bis. In the last three sentences of 149 Pascal
argues that it would have been unjust had God either revealed himself completely (thus abolishing man's freedom
to reject him) or hidden himself completely (thus removing
all external justification for a man's faith). Consequently
the believer can base his belief on God's presence, and
the non-believer can base his position on God's absence.
As God is both present and absent, both beliefs appear
to be justified.

Il y a assez de lumière pour ceux qui ne désirent que
de voir, et assez d'obscurité pour ceux qui ont une
disposition contraire (149 in fine = 241bis).

Pascal is of course not content to leave it there.
Many important fragments have been concerned precisely

with showing that dogmatic unbelief is unreasonable,
even unnatural, because it closes the door on the one
possibility of felicity. The test comes when the believer
has to explain God's absence, and the non-believer God's
presence. The non-believer, far from being on firm ground,
is actually in an impossible position, for even if God
is nearly always absent, he has only to be present once
for his existence to be known. 'L'être éternel est toujours s'il est une fois,' says Pascal in no. 440, a sentence assimilated into no. 448: 'S'il paraît une fois,
il est toujours.' The believer, on the other hand, is in
a very strong position, provided that he does not claim
that God is always manifest. Pascal has used this argument to answer an objection in the first paragraph of no.
427, and again in nos 3 (1°) and 781:[3] proof of God from
creation is not an argument the Christian sets any store
by. Once again the superiority of Christianity over deism
is manifest. We now have another test we can apply to the
different religions: do they teach that God is always
visible, or do they teach that God is a hidden God? Only
Christianity (and the Jewish faith on which it is based)
teaches the latter (242). The atheist's objection can
therefore be turned on its head. Like men's indifference
to religion, the very obscurity of God constitutes an
argument for, not against, Christianity:

> Reconnaissez donc la vérité de la religion dans l'ob-
> scurité même de la religion, dans le peu de lumière
> que nous en avons, dans l'indifférence que nous avons
> de la connaître (439).

The fragment immediately preceding that last one on
the Copies, no. 438, relies for its pithily expressed
point on the assumption that we are more conscious of
God's concealing himself, than of his revelation of himself, which is something to look forward to in the future:

> Que si la miséricorde de Dieu est si grande qu'il nous
> instruit salutairement, même lorsqu'il se cache, quelle
> lumière n'en devons-nous pas attendre, lorsqu'il se
> découvre?

The importance of the doctrine of the 'deus absconditus'
extends beyond the issue of whether or not man is given
any help in his quest for God. The doctrine illuminates

in fact every stage of the apologetic argument that we
have read to date.

First, the paradox of a God both hidden and revealed
corresponds to the fundamental duality of man. In secular terms, the duality was defined in section 7° as
'grandeur' and 'misère.' In theological terms, man is
able to know God because his first nature is not completely eradicated, but he is unworthy of such communion
because that original nature has been corrupted. We
therefore look for God and find that he is both accessible
and inaccessible, and we are reminded of our duality.

> Il est donc vrai que tout instruit l'homme de sa con-
> dition, mais il le faut bien entendre: car il n'est
> pas vrai que tout découvre Dieu, et il n'est pas vrai
> que tout cache Dieu. Mais il est vrai tout ensemble
> qu'il se cache à ceux qui le tentent, et qu'il se dé-
> couvre à ceux qui le cherchent, parce que les hommes
> sont tout ensemble indignes de Dieu et capables de Dieu:
> indignes par leur corruption, capables par leur pre-
> mière nature (444).

It is because of our contradictory nature that God is
hidden and manifest, not because of an arbitrary jest
on God's part.[4]

In section 7°, Pascal also argued that it was morally
dangerous to ignore one side of man's dual nature:

> Il est dangereux de trop faire voir à l'homme combien
> il est égal aux bêtes, sans lui montrer sa grandeur.
> Et il est encore dangereux de lui trop faire voir sa
> grandeur sans sa bassesse. Il est encore plus dangereux
> de lui laisser ignorer l'un et l'autre, mais il est
> très avantageux de lui représenter l'un et l'autre (121).

We have seen that Pascal frequently alleges that various
religions and philosophies have failed to avoid this danger. He said so in the first part of no. 149, and in section 17° went on to say that Christianity does meet the
double requirement.

> J-C. est un Dieu dont on s'approche sans orgueil et
> sous lequel on s'abaisse sans désespoir (212).

The doctrine of the 'Dieu caché' is relevant here too,
for a God who was never hidden would be ministering to

pride, while a God who was completely hidden would provoke despair.

> S'il n'y avait point d'obscurité, l'homme ne sentirait point sa corruption; s'il n'y avait point de lumière, l'homme n'espérerait point de remède. Ainsi, il n'est non seulement juste, mais utile pour nous que Dieu soit caché en partie, et découvert en partie, puisqu'il est également dangereux à l'homme de connaître Dieu sans connaître sa misère, et de connaître sa misère sans connaître Dieu (446).

By being partly hidden, God reminds us of our corruption. There can be only two reasons why we fail to reach God - either because he does not exist, or because we are unworthy of him. We know from the disclosures he has made of himself that the first alternative must be ruled out; therefore man is unworthy (445 and 448). A briefer, wittier proof of our unworthiness is given by 1114: either we think we are unworthy of God, or we do not; and if we do not, we show that we are presumptuous, and hence unworthy.

The obstacle lying between man and God is therefore not man's imperfect understanding (the fact that God has not disclosed the full truth), but his self-centred will (that he should prefer his selfish pleasures to a life dedicated to the search for God):

> Dieu veut plus disposer la volonté que l'esprit, la clarté parfaite servirait à l'esprit et nuirait à la volonté.
>   Abaisser la superbe (234).

This point of view is well argued in no. 835. The 'proofs' may not convince, but they make it not unreasonable to believe. The evidence for is stronger than the evidence against. Consequently a person who does not believe is influenced by concupiscence rather than by reason. There may not be enough evidence to convince, but there is enough to condemn.

The last sentence of no. 149 (241bis) is repeated at the beginning of no. 236, but with a significant change which echoes no. 835. Where no. 241bis was neutral in tone, and referred simply to the search for God, no. 236 uses the same formula in a more complex way to suggest first that believers are both illuminated and kept from

the dangers of pride, and second that non-believers are
baffled and also guilty:

> Il y a assez de clarté pour éclairer les élus et assez
> d'obscurité pour les humilier. Il y a assez d'obscurité
> pour aveugler les réprouvés et assez de clarté pour
> les condamner et les rendre inexcusables.

It follows from the first of these statements that instead of complaining that God is hidden, we should be
thankful that he has revealed himself to the extent that
he has done:

> Au lieu de vous plaindre de ce que Dieu s'est caché
> vous lui rendrez grâces de ce qu'il s'est tant décou-
> vert et vous lui rendrez grâces encore de ce qu'il ne
> s'est pas découvert aux sages superbes indignes de
> connaître un Dieu si saint (394).

The second paragraph of the *pensée* just quoted, no.
394, suggests, contrary to Pascal's usual view, that a
powerful intellect could attain to knowledge of God, in
spite of the resistance coming from self-will. It is
possible, though not certain, that the enigmatic no. 229
should be interpreted in the same sense:

> Ce que les hommes par leurs plus grandes lumières
> avaient pu connaître, cette religion l'enseignait
> à ses enfants.

Henri Gouhier's discussion of the position pagans occupy
in Pascal's vision of religion draws attention to a sentence from the second paragraph of no. 449 which may
serve to elucidate no. 229: 'Les sages qui ont dit qu'il
n'y avait qu'un Dieu ... ont vu par lumière naturelle
que s'il y a une véritable religion sur la terre, la
conduite de toutes choses doit y tendre comme à son
centre.'[5] But as the rest of no. 449 makes clear, mono-
theism is not enough. Ernst supposes no. 229 to refer to
the doctrines of the incarnation and the redemption, but
it is difficult to conceive of Pascal actually allowing
that natural reason could arrive at such an essentially
Christian doctrine.[6] Lafuma thinks that Pascal is thinking only of man's contradictory nature, but that was an
observation open to any thinking man to make, and it

would not have been associated with such a late section
in the Apologia as this.[7]

Returning to no. 236, the second sentence quoted ('il
y a assez d'obscurité ...') puts the blame firmly on the
shoulders of the unbeliever who has failed to seek diligently. The fact that the responsibility to seek is ours
makes the punishment God will mete out to the unbeliever
perfectly legitimate: the unbeliever will have brought
it upon himself. No. 461 gives another variation on the
same antithetical formula:

> il [leur] donne par grâce, assez de lumière pour
> revenir, s'ils le veulent chercher et le suivre, mais
> pour les punir, s'ils refusent de le chercher ou de
> le suivre.

The question of responsibility is theologically delicate. We have just read the words 'aveugler' and 'éclairer' in no. 236; no. 232 states that

> on n'entend rien aux ouvrages de Dieu si on ne prend
> pour principe qu'il a voulu aveugler les uns et éc-
> laircir les autres

This vocabulary is much stronger than 'Dieu se cache/se
découvre.' One can try to argue the embarrassing word
'aveugler' away, making it mean no more than 'confuse'
or 'leave some confused,' as in no. 149: 'il a voulu les
laisser dans la privation du bien qu'ils ne veulent pas.'
However, no. 427 and other texts make it clear that Pascal
believed indifference to be supernatural in origin. There
is, I think, no evidence that Pascal believed that God
chose in advance, by arbitrary fiat, who would be enlightened and who would not, but one cannot dodge the
issue that the will to seek is a gift of grace and that
consequently its absence is not due entirely to our own
shortcomings.[8] It is worth recalling in this connection
fragment 911 (mentioned in the previous chapter), which
contains in its second paragraph an objection to the
first paragraph, and the reply to that objection:

> J-C. rédempteur de tous. Oui, car il a offert comme un
> homme qui a racheté tous ceux qui voudront venir à
> lui. Ceux qui mourront en chemin c'est leur malheur,
> mais quant à lui il leur offrait rédemption.

Cela est bon en cet exemple où celui qui rachète et celui qui empêche de mourir font deux, mais non pas en J-C. qui fait l'un et l'autre. Non car J-C. en qualité de rédempteur n'est pas peut-être maître de tous, et ainsi en tant qu'il est en lui il est rédempteur de tous.

Pascal will say something about this in his conclusion. For the moment, it is appropriate to cite no. 235: 'J-C. est venu aveugler ceux qui voient clair et donner la vue aux aveugles...' This makes the act of 'blinding' part of the general reversal of the world's values which God effects. God blinds those who are confident that by the light of natural reason they enjoy perfect sight. Human values, based on pride and concupiscence, will be overthrown when the order of grace is restored.[9]

(c) que Dieu s'est voulu cacher (242)

With the phrase 'aveugler-éclairer' we have rejoined the last paragraph of section (a). The two quotations given there from nos 594 and 1115 implied that the argument about miracles and prophecies was connected with the other argument, about the hidden God.

In fact we find that the principle of the 'Deus absconditus' informs most of Pascal's argument about the 'fondement' of Christianity, that is, the record of Israel and the coming of the Messiah. No. 236 throws out, pell-mell, a number of different suggestions. The first I have quoted already, that there is enough light to convict the unbelievers. Pascal goes on in that fragment to speak of the genealogy of Jesus in the Old Testament, hidden among a host of other genealogies. He mentions difficulties in the Old Testament; if Moses was a clever man, there must be a satisfactory explanation for them. The examples he gives of difficulties in the Bible are, however, not from the Old Testament, but from the New: the contradictions in the gospel accounts which show, says Pascal, that there was no collusion between the evangelists. He also makes the point that there have to be several religions, in order that the truth of the one genuine religion shall be known only to those who seek. It will be seen that these thoughts are unified by the idea of ambiguities which will only be resolved by further enquiry and reflection.

Most of these ideas recur, either in the present section or in subsequent sections. No. 223, in this nineteenth dossier, is a note to the effect that a certain
fragment - no. 255 - filed under 'Figuratifs' (20°) should
be put here instead. Pascal identifies it by two questions:

Pourquoi J-C. prophétisé en son premier avènement,
pourquoi prophétisé obscurément en la manière.

No. 389 gives a variant of these two questions:

Pourquoi J-C. n'est-il pas venu d'une manière visible
au lieu de tirer sa preuve des prophéties précédentes?
Pourquoi s'est-il fait prédire en figures?

These questions break down into others, answered in no.
255. The first is why Jesus should have been predicted
at all, instead of coming 'd'une manière visible.' The
last word gives us the clue: if his claims were visible
and apparent to all, there would be no need to seek,
and seeking is, as we know, morally essential for man if
he is to avoid the danger of pride. The second question
is: why should the prophecies themselves be obscure? The
answer is the same: so that things are not made too easy.
The specific question 'pourquoi prophétisé obscurément
en la manière' is explained in no. 255: if all had been
obscure, nobody would have been able to use the prophecy,
so the time of his coming was made quite clear. What was
not so obvious was the manner of his coming. The imagery
of kingship and the promises of reward need to be interpreted. To take them literally, and expect them to be
fulfilled on the level of material possessions would be
to miss the point. They need to be interpreted spiritually, which requires some spirituality on the part of the
reader. Once again, the sheep and the goats are distinguished. The chapter in which this fragment was filed
gives many *pensées* on the subject of 'figures' or 'figu-
ratives.' One such fragment, however (238, 'Figures'),
is in the nineteenth dossier.[10] It offers an interpretation of the privations endured by the Jews. It is short,
and not explicit; the implication might be that the
material goods given to the Jews and then withheld are
a figure for God's gift of himself. As he has made the
gift once, we know that it is not because he is unable
to do so that he no longer gives himself.

> Dieu voulant priver les siens des biens périssables
> pour montrer que ce n'était pas par impuissance, il
> a fait le peuple juif.

The same principle governs Pascal's treatment of the
life of Jesus. The prophets did not say that Jesus would
be acclaimed by all, but that he would be in obscurity,
misunderstood. So there is no point in trying to criticize the Christian position by pointing to the obscurity
of Jesus' life, Christians would never deny that. The
prophets actually addressed their hearers with the words:
'Hear but understand not' (228). Jesus did not correct
the misunderstandings about him, 'pour laisser les mé-
chants dans l'aveuglement' (233). He lived largely un-
recognized; like truth, says Pascal, and like the bread
of the Eucharist, indistinguishable on the surface from
ordinary opinions and ordinary bread, as Jesus was not
outwardly different from ordinary men (225). Jesus did
not win the whole world, nor did he sow universal confusion. So the Christian is not vulnerable to the criticism
that Jesus did not win the whole world; the Christian
doctrine of Christ is absolutely in conformity with the
ambivalent facts (237).
　　No. 758, entitled 'Clarté. Obscurité' extends the principle to the Church herself. The Church is a visible witness to the truth. Just as there have to be several religions (cf. 236), so there have to be several opinions
within the Church, the truth being the opinion which has
always been held. Truth, that is, must be both visible
and ambiguous if man is to persist in the attitude of a
seeker, and not adopt the complacent outlook of one who
already knows the answer.
　　Doubt extends even beyond the grave: 'La peine du purgatoire la plus grande est l'incertitude du jugement.
Deus absconditus' (921).
　　I have left to the end fragment 793, which goes over
many of the points and might have served as a conclusion
to the section - except that it stands in need of considerable editorial tidying. The best way to tackle it would
appear to be to divide it into two, and in each half to
distinguish the basic text from the many additions.
　　The basic text of the second part ('Je trouve que depuis que la mémoire des hommes dure...') presents the
Jewish nation as having the longest history of all nations. Their teachers - not one, but several, over the

centuries - teach that man is corrupt but will be redeemed. The redeemer finally did come, fulfilling the precise details of the prophecies. The writer's personal reaction is to give himself to his redeemer, awaiting death in the confident hope of being united to him. It is thus a very personal text, in which Pascal offers the fulfilment of prophecies as the sure ground for accepting Jesus as his saviour.

The expansion to this second part elaborates at some length on the role of the prophecies:

> Un peuple entier le prédit avant sa venue, un peuple entier l'adore après sa venue; et ce qui a précédé et ce qui a suivi.

Even Christianity's enemies witness for its validity, as they were predicted too. And Pascal concludes:

> Je trouve cet enchaînement,[11] cette religion, toute divine dans son autorité, dans sa durée, dans sa perpétuité, dans sa morale, dans sa conduite, dans sa doctrine, dans ses effets et/
>
> /Ainsi je tends les bras à mon Liberateur, etc....

The first three lines of no. 793 read thus:

> Dès[12] là je refuse toutes les autres religions.
> Par là je trouve réponse à toutes les objections.
> Il est juste qu'un Dieu si pur ne se découvre qu'à ceux dont le coeur est purifié.

After the second sentence, Pascal had indicated: 'deus absconditus'; he was evidently thinking that the doctrine of the hidden God answers all the objections, including the accusation of unfairness. By deleting the words 'deus absconditus' and adding a fourth sentence, however, Pascal has made his meaning obscure. The fourth sentence, added later, probably to replace 'des absconditus'' is as follows:

> Dès là cette religion m'est aimable et je la trouve déjà assez autorisée par une si divine morale, mais j'y trouve de plus.

This appears to be leading into the sequel not from the 'deus absconditus' argument, but from section 17° in which the Christian religion was said to be 'aimable' because of its 'morale.' Perhaps this sentence implies the deletion of all the previous three. Whatever the correct interpretation is, it is clear that this fragment takes us from the matter of the first part of this chapter (a or b), through the matter of (c), to the ultimate goal, the acceptance of Christianity as one's personal religion. Subsequent sections will, however, explore further the implications of the proofs that have now been outlined.

20
Que la loi était figurative (245-76)

In the previous section, *Fondements*, Pascal argued that
Christianity has its roots in the Jewish faith, and that
we shall misjudge its claims if we fail to understand
that God deliberately reveals himself in such a way that
the evidence will easily be overlooked by a too hasty
enquirer. The twentieth dossier (Lafuma XIX) tackles one
particular aspect of that discussion. The Christian who
wishes to produce evidence of God's redemption of mankind
will argue that in the Old Testament God promised the
Messiah, and that in the life of Jesus, those prophecies
were fulfilled. But that statement is not a self-evident
truth. The Jews themselves, who lived in constant expectation of the promised saviour, rejected Jesus. How do
we get round this difficulty? Pascal's answer is that the
text of the Old Testament is ambiguous. If it is to be
interpreted literally, the Christian case is weak. But if
the text is wholly or in part figurative, it becomes perfectly reasonable to see Jesus as the Messiah.

The argument can be divided into three parts.
(a) that the Old Testament is to be read as figure can
be shown by applying principles of common sense, the
literal meaning being demonstrably inadequate. The prophets themselves invite us to understand their words in
this way.
(b) the key to the cipher was provided by Jesus, and
after him by the apostles. He indicated that there was
a 'true' as opposed to a literal meaning to several key
phrases in the Old Testament, and he showed that the
'kingdom' of God was a spiritual kingdom, and that the
Messiah was to live a life of humility and suffering.
With this key, many obscure details of the Old Testament
take on meaning.
(c) God's purpose in providing an ambiguous witness is
consistent with the thesis of the hidden God propounded

in the previous section. It is not an invitation to
flights of fancy; at times God's purposes are best served
by statements which are unambiguous. Interpretations must
all be tested by one unfailing criterion: do they increase
or diminish our understanding of the love of God? Pascal's
conclusion is that the Jews had the true religion, but
frequently failed to complement it with the true doctrine.

There are certain difficulties in presenting this chapter, because the more important fragments do not restrict
themselves to one point or to two successive points of
the argument, and they suggest that there is more than
one way to progress from one stage to another. The difficulty is beautifully illustrated by a variant to fragment
274. In the first version, this read:

> Que l'Ecriture a deux sens.
> 1. Preuve par l'Ecriture même
> ...
> 6. Preuves par la clef que J-C. et les apôtres nous en
> donnent.

In other words, the first proof would correspond to subsection (a) and would be based on a critical examination
of the text, and the last proof, corresponding to (b),
would support the conclusions by showing that the New
Testament interprets the Old in the same way. Pascal deleted the last sentence, however - not, as has been surmised, because that proof would only convince the converted, but because he saw it as in some way preceding
all the other proofs.[1] So he introduced the phrase into
his title, which now reads: 'Que l'écriture a deux sens,
que J-C. et les apôtres ont donné(s),[2] dont voici les
preuves.' It is no exaggeration to say that this hesitation over the position the New Testament should occupy
in the argument is mirrored in countless details. Some
fragments present the New Testament as solving an enigma
formulated through reading the Old Testament, while others
suggest that one reads the Old Testament in a certain way
because the words of Jesus and the apostles have alerted
us in advance to its ambiguity.

Twelve of the thirty-two classed fragments are entitled
'Figures' or 'figurat(ives),' as are six unclassed fragments, and also no. 238 from section 19°. In fact, twenty-
five unclassed fragments are included in the discussion:
nos 391 (I); 453 (VIII); 469, 475, 476 (XI); 488, 489

(XVII); 492, 495, 496, 497 (XVIII); 501, 502-3 (XIX);
566, 573, 575 (XXIII); 592, 593, 614, 615 (XXIV); 801,
807, 818 (XXIX); 826 (XXXI); 849 (XXXIII).[3]

(a) le vieux testament est un chiffre (276)

We know already that Pascal attached considerable importance to the messianic prophecies. Fragment 274, which
shows very clearly why he planned the present section,
is entitled 'Preuves des deux testaments à la fois.' Can
it be shown that Jesus fulfilled the prophecies of the
Messiah recorded in the Old Testament? If we take the
prophecies literally, it is quite clear that Jesus did
not fulfil them. But, before we jump hastily to a conclusion which would seriously embarrass the apologist, we
must ask: is the literal meaning the only one, or do the
prophets' words bear two different readings? The object
of this section will be to show that not only specific
prophecies, but the whole of Scripture has two meanings –
a literal one, and a figurative one. The title, preserved
on a slip of paper which Lafuma numbered 245 is clear:
'Que la loi était figurative.' Continuing fragment 274,
Pascal dictated a new heading, 'Que l'Ecriture a deux
sens,' and jotted down six proofs. Four of these (numbered two to five) are drawn from the Rabbinic writings,
and were to be further documented in a separate dossier
(21°). The first proof noted was that of Scripture itself,
and the sixth was the key given by Jesus and the Apostles.
I have already mentioned that this last proof was transferred to the title, which now reads 'Que l'Ecriture a
deux sens, que J-C. et les apôtres ont donnés, dont voici
les preuves.' The 'proofs' that Scripture has two meanings
will therefore be drawn primarily from an examination of
the text of Scripture itself. Pascal does not wish to impose on Scripture a meaning it cannot really bear. In no.
251 he quotes Saint Augustine:[4]

Qui veut donner le sens de l'Ecriture et ne le prend
point de l'Ecriture est ennemi de l'Ecriture.

Pascal believes that if we read Scripture carefully and
intelligently, we shall soon be convinced that it should
not be interpreted literally. He offers several proofs
to substantiate this statement. Three are given in no.
501. He wishes to prove that the prophets meant something

different from the immediately obvious interpretation of
their words, or (as he subsequently expressed it) that
when the prophets spoke of temporal goods, they had other
things in mind. Pascal's first argument was the one which
now comes second, that although the prophets promise
material goods very clearly, they say that their words
are obscure. This clearly implies that they were aware
of two meanings in what they had said.

A second proof is furnished by the contradictions
within the Old Testament. No author would contradict himself so blatantly, but if one supposes that there is both
a literal and a figurative meaning, the difficulties dissolve. Contradictions in a text might of course mean that
the author is not very bright, as Pascal readily admits
(257, 267, 276), but he will not allow that such is the
case here. There is too much good sense elsewhere for
us to take the contradictions as a sign of weakness (276).
Pascal's thinking is similar to what he had written in
the section on Mahomet about obscurity which could be
either incoherence or profundity (217-18); we give the
benefit of the doubt to those who impress us favourably
on other occasions where there is no ambiguity. I said
when presenting nos 217-18 in chapter 17 that the same
argument applied to the history of China in no. 822. In
that fragment Pascal writes significantly 'il y a de quoi
aveugler et de quoi éclaircir.' An interesting commentary
is found in fragment 566:

> Tout tourne en bien pour les élus, jusqu'aux obscurités
> de l'Ecriture, car ils les honorent à cause des clartés
> divines, et tout tourne en mal pour les autres jusqu'aux
> clartés, car ils les blasphèment à cause des obscurités
> qu'ils n'entendent pas.

Pascal then began a 'third' proof, though he wrote only
half a sentence, and we have to turn to another fragment
(no. 257) to follow his thought further. This so-called
third proof is an extension of the second, and Pascal
later deleted the indication that it was independent. He
also added a somewhat different proof earlier on, numbering it '1' and creating some confusion in the rest: 'que
cela serait indigne de Dieu.' But it is the argument from
the contradictions which we shall find most frequently
evoked and developed in other fragments.

The argument of no. 501 continues, as I have said, in
no. 257. Given the existence of contradictions in an
author we trust, we try to find a perspective which re-
conciles them. The Jewish (read: literal) reading of the
Old Testament does not do this.

Si on prend la loi, les sacrifices et le royaume pour
réalités on ne peut accorder tous les passages; il faut
donc par nécessité qu'ils ne soient que figures.

Specific instances are mentioned, here and in nos 258 and
263. The argument is pursued in no. 259. Remarks are made
concerning the law and sacrifice which cannot all be true
of the reality, but which could all be true of the figure.[5]
We must conclude that the prophets are speaking in figure.
Pascal also says, at the beginning of no. 259, that figures
will give both pleasure and displeasure, which again is
true of the law and sacrifices prescribed in the Old
Testament; they are both pleasing and displeasing to God.
His meaning here is clarified by a note added at the top
of fragment 260: 'Un portrait porte absence et présence,
plaisir et déplaisir. La réalité exclut absence et déplaisir.'
    In fragment 266 Pascal mentions another, human, aspect
of pleasure and displeasure. Taken literally, he says,
the Old Testament prophecies were flattering to their
hearers. But we know that the motive of the prophets was
not to court favour, because elsewhere they reversed the
prophecies, showing that the flattering sense was not the
correct one.
    Fragment 260, from which I have already quoted the
phrase written in above the title ('figures'), gathers
together several ideas, juxtaposing them in a slightly
different order from that implied by nos 501 and 257.[6]
There are now three parts.[7] The first two, separated by
a line, are anticipated by the very brief no. 265, and
the first sentence takes up a remark written in the margin of no. 267:

Savoir si les prophètes arrêtaient leur vue dans
l'ancien testament ou s'ils y voyaient d'autres choses.

No. 260 begins with the same question, in almost identical words. Did the prophets, for example, see something

of which the 'old covenant' was merely the 'figure'? When
they said the covenant would last forever, were they referring to the same covenant as the one which, they said
elsewhere, would be changed? The same prophets who said
clearly that the law was eternal, also said that their
meaning was veiled. Now, if a text which is perfectly
comprehensible, is said to be obscure, we naturally assume that it is 'un chiffre à double sens.' The argument
is close to the 'first proof' of no. 501.

All these arguments, threaded together, tend to strengthen the original contention, that there are two meanings
in Scripture, that the Old Testament is a cipher.

In the second part of no. 260, Pascal considers the
additional 'proof' of no. 501: 'que cela serait indigne
de Dieu.' There are intentions attributed to God in the
Old Testament which are either false or absurd if taken
literally (272). As they can be taken in a spiritual
sense, it would seem that this is the proper interpretation. Furthermore, there are some phrases which cannot
be taken any other way than spiritually. The clearest
instance of this argument comes in section 22° (no. 279),
but we are surely justified in quoting it here:

> Un mot de David ou de Moïse, comme que Dieu circoncira
> leur coeur fait juger de leur esprit.
>   Que tous leurs autres discours soient équivoques ou
> douteux d'être philosophes ou chrétiens, enfin un mot
> de cette nature détermine tous les autres comme un mot
> d'Epictète détermine tout le reste au contraire.
> Jusque-là l'ambiguïté dure et non pas après.

(b) *clef du chiffre*

There is therefore evidence in plenty that the Old Testament is a cipher. A cipher requires to be broken. The last
paragraph of no. 260 completes the argument by stating
that the meaning has indeed been revealed, by Jesus and
the apostles:

> Combien doit-on donc estimer ceux qui nous découvrent
> le chiffre et nous apprennent à connaître le sens caché,
> et principalement quand les principes qu'ils en prennent
> sont tout à fait naturels et clairs? C'est ce qu'a [sic]
> fait J-C. et les apôtres. Ils ont levé le sceau. Il a
> rompu le voile et a découvert l'esprit. Ils nous ont
> appris pour cela

que les ennemis de l'homme sont ses passions,
que le rédempteur serait spirituel et son règne
spirituel,
qu'il y aurait deux avènements
 l'un de misère pour abaisser l'homme superbe,
 l'autre de gloire pour élever l'homme humilié,
que J-C. serait Dieu et homme.

There is much of interest in this list, but a better
framework for discussion is provided by another fragment,
no. 253. No. 253 expands the opening of fragment 268, in
which Pascal noted various ideas relevant to the topic of
the revelation brought by Jesus. It begins with a quotation from St Luke's gospel (24:32): 'he opened to us the
scriptures,' and continues:

Deux grandes ouvertures sont celles-là.
1. Toutes choses leur arrivaient en figures.
2. Il a fallu que le Christ ait souffert pour entrer
   en sa gloire.
Deux avènements

Jesus has taught us by his use of the word 'true' that
there was a 'true' sense in the Old Testament which was
not the same as the literal sense. Three examples are
given in an addition made to no. 253. The list is repeated
and greatly augmented in nos 249 ('Clef du chiffre'), 268,
807, 818, and also in 835. Some of these lists mention
Jesus as the lamb of God, that is, the true lamb of which
the sacrificial lambs of the law were merely figures.
Pascal applies this principle to the Old Testament
generally, and not only to the specific instances author-
ized by the phrases cited in the fragments just mentioned.
His authority might be the writer of the Epistle to the
Hebrews, who described the law as 'a copy and shadow of
the heavenly things' (247, Hebrews 8:5). The first paragraph of no. 267 is particularly illuminating here:

Dès qu'on on a ouvert ce secret il est impossible de
ne le pas voir. Qu'on lise le vieil testament en cette
vue et qu'on voie si les sacrifices étaient vrais, si
la parenté d'Abraham était la vraie cause de l'amitié
de Dieu, si la terre promise était le véritable lieu
de repos? Non, donc c'étaient des figures.

Shorn of its first sentence, that paragraph would seem

to be another case of reflecting on the text of the Old
Testament. But the first sentence shows that the direction of such reflection was given by meditation on the
New Testament. The second paragraph of the same fragment
(267) tells us that if the ceremonies of the Old Testament have no bearing on the law of charity, they are to
be seen as figures. There are more developments of this
idea in a series of additions made to no. 270, and no.
849, written earlier, begins: 'La charité n'est pas un
précepte figuratif.' Although each of these fragments
presents the idea in a different context, we are probably
justified in assuming from the lay-out of no. 267 that it
is prompted in the first place by an 'opening' revealed
to us by the New Testament.

A very interesting case of this doubt as to whether
the conclusions Pascal draws stem from the evidence of
the Old Testament or from that of the New is given by
fragment 269. Here Pascal begins not from a word of Jesus,
nor from a reflection on the Old Testament, but from the
spiritual experience of an individual. Some people, he
says, have sufficient insight into their own nature to
be impatient with the Old Testament talk of enemies and
the promised land. They know that their only enemy is
concupiscence, and their only desire for God. (Such
people would probably agree with the 'proof' added to
no. 501: 'que cela serait indigne de Dieu.') Two other
fragments can be linked to this. In no. 475, Pascal says
that those who reject self-love are particularly ready
to know Jesus, and to understand the spiritual meaning
of the Old Testament. In no. 271, unconnected with the
main preoccupations of the section, Pascal says that
Jesus came to teach us that we are slaves of self-love,
and to free us from this bondage. No. 269, however, goes
on from there to furnish reasoned proof for the claim
that Jesus will free us from the sin of self-love.

Je ferai voir qu'un Messie a été promis pour délivrer
des ennemis et qu'il en est venu un pour délivrer des
iniquités, mais non des ennemis.

In other words, the 'enemies' of the Old Testament
must be understood figuratively: the enemies are our own
sins. Pascal's argument for this interpretation is along
the same lines as what we have already read: prophecies
made about enemies have not been fulfilled in their

literal meaning, but a figurative interpretation is possible. In other places the Old Testament prophets talk
of iniquities, and use the same vocabulary as when they
describe the conquest of enemies. This second group of
statements has only one meaning. It is therefore legitimate to assume that the figurative interpretation of the
first group is the correct one, because it removes all
the contradictions, and a manifestly false statement becomes a possibly true one. The words of Daniel (chapter
9) support this conclusion very precisely. Now in the
paragraph from no. 260 quoted above, we were told that
one of the things which Jesus and the Apostles taught us
was that 'les ennemis de l'homme sont ses passions.' The
deduction from the Old Testament is therefore anticipated
by the teaching of the apostles.

We may suspect that other points made about the Old
Testament have their roots in the New, like the problem
of phrases which are manifestly false, if taken literally
(272). Again, the history of the synagogue, which presents the same kind of anomalies as statements about the
law, can best be understood if we see the synagogue as
partly a figure of the Church (573). Other figures are
mentioned in 246 and 248.[8]

The second 'opening' provided by Jesus is that he had
to suffer ('Il a fallu que le Christ ait souffert pour
entrer dans sa gloire'). A note at the end of fragment
259 reminds us that the Book of Revelation speaks of
'the Lamb that hath been slain from the foundation of
the world' (13:8). Two phrases were added to the second
part of no. 253: Jesus was 'un Dieu humilié jusqu'à la
croix,' and he was to conquer death by dying himself.
In its final form, this paragraph is virtually identical
with a fragment filed in the previous dossier, no. 241,
but it is being used differently. In no. 241, entitled
'Source des contrariétés,' the Cross was seen to resolve
observable contradictions in man; here it resolves contradictions in the doctrine of the Messiah. The Jews expected the Messiah to be great as a king is great, arriving in spectacular fashion (264), and wielding a sword
(250); they were not prepared for a lowly person, subject
to death (256), ruler of a spiritual kingdom. The law was
thus a figure for the reign of grace, initiated by Jesus
(275); and Pascal adds that grace itself is but a figure of
glory, and the coming of Christ in glory is reserved for the
end of time (275; cf. 270, last sentence, on the Eucharist).

These are the points gathered together in the last part
of no. 260, which expands on just one of them, when it
defines the first and second coming as 'l'un de misère
pour abaisser l'homme superbe, l'autre de gloire pour
élever l'homme humilié.' This reminds us of earlier chapters which said that a true religion would need to provide the antidote both to pride and to despair.

(c) Raison pourquoi figures (502)

Jesus, then, by showing that there is a 'true' meaning
distinct from the literal one, and by showing that the
kingdom of which the prophets spoke was a spiritual one,
has revealed the correct way to read the Old Testament,
and when it is read in that way, Jesus' claims to be the
Messiah make perfect sense. Once the key has been given,
some of the curious details of the Old Testament fall
into place. Not that Pascal wants us to see symbols where
none exist. As in section 13° on the use of reason, he
issues a warning:

> Deux erreurs. 1. prendre tout littéralement. 2. prendre
> tout spirituellement (252).

Fragments 254 and 575 give instances of the second excess.
     There is one particular example which appears to have
preoccupied Pascal, and by following his references to
it, we shall be led to consider the reasons why the Old
Testament had to be ambivalent. Both the manner and the
time of the coming of the Messiah are prophesied, but
whereas prophecies concerning the manner are (as we have
seen) obscure, the prophecies which announce the time are
perfectly clear. One point taken up in a second part to
no. 272 needs to be settled first. In saying that the
time of the Messiah has been predicted, Pascal is not
thinking of the mystic significance attached by the
Talmudists to the sign ☐   (the closed mem substituted
without explanation for the correct open mem in a significant prophecy of Isaiah 9:6). That meaning is not revealed by Scripture and there are other graphic anomalies
which pass without comment. Fragments 476 and 492 allude
cryptically to the same phenomena.
     The important question is why there is a difference
between the two aspects of the prophecies. As only the
manner of the Messiah's coming is obscure, this question

resolves itself into this: why should there be any doubt
al all about his status? We can guess Pascal's answer,
because it has been fully prepared by the previous section. Man is not to be forced into belief. Nor is salvation automatic. Evidence can be found, but only by the
honest seeker. The incarnation is the most certain manifestation of God in the world, but he is still a hidden
God, likely to be missed by those whose hearts are hardened.

The first version of this explanation (to judge by the
difficulty Pascal had in expressing himself) comes in no.
270. The first two paragraphs summarize very clearly the
first two sections of the present chapter. The Messiah
was foretold in language which could be taken to announce
an age of material prosperity, and that is how the Jews
did, for the most part, understand the prophecies. The
time of his coming was predicted too. Then the Messiah,
Jesus, did come, 'dans le temps prédit, mais non pas dans
l'éclat attendu,' and it needed Saint Paul to explain how
the prophecies should have been understood. The examples
Pascal gives are familiar from other fragments. Then he
drew a line, and wrote:

> Mais Dieu n'ayant pas voulu découvrir ces choses à ce
> peuple qui en était indigne et ayant voulu néanmoins
> les produire afin qu'elles fussent crues, il en a
> prédit le temps clairement et les manières en figure.
> (Je ne dis pas bien.)

Again he drew a line, but subsequently he scratched out
the last five words, and replaced them with the following:

> et les a quelquefois exprimées clairement mais abondam-
> ment en figures afin que ceux qui aimaient les choses
> figurantes s'y arrêtassent et que ceux qui aimaient
> les figurées les y vissent.

'La chose figurée' is the sovereign good, 'les choses
figurantes' the diverse material goods which can be interpreted either literally or as a symbol of the former.
Other fragments (255, 502) will explain more clearly the
distinction Pascal is trying to make. The more immediate
task was to capture other ideas which this development
has suggested. One of them (the fifth) echoes again the
idea we are discussing:

> Les Juifs ont tant aimé les choses figurantes et les
> ont si bien attendues qu'ils ont méconnu la réalité
> quand elle est venue dans le temps et en la manière
> prédite.

The intervening jottings refer to charity. It is one way
of defining the key revealed by the New Testament. Anything which does not lead directly (on the literal level)
to charity is the figure of charity. In this way God
caters both for our need for the love of God, and our
need for diversity, for the one thing needful can be represented in countless different ways. The Rabbis interpret
the Song of Songs in this way. Even the Eucharist is a
figure – of the glory which is the ultimate destiny of
the Christian soul. We have seen the reflection of these
ideas in fragments quoted earlier in this chapter.

But we still have not been told exactly why predictions
of Christ's coming are ambiguous as to the manner. No.
255 explains it clearly: it is in order that 'les mé-
chants' (the spiritually dead, the servants of concupiscence) will not be corrected with no effort on their own
part. The pure of heart, we know already, will interpret
the references to the kingdom correctly; it must be possible for the hard of heart to misinterpret, not because
they are stupid, but because they are blinded by self-
love. By the same token, there would be no point in
having the time predicted in an unclear manner. Pureness
of heart does not help us to solve riddles. Further, the
very explicitness of the predictions concerning time
strengthen the case against the non-believers, who are
suppressing evidence which is really quite unambiguous.[9]

These considerations do not affect the second coming.
On that occasion, the signs will be irrefutable, and
there will be no need for the kind of guarantee provided
by the predictions of the date (261).

The ambiguity of the prophecies is thus one more illustration of God's intention to veil himself, in order to
sort out the sheep from the goats. The first part of no.
489 – which has a title in the margin omitted in practically all editions: 'Preuves par les Juifs'[10] – gives
several examples from the Old Testament to substantiate
this concept. Jesus removed the veil (260), but only in
part: 'Le voile qui est sur ces livres pour les Juifs y
est aussi pour les mauvais chrétiens' (475), and we must
await the second coming before God will completely vin-
dicate himself.

An important unclassed fragment, no. 502-3, probes
deeply into the advantages of having the prophecies mediated in this way.[11] There had to be a tradition of prophecy, the bearers of which had necessarily to be dili-
gent, active, and not suspect. All these conditions are
met by the ambiguities in the prophetic texts. Diligence
is ensured because the Jews are counting on tangible rewards. Their very self-love serves Jesus, who came to
cure men of self-love (614; the relative clause was later
crossed out). Even their hope in the Messiah serves to
harden their hearts, as it is grounded in concupiscence
(496). Their blindness then works in favour of the elect
(469). They are not suspect because when Jesus came, the
Jews rejected him, having expected the Messiah to behave
very differently. Consequently it is his enemies, not his
friends, who are witnessing for him. That point is expanded in no. 273. The prophets said he would be rejected,
so by rejecting him, the Jews are helping to fulfil the
prophecies made about him. This splendid Pascalian paradox recurs in no. 262: whether they accept or reject the
Messiah, they are proving his claims. This part of no.
502 is echoed also in no. 615:

> Rien n'est si semblable à la charité que la cupidité
> et rien n'y est si contraire. Ainsi les juifs pleins
> be biens qui flattaient leur cupidité étaient très con-
> formes aux chrétiens et très contraires. Et par ce
> moyen ils avaient les deux qualités qu'il fallait qu'ils
> eussent: d'être très conformes au Messie, pour le figurer,
> et très contraires pour n'être point témoins suspects.

The same point is made in no. 592 (the fact that the Jews
do not wish to witness for Christ only strengthens the
testimony they do unwittingly give.) In no. 593 Pascal
argues that the only reason the Jews give for rejecting
Jesus is that he did not measure up to their (carnal)
expectations 'Par ce refus, ils sont des témoins sans
reproche, et qui plus est par là ils accomplissent les
prophéties.' The idea recurs equally forcefully in nos
391 and 488. The Jews, witnesses and custodians of God's
revelation, do not understand the precious books they
look after so diligently (495).
    Yet the objection could be made: how can we be sure
that Jesus really was fulfilling the messianic prophecies?
Pascal's answer is that as not every passage is ambiguous,
those passages whose spiritual meaning is clear give the

key we need for the rest. Cupidity misled the Jews into
making the false interpretation. Had they been motivated
by charity and the love of God, they would have made the
correct reading, understanding 'enemies' as their passions.
We thus return to the argument of section (a). Pascal adds
some of the examples he had collected in no. 489.

And a further thought follows.

> Et cependant ce testament fait pour aveugler les uns et
> éclairer les autres marquait en ceux mêmes qu'il aveu-
> glait la vérité qui devait être connue des autres (503).

From the magnificence of the visible gifts God bestowed on
the Israelites, it was evident that he could make gifts
of an invisible, spiritual kind. For nature is an image
of grace, and the events of the Old Testament are images
of redemption. This idea is noted also in no. 238 (entitled
'Figures,' but filed in section 19°),[12] and expanded in
no. 275. The image of redemption is one strand of no. 392,
but despite the title ('Figures') I shall reserve fuller
discussion of that fragment until chapter 23.

Finally, God taught us the true meaning of a vocabulary
so often understood literally. (Here Pascal rejoins section b.) Those who interpret correctly avoid the contradictions which must puzzle those whose reading of the Old
Testament is literal and carnal. Pascal concludes that
the Jews had the true religion. They had the miracles,
the prophecies, the continuing tradition ('Perpétuité,'
see chapter 22), but this list would be insufficient if
the correct doctrine of the law did not add to it the
prescription to adore God alone. Copious jottings (taken
from Grotius)[13] to document this last point are found on
fragment 453, with one point echoed in 497.

No. 826 rounds the argument off neatly. The truth is
manifest only in heaven. The Jewish religion furnishes a
figure of the truth, and the truth of Christianity can
only be established by calling upon the figure provided
by the sacred texts of the Jewish faith. Or one might prefer to conclude with the link between the two testaments
which is made in an addition to no. 801:

> L'ancien Testament contenait les figures de la joie
> future et le nouveau contient les moyens d'y arriver.
> Les figures étaient de joie, les moyens de pénitence...

21
Rabbinage (277-8)

The twenty-first dossier (Lafuma XX) contains only two
fragments - two sets of notes taken from the *Pugio Fidei*
in the 1651 edition of Joseph de Voisin,[1] about the Rabbinic commentaries on the Old Testament. The first, no.
277, is entitled 'Chronologie du Rabbinisme' and is little
more than an attempt on Pascal's part to instruct himself
concerning a territory which must have been very unfami-
liar. No. 278 is more interesting. In it Pascal collects
examples which prove that there was a 'tradition ample
du péché originel selon les Juifs.' Discussion must therefore centre on just one fragment, eked out by two references to the rabbinic writings in section 20°, and by
one unclassed fragment, no. 616[2] (XXIV). Unpromising
material, one would think; but it yields a surprising
amount. Although the chapter is hardly long enough to
justify dividing it into subsections, and prefacing these
with a summary of the argument, the argument does have
two distinct parts to it, one linking this section with
the previous one, and the other linking it to the section
which follows.

Chapter 20 began with an analysis of fragment 274.
Proof of Christ's claims rests on the prophecies; these
can only be believed if it can be shown that Scripture
has two meanings, the literal and the spiritual. In no.
274 Pascal noted several ways in which this could in fact
be shown. The first, 'Preuve par l'Ecriture même,' was
elaborated at length in the other fragments in the twentieth dossier. The second read: 'Preuves par les Rabbins,'
and the remaining three appear merely to clarify that
remark:

Preuves par la Cabale
   Preuves par l'interprétation mystique que les Rabbins

mêmes donnent de l'Ecriture
   Preuves par les principes des Rabbins qu'il y a deux
sens.

None of these 'proofs' are really developed elsewhere.
All we have is a reference in no. 270 to the Rabbis'
fondness for 'figures,' and the long list of examples
from rabbinical writings which makes up fragment 278.
It is striking that all the examples listed in no. 278
are illustrations of the figurative approach favoured by
the rabbinical commentators.
   The first impulse behind no. 278 then, may well have
been to justify the figurative interpretation of the Old
Testament, by showing that it goes back to the learned
commentators of the Jewish tradition. That conclusion is
not explicitly drawn in no. 278, which makes no comment
at all on the examples listed. We cannot help wondering,
as we read it, just how seriously Pascal took the rabbinical arguments. The figurative interpretations which
Pascal himself put forward, in section 20°, were carefully justified, and a warning was issued against the
'trop grands figuratifs' (254) who did not take their
meaning from Scripture, but injected it from without (251,
etc.). Are the rabbinical commentators in this category
or not? I suspect they might be.
   Perhaps for that reason, Pascal's interest in what he
found out about the rabbinical writings seems to have
moved away from the manner to the matter. The title, originally just 'Du péché originel,' becomes 'Tradition
ample du péché originel selon des Juifs,' which invites
us to see in the long list which follows, not examples
of the figurative approach - sound or excessive - but
evidence of the strong pre-Christian history of Christian
thought. Original sin, the corruption of man, is a main
tenet of Christian doctrine. Pascal is at pains to show
that it was not invented by Christianity. Observation of
man's behaviour has suggested that man is corrupt (in the
first part of the Apologia), and now we find that the
Jewish faith taught the same thing. There is thus no need
for Christianity to prove the need for a redeemer - we
can agree about that - what we need to know is whether
Jesus Christ was the promised redeemer or not.
   The emphasis therefore shifts to the content of rabbinical teaching, and places Christian theology in a long-
continuing tradition. In fragment 616 Pascal we find a
characteristic observation on man's double nature.

La concupiscence nous est devenue naturelle et a fait
notre seconde nature. Ainsi il y a deux natures en
nous, l'une bonne, l'autre mauvaise.

Pascal then wrote the word 'Rabbins.'[2] Clearly he did
not need rabbinical authority for an idea he could justify on grounds much less esoteric; the word must imply
that in rabbinical teaching on concupiscence we have another case of a tradition preparing the way for Christianity.

There are also a number of additions to the text of no.
274, tending to show that key doctrines evoked in section
20° have their support from the writings of the rabbinic
commentators. Throughout section 20°, the Jews (only once
qualified explicitly as 'les Juifs charnels,' and that as
an afterthought, 256) were painted as blind to the hidden,
true meaning of Scripture, despite the hints from the prophets. In the fragments relating to the rabbinic writings,
we are reminded that there were 'spiritual' Jews as well
as carnal ones.

Pascal did not pursue the matter very far, either
through a lack of interest, or because he realized that
the apologetic value of technical details of interminable
and esoteric commentaries would be very limited.[3] But just
because there are so few trees, we are able to discern
the wood. Pascal has said enough to make a very neat
transition between his twentieth and twenty-second sections. The Rabbis not only strengthen the argument that
there is good precedent for a figurative interpretation
of the Old Testament; they also show how many of the
Christian insights were already grasped by the more discerning elements within the Jewish faith. The next section, entitled 'Perpétuité,' will draw important conclusions from the fact that the Christian religion was in
existence, though hidden from most men, from the beginning
of human history.

22
Perpétuité

In the preceding sections, Pascal has been very circumspectly establishing the objective claims of Jesus to be
the Messiah. The first peg was placed in section 13°, no.
180, in which Pascal told us that the Messiah was prophesied throughout the Old Testament, and that Jesus fulfilled
those prophecies, establishing his authority by miracles.
Touched upon in sections 14°, 15°, and 17°, the theme was
fully examined in section 19°, 'Fondements et réponse aux
objections.' The word 'Fondements' was explained in no.
243: in contrast to pagan religions, which have no firm
basis, or to Islam, whose basis is inadequate, Christianity is grounded in the Jewish faith, which is itself based
upon an authentic text. Pascal was careful to bid us distinguish between the true teaching of any religion and
the distortions we find in unworthy followers. The other
half of the title, 'Réponse aux objections,' was responsible for a long development elaborating the theory of
the 'hidden God.' It argued that the evidence was deliberately made obscure, though it could be discerned by
men of good will, and section 20° went into great detail
about one particular aspect of the obscurity - the need
to interpret prophetic utterances in the figurative, not
the literal sense, as God's meaning is 'hidden' in the
text, as indeed it is in all the Old Testament. This
method resolves difficulties which at first appear to
prevent us from attaching the life of Jesus to the messianic prophecies.

In section 21°, Pascal moved back from the exploration
of figures to the reality behind the figures. One thing
which emerges from the discussion is that while the majority of the Jews were content to believe the literal
meaning of the prophecies, and were misled by them, there
were always some men - the prophets themselves, and also
the Rabbinic commentators - who did understand the

spiritual implications. The rabbinical teachings show
that there was an 'ample tradition' of belief in original
sin, in corruption. Similarly, it could be argued that
there was a constant expectation of redemption.

Section 22° (XXI in Lafuma's numbering), while it incorporates some of the matter of the long digression, is
essentially a sequel to no. 243, a reflection on the tradition of basic Christian doctrine in the Jewish religion,
preserved in the authentic witness of the sacred writings.
Fragment 8, filed in the first *liasse*, read: 'Voir ce
qu'il y a de clair dans tout l'état des Juifs et d'incontestable.' Jewish tradition - referring of course to
their holy books and not to the beliefs of 'carnal Jews'
- has propagated since the beginning of time a doctrine
which the Jews believe to have been given by God himself,
that man is corrupt, but that God will send him a redeemer.
This teaching and this hope were preserved throughout the
centuries, despite many obstacles. The prophecies were
fulfilled in Jesus Christ, and the principles which pre-
side over Jewish history can still be seen to apply to
the Christian Church. In fragment 892[1] Pascal sums up the
advantages noted in no. 243 ('J'aime mieux suivre J-C.
qu'aucun autre parce qu'il a le miracle, prophétie, doctrine...') and continues: 'perpétuité, etc.'

The classified fragments are for the most part short,
with only no. 281 taking us to the heart of the matter.
There are, however, a number of important unclassed fragments (390, 451, 454, 456) which give a complete account
of Pascal's train of thought.[2] I also call upon nos 392
(I); 421, 425 (II); 452 (VII); 457 (X); 480 (XI); 492
(XVIII); 589, 590 (XXIII); 594 (XXIV); 776 (XXVII); 892
(XXXIV); and in a note mention 707 (XXV), 886, 871, and
894 (XXXIV).

I will mention first those few fragments where Pascal
seems still to be preoccupied with figures.

Les six âges, les six pères des six âges, les six merveilles à l'entrée des six âges, les six orients à
l'entrée des six âges (283).

This cryptic note is complemented by no. 590, which quotes
the Epistle to the Romans 5:14: Adam is a 'figure of him
that was to come' and the application is elaborated in
detail.

Another fragment, no. 279, was quoted in chapter 20.

Un mot de David ou de Moïse, comme que Dieu circoncira
leur coeur fait juger de leur esprit.

The obvious interpretation (the sequel leaves us in no
doubt) is that such phrases confirm the validity of a
figurative reading of the Old Testament. The circumcision
of the heart is also mentioned in no. 288, in a way which
leads us to believe that Pascal is doing again what he
did in no. 278 - moving from an example of a particular
method to the content of the statement to be interpreted.

Moïse, Deut. 30, promet que Dieu circoncira leur coeur
pour les rendre capables de l'aimer.

It thus forms part of the continuing record of God's promises to heal man's alienation.

But generally in this section Pascal retraces his steps
as far as the fragment originally entitled 'Fondement de
notre foi,' no. 243, summarized at the beginning of this
chapter. In that fragment he makes the necessary distinction between 'la tradition des livres saints' and 'la
tradition du peuple.' The idea that the average Jew has
carnal expectations and that the spiritual understanding
of religion has been restricted to a select minority has
become familiar to us, but understandably Pascal wishes
to remind us of it at the threshold of section 22°, lest
we should think we can refute his argument about the Jews
by referring to the criticisms Pascal himself has made
about them in previous chapters. Back in section 18° (no.
222) Pascal contrasted what he called 'les Juifs charnels'
with pagans on the one hand and Christians on the other,
and on the back of that fragment he wrote 'Voyez Perpétuité.' Meanwhile, in no. 256, Pascal added to the word
'Juifs' the qualifier 'charnels.'

The matter is amplified first of all in no. 287, the
first sentence of which repeats in almost identical words
the relevant passage from no. 243:

Qui jugera de la religion des Juifs par les grossiers
la connaîtra mal. Elle est visible dans les saints
livres et dans la tradition des prophètes qui ont assez
fait entendre qu'ils n'entendaient pas la loi à la
lettre. Ainsi notre religion est divine dans l'Evangile,
les apôtres et la tradition, mais elle est ridicule
dans ceux qui la traitent mal.

Le Messie selon les Juifs charnels doit être un grand
prince temporel. J-C. selon les chrétiens charnels est
venu nous dispenser d'aimer Dieu, et nous donner des
sacrements qui opèrent tout sans nous; ni l'un ni l'autre
n'est la religion chrétienne ni juive.

Les vrais Juifs et les vrais chrétiens ont toujours
attendu un Messie qui les ferait aimer Dieu et par cet
amour triompher de leurs ennemis.

It is very interesting to see Pascal here extending his
distinction between 'carnal' and 'true' Jews to Christians;
the thought thereby takes on a polemical aspect, and reads
like a pendant to the *Provinciales*.

No. 286 goes over the same ground, and also finds an
equivalent distinction among pagans.

No. 289, like no. 222, compares the Jews to pagans and
Christians. As in no. 256, Pascal added the epithet
'charnels,' and in a final sentence reminded us that there
are two kinds of Jews, the one fundamentally pagan, the
other fundamentally Christian.

'True' Jews, like true pagans and true Christians, must
be religiously sincere (480).

That distinction clearly made, Pascal can proceed with
his argument. No. 243 concluded: 'Notre religion est si
divine qu'une autre religion divine n'en a que le fondement.' No. 454 begins:

Je vois la religion chrétienne fondée sur une religion
précédente, où voici ce que je trouve d'effectif.

There would appear to be two versions of the sequel. In
the first, Pascal tells us that he will not insist on
the miracles (necessary, he had said in no. 180, to fulfil the prophecies), but will point out the indisputable
'fondements' of Christianity. He then gave the first:

Il est certain que nous voyons en quelques endroits du
monde un peuple particulier séparé de tous les autres
peuples du monde qui s'appelle le peuple juif.

He next wrote a different transition, leading to the same
point. Other religions show a bewildering variety of behaviour and belief. But among them there is one people

séparé de tous les autres peuples de la terre, le plus

ancien de tous et dont les histoires précèdent de plusieurs siècles les plus anciennes que nous ayons.

He goes on to make four points about the Jewish nation:

Je trouve donc ce peuple grand et nombreux sorti d'un
seul homme, qui adore un seul Dieu, et qui se conduit
par une loi qu'ils disent tenir de sa main. Ils soutiennent qu'ils sont les seuls du monde auxquels Dieu a
révélé ses mystères.

God's mysteries are, of course, the corruption of man
and the promise of a redeemer. The Jews are the guardians
of the promise made through them to all mankind.

No. 451, 'Avantages du peuple juif,' elaborates on the
same points: the single family, its antiquity, the perfection of the law. No. 456 reviews some of these ideas
briefly; it also mentions the dispersal of the Jews and
the long life of the Jewish nation (25°). No. 457 is a
marginal note in part absorbed by no. 456.

This great tapestry is all the more impressive when we
realize how extraordinarily improbable the story would
be if it were not authenticated. Fragment 284, echoing
no. 425 from the 'Infini rien' manuscript, tells us that

La seule religion contre la nature, contre le sens
commun, contre nos plaisirs est la seule qui ait
toujours été.

The law is exceptionally severe, yet it was never changed
(451); the record and the prophecies are unflattering,
yet they were scrupulously preserved (452). Israel, frequently persecuted or threatened by the lure of paganism,
has never actually succumbed (281). Fragment 492, entitled,
like no. 452, '(La) sincérité des Juifs,' notes that the
Jews were 'sincères contre leur honneur et mourant pour
cela. Cela n'a point d'exemple dans le monde ni sa racine
dans la nature.' This unnatural fidelity means that the
tales of the prophets are above suspicion, as we have
seen in chapter 20 (section c).[3] In no. 820 Pascal wrote:
'Je ne crois que les histoires dont les témoins se fe-
raient égorger' (quoted in chapter 17).

The Jewish faith, then, contains the two pillars of
Christian doctrine, and is of venerable antiquity. Consequently, one can say that Christian teaching is no
relatively modern invention:

Nulle secte ni religion n'a toujours été sur la terre
que la religion chrétienne (421, end).

The opening of no. 281, the longest fragment classified
in section 22°, originally read:

Cette religion qui consiste en l'adoration du Messie a
toujours été sur la terre

but it was expanded to read:

Cette religion qui consiste à croire que l'homme est
déchu d'un état de gloire et de communication avec Dieu
en un état de tristesse, de pénitence, et d'éloignement
de Dieu, mais qu'après cette vie nous serons rétablis
par un Messie qui devait venir, a toujours été sur la
terre.

In no. 281, Pascal is concerned to stress that the hope
of redemption persisted despite the strong lure of paganism and carnality. He mentions Enoch and Lemech, Noah,
'figure' of the Messiah, and the hope of Abraham, Jacob,
and Moses. Fragment 390, entitled 'Perpétuité' and evidently destined for this section, expresses the full wonder of the theme

Qu'on considère que depuis le commencement du monde
l'attente ou l'adoration du Messie subsiste sans inter-
ruption, qu'il s'est trouvé des hommes qui ont dit que
Dieu leur avait révélé, qu'il devait naître un rédempteur qui sauverait son peuple. Qu'Abraham est venu ensuite dire qu'il avait eu révélation qu'il naîtrait de
lui par un fils qu'il aurait, que Jacob a déclaré que
de ses douze enfants il naîtrait de Juda, que Moïse et
ses prophètes sont venus ensuite déclarer le temps et
la manière de sa venue. Qu'ils ont dit que la loi qu'ils
avaient n'était qu'en attendant celle du Messie, que
jusques là elle serait perpétuelle, mais que l'autre
durerait éternellement, qu'ainsi leur loi ou celle du
Messie dont elle était la promesse serait toujours sur
la terre, qu'en effet elle a toujours duré, qu'enfin
est venu J-C. dans toutes les circonstances prédites.
Cela est admirable.

No. 282 summarizes this, but adds two new ideas:

> Le Messie a toujours été cru. La tradition d'Adam était
> encore nouvelle en Noé et en Moïse. Les prophètes l'ont
> prédit depuis en prédisant toujours d'autres choses dont
> les événements qui arrivaient de temps en temps à la
> vue des hommes marquaient la vérité de leur mission et
> par conséquent celle de leurs promesses concernant le
> Messie. Jésus C. a fait des miracles et les apôtres
> aussi qui ont converti tous les païens et par là toutes
> les prophéties étant accomplies le Messie est prouvé
> pour jamais.

The two new ideas mentioned here (the tradition of Adam,
still fresh at the time of Moses, and the miracles of
Jesus and the apostles) will be the subject of the next
two sections, 'Preuves de Moïse' and 'Preuves de Jésus
Christ.'

The second of these ideas reappears in the same context
in fragment 594, and the first in no. 392. This latter
fragment bears the title 'Figures,' no doubt because the
second of its three paragraphs is about Noah, whom fragment 281 called a 'figure' of the Messiah (here he is
'l'image'). But whereas other fragments entitled 'Figures'
go naturally with section 20°, ('Loi figurative'), there
is no doubt that no. 392 should be bracketed with nos
281 and 282. The first sentence reminds us of other points
already made:

> Dieu voulant se former un peuple saint, qu'il séparerait
> de toutes les autres nations, qu'il délivrerait de ses
> ennemis qu'il mettrait dans un lieu de repos, a promis
> de le faire et a prédit par ses prophètes le temps et
> la manière de sa venue.

The continuation notes various ways in which God strengthened the hope of his elect.

A final group of *pensées* in this section looks beyond
the time of Jesus to the Christian era. Events have followed the same pattern, with 'le peuple juif moqué des
Gentils, le peuple chrétien persécuté' (589 b). The Jews
have survived despite their dispersal since the time of
Christ. The last part of no. 281 goes on to trace the
history of the Christian Church, which never compromised
with tyrannical rules, whereas (adds fragment 280), political states have to bend their laws now and again, and
they do not last anything like so long. History is full

of great nations which have disappeared (451, cf. 281: 'Toutes choses ont passé et celle-là a subsisté pour[4] laquelle sont toutes choses'). The hand of God is evident in this: 'Dieu n'a jamais laissé ses vrais adorateurs' (892).

The Christian Church has the incomparable advantage of being able to call upon the age-old tradition (285). 'L'histoire de l'Eglise doit être proprement appelée l'histoire de la vérité' (776).[5]

23
Preuves de Moïse (290-7)

The twenty-third dossier (Lafuma XXII) is very short, and
I am calling on seven unclassed fragments to amplify it:
nos 384 (I); 435 (IV); 436 (V); 474, 481 (XI); 589
(XXIII); 1102. The majority of relevant fragments present no real problems, but there are a couple of classified fragments (291 and 293) which seem unrelated to the
rest of the section. They are discussed at the end of
this chapter.

In the previous section (no. 282), we read: 'Le Messie
a toujours été cru. La tradition d'Adam etait encore nouvelle en Noé et en Moïse.' The essential idea in that
section, expressed in nos 281, 390, and 392, was that man
has never been without assurances of his eventual redemption. The promise was made to Adam directly, the Flood
was a 'figure' of the same truth, and the story continued
through the faith of various leaders like Abraham and
Jacob, until the day when Moses recorded the different
examples. One recalls also 1115, used in chapter 19, which
spoke of the signs of God available to those who lived at
the time of the Flood, or at the time of Moses.

The point of the present section is to explain how and
why the authentic tradition has been preserved, first
orally and then in a written record we can trust. Pascal
accepts the current assumption that Moses was the author
of all the books in the Pentateuch, and he shows a touch-
ing faith in the literal accuracy of details such as the
ages ascribed in those books to the patriarchs, indeed
he bases part of his argument upon them. There is therefore no textual criticism in the present section.

Pascal's argument falls into three parts, but I have
not thought it necessary to split the chapter into subsections. First, Pascal argues that the longevity of the
patriarchs guarantees the witness of the Creation and the
Flood. From that he goes on to explain why a reliable

written record had to be established, and then he shows
how God ensured that the record would be preserved.
    Fragment 292 sketches the question and the answer:

Preuves de Moïse.
    Pourquoi Moïse va-t-il faire la vie des hommes si
longue et si peu de générations.
    Car ce n'est pas la longueur des années mais la mul-
titude des générations qui rendent les choses obscures.
    Car la vérité ne s'altère que par le changement des
hommes.
    Et cependant il met deux choses les plus mémorables
qui se soient jamais imaginées, savoir la création et
le déluge, si proches qu'on y touche.

The first part is explained in no. 290. People then had
plenty of time to live in the company of their ancestors,
and hear their authentic reminiscences. There was therefore little likelihood of any distortion in the story,
which passed through few hands and which was heard many
times over. Pascal even invokes Montaigne for support;
Montaigne had said he would be most attentive if someone
could give him a first-hand account of his ancestors.[1]
    Fragment 292 is continued by 1102:[2]

Car quoiqu'il y eût environ deux mille ans qu'elles
avaient été faites, le peu de générations qui s'étaient
passées faisaient qu'elles étaient aussi nouvelles aux
hommes qui étaient en ce temps-là que nous le sont à
présent celles qui sont arrivées il y a environ 300 ans.
Cela vient de la longueur de la vie des premiers hommes.
En sorte que Sem qui a vu Lamech, etc.

The word 'etc.' is a reminder to copy a sentence recorded
as no. 296:

Sem qui a vu Lamech qui a vu Adam, a vu aussi Jacob qui
a vu ceux qui ont vu Moïse: donc le déluge et la création sont vrais. Cela conclut entre de certaines gens
qui l'entendent bien.

That last sentence (added by Pascal himself; the first
sentence was dictated) is picked up in the continuation
of 1102:

> Cette preuve suffit pour convaincre les personnes rai-
> sonnables de la vérité du Déluge et de la Création, et
> cela fait voir la Providence de Dieu, lequel, voyant
> que la Création commençait à s'éloigner, a pourvu d'un
> historien qu'on peut appeler contemporain, et a commis
> tout un peuple pour la garde de son livre.

Certain unclassed fragments expand on this paragraph.
No. 474 uses a very similar vocabulary:

> La création du monde commençant à s'éloigner, Dieu a
> pourvu d'un historien unique contemporain, et a commis
> tout un peuple pour la garde de ce livre, afin que
> cette histoire fût la plus authentique du monde et que
> tous les hommes pussent apprendre par là une chose si
> nécessaire à savoir, et qu'on ne pût la savoir que par
> là.

No. 435 introduced two other nuances into the same idea:

> La création et le déluge étant passés, et Dieu ne de-
> vant plus détruire le monde, non plus que le recréer,
> ni donner de ces grandes marques de lui, il commença
> d'établir un peuple sur la terre, formé exprès, qui
> devait durer jusqu'au peuple que le Messie formerait
> par son esprit.

The third paragraph of 1102 adds something not mentioned
in the other fragments: the respect with which the Old
Testament has been treated by people outside the Jewish
tradition.

Two of the classified fragments (294, 297) tell us how
the law, once recorded, was kept for another 2000 years.
In the first place there were the prophets, who fought
any signs of defection in the Jews. Once the line of
prophets ended, a reawakening of zeal among the Jewish
people ensured their fidelity (cf. 589 first sentence,
and 384, echoing a note added to 492: 'Depuis qu'ils
n'ont plus de prophètes. Machab. Depuis J-C. Massorett').

So far, only fragment 1102 has mentioned the role of
Moses in establishing the text of the law. The words
Pascal uses to describe him, 'historien qu'on peut appeler
contemporain' remind us of no. 436, 'Antiquité des Juifs,'
in which Pascal argues that many so-called histories
(Greek, Egyptian, Chinese) are written by people with no

first-hand knowledge of the events they are describing,
and the result is unreliable.

> Il y a bien de la différence entre un livre que fait
> un particulier et qu'il jette dans le peuple, et un
> livre qui[3] fait lui-même un peuple. On ne peut douter
> que le livre ne soit aussi ancien que le peuple.

What Pascal had written about the generations from Adam
to Moses helps us to understand what he means by this
rather oblique allusion. A similar phrase comes also in
no. 481, entitled 'Contre l'histoire de la Chine': 'Différence d'un livre reçu d'un peuple, ou qui forme un
peuple.' 'La Chine obscurcit, mais il y a clarté à trouver,' he writes in no. 822. Fragment 295 mentions Moses
too. In contrast to Josephus, Moses does not hide the
discreditable aspects of Jewish history. This argument
from sincerity (cf. 452 and 492 'Sincérité des Juifs'
quoted in the previous chapter) will be paralleled by
some of Pascal's thoughts on the evangelists in section
24°.
   Two fragments stand apart from the others:

> Si on doit donner huit jours on doit donner toute la
> vie (293).

> Cette religion si grande en miracles, si grande en
> science, après avoir étalé tous ses miracles et toute
> sa sagesse, elle réprouve cela et dit qu'elle n'a ni
> sagesse, ni signe, mais la croix et la folie (291).

The first of these fragments comes, in one form or another, four times in the *Pensées*: here, in section 12°
(159), in section 25° (326), and in the first set of unclassed fragments (386). The clearest indication of what
it means is no. 326, quoted in chapter 12. Pascal urges
us to conduct ourselves as if we have only eight days to
live. Fragment 291, anticipated by a passing remark on
the 'Infini rien' fragment ('*stultitiam*'), can best be
understood in the context of section 28°. One is tempted
to attribute the presence of these two fragments in this
dossier to a mistake. Lafuma has no hesitation in the
case of no. 293, which follows directly fragment 292,
separated from it by a line; in Lafuma's view, Pascal
simply neglected to take his scissors and cut along the

line.[4] Pol Ernst, however, unwilling to take the easy
way out, interprets nos 291 and 293 together as a salutary
reminder that all these proofs are not meant to convert,
only to show that there are rational grounds for accepting
Christianity.[5] True faith involves the personality at a
totally different level. If we share Ernst's unwillingness
to allow that Homer sometimes nods, this is probably the
best justification; but it has a somewhat specious look,
and it is difficult to understand why Pascal should place
his reminder in this particular section, before he has
reached the end of the closely knit block of dossiers on
historical evidence, which extend as far as section 26°.
Certainly the next section, with its title 'Preuves de
Jésus-Christ' clearly balancing 'Preuves de Moïse' cannot
be seen as marking a radical new departure in the apologetic argument.

24
Preuves de Jésus-Christ (298-322)

The previous chapters have asserted that the Old Testament teaches man's need of redemption, and expresses
man's hope that God will send a redeemer, the Messiah.
In 'Preuves de Moïse,' Pascal demonstrated the authenticity of the Old Testament record, and explained the
reason for some unusual features.

The twenty-fourth section, 'Preuves de Jésus-Christ'
(Lafuma XXIII), aims to show that Jesus was indeed the
promised Messiah. It does so in two ways. First, Pascal
links the coming of Jesus with Old Testament prophecies
concerning the Messiah and the Jewish people. In a second
part he breaks free of this reliance on prophecy, and
argues that the New Testament affords independent proof
of the claims of Jesus. Finally, he answers the predict-
able objection: why, if the case can be proved, was Jesus
not universally acclaimed?

The details of the argument can be summed up in this
way:

(a) the Old Testament points to Jesus as the promised
redeemer, in the general tenor of the Scriptures, and
the genealogy of the Old Testament, as does the evidence
of the secular historians, and the later history of the
Jewish people and the Church.

(b) certain features of the New Testament make it impossible seriously to doubt that it too is an authentic
record. And in the New Testament we read of the miracles
of Jesus, which established his claim by fulfilling the
prophecies, and of the person of Jesus, clearly both
divine and human.

(c) if this is none the less not self-evident, it is
because Jesus, being divine, has concealed his divinity
from the unfaithful. He did not fulfil expectations,
because people had the wrong expectations, carnal and
not spiritual. A careful distinction must be made between

three 'orders' - flesh, mind, and heart. There are parallels between them, which enable us to understand by analogy the highest order, the order of charity, but there is
no interference.

Unclassified fragments called upon in this chapter are:
388 (I); 433 (IV); 454 (IX); 457 (X); 487 (XVI); 499
(XVIII); 500 (XIX); 568, 574 (XXIII); 607, 608 (XXIV);
746, 753 (XXVI); 790 (XXVII); 811, 812 (XXIX); 832, 834,
846 (XXXIII); 865, 903 (XXXIV); 933; 970-2.[1]

*(a) J-C. que l'ancien testament regarde comme son attente
(388)*

Ever since the Fall, man has lived in hope of redemption.
Is Jesus the redeemer whom God promised? Fragment 388
tells us that both Testaments regard Jesus as their centre,
'l'ancien comme son attente, le nouveau comme son modèle.'
The prophecies recorded in the Pentateuch and the hope of
Job are mentioned in no. 811; both Moses and Job 'regardent J-C. comme leur centre commun et leur objet.' Three
Latin phrases (312) bid us to read the prophecies, see
what has been fulfilled, and note what remains to be fulfilled.

This may remind us of the recurring phrase, 'ce qui a
précédé, ce qui a suivi,' commented on in chapter 19.
One of its occurrences is in an addition squeezed between
nos 608 and 609. The main text of no. 608 is a note of
all the various tasks expected of the Messiah; it expands
no. 607 entitled 'Fig.' Countless prophecies of the Messiah
are collected in no. 487.[2] In fragment 315 Pascal reminds
us that the Messiah is clearly announced in the Pentateuch
and the Psalms, and in no. 319, that the synagogue and
the Jews are forerunners of the Christian Church and
Christians, whom the prophets predicted. Both these fragments refer also to Saint John the Baptist.

Jacob prophesied that the Messiah would be born of the
line of Judah. In fragment 236 the genealogy of Jesus was
given as an example of clarity/obscurity in God's dealings
with man:

Si Moïse n'eût tenu registre que des ancêtres de J-C.
cela eût été trop visible; s'il n'eût pas marqué celle
de J-C. cela n'eût pas été assez visible, mais après
tout, qui y regarde de près voit celle de J-C. bien
discernée par Thamar, Ruth etc.

The story of Tamar and the book of Ruth have been preserved by the Jews to show that Jacob's prophecy was fulfilled (304). The name Jesus belongs to the Messiah as
the last of the line initiated by Joshua (790).

The secular historians supply evidence which shows that
Jesus did indeed fulfil the prophecies, properly understood. That is the plausible interpretation advanced by
Ernst for no. 317, a collection of ideas whose unity is
not immediately apparent.[3] The ideas look back to earlier
chapters, and the fragment was probably written at a time
when the distinctions to be made within this block were
not clear to Pascal.[4] On the manuscript of no. 501,
'Figures,' which I used to launch the discussion of
chapter 20, Pascal wrote: 'Beau de voir des yeux de la
foi l'histoire d'Hérode, de César' (500). The thought
reappears as the fifth of the five sentences, each separated by a line, which make up no. 317 (itself originally
entitled 'Figures'). The fourth sentence reads: 'Qu'on
est heureux d'avoir cette lumière dans cette obscurité.'
The first three sentences were added later. The third
cited the visions of Jacob and of Daniel, and is presumably the 'light' referred to: 'J-C. prédit quant au
temps...'; the notion will be explained fully in section
25°. The first two sentences have to do with the zeal of
the Jews, which we came across in the previous chapter;
Josephus and Philo the Jew are invoked as witnesses.
Ernst draws our attention also to no. 320, which quotes
Macrobius on the massacre of the innocents (on which see
also no. 753).[5] Ernst takes it to mean that Herod knew
very well that the time had come, and took steps to fore-
stall the end of the monarchy predicted by Daniel.

In two fragments (305 and 314), Pascal talks of the
dispersal of the Jews. In Old Testament times, temporary
exile, undergone in the knowledge that it would not last
forever, did not constitute dispersal. God promised the
Jews that if they were faithful he would reunite them.
Since the time of Jesus there have been no signs of re-
union. That is because the new law has replaced the old,
and the Jews are no longer living in obedience to the
operative law.

The very fact that the Jews have continued as a nation,
despite their present misery, is itself worthy of reflection. It is necessary

pour la preuve de J-C. et qu'il subsiste pour le

prouver, et qu'il soit misérable, puisqu'ils l'ont crucifié. Et quoiqu'il soit contraire d'être misérable et de subsister il subsiste néanmoins toujours malgré sa misère (311).

Finally, fragment 301 refers to a prophecy not of Jesus himself, but of his effect on others: 'I will pour out my spirit upon all flesh, and your sons and your daughters shall prophesy, your old men shall dream dreams, your young men shall see visions' (Joel 2:28)

> *Effundam spiritum meum.* Tous les peuples étaient dans l'infidélité et dans la concupiscence, toute la terre fut ardente de charité: les princes quittent leur grandeur, les filles souffrent le martyr. D'où vient cette force? C'est que le Messie est arrivé. Voilà l'effet et les marques de sa venue.

An unclassed fragment, no. 433, stresses the strong opposition the reign of charity naturally encountered. 'Et tout cela se fait par la force qui l'avait prédit.'

(b) J-C. que le nouveau testament regarde comme son modèle (388)

The record of Jesus is contained in the four gospels of the New Testament. I have already quoted no. 388, which says that both Testaments regard Jesus as their focal centre, and Pascal has fully documented that statement for the Old Testament. On this aspect of the New Testament we have only no. 299, observing the biblical references to the virgin birth: 'Tout par rapport à J-C.'
    In this section Pascal wishes first of all to authenticate the gospel records.[6] He does so by psychological rather than by critical arguments. If the evangelists had made it all up, he says, then they would have done it differently. They would surely have ironed out discrepancies in their accounts (318), presented Jesus in his agony with no trace of weakness (316). Why should they maintain that Jesus had risen from the dead if he had not? It would have been much too dangerous, and they could hardly have been themselves deceived in such an extraordinary matter (322 and 310, developing a hint in no. 457). Would they have had the understanding of God which Jesus shows (303)? Would they have had of their own the charity to treat enemies without invective (812)?

We must therefore accept that what is said of Jesus
constitutes an authentic record. In it we are told both
of the acts and the person of Jesus. Among the acts,
particular importance attaches to the miracles because
it was by his miracles that Jesus established his claim
in the eyes of his contemporaries, and thereby fulfilled
the prophecies. This contention has been made already,
beginning with an important *pensée* in the section on the
right use of reason (13°), no. 180. The terms of no. 180
are echoed in no. 282 (22°) and in the second part of no.
594 (which we attached to section 22°). The miracles were
necessary for the fulfilment of the prophecies, but once
the prophecies were fulfilled, it is the prophecies, not
the miracles, which carry the burden of proof. For those
who accept tradition, 'les miracles ne sont plus nécessaires à cause qu'on en a déjà' (865).

Nevertheless, historically the miracles were important
and constitute one of the ways in which Christianity has
a much stronger case than Mahometanism. The point was
made in no. 243 (19°), and it recurs in this twenty-
fourth section, with no. 321.

> Tout homme peut faire ce qu'a fait Mahomet. Car il n'a
> point fait de miracles, il n'a point été prédit. Nul
> homme ne peut faire ce qu'a fait J-C.

Would Pascal have chosen to expand on his ideas, and what
would he have wished to add? We can only speculate. Editions of the *pensées* all include several pages on the
subject, but the fragments in question (Units XXXII,
XXXIII, XXXIV in the Lafuma classification, nos 830–912)
are for the most part not suitable, in the form Pascal
wrote them, for an apologia.[7]

Pascal was perfectly well aware of the limited usefulness of the topic. He described miracles in no. 454 as
not immediately convincing, as not beyond dispute.[8] And
although he wrote that 'il n'est pas possible de croire
raisonnablement contre les miracles' (568; the context
is, however, polemical, not apologetic), he recognized
that reason always finds excuses for not believing such
unusual evidence (574, and cf. 834, title: 'Raisons pourquoi on ne croit point').

Nevertheless, we have seen that he could not keep them
out of his apologetic argument altogether, and the case
for miracles is put in some classified fragments. One can
understand therefore why Pascal said that miracles were

the 'Fondement de la religion' (832, 834) and why he made
notes on the importance Jesus himself attached to the
miracles (846, and 903 para. 3). Louis Lafuma, arguing
that some fragments on miracles were written years after
the dispute with the Jesuits about the Holy Thorn, believed that there would have been something on miracles
in the chapter entitled 'Fondements,' but that Pascal
would have excluded anything which prolonged the quarrel
within the Church.[9] I would agree with this, except that
my own analysis of the *liasses* suggests section 24° as a
more appropriate location than 19° despite the title. In
section 19° Pascal spoke generally about the 'fondements,'
and answered objections, and we have seen that he there
argued that miracles were not a stumbling-block to reason. The present section would seem to be the best place
in which to mention specifically the miracles of Jesus,
that is, after a long discussion of the first 'fondement,'
the Old Testament, at the point where Pascal is ready to
discuss the New. Textual support for this view that the
miracles would have been discussed in section 24° is
restricted - no. 321 apart - to one brief and enigmatic
fragment, no. 302, 'Les combinaisons des miracles.'

As well as presenting the miracles, the New Testament
gives us our only full portrayal of the person of Jesus,
both divine and human. The gospel record is that of a man
who was surely divine, who spoke of the things of God
with authority (303), in words both simple and clear (309).
Pascal draws from the sayings and actions of Jesus several
texts for meditation; here we are on the border, difficult
to define, between apologetic and private text.

Fragment 307 reminds us that the Church has taken as
much trouble to affirm Christ's humanity as it has his
divinity. His humanity is finally proved by his dying.[10]
That thought leads to a characteristic paradox:

Les Juifs en éprouvant s'il était Dieu, ont montré
qu'il était homme (306).

Do the early heretics weaken the case for Jesus as
Messiah? No, replies Pascal (313), because they draw
their heresies from a particular interpretation of the
gospels, so they do accept the gospels themselves.

(c) l'éclat de son ordre (308)

Jesus therefore not only came at the time and in the way

the prophets (correctly understood) predicted, he showed
in his life, recorded in the four gospels whose authority
cannot be seriously questioned, the kind of spirituality
a man of discernment would expect. Yet his claims have
been disputed, as nothing of what has been said is self-
evident. Is there a potential difficulty here?

Only, says Pascal, if we forget that God is both hidden
and also accessible to men who are willing to fulfil certain conditions, and Jesus must necessarily share this
double characteristic. This was made clear as early as
section 19° with no. 228:

> Que disent les prophètes de J-C.? qu'il sera évidemment
> Dieu? Non mais qu'il est un Dieu véritablement caché,
> qu'il sera méconnu, qu'on ne pensera point que ce soit
> lui, qu'il sera une pierre d'achoppement, à laquelle
> plusieurs heurteront, etc.

That Jesus is the promised Messiah is therefore beyond
reasonable doubt, but his life was so obscure, so humble
that it was missed by the Jewish historians (300). (In
no. 746 Pascal contradicts this statement, saying that
the historians noticed him all right, but thought it
advisable to keep quiet.) The full paradox is set out
by no. 499, which concludes that the 'éclat' will aid us
who need to know Jesus, but it was not used by Jesus for
his own benefit.

> Quel homme eut jamais plus d'éclat? Le peuple juif tout
> entier le prédit avant sa venue. Le peuple gentil l'adore
> après sa venue. Ces deux peuples gentil et juif le
> regardent comme leur centre.
>
> Et cependant quel homme jouit jamais moins de cet
> éclat? De 33 ans il en vit 30 sans paraître. Dans 3
> ans il passe pour un imposteur. Les prêtres et les
> principaux le rejètent. Ses amis et ses plus proches
> le méprisent, enfin il meurt trahi par un des siens,
> renié par l'autre et abandonné par tous.
>
> Quelle part a-t-il donc à cet éclat? Jamais homme
> n'a eu tant d'éclat, jamais homme n'a eu plus d'igno-
> minie. Tout cet éclat n'a servi qu'à nous pour nous
> le rendre reconnaissable, et il n'en a rien en pour lui.

The paradox of the 'éclat caché' leads Pascal to make,
in one of his most justly famous *pensées*, no. 308, a
rigorous distinction between the three 'orders' of flesh,

mind, and heart (charity, *sagesse*).[11] Jesus came with the 'éclat de son ordre,' which has nothing to do with the splendour of intellectual strength or of dazzling riches and power. Differences between the orders of the flesh and of the mind we can understand, and these can help us to conceive the supernatural order of charity. A sentence added at the head of the manuscript brings in the theme of 'figures,' and also the mathematical analogy with infinity familiar from the first part of no. 418:

La distance infinie des corps aux esprits figure la distance infiniment plus infinie des esprits à la charité car elle est surnaturelle.

A different treatment of the same distinction comes in fragment 933 on the 'three concupiscences.' The concept has an unexpected development in no. 298, which applies the distinction between heart and mind to the different styles required by gospel narrative and rational presentation, a fragment which naturally has been seen as a vital clue to Pascal's own approach in the Apologia:

L'ordre. Contre l'objection que l'Ecriture n'a pas d'ordre.
Le coeur a son ordre, l'esprit a le sien qui est par principe et démonstration. Le coeur en a un autre. On ne prouve pas qu'on doit être aimé en exposant d'ordre les causes de l'amour; cela serait ridicule.
J-C., Saint Paul ont l'ordre de la charité, non de l'esprit; car ils voulaient rabaisser, non instruire.
Saint Augustin de même. Cet ordre consiste principalement à la digression sur chaque point qui a rapport à la fin, pour la montrer toujours.[12]

25
Prophéties

Pascal's definition of the order of what might be termed
'charitable discourse' - 'Cet ordre consiste principalement à la digression sur chaque point qui a rapport à la
fin, pour la montrer toujours' (298) - is illustrated
perfectly in the shape of this third block which has proceeded, at least since section 19°, in this very way. The
title of section 25° (XXIV in Lafuma's numbering) shows
us that Pascal has not yet exhausted the theme of the
prophecies. It is here that Pascal properly completes
the argument begun in section 20°, itself picking up a
remark from 13° (fragment 180). We were told there that
the objective claims of Christianity rested above all on
the prophecies. The intervening chapters have attempted
to educate us, and show how the Bible should be read.
Woven throughout the Old Testament, not always visible,
but quite apparent if we take up the correct vantage-
point, is the faith in a redeemer, together with prophecies of the coming of the Messiah. When Jesus came, he
established his claim by miracles and by his person, but
the proof was cemented by his thereby fulfilling the prophecies. Consequently, the last word must be with the
prophecies as the final authority for the Christian's
faith in Jesus.
  Four related points act as focus for the twenty-six
fragments filed in this dossier:
(a) the strongest argument for Jesus is in the prophecies,
which, many and diverse, all converge on his ministry
(b) the predictions concerning the time of his coming
create four independent conditions
(c) the prophets foretold, with the coming of the Messiah,
that the Jews would be rejected and Gentiles converted
(d) all these prophecies were in fact fulfilled by Jesus,
or by the apostles acting on Jesus's authority.

Nine unclassed fragments can be fitted into this scheme with little difficulty: 385 (I); 447 (V); 455 (IX); 456 (X); 462 (XI); 490, 493 (XVIII); 544 (XXIII); 819 (XXIX). In addition, Pascal draws upon nos 483 (XII), 485 (XIV), 486 (XV), 489 (XVII) with 459 (XI), 498 (XVIII), 550 (XXIII), 609 and 624 (XXIV), 763 (XXVI) and 840 (XXXIII).[1]

(a) *la plus grande des preuves (335)*

The person of Jesus and the miracles he wrought would be enough, indeed were enough, to establish his claim. That was the burden of section 24°. But as Pascal has said before, acceptance on these grounds was necessary for the prophecies to be fulfilled; once fulfilled, the prophecies themselves constitute the major argument. One of the notes on miracles (no. 840) contains an interesting paragraph on the relation of prophecy and miracle:

> Les preuves que J-C. et les apôtres tirent de l'Ecriture ne sont pas démonstratives, car ils disent seulement que Moïse a dit qu'un prophète viendrait, mais ils ne prouvent pas par là que ce soit celui-là, et c'était toute la question. Ces passages ne servent donc qu'à montrer qu'on n'est pas contraire à l'Ecriture et qu'il n'y paraît point de répugnance, mais non pas qu'il y ait accord. Or cela suffit: exclusion de répugnance avant miracles.[2]

A note on the New Testament (550) mentions one isolated example of a prophecy fulfilled:

> Le mot de Galilée que la foule des Juifs prononça comme par hasard en accusant J-C. devant Pilate donne sujet à Pilate d'envoyer J-C. à Hérode, en quoi fut accompli le mystère qu'il devait être jugé par les juifs et les gentils. Le hasard en apparence fut la cause de l'accomplissement du mystère.[3]

But when the examples are multiplied, chance is ruled out as an explanation:

> Et ce qui couronne tout cela est la prédiction afin qu'on ne dit point que c'est le hasard qui l'a fait (326).[4]

No. 385 gives in its second sentence (added later) another
version of the same idea:

Et afin qu'on ne prenne point tout cela[5] pour un effet
du hasard il fallait que cela fût prédit.

The original sentence to which that one was added states
that the prophecies needed to be widely known, and preserved as a witness for later generations.

Mais ce n'était pas assez que ces prophéties fussent,
il fallait qu'elles fussent distribuées par tous les
lieux et conservées dans tous les temps.[6]

This idea is expanded by no. 335, allocated to the present section:

La plus grande des preuves de J-C. sont les prophéties.
C'est aussi à quoi Dieu a le plus pourvu, car l'événement qui les a remplies est un miracle subsistant depuis
la naissance de l'Eglise jusques à la fin. Aussi Dieu
a suscité des prophètes durant 1600 ans et pendant 400
ans après il a dispersé toutes ces prophéties avec tous
les juifs qui les portaient dans tous les lieux du
monde. Voilà quelle a été la préparation à la naissance
de J-C. dont l'Evangile devant être cru de tout le
monde, il a fallu non seulement qu'il y ait eu des
prophéties pour le faire croire mais que ces prophéties
fussent par tout le monde pour le faire embrasser par
tout le monde.

It is therefore on the prophecies which the claims of
Christianity must ultimately rest, and the sign of God's
hand in the preparation of Christ's coming through the
prophets is clear. (In fragment 763, however, Pascal
paradoxically asserts that the evangelists quote prophecies not to convince us, but to put us off.) In fragment
344, Pascal speaks of a prophet who clearly predicts
certain things, and they come to pass; who says that he
wants to illuminate but also leave areas of darkness,
and his prophecies do have obscurities. One could not
withold one's veneration for such a man. Pascal is obviously thinking here not of any one individual prophet,
but of the whole prophetic tradition. And that is even

more extraordinary: the predictions, concerning both the
time and manner of the Messiah's coming, were made not
by one man alone, but by a succession of men whose witness has been preserved, in spite of all the obstacles,
for 4000 years (332).

This section, then, explores the prophetic fact. It is
relevant to quote the last part of no. 456 (the first
part of which was linked to the theme of perpetuity [22°]:
'toutes les autres sectes cessent, celle-là dure toujours
et depuis 4000 ans'):

> Que durant 1600 ans ils ont eu des prophètes[7] qui ont
> prédit le temps et la manière.
> Que 400 ans après ils ont été épars partout, parce
> que J-C. devait être annoncé partout.
> Que J-C est venu en la manière et au temps prédit.
> Que depuis les juifs sont épars partout en malédic-
> tion, et subsistants néanmoins.

(b) Le temps prédit (333)

Enough has been said already about the manner in which
the Messiah came, notably in the previous section with
the *pensées* on the 'éclat' of Jesus. There have also
been several allusions in previous sections to the fact
that the time was clearly predicted. For the most part,
however, the allusions in question were rather vague
(although no. 317 mentioned 'le duc ôté de la cuisse, et
la quatrième monarchie'), and the matter is examined more
thoroughly in this section.

Fragments filed here stress that the predictions of
the date were not single lucky guesses, but a web of
converging statements:

> Le temps prédit par l'état du peuple juif, par l'état
> du peuple païen, par l'état du temple, par le nombre
> des années (333).

It would not be enough for merely one of these four kinds
of prophecy to be fulfilled:

> Les prophètes ayant donné diverses marques qui devaient
> toutes arriver à l'avènement du Messie il fallait que
> toutes ces marques arrivassent en même temps. Ainsi il
> fallait que la quatrième monarchie fût venue lorsque

les septante semaines de Daniel seraient accomplies et
que le sceptre fût alors ôté de Juda (339).

Il faut être hardi pour prédire une même chose en tant
de manières. Il fallait que les 4 monarchies, idolâtres
ou païennes, la fin du règne de Juda, et les 70 semaines
arrivassent en même temps, et le tout avant que le 2e
temple fut détruit (336).

The conjunction of events fulfilling these diverse conditions predispose one in the prophets' favour, make one
ready to believe that with all the circumstances realized,
the Messiah very likely did indeed come (329). And that
is what happened; no. 339 continues thus:

> Et tout cela est arrivé sans aucune difficulté et qu'-
> alors il arrivât le Messie et J-C. est arrivé alors
> qui s'est dit le Messie et tout cela est encore sans
> difficulté et cela marque bien la vérité de prophétie.

Fragment 341 allows that there is a certain ambiguity
in the application of the 'seventy weeks' of Daniel, but
Pascal thinks it makes little difference, a 200-year margin at the most. A detailed commentary on Daniel's prophecy is given in fragment 485. Fragment 342 silences
further quibbling about the years of captivity in Babylon,
but it only repeats what we knew from the previous section
(no. 314).

(c) réprobation des Juifs et conversion des Gentils (489)

Several fragments in this chapter note things prophesied
in the Old Testament. The emphasis now is on the fate of
the Jewish nation and the Gentiles, who will inherit the
kingdom from which the Jews will be banished. Once again,
Pascal is using the word Jews in the sense of the carnal
Jews, faithful to a literal and uncomprehending reading
of their scriptures:

> Au temps du Messie ce peuple se partage. Les spirituels
> ont embrassé le Messie, les grossiers sont demeurés
> pour lui servir de témoins (331).

The Jews will be rejected, and they will be struck with
blindness (Deut. 28:28-9, fragment 347). The same fragment

mentions Malachi's prophecy (3:1) of the messenger who
shall prepare the way. Some relevant references are noted
in no. 334, and the unclassed fragments contain ample
documentation on the subject (notably nos 483 and 486).
The list of things prophesied of the Messiah in fragment
609 (Prophéties') concludes:

> que son peuple qui l'aurait renié ne serait plus son
> peuple, que les idolâtres le recevraient et auraient
> recours à lui, qu'il quitterait Sion pour régner au
> centre de l'idolâtrie, que néanmoins les Juifs subsis-
> teront toujours, qu'il devait être de Juda et qu'il
> n'y aurait plus de roi.[8]

Coupled with the rejection of the Jews is the conversion of the Gentiles, predicted by Isaiah (chap. 19) who
spoke of the altar in Egypt (330). Fragment 323, entitled
'Ruine des Juifs et des païens par J-C.,' collects a number of quotations on the salvation of the nations. One,
'parum est ut' (Is. 49:6, 'I will also give thee for a
light to the Gentiles, that thou mayest be my salvation
unto the end of the earth') is repeated in no. 345, with
the additional note, 'Vocation des Gentils par J-C.,'
and a reference to Isaiah 52:15: 'So shall he sprinkle
many nations; kings shall shut their mouths at him, for
that which had not been told them shall they see, and
that which they see, and that which they had not heard
shall they understand.' No. 447 notes that the grace of
Christ accomplished what the Jews had never been able to
do: the conversion of pagans. More documentation can be
found in no. 489, pages 6-9 of the original manuscript
(I have borrowed the title for the title of this part
of the present chapter), completed by no. 459; and in
other fragments. No. 493, originally entitled 'Prophéties,'
but subsequently given the precise title 'Prophéties
accomplies,' groups examples of prophecies fulfilled
within Old Testament times, but it also quotes Deuteronomy
32:21, 'I will move them to jealousy with those which are
not a people,' and Pascal notes: 'Moïse prédit la vocation des gentils.' This combination of short-term prophecies, the fulfilment of which strengthens the credibility
of the prophets, with the long-range prophecies of the
upset caused by the coming of the Messiah, is explained
in no. 819:

Les prophéties mêlées des choses particulières et de
celles du Messie afin que les prophéties du Messie ne
fussent pas sans preuve et que les prophéties particulières ne fussent pas sans fruit.

Ezekiel and Malachi spoke of the end of idolatry and
the installation of true worship (foretold in Psalm 50);
Psalm 72 says that kings will do hommage to him (324).
Fragment 328 speaks of the prophecies of Jeremiah (33:33-4)
and Joel (2:28); in that time, the prophets will not be
necessary, as all men will understand the things of God.
The same prophecy, along with others, is summarized with
the words 'Vocation des gentils' in no. 498.

(d) et cela est arrivé alors (327)

Then Jesus came, and announced the imminent realization
of these things (327). And Pascal adds: 'et cela est
arrivé alors.' Jesus is both the fulfilment of the prophecies and the last of the prophets (462).
    An illustration of the blindness of the Jews (and their
deafness; Pascal quotes Is. 6:0, 'Hear ye and understand
not')[9] is afforded by the fact that Herod was believed
the Messiah by some, and there were other unlikely candidates, as historians testify (337).
    When the Jews rejected Jesus, they said their only king
was Caesar, an admission that the 'eternal line of David'
was extinct (340, 490, 348, and the deleted no. 455),
thus opening the way for the spiritual reign of Jesus.
    No. 324 does not simply state the prophecy 'Qu'il
serait roi des juifs et des gentils'; it continues:

et voilà ce roi des juifs et des gentils opprimé par les
uns et les autres qui conspirent à sa mort dominant des
uns et des autres, et détruisant et le culte de Moïse
dans Jerusalem, qui en était le centre, dont il fait sa
première église et le culte des idoles dans Rome qui en
était le centre et dont il fait sa principale église.

Likewise no. 325, which begins by recalling another prophecy of Isaiah (2:3), that 'He will teach us of his ways':

Et jamais il n'est venu ni devant ni après aucun homme
qui ait enseigné rien de divin approchant de cela.

We know that Joel's prophecy has been fulfilled from no. 301. The line 'je mettrai mon esprit et ma crainte en votre coeur' (328, quoting Jeremiah) is repeated in no. 346, which adds: 'Qui ne voit la loi chrétienne en tout cela?'

The predictions about the conversion of the world are summarized in the first paragraph of no. 338:

> Qu'en la 4e monarchie, avant la destruction du 2e temple, avant que la domination des Juifs fût ôtée, en la 70e semaine de Daniel, pendant la durée du 2e temple, les païens seraient instruits et amenés à la connaissance du Dieu adoré par les Juifs, que ceux qui l'aiment seraient délivrés de leurs ennemis, remplis de sa crainte et de son amour.

And that, says Pascal, is just what happened. People voluntarily renounced self-love, idolatry is destroyed, and kings worship the Messiah. 'C'est l'esprit de Dieu qui est répandu sur la terre.' Pagan testimony supports this evidence, Plutarch reporting the belief that the great Pan is dead (343). The gospels speak of all men being baptised by John, the precursor (544).

Objections to the claims of Jesus are met elsewhere. One is, however, noted in a fragment entitled 'Prophéties' (624): a prophecy from the Psalms implies that Christ would not subdue his enemies during his lifetime.

26
Figures particulières

Comprising only two short sentences, the twenty-sixth
dossier (Lafuma XXV) is necessarily enigmatic in appearance. The title, 'Figures particulières,' recalls the
title of section 20°, 'Que la loi était figurative,' and
some readers have hastily assumed that it is an offshoot
of that section, manifestly out of place in its present
position. It is, however, a necessary complement to section 25°.[1] In section 25° the emphasis had been on the
state of the world. Jesus came at a point in the world's
history which had been clearly foretold by the prophets,
and he transformed the world, again in a way which had
been predicted. But there are other ways in which Jesus
fulfilled the prophecies. We must not forget that the
Old Testament is a figurative text, and one more indication that Jesus was the Messiah is that in him many of
the implications are realized and revealed.

   The two fragments which found their way into this dossier suggest that Pascal would have tackled the question
in at least two distinct ways. The first, itself entitled
'Figures particulières,' reads:

   Double loi, doubles tables de la loi, double temple,
   double captivité (349).

The meaning must be that certain key motifs in the Old
Testament have two applications, the literal one described
in the Old Testament, and the symbolic one revealed by
the New, where, for example, Jesus speaks of the 'temple
of the body' and of deliverance from the bondage of sin.
   The other fragment (no. 350) is specific:

   Joseph croise ses bras et préfère le jeune.

'Joseph' here is a slip; it was of course Jacob who, when
Joseph presented his sons Manasseh and Ephraim, crossed

his arms over so that his right hand blessed the younger one, Ephraim (Gen. 48). As Ernst says, this could be seen as prefiguring both the cross of Christ, and (more plausibly, in my view), the Gentiles taking the place which one would have expected to fall to the Jews.[2]

The story of Joseph is told more fully in no. 484 (XIII), entitled 'Prédiction des choses particulières.' Joseph himself as a figure of Jesus is the subject of no. 570 (XXIII). I have nothing else with which to amplify this disappointingly slender section, although my reading of earlier chapters can suggest ways in which it might have been expanded. Nor is there any obvious conclusion to be slotted in. This is none the less the end of the long and intricate group which has argued that for the man prepared to read the Scriptures with understanding, there is clear evidence that Jesus was the Messiah and that where other religions are false, Christianity is indubitably true.

Morale chrétienne

Earlier parts of the Aplogia had accustomed us to the
twin headings of 'le vrai' and 'le bien.' Once the way
was clear for an exposition of the objective claims of
Christianity, Pascal devoted many sections to exploring
these claims and this part of the Apologia could be called
the last stage in the discussion of 'le vrai,' corresponding to the 'et puis montrer qu'elle est vraie' of
no. 12. The penultimate dossier of the Apologia (XXVI
in Lafuma's numbering, but 27° in ours) shows that Pascal
has not forgotten about the important issue of 'le bien.'
The time is now ripe to crown the argument by showing
that all the problems involved by man's search for fulfilment are solved by Christianity. We have been told,
notably in nos 148 and 149, that the happiness man desires
can only be found in God, and that since men have turned
their back on God - without losing the longing for para-
dise, on which Pascal built part of his argument - they
have found innumerable substitutes, all inadequate. A
true religion must restore man's contact with God. Pascal
does not need to go over again the separate questions
raised by no. 149: the existence of God, the obligation
to love him, God as the unique source of felicity, the
reasons why we turn from him, the remedies and the way
to obtain them, the dangers of one-sided philosophies,
leading to despair or to presumption. What Pascal does
in this twenty-seventh section is to paint the Christian
life in such a way that we recall the moral deficiencies
of the alternatives and appreciate the manner in which
Christianity has harmonized the warring elements.
    The argument can be divided into four parts:
(a) by serving God and not self, the Christian finds perfect happiness and virtue.
(b) the City of God can be understood through the Pauline
analogy of the parts of the body, functioning properly
and sustained only when they serve the body as a whole.

(c) a society which is guided by grace will not fall into the trap of formalistic obedience of an elaborate law, but it will not despise law, as human nature will always require regular discipline.

(d) Christianity neither flatters nor abases human nature, and so avoids the dangers inherent in the various philosophies.

We are citing sixteen unclassed fragments: 426 (II); 460 (XI); 536, 545, 562 (XXIII); 618 (XXIV); 693, 713 (XXV); 800 (XXIX); 824 (XXX); 897, 912 (XXXIV); 918, 936, 944, 948.[1]

(a) nul n'est heureux comme un vrai chrétien (357)

The claim Pascal makes in this section is stated without frills in no. 357:

> Nul n'est heureux comme un vrai chrétien, ni raisonnable, ni vertueux, ni aimable.

That the Christian is alone 'reasonable' has been argued in the previous sections; this one concentrates on the assertion that he is also incomparably 'heureux, vertueux, aimable.' Happiness means to most people self-gratification, but a selfish person is not 'vertueux' and 'aimable.' It is the great strength of *honnêteté* that it has elaborated a code in which pride of place is given to the art of pleasing others, but without the religious dimension curbing self-love, an *honnête homme* can never be completely happy in his role:

> Il n'y a que la religion chrétienne qui rende l'homme aimable et heureux tout ensemble; dans l'honnêteté on ne peut être aimable et heureux ensemble (426).

In the 'Infini rien' fragment (and no. 426 comes from that manuscript), Pascal had advised the unbeliever who was attracted to suspend disbelief and begin by going through the motions: 'Quel mal vous arrivera-t-il en prenant ce parti? Vous serez fidèle, honnête, humble, reconnaissant, bienfaisant, aimable, sincère, véritable' (418). At the stage in the argument we have now reached, there should be no more resistance on the grounds that 'je suis fait d'une telle sorte que je ne puis croire' (ibid.). Pascal is no longer merely inviting the non-

Christian to try it, he is confidently asserting the
superiority of Christianity over all other prescriptions
for living.

The Christian is not only 'vertueux' and 'aimable' in
the eyes of the world; he is also 'heureux.' This is because he has renounced self-will, and no longer makes the
fundamental mistake of expecting to be his own supplier
of satisfaction (362). A slave who is liked and flattered
by his master (361), a soldier who obeys his superiors
but lives in daily hope of liberty (356) are deceiving
themselves; only the Christian who has accepted that he
is always subject to the will of God can know happiness.
(In no. 693, Pascal reminds us that the religious life
is conducted according to a totally different set of
values from what obtains in ordinary society.)

The Christian is happy because he seeks the Sovereign
Good in the one place where the true good exists. And it
is a property of the Christian God that he should invite
and enable man to undertake this quest.

> Le Dieu des chrétiens est un Dieu qui fait sentir à
> l'âme qu'il est son unique bien; que tout son repos
> est en lui, qu'elle n'aura de joie qu'à l'aimer; et qui
> lui fait en même temps abhorrer les obstacles qui la
> retiennent et l'empêchent d'aimer Dieu de toutes ses
> forces. L'amour-propre et la concupiscence, qui l'ar-
> rêtent, lui sont insupportables. Ce Dieu lui fait
> sentir qu'elle a ce fonds d'amour-propre qui la perd,
> et que lui seul la peut guérir (460).

It follows that 'il faut n'aimer que Dieu et ne haïr que
soi' (first sentence of no. 373). The self one is to
hate is the self which is a prey to concupiscence. Put
in a more positive way, this moral command becomes the
double law of Christ, referred to in no. 376, to love
God and to love one's neighbour. Loving God is the first
law of the Christian (and of the Jewish) republic (369).
We should love God, and not be attached to fellow creatures (618); at the same time we should approach our
fellow beings in a spirit of love and charity. Christian
devotion (which must include charity) is thus of a higher
order than the 'goodness' of secular society (365).
Charity does not stop with one's own kin and friends, it
extends to our enemies as well (355). And so it produces
'des fruits contre la concupiscence' (last phrase of no. 536).

(b) membre de Jesus-Christ (372)

Pascal had earlier portrayed society as at best a precarious balance of concupiscences. In this section he
gives the contrasting model for the Christian community,
derived from Saint Paul's analogy with parts of the body.
This model will help us to understand what is legitimate
in self-love:

> Membres.
> Commencer par là.
>   Pour régler l'amour qu'on se doit à soi-même il faut
> s'imaginer un corps plein de membres pensants... (368,
> absorbing 371).

A full explantion comes in fragment 360 (the only fragment actually to bear the title 'Morale,' and that only
as an afterthought). The parts of the body work together
for the good of the whole, but they do not have any awareness. Man, who has the awareness and hence the possibility
of rejoicing in the harmonious scheme of which he forms
a vital part, does not have the 'good will' to agree to
serve the interests of the whole. He is like a part of
the body trying to take all the food for itself, a self-
defeating action,

> leur béatitude aussi bien que leur devoir consistant
> à consentir à la conduite de l'âme entière à qui ils
> appartiennent, qui les aime mieux qu'ils ne s'aiment
> eux-mêmes.

To be happy one needs first to have a will, and secondly
to use it properly, that is, to the general good (370,
374). Failure to do this leads to an individualism which
is totally inappropriate, and so 'le membre séparé' becomes a good analogue for the self-loving individual
(372). In fragment 373, beneath the line he had drawn
under the sentence already quoted, Pascal evokes a foot
which discovered only very late that it depended on a
body who would have abandoned it if the foot had really
separated from it.
  What the body is, and just how all this affects the
'amour qu'on se doit à soi-même,' is shown by an addition
to no. 372. Pascal quotes Saint Paul (1 Cor. 6:17), 'He
that is joined unto the Lord is one spirit.' The body
of which we are members is Jesus.

On s'aime parce qu'on est membre de J-C.; on aime J-C.
parce qu'il est le corps dont on est membre.

And so the Christian God consecrates human virtues - unlike the pagan gods to whom were attributed human vices
(375).

The concept of the body illuminates Pascal's examples
of sympathy; he says that the death of the Christian
martyrs affects us in a way the deaths of the Stoics of
antiquity do not (359). And when sacrifices are made,
feelings are not denied. Corneille's Horace said 'Albe
vous a nommé, je ne vous connais point'; Saint Paul at
Caeserea, besought by his friends to avoid Jerusalem
where his duty called him, acknowledged that his heart
was breaking (897, Acts 21:13).[2]

(c) point formalistes (367)

In place of self-will as a guide for us to follow, the
Christian substitutes the will of God. Fragment 948,
which Lafuma believed to be a draft for a letter to Mlle
Roannez, gives the answer to the bewildered question formulated in section 2° (no. 21 and related fragments):

> Changeons la règle que nous avions prise jusqu'ici
> pour juger de ce qui est bon. Nous en avions pour règle
> notre volonté; prenons maintenant la volonté de Dieu;
> tout ce qu'il veut nous est bon et juste, tout ce qu'il
> ne veut pas [mauvais et injuste].[3]

The grace of God is greatly superior not merely to our
own wills, but to the law, even if the law is divinely
ordained. It is enabling where the law is merely pres-
criptive (824). The Jews attached the greatest importance
to the law, but Christians have interpreted the law as
a manifestation of the Holy Spirit under which the guidance of the same spirit we can transgress (367). There
is a parallel in the *pensée* on the conception of children
outside wedlock (713).

The issue of formal obedience takes a new form in the
life of the Christian Church. Pascal reminds us in fragment 366 that there are two kinds of person in every
religion, giving a cross-reference to 'Perpétuité' to
explain what he means. The fragment in question is evidently no. 286 where we read: 'les chrétiens grossiers
croient que le Messie les a dispensées d'aimer Dieu ...

les vrais chrétiens adorent un Messie qui leur fait aimer
Dieu.' It is of course 'le *vrai* chrétien' who knows true
happiness (357). But the distinction noted in no. 366 is
not between formalist and genuine, it is between 'superstition' and 'concupiscence.' No. 363 also opposes superstition and concupiscence, but without illuminating further the concept of 'le vrai chrétien.' Pascal speaks of
those who leave concupiscence untrammeled while retaining
scruples - he must have Jesuits in mind - and we can
surely associate the scrupulous with the superstitious
or with the 'carnal' whose spiritual understanding is
severely limited. No. 364 contrasts the superstitious
formalist and those who, rejecting formalism altogether,
are guilty of pride.

> C'est être superstitieux de mettre son espérance dans
> les formalités, mais c'est être superbe de ne vouloir
> s'y soumettre.

The idea is beautifully expressed in no. 944, which picks
up an incomplete sentence from no. 936:

> Il faut que l'extérieur soit joint à l'intérieur pour
> obtenir de Dieu; c'est à dire que l'on se mette à
> genoux, prie des lèvres, etc. afin que l'homme orgueil-
> leux qui n'a voulu se soumettre à Dieu soit maintenant
> soumis à la créature. Attendre de cet extérieur le se-
> cours est être superstitieux; ne vouloir pas le joindre
> à l'intérieur est être superbe.

This same notion is echoed in 912 ('on s'accoutume ainsi
aux vertus intérieures par ces habitudes extérieures'),
which leads into it by saying that the idea that 'J-C.
n'est pas mort pour tous' favours despair instead of
winning people away from despair by offering hope.[4]
   For another way of dividing mankind into two, we can
turn to no. 562: 'Il n'y a que deux sortes d'hommes, les
uns justes qui se croient pécheurs, les autres pécheurs
qui se croient justes.'

(d) point de doctrine plus propre à l'homme (354)

The vocabulary of those last examples, defining the danger
of excessive pride, will necessarily remind us of a refrain
from earlier sections in the Apologia. The philosophers,

we were told, ministered to either pride or despair, and
already in section 14° Pascal informed us that Christianity escaped from that particular dilemma:

La connaissance de Dieu sans celle de sa misère fait
l'orgueil.
La connaissance de sa misère sans celle de Dieu fait
le désespoir.
La connaissance de J-C. fait le milieu parce que nous
y trouvons et Dieu et notre misère (192).

In no. 449, which we attached to section 15°, the idea
was fully developed. It is dangerous to know only one of
the two fundamental Christian doctrines, as we are then
led either to 'la superbe des philosophes' or to 'le
désespoir des athées,' and 'la superbe' must be brought
low (cf. 234/19°). A fragment in section 17° pointed to
the same reconciliation in a person's spiritual life:

J-C. est un Dieu dont on s'approche sans orgueil et
sous lequel on s'abaisse sans désespoir (212).

It is very fitting that we should be reminded in this
penultimate section, on 'la morale chrétienne,' that
Christianity avoids both excesses, not by ignoring them,
but by absorbing them both and neutralizing them.

Le christianisme est étrange; il ordonne à l'homme de
reconnaître qu'il est vil et même abominable, et lui
ordonne de vouloir être semblable à Dieu. Sans un tel
contrepoids cette élévation le rendrait horriblement
vain, ou cet abaissement le rendrait horriblement ab-
ject (351).

Avec combien peu d'orgueil un chrétien se croit-il uni
à Dieu. Avec combien peu d'abjection s'égale-t-il aux
vers de la terre... (358).

Nos pas un abaissement qui nous rende incapables du
bien ni une sainteté exempte de mal (353).

Il n'y a point de doctrine plus propre à l'homme que
celle-là qui l'instruit de sa double capacité de rece-
voir et de perdre la grâce à cause du double péril où
il est toujours exposé de désespoir ou d'orgueil (354).

> La misère persuade le désespoir.
> L'orgueil persuade la présomption.
> L'Incarnation montre à l'homme la grandeur de sa
> misère par la grandeur du remède qu'il a fallu (352).

In an unclassed fragment (800), Pascal finds a parallel
in nature for this permanent corrective afforded by Scripture.

> L'Ecriture a pourvu de passages pour consoler toutes
> les conditions et pour intimider toutes les conditions.
> La nature semble avoir fait la même chose par ces
> deux infinis naturels et moraux. Car nous aurons tou-
> jours du dessus et du dessous, de plus habiles et de
> moins habiles, de plus élévés et de plus misérables,
> pour abaisser notre orgueil et relever notre abjection.

One of the most poetic fragments of all, no. 545 (expanding on no. 918),[5] talks of those who ride unharmed
on the waters of concupiscence, weeping not for the
pleasures they have renounced, but for the heavenly home
from which they are at the moment excluded. It is probably too personal and too intense for inclusion in the
Apologia, but the ideas it enshrines make a wonderfully
appropriate conclusion for this section on the Christian
life.

28
Conclusion

Pascal has never forgotten, even during the intricate elaborations of the historical proofs, that his argument is addressed to a man who began by being indifferent to religion. Assuming enough good will to enable him to move on to new stages in the argument, Pascal has taken us beyond indifference and open resistance through sympathetic interest. With the twenty-seventh chapter, 'Morale chrétienne,' the demonstration is as complete as Pascal needs to make it. The case for the objective claims of Christianity has been expounded at length - in Christianity we find 'le vrai' - and in the last chapter, Pascal assured us that Christianity also brings the satisfaction for which we crave as moral beings ('le bien').

Does Pascal now dare to assume that he has taken the interlocutor with him on the final stage, and that the *honnête homme indifférent* of the opening has become a convert? Pascal makes no such claim, for two reasons. The first is that there is no need to assume total success in the missionary enterprise. Partial success was necessary to keep the discussion moving, but to announce now that the argument had actually produced a convert to Christianity would appear as a facile and complacent solution, and diminish the effect of the Apologia on the reader himself. The second reason is that Pascal does not want to give the impression that Christians are created by arguments, however sound. All we can do is to help others and ourselves to remove obstacles of our own creating, but if Christianity is right in its insistence on man's corruption and God's initiative in restoring the broken relationship, then the last step can only be taken with God's grace; the apologist retires before the last round, like a trainer who has to leave his charge to run the race itself on his own.

The concluding section will therefore make the apologist's position quite clear. It is convenient to divide it into three.
(a) although Christianity can appeal to reason, and show unbelief to be unreasonable, conversion operates at a deeper level than that of natural reason.
(b) some believers remain ignorant of the arguments for the objective truth of Christianity's claims, but their faith is not for that reason suspect.
(c) reasoned arguments of the kind expounded in this Apologia can break down prejudice, and we can then discipline our natural concupiscence and develop habits which will encourage growth in the Christian life. But for the crowning gift of faith we are dependent on the grace of God.

A number of unclassed fragments are indispensable to the argument of this conclusion: nos 458, 482 (XI); 574, 588 (XXIII); 695, 703 (XXV); 808 (XXIX); 821 (XXX); 835, 842, 846 (XXXIII); 869, 874 (XXXIV); 975.[1]

(a) assez d'évidence pour condamner, et non assez pour convaincre (835)

The interlocutor has now heard the full argument. What if he is still unconvinced? Pascal is prepared for this possibility. The role of argument is negative; it shows that there is nothing unreasonable about being a Christian, and nothing especially reasonable about being an unbeliever. The point had been made at the outset (no. 12): the obstacles in the way of faith are suspicion and fear, not pure intellectual conviction. The enemy of faith is not reason, but concupiscence; and conversely, the source of faith is not reason, but grace. After listing twelve 'proofs' in fragment 482 (a list somewhat modified in the plan as we know it), Pascal added:

> Il est indubitable qu'après cela on ne doit pas refuser, en considérant ce que c'est que la vie et que cette religion, de suivre l'inclination de la suivre, si elle nous vient dans le coeur; et il est certain qu'il n'y a nul lieu de se moquer de ceux qui la suivent.

The fullest statement of Pascal's thinking on this vital topic is found in another unclassed fragment, no. 835, summarized in chapter 19 (b), where it was linked with

no. 236. The proofs which Christianity can produce are
not strictly speaking convincing, but they put the onus
of proof on the non-believer. Like so much evidence of
the divinity, it is both manifest and obscure, according
to the attitude we have. And this attitude depends not
on objective reason, but on the degree to which our wills
are turned towards God.

> Les prophéties, les miracles mêmes et les preuves de
> notre religion ne sont pas de telle nature qu'on puisse
> dire qu'ils sont absolument convaincants, mais ils le
> sont aussi de telle sorte qu'on ne peut dire que ce
> soit être sans raison que de les croire. Ainsi il y a
> de l'évidence et de l'obscurité pour éclairer les uns
> et obscurcir les autres, mais l'évidence est telle
> qu'elle surpasse ou égale pour le moins l'évidence du
> contraire, de sorte que ce n'est pas la raison qui
> puisse déterminer à ne la pas suivre, et ainsi ce ne
> peut être que la concupiscence et la malice du coeur.
> Et par ce moyen il y a assez d'évidence pour condamner,
> et non assez pour convaincre, afin qu'il paraisse qu'en
> ceux qui la suivent c'est la grâce et non la raison qui
> fait suivre, et qu'en ceux qui la fuient c'est la con-
> cupiscence et non la raison qui fait fuir.

The whole of the conclusion is essentially an elaboration
of that fragment.

Two of the classified fragments (378 and 379) refer
specifically to miracles, which 'ne servent pas à convertir mais à condamner' (379, referring to Saint Thomas).[2]
Lafuma and Tourneur cite no. 846[3] in this connection:
the Jews would not be guilty if they had not seen the
miracles. The miracles, then, condemn unbelief; in what
sense do they fail to convert? Two fragments illustrate
their ineffectiveness, nos 574 and 378. Both ridicule
the statement: 'If I could but see a miracle, then I
would be converted.' Not at all, says Pascal in no. 574:
reason will always find a way out if it wishes to. And
in no. 378 he says that such statements show a complete
misunderstanding of the meaning of conversion, which involves genuine self-abnegation and total trust in the
mediator without whom man can never reach God.

Reason, then, has the negative role of condemning unbelief; it also has a limited positive role, in preparing
the way for God's grace. The teaching of the Church works
in this way:

L'Eglise enseigne et Dieu inspire l'un et l'autre
infailliblement. L'opération de l'Eglise ne sert qu'à
préparer à la grace, ou à la condamnation. Ce qu'elle
fait suffit pour condamner, non pour inspirer (874).

Elsewhere:

La foi est un don de Dieu. Ne croyez pas que nous
disions que c'est un don de raisonnement (588).

The point was made very clearly in a fragment Pascal assigned to his introduction, no. 7:

Lettre qui marque l'utilité des preuves.
   La foi est différente de la preuve. L'une est humaine
et l'autre est un don de Dieu. *Justus ex fide vivit.*
C'est de cette foi que Dieu lui-même met dans le coeur,
qui fait dire non *scio* mais *credo.*[4]

Christianity has reason on its side, but if it were
merely a matter of marshalling arguments, the central
fact of Christianity - the crucifixion - would be of 'no
effect' as Saint Paul put it. The fragment which makes
this point refers, again, to the antithesis condemn/con-
vert:

Notre religion est sage et folle, sage parce que c'est
la plus savante et la plus fondée en miracles, prophéties, etc., folle parce que ce n'est point tout cela
qui fait qu'on en est. Cela fait bien condamner ceux
qui n'en sont pas, mais non pas croire ceux qui en
sont. Ce qui les fait croire est la croix, *ne evacuata
sit crux.*
   Et ainsi St Paul qui est venu en sagesse et signes
dit qu'il n'est venu ni en sagesse ni en signes, car
il venait pour convertir, mais ceux qui ne viennent
que pour convaincre peuvent dire qu'ils viennent en
sagesse et en signes (842).

A reminder of this fragment (458: 'Sagesse infinie et
folie de la religion') has the title 'Contrariétés,' and
we recall that wisdom and folly were contradictory and
complementary aspects of human nature (412, quoted in
chapter 2). On the folly of Christianity, we can compare
418 ('*stultitiam*'), 291 ('la folie de la croix') and 695
('Le péché originel est folie devant les hommes').

(b) inspiré de Dieu (382)

Because faith is a God-given thing, not dependent on reason, it should not surprise, or offend, if there are
people who believe without being able to justify themselves intellectually. They have what is needful: a love
for God, and a loathing of themselves.

> Ne vous étonnez pas de voir des personnes simples croire
> sans raisonnement. Dieu leur donne l'amour de soi et la
> haine d'eux-mêmes. Il incline leur coeur à croire. On
> ne croira jamais, d'une créance utile et de foi si Dieu
> n'incline le coeur, et on croira dès qu'il l'inclinera
> (380).

At various stages in the Apologia Pascal has qualified
what he says by reminding us that there are always those
who by-pass the reasoned arguments, and so we should be
prepared to find them again in this final section.

> Ceux à qui Dieu a donné la religion par sentiment de
> coeur sont bienheureux et bien légitimement persuadés,
> mais ceux qui ne l'ont pas nous ne pouvons donner que
> par raisonnement en attendant que Dieu la leur donne
> par sentiment de coeur, sans quoi la foi n'est qu'hu-
> maine et inutile pour le salut (110/6°; cf. no. 7).

> Il y a peu de vrais chrétiens. Je dis même pour la
> foi. Il y en a bien qui croient mais par superstition
> ... Je ne comprends pas en cela ceux qui sont dans la
> véritable piété de moeurs et tous ceux qui croient par
> un sentiment du coeur (179/13°).

> Il y en a qui voient bien qu'il n'y a pas d'autre
> ennemi de l'homme que la concupiscence qui les détourne
> de Dieu ... ni d'autre bien que Dieu ... Qu'ils se
> consolent, je leur annonce une heureuse nouvelle: il
> y a un Libérateur pour eux ... (269/20°).

The last fragment is echoed in no. 381:

> Ceux qui croient sans avoir lu les Testaments c'est
> parce qu'ils ont une disposition intérieure toute sainte
> et que ce qu'ils entendent dire de notre religion y est
> conforme. Ils sentent qu'un Dieu les a faits. Ils ne
> veulent aimer que Dieu, ils ne veulent haïr qu'eux-
> mêmes. Ils sentent qu'ils n'en ont pas la force d'eux-
> mêmes, qu'ils sont incapables d'aller à Dieu et que si

> Dieu ne vient à eux ils sont incapables d'aucune com-
> munication avec lui et ils entendent dire dans notre
> religion qu'il ne faut aimer que Dieu et ne haïr que
> soi-même, mais qu'étant tous corrompus et incapables
> de Dieu, Dieu s'est fait homme pour s'unir à nous. Il
> n'en faut pas davantage pour persuader des hommes qui
> ont cette disposition dans le coeur et qui ont cette
> connaissance de leur devoir et de leur incapacité (381).

And in no. 382 Pascal says that those Christians who have
no knowledge of proofs and prophecies are nevertheless
discerning believers.

> ...C'est Dieu lui-même qui les incline à croire et
> ainsi ils sont très efficacement persuadés...

These are indeed the people of whom the prophet Joel
spoke when he said 'your sons and daughters shall prophesy.'[5] They may not be able themselves to prove that
they are inspired, but there are others who can prove it
for them.

*(c) Qu'il y a loin de la connaissance de Dieu à l'aimer
(377)*

That last fragment (382) is entitled 'Connaissance de
Dieu,' and the brief fragment 377 - 'Qu'il y a loin de
la connaissance de Dieu à l'aimer' - may be interpreted
as an alternative title to the dossier, especially once
it is shorn of the exclamation mark arbitrarily added
by several editors.[6] So far we have assumed a continuing
scepticism on the part of the interlocutor. He is not
convinced by the proofs, at least not to the point of
considering himself a convert, and he is suspicious when
told that some believe without knowing the arguments.
Pascal has answered these objections to the best of his
ability. But what if the interlocutor declares himself
satisfied, and says that he wants to join the faithful?
   First, a warning. There is still a long way to go (377),
and willingness is not the same thing as actually being
converted (975). The mind can accept God, but to turn
the will so that it becomes properly God-centred and not
self-centred (the true meaning of conversion) does not
necessarily follow immediately. If the 'transition de la
connaissance de l'homme à Dieu' (14°) was possible, thanks

to the initiative God took in Jesus, the final transition
from 'la connaissance de Dieu' to the life of a devoted
servant of God is less easy to guide a person through.
Faith, we know, is a gift of God, and we cannot force
God's hand.

What we can do, however, is to do all in our power to
discipline the concupiscence which is the chief obstacle
standing between ourselves and God. We know from the sections on the 'misère de l'homme sans Dieu' that our beliefs
are often conditioned by our habits, of behaviour and of
thought. In the 'Infini rien' fragment (418), Pascal saw
the importance of deliberately taking on new customs to
help make us properly receptive towards Christianity:

> ...Travaillez donc non pas à vous convaincre par l'aug-
> mentation des preuves de Dieu, mais par la diminution
> de vos passions. Vous voulez aller à la foi et vous
> n'en savez pas le chemin ... Apprenez de ceux qui ont
> été lies comme vous ... Suivez la manière par où ils
> ont commencé. C'est en faisant tout comme s'ils croy-
> aient, en prenant de l'eau bénite, en faisant dire des
> messes, etc. Naturellement même cela vous fera croire...

The importance of developing habits which will confirm
decisions taken by reason is stressed in fragment 821.

> Car il ne faut pas se méconnaître, nous sommes automate
> autant qu'esprit ... Quand on ne croit que par la force
> de la conviction et que l'automate est incliné à croire
> le contraire ce n'est pas assez. Il faut donc faire
> croire nos deux pièces, l'esprit par les raisons qu'il
> suffit d'avoir vues une fois en sa vie et l'automate
> par la coutume, et en ne lui permettant pas de s'incliner
> au contraire.

The word *incliner* reminds Pascal of Psalm 119, verse 36,
also quoted in fragment 380, 'Incline my heart unto thy
testimonies.' It is God who makes the believer - as it
is God who makes the saint (869).

Fragment 808 sums the whole matter up very succinctly,
reminding us that belief involves reason, custom, and
God's inspiration - that is, each of the three 'orders'
memorably described in section 24°. Faith is quite distinct from reason, as it is from works - as Saint Paul
recognized (see 703, and 842 already quoted).

Il y a trois moyens de croire: la raison, la coutume, l'inspiration. La religion chrétienne qui seule a raison n'admet point pour ses vrais enfants ceux qui croient sans inspiration. Ce n'est pas qu'elle exclue la raison et la coutume, au contraire; mais il faut ouvrir son esprit aux preuves, s'y confirmer par la coutume, mais s'offrir par les humiliations aux inspirations, qui seules peuvent faire le vrai et salutaire effet, *ne evacuetur crux Christi*.

No more appropriate final word could be imagined. Pascal justifies his own activity, but sets it in its true perspective, as a human preparation which can reduce the obstacles to grace, but which cannot automatically guarantee it. Pascal silences argument, and quietly removes himself, concluding with a quotation from holy Scripture, of which the last pair of words is significantly 'crux Christi,' 'the Cross of Christ.'

29
Conclusion to Part One:
the argument of the Apologia
summarized

The previous chapters have presented the reasons for interpreting the fragments in a particular way. Although
each chapter was prefaced by a summary of the conclusions
reached, there has been no résumé of Pascal's arguments
as such. The present chapter assumes the debate about the
order of the fragments now to be closed, and outlines the
kind of argument Pascal must have envisaged, if my reasoning in the previous chapters is correct. No attempt
is made to lend this account the warmth of Pascal's own
style, but I have avoided as far as possible intrusive
phrases of the kind 'Pascal (would have) continued,' pre-
ferring to use the first person quite openly to engineer
transitions. The order followed, allowing for a few overlaps, is that of the twenty-eight dossiers, incorporating
the modifications we proposed for 14°, 15°, and 16°. At
the beginning of paragraphs numerals indicate the section
about to be summarized.[1]

   1°: This is an attempt to present the Christian religion to those who are sceptical about religion, or indifferent to it, or openly hostile. Religion is both despised and feared, for it is seen as a threat both to our
ideal of truth and to our desire for a happy life, free
from anguish. My first task, then, is to show that that
scorn is not justified, because religion is not the enemy
of reason, and to allay the fears, on the grounds that
the devout life produces a peace and happiness and ultimately bliss, which cannot be found outside it. There is
strong evidence to support the claims Christianity makes
for itself, but I shall not disclose it until I feel that
my opponent is ready to embark on a willing search for it.
   My argument can therefore be divided into two. I shall
first evoke the wretchedness of man without God, and show
that nature, including man, is corrupt. Then I shall paint

man's felicity once he allies himself to God, and show, with the aid of holy Scripture, that corrupt and fallen man has been redeemed by God, in Jesus.

Some general remarks about the first part before we move to details. Man's understanding of life has been the subject of many books, including Montaigne's *Essais* and various compilations of Charron. Charron's rigid categories do not do justice to the subject, which cannot be contained in this way. The free method of Montaigne is the only suitable approach. I do find things to reproach Montaigne with, and I do not think it is a laudable ambition to spend all one's energies on portraying oneself. But Montaigne certainly reveals the complexity of human history, and even his self-portraits open our eyes to our own existential situation.

I have wished to bring my unbelieving reader to make similar discoveries about himself and the human condition, by following Montaigne's lead and collecting examples of human vanity, and pointing out the contradictions, the incomprehensibility even of our destiny, problems which the philosophers have not solved, and which we have tended to run away from, as if that course of action solved anything. I hope that this confrontation with his own wretchedness will encourage my reader to search for a God whose presence in the world is not by any means immediately apparent. I shall try to show that some of the obstacles are of our making, and that by self-discipline they can be reduced. Ultimately, of course, faith is given by God, but there is a large area which is man's responsibility and there is much in that area to explore.

2°, 3°, 4°: Without the perspective of religion, human life is characterized by wretchedness, *misère*. One has only to turn to Montaigne's *Essais* to see this illustrated on all sides. A man is wretched if he can neither quench nor satisfy a strong desire. We have two profound impulses, which we are unable to satisfy: the desire to find happiness, and the desire for truth. We need happiness, but cannot attain it; we desire truth, but can never be sure that we have reached it. The two impulses function in a similar way and indeed are often linked. But in the last analysis our deeper need is for *le bien*.

If it were all a simple matter of pain and pleasure, it would be easier to understand. The classic statement of human suffering is the Book of Job, but another book

of the Old Testament, Ecclesiastes, shows how complex is
the matter of human happiness, if happiness is sought
amid things of the world. Ecclesiastes was written by a
great and powerful king, Solomon, who had discovered that
pleasure, power, and riches do not in fact bring happiness, as we come to see that 'all is vanity,' that we
attribute to things an importance they do not deserve,
that our existence is governed by trivia. We do not even
have the consolation of knowing that we can use our minds
to raise ourselves above the ills of the body, and attain
truth. Doubting is our natural state, yet doubt cannot
satisfy us either. The search for truth is thus in a sense
one aspect of our search for happiness. But we can take
it separately, and see where our reflections lead us.

That we are unable to devote our lives to pursuing
truth should occasion no surprise. Reason is sabotaged
on all sides. Its authority is sapped notably by imagination, imperiously demanding its own satisfaction. Imagination is equally responsible for our experience of
beauty, of happiness, and, together with the senses, of
love.

Sabotaged by the imagination, reason is threatened also
by the senses, by illness, by our desire for novelty
(which is no guarantee of truth), and by self-interest:
vanity, *gloire*, ambition all lead to actions difficult
to justify rationally. More insidious even than self-
interest is self-love. We put ourselves at the centre of
life, which is plainly unreasonable. Consequently we are
committed to opposing the truth about ourselves, the truth
being that we are one of an infinite number of egos, all
fighting for the place we covet for ourselves. So deeply
rooted is this self-love that it becomes second nature.
Social codes like *honnêteté* very successfully disguise
it, but they cannot remove the basic injustice of amour-
propre, which is omnipresent, and which takes widely diverse forms.

Even without being attacked from outside, reason itself
is flawed. The sceptics' case is irrefutable - without
God, we have no authority for any belief, as reason cannot justify the ultimate authority it gives itself without tautology.

But even if we admit that we can never be sure of the
foundations on which reason builds, we can nevertheless
pragmatically try to understand our present situation.
It needs some courage. We become quickly conscious of

our fickleness towards things we say we honour, and of
the vanity of our values, and our activites. And if we
look at the basis of society, we come to similar conclusions. We have a hankering after justice, as we have a
longing for truth, but we have no criteria for deciding
what is absolutely just any more than we have criteria
for knowing what is absolutely true. As it is concupiscence, not reason, which really governs our actions, so
it is force, not justice, which dictates the way society
has been organized. We cannot know justice, but force is
unanswerable, and the best modus vivendi society has found
has been to give the strong man the title of just man.
Thereafter, society is preserved by myths, imagination,
and custom.

Our first reaction is to defend ourselves against these
unpalatable conclusions. Sensing that all our reflection
leads to nihilism and despair, we find ways to evade the
truth. We sometimes pride ourselves on having thought so
deeply, and our self-satisfaction protects us from the
anguish. More often, we seek in distraction a measure of
consolation, although by throwing ourselves into pointless activities, we are only increasing the grounds for
despair, and postponing the day of reckoning.

5°: Nevertheless, we should try to think the question
through, to the other side of despair, if necessary. How
do we understand our predicament? If our thinking has
gone no further than observing that all is vanity - finding distraction in pointless activities, pursuing *gloire*,
relying on hereditary monarchy as a system for choosing
a ruler - we may begin by feeling agreeably pleased with
ourselves. But these 'vain' views are in fact not so
stupid. The people who subscribe to them may do so for
the wrong reasons, but as practical guides to living,
they have their point. Many idealistic opinions are so
impractical as to be actually dangerous, and the people
who scorn the views of the majority are often not clever
enough to understand the profound reasons which justify
those views. We talk of the vanity of much generally accepted conduct, but we should perhaps rather talk of the
sanity of these widely held views.

Yet we are right to denounce vanity, because most people
do not understand why their conduct is justifiable, and
if their conclusions are right, their reasoning is quite
wrong. What passes for justice or merit is frequently a
disguise for force, but we would be imprudent if we

undervalued force, or if we allowed brute force to control our lives directly. It is because of their lack of
insight that the accepting attitude of the majority is
to be applauded. For the man deprived of Christian understanding, custom and majority opinion are the safest
guides, because they do at least preserve society from
disorder and individuals from despair. We need to find a
solution which preserves the virtues of the present arrangement - civil and psychological peace - but bases
them on a true apprehension of justice and the human condition.

So far, we have not been able to find any such grounds,
but we must pursue our reflection.

6°: Everything to date - vanity, injustice, anguish -
has pointed to *misère* as the key to human life. But that
is by no means the whole picture. Life is ultimately
controlled by force and concupiscence, yet man has created,
on this unpromising foundation, an ordered society which
could even be called an image of charity (charity being
the Christian prescription for society). We are wretched,
but we have an impulse towards elevation, and even the
word 'wretched' implies some tension between the reality
of our existence and our calling, dimly sensed. We are
at the mercy of our senses, but we know that our nature
cannot be confined to the material realm.

So wretchedness is only half the story: the very things
which compose our wretchedness are counterpointed with
aspects which draw us higher. Our greatness is shown
above all by reason, something which makes us superior
to the whole universe. We are wretched, but we know that
we are. We use our reason badly, but reason itself is
good - as our wish to be judged well by others perhaps
implies. Doubting is natural to us, but it can never be
total; there are things we know to be true, although we
can never get the other side of them in order to prove
them from distinct, rational premises. Sceptics and dogmatists continue their interminable debate.

What if faith were one of these unprovable but indubit-
able first principles? Those who have it believe it is,
but those who do not cannot accept their point of view.
Thus we are obliged to rely on our reason, however inadequate. Man without God is caught in a vicious circle,
unable to depend on his reason but having no other instrument to master his situation. Because of this limitation
in reason, we can never hope to prove that God exists.

Indeed, the Christian concept of God as the source of love sets him outside the range of rational enquiry anyway, identified with 'le bien' more compellingly than with 'le vrai.' But let us not pursue that idea for a while. What has this examination of man's quest for truth taught us about the nature of man himself?

7°: It has taught us, surely, that man is characterized by both wretchedness and greatness; he is obviously contradictory. His contradictory nature is evident in countless tiny matters. The more carefully we observe man, the more evidence we find both of his wretchedness and of his greatness. The exercise is salutary; self-knowledge means recognizing both, and recognizing that man is simultaneously wretched and great. Recognizing this, we shall avoid the moral dangers of despair on the one hand and pride on the other. There is much to admire in man, particularly in his performance. Self-knowledge enables us to identify the passions as the enemy which prevents us from realizing our potential, and resisting them.

Philosophers have always taken sides, attaching an excessive importance to either one aspect or the other. Can we hope to find from them the true analysis and explanation of our condition? Here we meet the pyrrhonian and the dogmatist again, perfect examples of two schools perpetually at war with each other. We say we believe in certain first principles, but there is always a suspicion of doubt. In practical terms, however, nobody is a thoroughgoing sceptic. But we can never be quite sure of what we believe; natural reason fails us.

But if the philosophers are of no use in our quest, religions seem to get nearer the crux. There is one explanation, that of Christianity, which teaches that man has fallen from his true state without losing all traces of it. The explanation is incomprehensible, but at least it recognizes the facts, the duality of human nature. At this stage, we can say no more. We must turn from the search for truth and look equally carefully at the other impulse, man's desire for happiness, for what the philosophers call the Sovereign Good.

8°: Just as man without faith cannot know the truth, so he cannot know the true good. In a way the two are connected. We know we have a potential for reasoned thought, yet we cannot realize it. The chances of physical existence pull us down from our intimations of

immortality. As soon as we start thinking seriously about
ourselves, we become anxious. Better not to think, better
to distract ourselves. Distraction is vain, but it is
justified. As it is the activity which distracts, there
is no point in being practical and mocking the activity
for accomplishing nothing. If people who distract themselves - and few are exempt - are to be criticized, it
is for deluding themselves with the thought that they
will one day be able to give up the feverish activity
and find happiness in repose.

In fact, repose is the last thing we want. We would
find it unbearable, or at best would be bored, and would
seek for fresh distractions, spurred on by the hope of
being able to impress others with our achievements. But
we still believe that what we really want is rest, and
this is a sign that we do need it, but we cannot - can
no longer - bear it. Yet we would be better advised to
shun distraction, contemplate our mortality, and advance
in self-knowledge.

The truth is that we cannot reach happiness on our own.
We have lost touch with our true nature. We try to cover
the void by vain activities, but only God can fill it.
Infinitely diverse are the substitutes we have found:
authority, intellectual endeavours, and voluptuousness,
popularly associated with the Epicureans.

9°, 10°: The Stoic philosophers taught that God alone
is worthy of admiration. But they have failed to understand that man, in his wretchedness, cannot reach God by
an act of will alone, and so their counsel of perfection
serves to increase man's pride, a form of concupiscence.
They bid us seek happiness inside ourselves, by an effort
of will, but we know (though we interpret the conviction
wrongly) that happiness must come from outside ourselves.
Where we go wrong is in fixing on some trivial external
source for our happiness, and expecting it to prove the
happiness we want. The Platonists saw that the Sovereign
Good must be something which all men can attain and possess. Only God fulfils those conditions. But as we are
at present constituted, we cannot reach God without faith.
So all the natural philosophers fail to give man the
practical help he needs, however valid their theoretical
pronouncements. There is no access to God without faith;
Jesus, not Epictetus, is the only Way.

The two main philosophical schools, Epicureans and
Stoics, fail therefore to satisfy our craving. We are

not wholly flesh, nor are we wholly will. We are double, and the contradictions cannot be suppressed. Our animal nature needs to be elevated, our pride needs to be humbled. Our double nature implies that we are alienated, that we have lost contact with the situation for which we were created, and philosophers are no help to us here. After we have searched for the Sovereign Good, we are ready to turn to Jesus.

Our desires for the truth and for the good are thus both unsatisfied. It is as if we are being punished for our shortcomings; we know that we are not fulfilling ourselves.

11°: The philosophers have failed to account for the diversity which is the most profound characteristic of man and for his failure to satisfy his deepest needs. What of religion? We know now what we have a right to expect of any religion worthy of the name. It has to teach that man is both wretched and superior, and to account for this duality; it has to offer the possibility of felicity and an antidote to concupiscence. The inner conflicts of mankind suggest that man is not in the state for which he was created, and that he has a memory, imperfectly understood, of his former state. The philosophers contradict each other because they have partial views only, and so they do not have the explanation. Nor have they brought any remedy, as those who destroy pride increase concupiscence, and those who would conquer concupiscence minister to pride.

Christianity, whose explanation of man has already been hinted at, fulfils the conditions as no other. The doctrine of the fall accounts for man's duality, and the doctrine of redemption - known as a real possibility, not as an immutable certainty, for each one of us - elevates and humbles us at the points where elevation and humiliation are necessary. It is incomprehensible, but that merely indicates the limitations for reason, not the flaw in the system; life is no less incomprehensible without the Christian explanation. It may seem quite improbable, that God should 'so love the world' that he sent a redeemer; but we who do not know what is true justice cannot judge what God is likely or unlikely to decide; our task is simply to love him. If we ask him, in an attitude of trust, to give us evidence of his word, we shall find that he supplies just enough proof to quiten our doubts, and that thereafter he asks for our confidence.

12°: Certainly we cannot expect incontrovertible, universally binding proof; if we could, there would be no dispute in the first place. But there is a very real distinction to be made as regards the attitude of the enquirer, between the man who hopes to find and is open to the evidence, and the hostile sceptic who turns a blind eye to the evidence provided. The search must be serious. There is evidence, but it is placed in such a way that some effort is required on our part. The question therefore resolves itself into this: should we make the effort required?

The answer cannot be in doubt, once we have realized the important stakes which are involved. For the search is bound up with the issue of eternal life and our own mortality or immortality. What awaits us at death? For the agnostic, there are only two possibilities: annihilation or an eternity of *misère*. In life on earth, *misère* is inescapable, and all we have effectively to balance it is the hope of eternal bliss. Is this hope justified? That is how the question presents itself to us.

Evidently it is unreasonable not to enquire further. Self-interest demands that we do so. To refuse therefore goes against self-interest, and that is unnatural. It may even be supernatural in origin, so difficult is it to find any normal explanation.

It follows that indifference is not a reaction be be proud of. We should not be tempted to imitate it. Those who are indifferent should recognize that it is an unreasonable attitude, and try to reflect further, for example by reading this Apologia. As for those who are already seeking, or those who are now ready to seek, they can be assured that there are proofs, which I hope to expose later on in this book.

I readily allow that even if the reader is interested, he will have various objections which will have to be met before he is ready for the so-called proofs. One arises out of a point made earlier, when I argued that by the very nature of reason and of God as Christianity conceives him, we cannot know God by reason. The enterprise must therefore be methodologically unsound. This argument is plausible, but it can be answered on its own terms. If reason cannot lead to God, we can agree to put the quest for 'le vrai' completely to one side, and to use reason for another purpose, to discover 'le bien.'

We have to choose one way or another, and fashion our lives on one of two assumptions, either that Christianity's claims are sound, or that they are not. If they are sound, it is clearly sensible to choose for and not against. If they are not, nothing is lost by choosing it (except that our lives will not be in accordance with 'le vrai,' but we have agreed to put that consideration out of court). In our search for 'le bien' we will have gained, because morally Christianity provides the antidote to selfishness (which *honnêteté* cannot), by its doctrine of original sin and the remedy offered in the redeeming work of Christ. And nothing is lost: by living the Christian life we shall discover that only our selfishness suffers, and there are compensating rewards - joy, fulfilment - which no self-centred ethos can provide.

Plainly, then, we should choose for, rather than against, Christianity. How do we go about acquiring Christian convictions? We must understand that unbelief does not come from rational certainty about the non-existence of God, but from our self-love. We should therefore start by disciplining the passions. As we are creatures of custom, we should create new habits for ourselves, spiritual disciplines, including prayer, which we shall discover does create that link between man and God which reason is unable to forge. And through this new habit of Christian living, we shall acquire the desired quality, Christian hope.

So, on grounds of prudence alone, one can come to want fervently to be Christian. And once one has reached that stage, one will be less interested in using the argument about the inaccessibility of God to reason in order to discredit the apologetic endeavour.

13°: In fact, there is no need to assume, other than provisionally, that reason has no part to play in the process. Faith does not fly against reason and observation, and it has nothing to do with superstition. But if we use our reason properly, as we should, we shall see that reason does have its limitations. There are things which go beyond reason, indeed which go beyond what we normally call 'nature.' Reason can always be disputed, and religion needs a firmer basis than that. The authority for religion is found in holy Scripture. There we find that the case rests on miracles and prophecies. To these we shall return, in due course.

Not everybody will react in the same way to the problems of human destiny as the relatively cool and 'rational' person just addressed. Some people will experience

genuine anguish, and this will prompt them to begin
searching immediately. But where are they to search for
evidence of God? They should not expect to find incontrovertible proof in nature. The place to seek is the
Christian Church, and in the record of other religions.

14°: Scrutiny of nature does, however, produce some
results. It shows us the enormity of creation, it reveals
our own position in that universe, occupying one point
on an infinite scale, yet having the inestimable advantage of possessing reason. By using reason and considering our place in the universe, we can understand that
there must be a Creator, able to embrace the whole of
this creation which far outstrips our mental faculties,
even our imagination. But as our reason is unable to
comprehend the totality, our understanding must remain
woefully incomplete. What then are we to do? We can learn
humility. And we can use our mind to think correctly;
we can trust God, and we can examine, critically but without unfair prejudice, the religions of the world.

15°, 16°, 17°, 18°: I have tried by these different
arguments to bring readers of differing temperaments to
the point where they can be assumed both to admit the
supernatural as part of experience, and to be ready to
examine critically the various possibilities which have
been advanced from that premiss. This is really the second
main division of my argument. I want to show that Christianity satisfies all the requirements we have laid down
for an authentic religion, that it has credentials we can
justify rationally, and that it possesses the secret of
the good life for which we long.

15°: We must first of all rid our minds of any confusion between Christianity and other religions, which have
at best a partial understanding of God. Deism, for example, identifies God with the creator, and attempts to
prove his existence rationally. The Christian God is
creator too, of course, but he is also Father, a God of
love. Christian doctrine consists essentially of two
points: man is fallen, man has been redeemed. It is a
doctrine which both explains man's predicament, and offers a remedy. At the centre is the person of Jesus, who
made certain specific claims for himself, and these claims
can be tested by reason - provided we accept the premiss
that natural explanations are not necessarily the only ones.

The doctrine of the fall accounts for what we have already observed to be the reality of the human condition - our inadequacy, and our sense that we are not realizing our own potential. It may be difficult to find evidence of God in nature, but there is evidence in plenty of corruption.

16°: Moreover, the vision Christianity has of man's ultimate destiny increases our awareness of our corrupt present nature.

17°a: For Christianity teaches that fallen man has been redeemed. This complementary doctrine preserves us from the moral dangers which the philosophers have been unable to avoid: pride on the one hand and despair on the other. Our need of redemption is clear; Jesus has given us the means of redemption. Only through him can we have access to God, and fulfil our basic duty, to worship and love God. Rational arguments for the existence of God, as well as failing to convince us totally, by-pass the essential doctrine of the redemptive work of God. A Christ-centred faith, on the other hand, gives us a constant experience of God's love.

18°: Not that we are to take redemption as automatic. That would remove the drama from the theatre where it has to be played out - in our own lives as fallen, yet redeemable individuals. God has offered the possibility of redemption, and it is up to each one of us to make it real, by becoming followers of Jesus, and practising humility, mortification, prayer, love.

19°, 17°b: Christian doctrine, then, harmonizes so well with human experience and human needs that we are ready to subscribe to it rather than to other religions. But there must be more solid evidence, if doubts are to be silenced completely. There are for instance three main objections that can be made to the doctrine of the fall and redemption of man: that it is incomprehensible, that God would never so descend to man, and that there is no evidence for it. To the first two objections, already touched on earlier, one can answer simply by questioning the objector's grounds, but the third objection is more challenging. One can concede a certain truth in it: we have already agreed that God cannot be proved conclusively from observing nature. What is obvious from nature is the world's corruption, which is one part of Christian doctrine. But we must not say that there are in nature no signs whatsoever of God's presence. If man is corrupt, needing always to force his will to do what is right because right behaviour and right thinking do not come naturally, one might expect God to give clues rather than clear unambiguous statements, enough to encourage us in our search, but not making it so easy that we can find solutions without effort. He would thus be hidden, but not totally inaccessible. And this is the view of God advanced by Christians. Rather than atheism, rather than other religions, it is Christianity which meets the objections put forward by the agnostic.

The view of God as both hidden and revealed constantly reminds us of our duality, fallen yet capable of redemption. As he is in part revealed, we can trust him, but as he is in part concealed, we will not be over-confident. We thus avoid the dangers of despair and pride. Our duty is to seek further, not to use God's concealment of himself as an excuse. Not to seek is, we have said, a form of blindness - blindness inflicted by God as a punishment on those who trust their own perception to a presumptuous degree.

If nature provides no conclusive proof of the Christian God, where should we continue our search? Christianity teaches that God can be known only through Jesus. Jesus entered human history, and the Christian religion claims that he was the Messiah, the redeemer promised by God to the Israelites. We should therefore look, as carefully as we are able, at his credentials.

Even before we consider the specific problems which such a scrutiny poses, we will be struck once again by the superiority of Christianity over other faiths. No other religion can make so impressive a case. Other religions claim authority, but the claim is empty. Mahomet was his own witness and he called himself a prophet; but the witness for Jesus, and the argument from the Hebrew prophets are altogether more telling - and there are other points in Mahommedanism which compare unfavourably with Christianity. Christianity is the fulfilment of the Jewish religion, which is itself firmly grounded. When Jesus is replaced in his historical context, as the Messiah expected by the Jews, we find a series of interlocking proofs. He proved his divinity to his followers by miracles, and by this means he fulfilled the prophecies. As well as the fulfilment of the prophecies, we have the growth of the Christian Church as further evidence that Jesus was the son of God.

When we come actually to examine in detail the objective evidence for Christianity, we shall not forget that God is hidden from our immediate vision, for the notion helps us to resolve many difficulties. Obscurities and contradictions in the Bible, the multiplicity of religions and of opinions within the Church are all an invitation to search. Jesus did not strike everyone as being what he claimed to be. His validity rests on the fact that he was predicted. Yet the prophecies themselves were obscure, clear as to the time, but ambiguous as to the manner of his coming. The Messiah was expected to be a king, whereas Jesus's kingdom, it turned out, was not of this world. Jesus lived in obscurity. In all ways truth is visible yet ambiguous, a stimulus to further thought. With this approach the way is clear to seeing that Jesus did fulfil the messianic prophecies, and to accepting him as a saviour.

20°: The argument for God's redemption of mankind rests on the Bible: in the Old Testament God promised the Messiah, and these prophecies were fulfilled in Jesus. But this sequence is by no means self-evident. It is so only if we read the Old Testament as a figurative text. We are justified in doing so by Scripture itself. The prophets talk of obscurity, even when their literal meaning is clear. There are contradictions in the literal sense too blatant for us not to want to explain them away. These contradictions vanish if we see the text as sometimes figurative. The prophets themselves interpreted their own words in this way. There are also absurdities in the Old Testament, and phrases which have no sense taken literally. A literal reading is thus manifestly inadequate.

Jesus did not fulfil the prophecies in their literal sense. He gave us the keys to the cipher of the Old Testament, showing us that the 'true' sense was often not the literal one, and that we need to look beyond the literal sense if the literal sense goes against the law of charity. The enemies we are to fight and kill, for example, are our own passions. This can be proved by careful exegesis as well as supported by appeal to spiritual intuition.

Another key given by Jesus was that the Messiah was to suffer. The time of the Messiah was always predicted clearly, but the manner of his coming was ambiguous, leading the carnal-minded to expect a spectacular king. But in defiance of the world's values, Jesus came to

suffer. The prophets said he would be rejected, and rejected he was - by the Jews who had not understood the
prophets correctly. They were guardians of the authentic
religion, but by being attached to the literal meaning
instead of relating every word to the fundamental precept
of the love of God, they betrayed their trust, and paradoxically thereby fulfilled the prophecies. The Old
Testament therefore reflects faithfully God's intention
to reveal himself only to those willing to seek him in
humility.

21°: The rabbinical writings show that there was authority within the Jewish tradition for the figurative
approach. The comments made show also that the Jewish
tradition admitted the concept of the fall, of original
sin. Christian doctrine was thus prepared from the beginning of time.

22°: We are now equipped to look more closely at the
Christian tradition. Christianity is based on the Jewish
religion, which teaches that man is corrupt and will be
redeemed by a Messiah who will restore to man his natural
inclination to love God above all things. The doctrine
should be studied in its truest form, not in the distorted
version found in the 'carnal' practitioners - in the Jews
who understand spiritual things, for example, and not in
those who expected a political advantage.

The Jewish people, in whom Christianity is grounded,
is a race of venerable antiquity, worshipping a single
God, living according to an ancient and perfect law which
they derive from God, guardians of a revelation which
teaches corruption and promises redemption. They have
been faithful to the law despite provocation and persecution, and they have a history far exceeding in length
that of any other nation. Their credentials are beyond
reproach.

Consequently the Christian religion has a very long
history. The hope of redemption goes back to the fall of
Adam. The prophets spoke of the coming of a Messiah, and
we believe the Messiah to have come in the person of Jesus
who by his miracles converted pagans and thus fulfilled
the prophecies about him; in this fulfilment is the permanent proof of Jesus's claims. What has happened since,
both to Jews and to Christians, has followed the same
pattern of persecution, dispersal, survival.

23°: The two fundamental doctrines of Christianity
were thus known from the beginning of time. The longevity

of the patriarchs recorded in the Old Testament ensures
that the witness of the Creation and the Flood was not
distorted by being transmitted through countless generations. When memories became faded, Moses set the record
down. The Jewish people were entrusted with the task of
preserving the record, and were kept to this by the prophets and by their own divinely inspired zeal.

24°: The Old Testament confidently looks forward to the
coming of the Messiah, born of the line of Judah. The
history of the Jews can be interpreted in such a way as
to suggest that the prophecies were indeed fulfilled in
Jesus. To support what is claimed for Jesus, we can thus
point to his doctrine, the perpetuity of the Jewish witness, and the prophecies.

The New Testament gives complementary evidence that he
was indeed the Messiah. We need not doubt that the New
Testament is authentic. That record tells us of his
miracles, by which he established his claim and fulfilled
the prophecies that he would convert the Gentiles, and
it paints a man clearly divine and at the same time fully
human.

Yet he has not been universally recognized. But we know
that God conceals himself as well as reveals himself, and
so it has been with Jesus. The obscurity of Jesus was
foretold; it is an argument which tells in his favour,
not against him. We must realize that there are different
'orders' in existence: the flesh, the mind, and the heart,
and Jesus' supremacy lay in the highest order, the spiritual, not in the physical or intellectual realm. Rational
clarity, excellent in its own sphere, is not required in
matters of the spirit.

25°: The effect of all this (the miracles, the person
of Jesus, both God and man) was for Jesus to be accepted
by many (but not all), and messianic prophecies were
thereby fulfilled, constituting the final proof. Scripture shows the life of Jesus in agreement with the prophecies made of the Messiah, and if we scrutinize the
details, this circumstantial evidence becomes very significant. The remarkable thing is that so many details
combine. One notices the extreme diversity of sources,
producing a multiplicity of prophecies which converge on
Jesus.

These prophecies were widely disseminated before his
advent. The time of his coming was similarly predicted
in various ways, making a number of distinct conditions

which had to be, and were, met. The prophets spoke of
the rejection of the Jews and the conversion of the Gentiles. This too happened, once Jesus had been accepted
by the nucleus of believers who then went out and converted the world.

26°: Finally, certain Old Testament motifs and characters can be interpreted as figures of Jesus; he made actual not only the specific prophecies, but many hidden
implications of the Old Testament.

27°: We can thus legitimately argue that in Christianity man does find the truth for which he is searching.
The only premiss which can underlie all the complex observable facts is the Christian one. But we know that
man longs equally for 'le bien'; and that too he can find
in Jesus, who restored man's contact with God.

The Christian serves God, not himself, and in this ser-
vice finds both happiness and virtue, a combination difficult within the ethos of *honnêteté*. A Christian accepts
the will of God, and seeks the true good. He loves God
and his fellows, and conquers self-love. He lives with
his fellow Christians in a way analogous to that in which
the limbs co-exist in the body, the Christian's 'body'
being Jesus. His behaviour is guided not by his own will,
but by the will of God. Formal obedience can be superstition merely, but discipline is nevertheless necessary to
our moral life, as it saves us from the dangers of pride
and despair. We are surrounded by things which console
us, but which also warn us. Of all religions, Christianity is the only one which is demonstrably perfectly
suited to the complexities of the human condition.

28°: That is as far as we can go in making a well-
presented case. The final stage, conversion, lies beyond
the scope of an apologia. Unbelief is unreasonable, but
that does not mean that belief is reasonable and nothing
more. If our will is turned towards God, we will see
things differently from the rationalist who has not
fought self-will. Reason can pave the way, but sooner
or later the individual must face the fact of the Cross
and make a leap into faith. Faith is God-given, and may
come to people quite unable to justify themselves intellectually.

It is not easy for us to make the final step. After
accepting with our mind, and working to turn our will
towards God, all we can do is discipline ourselves by
building new habits, and wait for God's grace.

PART TWO: GROWTH

30
The genesis of the Apologia

In the previous chapter I presented Pascal's argument as
it can be deduced from the twenty-eight *liasses*, liberally
supplemented by material from the thirty-five 'Units,'
that is, the collection of *pensées* which Pascal did not
himself divide out among the *liasses*. I did not try to
force all of those fragments into the framework of twenty-
eight sections, but acted as if the great majority of
them were relevant to the Apologia, and as if it were
only for contingent reasons that Pascal did not actually
incorporate them. I have assumed that he stopped filing
before he had sorted all the fragments already extant,
and that he subsequently amassed additional fragments,
which the twenty-eight sections could have accommodated
with ease.

One would like to be able to test this assumption further, first by examining the constitution of the *liasses*
(or at least putting them in sequence), and then by dating
the Units and examining the alternatives to the hypothesis
I have accepted. This will be the aim of the thirty-first
and thirty-second chapters. The present chapter prepares
for this by showing the direction Pascal's thinking had
taken before he gave his energies over to the Apologia.
Most major works have a subterranean pre-history, and the
Pensées are no exception. The ten years before 1657 (the
year in which Pascal set his sights squarely on the
Apologia) are marked by intense activity and in his writings
from that decade there are many hints of what was to come
- emerging attitudes, formulation of themes and motifs,
sometimes in ways which strikingly anticipate phrases in
the *pensées* legitimately associated with the Apologia.
Careful examination of papers compiled in the latter part
of 1656 shows themes coalescing into new patterns, and
reveals the increasingly apologetic colour of Pascal's
writing.

The chapter is divided into seven sections:

(a) In the period between his two 'conversions' (1646-54)
Pascal was active as both scientist and neophyte. Though
the two domains are distinct, and though theological
truths are known to faith and not to reason, Pascal sees
a role for reason in the war against rationalism. In his
spiritual letters, Pascal writes that corporal things are
a figure of things spiritual, but that their spiritual
meaning is only made clear to those who know and love God.
As both fallen and redeemed, we belong to two realms. God
must be at the centre of our lives.
(b) After his profound religious experience of November
1654, Pascal discussed with M. de Sacy of Port-Royal a
project which we can call apologetic. By playing off
Epictetus and Montaigne against each other, the *honnête
homme* can be brought to realize the inadequacy and the
inconsistency of his world-view, and shown that the contrasting insights are harmonized only by the Christian
doctrine of the fall and redemption. The strategy will
be refined considerably, but the seeds of the first part
of the Apologia are here, and many ideas from the
Entretien avec M. de Sacy will be taken over by the
Apologia.
(c) An opuscule entitled *De l'esprit géométrique* (1655)
examines the basis of geometric method. One has to accept,
says Pascal, that certain things are given. Geometric
method, rigorously applied, allows us to build on those
foundations and reach certainty. As an answer to out and
out scepticism, Pascal's argument is powerful. But he is
himself aware that it leaves a lot unsaid. Men are not
persuaded by rational arguments alone; we find ways of
not receiving what we do not wish to receive, and where
mind and heart clash, we need a method which will convince
the heart as well as the head. Subsequently, Pascal will
ask how the phenomenon of faith fits into his picture.
Can we talk of accepting the premiss of religious faith
the way we necessarily accept the existence of time, number, and dimension? These questions are developed in a
series of essays which it is reasonable to assume were
written not long after the two projects of 1655.
(d) The important manuscript 'Infini rien' (Unit II)
takes as its starting-point the basic contention of the
first part of *De l'esprit géométrique*. Reason can prove
that infinity exists, but not that God exists. God is

known to the heart. Yet the heart, seat of self-love, re-
sists. Reason can show that the heart is foolish to resist,
because true happiness comes only in the Christian life.
The natural resistance of the heart can be reduced by
consciously adopting new habits. Once this resistance is
overcome, a person can see that there are in fact reasons
for believing in God, for he has entered our finite world.
Some of these ideas are greatly expanded, often in directions which appear unrelated to the main argument, but
which greatly enrich Pascal's conception of faith (the
role of habit, 'Dieu sensible au coeur,' the attraction
of concupiscence) and of the credentials of Christianity
(it goes right against our inclinations, yet appears in-
destructible).We cannot date this manuscript exactly, but
it is probably roughly simultaneous with the many papers
which together give the material of my remaining sections.
(e) The year 1656 brought Pascal into the conflict between
Port-Royal and the Jesuits. He was writing the *Provinciales* throughout the year, and from late August was also
involved in a dispute with the Jesuits over the status
of miracles. He wrote many fragments on the latter subject. Some were intended to show that the attitude of
the Jesuits to the miracles being performed that year at
Port-Royal was indefensible, and they have no relevance
to a modern Apologia. But when Pascal discusses the role
played in the establishment of Christianity by the miracles
of Jesus himself, he introduces a theme which the Apologia
will have to include, although he places less importance
in the Apologia on miracles than he does on two other arguments which also emerge from the reflections of these
months – prophecy and perpetuity.
(f) Consideration of miracles also leads Pascal to write
more about the nature of reason and faith. Two main areas
are explored. First, God usually conceals himself from
senses and reason, making himself accessible only to
faith. There are many implications to this notion, worked
out here and fully developed in the Apologia. Second,
Pascal considers reason and faith from the human point
of view. This too is fundamental to the design of the
Apologia.
(g) Finally, other themes can be traced to these months,
themes which have no apparent connection with miracles or
with the Jesuits, but which appear on the same pages, or at
least on identical paper, as the thoughts on miracles. Chief
among these are the elusiveness of truth and of happiness.

(a) les secrets de la nature sont cachés[1]

Two distinct fields of activity occupied Pascal in the
late 1640s. As a scientist he was conducting his experiments on the vacuum, and defending the conclusions he had
reached. As a recent convert to Jansenism, he played a
significant part in opposing the ambition of a heterodox
theologian, Jacques Forton, sieur de Saint-Ange, and as
his letters to his sister and her husband show, he reflected deeply and long on the Scriptures and on such
commentators as Saint Augustine, Jansen, and Saint-Cyran.
He thought also about the relation of science and theology. The documents in which his thinking has been preserved contain several insights in which we can recognize
the future author of the *Pensées*. But there is as yet no
sign of an apologetic mission, and it would be wrong to
find 'first versions' of any of the *pensées* in the
writings of 1647-51; they are indications of the nature
of Pascal's spirituality and of his major preoccupations.

The two major interests of these years occasionally
come together, as Pascal carefully maps out the demarcation line between science and theology in the *Préface
sur le Traité du Vide* (1651), or as he wonders how far
reason could be implicated in theology, while admitting
that faith transcends reason and nature. The three levels
of experience, which Pascal will later call the three
'orders' (nature, reason, faith), provide a key to his
thought, and I shall frequently relate his ideas to this
model.

Pascal discussed his ideas on the use of reason in
theological discussion with M. de Rebours of Port-Royal
early in 1648. He informed his sister Gilberte of the
conversation:

> Je lui dis ensuite que je pensais que l'on pouvait,
> suivant les principes mêmes du sens commun, montrer
> beaucoup de choses que les adversaires disent lui être
> contraires, et que le raisonnement bien conduit portait
> à les croire, quoiqu'il les faille croire sans l'aide
> du raisonnement.[2]

Jan Miel has argued that the 'adversaries' here are not
unbelievers, but Molinists, that is, Catholics whose
theological position is outside the tradition stemming
from Saint Augustine.[3] In the opinion of Henri Gouhier,

the reason why Pascal visited M. de Rebours was that he
needed the priest's advice, if he was to do what he felt
called to do: to act as lay director to Gilberte.[4] Rebours
demanded that he first scrutinize his own motives. Pascal
did so, and assumed the role, but without M. de Rebours's
blessing.

He took the role very seriously, and wrote several letters of edification to Gilberte and to other members of
his immediate family. Here, the distinction is less
between reason and faith as between the flesh and faith.
In a letter of 1 April 1648, he develops the idea that
the world is only a figure, 'les choses corporelles'
being 'une image des spirituelles.' We are like prisoners
to whom the means of escape have been shown, but only
indirectly. Here is the 'Dieu caché' theme, of which
Pascal will make so much later, and with it the 'aveugler/
éclaircir' motif:

> on ne peut apercevoir ces saints caractères sans une
> lumière surnaturelle; car comme toutes choses parlent
> de Dieu à ceux qui le connaissent, et qu'elles le
> découvrent à tous ceux qui l'aiment, ces mêmes choses
> le cachent à tous ceux qui ne le connaissent pas.[5]

The letter is a meditation on the necessity to honour
God and not creatures, 'car il n'y a que Dieu qui doive
être la dernière fin comme lui seul est le vrai principe.'
We are to avoid 'cet aveuglement charnel et judaïque qui
fait prendre la figure pour la réalité.' If we have been
redeemed by God, we have a double obligation, corresponding to our status as members of both 'l'ordre des créa-
tures' and the Body of Christ. A meditation on Saint Paul
and Saint Augustine, possibly through the meditation of
Jansen and Saint-Cyran, is thus at the origin of what
will become a principal strand of the Apologia. We shall
see that it surfaces again in 1656; at that point we
shall be able to discuss it more fully.

Jean Mesnard remarks of the letter which Pascal sent
to M. Périer shortly after the death of his father, on
17 October 1651,[6] that 'quelques thèmes majeurs des
Pensées sont déjà magnifiquement esquissés.'[7] Certainly
it witnesses to the intensity of Pascal's spiritual life
at this time, with its argument that the death and resurrection of Jesus have set our natural reactions of
amour-propre in a new perspective.

> Ne quittons donc pas cet amour que la nature nous a
> donné pour la vie, puisque nous l'avons reçu de Dieu;
> mais que ce soit pour la même vie pour laquelle Dieu
> nous l'a donné, et non pas pour un objet contraire.[8]

Viewed as a germ of the Apologia, however, it yields less
than the other texts I have cited.

One further example may be taken from the first paragraph of the sketch for a preface to the *Traité du Vide*
in 1651:

> Le respect que l'on porte à l'antiquité étant aujour-
> d'hui à tel point, dans les matières où il doit avoir
> moins de force, que l'on se fait des oracles de toutes
> ses pensées, et des mystères même de ses obscurités.[9]

The distinction made here between meaningful and meaning-
less obscurity will be used later to answer criticisms of
the Old Testament. The principal lesson one gleans from
the preface, however, is more general: it is the very
lucid distinction Pascal draws between the domain of reason and the domain of faith, as he discusses the nature
of authority. The principles of theology are 'au-dessus
de la nature et de la raison,' and we need to have the
authority of Scripture; in matters which do fall 'sous
les sens ou sous le raisonnement,' we require a very different set of rules by which we can hope gradually to un-
cover 'les secrets de la nature.'

A rather different, indeed a caricatural view of the
'orders' is made in the flattering letter which accompanied
the arithmetical machine Pascal sent to Queen Christiana
of Sweden in 1652.[10] There the only distinction is between
reason and the senses. In marked contrast to the letter
to Gilberte about figures, the reality of the spiritual
order is nowhere implied.

Pascal's scientific work continued, and in 1654 intense
reflection on the mathematics of gambling led to the Law
of Probability and the *Traité du Triangle arithmétique*.
The treatise was printed but never published, presumably
because after his definitive conversion Pascal renounced
the pleasures of scholarly prestige.[11] The thinking enshrined in the treatise and in his correspondence of this
period does, however, make its mark on the Apologia, with
the motif of the 'partis' in section 12°.

Together with the general notion of three levels or
orders, I shall retain from these years two particularly
significant notions: that there is a place for rational
argument with people who are outside the faith; and that
as God is 'hidden,' discernment is needed if physical
phenomena are to point to spiritual realities and not
obscure them.

*(b) Ils s'anéantissent pour faire place à la vérité de
l'Evangile*[12]

After November 1654, the date of the so-called 'second
conversion,' recorded in a document known as the Mémorial,
Pascal's desire to reach the unbelievers of his milieu
manifests itself more clearly.[13] The Mémorial itself,
with its fervent affirmation of the nature of the Christian God of love, is a first step in this direction. The
strongly Christocentric tendency of Pascal's theology
was evident in his letter on death, in 1651, but it is
the Mémorial which reveals the guiding thought behind
Pascal's apologetics: an overwhelming experience of God,
which will make him burn to show other men not merely
that God exists, but that their lives can be transformed
if only they open themselves to God's holy spirit.[14] The
words of the Mémorial ('Dieu d'Abraham, Dieu d'Isaac,
Dieu de Jacob, non des philosophes et des savants. Certitude, certitude, sentiment, joie, paix') are echoed in
449 (Unit V), whose crucial important in the Apologia
has been underlined in chapter 15.

In 1655 Pascal's apolegetic mission took shape, and he
discussed with M. de Sacy of Port-Royal an argument which
he had conceived.[15] He would take two authors revered by
the *honnête homme*, Epictetus and Montaigne, and show that
as they stand, their views are irreconcilable.

Epictetus taught that God was the principal object of
man's moral endeavour. Life comes from God; we should
accept what God has chosen for us, recognize God's will,
and follow it. Pascal criticizes Epictetus not for his
fundamental insight into the primacy of God, which Pascal
naturally accepts (he had said the same in his letter to
Gilberte of 1 April 1648), but for the assumption that
what he prescribes is within man's power. Epictetus writes
as if the mind and will are free, so that we have the
means to do our duty and find felicity.

Montaigne is presented as a 'pur pyrrhonien.' His object
is to demonstrate that if one fails to acknowledge the
authority of revelation, it becomes quite impossible to
find certainty anywhere. One cannot be sure that one is
right, nor can one be sure that one is wrong. The soul
cannot understand its own nature; the assumption that it
is spiritual creates as many problems as the assumption
that it is material. Reason can never attain certainty
if truth is regarded as independent of God. This irrefutable onslaught on the claims of natural reason, Pascal
says, gave him great joy. Nevertheless, Montaigne is
seriously at fault for he applies the same critical
method to man's search for 'le bien,' concluding that
when we are faced with a choice, only example and com-
modity can help us choose wisely. Happiness consists in
taking the line of least resistance. What Montaigne, as
a Catholic, should have said, was that in view of the
uncertainties that surround us, we must take care to dis-
please God as little as possible.

In effect then, Montaigne writes as if man has no access
to God, and is condemned to an infernal circle of perpetual doubt. Together, Montaigne and Epictetus illustrate
the two paths open to man if he places himself outside
the Christian revelation, trusting his reason alone.

On ne peut suivre qu'une de ces deux routes, savoir:
ou qu'il y a un Dieu, et lors il y place son souverain
bien; ou qu'il est incertain, et qu'alors le vrai bien
l'est aussi, puisqu'il en est incapable.

Pascal then formulates his critique of the two authors.
Both systems leave out of account the essential understanding of Christianity, that man is both fallen and
redeemed. Epictetus's man is not fallen, Montaigne's is
not redeemed. As a consequence, the teaching of Epictetus
encourages pride and presumption, that of Montaigne laziness and moral cowardice. Both authors are useful, both
are dangerous; taken together, they could be salutary,
as each points to the inadequacies of the other. But it
is impossible, Pascal says, to reconcile naturally the
two doctrines. Reconciliation is found only in the perspective of the Christian gospel, which admits both sides
of man's nature, and explains the apparent incompatibili-
ties by the doctrine of the fall and redemption of man.

Although Jean Mesnard may be right in saying that this
is strictly speaking a pedagogic, not an apologetic text,
which could well be entitled 'l'utilité des lectures,'
it is clearly of great importance in tracing the genesis
of Pascal's Apologia.[16] If Epictetus manifests 'un art
incomparable pour troubler le repos de ceux qui le cherchent dans les choses extérieures,' forcing them to recognize the extent of their corruption, and if Montaigne is
'incomparable pour confondre l'orgueil de ceux qui, hors
la foi, se piquent d'une véritable justice,'[17] and if,
moreover, 'ces lectures doivent être réglées avec beaucoup de soin,' we are obliged to conclude that Pascal had
in mind readers who would be more ready to believe
Epictetus and/or Montaigne than the Gospels, but who would
be ready to allow someone to guide their reading. In other
words, Pascal seems already to be thinking of a person
willing to listen to the Christian case, without yet
abandoning his own predilections.

The confrontation of Epictetus and Montaigne has ultimately a psychological effect, that of worrying the
reader who, conscious of having been led into an impasse,
will look elsewhere. The process is well described by
Gouhier:

> Il ne s'agit pas d'une recherche de la vérité avec une
> zone de vérités rationnelles à traverser avant d'entrer
> dans celle des vérités de foi: il s'agit d'une prépara-
> tion à la conversion en créant une situation propice
> à l'action de la grâce s'il plaît à Dieu de l'envoyer.[18]

It occurs in the Apologia as a fundamental strategy: 'le
faire chercher chez les philosophes ... qui travailleront
celui qui le recherche' (4/1°).

The organization of the argument already shows some of
the fundamental characteristics of the Apologia, even if
the details are often quite different. Chief among the
differences is that in the paragraphs on Epictetus the
emphasis falls on what Pascal was later to call the 'recherche du bien,' whereas with Montaigne, Pascal distinguishes between his attitude to *le vrai* and his attitude
to *le bien*, reproaching Montaigne with putting them on
the same level. In the Apologia proper, this distinction
governs the internal ordering of the *liasses*.

When Pascal comes to a confrontation of Epictetus and Montaigne, however, the patterns he makes are virtually the same as in the Apologia, and they are clearly much more intuitively felt than the distinction between *le vrai* and *le bien*, which is really only a convenience for the clear presentation of his case. In identifying the parallel dangers inherent in the two systems, and showing that Christian doctrine accommodates the dual portrait by its dogma of the two states of man, Pascal reveals the coherent central tenet which will animate many a paradox.

There is reason to believe that a handful of *pensées* draw on the *Entretien* not only because Pascal went on to refine the framework he had expounded here, but because there are precise textual parallels.[19] The paragraph beginning 'Voilà, monsieur,' for example, contains in germ most of the material of section 9°, though the tone is less virulent, and we are at liberty to believe that the ninth *liasse* collects together notes taken during the same period as the *Entretien*. The critique of reason and the exposure of the relativity of justice (one example in the *Entretien* of the 'vanité des opinions les plus reçues') are developed in fragments 76 and 60, found on the same two sheets. Another group of important *pensées* (109, 110, 131, 208, maybe 149) develops the *Entretien*'s unifying frame, and uses a very similar vocabulary.[20] As this group contains echoes of another work of the same period yet to be examined, I postpone discussion of all this until the end of the next section.

(c) non seulement par la raison, mais par le coeur (110)

The pedagogical concerns of 1655 come to the fore in the opuscule to which Jean Mesnard has restored the title *De l'esprit géométrique*.[21] Pedagogy was one of the principal tasks of Port-Royal, and not surprisingly Pascal's talents were drawn upon. *De l'esprit géométrique* attempts to iden-tify the strengths of mathematical reasoning and give guidance as to how it can be acquired. The first of its two parts ('Reflexions sur la Géométrie en général')[22] treats of the perfection of geometric method. The ideal method, says Pascal, would be the perfection of geometric method. The ideal method, says Pascal, would be to define everything and to go on to prove everything. But this is impossible, as in order to formulate our first definition, we would be obliged to use words we had not defined.

'D'où il paraît que les hommes sont dans une impuissance
naturelle et immuable de traiter quelque science que ce
soit, dans un ordre absolument accompli.' Geometric method
is the best we have, as the premisses it has to accept
are simple and will not be doubted by anyone of good will.

> Il ne suppose que des choses claires et constantes par
> la lumière naturelle, et c'est pourquoi il est parfaite-
> ment véritable, la nature le soutenant au défaut du
> discours ... La géométrie ne définit aucune de ces
> choses, espace, temps, mouvement, nombre, égalité...

The words we use for these basic elements simply designate universally known phenomena; they have nothing to
tell us about the nature of these phenomena. Definitions
of things which are known to everyone, as they are the basic
data of existence, are confusing and foolish. These things
need neither definition nor proof. Conversely, geometry will
prove step by step everything which lies outside the category of universally recognized phenomena, 'de sorte que
tout ce que la géométrie propose est parfaitement démontré,
ou par la lumière naturelle, ou par les preuves.'
Our reflection rests therefore on three fundamental
data: movement, number, and space. By rigorous reasoning
we can arrive at conclusions which far outstrip the evidence of the senses alone. Thus, the concept of number
implies a double infinity, as any number can theoretically
be increased or decreased indefinitely. Pascal's position
on the truths known to 'la lumière naturelle' might seem
like an answer to the scepticism of the *Entretien*[23] (from
which he borrows one example of words impossible to define)[24] if we did not know that the principles he enunciates had guided him for several years in his scientific
and mathematical work. The scope and relation of the two
lower 'orders' (senses and reason) are clarified in a
definitive manner.
Pascal summarizes his position by saying that geometry
gives certainty but not conviction. The geometric method,
as he conceives it, is an antidote to our tendency to dismiss what we cannot understand. We can reasonably dismiss
a statement only when it is irreconcilable with something
certain. He illustrates this with a long development on
divisibles and indivisibles. This passage contains the germ
of the celebrated fragement on 'les deux infinis' (199) and
also of the orders (here the 'grandeurs homogènes' of Euclid).

> Toutes ces grandeurs sont divisibles à l'infini, sans
> tomber dans leurs indivisibles, de sorte qu'elles
> tiennent toutes le milieu entre l'infini et le néant.

This mathematical argument leads Pascal to a conclusion
on man's place in the universe, which is echoed in fragment 199 and elsewhere (eg, 119 'Que l'homme maintenant
s'estime son prix').

> Mais ceux qui verront clairment ces vérités pourront
> admirer la grandeur et la puissance de la nature dans
> cette double infinité qui nous environne de toutes
> parts, et apprendre par cette considération merveilleuse
> à se connaître eux-mêmes, en se regardant placés entre
> une infinité et un néant d'étendue, entre une infinité
> et un néant de nombre, entre une infinité et un néant
> de mouvement, entre une infinité et un néant de temps.
> Sur quoi on peut apprendre à s'estimer à son juste prix,
> et former des réflexions qui valent mieux que tout le
> reste de la géometrie.

The second part of *De l'Esprit géométrique* is entitled
'De l'Art de persuader,'[25] and it brings in the third
'order' and also what I must call its diabolic counterpart. Setting aside the acquisition of religious faith
(I shall return to this), Pascal starts by positing that
we give our assent either to something which our minds
acknowledge as true, or else to something which our wills
find pleasing. Problems arise when these two influences
conflict with each other. Anyone wishing to persuade another person of something needs to understand what the
recipient will respond to on both levels, 'de sorte que
l'art de persuader consiste autant en celui d'agréer
qu'en celui de convaincre, tant les hommes se gouvernent
plus par caprice que par raison!'
He feels himeself able to indicate how an argument can
be presented persuasively to reason, but incapable of
teaching the subtle art of *agrément*. We are back then
with the mathematical order of part one, and Pascal formulates a number of rules we should follow if we are to
master the art of persuading other people that our case
is intellectually sound. At the same time, we are left
with an uncomfortable feeling that the art of persuasion
is vastly more complex, and that to be wholly convincing
and effective, Pascal will have to integrate both our need

to be captivated, and also the issue of religious faith.
When he does so, he will have less confidence in the effectiveness of geometric method.[26]

In the first part of 'De l'Art de persuader,' Pascal
excludes the transmission of divine truths from this art
of human persuasion. 'Dieu seul peut les mettre dans l'âme,
et par la manière qu'il lui plaît.' He elaborates for a
few paragraphs. In human affairs it is prudent to pass
from knowledge to enjoyment, from the mind to the heart.
God, wishing to humiliate human reason, for the perfection
of its method risks circumventing the need for faith,
conveys the truth about himself to the heart, whence it
must be transmitted to the mind. Now men have in fact
done the same, though they are reluctant to admit it; we
accept or reject a thing according to whether it appeals
to us. It is understandable then that we should reject
the Christian religion, 'tout opposée à nos plaisirs.'
God is therefore obliged not only to humiliate reason,
but also to tame the rebellious heart or will.

Although 'De l'Art de persuader' then moves off in another direction, identifying the rules by which an argument will convince the mind, and neglecting both the heart
and the issue of faith, these opening paragraphs are
manifestly very important for the pre-history of the
Apologia. Once Pascal has the motivation to compose a
fully-fledged apologia, he will necessarily have to bear
in mind what he says here, that Christian truths mediated
directly to the reason will be resisted by the heart, and
that God converts by attacking the heart first, by delec-
tation.

This further meditation was in all probability not long
in coming. It is natural to pass from the discussion of
the *Entretien* and *De l'esprit géométrique*, believed to
have been written in 1655, to a small number of substantial *pensées* which reflect them: nos 60, 76, 109, 110,
131, 149, 208, and 418, with its satellites 419-26. Even
if several months elapsed between the writing of *De l'esprit géométrique* and these other fragments, there is no
logical hiatus.[27] The fact that they echo both the texts
we have been discussing makes it difficult to believe
that they were written significantly later. Had it been
a case of Pascal's going back after a couple of years to
the Sacy notes and elaborating them, we would not expect
to find so many parallels with the *Esprit géométrique*.

Let us first summarize the points Pascal has made in these writings of 1655, fitting the two parts of *De l'esprit géométrique* in a frame provided by the *Entretien*. Natural reason, acting outside any framework of revelation, produces total scepticism. The geometric method, which builds from certainty to certainty, has to accept the existence of certain fundamentals which no man can seriously call into question. But man cannot live by geometry alone. Such is the power of concupiscence that our inclination is to find reasons to justify what appeals to us, rather than to relish what we know to be true. And because of that, religious truths are vouchsafed directly to the heart; God addresses himself to what is really opposing him, and by doing so humiliates reason, source of pride. It is thus quite inadequate to hope with the Stoics that man will be able to recognize God and to live in conformity with him. Man is a fallen creature. But he is also redeemed, and must not let his weakness sap his moral life.

The sceptical argument is developed in two fragments contained on a pair of pages, covered on both sides. The fact that they are written in this way shows that Pascal had not realized that he would need to file his papers under distinct headings. Two and one-half sides are taken up with a long reflection on laws, filed in *liasse* 3° (Lafuma 60). The remaining one and one-half sides contain a very different development, which it is reasonable to identify with the 'lettre de la folie humaine' of no. 408;[28] they have been crossed out. Lafuma, following the example of Copy 9203, puts this development at the end of the section, and gives it the number 76. The manuscript presents editors and commentators with several knotty problems. It is not at all clear either how Pascal came to combine two such different reflections on the same sheets,[29] nor what he meant by a marginal indication which seems to link them together.[30] When he filed them, however, he left only no. 60 intact, deleting the whole of no. 76.

Whatever the facts of the matter, it is clear that we have here two essays, probably written at about the same time, which develop ideas touched on in the Montaigne section of the *Entretien*, and drawing, like the *Entretien*, principally on the *Apologie de Raymond Sebond*.

The top of the first page is missing,[31] which explains why both *pensées* begin by alluding to something which has

just preceded. No. 60 begins: 'en vérité la vanité des
lois il s'en délivrerait, il est donc utile de l'abuser.'
Pascal has evidently been saying that if men realized
how vain laws turn out to be, they would ignore the laws.
But what could be substituted for them? Justice is not
known to man; the variety shown by different, even neigh-
bouring countries, in the kinds of behaviour they permit
is ample evidence of that. It is impossible even to speak
of natural laws. All we can go on is custom; it is foolish
to try to go beyond this, as we shall never arrive at any
universally acceptable conclusion.[32]

Fragment 76 is a critique of reason in general. Pascal
has been dealing (either in the first few lines, or in a
previous passage to which this is the sequel) with a subject which 'passe la portée de la raison,'[33] so he will
turn now to subjects where reason is more likely to feel
at home. Where do men locate the Sovereign Good? There
is so great a diversity in the answers which have been
given that we must conclude that we do not know. Second
enquiry: what do philosophers say of the nature of the
soul? That too proves fruitless. Third enquiry, on the
other sheet: can the mind understand the body, and matter?
The conclusion must be, that reason is a very limited
instrument. But reason will not accept that conclusion,
it continues to search, hoping one day to find the answers.
So the enquiry must continue, with the question: has reason the capacity to 'saisir la vérité'?

There is no identifiable sequel to no. 76, but we know
where this fourth enquiry would have led us: to a radical
scepticism tempered only by the observation that no man
can actually live according to the tenets of an absolute
scepticism. With this we join nos 109, 110 and 131. These
three fragments all begin from what Pascal calls the
sceptics' strongest suit: our inability to find independent proof of the certainty of what he now calls 'les
premiers principes.'

The first sentence of no. 109, subsequently crossed
out, read: 'C'est donc une chose étrange qu'on ne peut
définir ces choses sans les obscurcir.'[34] The *pensée*
thus followed on some such idea as that defining first
principles introduces words less certain than the words
for the principles themselves. The argument is familiar
from the 1655 texts. In no. 109 Pascal goes as far as to
say that the fact that a certain basic vocabulary is
universally accepted does not mean that everyone conceives

the notions in the same way.[35] 'La clarté naturelle' is
not on that account extinguished, but it is less bright
than we might think. One can reasonably assume 'une con-
formité d'idée,' but 'cela n'est pas absolument convaincant, puisqu'on sait qu'on tire souvent les mêmes conséquences des suppositions différentes.'

In no. 110, Pascal repeats what he said in the 'Réflexions sur la Géométrie' but slants it more directly towards the sceptics. The sceptics cannot call first principles into question, they can only indicate the weakness
of reason, unable to prove the existence of these basic
data. Reason has to build on 'ces connaissances du coeur
et de l'instinct,' and thus certainty is possible.

A second paragraph shows that Pascal has been trying
to adapt the problem of faith to his scheme. Faith is a
basic principle too, though not one universally shared,
as a consequence of the fall. 'Et c'est pour quoi ceux
à qui Dieu a donné la religion par sentiment de coeur
sont bienheureux et bien légitimement persuadés.' Furthermore, he has been wondering if a reasoned exposition cannot help a man to find faith. This is very like the point
he made in 1647 to M. de Rebours,[36] and it has the same
qualification now as then:

> Mais ceux [sic] qui ne l'ont pas nous ne pouvons la
> donner que par raisonnement en attendant que Dieu la
> leur donne par sentiment de coeur, sans quoi la foi
> n'est qu'humaine et inutile pour le salut.

Fragment 131 takes us much further than these reflections on the limits of scepticism, but it begins in the
same way. We have no certainty of the truth of these
principles, other than an inborn feeling that they are
so. But if we do not have the conviction born of faith,
that we are the creatures of God, we cannot trust our
instincts to lead us to truth: 'ce sentiment naturel n'est
pas une preuve convaincante.' Nevertheless we cannot
doubt such deeply ingrained convictions. The text is very
close to one part of the *Entretien*, and it also mirrors
the 'Réflexions' in its distinction between conviction
and certainty.[37] Pascal here defines those who hold that
'en parlant de bonne foi et sincèrement on ne peut douter
des principes naturels' - the very attitude he had himself advocated in the 'Réflexions' - as 'dogmatists.'
Now this is different from the *Entretien*, where the

contrast was between the Stoics, who accept that God
exists and that he is necessarily our Sovereign Good,
and the sceptics who say that we cannot know God and
consequently we cannot identify *le vrai bien*. There is
a certain confusion here, which Pascal sorted out in the
pensées we are discussing, between the two searches, for
'le vrai' and for 'le bien.' Montaigne's initial question,
as it is presented in the *Entretien*, concerns 'le bien'
('quelle morale la raison devrait dicter sans la lumière
de la foi'), while the argument concentrated on the impossibility of finding truth. Epictetus was presented
as a searcher for the Sovereign Good, though it was mentioned that he held that 'l'esprit ne peut être forcé de
croire ce qu'il sait être faux.' Only at the end did
Pascal find a connecting formula which implies an even
balance between the two strands of his exposé:

> il arrive que l'un, connaissant les devoirs de l'homme
> et ignorant son impuissance, se perd dans la présomp-
> tion, et que l'autre, connaissant l'impuissance et non
> le devoir, il s'abat dans la lâcheté ... l'un établis-
> sant la certitude, l'autre le doute, l'un la grandeur
> de l'homme, l'autre sa faiblesse.[38]

Pascal is still unable to dissociate the two searches
completely; in no. 131, arguing that life may be a dream,
and really addressing himself to the issue of truth, he
argues that life may be a dream 'pendant laquelle [sic]
nous avons aussi peu les principes du vrai *et du bien*
que pendant le sommeil naturel.' But in no. 131 and the
other fragments we are considering, the opposition of
sceptics and Stoics is replaced by the more precisely
focused contrast of sceptics and dogmatists. No. 208
specifically identifies two pairs: Stoics and Epicureans,
Dogmatists and Academicians. The second page of no. 149
elaborates on the opposition Stoic/Epicurean in a way
which balances the Dogmatist/Pyrrhonian antithesis developed
elsewhere. The Stoics are defined in the same way as the
Entretien ('S'ils vous ont donné Dieu pour objet, ce n'a
été que pour exercer votre superbe'), while the Epicureans
are said to encourage concupiscence and make man like the
beasts.
By opposing Stoic and sceptic Pascal wished to show
that two plausible views of man were irreconcilable without the Christian doctrine of the double nature of man:

his original, true nature, and his present, fallen nature.
Epictetus forgot the second, Montaigne the first:

> l'un remarquant quelques traces de sa première grandeur,
> et ignorant sa corruption, a traité la nature comme
> saine et sans besoin de réparateur, ce qui le mène au
> comble de la superbe; au lieu que l'autre, éprouvant la
> misère présente et ignorant la première dignité, traite
> la nature comme nécessairement infirme et irréparable,
> ce qui le précipite dans le désespoir...[39]

He makes exactly the same point in no. 131, now opposing
sceptics and dogmatists, and he again describes the situation as a 'war.' Neither side can maintain its position
totally. 'La nature confond les pyrrhoniens et la raison
confond les dogmatiques.' Reason and nature cannot provide the answer; we must listen to God. In the *Entretien*,
the Christian resolution was outlined in the concluding
lines; in no. 131 there is a longer development which
takes us temporarily away from the *Entretien*, and which
also raises some difficult textual questions.

The following page starts not with the words of God,
but with these three sentences:

> N'est-il donc pas clair comme le jour que la condition
> de l'homme est double? Certainement si l'homme n'avait
> jamais été corrompu il jouirait dans son innocence et
> de la vérité et de la félicité avec assurance. Et si
> l'homme n'avait jamais été que corrompu il n'aurait
> aucune idée de la vérité, ni de la béatitude.

One notices that truth and felicity are given equal rights
in this part of the argument, which was hardly the case
in all that went before; that the key notion of man's
corruption has been introduced out of the blue; and that
Pascal seems to be presenting an argument, in his characteristic manner, rather than writing a Prosopopoeia. As
the passage quoted begins a new page, we may wish to believe that it was written at a different time. The handwriting, however, does not give any support to this
theory, nor is the watermark different.

The thought of the paragraph just quoted is completed
by saying that we are 'malheureux,' haunted by ideals
which are unattainable. Conclusion: man is incomprehensible to himself without the insights given by faith.

Yet, Pascal continues, the doctrine which removes the
difficulty is itself incomprehensible, even apparently
unjust. God has chosen thus deliberately, so that we will
learn to submit, rather than to trust our reason in all
things (cf. 'De l'art de persuader'). Two truths are
taught by religion: that man in the state of Creation,
or of grace, is like God himself, and that in the state
of corruption, he is like the beasts.

No. 131 has a sequel: no. 208, which began 'Nous pouvons marcher sûrement à la clarté de ces célestes lumières.'[40] Without an understanding of his double nature,
man has seen himself in either his corrupt or his redeemed state, and this accounts for the diversity of
philosophical positions, 'les diverses sectes des stoïques
et des épicuriens, des dogmatistes et des académiciens,'
which have engendered either pride or despair. Only
Christianity has been able to expel these vices, elevating
without pride, humbling without despair. The truth of this
diagnosis is something we can all experience within ourselves. All this page of no. 208 uses the precise vocabulary of the last part of the *Entretien*, and the similarities cannot be fortuitous, even if the ideas are common in Pascal's work.

The fragment ends:

Que nous crie donc ce chaos et cette confusion monstrueuse sinon la vérité de ces deux états avec une voix
si puissante qu'il est impossible de résister? Car
en[fin]

If we now turn back to no. 131, we find at the end of
the first part that Pascal asks 'Quelle chimère est-ce
donc que l'homme? quelle nouveauté, quel monstre, quel
chaos, quel sujet de contradictions? ... Qui démêlera
cet embrouillement?' The sequel, seven lines in the
Luxembourg edition, was rewritten, twice, in the right-
hand margin.[41] On the next page come the three sentences
quoted earlier. The first is crossed out, and the word
'Certainement' replaced with 'Car enfin.' It is usually
assumed that this page is to follow on from no. 208,
which can therefore no longer follow on from no. 131.[42]
The matter is very complicated, and it is not made any
easier by a similarly involved set of clues which lead
us to no. 149.

No. 149 is of course the important development subsequently headed 'A P.R.' Now the second page of this no.
149 is entitled 'Prosopopée,' and we remember that no.
131 bade us 'listen to God.' Though the ideas are of the
same general purport as the ones we have been looking at,
the emphasis here is all on felicity rather than truth.
There are several reminiscences of the last part of no.
131, both in the text itself (where we have the opposition God/beasts as well as the theme of felicity, which
is difficult to account for in no. 131), and in the notes
which complete the verso side of the page:

Vous n'êtes pas dans l'état de votre création.[43]

Tant de contradictions se trouveraient-elles dans un
sujet simple?

Incompréhensible.
Tout ce qui est incompréhensible ne laisse pas d'être.

This last fragment turns up again in fragment 809 (Unit
XXIX), where Pascal writes: 'Incompréhensible que Dieu
soit et incompréhensible qu'il ne soit pas'; it hearks
back to a remark in the 'Réflexions sur la Géométrie,'
that we cannot dismiss a concept simply because it is
'incomprehensible.'
    These parallels are troubling. But whatever the precise
filiation from one text to another, we can surely infer
that the thinking of the *Entretien* and *De l'esprit géométrique* was continued in the months that followed, opening up vistas which take us, all too rapidly, to the
period of the Apologia proper, subject of chapter 31.
    Pursuing traces of the 1655 projects, we have alighted
on a number of well developed texts which look as if they
once belonged to a single argument, part of which is now
missing. Shortly after the Second World War, P.L. Couchoud
attempted to reconstruct a *Discours sur la condition de
l'homme* which he saw as a first version of the Apologia.[44]
The scepticism with which his efforts were greeted shows
how perilous the enterprise was.[45] He was criticized
chiefly for believing that reflections on large sheets
were somehow different in origin from the fragments which
have been preserved on small sheets. What Couchoud did
not realize, it was said, is that Pascal *always* wrote on
large sheets. But that is really a rather silly objection,
because Pascal did *not* always write passages of sustained

prose, and the existence of a dozen or so draft 'chapters' implies that as well as noting down short reflections and later filing them, he did sometimes think in larger sequences. It is not unreasonable to go on from there and wonder if these are part of a single enterprise. In view of the highly speculative nature of Couchoud's reconstruction, I prefer to limit my chronological survey to those texts which do appear to be written in the wake of the writings of 1655, but I ought briefly to mention what other fragments Couchoud associated with the *Discours*.

Couchoud quoted no. 199 first, following on from eight chapters which, he says, are lost.[46] This the famous *pensée* now known as the 'Disproportion de l'homme,' and originally beginning: 'Voilà où nous mènent les connaissances naturelles.[47] Si celles-là ne sont véritables il n'y a point de vérité pour l'homme, et si elles le sont, il y trouve un grand sujet d'humiliation, forcé à s'abaisser d'une ou d'autre manière.' It clearly belongs to the same sceptical current as the rest of the group we have looked at. One sentence is almost identical to a sentence in no. 131.[48]

In Couchoud's scheme, no. 76 would have been chapter 13,[49] and would have been followed by no. 148: 'Seconde partie. Que l'homme sans la foi ne peut connaître le vrai bien, ni la justice.' Again one is obliged to salute what seems to be a good hunch, but express reservations as to the details of the working out. The phrase 'sans la foi' brings no. 148 into the same orbit as the other fragments on the fruitless quest for 'le vrai.' But no. 76 began with a section on the contradictory claims to have found the Sovereign Good.

Fragment 408 notes that a 'letter' which it is easy to identify with the first part of no. 76 should be placed 'avant le divertissement.' This may well mean that the parts of no. 76 were to have been expanded separately. Couchoud places after no. 148 various long fragments on *le divertissement:* 47,[50] 137, 139, 136. No. 148 announces as the next theme, 'la justice.' This is clearly no. 60, to be followed, Couchoud says, by the second part of no. 76 ('transposez après les lois...') - although this part of no. 76 (on differing views of the soul) sends us back to no. 199.

The third part, Couchoud says plausibly, was to have shown that reason was viciated. Here we would have nos 44 and 45 on imagination.[51] Couchoud here introduces

the anti-pyrrhonist nos 109 and 110, followed very properly
by no. 131 (incorporating no. 208), which passes from the
dilemma of natural philosophy to the Christian resolution.
It seems to me that, while Couchoud's 'reconstruction' may
have been overambitious, his intuition that Pascal developed
the *Entretien* into a longer discourse of which several significant parts remain, is probably sound. Other developed
passages, not used by Couchoud, could reasonably be associated with the project, such as 117, 119, and 121. Couchoud
concludes with 'Infini rien' (418), which is a reasonable
suggestion, even if, as Couchoud admitted and Béguin underlined, the large sheets which make up this essay are quite
different from the other large sheets which were Couchoud's
prime justification for claiming that there was once an
independent *Discours sur la condition de l'homme*. I would
agree that 'Infini rien' is another development made in
the wake of the *Entretien* and *De l'esprit géométrique*.
More obviously than the other *pensées* we have been considering, however, it explodes in new directions, and it
has seemed to me sufficiently rich and complex to merit
being treated in a separate section.

(d) Infini rien

If the fragments we have been discussing hardly step outside the range of themes touched on in the writings of
1655, fragments 418-26 (Unit II in the accepted numbering)
open up exciting new possibilities.

No. 418, headed 'Infini rien,' takes as its starting-
point one of the longer developments in the 'Réflexions':
that finite quantities can all be increased or reduced.[52]
It makes the by now familiar points, that we have to accept the basic data and construct our rational systems
upon them, and that by reflection on the nature of finite
quantities, we can conceive that infinity must exist,
although we cannot understand its nature.[53]

Our knowledge of God can be described in analogous
terms. As God has no point of contact with us, we cannot
know his existence in the way we can know the existence
of infinity. We know God not by geometric reason working
on the given elements of our corporal existence but by
faith. A small number of additions prepare for this conclusion, while at the same time obscuring the march of
the argument. One concerns God's justice.[54]

Having established that reason cannot know God, Pascal
continues his argument solely according to the desires of
the heart. If faith is of the heart, and if the heart is

the seat of concupiscence, can we persuade ourselves to effect a change of heart? The argument which follows this formulation of the problem illustrates Pascal's contention that reason can be used in matters of faith, although it can never replace it. We desire happiness; how do we achieve it, through accepting Christianity, or through rejecting it? By accepting it, says Pascal; for Christianity promises that after death we will be eternally blessed or damned. But if this claim is false? In that case, says Pascal, we will stand to gain, because although the austerity of Christianity seems inimical to self-will, it in fact produces a more lasting happiness than any amount of pleasure-seeking.

This basic argument is greatly expanded. First of all, of course, there is the mathematical argument with which Pascal weighs the finite against infinity. Here we meet again the kind of arguments Pascal had developed in 1654 in connection with the mathematics of gabmling, now applied to a religious issue.

The expansion of the last part touches on a variety of matters. That there are in fact reasons for belief: the Scriptures. That the real reason for not believing comes from the passions. That the passions can be tamed by going through the outward motions of Christian devotion. This is all quite consistent with the first part of 'L'Art de persuader,' but it is now being given specific direction. The thoughts which Pascal scribbled below no. 418, and in the margin, strengthen this impression, as we shall see.

If no. 418 is integrated into the Apologia (and I have shown in chapter 12 that it can be, without strain), the uncompromising stand it takes appears to be softened somewhat. In the Apologia Pascal does not put reason out of court, except in so far as saving grace is of God, not of man. But his chief positive proof is historical; that is, by the Incarnation, God entered the world of finite man and gave reason something to work on. This aspect, implied in the word 'l'Ecriture' in 418, but not explained further, will give the necessary counterbalance to the first page of 'Infini rien.'

The fourth and last page of that essay contains various separate fragments, numbered 419-26 by Lafuma.

The first is a gloss on the first sentence of no. 418, summarized above, about the soul having to accept certain data of experience. It is impossible for us not to believe them. In no. 419 Pascal calls this 'custom,' and makes three points: that we can accustom ourselves to faith and then find ourselves incapable of disbelief; that in daily life, once we grow used to an idea, [we firmly believe it];[55] that consequently our soul, accustomed to number, space, movement, necessarily believes them. The interest of this *pensée*, replaced in its context, is that the notion of custom, implied in the advice to the non-believer to adopt new habits, becomes a focal centre unifying ideas about faith, day-to-day experience, and epistemology; and also that the last of these applications, which one would think the best established (it was after all the starting-point for this manuscript) is presented as a consequence of the other two.

Beneath that, and separated from it by a line, comes a finite analogy to show that it is possible to conceive an infinite being (420), clearly another gloss on page 1, in the same vein as *De l'esprit géométrique*.

The next idea to be noted down was probably no. 424, written in the left-hand margin. Again it grows out of the concerns of page 1, where Pascal had said that God is known only by faith. Pascal finds a formula with which to define faith, using the distinction between reason and heart familiar from no. 110 and the 'Art de persuader':

> C'est le coeur qui sent Dieu et non la raison. Voilà
> ce que c'est que la foi. Dieu sensible au coeur, non
> à la raison.

There are two more fragments below no. 424, and a sign indicates that the uppermost one is the continuation of the lower. Lafuma gives the double fragment the number 421; Brunschvicg kept them separate (Br. 447 and 606). The theme is self-love. We are born with the will to place ourselves in the centre, which is clearly unjust, a negation of order. The sequel appears unrelated: only Christianity teaches that man is born in sin. The connection is probably in the unspoken thought that if our will is depraved, a religion must include this as part of its teaching about man. Then Pascal adds another idea, triggered off, one supposes, by the phrase 'nulle religion que la nôtre': no other religion or sect, he says, has been in existence since the beginning of time. The remark is very cryptic, but there are other fragments which elucidate it. The idea will become a major argument in the historical part of the Apologia.

Three more *pensées* need to be mentioned. Above no. 424, moving out towards the top left-hand corner, is no. 426, on the contrast between Christianity and *honnêteté*. Christianity is the only way to realize the idea of *honnêteté*,

making man both 'aimable et heureux.' This is a gloss on
the conclusion to no. 418.

No. 423 is written at the top of the page, the page having now been turned through 180°. It is another reflection
on the heart, which has its own 'reasons,' quite different
from those of reason. In the 'Art de persuader,' heart and
will were more or less interchangeable. Subsequently, the
heart has tended to be reserved for the intuitive acceptance
of the fundamentals of life - including faith for those
blessed enough to have it - while the will (as in no. 421)
is the seat of self-love. Bring them together again, and
you can say that the heart will love either God or the self,
both naturally. What influences the choice? Not reason,
surely, as it is not by reason that a man loves himself (as
no. 421 has made clear).

Page 4 being full, Pascal finds a space on page 3 to set
down his final thought. Like no. 421, it unites the theme
of perpetuity with the theme of concupiscence, seen as an
obstacle to religion:

> La seule science qui est contre le sens commun et la
> nature des hommes est la seule qui ait toujours sub-
> sisté parmi les hommes (425)

The 'Infini rien' manuscript is evidently of capital importance in the gestation of Pascal's Apologia. Beginning
with a theological consideration of the positions taken in
De l'esprit géométrique (1655), passing through an argument
ad hominem which involves mathematical considerations closely
related to the problems which exercised him in 1654, and
concluding with an exhortation to the interlocutor to change
his way of life, the four pages of Unit II touch upon countless motifs which will have to be amplified, but which are
recognizable as early versions of essential strands in the
Apologia. Thus we encounter the pre-rational nature of faith,
the argument from self-interest, applied both to the here-
after and to the here and now, the proof from Scripture, the
need to discipline the passions, and the way that can be
done. Further jottings isolate the theme of custom (in
faith, in daily living, and in the acquisition of certainty), the superiority of Christianity, both in the diagnosis it makes of man's sinfulness and in its long history,
the role of the heart as the recipient of grace and as the
centre of concupiscence, the self-centredness and the power
of the depraved will. Amplification of these ideas will
produce much of the basic material of the Apologia. But
the Apologia is fed, in all probability virtually simultaneously, from another source which we must now examine.

(e) *les malheureux qui nous ont obligé de parler du fond de la Religion (862).*

During the year 1656 Pascal was deeply involved in the conflict which opposed Port-Royal and the Society of Jesus. The first of his *Provinciales* was published on 23 January, and in the next fourteen months he was to write eighteen of these public letters. The first letters discuss the condemnation of Antoine Arnauld by the Sorbonne, and in effect accuse the Jesuits of transgressing the laws of authority and evidence which Pascal had defined in the *Préface sur le Traité du Vide*.[56] With the fourth letter (25 February) Pascal moved to the offensive, and attacked Jesuit casuistry and the doctrine of probability. Beginning in the summer of 1656 Pascal was increasingly the object of attack by the Jesuits, and from letter 11 he defended himself vigorously, addressing the 'Révérends Pères jésuites' directly.

Les Provinciales are not in themselves any more relevant to the Apologia than was the preface Pascal drafted for the *Traité du Vide*,[57] but manuscript notes which have survived show that in working at the *Provinciales*, Pascal was sometimes led to ideas which do point to the Apologia. This process is very clear in the pages which tackle the subject of miracles. These were written while the anti-Jesuit campaign was at its height, and were prompted by Jesuit criticisms of Port-Royal's attitude, and although Pascal did not publish a *Provinciale* – or anything else – specifically about miracles, his reflections took him to the point where we can virtually say that the Apologia, which will absorb a number of the thoughts on miracles, has come into focus.[58]

The Jesuit attacks began two days after the publication of Letter 11, on 20 August. In March 1656, Pascal's niece and goddaughter, Marguerite Périer, who was suffering from a malignant fistula on the left eye, had been miraculously cured by the application of what was believed to be a relic of Jesus' crown of thorns. This miracle was naturally understood as a sign that God was intervening to encourage the Jansenists, and was the cause of much rejoicing.[59] The Jesuits responded with a pamphlet entitled *Le Rabat-joie des jansénistes* (20 August), saying that as it is inconceivable that God would sanction a group whom he had condemned through the voice of the Church, the miracle must be taken as an appeal *in extremis* to the Jansenists to turn from their errors. The *Rabat-joie* sparked off a bitter exchange of pamphlets.[60] The Port-Royal reply was drafted immediately, but witheld until the miracle had been authenticated by an official pronouncement. There was a Jesuit reply to this, and Arnauld himself began an answer, which he did not complete. Then, on the Wednesday following the first Sunday in Lent (21 February 1657), another Jesuit, le Père de Lingendes, preached a sermon on miracles wrought by magicians and heretics, which though it did not name Port-Royal, clearly contained an implied criticism of their position.[61]

Althouth the prolonged debate did not involve Pascal directly - there is only one reference to it in the *Provinciales*, and that is quite discreet[62] - the papers preserved by the two Copies show that Pascal reflected intensely on the matter.[63] He himself made a dossier, perhaps two dossiers, out of papers which contain thoughts on miracles; these constitute the thirty-third and thirty-fourth Units of Copy 9203.[64] There are also a few other thoughts, undoubtedly written at the same period, which have escaped the two basic dossiers.[65]

It is not possible to date these papers with rigorous precision, although some of them can be set within fairly clear limits. None of them, certainly, is earlier than the *Rabat-joie des jansénistes* (August 1656), and it is not likely that Pascal continued to reflect on the polemic aspect of miracles (as opposed to the apologetic) long after the Lenten sermons of Ligendes in 1657, which marked the end of public debate on the subject. The difficulty is to place individual papers within these six months. The close interrelatedness of theme suggests that they were written in a single concentraded spell, say of two or three weeks. But if we try to decide between October-November 1656 and February-March 1657, we find that the clues conflict. It hardly affects the present argument, however, if we assign the two Units, rather vaguely, to the winter of 1656-7.[66]

Pascal's reflections start from the situation in which Port-Royal found itself in the autumn of 1656, accused of heresy, the miracle being interpreted by the Jesuits not as a confirmation but as a warning. Pascal's argument is scattered among countless fragments, but the main thrust is clear. A miracle is not necessarily a sign of orthodoxy. Faced with a declared enemy, God, who will not

permit anything which would lead men into error, can allow a miracle in the knowledge that nobody will take it
as a sign of his favour. Either it will be a false miracle, or else it will be a miracle whose significance
will not be to confirm but (for example) to call to re-
pentance. If, however, there is a dispute between two
individuals or two groups who both claim to be with God,
the normal method for discerning true miracles is not
available, and therefore any miracle which is not manifestly false can be assumed to be true. Further, in these
circumstances we would have no criterion for distinguishing a miracle meant to confirm from a miracle meant to
correct. The obvious assumption most people would make
would be that if there was a miracle on one side of a
dispute, God was thereby showing us where the truth lies,
and helping us out of our dilemma. If that were not the
case, we would fall inescapably into error. But God will
not permit that. Therefore, if the miracle is not obviously false, we can trust it, and consequently accept
that the people on whom the miracle has been performed
are in fact orthodox. And such, clearly, is the case with
Port-Royal.

If one does not admit that in these circumstances miracles discern doctrine, then miracles serve no purpose,
and one cannot build on any miracles, including the miracles of Jesus himself.[67] This would destroy the very
basis of Christianity, for it was by miracles, which all
but the spiritually blind could see were the work of God,
that Jesus established his claim to be the Messiah. Normally, once the Church was established, the need for miracles ceased, but when the voice of the Church errs, miracles are once again needed, to indicate that dissidents
are in fact defenders of the truth.

It would clearly be inappropriate to include in an apologia addressed to the unbeliever a section defending the
Port-Royal interpretation of miracles against the Jesuits.
But there are other ways in which the ramifications of
the subject lead to areas which are very relevant to the
Apologia. We have seen that the notes on miracles include
some discussion of the role miracles played in the establishment of Jesus' claims to be the Messiah. Here certainly
is a point which will have to be raised in the Apologia.
But it is not given much prominence there, and we can see
from the papers preserved in Units XXXIII and XXXIV how
the reflections on miracles themselves provoked further

thoughts which then put the subject of miracles into
broader perspective.

In the notes on miracles, Pascal insists that in establishing Jesus as the Messiah, miracles were more important than the fulfilment of prophecy. The prophecies
paved the way, but they could not point unequivocally to
Jesus as the Messiah (840). There would have been no
proof of that without signs or miracles (841, 846). The
prophecies are never called miracles (ibid.). Hence,
Jesus attached the greatest importance to his miracles
(903). Nevertheless, once Jesus had been accepted as
Messiah, the prophecies were fulfilled, and they became
much more important to later generations.[68] They are a
'miracle subsistant' (180, 335, 593 [deleted], 594).
Consequently in the Apologia the roles are reversed, and
prophecies overshadow miracles.[69] There are other references to miracles in the twenty-eight *liasses à titres*,
but they are not emphasized, even in the section 'Preuves
de Jesus Christ' (24°, see 302, 321, and cf. 243/19°).
The miracles of Jesus are mentioned in passing in 264
(20°). Section 13°, on the use of reason, quotes Saint
Augustine, that without miracles there are no grounds
for Christianity (169, cf. 184). God will have his authority recognized 'par des merveilles et par des preuves
que vous ne puissiez refuser' (194). The miracles of
Jesus were necessary (180), they form part of the scheme
of things (282/22°). Pascal no doubt thought that, despite their very great historical importance for the establishment of Christianity, miracles were too unusual
in the modern world to be of interest to a non-believer.
He would none the less have had to say more about them
than is recorded in the classified fragments, and I have
already suggested, in chapter 24, how and where that
amplification might have taken place.

In the Apologia, miracles are overshadowed not only by
prophecy but by 'Perpetuity.' It is interesting to discover that it too grows from the campaign against the
Jesuits, and that in some fragments of Unit XXXIV it is
put parallel to the issue of miracles. The idea was already touched on in nos 421 and 425, discussed in the
previous section. The first use of the word appears to
be in connection with the tradition which the Jesuits
are destroying (cf. 866, 877): 'Perpétuité. Votre caractère est-il fondé sur Escobar?' (866), and later down
the same page: 'Perpétuité-Molina-Nouveauté' (871).

Fragment 870 says that 'les hérétiques ont toujours com-
battu ces trois marques qu'ils n'ont point.' This is explained elsewhere, by 894: 'Les trois marques de la religion: la perpétuité, la bonne vie, les miracles. Ils
détruisent la perpétuité par la probabilité, la bonne vie
par leur morale, les miracles en détruisant ou leur vérité,
ou leur conséquence.' A *pensée* to be found in Unit XXV
(707) reads: 'Ils ne peuvent avoir la perpétuité et ils
cherchent l'universalité et pour cela ils font toute
l'Eglise corrompue afin qu'ils soient saints.'

In fragment 892 we read: 'J'aime mieux suivre J-C. qu'aucun autre parce qu'il a le miracle, prophétie, doctrine,
perpétuité, etc.' Perpetuity thus joins other credentials
of Jesus. Here it clearly means more than the tradition
of the Catholic Church, and we are reminded of a deleted
sentence on fragment 878: 'Depuis le commencement du monde
J-C. subsiste, cela est plus fort que tous les miracles
de l'Antéchrist.'[70]

In fragment 895, perpetuity is seen as only one of the
different proofs that can be given for Christianity. Some
proofs are more appropriate for certain people than others.

> La religion est proportionnée à toutes sortes d'esprits.
> Les premiers s'arrêtent au seul établissement, et cette
> religion est telle que son établissement est suffisant
> pour en prouver la vérité.

In other words, the fact that Christianity was established at all is a guarantee of its validity. But there
are other proofs, if one cares to look further. Some believers, more learned, 'vont jusqu'au commencement du
monde.' Pascal will retain from this fragment not only
the argument of perpetuity, but the idea that different
people have different grounds for their faith. He is already moving into the realm of apologetic psychology.

(f) aveuglement surnaturel (964, Lux. *966)*

The miracles of Jesus raise a psychological question also.
Why were they not universally believed? A sketch of an
answer comes in no. 840, in which Pascal says that Jesus
'aveuglait les pharisiens qui disaient qu'il fallait
juger des miracles par la doctrine' and that 'l'incrédu-
lité de Pharao et des Pharisiens est l'effet d'un endur-
cissement surnaturel.'[71] In the context of the polemic,

the answer to this question brings us back to the Jesuits, who are behaving like the Philistines of Old.[72] But Pascal's thinking on the matter of unbelief is fully developed only in a wider context where the question is not why the Pharisees did not believe the miracles of Jesus, but why men everywhere turn their back on God. Having thus started with the present – the Jesuits – and moved back in time to the miracles of Jesus, Pascal, by generalizing the question of unbelief, is brought back to the present. And it is with this third movement, even more than with the treatment of the miracles of Jesus, that we approach the very heart of the Apologia.[73] Pascal finds two main focuses for his thinking: the nature of certainty and nature of belief.

This development in his thought thus brings Pascal back to the subjects he had discussed in *De l'esprit géométrique* a year before. There he had written that provided we accept certain data, we can use reason to reach truths inaccessible to the senses directly. If we do not accept the data, we are doomed to perpetual scepticism. But he had also said that the heart needs to be convinced as much as reason does, and in fragment 110, linked by theme if not by date, he remarked that matters of faith went beyond what could be deduced by reason acting on universal basic assumptions.

These notions reappear in the reflections on miracles. In fragment 837, for example, Pascal says that we cannot expect all miracles to be true, as there must be an element of doubt, there being no such thing as absolute human certainty.

The long fragment no. 840 begins by considering why it is that 'le lieu est ouvert au blasphème et même sur des vérités au moins bien apparentes.' He explains it thus:

Ce n'est point ici le pays de la vérité;[74] elle erre inconnue parmi les hommes. Dieu l'a couverte d'un voile qui la laisse méconnaître à ceux qui n'entendent pas sa voix.

It is at first surprising to find the author of *De l'esprit géométrique* saying that truth is accessible only to those who listen to the word of God. But in writing his opuscule on geometric method, Pascal was concerned only with rational truth. He had already made a clear distinction between reason and theology, and in the second part

of *De l'esprit géométrique*, he admitted that the heart
makes demands often in conflict with those of pure reason.
Geometry attains certainty, but only in its own sphere,
and Pascal is not thinking of that sphere now. Miracles
occupy an ill-defined no man's land between the world
of ordinary experience and theology. Pascal's first task,
indeed, is to find a way to ascertain which set of rules
applies.

Although he may not have realized it, the phrase just
quoted from no. 840 recalls something Pascal had written
eight years earlier, to his sister Gilberte. There he was
talking not about rational enquiry, but about the spiritual truths which are conveyed to us by physical phenomena.
These truths are not visible to the naked eye, they are
to be discerned by 'une lumière surnaturelle' which God
grants to those who know him and love him. For those who
do not know him, the objects they see appear as objects
merely, actually obscuring the spiritual meaning they
convey to others.

The two ideas - the ambivalence of physical phenomena,
and the specific motif of the veil - come together in
the important letter which Pascal wrote to Mlle de Roannez
at the end of October 1656. The occasion is the official
Sentence affirming the authenticity of the miracle of
the holy thorn.[75] This miracle, Pascal writes, is one of
the rare instances of God '[sortant] du secret de la
nature qui le couvre.' Normally, then, the world of appearances, of nature, conceals God, who remains hidden.
In a phenomenon like the miracle, God momentarily lifts
the veil. This notion of God as a 'hidden God' (The 'Deus
absconditus' of Isaiah)[76] can be extended in several ways.
It applies to Jesus, whose divine nature was concealed
from many of his contemporaries, to the elements of the
Eucharist, which even many Christians deny contain the
divine presence, and to the words of Holy Scripture,
which taken literally seem not to point to divine truth.

The letter to Mlle de Roannez is echoed by the sixteenth
Provinciale, dated 4 December 1656.

Les bienheureux possèdent Jésus-Christ réellement,
sans figures et sans voiles. Les Juifs n'ont possédé
de Jésus-Christ que les figures et les voiles, comme
étaient la manne et l'agneau Pascal. Et les chrétiens
possèdent Jésus-Christ dans l'Eucharistie véritablement
et réellement, mais encore couvert de voiles.

Pascal quotes Saint Eucher.[77] This is how we know God,
not as of a certainty, visible, nor by the law only, but
by faith, God being real but veiled. Always ambivalent,
the world of appearances functions as both reality and
as figure of a higher reality.

In no. 859, Pascal cites the prophet Ezekiel, who said
that the Israelites were talking like heathens.[78] That
does not mean, says Pascal, that the Jewish religion was
in all respects like the heathen. 'Tout cela se passait
en figure. Les autres religions périssent, celle-là ne
périt point.' An addition elaborates on the synagogue,
both truth and figure.

> La synagogue était la figure et ainsi ne périssait
> point; et n'était que la figure, et ainsi est périe.
> C'était une figure qui contenait la vérité et ainsi
> elle a subsisté jusqu'à ce qu'elle n'a plus eu la
> vérité.[79]

Broadened immeasurably in scope, the notion of the figure
becomes a major element in the structure of the Apologia.

It also enables Pascal to reformulate a criticism made
in the tenth *Provinciale* (2 August). There he had written:

> Cette dispense de l'obligation fâcheuse d'aimer Dieu
> est le privilège de la loi Evangélique par-dessus la
> Judaïque ... O mon Père, il n'y a point de patience
> que vous ne mettiez à bout et on ne peut ouïr sans
> horreur les choses que je viens d'entendre.

Now (fragment 849) he can say:

> La charité n'est pas un précepte figuratif. Dire que
> Jésus-Christ qui est venu ôter les figures pour mettre
> la vérité ne soit venu que mettre la figure de la
> charité pour ôter la réalité qui était auparavant,
> cela est horrible.

These extensions of the 'hidden God' motif are of a
different order from miracles. Miracles challenge our
normal experience of body and mind. Were these the only
levels of experience, we would probably need miracles
more frequently. Fragment 848 reads: 'Les miracles et la
vérité sont nécessaires à cause qu'il faut convaincre
l'homme entier en corps et en âme.' But there is a third

level or 'order,' that of grace operating on the heart.
'Les deux fondements: l'un intérieur, l'autre extérieur,
la grâce, les miracles, tous deux surnaturels' (861).
Grace works through the heart, where it has to overcome
self-love. Once grace has entered the heart, a man is
able to discern the spiritual reality which lies behind
physical phenomena. God may be normally hidden from the
naked eye, but his spirit directs the mind to understand
the evidence of the senses in a new light.

It is not surprising to find that when Pascal wrote
his eighteenth *Provinciale* (24 March 1657) he was in
full possession of his doctrine of the three orders. The
eighteenth *Provinciale* reverts to the matter of the early
letters, as the Jesuits persist in confusing the levels
of fact and doctrine in their pronouncements on the five
propositions of Jansen. Citing Saint Paul, Saint Augustine,
and Saint Thomas, Pascal says that the superior orders do
not annul the lesser, and if the legitimate certainties
acquired by the lower orders are sabotaged, faith itself
is weakened.[80]

God then has chosen to hide himself, yet on occasion
to reveal himself. Why? The letter to Mlle de Roannez
shows Pascal's thinking on this. Normally God remains
hidden. If he never revealed himself, we would have no
cause to believe that he was there at all. If he were
always manifest, on the other hand, there would be no
merit in believing him. The word merit, unexplained, implies a complex theology. In *De l'esprit géométrique*
Pascal had said that reason can go beyond the senses,
yet we do not act according to the dictates of reason
alone. Faith in God is not something to be attained
simply by reasoning. Faith being a cardinal virtue, in
conflict with the inclinations of natural fallen man, it
is important that we should not be able to bypass it by
reaching all truth - God - by reason alone. Faith belongs
to the heart, and the heart is the seat of concupiscence.
It is the heart which holds us back from believing what
it is perfectly reasonable to believe, so it must be the
heart which enables us to believe what reason cannot
totally convince us of. This was the conclusion reached
in section (c) of this chapter, and it is further explored
in two fragments from Unit XXXIII, nos 835 and 842.

Miracles, like the prophecies and Scripture, are not
'absolument convaincants' (835). Certainly they are sufficiently convincing for us to have no reason to refuse

them. But it is not reason which makes the final decision
in these cases. Something clouds the judgment, they are
not self-evident truths. The evidence is not strong enough
to convince, but it is strong enough for those who do not
believe to stand condemned. They reject Christianity because they are activated by concupiscence, whereas believers owe their faith ultimately to grace. Grace too
is a 'miracle subsistant.' (In no. 874, Pascal substitutes
the whole teaching of the Church for miracles: 'L'opération de l'Eglise ne sert qu'à préparer à la grâce ou à
la condamnation.')

No. 842 takes this further. The Christian religion has
the best credentials, but they are not what ultimately
counts. They merely serve to condmen unbelievers. What
then does bring about belief? Belief is given by the Cross
of Christ. Faith is a matter of conversion, not conviction.
Christianity possesses wisdom, but it preaches Christ
crucified, this 'folly.'

In sum, we cannot attain certainty because God has not
willed it. He wants our faith to be a victory over self-
love, not a matter of intellectual conviction only. The
Cross of Christ, the grace of God, these are what determine faith. But the evidence of God, though not conclusive, is so strong that nobody can produce sound reasons
for not believing. Disbelief is therefore caused by concupiscence, not reason.

It follows from this that unbelief is unnatural. If it
is reasonable to believe something, not to believe means
that another level is interfering with the level of reason and preventing it from functioning naturally. Reason
will normally accept the truth when it sees it. On the
level of reason, therefore, unbelief is a form of blindness. This would seem to be the implication behind
Pascal's frequent recourse to the word 'aveuglement,'
sometimes coupled with the word 'surnaturel.'[81] Supernatural, and not just unnatural, because the explanation
must be sought in the idea of the fall. In fact, on occasion Pascal even says that men are blinded by God, a
phrase as difficult as the implication of the Lord's
prayer that God might lead us into temptation. But it is
justifiable, if we agree that God has willed the consequences of man's disobedience, and if we admit that the
veil which hides spiritual reality from us, also obscures
truth. Not very much, in fact, can be elicited by the
geometric method.

This cluster of thoughts on different aspects of the psychology of belief invites us to consider the subject as a meeting-place for a number of essential Pascalian themes. We have seen that some go back to 1648 and others to 1655. It is as if the thinking on miracles brought them back into consciousness and gave them a new focus. Fragment 110 (discussed in section c) and Unit II (section d) cannot be dated, but it seems highly probable that both belong to the same period as the papers on miracles.[82] Rereading Unit II, we are struck by the number of links with the themes which we have seen emerge from the papers on miracles. In the 'Infini rien' essay, Pascal refuses to give a rational justification for Christianity which Christians declare to be 'une sottise, *stultitiam*.' The reference is to the first Epistle to the Corinthians, and is obviously akin to no. 842. At the end of 'Infini rien' Pascal discloses that there is a way to see 'le dessous du jeu,' and that is Scripture. If the reader 'cannot' believe, that is due to his passions and not to his reason. It is noteworthy too that the same manuscript includes fragments on faith mediated through the heart, which has its own 'reasons' different from those of reason, on concupiscence, on the heart as battle-ground of the war between self-love and the love of God, and also on perpetuity.

If the topic of miracles is relatively subdued in the Apologia, the psychological themes discussed in this section play a very important role. Virtually the whole of the second part rests on the premiss that God is hidden, though not totally – in nature, in the Incarnation, in the Scriptures; and that such concealment is God's response to the fall of man to whom redemption is open although it cannot be automatic.[83] As for Pascal's theories of unbelief, on the role of reason and the transcending of reason by conversion to the Cross, they determined Pascal's entire tactic in the Apologia. There is thus no need to illustrate these themes in the Apologia, they are all-pervasive.[84] Section 19° offers the closest parallel to the fragments on the 'Deus absconditus' (see section b of chapter 19), and section 28° (conclusion) to those on conversion. A fragment found in Unit I draws together several of these preoccupations, though it does not mention Perpetuity: 'Preuves de la religion. Morale/ Doctrine/ Miracles/ Prophéties/ Figures' (402).

There is another *liasse* which is even more intimately
connected to the reflections on miracles, and that is
the thirteenth, 'Soumission et usage de la raison.' When
I presented it in chapter 13, I was able to relate the
content to the argument of the Apologia, though I noted
that one or two fragments struck a polemical rather than
an apologetic note. If we reread the fragments of *liasse*
13° in the light of Units XXXIII and XXXIV, we are led
inescapably to conclude that the entire *liasse* must have
arisen out of the preoccupations of the latter part of
1656.

The title itself is revealing. The 'usage de la raison'
was explained in *De l'esprit géométrique*; the word 'soumission' implies Pascal's familiar distinction between
the realms of reason and theology. There is a proper place
for scepticism, a proper place for rationalism, and a
proper place for faith. Fragment 170 reads like a conclusion to the whole discussion. Pascal insists that reason
itself will conclude that it has its limits, and must
not go beyond them (174, 182, 188). He says also that
faith transcends reason, but does not annul it (173, 185).
This is the point made in the eighteenth *Provinciale*.
There are thus two levels relevant to faith (reason and
the heart), and it is out of place to introduce force
and threats, which belong to the order of the flesh[85]
(172; Pascal does not mention signs as an aid to faith
on the carnal level, as he did in no. 848).

This last remark is clearly aimed at the Jesuits. And
when Pascal makes the title of the section explicit (167),
he adds: 'en quoi consiste le vrai christianisme.' Fragment 181 draws a distinction between piety and superstition. The example of superstition is 'de croire des
propositions': in other words, the Jesuits are applying
faith to the order of reason, and that is superstition.
Many Christians, says Pascal, are superstitious in this
sense (179). He is careful to except 'ceux qui sont dans
la veritable piété de moeurs et tous ceux qui croient
par un sentiment du coeur.' The same phrase occurs in
no. 110. Fragment 178 gives a clue which it is illuminating to follow up. It is simply a note to say something
here about 'les deux sortes d'hommes' in the bundle entitled 'Perpétuité.' That leads us to no. 286, which
talks of 'les chrétiens grossiers' who 'croient que le
Messie les a dispensés d'aimer Dieu,' which brings us

right back to the Jesuits and to fragment 849.[86] I suspect that fragment 286 is contemporary with the fragments
we are discussing, but that Pascal later moved it to
liasse 22°, leaving a cross-reference in his thirteenth
bundle.

Now, the same cross-reference appears also in the
twenty-seventh bundle, no. 366. There we have also the
words, 'Superstition, concupiscence,' which takes us
back to Unit XXXIV and fragment 908 'Superstition et
concupiscence.' The subject is holy and unholy fear, and
it articulates a criticism of Jesuit practice implicit in
several of the *Provinciales* of this period.[87]

As well as giving an example of superstition, fragment
181 illustrates impiety: 'Impiété de ne pas croire
l'Eucharistie sur ce qu'on la voit pas.' This clearly
ties in with the letter to Mlle de Roannez of late
October 1656. Fragment 168 likewise expresses disapproval
of those who refuse to believe in the Eucharist. In
fragment 179 Pascal makes a parallel between those
Christians who believe by superstition and unbelievers
whose unbelief is based not on reason but on 'libertinage.'
Men refuse the truth, and then find specious reasons for
doing so, such as invoking the sceptic argument from the
diversity of opinion (176-7). Unbelievers are misusing
their reason, and reason will condemn them (175).

Finally there is a group which refers directly to miracles. Saint Augustine said that without the miracles
he would not be a Christian (169). Without the miracles
it would have been no sin not to believe Jesus (184,
echoing the last part of 846). And in no. 180 Pascal
makes his clearest statement about the relation of miracles and prophecies.

An appendix to this section could be added: fragments
where Pascal considers the contemporary non-believer's
attitude to miracles. There is first the sceptic who
will not believe the Virgin Birth and the Resurrection.
Yet the only reason why he accepts natural birth and not
virgin birth is that he is used to it. There is no absolute reason why one should be miraculous and the other
not (882, entitled 'Athées'). Two other fragments which
are found outside Units XXXIII and XXXIV show Pascal answering the unbeliever's statement that he would believe
if only he could be shown a miracle. In no. 574 (XXIII),
Pascal replies that the permanent possibility of scepticism belies this optimism.

Il n'y a point, dit-on de règle qui n'ait quelque
exception, ni de vérité si générale qui n'ait quelque
face par où elle manque. Il suffit qu'elle ne soit pas
absolument universelle pour nous donner sujet d'appliquer l'exception au sujet présent, et de dire: cela
n'est pas toujours vrai, donc il y a des cas où cela
n'est pas.

And if the unbeliever says he would be converted if he
could see a miracle, he clearly has not understood the
nature of conversion (378/28°). Conversion is not conversation; 'la conversion véritable consiste à s'anéantir
devant cet être universel ... Elle consiste à connaître
... que sans un médiateur il ne peut y avoir de commerce.'
  Let us note finally that T. Shiokawa remarks that disbelief in the miracles becomes a proof of man's corruption, and he argues that this change of perspective is
of crucial importance in the birth of the Apologia.[88]

(g) 'Pensées' (889)

Two lines of thought have thus brought us to the threshold
of the Apologia, one issuing from the project Pascal announced to Sacy and one from the intense reflection on
miracles.[89] The two could not remain distinct for long,
and indeed the papers on miracles themselves, as well as
gathering together many separate strands, strike off in
new directions and re-establish contact with the earlier
ideas. Two sheets are of particular interest here, those
containing fragments 882-91 and 903-12. The second one
is probably earlier than the first. Most of the fragments
it contains relate to the quarrel with the Jesuits, and
no. 903 (eighteen separate fragments) is about miracles.
No. 905, however, headed 'Pyrrhonisme,' is about neither.
We do not have access to truth, because everything we
experience is partly true, but debatable. We can say that
it is true that homicide is bad because we do know 'le
mal et le faux.' But we cannot say of any action that it
is unequivocally true that it is good. Hence the conclusion: 'Nous n'avons ni vrai, ni bien que en partie, et
mêlé de mal et de faux.' This argument, possibly suggested
in the first place by the loopholes of Jesuit moral theology, unites *le vrai* and *le bien*, reintroducing a theme
adumbrated in the *Entretien avec M. de Sacy.*[90]
  The paper containing nos 903-12 brings one other clue:

the watermark. One has to tread circumspectly, as nobody
can be expected always to complete a given stock of writing paper in a specific period.[91] It is, however, noteworthy that there are only a handful of sheets bearing
the same watermark as 903-12, a B and a C separated by a
heart, and that they show a marked similarity of theme.[92]
And they take us out of Unit XXXIV to other Units and
even in one instance to the *liasses*.

I have already mentioned that Unit II ('Infini rien')
has this watermark. The link does not enable us to answer
the question about the relative chronology of Unit II and
the work on miracles, but it does tend to confirm what
thematic analysis had suggested, that the two projects
belong to the same period.

Another page with the same watermark contains fragments
515-24 (XXIII).[93] The verso (519-24) has been crossed
out. One of these fragments, crushed in at the bottom
right, plainly after the rest of the page was full, reads:
'Il faut sobrement juger des ordonnances divines, mon
Père. Saint-Paul en l'île de Malte.' The analogy with a
part of no. 840 seems clear.[94]

On the recto side are four fragments written one below
the other. The first (515) has to do with style. The
second and third (516-17) are once again on the dissension within the Church.[95] The last (518) is entitled
'Pyrrh.' and develops the idea that man's place is to be
in the middle; we must shun the extremities. The idea is
continued overleaf with 519; in all things we are poised
between two contradictory movements. Beneath it, in no.
520, Pascal says that he once believed in human justice,
but the diversity of opinions made him sceptical. Divine
justice exists, which God may or may not choose to reveal
to us. No. 523 is added at the right. We cannot think of
two things at once. In setting down these thoughts, Pascal
has left a lot of space at the right-hand side of his
page. So he now fills it up, beginning with no. 522. A
man with cause for real distress of mind can nevertheless
distract himself with some trivial occupation. Likewise
a man who can understand profound questions and decide
momentous issues will, because he is a man ('ni ange, ni
bête, mais homme'), be distracted by unimportant things.
No. 524 comes in the bottom corner, beneath 522.[96] Finally
in the top right-hand corner, no. 521: we cannot be certain that anything is certain, so we cannot be certain
that anything is absolutely uncertain. 'A la gloire

du pyrrhonisme.' (There is an echo of this in no. 33/2°:
'Rien ne fortifie plus le pyrrhonisme que ce qu'il y en
a qui ne sont point pyrrhoniens. Si tous l'étaient ils
auraient tort.')

We can thus interpret paper 515-24 as a series of reflections on Pyrrhonism, to be linked with no. 905. Plu-
rality marks the human condition (518), and as soon as
we get out on a limb, we fall into error. Opinions are
multifarious and contradictory. Certainty is beyond us.
So is emotional stability; we are always prone to distraction, which has its good side and its bad side.

If this paper was put aside, and if the writing on the
verso was all crossed out, we are bound to conclude that
Pascal wished to preserve one (at least) of the *pensées*
on the recto for another purpose, probably for the Apologia. In the case of fragments 390 and 190, which also
have the watermark BC,[97] Pascal went further, and cut
them in order to file them separately. No. 390 is found
in Unit I, the connection of which with the argument of
the Apologia is undoubted. It is entitled 'Perpétuité'
and develops the theme that the coming of Christ was
awaited from the dawn of time. Over the ages the prophecies became more specific, and Jesus fulfilled them all.
This fragment clearly is a development of a theme mentioned in the previous section. The opening phrase 'depuis
le commencement du monde' comes straight from 878 and 895.
It recurs in 281 (22°, section entitled 'Perpétuité')
and is echoed in a later fragment, no. 489.

The one example of this watermark which found its way
into the *liasses à titres* is 190. It is far removed from
the preoccupations of other fragments we have been considering, and in it we suddenly glimpse again the criticism of the Stoics which Pascal had made two years earlier
in his *Entretien avec M. de Sacy*. Rational demonstrations
of God will only be understood by a few, will be retained
by fewer, and they encourage the false belief that we
can know God without a mediator. 'Au lieu que ceux qui
ont connu Dieu par médiateur connaissent leur misère.'[98]

This example has taken us well beyond the scope of the
other papers associated, directly or indirectly, with
Units XXXIII and XXXIV, both in idea and also perhaps in
time.[99] But before I conclude this long chapter, I must
mention the other paper which records thoughts that have
nothing to do with either Jesuits or miracles: the one
containing fragments 882-91. It may be later than most

of the other papers (no. 891, written low down on the
left-hand side, formulates a definition of miracles which
recurs in the questions Pascal put to Barcos), but we
cannot be sure.[100] I have already quoted no. 882, which
is the first fragment on the verso side of the page. On
the recto, two cryptic sentences about Pyrrhonians and
Descartes respectively, which it may not be correct to
associate with the page on Pyrrhonism just analysed.[101]

Much more interesting are the two fragments located towards the bottom right-hand corner. The first is actually
entitled 'Pensées.' It reads as follows:

In omnibus requiem quaesivi[102]
   Si notre condition était véritablement heureuse, il
ne nous faudrait pas divertir d'y penser pour nous
rendre heureux (889)

The title clearly refers to the content, and means 'What
we do with our thoughts.' The idea itself - that we are
not truly happy, that we find distractions to keep us
from thinking about our situation - will become a key
strand of the first part of the Apologia.

Beneath no. 889 comes no. 890:

Toutes les occupations des hommes sont à avoir du bien
et ils n'ont ni titre pour le posséder justement, ni
force pour le posséder surement. De même, la science,
les plaisirs: nous n'avons ni le vrai ni le bien.

One can see the connection with no. 889: man's ability
to find happiness, which in no. 889 prompted a remark on
distraction, now suggests an analysis of that inability.
And when he says 'nous n'avons ni le vrai ni le bien,'
it is as if he is joining these recent thoughts on happiness with those earlier thoughts on our inability to
reach certainty. The phrase recalls no. 905.

Pascal is clearly in a very different area here from
when he was discussing miracles and faith. But these reflections on happiness are equally relevant to the Apologia. In fact, Pascal copied both of them onto another
sheet, very slightly varied, and they found their way into
the *liasses à titres*, as nos 70 (3°) and 28 (2°). With
these examples, an idea is being transferred from an abortive study on miracles - the material for which Pascal
wished nevertheless to keep intact - to the Apologia which
was to be Pascal's next major project after the demise of
the *Provinciales* in March 1657.[103]

31
The evolution of the plan

In the previous chapter we traced the growth of various preoccupations which came to feed the Apologia. Pascal must have begun working seriously at this early in 1657, for he had clearly accomplished a great deal before he fell ill two years later. In this chapter and the next one, we examine the evidence to see if anything of the chronological sequence can be established. The two chapters do not correspond to two stages in the growth of the plan, but to the two different sets of evidence we have: the classified fragments, stored in bundles ('*liasses*'), and the 'unclassified' fragments, housed in a number of 'Units.' At the end of this enquriy, we shall see to what extent it is possible to answer the initial question. In this introductory portion of chapter 31, I shall briefly characterize Pascal's thinking as he moves from polemics to apolegetics.

Even before Pascal was consciously thinking of planning an Apologia, his thoughts frequently take an apologetic turn, as if he never really ceased to reflect on that conversation with Sacy which presents the first rough outline of an apologetic method. Indeed, I have argued that some of the key fragments in the classified bundles began as a simple elaboration of the Sacy argument, and go back to the years 1655 and 1656. Unit II, which I assigned to the year 1656, is clearly the text of an apologist in a specific situation. Several ideas noted there, and on the dossiers on miracles (Units XXXII to XXXIV, winter of 1656-7) announce or even reappear in other Units, notably XXIII to XXV. And while *pensées* in these Units are technically not necessarily part of the Apologia, they are formally indistinguishable from other thoughts which indubitably do belong to the projected Apologia. I was also led to ascribe *liasse* 13°, on the use of reason, to this early period.

As Pascal emerged from the period of the *Provinciales*, and entered what we must regard as the period of the

Apologia, he had therefore already given much thought to
the problem of unbelief. He was fully aware of the threat
which scepticism poses to faith, and was steeped in
Montaigne's *Apologie de Raymond Sebond*. He had sketched
one answer to the sceptical when he set in opposition
their view of man, which humiliates him, and the Stoic
view, which elevates him, and argued that the Christian
view both humiliates and elevates, at the points where
humiliation and elevation are necessary. He had elaborated
on this argument in a series of fragments which were to
become key moments in the Apologia. But that fuller version of the *Entretien* was far from exhausting the topic.
Several issues continued to preoccupy him.

Pascal's own thinking on the matter of scepticism and
faith was clear. Reason, even in the natural sphere, has
to build on certain basic principles, which are known
intuitively. Knowledge of God is intuitive knowledge of
this sort, the only difference being that it seems to be
an intuition which is not universally shared. Pascal does
not want to undervalue reason, only to limit it to its
proper domain. In that domain, its principles must not
be slighted.

In the 'Infini rien' fragment, Pascal pursued some of
the consequences of his stand on reason. If reason is
irrelevant to faith, scepticism is irrelevant too. Let
us therefore use reason to argue not about the grounds
of faith, but about the consequences of faith in normal
experience. Which is more likely to lead us to happiness,
belief or unbelief? Second, what does one say to the man
who would like to have that assurance, but cannot? One
answers first, that the opposition comes from his will,
and from the power of habit, and can be tackled at that
level; second, one can make a concession to reason saying
that although reason cannot produce faith, it can justify
the faith of those who have it, by showing reasonable
grounds for accepting the claims Christianity makes.

That fragment expresses in paradoxical form a point of
view which is formulated more discreetly elsewhere. A
man's moral experience can lead him to Christianity. If
he is not blind, he will recognize his inadequacy, his
need for redemption, and welcome a religion which speaks
so eloquently to his deepest need.

But are there proofs to substantiate the promises
Christianity makes? Is it more than an elegant paraphrase
of human experience? Yes, Pascal says, there are proofs,

and they have to do with the history of Christian teachings. Christianity tells us that man was created in the
image of God, has fallen, and that God has sent us the
means of redemption. That this is not a poetic metaphor
is shown by the pre-history of Christianity: the long
period during which the Jewish nation waited for the
promised redeemer, and the way the prophets spoke of him.
That the redeemer did come, in the person of Jesus, is
shown by the way he fulfilled the prophecies.

There remains one question. If there are indeed proofs
that Jesus was the Messiah, why is it that they are not
universally accepted, and not productive of faith? The
answer to this is bound up with the purposes of God, and
again Jewish and Christian teaching suggests an answer:
God has concealed himself from us, so that a moral effort
is required of us to fight concupiscence, and attain the
vision of faith.

Such, in a nutshell, is the answer Pascal would have
made to the difficult question of unbelief. Although he
never gave a complete bird's-eye view, the fragments that
he did write all imply such a framework - partly because
pensées written simultaneously pass from one part of the
argument to another freely, and partly because several
fragments join different parts of the argument in one
single statement.

Pascal's concern in writing an apologia was, however,
not with clarifying his own views on reason and faith,
but with using them in an attempt to convert his contemporaries. A paradoxical enterprise, if faith is God-given.
But it is not inconsistent to wish to remove some of the
obstacles, such as complacency and misunderstanding. And
so the ordering of the fragments, classifying them according to twenty-eight headings, and increasingly the formulation of the ideas themselves, will be governed by
Pascal's concept of himself as an apologist.

At the same time, the impulse is strongly artistic. In
forming his Apologia out of countless diverse fragments,
Pascal was doing what all artists are doing, searching
for that which gives unity to the parts of experience.
Basic patterns, such as conflict and resolution,[1] govern
not only the syntax of individual sentences, but the relationships between one phase and another. The form, that
is, is both rhetorical and imaginative.

Although Pascal had, from the start (the *Entretien avec
M. de Sacy* antedates the period of the Apologia proper by

a couple of years), a framework which he appears to have worked on and expanded, he does not seem to have tackled the problem of organization systematically until he had collected more material with which to work. A systematic approach at this stage would have closed the door on his deepest inspiration. This is implied by *pensée* 532, in Unit XXIII:

> J'écrirai ici mes pensées sans ordre et non pas peut-être dans une confusion sans dessein. C'est le véritable ordre et qui marquera toujours mon objet par le désordre même.
> Je ferais trop d'honneur à mon sujet si je le traitais avec ordre puisque je veux montrer qu'il en est incapable.

But though that might be an accurate description of Pascal's way of writing, it would be a mistake to use it to argue that Pascal believed that disorder was the truest order. Out and out disorder is not order, in any sense; the author of *De l'esprit géométrique* would never subscribe to that. So Pascal will avoid the over-systematic exposition of a Charron, but he will search for some viable substitute – a form which will both make the best case for Christianity to the contemporary reader, and also do justice to his own vision.

And so, for the next two years or so, Pascal wrote down, on large sheets, using one side only, all his ideas on the subjects which seemed to him relevant to his project.[2] Some ideas needed to be made more precise, and that necessitated reading and documentation. And as he collected more and more separate thoughts, he became taken up with the relation between different stages of the argument, sometimes experimenting with different possibilities. He made the decision to sort his ideas into bundles, and he divided the separate fragments up by cutting between them. He did not cut up all his papers, and he did not file all the resulting pieces, but we know that nearly 400 of them were distributed among twenty-eight bundles, staked and tied. The way the material was copied after Pascal's death enables us to reconstitute the bundles, and also to see that the rest divides into thirty-five blocks or 'Units.' There is also additional material not recorded by the official copies, which has survived.

One would like to be able to trace the stages by which
the unconnected ideas and the embryonic plan which we
know to have existed by the spring of 1657 evolved into
the intricate design represented by the twenty-eight
liasses. In order to do this properly, we should have to
know when each fragment was written and when each classified fragment was classified. There is no hope of ever
attaining this kind of precision. A few fragments can be
approximately dated, or some limit set, by external
criteria (references to events, or recent books; date of
the paper; in one instance, a fragment is written on the
back of a dated letter), but they do not amount to more
than a handful.[3] Are there any other criteria we can use?
In chapter 30 I based some groupings on similarity of
theme, but as the Apologia becomes more and more intricate, this method has less and less validity. I also had
recourse to watermarks. But that is not a foolproof method
either, and in any case the amount of information we have
about watermarks is relatively scanty.[4]

There are other possibilities, concerning the Units on
the one hand, and the *liasses* on the other. Recent research on the composition of the Units has in my view
been pressed a little too hard. Strictly speaking, the
presence of a dateable fragment in a particular Unit gives
only a *terminus ab quo* for the constitution of the Unit;
it does not mean that all the fragments in the Unit are
of the same approximate date, yet this assumption has
been widely made. This matter is treated in chapter 32.

If scholars have been a little precipitous in their
conclusions concerning the Units, they have been over-
tentative in their treatment of the *liasses*. One sometimes has the impression that Pascal is thought to have
sat down with several hundred fragments, which he calmly
distributed in twenty-eight separate bundles. Naturally,
it cannot have happened that way. It is much more likely
that Pascal began sorting his fragments according to certain broad headings, that he worked on the individual
parts sometime later, devising new subdivisions, and that
at the same time he continued to write. Indeed, one would
expect the process of classifying to inspire new thoughts,
particularly ones concerning the way the parts could link
together. Is there any way in which this hypothesis could
be tested? It is always assumed that Pascal placed his
fragments face upwards onto a spike, so that the lowest
paper in each bundle (the last to be copied) is the first

to have been filed. Now, if we read each section in the order in which the fragments were filed, we find frequently that the character of the *liasse* changes subtly, becoming more sharply focused, and that ideas mentioned in the lowest fragments are often further developed elsewhere. From this I have been able to suggest how the complexities of the design grew gradually, suggested very often by the experience of finding the initial categories too simple. This is the moment where the dynamic, imaginative shape comes into focus.[5]

The chronological problems of the *liasses* and of the Units, while methodologically distinct, do of course overlap. Indeed they interlock, creating for the researcher the very real danger of using circular arguments. For if the stages of the plan can be deduced in part by evidence from early fragments in the Units, conversely, fragments in the Units can sometimes be put in order by reference to the changing plan. Consequently, although I am leaving a full discussion of the Units until the next chapter, I ought to mention here that there is no reason to doubt that all the fragments in Units I, XXIII, XXIV, and XXV were extant before Pascal set his twenty-eight bundles aside. They can therefore be cited in support of some of my contentions concerning Pascal's struggle with his plan, as well as Units II ('Infini rien') and XXXII to XXXIV (on miracles), which were discussed in chapter 30. Unit I is of particular significance.

This analysis of the shifting plan concealed inside the twenty-eight *liasses* will be the main business of the present chapter. I shall treat separately the three divisions of the Apologia: the human condition (2°-10°), the bridge between this and what is usually called the second part (11°-18°) and the proofs themselves (19°-26°). The bridge section I shall treat on two different occasions, as there are signs of a first version much simpler than what Pascal finally devised. The concluding chapters (27°-28°) belong to this first version.

My conclusions are as follows:
(a) Whatever ideas Pascal may have once had for a general introduction (a problem he seems to have put to one side), the *liasses* show that his first major concern was to find a way to organize the large number of fragments which constitute part one. The intricate subdivisions of this first part - the 'misère de l'homme sans Dieu' - were not apparent to Pascal as he began classifying, and the

first fragments filed in *liasse* 3° ('Misère') probably
represent his first thoughts concerning this stage of the
work. In time he added 'Vanité' (2°), and neglected 3°.
A separate section for 'Ennui' was soon abandoned, as
the plan took a new direction, marked by a dialectic –
different perspectives on the theme of justice (5°),
'Grandeur' as a necessary complement to 'Misère' (6°).
At this point he came across no. 131 again, and used it
to start a provisional conclusion, entitled 'Contrariétes.'
Meanwhile, a growing number of thoughts were not accommodated in the evolving structure; some of these were put
to one side (13°, 14°), while others now form *liasses*
8°-10°. They gather ideas which might at one stage have
been housed in the opening chapters, and other ideas collected in 1655. Pascal was probably still working on the
internal ordering of this group, which has no formal conclusion, when he abandoned the task, either definitively,
or else in order to tackle the later parts. Unit I, which
appears to record in chronological sequence the evolution
of the overall plan, gives many suggestions for a conclusion which would open the way to a second part, on
Christianity's claims.
(b) Pascal's first idea of the sequel (adumbrated in no.
12) was to lead the non-believer to overcome his fear of
Christianity by making him wish it were true, and then
to produce the objective evidence. The so-called 'moral'
proofs were already sketched out in the amplification
Pascal made of the Sacy discourse, discussed in chapter
30. Christianity alone has correctly diagnosed man's
need and offered a remedy. In the Apologia that we know,
this text is dispersed among a number of chapters. One
can trace the next stage in its development. Framed by
no. 149 (page 2) and the conclusion (28°), it is expanded in *liasse* 17° ('Fausseté des autres religions'),
in the page added to no. 149 (now page 1), and in 27°
('Morale chrétienne'). One can also see it gradually dis-
appearing from view, as fragments are filed in Bundle
17° which have more to do with the historical than with
the 'moral' proofs.
(c) The section on historical proofs began like the first
part, with a simple heading, 'Fondements de la religion
et réponse aux objections' (19°). But it quickly expanded.
The theme of the 'fondements,' continuing 17°, gives
material for several separate divisions, probably opened
in the following order: 'Perpétuité' (22°), which grows

out of thoughts expressed in the papers on miracles,
'Preuves de Jésus-Christ' (24°), out of which evolved
'Preuves de Moise' (23°, a kind of appendix to 22° in
effect), 'Figures particulières' (26°) and 'Prophéties'
(25°). This in turn provokes a theoretical chapter (20°,
'Que la loi était figurative'), some reading for which
yields 21° 'Rabbinage.' Apart from a couple of thoughts
on miracles, for which there is no obvious home, fragments on the theme of 'Fondements' go into these other
dossiers, once they are set up, leaving 19° for the
crucial 'Réponse aux objections.' The reply is the concept of God as a *deus absconditus*, a concept already
very familiar to Pascal, which he elaborates on fragment
149 (pages 3 to 4) as well as in the other fragments
filed in *liasse* 19°.

(d) The transition envisaged in no. 149 did not survive
long. Pascal wished to say much more about the attitude
of the unbeliever. The *liasses* on the right use of reason (13° and 14°, put to one side when Pascal was expanding part one) together with a new section on indifference
(12°) are placed at the head of part two, prefaced only
by no. 149, or part of it. Second, Pascal wished to write
a kind of doctrinal preface before going into the details
of the Christian case. This gives us *liasse* 15° (placed,
for some reason, before 14° and not after it), and two
appendices, on the key doctrines of corruption and redemption. The first of these (16°) was not put in place,
though it was indicated on the table of titles Pascal
drew up before abandoning his work of classifying; the
other is the brief 18°, placed a little oddly between
17° and 19°. Both of these abortive dossiers had possibly
started out as part of a general introduction to part
one. Once he had grafted them onto part two, Pascal put
his twenty-eight bundles aside.

(e) Pascal's elaboration of his plan, by classifying 400
fragments in a scheme which gradually expanded as he did
so, took place during the year 1658. Sometime during the
first half of that year, he expounded it to a group of
friends; he may also have spoken on the subject at Port-
Royal. The account of the talk published by Filleau de
la Chaise in 1672 (following in part indications supplied
by the Duc de Roannez) is probably reliable as far as
the first part of the argument is concerned, and his version corresponds closely to what we have surmised of the
shape of the Apologia at one moment - before the last

portion of part one was in place, and when no. 149 led
straight into 17° and from there to the historical proofs.
On the historical proofs, Filleau expands at length,
using texts of Pascal with which he was familiar and
which interested him particularly. In this instance, his
witness does not tell us anything about Pascal's thoughts
in 1658 as opposed to 1661 or 1662. Etienne Périer's
version of the talk, which forms part of the preface to
the first edition, is much shorter than Filleau's, and
occasionally different, but nothing allows us to believe
his version closer to the actual thoughts of Pascal when
he addressed a group of interested friends in 1658.

(a) première partie: la misère de l'homme sans Dieu (6)

Before embarking on the detailed analysis of part one, I
must say something about Unit I, which differs from other
Units in that it consists of papers already cut. How it
got put together we cannot be sure, but it is striking
that if we put the first two fragments aside temporarily,
we have a summary of various salient points of the Apology,
in more or less the order in which they are developed.
What that order is will be the subject of this chapter.
My presentation will be based on the evidence of the
liasses themselves. Time and time again corroboration is
brought by a retrograde reading of Unit I, and I shall
cite it whenever possible.

Fragments 417 and 416 constitute a special case. Jean
Mesnard believes that they are not really part of Unit I,
but that that they are in fact the missing sixteenth
liasse, identified on the table of contents as 'La nature
est corrompue.' The Copies give no. 416 that title. As
the extant manuscript does not record it, it was most
likely on a separate piece of paper, marking the chapter-
heading. Mesnard believes that Pascal was in the process
of amplifying this dossier when he stopped work, and (for
a reason which is obscure) he placed the notes which make
up Unit I on top of it.[6] This is certainly plausible,
particularly as we shall find that other arguments lead
us to believe that this part of the Apologia was the last
one Pascal attended to. It is just possible, however,
that fragments 416-17, instead of being a misplaced
liasse, are genuinely part of Unit I, and correctly posi-
tioned. If Pascal started this series of fragments with
two *pensées* on the corruption of nature, it would mean

that he once envisaged beginning the Apologia there. Two
pieces of evidence could be given in support of this.
One is that the first part is defined in no. 6 (alternative framework) in the self-same words, 'Que la nature
est corrompue.' The other is that fragment 190, which it
is not difficult to relate to nos 416-17, is entitled
'Préface.'[7] It is admittedly like another fragment entitled 'Préface de la seconde partie' (781), but the fact
remains that the word is not qualified on no. 190. The
implication would be that Pascal thought at one moment
of putting the first part of his Apologia under a doctrinal heading, with a preface stating the Christian
position.[8] Later, when he saw how part one was shaping
up, he reconsidered the psychological tactics, and the
statement was moved to part two, under the general heading of doctrine (402, in Unit I). The weakness of this
argument is that it does not account for the independent
heading ('La nature est corrompue') given, if we are to
trust the Copies, to no. 416, and corresponding to the
sixteenth title recorded on the table.

Fragment 6 is probably a stronger argument for the
hypothesis of a doctrinal preface than is the location
of Bundle 16° at the bottom of Unit I. I have already
argued that *liasse* 1° constitutes the basis of a preface.
Placed in that *liasse*, therefore, fragment 6 is not merely
an outline of the plan; it implies that Pascal would have
said something in his preface about it. Now, the phrase
'Que la nature est corrompue,' is balanced by another:
'Qu'il y a un Réparateur.' And that idea, like that of
'la nature corrompue,' is extended slightly in an abortive
liasse: the eighteenth, to which Pascal gave the title
(echoing no. 12 rather than no. 6) '(La) religion (est)
aimable.' The parallelism of 16° and 18°, and the link
of both with no. 6 cannot be a coincidence. The parallelism is not complete, however; there is no trace of 18°
among the papers of Unit I.

Indications of Pascal's hesitations about his preface
are to be found elsewhere, notably in the first of the
twenty-eight *liasses à titre*. I stated the problem in
chapter 1, but I was there more concerned with what might
have been, had Pascal been able to expand the fragments
contained in this dossier, than with what might have
happened which would explain its unusual features. I
noted that nearly all references to the divisions of
the Apologia as 'letters' come in this *liasse*, although

it must have been constituted on the grounds of the content of the 'letters.' I noted also that fragment 6 records, in two ways, a simple bipartite structure, whereas
no. 12 shows Pascal in command of the outline of his
final, more complex scheme. The sentences he added to
no. 12 put the emphasis on the psychological reasons for
his approach. Looking at this evidence afresh from the
point of view of chronology, it seems that three assumptions can be reasonably made. First, that *liasse* 1° was
opened by a relatively late note - fragment 12, in its
augmented form. (Fragment 12 is entitled 'Ordre,' and
that title was used for the whole *liasse*.)[9] Second, that
the fragments stored with no. 12 were to have been used
for a general preface.[10] And third, that some of these
other fragments went back to an earlier phase, and had
stayed together.[11] At what stage the others had joined
them, I cannot tell. I suggested in chapter 1 that Pascal
had planned and then abandoned a first preface, and that
he subsequently considered writing a preface for each of
his two parts. Evidence for that hypothesis is not found
in the first *liasse*, and I shall have to return to it.[12]

I turn now to the elaboration of the sequence of chapters which develop the idea of the 'Misère de l'homme
sans Dieu.' I shall begin my reading not with *liasse* 2°
('Vanité) but with *liasse* 3°, which has the fundamental
title, 'Misère.'

The first fragment we find is no. 75:

L'Ecclésiaste montre que l'homme sans Dieu est dans
l'ignorance de tout et dans un malheur inévitable,
car c'est malheureux que de vouloir et ne pouvoir.
Or il veut être heureux et assuré de quelque vérité.
Et cependant il ne peut ni savoir ni ne désirer point
de savoir. Il ne peut même douter.

The close connection of this with *pensées* already discussed is clear: not only with no. 6 ('Misère de l'homme
sans Dieu') but with the longer passages which expand
the *Entretien*. They drew our attention to the impossibility
of either being totally certain or even totally uncertain;
and they too made a parallel between our longing for
truth and our longing for happiness. It is very appropriate
that the first fragment filed under 'Misère' should see
the subject whole like this.

No. 74 is entitled 'Injustice,' as are nos 67 and 66;[13]

we recall that no. 9 speaks of a 'lettre de l'injustice.'
This too, evidently, is subsumed under 'Misère.' No. 74
is cryptic, it refers simply to Job and Salomon. So does
no. 69, entitled 'Misère.' For the explanation we have
to go to no. 403, in Unit I:[14]

> Salomon et Job ont le mieux connu et le mieux parlé
> de la misère de l'homme ... l'un connaissant la vanité
> des plaisirs ... l'autre la réalité des maux.

Here 'Misère' and 'Vanité' are paired. No. 73 also talks
of 'la vanité des plaisirs'; can we assume from its inclusion in a bundle entitled 'Misère' that the corresponding bundle for 'Vanité' was not yet constituted? Or
does this announce two chapters, one on 'Misère' and one
on 'Vanité'?

No. 72 says that if the search for truth is unavailing,
we still need a guide for conducting our life. No. 71 is
entitled 'Contradiction'; was there not yet a separate
category 'Contrariétés'? Similarly with no. 70, which
one imagines could have gone into a file marked 'Divertissement' had there been one ready:

> Si notre condition était véritablement heureuse il ne
> faudrait pas nous divertir d'y penser.

(This copies a note made at the time Pascal was working
on miracles, 889/XXXIV, and is echoed by no. 414 in Unit
I. No. 415 is also on our need for activities which offset boredom.) No. 68 on the frightening enigma of man,
lost in 'l'infinie immensité des espaces' reminds us of
no. 199, to be filed elsewhere, and probably already
written by this time.[15]

I have mentioned that three of these fragments are entitled 'Injustice'; no. 61 is called 'Justice,' and no.
60 is of course the long development on laws already
discussed at some length. It has parallels in 520 (XXIII)
and 645 (XXV). The original first sentence of no. 60
spoke of 'la vanité des lois,' and the ideas go right
back to the section in the *Entretien* on 'la vanité des
opinions les plus reçues.' But it is not placed in the
dossier which has the specific title 'Vanité.'

Of the other fragments included here, the most interesting is no. 58 on tyranny, explained as a confusion of
the autonomy of the three orders. Pascal is here picking

up a distinction which marked much of his earlier thinking, which was noted many times in chapter 30.

The first thing that strikes us when we turn to *liasse*
2° ('Vanité') is that a number of fragments filed here
are curiously close to fragments in 3°. The bottom fragment, for example, no. 52, is a gloss on no. 58, and no.
51 belongs with no. 60 (as does no. 20). No. 47 could
possibly absorb no. 73, while no. 23 is allied to no. 72.
We might wonder if Pascal opened this 'second' dossier
only after certain fragments were already firmly placed
in section 3°. This idea is possibly confirmed by an observation of Tourneur, that no. 59 was written straight
after no. 49[16] - and therefore in all probability filed
at the same time. That would mean that by the time Pascal
was filing no. 59 (the seventeenth fragment in the third
liasse) he had only put three fragments into *liasse* 2°.
After that the proportions are reversed, Bundle 3° containing only five more, while Bundle 2° goes on to a
grand total of forty. Fragment 46, which has the title
'Vanité,' refers to the next fragment we find when we
pursue our retrograde reading of Unit I: no. 413.[17]

It is thus *liasse* 2° which will take care of several
important ideas. As with nos 60 and 76, Pascal explores
both the general workings of reason and imagination (48,
44-5, referring to a 'chapitre des puissances trompeuses;
which goes back perhaps to the embryonic apologia discussed
in the last chapter) and also specific instances, notably
in the realm of social institutions. There are many fragments on this theme, which ties in naturally with no. 60
(44, 35 - a shorter version of no. 634 in Unit XXIV - 32,
30, 26, 25, 20, 19, 16). One of them, no. 26, is on the
verso of a page apparently containing a note on simony,
and so is very likely contemporary with the sixth or
twelfth *Provinciale*.[18]

The first fragments in this Bundle recall the preoccupations of 1655-6. Two dictated *pensées* (33-4) take us
right back to the debate on pyrrhonism, our reluctance
to admit that we will never be able to attain reason and
justice (cf. 60, 76, and 521/XXIII).[19] Three interesting
fragments pair off 'le vrai' and 'le bien' and are
probably part of the early process of bringing these concepts into focus. No. 28 arrives at the conclusion 'nous
sommes incapables et de vrai et de bien' after beginning
with the difficulty of having 'du bien' (cf. no. 60). It
follows closely a note made during the period when Pascal

was writing on miracles (890/XXXIV; cf. 905/XXXIV, also 661/XXV).

No. 21 is linked with the reflections on man's position between two infinites (akin to nos 38 and 41, which are closely related to a paragraph in no. 199). Again, Pascal concludes by linking 'la vérité' and 'la morale.' No. 23 links them in another way, trying to assess the relative importance of the two.[20]

I suggested that *liasse* 2° was born of a need to diversify *liasse* 3°, but it now looks as if it simply became the new catch-all, replacing 3° without profiting from the possibility of discrimination. In time *liasse* 2° itself suggested new section headings, with the difference that this time, after one false start, a much more fruitful plan emerged.

The false start is of course *liasse* 4°, 'Ennui et qualités essentielles à l'homme.' This takes over some of the material which had been going into 2° (fragment 77 is akin to nos 31 and 42, and no. 24 would fit the new dossier well enough). No. 79 is on 'Ennui.' No. 662 (XXIV) seems admirably well suited, but it was never filed. It has some similarity to no. 36, a most interesting *pensée* which stands at the crossroads of sections 2°, 3°, 4°, and 8°. But the motif of 'Ennui' quickly yields to the motif of 'Divertissement,' and a new *liasse* will be set up for this theme alone.

However, 'Divertissement' does not appear as simply the next subdivision. It is placed eighth, after 'Opinions du peuple saines' (original designation of 'Raison des effets'), 'Grandeur' and 'Contrariétés.' Somewhere in this transformation of a simple scheme into a more complex one lies the secret we are seeking, the change from a means of classifying pieces of paper to a dynamic imaginative scheme. There would appear to be three distinct factors at work, which will be considered in the order in which we come across them in the printed text.

The idea contained in the words 'Opinions du peuple saines' is latent in several *pensées* in 3° and 2°, as when Pascal says that the people must now be told that the laws are unjust, or they will have no cause to obey any more (66, 67, 60) or that the monarchy is built on 'la folie du peuple' (26). In no. 14 Pascal noted that Christians were obliged to accept human folly:

Les vrais chrétiens obéissent aux folies néanmoins, non pas qu'ils respectent les folies, mais l'ordre

de Dieu qui pour la punition des hommes les a asservis
à ces folies.

One wonders if this *pensée* would have gone into 2° if the
idea of section 5° had been already clear. In section 5°
(no. 90) Pascal again evokes 'perfect' Christians, who
honour the nobility 'par une autre lumière supérieure.'

In section 5° Pascal finds many examples to prove that
though the opinions held by most people do not have their
basis in reason, those opinions make practical sense.
The idea is clearly spelled out in no. 525 (XXIII). Many
of these fragments are clearly meant as the sequel to
thoughts put out in section 2°, particularly but not
exclusively on justice. There are several precise allusions. This raises a very difficult question. On the one
hand, it looks as if Pascal wrote these fragments, or
came across them, only after he had put together much of
Bundle 2°. The presence of fragment 32 half way through
2° would appear to support this view. It is clearly a
reminder to develop a particular idea in this chapter.
But by the time he actually came across (or wrote) the
development, he had set up Bundle 5°, and that is where
he places his paper (no. 80).[21] On the other hand, the
existence of no. 525 (and others) shows that the basic
idea of *liasse* 5° was not very new, and that instances
had already been noted down. Are we then to believe that
Pascal happened to come across them late on in his sorting? There are so many fragments filed in Bundle 5° that
that explanation looks implausible. Nor do the titles
attached to a number of the fragments help to solve the
riddle. The presence of a title might be held to imply
that the chapter-heading was already known, and that the
fragment was written with the specific chapter in mind.
In the present case, the chapter has two titles,[22] and
both appear on the fragments, jostling each other on
equal terms. Furthermore, if all the fragments were written after the idea for this new development had struck
Pascal, would not they tend to be grouped on the same
few sheets of paper, instead of being divided up like the
other independent *pensées*?

This doubt dogs the whole of the present chapter, and
there is no clear solution. It makes it very difficult
to envisage exactly how Pascal was proceeding. My inability to provide a satisfactory answer does not, however,
invalidate the conclusions I am drawing from the order
of the classified fragments, namely that the plan evolved

and that sufficient traces remain to tempt me to give a sketchy account of that evolution.

Certainly, the fifth section has a different character from 3° and 2°, because the ideas seem to be part of an argument. The scepticism about justice (going back through no. 60 to the *Entretien avec M. de Sacy*) is now structured according to a series of antithetical positions, reaching out finally to the altogether superior understanding of the 'chrétiens parfaits.' This development is not really surprising; the antithetical bias of Pascal's imagination is clear from the *Entretien* and the texts written in its wake, as well as from no. 576 (XXIII).

Pascal insisted in the *Entretien* and elsewhere that writers have repeatedly given a one-sided view of man, in whom 'la misère présente' is countered by 'quelques traces de sa première grandeur' or 'la première dignité.'[23] Naturally then, if the 'misère de l'homme sans Dieu' part of his apologia is going to divide into separate sections, there will have to be one section called 'Grandeur.' In the *Entretien* the example of greatness is Stoic philosophy, the ideal which man is invited to aspire to. A file marked 'Philosophes' gathers many reflections which may well date from the year of the *Entretien* and Pascal's reading of Epictetus (not an author Pascal went back to, one surmises).   But for a reason that shall become clear shortly, Pascal does not make Stoicism the linchpin of his chapter on Greatness.[24]

There is another possible basis for the chapter: in the embryonic 'discours,' Pascal made a lot of the unending argument between sceptics and dogmatists, and said that the former could never entirely destroy the credibility of reason. But the case was not strongly made, and was no match for the carefully argued defence of scepticism which fills these early sections of the Apologia.

More fundamental, to Pascal, is the notion of the 'traces de sa première grandeur.' Convinced as he is of the radical duality of man, and strongly drawn by anything which smacks of antithesis and paradox, Pascal wishes to discern traces of original greatness in the portrait of wretchedness itself. The very fact that we call ourselves wretched implies that we think we were born for something better. The second, third, and fifth fragments filed in the sixth *liasse* (117, 116, 114) link *misère* and *grandeur* in a more organic way than the texts (such as 131) which prepare the way for this development.[25]

The first fragment filed (118) similarly makes *grandeur* a function of *misère* (here in the form of concupiscence: this concentrates the essence of various unclassed fragments on *honnêteté*). Another fragment, filed quite late, repeats this idea, mentioning 'la raison des effets,' which is the revised title of *liasse* 5° (106). The fragment in *liasse* 3° entitled 'Contradiction' (no. 71) is similar. An interesting unclassified fragment (no. 613/XXIV) relates this section to the antithetical rhythms of the previous one and sees it leading to the full perspective of the Christians who 'étonnent les philosophes.' It is entitled 'Grandeur, misère.' In Unit I we find no. 411, deducing our belief in human greatness from man's vanity. The title 'Grandeur de l'homme' looks like an afterthought.

The conviction exemplified by the dogmatists does fit in here. Pascal dictated a note: 'Nous avons une idée de la vérité invincible à tout le pyrrhonisme' (406/I).[26] He subsequently added in his own hand a phrase which formulates the corresponding 'demi-vérité' which favours the sceptics, and a title: 'Instinct, raison.' In *liasse* 6° we find 'Instinct et raison, marques de deux natures' (112). Man is great because he has thought (113, 111), which distinguishes him from animals (107, 105). And Pascal places in this section fragments 109 and 110 from the longer argument from scepticism, the ones concerning 'la clarté naturelle.'

Along with nos 109 and 110 Pascal very likely found no. 131, which covers the next stages of the argument: the way out of the dilemma posed by the interminable arguments of sceptics and dogmatists. This important essay - shorn of its last page and its sequel (208), which would take us much too far at this stage - is used to open a new dossier, entitled 'Contrariétés.' Pascal's perception of man has always been that he is double, and that philosophers have erred by being too exclusive. 'Grandeur' can therefore be no resting-point, but only a stage leading to the real conclusion, that man is a mass of contradictions. Once this new dossier is set up, it can absorb fragments which earlier would have gone into 'Vanité': no. 129 corresponds to no. 35 (the earlier classification is happier). No. 128 is very like no. 112, quoted above and put into section 6°.

The most impressive fragments here are the ones which refer to the wider argument: nos 122, 121, 119. No. 122

continues the point made in no. 117, that *misère* and
grandeur are sides of the same coin. No. 121 contains
the kind of antithesis I have noted in those early texts,
emphasizing the danger in embracing a view which stresses
either *bassesse* or *grandeur* exclusively. Man is both
angel and beast. (This particular pairing goes back to
the fragment on distraction, 522/XXIII 'ni ange, ni bête,
mais homme.')

Before we look at the last fragment filed in *liasse* 7°
(no. 119), I should mention that there are indications
that it was at this stage - when the 'recherche du vrai'
figured more prominently than the 'recherche du bien' -
that Pascal first gave some thought to thinking his argument through to the end, and introducing the principal
'proof' of Christianity, namely the prophecies, fulfilled
by Jesus. *Pensée* 110 had moved from knowledge of first
principles to the problem of faith, and those who believe
without any intellectual understanding of the grounds of
their faith:

Ceux à qui Dieu a donné la religion par sentiment de
coeur sont bienheureux et bien légitimement persuadés,
mais ceux qui ne l'ont pas nous ne pouvons la donner
que par raisonnement, en attendant que Dieu la leur
donne par sentiment de coeur, sans quoi la foi n'est
qu'humaine et inutile pour le salut.

Now there are two dossiers which appear to expand on
this paragraph; they now occupy the thirteenth and twenty-
eighth place. The first of these is the one entitled
'Soumission et usage de la raison.' I have already shown
that this dossier reflects Pascal's preoccupations during
his campaign against the Jesuits; it is very much concerned
with the limits of reason, and to a lesser degree with
the reconciliation of reason and faith. In the case of
one of the last to be filed, no. 170, Pascal originally
wrote the title 'Miscell,' as on 515, the top fragment
of Unit XXIII. At the centre of the *liasse* is a statement
on the role of miracles, which enable the prophecies to
be fulfilled.

The other *liasse* has the neutral title 'Conclusion.'
The first fragment filed (382) is entitled 'Connaissance
de Dieu'; it follows the last paragraph of no. 110 quite
closely, giving in addition a 'proof' that instinctive
believers are inspired by God. Elsewhere (381, 380)

Pascal explains why these people believe: because they know their own corruption and their need of redemption, and respond naturally to the teachings and promises of Christianity. No. 595 in Unit XXIV is similar. Fragment 379 on miracles is close to no. 835 in Unit XXXIII.

I suspect that there is a third *liasse* to be considered here: the one entitled 'Transition de la connaissance de l'homme à Dieu' - the echo of the title of no. 382 is probably no accident. Many problems concerning this *liasse* dissolve if we think of it as constituted relatively early, before the second half of part one and the rest of the Apologia were in place. That hypothesis explains notably the number of parallels with the early *liasses* brought out in the analysis (chapter 14). There is no need to assume that Pascal dismembered any of his bundles; he could still have been sifting his material as he constituted this one along with the others. That would explain why it includes another excerpt from the hypothetical post-Sacy *Discours*: no. 199, 'Disproportion de l'homme.' There is no reference to the 'recherche du bien' here; Pascal is still concerned with reason, which surveys the universe and is frightened at the overwhelming vastness. Another indication that these fragments are early: nos 195-7 are found on the verso of no. 194 (as no. 76 backed no. 60). Pascal had not discovered the inconvenience of using both sides of a sheet. He was to do so with this very example. No. 197 belongs to 'Vanité' and Pascal wrote a reminder to include it in that *liasse* (no. 46).[27] That may be a clue as to the chronological sequence. A little earlier, and no. 194 would surely have gone into section 3°, along with no. 68. But 35, which is akin to 193, goes into 2°, not 14°. As we suggested in chapter 14, Pascal was here reviving a theme from earlier sections, and looking at it from a new perspective which gave him the idea of opening a separate dossier. Man is blind, wretched, abandoned in a world which does not disclose its secret. Nobody seems to know if there is an answer. But there is a clue, says Pascal, which comes from a comparison of the different religions, their various claims for authority, with only Christianity producing fulfilled prophecies. This fragment ties in with other ideas to be developed in later sections, notably 17°, 'Fausseté des autres religions.' There were in fact many more developments before 'Transition' would find its proper place, and we must imagine that Pascal put these two bundles to one side.

The first fragment filed in this *liasse* is unexpected:

Consolez-vous; ce n'est point de vous que vous devez
l'attendre mais au contraire en n'attendant rien de
vous que vous devez l'attendre. (202)

I was able to justify it in chapter 14; maybe in its original context it was to console those who were dismayed to
find reason so limited, and Pascal decided to be more specific about the use to which reason could be put.

We return now to the seventh *liasse* and the elaboration
of the complete version of part one. The last fragment
filed in the seventh bundle (no. 119) is itself entitled
'Contrariétés' and it has the characteristics of a conclusion. The portrait given so far will lead the reader to
make a balanced assessment of his strength and weakness,
calling forth a response of self-love and self-loathing.
We are not far from nos 382 and 595. The curious thing
about finding it placed here is that this fragment talks
equally of *le vrai* and *le bien*, whereas very little has
been said yet about *le bien* apart from the equally unexpected references, discussed in the previous chapter, in
no. 131; and it announces a sequel which takes us out of
this part of the Apologia altogether, on the psychological
conditions for belief, once we have realized the impasse
we are in.

It is possible that the presence of no. 119 at this
place indicates that Pascal had hesitated about his exact
plan and the location of what are now sections 8°, 9°,
and 10°. We must assume that while he was setting up
Bundles 5°, 6°, and 7° he came across many other fragments,
including several now found in the three following sections. 'Divertissement,' I have suggested, took over from
liasse 4°, 'Philosophes' simply gathers together the
Epictetus material,[28] and 'Le Souverain Bien' almost certainly goes back to the same enterprise as nos 110 and 131.
Grouped together, they form an argument about *le bien* which
corresponds to the discussion of *le vrai* in sections 2°
to 7°. No. 148 significantly includes the words 'seconde
partie,' which must mean second division of the first part,
as we are still dealing with the *misère de l'homme*.[29]

This group shows signs of uncertainty over the internal
ordering. The case of no. 148, which seems more an introduction and frame than a conclusion to the section, was
discussed in chapter 10. The fragment included with it in

the undeveloped tenth *liasse* is about the 'Dispute du Souverain Bien,' and no. 408, which contains three brief notes on the same subject, states that a certain 'letter' should come 'avant le divertissement.' Two of the notes enable us to identify the 'letter' in question ('une lettre de la folie de la science humaine et de la philosophie') with fragment 76, crossed out when no. 60 was filed in *liasse* 3°.[30] The fragment which jostles no. 408 in Unit I (407) gives a bird's-eye view of the group we are discussing, and again, the order is 'Philosophes' before 'Divertissement':

Les stoïques disent: rentrez au dedans de vous même, c'est là où vous trouverez votre repos. Et cela n'est pas vrai.
   Les autres disent: sortez dehors et cherchez le bonheur en un divertissement. Et cela n'est pas vrai, les maladies viennent.
   Le bonheur n'est ni hors de nous ni dans nous; il est en Dieu et hors et dans nous.

The fragment which follows this one into Unit I (406) gives the balancing view of sceptics and dogmatists. I cited it in connection with section 6°. Its position in Unit I, after 410-407, may well imply that the true function of 6°, concentrating on 'le vrai' where 8°-10° concentrate on 'le bien,' struck Pascal only after his first experiments with the latter block.
   The *liasse* on 'Divertissement' is manifestly an offshoot of Bundles 2° and 3°, and the idea goes on back to the winter of 1656-7. No. 889, from Unit XXXIV, notes distraction as a proof that our condition is not happy; this recurs as the one of the earliest fragments to be filed: the sixth in *liasse* 3°, no. 70. No. 522 (XXIII, crossed out) speaks scornfully of the bereaved husband and father who can nevertheless forget his sorrow in the pleasures of playing a ball game; there is an echo of this in no. 39 (2°). Also in the second Bundle is the fertile no. 36, which contains the sentence 'Otez leur divertissement vous les verrez se sécher d'ennui,' which is echoed in no. 622, candidate for section 4°, but left unclassed, in Unit XXIV. Two other fragments from Unit XXIV place the motif of 'Divertissement' in relation to two main preoccupations of this part of the Apologia, thought and the Sovereign Good. No. 620, written on the same kind of paper as no.

622, states that thought is the source of man's dignity and merit, but that instead of thinking of important matters, he thinks only of amusing himself. No. 626 says that men have mistakenly looked for 'le vrai bien' in fortune, possessions, 'ou au moins dans le divertissement.'

The ideas are all picked up in the section entitled 'Divertissement.' Now, the longest essay on the subject (no. 136) was originally entitled 'Misère de l'homme' before this was changed to 'Divertissement.'[31] No. 414, one of the earliest fragments of Unit I, has the same title, and it too is a reflection on *le divertissement*. In *liasse* 1°, fragment 10 links *divertissement* and *misère*. It might have been fragment 136, important enough to stand on its own as illustrating a specific theme, which suggested to Pascal that a separate dossier was called for - although it was not the first paper to go into the file. We distract ourselves to avoid having to face the truth. Thus we can understand why 'Divertissement' follows soon after 'Grandeur'; it undercuts, with characteristic dialectic, the claims made for thought in that section.[32]

But although 'Divertissement' fits into the continuing argument about reason, Pascal must have seen around this time that a more flexible framework would be obtained by distinguishing the search for 'le vrai' from the search for 'le bien,' and exposing both according to the same pattern: illustration of *la bassesse* and *la grandeur*, both sides inadequate. So 'Divertissement,' as well as continuing from 'Grandeur,' will be another proof of our *misère*,[33] to be offset in its turn by the moral claims of the philosophers. The first subdivision had its conclusion in the listing of the contradictions involved ('Contrariétés'); as indicated in the main body of this book, there are plenty of unclassed fragments which could provide a general conclusion on the same lines. No. 119, already filed in 'Contrariétés,' could be counted among them.

Many of the others come in Unit I. No. 410 identifies the two sects and finds their prescriptions for living both inadequate, for complementary reasons.[34] No. 407, already quoted, finds their location of happiness inadequate in the same way. No. 405 inculpates those who blame man, those who praise him, those who urge him to distract himself. No. 404 concludes: these diverse contradictions have taken him further on the road which leads to religion.[35] The theme is picked up a little further back in the Unit, but there it is slanted more to the Christian account of the phenomena outlined, taking us into the first stages of part two. No. 403, which follows no. 404 in Unit I, is the definition of *misère* and *vanité* with which we began; one is surprised that it had not been filed in Unit I from the start.

The conclusion of this account of part one is that the internal ordering had evolved while Pascal distributed his fragments, and that when he abandoned it, he had not put the last phase into shape. He did, however, note the ten titles down, in order, on a sheet that was not filed immediately.[36]

(b) Seconde partie: félicité de l'homme avec Dieu (6)

Meanwhile, simultaneously, the other two parts of the Apologia had been evolving in a somewhat similar way. Because the history of the transition is particularly complicated, I shall begin by isolating a first and simpler version.

The next note filed in Unit I reads:

Preuves de la religion.
Morale/Doctrine/Miracles/Prophéties/Figures (402)

One notices that the list joins together two quite distinct kinds of proof, which we might term subjective or moral, and objective or historical. The twofold distinction is a valid one, and will help unravel the next part of the puzzle. Faith, Pascal will always maintain, is God-given. But there are certain receptive states of mind which we can actively encourage.

The moral argument for Christianity is that it alone caters to man's deepest need. We sense our present inadequacy and our need to be rescued from it, and Christianity alone claims to have the remedy. What the remedy is can be expressed in doctrinal terms: man is seen as having fallen from grace, but he is not abandoned by God, who has given each man the possibility of redemption through faith in Christ. Because this doctrine hinges on the witness of the historical figure of Jesus, the 'objective' proofs amount to a scrutiny of the credentials of Jesus, the way he fulfilled the prophecies of the Messiah, and the hopes of the Jewish religion. The sequence is therefore perfectly logical and easy to follow.

The two parts are, however, quite distinct in character, and must have been elaborated independently of each other, even if Pascal worked on both simultaneously. In the Apologia as it stands, the 'moral' argument has been largely concealed by other matter which Pascal grafted onto this part of his book, and it is concentrated in a fairly small number of fragments. It is important to consider these before passing to the historical proofs, because although Pascal undoubtedly gave much thought to the historical proofs from the beginning, it is in the course of elaborating his moral argument that he hit on the guiding theme for the following block.

The moral argument goes back to the *Entretien avec M. de Sacy* and its subsequent developments. The simplest statement is found in *liasse* 28°, no. 381:

> Ceux qui croient sans avour lu les Testaments c'est parce qu'ils ont une disposition intérieure tout sainte et que ce qu'ils entendent de notre religion y est conforme.

That this 'disposition' or 'inclination' comes from God is made clear by no. 380.[37] In order to encourage this attitude in his hearers by human means, the apologist needs to use the tools of rhetoric, and the pattern which Pascal finds particularly congenial is that of conflict and resolution. We saw the first rough outline of such a movement in the *Entretien*, soon to be fleshed out in the group of *pensées* discussed in the previous chapter: 131, 149 (page 2), 208. When Pascal came to file these *pensées*, he separated them, and he greatly amplified no. 149. This amplification leads us directly to the first stages of the block on historical proofs.

The argument in this post-Sacy *Discours*, as I have termed it, is that if a man has any understanding of, or feeling for, the complexities and the inadequacies of ths human condition, and if he is presented with the Christian doctrine of the duality of man and the redemption of mankind in Jesus, he will surely respond, and accept Christianity's claims. We have found this argument in fragment 131. Although no. 131 touches on our inability to find felicity, it is filed in 'Contrariétés' (7°), where the emphasis has fallen on the strength and weakness of reason, our inability to find truth.

In no. 149 (page 2) the stress fell rather on the search
for *le vrai bien*, although here again both categories are
mentioned (in the first paragraph: 'vous trouverez ni la
vérité ni le bien'). For the moment, we may surmise,
Pascal put this sheet to one side, intending to amplify
it further. Meanwhile, another dossier was set up, destined to be the seventeenth, called 'Fausseté des autres
religions.'[38] In this dossier Pascal filed a number of
fragments concerning the moral superiority of Christianity.
The first one echoes the sentiments of no. 381:

> Nulle autre religion n'a proposé de se haïr, nulle
> autre religion ne peut donc plaire à ceux qui se
> haïssent et qui cherchent un être véritablement aimable.
> Et ceux-là s'ils n'avaient jamais ouï parler de la
> religion d'un Dieu humilié l'embrasseraient incontinent
> (220).

Christianity, unlike other religions, can appeal to both
intellectuals and to ordinary folk (219). Over and over
again in this chapter we are told that Christianity has
the true knowledge of the human condition, and that it
brings the necessary remedies. It is into this dossier
that Pascal will put the remaining extract of his original
sequence, no. 208.

The first page of no. 149 represents a conscious attempt on Pascal's part to link the sections on the human
condition (2° to 10°) with section 17°. It draws on some
of the notes which we find on the verso of page 2.[39] It
takes into account the diversification of the argument
of part one, with sections on the *recherche du vrai* and
sections on the *recherche du bien*. It opens with a summary not only of the different sections immediately preceding, but of the symmetrical positions reached in both
enquiries. A true religion must acknowledge in man 'un
grand principe de grandeur' and 'un grand principe de
misère' and must account for 'ces étonnantes contrariétés'
– an indication that part one had already been elaborated
as far as *liasse* 7° when Pascal wrote this page of no.
149 – and it must teach that God is the Sovereign Good,
and account for our unwillingness to accept the consequences. The philosophers and Mahomet, says Pascal, have
failed to do this. Christianity has succeeded in explaining the present state of man by the doctrine of the fall.

There is a conclusion to this argument, now forming
the twenty-seventh section, 'Morale chrétienne.' It explores the Christian idea of felicity. One fragment (357)[40]
is simply a transcription of something Pascal said in the
'Infini rien' fragment (426). The last four papers filed
repeat the theme of section 17°, that Christianity harmonizes impulses which the different philosophical schools
developed in isolation and to excess.

With this, we might suppose, the first two parts of
the tripartite design delineated in no. 12, are complete,
and there remains only to link them to the third part
(already, one could assume, well under way). No. 12 is
expanded in fragment 595 (Unit XXIV), and the line of
demarcation is clear:

Si l'on ne se connaît plein de superbe, d'ambition, de
concupiscence, de faiblesse, de misère et d'injustice,
on est bien aveugle. Et si en le connaissant on ne
désire d'en être délivré que peut-on dire d'un homme?
  Que peut-on donc avoir, que de l'estime pour une
religion qui connaît si bien les défauts de l'homme,
et que du désir pour la vérité d'une religion qui y
promet des remèdes si souhaitables?

But if it might have been a simple matter to proceed
from the 'desire' that Christianity be found true, to
the actual proofs, three factors have confused the issue
somewhat. The first took place within the seventeenth
liasse itself, before no. 208 was ever filed there. All
manner of comparisons between Christianity and Mahometanism are now lodged in that dossier, whether of a moral
nature or not. Thus nos 218 and 217 have to do with the
differences between 'mysteries' and 'obscurities' in
sacred texts. No. 209 taxes Mahomet with inconsistency
in his attitude to the Gospels, and the last two to be
filed note that other religions lack witnesses and lack
the authority of Christianity (204, 203). Evidently the
theme of the 'fausseté des autres religions' has become
all-important, outweighing the consideration that these
are historical, not moral arguments, and would be better
located in the next block.

The other two complicating factors will be treated in
the two following parts of this chapter. The first concerns the way in which the third part of the Apologia is
introduced. Pascal sketches this introduction as a continuation of no. 149, leaving an editorial problem which

is not perhaps very difficult to solve. The second concerns a mass of material for which there is no place in
the present scheme; inserted as sections 12°, 13°, 14°,
15°, 16°, and 18°, it makes a very different bridge from
the one originally planned.

(c) part two: the historical proofs

We move now to the second main part of the Apologia. As
it stands now, the second part is prefaced by a long and
intricate transitional section, with the result that it
is not quite clear where it really begins: 11°? 12°? 15°?
17°? The difficulty is caused in part by the fact that
Pascal envisaged at different times several different
sequels to his first part, and these were eventually
meshed together in the pattern analysed earlier in this
study. We can distinguish four strains:
     (1) I discussed above *liasses* 13°⁻ and 28°, on the use
of reason and the possibility of justifying unreasoned
faith, thoughts which are linked in Pascal's mind with
his reflections on miracles, and also with *De l'esprit
géométrique*. I associated with these two *liasses*, *liasse*
14°. All three *liasses* mention that there are proper
proofs for Christianity, involving the miracles and the
prophecies of Jesus.
     (2) there are other fragments on the 'proper proofs,'
which include the permanence of Christian doctrine
('perpétuité'), and which rest on the authority of Scripture. These will have to be documented and expanded.
     (3) the *Entretien avec M. de Sacy*, subsequently elab-
orated in a series of important *pensées*, argues from the
duality of man and the appositeness of Christian teaching.
     (4) although Pascal had chiefly in mind the genuine en-
quirer, he was aware that resistance to his arguments
could come from various sources, and he sometimes slanted
his thoughts towards unnerving the adversary whose indifference was, he thought, unnatural. 'Infini rien' would
be an example.
     As we know, Pascal thought along different lines simul-
taneously, and there can be no question of indicating a
strict chronology. We can, however, see, once again, how
the evolving design made some connections unworkable, and
brought others into prominence. A crucial piece of evidence is afforded by fragment 149, originally part of the
post-Sacy *Discours* which I have posited, but soon expanded,
and its ideas developed in other parts of the Apologia.

This expansion, which lead easily enough to the *liasses* elaborating the proofs, made it much less easy to accommodate some of the other developments; the structure is later opened up in order to do this, leaving some loose ends.

The logical order to follow here is: (3) (2) (4) (1). This section deals with the first two of these.

I have discussed the first expansion Pascal made to no. 149 (page 1 of the manuscript) in an attempt to link the first part of his Apologia to the part explaining the 'moral' proofs. In this part of the chapter I have to discuss a second expansion, contained on pages 3 and 4, which leads into the section on the historical proofs. The sequence is very complicated, as it appears to have involved several examples of fission, that is, of new dossiers being created to relieve the growing complexities of the first ones planned. Thus, the title of the first *liasse* we shall mention (19°: 'Fondements de la religion et réponse aux objections') explicitly declares its thematic content to be double, and the *liasse* early proves inadequate for the first of the two themes mentioned.

The first fragment filed in *liasse* 19° states the fundamental objection to which Pascal feels obliged to provide an answer: 'Objection des athées. Mais nous n'avons nulle lumière.'[41] The second page contains two fragments, numbered 242 and 243 by Lafuma.[42] The first of these sketches an answer to no. 244; the other one continues in the vein of chapter 17°, and clearly corresponds to the first part of the title, 'Fondements.' I shall discuss this aspect of the chapter first, and follow it through the seven supplementary dossiers which record Pascal's full treatment of the theme. I shall then return to *liasse* 19° and discuss the other theme, as it is presented both inside the *liasse* and on the manuscript of no. 149. I shall ask why Pascal placed this bundle where he did, and finally I shall attempt to relate the development of the two themes chronologically.

Fragment 243 continues the argument with Islam:

La religion mahométane a pour fondement l'Alcoran, et Mahomet. Mais ce prophète qui devait être la dernière attente du monde a-t-il été prédit? Et quelle marque a-t-il que n'ait aussi tout homme qui se voudra dire prophète? Quels miracles dit-il lui-même avoir faits? Quel mystère a-t-il enseigné selon sa tradition même? Quelle morale et quelle félicité?

The 'fondement' of the Christian religion, on the other hand, is much more solid, 'c'est le plus ancien livre du monde et le plus authentique.' This remark is prefaced by a caution: we must judge the Jewish faith by the Scriptures, not by popular tradition; and in the margin he added a swipe at the modern equivalent of popular falsification: the writings of the casuists. We can be sure that this is an early fragment.[43]

If we read a little further back into this *liasse* in search of other examples of 'fondements,' we find only four brief fragments. No. 240 is entitled 'Preuve,' the proof noted being 'Prophéties avec l'accomplissement...' No. 238 is entitled 'Figures,' and is on the Jewish people. There are also two on miracles (227, 224). To trace the further development of these ideas, and other themes noted in no. 243, we need to look first at the *liasses* following 19°. Two of these *liasses* pick up the argument of 17°, as does no. 243 itself. But as these *liasses* call upon material which may have been temporarily envisaged in a different way, we ought here to review this other evidence.

It comes in Unit I. Our retrograde reading of that Unit had brought us to no. 402, which is entitled 'Preuves de la religion,' and lists five headings: 'Morale/Doctrine/ Miracles/Prophéties/Figures.' The first heading ('Morale') is treated in nos 401 to 397; only Christianity offers a way out of the impasse of the philosophers. We could go further back, and cite 393:[44] 'La vraie nature de l'homme, son vrai bien et la vraie vertu et la vraie religion sont choses dont la connaissance est inséparable.' The fragments corresponding to 'Doctrine' are out of place, and will be discussed separately.[45] The other three headings - miracles, prophecies and figures - do not seem to have borne the weight of the argument for long. We have already studied the fragments on miracles, and noted that very few of them find their way into the classified bundles, because Pascal did not consider them very convincing to the unbeliever. It is true that they have crucial historical importance, in that without them Jesus would not have been able to have staked his claim to be the Messiah, and hence would not have fulfilled the prophecies (cf. 180). But the emphasis falls immediately on the prophecies, and no separate dossier is created for miracles.

There will be a dossier for prophecies, and there will be a dossier for figures. But independent evidence leads

us to believe that these dossiers arose – and were further split and refined – not because of the idea Pascal
had when he wrote no. 402, but by the way the logic of
the argument took him after revising no. 149. It is
probably Unit I itself which preserves the first sound-
ings of this territory, in which figures and prophecies
are closely connected. The expansion of no. 149, as we
shall see shortly, brought Pascal to the motif of the
'Dieu caché' and his justification of this fundamental
choice God has made; it is crystallized in no. 394. No.
392 bears the title 'Figures,' and so gives us a clue as
to what Pascal meant by the fifth heading recorded in
no. 402. In no. 392 Pascal talks of the Jewish nation,
God's promises of redemption, and the precise predictions
as to the time and the manner of the redeemer's coming.
To strengthen the hope of the elect, God has given a
number of figures, or images of the eventual redemption,
such as the Flood. The role of Abraham and Moses fits
into the same pattern and purpose. But the objection can
be put: why did the Jews not believe, and why were they
permitted to get away with it? Answer: all this was part
of the prophecy, and their disbelief was needed as a foil
to the witness of the believers. They are independent
witnesses, who are not suspect (391). No. 317, which is
the sixth fragment filed in *liasse* 24° (set up, I shall
argue, soon after Pascal began to amplify 19°) was entitled 'Figures' too, and it comprises diverse jottings,
on the witness of both Jews and pagans, and on the predictions as to time. It is clear from all this that the
themes of figures and prophecies overlap, and we receive
the same impression from a handful of related fragments
in Unit XXIV. Nos 592-4 are on the theme of the Jews as
witnesses. So are nos 614 and 615, both headed 'Figuratif.'
Nos 607-9 (together on one sheet) mix together themes of
the Old Testament which may be said to prefigure Jesus
(607, 'Fig.'), tasks assigned by prophecy to the redeemer
(608, 'J-C. offices,' echoed in the opening of 392), prophecies of Christ's mission and life (609, 'Prophéties').
In the space between 608 and 609, Pascal has added a few
lines, including the phrase 'Ce qui a précédé, ce qui a
suivi, tous les juifs subsistants et vagabonds.' It is
the theme of the continuing witness again; the opening
words recur in no. 793[46] and in the note which found its
way into *liasse* 19°: 'Preuve. Prophétie avec l'accomplissement. Ce qui a précédé et ce qui a suivi J-C.' (240).

In the light of this close connection of prophecies and
figures, it is not surprising to find a little further
on in *liasse* 19° no. 238, with the title 'Figures.'

Reading back in Unit I, we find no. 390, entitled
'Perpétuité.' This theme was not mentioned in no. 402,
and the omission is surprising. In other lists, we find
perpetuity mentioned more frequently than figures.[47] The
idea expressed in no. 390 reads like a continuation of
the idea of no. 392. People have said from all time that
God promised a redeemer, and Abraham, Jacob, and Moses
have repeated this promise, saying that the Law would
last until the Messiah arrived to fulfil it. Jesus then
came, exactly as predicted. No. 389 is a note to explain
why the Messiah chose this obscure way of establishing
his identity - by prophecy rather than by obvious credentials, and by prophecies which were to be understood
figuratively. So we move back from perpetuity to prophecies and figures. Prophecies are the theme of no. 385
also.

With this we can resume our examination of the *liasses*.
Several new ones were created to take over the theme of
the 'Fondements.' The two fundamental *liasses* in this
block are 'Perpétuité' (22°) and 'Preuves de Jésus-
Christ' (24°), and clearly follow on from the group in
Unit I we have been discussing.

The argument from perpetuity - the idea that the ground
of Christianity, the Jewish religion, goes back to the
dawn of time - achieved independence quite early, it
seems. It was clearly adumbrated on the papers on miracles
(892 - 'J'aime mieux suivre J-C. qu'aucun autre parce
qu'il a le miracle, prophétie, doctrine, perpétuité,
etc.' - 878, 895) and on the 'Infini rien' manuscript
(421, 425). No. 425, slightly reworded, is copied and
put into section 22° (no. 284, the sixth from the bottom).
No. 283 is glossed in no. 590 (XXIII). The opening of
no. 282, which surveys the whole spectrum (perpetuity,
miracles, prophecies) is elaborated in no. 392, already
discussed. No. 281, remarking how extraordinary the
pehnomenon is, recalls no. 390, which is entitled 'Perpétuité,' and which has the same watermark as 'Infini
rien.'

The constitution of the *liasse* suggests that Pascal
intended to preface the argument itself with a cautionary
note, on the same lines as no. 243. There are two kinds
of Jews, carnal and spiritual, and we must judge the

Jewish faith as it is found in the latter kind, not the
former (289, 287, 286).[48] We have seen that the idea goes
back to the time of the quarrel with the Jesuits, who
were seen as 'carnal Christians.' The distinction is also
made in three fragments in other *liasses* which allude to
the *liasse* 'Perpétuité,' showing that this layer of the
dossier, if no more, was already constituted. These are
nos 178 (13°) and 366 (27°) which refer to no. 286, and
no. 222 (18°) which refers to the bottom fragment in the
pile, no. 289.[49] What this implies for *liasses* 13°, 18°,
and 27° we shall see in due course.

The heading of section 24° - 'Preuves de Jésus-Christ,'
amplifying the 'Preuve' of no. 240 - indicates its fundamental importance. More than any other, this is the logical sequel to the section on the 'fausseté des autres
religions' (17°). The second fragment to be filed (321)
makes the same contrast with Mahomet which we have met
in the earlier section, and in no. 243:

> Tout homme peut faire ce qu'a fait Mahomet. Car il n'a
> point fait de miracles, il n'a point été prédit. Nul
> homme ne peut faire ce qu'a fait J-C.

We recall that the last two fragments filed in section
17° said that Mahomet had neither authority nor witnesses.
These four points of difference - miracles, prophecies,
authority, witness - are all picked up, in a positive way,
by the present section, which is well summed up by a
fragment filed in Unit I: 'J-C. que les deux Testaments
regardent, l'ancien comme son attente, le nouveau comme
son modèle, tous deux comme leur centre' (388).

The Bible is of course the 'authority' which Mahomet
lacked. Many fragments, beginning with the very first
one filed, defend the New Testament from criticims, or
reflect on the authentic portrait of Jesus to be found
in its pages. The themes of miracles, and of pagan witnesses, can perhaps be seen as an extension of this approach. Miracles are in fact mentioned only once (apart
from no. 321), in no. 302. We have seen that fragments
concerning miracles are dispersed as the theme is divested
of particular significance. Pagan witnesses are mentioned
in nos 320 and 317, the first version of which was solely
on that theme. There are, however, other witnesses for
Jesus: the Jews themselves. That theme, and that of prophecies, are also found in this section, but they are

sufficiently important to Pascal to merit being developed
elsewhere. The fundamental question, why Jesus should
rest his claim on prophecies, and figurative prophecies
at that, is posed in no. 389 (I), but the dossiers I am
discussing give examples rather than explanations.

Fragment 319 sees the Jewish nation as a prefiguration
of Christianity, and it specifically mentioned prophecies,
or predictions: 'La synagogue a précédé l'Eglise, les
Juifs les chrétiens. Les prophètes ont prédit les chrétiens. St. Jean J-C.' These themes can be found elsewhere,
and are generally early. The synagogue is mentioned on
two of the miracles papers (859, 903), on 573 in Unit
XXIII and on no. 793 in Unit XXVIII.[50] The prediction of
the Christians is found also in no. 301, at the end of
no. 131 (the page that was crossed out), and in no. 382
in *liasse* 28°. The same *liasse* includes no. 379, which
Tourneur tells us was written on the same sheet as no.
301.[51] We have given our reasons for assigning an early
date to that *liasse*. A couple of specific prefigurations
of Jesus go into a separate dossier (26°, 'Figures particulières'), but the fuller development of the theme of
prediction and prophecy is elsewhere.[52]

More fruitful than no. 319 is no. 317. The original
layer, as we have said, is about pagan witnesses, and
expands a note added to the top of no. 501 (500/XIX).
Pascal deleted the title ('Figures'), and added three
thoughts. The first two read:

Le zèle des juifs pour leur loi et leur temple. Josèphe
et Philon juif, *ad Caium.*
    Quel autre peuple a un tel zèle, il fallait qu'ils
l'eussent.

By their zeal, the Jews witness to Christianity. Looked
at slightly differently, this theme produces no. 297[53]
and no. 294. No. 297 initiates a new dossier, to which
Pascal gave the title 'Preuves de Moise,' which clearly
echoes the title of *liasse* 24°; indeed, as a heading for
these two fragments, it seems to owe more to the sound
than to the sense. The title is more appropriate to other
fragments which go into the same dossier: remarks on the
longevity of the patriarchs.[54] The new dossier thus becomes a documentary appendix not to 24° but to 22° ('Perpétuité').

Moses, meanwhile, is cited in no. 315, principally on
another 'witness,' David. The next fragment in *liasse* 24°,
no. 314, speaks of the two destructions of the temple and
the dispersal of the Jews. The dispersal as a proof of
Jesus is the theme of no. 311, and the ideas of nos 314
and 311 are brought together in no. 305. The same ideas
recur in another dossier, 'Prophéties' (25°). The third
addition to no. 317 is about the precision of the predictions concerning the time and the political situation of
the First Coming, and it too will be developed in *liasse*
25°. We can therefore say that a separate dossier on
prophecies evolved naturally as Pascal saw where some of
his ideas on the 'Preuves de Jésus-Christ' would lead
him. The only other mention of prophecies in 24° is the
general injunction to study them carefully (312). There
is, however, a hidden connection between the theme of
the prophecies, and the most important fragment in *liasse*
24°, no. 308 on the 'three orders.' Pascal is showing
that Jesus fulfilled the messianic prophecies on a wholly
different level from the level on which the carnally-
minded Jews understood the biblical texts. The theme of
the three orders, as we have seen, has long been characteristic of Pascal's thinking, and Pascal also draws, in
no. 308, on the analogy of the finite and the infinite
realms made in the fragment which is entitled 'Infini
rien.'

The new dossier on prophecies is relatively straightforward, though long. Pascal seeks out messianic prophecies from the Old Testament, dwelling on the remarkable
fact that so many different predictions should have con-
verged onto Jesus. To him, the argument is conclusive
(329), the greatest of all the 'preuves de J-C.' (335),
the crowning argument (326). No. 326, which rather mys-
teriously connects prophecies with the idea that our
thinking should be governed by a constant awareness of
our mortality, echoes in this last remark no. 386 in
Unit I,[55] and its opening sentence is echoed in an addition made to no. 385, on the way the Jews have faithfully
preserved the prophecies. The prophecies include, then,
the witness of the Jews, and the gift of the Holy Spirit.
One fragment on the Jews makes the same distinction
between carnal and spiritual that was made for the fragments on perpetuity: 'Au temps du Messie, ce peuple se
partage. Les spirituels ont embrassé le Messie, les
grossiers sont demeurés pour lui servir de témoins' (331).

This same research and documentation prompted a large number of reflections where the emphasis falls differently. We have seen that the time and the context of Christ's coming were predicted 'clearly'; the manner, however, was ambiguous. The Old Testament is often a figurative text, which has to be deciphered. Many difficulties - notably, that the prophecies were not fulfilled in a literal sense - disappear if we admit a figurative reading. For fragments illustrating this argument, another new dossier was opened: 'Que la loi était figurative' (20°). The first fragment filed recalls a couple of fragments in 'Fausseté' (217-18). There Pascal had contrasted the Bible and the Koran, both of which are obscure in places, by saying that the amount of good sense in the former predisposes us to find the obscure passages mysteries, whereas those in the Koran we are ready to believe nonsensical (218). The first fragment placed in the twentieth dossier makes the same general point, and concludes that 'Le vieux testament est un chiffre.' Pascal reflected long on the problems of interpreting Scripture, and the key, to him, was that the Old Testament - specifically, the Law - was figurative. This provides all manner of insights concerning the meaning of scriptural texts.[56]

Another fragment in 20° (269) interestingly joins the argument about the Old Testament being figurative with the previous stage, the 'moral' proof of Christianity. Pascal is here addressing directly the people who intuitively understand their need for redemption. He has good news for them: there is a liberator, there is a God. Jesus came to deliver us from our 'enemies' and by this is meant precisely the concupiscence and self-love which such good people have already identified as the real enemy. (A fragment on Jesus as satisfying man's moral hunger has strayed into this *liasse*, as no. 271.)

The brief twenty-first *liasse* ('Rabbinage') arises out of a note (no. 274, the third fragment filed in 20°) on rabbinical evidence for the double reading of Scripture (literal and figurative) which Pascal is proposing. It clearly witnesses to a piece of research conducted somewhere along the line.

The section on the figurative interpretation of the Old Testament (20°) is put at the head of the block of proofs, because it explains the method to be used. Another substantial dossier is placed with it, one which answers the objection that none of all this is self-evident.

This is of course *liasse* 19°, which takes its real character not from that part of its title which reads 'Fondements,' but from the other part, 'Réponse aux objections.' I have already cited fragment 244, and remarked that the answer to that 'objection' was sketched in no. 242. We are now in a possition to examine the ramifications of this element further.

The text of no. 242 is as follows:

Que Dieu s'est voulu cacher.
   S'il n'y avait qu'une religion, Dieu y serait bien manifeste.
   S'il n'y avait des martyrs qu'en notre religion, de même.
   Dieu étant ainsi caché, toute religion qui ne dit pas que Dieu est caché n'est pas véritable, et toute religion qui n'en rend pas la raison n'est pas instruisante. La nôtre fait tout cela. *Vere tu es deus absconditus.*

Although this reply to an objection is couched, like no. 243 and the corresponding fragments in *liasse* 17°, as an implied contrast between Christianity and other religions, turning an objection into a positive argument, the notion of the hidden God enshrines a basic religious insight which need not be tied to a polemical context.

The 'objection' noted in no. 244 is ineed a very fundamental one, and Pascal had his answer ready. It is contained in the famous letter to Mlle de Roannez written in 1656, as well as in sundry other observations made at the same time; they have all been discussed in chapter 30.[57] He makes three related points. The first is that certainty is unknown to us, we have to accept the existence of certain principles on which reason builds. (This idea belongs to part one of the Apology.) The second is that spiritual truths fall into the same pattern, known to the heart through grace, mediated often through physical phenomena which have a distinct meaning on their own physical level. Thus there is evidence, but it is ambiguous. The third point is a proposed explanation of God's purpose in withdrawing certainty from us. The problem has to be tackled where man's rebellion against God is most concentrated: in the will. If reason could find God unaided, we would be more proud still. Reason therefore has to be put in its place, and the will brought

into subjection. It is the will, not reason, which ultimately has to decide, by conversion and not conviction.
God, then, conceals himself, though he can be found.

The development of this idea in the Apologia is to be
found in the latter half of no. 149 and in various fragments filed in *liasse* 19°. Indeed, the last page of no.
149 is itself filed in 19°, immediately after no. 242.
To understand the steps which led from the parts of no.
149 we have already discussed to this development of
liasse 19°, we have the clear evidence of the manuscript
itself.

It will be recalled that to the original layer of no.
149 (now page 2: a text and some jottings) was added a
first page, which led to section 17°. Some of the jottings
were absorbed at that time. The manuscript of no. 149
contains no fewer than three more developments, in different handwriting. We cannot tell how long a gap separated them. The first, like the one just cited, is an
objection followed by a reply. But this time the reply
is quite long, and it goes immediately onto a new (third)
page, filling three-quarters of it. The objection is:
'Incroyable que Dieu s'unisse à nous,' which Pascal says
is logically not justified.[58] The second new development
completes the available space, and once more uses the
convention of the prosopopoeia. It ties in with what
Pascal has always said about the use of reason in religious matters: it will not be spurned, but its use will
be very limited. The convention is abandoned again in
the final development, to be found on the *verso* of page
3, and spilling onto a fourth page.[59] In this, Pascal
sketches an explanation of God's purpose. The focus is
still the issue of faith as something God-given, and it
is now linked to another motif we shall be discussing
later, that of the seeker after God. God, we are told,
wishes to redeem and save those who seek him. But we can
never merit divine grace, and it is right that grace
should be refused to us for our hardness of heart. So
God has not declared himself in an unambiguous manner.
He can be found only by those who seek him. He allows
enough light to help those who genuinely search. He is
not toally invisible, but he is not visible to all.

The last two developments just described can be seen
as answers to the fundamental objection recorded in the
first fragment placed in *liasse* 19°; 'Mais nous n'avons
nulle lumière' (244). And when Pascal reflects on the

proper location for what he has added to no. 149, he sees
that here is, in fact, the nucleus of section 19°. And
so, after no. 242-3, Pascal filed the last page (4) of
no. 149, which we can number 241bis. If no. 244 states
the main objection, no. 242 and 241bis sketch the reply,
calling on the biblical notion of the hidden God.

It is surprising that Pascal did not include the third
page along with the fourth in this nineteenth *liasse*.
Very likely it was an oversight, for many of the separate
fragments he wrote and filed in this nineteenth *liasse*
are based on what he had written earlier in no. 149. The
reflections on God's joining himself to us (ie, page 3
recto) inspire nos 239 and 231 (scored out).[60] We even
find a couple of the jottings of page 2 in *liasse* 19°.
The one on incomprehensibility is here, shorn of the
geometrical example (230), and the first one is expanded
into no. 226. But the key to it all is the important
development of page 3 verso. The emphasis throughout this
liasse is on the relative clarity and obscurity of God,
above all on the ambiguity of the evidence, seen as part
of God's design. Many fragments speak of Jesus, whose
divinity was concealed, and who himself gave light to some
and kept others in the dark (241, 237, 236, 235, 233, 228,
225). Another fragment (234) touches on the need for God
to address the will rather than reason, which we saw was
the natural conclusion to a sequence on the hidden God.[61]

We have accounted now for the block of *liasses* from
19° to 26°. At the end of the sequence (27°) comes a
section entitled 'Morale chrétienne.' This is evidently
to be distinguished from the *pensées* on 'la Morale.' It
is for the most part quite different in tone, being a
hymn to felicity. The theme was touched upon towards the
end of no. 418. Only with the last four fragments filed
(351-4), and also perhaps with no. 358, is the distinction
between this *liasse* and 17° blurred. We know incidentally
that *liasse* 22° already contained no. 286 by the time
Pascal filed no. 366, which refers to it. The manuscript
of no. 366 having unfortunately disappeared, we cannot
know if the words 'Voyez Perpétuité' were a later addition.

To round the Apologia off, Pascal had recourse to a
brief dossier discussed in connection with no. 110 earlier
in this chapter. Although it could conceivably have served
to introduce the section on proofs, it fits equally well
as a conclusion, and that is what Pascal called it,

rather than 'Connaissance de Dieu.' Indeed, the last
fragment filed (an afterthought?) goes beyond that subject: 'Qu'il y a loin de la connaissance de Dieu à
l'aimer' (377). Using this *liasse* in this way may have
reminded Pascal of the related bundles, now 13° and 14°.
Those two will be used to introduce the proofs, taking
their place in an extremely elaborate bridge passage
which replaces the expansion of no. 149 discussed in the
present section.

It is not difficult to see why *liasse* 19° was placed
before the treatment of the historical proofs. If it had
been conceived only as a way of answering objections
which might cross the mind of a man reading the proofs,
it might have been left to the end - although there is
an advantage in forestalling the major objection from
the start, thus ensuring that the section on the proofs
would be read more sympathetically. But the answer Pascal
gave contained the key to how difficult evidence should
be interpreted, and it is natural to explain one's approach before embarking on details. Moreover, Pascal knew
he did not have to pretend that it was only by considering the historical proofs that the atheist would be
brought to observe that 'nous n'avons nulle lumière.'
This doubt Pascal sees as always present in the mind of
the unbeliever. Indeed, so basic is it, that he will
tackle it from a different perspective, and plan a new
linking section which will completely transform this
part of the Apologia.

Before we consider that problem, we should observe that
the place of some fragments gives us a clue as to the
order in which the passage we have been studying expanded,
and supports some of the conclusions arrived at logically.
The presence of no. 240 ('Preuve') and no. 238 ('Figures,)
implies that Pascal began to constitute *liasse* 19° before
he had set up 24° and 20°, for no. 240 would be more at
home in *liasse* 24° ('Preuves de J-C.'), and the second
fragment filed in *liasse* 20° is an expansion of no. 238.
If two fragments on miracles (227, 224, both filed relatively late) go here, it is because there is no obvious
home for the thoughts on miracles, and Pascal has not
completely abandoned the idea that *liasse* 19° should say
something about the 'fondements.' Indeed, the last fragment filed (223) implies some degree of retraction on
Pascal's part, regretting that he had put into the section on 'la loi figurative' something which should be

announced in 19°. The reference is to no. 255, and we
can understand Pascal's hesitation: the explanation ac-
cords with the general theory of enlightenment and obscurity, which is the unifying motif of 19°. This shows
that by the time Pascal completed *liasse* 19°, *liasse* 20°,
begun after 19° had been started, was almost complete
(*liasse* 20° runs from 276 to 245). The two bundles were
therefore constituted simultaneously, but that did not
prevent Pascal from having second thoughts about the
place he had assigned to one of his *pensées*. That he made
a note about it, rather than searching for the relevant
piece of paper and moving it, suggests that time was short.

(d) *Transition de la connaissance de l'homme à Dieu (14°)*

We have discerned in no. 149 the vestiges of a transition
between parts one and two, with only section 17° separating section 11° from section 19°. We must now look at the
more complex transition which Pascal conceived subsequently
There are many ideas which somehow have not found a niche
in the bipartite scheme just presented, and what Pascal
does is to open out the structure at the point where the
two parts join, in no. 149. This creates a problem which
he did not try to solve: the last page of no. 149 is now
eight sections away from the previous pages, and the
break actually occurs in mid-sentence.

The inserted sections fall into two groups: 12°, 13°,
and 14° on the one hand; 15°, 16°, and 18° on the other.
I suggested earlier that *liasses* 13° and 14° belong
(like *liasse* 28°) to an early phase in the growth of the
Apologia. Both have to do with the right use of reason,
and they would have fitted well enough on the end of part
one when part one went only to section 7°. Developments
since then have made the march of the argument much less
simple, and the relationship between the two parts has
been greatly modified by the expansion of fragment 149.
That expansion has left no obvious place in which to
lodge the *liasses* in question, but they cannot be ignored.
If the role of part two had once been to implant spiritual
longings in the hearts of *les bons* who have 'une disposition intérieure toute sainté' (381),[62] it has become a
way of replying to the objections one would expect an
agnostic to make. In the last analysis, this is not a
matter of reasoning, good or bad, but of a reluctance to
accept the limitations of reason, and make a leap of faith.

The reason for doubting is in Pascal's view psychological
rather than intellectual. The notion is expressed in the
sentences added at the beginning of no. 12: 'Les hommes
ont mépris pour la religion. Ils en ont haine et peur
qu'elle soit vraie. Pour guérir cela il faut/connaître
(etc.).' So his two dossiers on the limitations and the
correct use of reason should go in early in part two.

The theme opens onto others. The psychological argument,
as opposed to a reasoned account of faith, is at the basis
of 'Infini rien,' already written, and one of the last
fragments filed in Unit I refers to it: 'J'aurais bien
plus peur de me tromper et de trouver que la religion
chrétienne soit vraie que non pas de me tromper en la
croyant vraie' (387). It is not clear when *liasse* 12°
was constituted, but I would be surprised if it were as
early as 13° and 14°.[63] The title, mentioned (according
to the Copies) on the third fragment filed, is 'Commencement,' which probably meant originally (however we may
interpret it in the larger context of the Apologia) that
this would be the starting-point of the part of the
Apologia Pascal was now addressing himself to. The basic
theme is that in the perspective of our mortality, indifference about religious teaching is unnatural, and
this too is noted in Unit I, on the last paper to be
included, no. 383: 'D'être insensible à mépriser les
choses intéressantes, et devenir insensible au point qui
nous intéresse le plus.'[64] We are creatures of passion,
sobered only by the prospect of imminent death - as if
death is not at all moments a real threat. This is implied
by no. 386. Other fragments in the same *liasse* echo the
mathematics of the 'Infini rien' passage.

Reading the seventeen fragments of liasse 12°, one
has the impression of a discourse addressed directly to
the unbeliever, alerting him to the importance of the
religious question in life, and accusing him of unnatural
and unreasonable behaviour. We are no longer talking to
the genuine seeker - 'ceux qui cherchent en gémissant,'
he said in no. 405 - but to the man who refuses to bother,
and some fragments in 12° make the distinction clearly.

This urgent appeal to the unbeliever can serve as a
kind of preface to part two, hence the title, known from
the start, of 'Commencement.' Very approximately, it can
be made to tie in with the agnostic's objections noted
on fragment 149, which hitherto has provided the link
between the first part and sections 17° and 19°. And so

Pascal places no. 149 on the top of his twelfth bundle, and writes on it 'Commencement. Après avoir expliqué l'incompréhensibilité.' It is even doubtful whether no. 149 would have been maintained as an independent section.[65]

With the original argument disrupted, Pascal saw the possibility of a separate introduction to part two, announcing the main theme (Jesus the redeemer). This gives us *liasse* 15°, 'Excèllence de cette manière de prouver Dieu.' The first fragment filed (192) resolves the pride/despair dichotomy in Christ, and the others insist that Christ is our only access to God. Something else might go in here. No. 402 had listed five 'Preuves de la religion,' of which the first two were 'Morale' and 'Doctrine.' 'Morale' I have already discussed; but what did Pascal mean by doctrine? The basic Christian doctrine is that man is both fallen and redeemed, and we know from the table of chapter-titles that Pascal contemplated two sections which would correspond to the themes of corruption and redemption. Title 16° is 'Que la nature est corrumpue,' and 18° is 'Rendre la religion aimable.' The sixteenth *liasse* is not constituted as such, but the contents are indicated by the first two fragments in Unit I, nos 417 and 416. No. 417 seems to follow directly on the heels of no. 189, the last fragment in 15°. We have already surmised that we have in nos 416 and 417 (and in no. 190) the vestiges of an early general introduction;[66] be that as it may, it makes good sense to use them to pave the way for the full consideration of the Christian case.

Liasse 18° which balances 16° (and which may also go back to an earlier projected introduction) does exist, but it too is very short, comprising two fragments only, on the issue of the universality of Christ's redemption. The theme goes back to the dossiers on miracles (910-12/ XXXIV) and to no. 544, in Unit XXIII. No. 222 makes the same distinction as the first fragment filed in 'Perpétuité' (no. 289); both were dictated, maybe at the same time. Later, probably when they were put into place before *liasse* 19°, Pascal added on the back the words 'Voyez Perpétuité.'[67]

We can be sure that it was at this stage of his work that Pascal stopped setting up his dossiers, giving each Bundle its title, inscribed on a separate flyer. The problem of no. 149 is not resolved; the amplifications of 12° and 15° (in fragments 427-8 and 449) are not

incorporated; the embryon of 16° is not put in place, and
18° is nowhere developed. In addition, Pascal seems to
have been careless in his actual ordering, putting 15°
before 14°, and 18° after 17° rather than before it. This
order is preserved on the list of titles, which he added
as a complement to the titles already noted of the first
ten chapters. This list includes the title of 16°. Was
it at this time that Pascal, rereading the ten titles
already noted, decided to change the title assigned to
his fifth *liasse*?

The complete list is then put at the top of Unit I.[67]
We thus end as we began, with Unit I, which appears to
have recorded the steps through which the Apologia passed
with remarkable fidelity. Remarkable because it is not
at all clear why Pascal should have constituted a *liasse*
in this way. Mesnard calls it 'une sorte d'esquisse de
l'*Apologie*, analogue, quoique sommaire et non ordonné,
à celle des 27 chapitres'[68] – although it does have some
order, as we have seen. Sellier's label is 'liasse-table,'[69]
although the fragments are surely too precise to fit that
description exactly. It remains something of an enigma,
all the more so as Pascal occasionally made a note to include in a *liasse* a thought which is located in Unit I.

(e) Pascal's lecture

We cannot close this chapter without looking at one more
problem, or group of problems. One would like to know
when Pascal undertook the classification. The last five
years of Pascal's life were divided into three distinct
parts, as he was seriously ill for eighteen months, from
early in 1659 to the summer of 1660.[70] Did he classify
his fragments before he fell ill, or after he recovered?
There can be no reasonable doubt that the former is much
the more likely. We have seen that classifying the fragments was part of the creative process, suggesting new
ways for the Apologia to develop, and it would seem to
be a natural outcome of the first phase, beginning early
in 1657, in which Pascal noted down so many thoughts,
expanding them in different directions. When we look at
the unclassed fragments, we shall find that some of them
are late, whereas the same cannot be said for any of the
classified fragments.[71] For the last half of 1658 Pascal
was also engrossed with the 'affaire de la roulette,'[72]
and it is perfectly understandable that sensing that he

would not have the time or the strength to go much further with his work on the Apologia, he should at least
put the papers in order and put them away tidily. So,
even if we had no other grounds, we could assume that
most of the work on the bundles was done during the year
1658.[73]

Writers on Pascal, however, speak of the matter somewhat differently. Combining different accounts, and
suppressing sundry nuances which different scholars have
introduced, one might say that it is widely assumed that
Pascal classified his fragments in preparation for a talk
he gave at Port-Royal, the outline of which was reported
first by Filleau de la Chaise and then by Etienne Périer,
in texts which they wrote to serve as preface to the
first edition of the *Pensées*.[74] The matter is however
much more complex and more problematical than that, and
in examining it we need to distinguish three questions:
the lecture at Port-Royal, a talk Pascal gave to some
friends, and the reliability of Filleau and Etienne Périer.
We can ask how relevant this talk or these talks were to
the business of classifying the fragments; and when this
is done, we can ask if the enquiry has helped at all to
date the different stages of the work Pascal did.

The first thing to say is that the evidence for a lecture at Port-Royal is slender. Filleau and Etienne Périer
do not mention it. They say only that Pascal expounded
his ideas to a group of friends. This is how Filleau de
la Chaise describes it:

> On le (le dessein de M. Pascal) sait par un discours
> qu'il fit un jour en présence de quelques-uns de ses
> amis, et qui fut comme le plan de l'ouvrage qu'il
> méditait. Il parla pour le moins deux heures; et
> quoique ceux qui s'y trouvèrent soient des gens d'un
> esprit à admirer peu de choses, comme on en conviendrait
> aisément si je les nommais, ils reconnaissent encore
> présentement qu'ils en furent transportés...[75]

Etienne Périer says much the same:

> Il se rencontra néanmoins une occasion, il y a environ
> dix ou douze ans, en laquelle on l'obligea, non pas
> d'écrire ce qu'il avait dans l'esprit sur ce sujet-là,
> mais d'en dire quelque chose de vive voix. Il le fit
> donc en présence et à la prière de plusieurs personnes

très considérables de ses amis. Il leur développa en
peu de mots le plan de tout son ouvrage ... et les
personnes, qui sont aussi capables qu'on le puisse être
de juger de ces sortes de choses, avouent qu'elles
n'ont jamais rien entendu de plus beau, de plus fort,
de plus touchant, ni de plus convaincant; qu'elles en
furent charmées; et que ce qu'elles virent de ce projet
et de ce dessein dans un discours de deux ou trois
heures, fait ainsi sur-le-champ sans avoir été prémé-
dité ni travaillé, leur fit juger ce que ce pourrait
être un jour, s'il était jamais exécuté...[76]

This talk which Filleau and Etienne Périer claim to be
reporting was at some point identified with another talk,
knowledge of which comes from a very different source.
Four times - once on no. 122, three times on no. 149 -
Pascal's manuscript records the initials 'A P.R.' and
on two occasions (both on fragment 149) the phrase reads
'A P.R. pour demain.' Clearly, then, Pascal wrote no.
149 with a specific occasion in mind, presumably for some
kind of talk he was giving the next day. Given this, it
is reasonable to interpret the initials as meaning 'A
Port-Royal.'[77] This reading is not beyond doubt - Pol
Ernst has made the nice point that twice the letter 'A'
seems to be followed by a full stop, which would mean
that it is an abbreviation[78] - but no satisfactory alternative has been proposed.[79] One of the most attractive
('Apologie pour la religion') is open to the objection
that 'P' is not Pascal's way of abbreviating 'pour.' So
the traditional interpretation has never really been
challenged. It is disquieting nevertheless to find that
no other mention has been found, in any document, of such
a lecture.[80]

Even if we accept the hypothesis of a lecture given at
Port-Royal, can we go on from that to assume that the
fragments were classified in view of that lecture?[81]
Nothing is less likely. The bundles could certainly be
used for the writing of a book, but they would be impos-
sibly cumbersome as lecture-notes. As for Lafuma's remark
that once the lecture was over, Pascal saw no reason
to continue classifying his fragments,[82] this can be
fairly easily disproved by noting the place of the papers
marked 'A P.R.' in the *liasses*.[83]

Fragment 122 is the fourth from the top of *liasse* 7°;
it is entitled 'Grandeur et Misère,' and it shows how

those two notions mutually support each other. No. 149
forms a separate unit, added (subsequently?) to the top
of *liasse* 12° ('Commencement'). It has a title, visibly
added later: 'Commencement: Après avoir expliqué l'incompréhensibilité.' The last page of no. 149 goes early into
liasse 19°, as we have seen. This suggests that whatever
else Pascal may have said to his audience 'à Port-Royal,'
he gave his bacic conclusions on the themes of 'Contrarié-
ties' (perhaps adding to no. 122 the allied fragments 121
and 119, which develop the same antithesis), and showed
how they led to a rejection of many religions and acceptance of the basic positions of Christianity. He was ready
to present not only the first version of this crucial
part of his argument (149 page 2, 'Prosopopée'; 'A P.R.
pour demain' is added), but also the interesting developments which stem from it: pages 1 ('A P.R.'), 3, and 4
('A.P.R. pr demain').

The place of page 4 in *liasse* 19° shows also that Pascal
had yet to work out the remifications of that part of his
argument. The preparation of the lecture (or whatever
else may be lurking behind the phrase 'A P.R. pour demain')
was therefore closely connected with the linking together
of the two parts of the Apologia and the consequent expansion, and this preparation took place before *liasse*
7° was complete. Whatever the exact calendar date concealed behind the word 'demain,' it is clear that this
conclusion fits nicely with what we saw to be the evolution of the plan in a previous portion of this chapter.[84]

What of the talk reported by Filleau, and after him by
Etienne Périer? Again there is no independent source, and
Filleau's credibility has been questioned. He does not
claim to have been present himself. He says he is presenting the memories of a first-hand witness, although
he forgets this at times, and writes more in the direct
style of one composing a preface to a collection of written texts. The talk and the witness may therefore be no
more than a convenient literary device, in the manner of
Fontaine's dialogues.[85] This scepticism is probably excessive. Filleau was a member of the editorial committee,
of which Pascal's closest friend, the Duc de Roannez, was
president; his text was read by the family, who disapproved
of it, and commissioned Etienne Périer to write another
one.[86] The fact that Etienne Périer left in the account
of the talk shows that they did not disapprove of that,
and given the fanatical loyalty of all these people to

Pascal's memory, it is doubtful that they would have accepted a fictitious statement of this kind.[87] It is more
straightforward to believe that Pascal had spoken to his
intimates, in the manner described, and that this tradition was still alive. Nor is it difficult to identify
the person by whom it was transmitted. We know that Pascal
was very close to the Duc de Roannez. If he was the source
of Filleau's knowledge, then we can say that the talk
must have taken place before the mid-point of 1658, for
the Duke left Paris for Poitiers in July of that year.[88]
This again tallies with what has emerged from a study of
the other evidence. But we cannot seriously maintain that
this talk was the *raison d'être* of the classification;
it is far more reasonable to connect the classification
with the book Pascal was planning, rather than with something as ephemeral as a few hours discussion with a group
of friends.

But even if we accept the fact of the talk Pascal gave
to his friends, can we believe Filleau's account of the
content? Here, critical opinion has been sharply divided.
On the one hand have been those who accept Filleau at his
word, and even use his detailed summary as the basis of
editions of the *Pensées*.[89] On the other hand are those
like Lafuma, who, discounting Filleau's claim to be preserving the outline of a talk Pascal gave back in 1658,
argue that Filleau was simply following Copy 9203.[90]

It is perfectly true that Filleau must have been doing
more than just following the memories, or the notes, of
someone present at the talk which he evokes at the beginning of his *Discours*.[91] Common sense dictates as much:
the account is just too long, too detailed, and the vocabulary shows that Filleau was steeped in Pascal. Some
kind of interference would be only natural. In fact it
can be proved, said Lafuma, as some of the ideas used
were developed by Pascal after 1658.[92] Moreover, Filleau
is not above introducing ideas of his own. Does this invalidate his evidence completely?

In fairness to Filleau, it must be pointed out that he
does not claim that he is reporting the talk just as it
was given. What Filleau says is that Pascal's fragments
give no idea of the magisterial power of his great project. After giving a brief outline of 'le dessein de M.
Pascal' ('il voulait rappeler les hommes à leur coeur,
et leur faire commencer par se bien connaître eux-mêmes'
- the point being that proof of God's existence rests on

principles known to the heart, such as the vestiges we
can still sense of our former greatness, but that sin
had made us deaf to the voice of the heart and blind to
the evidence of God in nature), Filleau says that the
design emerges not only from the fragments to be published
('ces fragments') and from those it has been decided not
to publish, but also from 'un discours qu'il fit un jour
en présence de quelques-uns de ses amis, et qui fut comme
le plan de l'ouvrage qu'il méditait.' Then he adds: 'C'est
d'un d'eux que plus de huit ans après on a appris ce qu'on
va en dire.' That would seem to be a formal indication
that everything that follows goes back to the recollec-
tions of a first-hand witness. But although he says he
took what he is going to say from someone who was present
at the original talk, he does not in fact push this very
far. This is what he says about the talk itself:

> Après donc qu'il leur eut exposé ce qu'il pensait des
> preuves dont on se sert d'ordinaire, et fait voir com-
> bien celles qu'on tire des ouvrages de Dieu sont peu
> proportionnées à l'état naturel du coeur humain, et
> combien les hommes ont la tête peu propre aux raison-
> nements métaphysiques, il montre clairement qu'il n'y
> a que les preuves morales et historiques, et de certains
> sentiments qui viennent de la nature et de l'expérience,
> qui soient de leur portée; et il fit voir que ce n'est
> que sur des preuves de cette sorte que sont fondées les
> choses qui sont reconnues dans le monde pour les plus
> certaines.

He adds an example and comment of his own.[93]
Then comes the key sentence for our present enquiry:

> M. Pascal entreprit donc de faire voir que la Religion
> chrétienne était en aussi forts termes que ce qu'on
> reçoit le plus indubitablement entre les hommes; et
> suivant son dessein de leur apprendre à se connaître,
> il commença par une peinture de l'homme...

Does he mean 'in the talk,' or 'in the work (as the talk
confirmed'? It was surely his readers, not his friends,
to whom Pascal would teach self-knowledge. The next paragraph begins: 'Que chacun s'examine sérieusement sur ce
qu'il trouvera dans ce Recueil.' Again, Filleau is not
thinking of the talk (still less of relaying its contents

precisely) but of the book to which he is writing a Preface - as instanced also by the phrase 'ces fragments,'
quoted earlier.[94] The point is even clearer on the next
page.

> C'est à cet étrange repos que M. Pascal en voulait
> principalement: et on le trouvera poussé dans ses
> écrits avec tant de force et d'éloquence, etc. ... Et
> après avoir supposé qu'un homme raisonnable n'y pouvait
> demeurer, non plus que dans l'ignorance de son véritable
> état présent et à venir, il lui fit chercher tout ce
> qui lui pouvait donner quelque lumière, et examina pre-
> mièrement ce qu'en avaient dit ceux qu'on appelle Philo-
> sophes.

Filleau de la Chaise, then, sets Pascal's argument in
the framework of an attempt to make men change their attitude. He gives a brief, but adequate, summary of part
one, concentrating on the conclusion: lucidity about the
questions which need to be answered, and dissatisfaction
with the explanations currently offered by philosophers
and by many religions. He pushes the enquirer to the
verge of despair,[95] before allowing him to find the way
out of the impasse by discovering 'le peuple Juif.'
  With the second part, however, Filleau is much less
discreet, and he expands Pascal's biblical argument at
great length. For all its length, the outline is clear,
and in most respects valid as a representation of Pascal's
thought. He begins by stressing the odd features of Jewish
history which command respect, and then examines the Old
Testament. He discusses the credibility of the Bible account of the Creation and of the Fall, of its concept of
God, and of man's relationship with God. He talks of the
biblical understanding of the Fall and its consequences,
and of God's promise of liberation. This corresponds to
the 'moral' argument of the Apologia; the superiority of
the Jewish religion acts as a kind of guarantee, Filleau
says.
  He then passes to the historical proofs: to those elements, like miracles and prophecies, which are not in
the natural order of things. He talks at length about
Moses, whom it is difficult to see as an impostor. Anyone
who rejects the claim of the Old Testament has a number
of awkward facts to explain, particularly in the way it
converges on the ministry of Jesus, who fulfilled so many

diverse prophecies, and fulfilled them in a way which
squares with the spiritual insights into the human condition which we have been considering.

Throughout his exposition, Filleau has at times raised
the question of disbelief and non-acceptance. In a double
conclusion, he argues that Pascal has shown that the
Christian religion is well established, and that what
needs explanation is not belief but disbelief, and secondly
he mentions the different attitudes which are likely to
lead men to reject Pascal's case. He finishes with a
point which Pascal himself stresses much more than Filleau
does: that it is to be hoped that people will give some
time and thought to the matter, because a bad choice now
may mean an eternity of regret.[96]

In summary, this is an interesting text, an intelligent
attempt to present Pascal's thought to his very first
public, using as a framework the memories of an address
Pascal had given, and filling it out with a reasonably
judicious use of the material Pascal had left at his
death, which had been copied, and which was in the process of being sifted and edited.[97]

Can we say more? In particular, is there any way in
which Filleau's record can contribute to our knowledge
of Pascal's thought in 1658, as opposed to 1661 or 1662?
If Lafuma is right, and Filleau's only source is Copy
9203, his usefulness is clearly very limited. Annie Barnes
challenged Lafuma's conclusions.[98] She argued that if
Filleau had based his *Discours* on the Copy, he would not
have omitted such important chapters as 'Raison des
effets' (5°), 'Divertissement' (8°), and 'Transition'
(14°), nor would he have moved straight from 'Philosophes'
(9°) to 'Fausseté des Religions' (17°). In the second
part, Filleau developed some ideas (miracles, and the
theory of 'les apôtres fourbes'), which are not given
any emphasis in the Copy. Mrs Barnes also spotted a source
- fragment 948, a draft used in two letters to Mlle de
Roannez - which was not on the Copies. The only point
here that Lafuma was able satisfactorily to answer was
the last one: the letters themselves were printed in the
Port-Royal edition, which would explain Filleau's familiarity with the ideas in them. Lafuma's comment that the
edition also plays down sections 5° and 8°, and that the
ideas of 14° are found elsewhere, does not really weaken
Mrs Barnes's argument.

Mrs Barnes's observations on Filleau's abbreviated
version of part one and of the transition to part two
have other implications. I have said that Filleau seems
much more interested in part two of Pascal's argument
than in part one, and it is his expansion of the second
part that makes use of such a wide variety of material.[99]
What is striking about his account of part one is that
it conforms quite closely to what I surmised was an
earlier stage in the development of that portion of the
argument. The omission of 'Divertissement,' the placing
of the section on 'Philosophes' after the interlocutor
has begun his search (cf. no. 4), the transition from
that to section 17°, using the argument of no. 149 (Mrs
Barnes omits this significant link, writing merely that
the one 'follows immediately' on the other),[100] and the
dispersal of 14°, all ties in with our reading of the
manuscript evidence earlier in the chapter.

My view of Filleau is therefore rather more nuanced
than the view of those who hold on the one hand that he
is a wholly reliable witness, and on the other that he
is simply summarizing, or glossing, the text of Copy 9203.
It seems to me that his interpretation does owe something
to a tradition which goes back to Pascal's presentation
of his Apologia to the Duc de Roannez and other friends
in the first half of 1658, and that this comes out most
clearly in the account he gives of part one of the Apologia. The difference between his account and the full version we can infer from the *liasses* corresponds to what I
was able to deduce from internal evidence and from the
key fragment 'A P.R.' about the earlier stages of the
plan, suggesting that there may be foundation in fact in
the connection often made between the talk to friends
and the lecture planned for Port-Royal. At the same time,
Filleau himself knew Pascal well during the last two
years of the writer's life; he was clearly very familiar
with Pascal's text; he was himself particularly intrigued
by the so-called historical proofs, and with Pascal's
theory of unbelief, and he expanded those parts of his
Discours from his knowledge of Pascal and from his own
Pascal-inspired reflections.[101] As a consequence, I would
be prepared to say that while Filleau's testimony is not
so reliable that we could use it to challenge the validity of other evidence, the fact that it appears to support
other evidence is comforting. It strengthens my case that

the sorting was under way, but not completed, by about
June 1658, and that if Pascal did give a detailed exposition of his argument, to friends or at Port-Royal, it
must have been at that stage in the evolution of the
Apologia.

Filleau's *Discours* was rejected by Gilberte Périer,
either because it was too long, or because it was recognized that in some important respects Filleau was distorting Pascal's views. A new preface was commissioned from
Gilberte's son Etienne.[102] It is often said that the
pages of Etienne Périer's preface which report Pascal's
talk are no more than a well edited summary of Filleau's
Discours.[103] If so, they would clearly have little to
offer us. Certainly, there can be no reasonable doubt
that for much of his text, Périer had Filleau's words
before him. Pol Ernst reduced Périer's account to a
schema, and found that it fitted Filleau's discours very
well.[104] Annie Barnes had pointed out that the same ab-
sences which we noted in Filleau's summary of part one
apply to Périer's version.[105] The very large number of
exact textual echoes underlines his debt.[106] If these
were limited to key words, the hypothesis of a common
source would be very plausible, but very often they are
the purely functional elements, which at times Etienne
Périer rearranges, so as not to follow Filleau too
closely. If we were to imagine a source document which
Etienne Périer reduced, and which Filleau inflated,
these parallels would be less evenly distributed.

Why then should we not accept the notion that Etienne
Périer's sole source was Filleau? One impressionistic
argument can be discounted from the start: we are sometimes asked to believe that Filleau's version is so im-
possibly diffuse that it would need a genius to reduce
it to the crystalline order of Etienne Périer's version.[107]
This does injustice to both parties. In fact it is not
particularly difficult to summarize Filleau, and if one
decides, as Etienne Périer or his superiors evidently
did, to cut out the theme of the different responses the
apologetic case could be expected to produce, one could
well end up with a text like Périer's.

There are nevertheless one or two passages which raise
doubts. Lafuma pointed out one instance of Etienne Périer
drawing on his mother's Life of Pascal, but there was
not much to be gleaned from that source.[108] More disquieting are the observations of Annie Barnes, to the
effect that a crucial paragraph in Périer has no corres-

ponding passage in Filleau.[109] This is the transition
from the willingness to believe, to the exposition of
the historical proofs. Mrs Barnes concluded that Périer
and Filleau were both following the same written text.
A different hypothesis seems more likely: that Périer
was in the main following Filleau, simplifying the argument quite ruthlessly, and that he discussed some of his
difficulties with other *pascalins*, perhaps with Arnauld
and Nicole, who were collaborating with the committee at
the time Etienne Périer wrote his preface. The new paragraph would be the result of one of those discussions.
There is finally the point made by Gilbert Chinard.
Filleau, he says, did not properly grasp Pascal's view of
certainty, and Etienne Périer's text provides a clear
corrective on this point.[110]

Etienne Périer has done an impressive job, omitting all
reference to the different types of seekers, to the explanation of difficulties in discerning God's presence,
tidying up the loose ends, making the text consistent.
Although the result is generally admitted to be an improvement on the original,[111] one cannot feel wholly satisfied
with it. If Filleau is too prolix, Périer is too dry; if
one lacks clarity of focus, the other lacks warmth and
presence.

On the matter of Pascal's talk, Etienne Périer is less
ambivalent than Filleau, though only by dint of a neat
device. He begins: 'Après qu'il leur eut fait voir quelles
sont les preuves...' ('leur' being 'plusieurs personnes
trés considérables de ses amis'). Then he introduces a
fictitious character ('Il supposa ensuite un homme...'),
and the rest of the argument is addressed directly to
this man, up to the point where he is ready to listen to
the proofs.[112] From then on, the fictitious listener is
not mentioned, and we are given to understand that Périer
is summarizing 'un simple discours' which is itself very
sketchy compared to the 'grand ouvrage qu'il méditait.'
It would be imprudent to argue that Pascal himself must
have changed tack when he expounded his ideas to the
group of friends.

However we resolve the question of the differences
between Filleau and Périer, this study of Etienne Périer's
preface has thus brought us no nearer to reconstructing
the talk, nor to dating it. In this, the *Discours* of
Filleau has yielded a little more than does the preface.
From all the issues examined in this chapter, however,
something has emerged. I see no reason to doubt, and

several reasons to accept the notion that as well as
continuing to elaborate his ideas, and pondering on the
mathematics of the cycloid, Pascal devoted much of his
energies in the year 1658 to developing a plan for his
Apologia, and that there are vestiges - in the manuscript,
in the location of some of the classified *pensées*, and
in the later account of what Pascal told his friends -
of some of the intermediary stages, evidence which seems
remarkably consistent.

32
The unclassed papers

In chapter 30 I discussed those fragments which can confidently be assigned to the years 1656-7. In chapter 31
I examined the constitution of the twenty-eight *liasses*
à titres and discerned traces of an evolution and refine-
ment of Pascal's design. These two enquiries neglected a
large number of unclassed fragments, and have left two
major gaps in this account of the growth of the Apologia.
First, we cannot assume that all the relevant fragments
available to Pascal in 1658 found their way into the
liasses; if some of the unclassed fragments were written
in 1657-8, what light do they shed on the genesis of the
Apologia? Second, assuming that some of the unclassed
fragments were written after the twenty-eight bundles
had been tied up, what do they tell us about Pascal's
later thoughts? In particular, do they reveal any inadequacy in the scheme which seemed to work in 1658?

In order to answer these questions, we have first to
know which fragments were extant in 1658, and which were
written later. Apart from a handful of instances, incontrovertible external evidence hardly exists, and so we
are thrown back on hypotheses. Some of these arise from
the material constitution of the thirty-five 'Units' in
which the unclassed fragments are housed, and some from
verbal similarities between different *pensées*. The two
sets of clues do not always match, teaching us to be prudent about the extent to which we can push our hypotheses,
but not, I believe, invalidating them entirely.

In the introductory portion of this final chapter, I
shall state the problem, indicate what conclusions have
been drawn by other scholars, and define my own approach.
The main body of the chapter will be divided into two
parts, dealing with the Units probably constituted before
Pascal's illness, and with those generally assumed to
have been made up later. The distinction is a little

390 The Composition of Pascal's Apologia

arbitrary, as I do not agree with all these assumptions,
but it breaks the chapter up conveniently. In each part
I shall review the evidence carefully, propose hypotheses,
and indicate what conclusions could be drawn, if those
hypotheses were true. As in the previous chapters, a summary of my findings is given at the end of this introduction.

On Copy 9203, which was used by Lafuma as the basis for
his editions, the so-called 'unclassed' papers comprised
thirty-four 'Series' or 'Units,' which follow the twenty-
seven *liasses à titres*.[1] It was never easy to see the
rationale behind the contents or the order of these
thirty-four Units, except that the last three give us
the two dossiers on miracles (discussed in a previous
chapter), preceded by the questionnaire on the same subject which Pascal submitted to Barcos. Roger Pons wrote
that 'un rangement, sinon un classement, s'y ébauche'[2] -
but whose arrangement was it? Lafuma was less optimistic:
'à part ceux des miracles, aucune idée ordonnatrice ne
se dégage.'[3] Anzieu noted that the first nineteen Units
were obviously made up of apologetic material, while the
next eleven mixed apologetic matter with notes for the
Provinciales and other writings.[4] There were a few attempts to give titles to the Units,[5] but these do not
really indicate that there was any firm guiding principle
behind the constitution of the Units. The general impression left by Copy 9203 was well summed up by Philippe
Sellier: 'Après la liasse-table[6] ... il a placé les fragments les plus étendus, puis d'autres dont le contenu
correspondait encore bien aux rubriques du projet
d'*Apologie*, et en dernier lieu des dossiers qui lui ont
paru sans unité. Les liasses 'Miracles,' extérieures à
l'Apologie, ont été rejetées tout à la fin. Du point de
vue matériel, on trouve une liasse, puis une double
feuille, un cahier ... de nouveau des liasses.'[7]

Progress in this matter was not possible until scholars
had taken account of the complementary evidence, that of
Copy 12449, which presents the Units in a different order.
(It also includes one Unit not recorded by the First Copy,
so that we now speak of thirty-five Units, not thirty-
four.)[8] Two scholars (Philippe Sellier and Jean Mesnard)
subjected Copy 12449 to a thorough examination, and carefully compared the order of the Units in the two copies,
with extremely interesting results.

On Copy 12449 Unit I precedes the twenty-seven *liasses*
and the rest follows them. They divide into six groups -
or rather seven, for as we shall see, internal evidence
obliges us to split one group into two. Using the familiar First Copy numbering, the order of the Second Copy
is as follows:

XXXV	C[9]
XXXII-XXXIV	D
XXIII-XXV	E
XXVI-XXXI	F
XXI-XXII	G
XX	H
II-XIX	J

Is there perhaps a chronological pattern to be discerned here? That was the view of Philippe Sellier, who
edited the Second Copy in 1976. He presents the seven
groups as 'Les dossiers de la phase préparatoire, été
1656 - mai 1658'[10] (Groups C, D, and E), 'les liasses de
1659-1662' (F, G, and H), and 'les développements de
1659-1662' (Group J).[11] Unit I (A), in which the *pensées*
are already divided into fragments, as in the *liasses à
titres*, belongs, with the *liasses* (B), to the period
between the first and the second phases noted. This is
an attractive hypothesis; the only thing which is immediately surprising is to find Unit II assigned to a late
date.[12]
    Jean Mesnard, on the other hand, reads the evidence
differently.[13] If he seems unwilling to accept Sellier's
explanation of the pattern behind the order of the Units
in Copy 12449,[14] it is because it does not fully explain
why the Units should follow that precise sequence. Why,
notably, should Units XXVI-XXXI (Group F) follow XXV
(which is early) rather than XIX (which, like them, is
late)? The answer is double: first, because, like Units
XXIII-XXV (Group E), they are not exclusively apologetic,
whereas the other group (II-XIX, Group J) is, and also
because they are for the most part complex - that is,
they comprise more than one material element - again like
Group E. Units II-XIX, on the other hand, are 'simple' -
that is, each Unit comprises only one sheet (single or
double), or one exercise-book, or one development.[15] It
is true that Unit XI is complex,[16] and that Unit XIX has

two elements, not one, and that Unit XXXI, unlike the
rest of Group F, is 'simple.' But Mesnard has an explanation ready. In these cases, he says, the principle of
material constitution has been overweighed by the principle of intention – both XI and XIX are apologetic, like
the rest of Group J, and likewise, Unit XXXI, like the
rest of Group F, is not exclusively apologetic.[17] The
Units which lie outside these two major groups are independent, although Units XXI and XXII (G) both have to
do with *l'esprit de géométrie*, and Units XXXII to XXXIV
(D) have all to do with miracles. Unit XXXV, on Esdras
(C), has links with the papers on miracles, as we shall
see.

   These different ways of looking at the Units – format,
intention, chronology – are not mutually contradictory.
We are presented with one group which is only partly apologetic, in which the Units are for the most part complex,
proceeding from the more complex to the less, and set
out in chronological order; and another group which is
predominantly apologetic, the individual Units 'simple'
in composition, and possibly later than the work of
classification. If Sellier's theory about the chronological sequence could be supported by independent evidence,
we would have a very elegant solution to the whole problem of the Second Copy. Unfortunately, what evidence we
have does not always support that theory, and not only
because of what has been said already about Unit II. I
propose to accept as a provisional starting-point Sellier's
division of the Unit-groups into pre-1659 and post-1659,
but to test the hypothesis by asking what confirms, and
what invalidates it? In the case of the first group, we
shall find a great deal of confirmation. But with the
second group, we shall find that while some of the fragments can be shown to have been written in 1660 or there-
abouts, it is difficult to believe this to be true of all.
The two dates therefore at best apply only to the constitution of the Units, not to the composition of the fragments they contain.

   In trying to date the *pensées* by external means, three
assumptions are generally made. The first is that all
fragments written on the same page belong to the same
period. The second is that all papers filed in the same
Unit are contemporary. And the third is that all Units
grouped together in the same way on the two Copies are
likewise contemporary. It is obvious that these three

assumptions do not have equal validity. The first is reasonable, especially when the handwriting looks to be consistent.[18] At times Pascal has added phrases in a different style, or in different ink, and there is no way to
tell how much time elapsed between the original text and
the gloss. Also, of course, what were once single pages
have been cut up and redistributed; reconstituting the
original pages is a risky undertaking. But as we have already seen in chapter 30, some pages were not cut, and
quite a lot can be established by looking at the *pensées*
Pascal set down on the same sheet.

To assume that all the papers in a given Unit were
written at the same period is a different kind of assumption altogether. Admittedly, it is very likely that once
all the papers were arranged (in 1658), they would not
be disturbed when Pascal wrote new *pensées* and subsequently filed them. But that is not necessarily the way
it happened, and we must be cautious. The presence of a
known late fragment in a Unit shows that the Unit was
constituted late; it does not signify that it was made
up exclusively of late fragments. This is, however, what
Jean Mesnard implies.[19] A fortiori, to extend that argument to the Unit-groups, as Sellier does, leaves even
more room for error.

Other kinds of argument are stronger. They are basically
two. Just occasionally a fragment can be dated within
quite specific limits, but the number of such instances
is very small. Some scholars have argued about whether
Pascal could or could not have worked after the worst of
his illness was past, and how much he could have managed
to do.[20] Such arguments are inconclusive. We know he did
some work; we just do not have enough information to be
able to say what limits his health imposed.[21] It would be
better to err on the side of caution.[22]

We are thus forced to have recourse to the final kind
of argument: that of internal evidence. It has to be
handled discreetly. But a lot of material can be approximately dated (including, of course, all the classified
fragments, which we must believe to have been written
before the end of 1658), and other fragments can be
fruitfully compared with this material. Comparison of
two texts can reveal that an unclassified fragment antedates a classified one. Or else an undated fragment is
formulated in a way so close to a dated fragment that we
cannot believe it to have been written at a later period.

Thus by a patient uncovering of these different clues,
certain tentative conclusions can be reached. Summarized,
they are as follows:
(a) As well as Units II, XXXII, XXXIII, and XXXIV (already
discussed), five Units appear to have been constituted
for certain before 1659: XXXV, XX, XXIII, XXIV, and XXV.
The most important of these are XXIII to XXV. Some of the
fragments contained in them go back to the year 1656,
others are evidently contemporary with fragments classified in the twenty-eight *liasses*. Many continue further
the lines of thought opened on some of the papers on
miracles, and the apologetic thrust - with even, in the
case of Unit XXIV, some unambiguous references to the
plan - is marked. The observations on man are so frequently
related to the apologetic enterprise that one suspects
that one reason for Pascal not classifying them is that
they go against his decision to keep part one of the
Apologia neutral in doctrine. Biblical fragments move
from the personal (Unit XXIII) to the apologetic (XXIV).
Here the emphasis is on the witness of the Jews, and the
developments Pascal makes see the subject whole, rather
than parcelled into separate topics, as is the case of
the full version of part two. There are also fragments on
style and organization. There is no doubt that many
pensées in these Units could have been salvaged and
worked into the Apologia. But Pascal closed his twenty-
eight dossiers, and put these Units to one side, and
while he might have looked at them again, after his illness, no later fragment has found its way into these Units.
(b) There are other Units, however, which do contain
papers believed to have been written after 1659. The number of cases where a late date can be assigned with anything like certainty is surprisingly small. By inference
the number can be extended. But we have to be cautious,
because many of the *pensées* in these Units - far more,
in fact, than has been generally admitted - are closely
paralleled by texts from before Pascal's illness. In
some instances we can relate them to precise moments in
the evolution of the design, and it is almost impossible
to believe that these, at least, are late. Even if the
case for an earlier dating than is customary for these
fragments cannot be said to be watertight, the fact that
it can be made raises questions which the proponents of
the accepted view have to answer. In this category are
(1) the miscellaneous thoughts of Units XXVI to XXXI,

among which are to be found early and late fragments,
and Units XXI and XXII;[23] (2) longer fragments on the
impious (III to V, XI),[24] which very likely were drafted
when Pascal was planning a general preface; (3) other
long fragments on the Jewish nation (VI to X, XII to XIX),
some of which are reflections on the meaning of the Jews
who, like the impious, are unconscious witnesses to
Christianity, and some show Pascal documenting himself
from the Old Testament. They are generally held to be
late, but the evidence is inconclusive, even contradictory.

I conclude that even if we cannot give a complete account of the evolution of Pascal's thought after the
middle of 1657, the fact that one can argue for the earlier dating on the basis of internal evidence makes it
very difficult to maintain that there was any radical
change in Pascal's conception of his Apologia after 1658.
And that is, essentially, all we needed to know.

(a) j'écrirai ici mes pensées sans ordre (532/XXIII)

We have already studied (in chapter 30) the beginning of
the Apologia in the papers primarily about miracles
(Units XXXII to XXXIV), in certain developments of the
conversation Pascal had with Sacy, and in the 'Infini
rien' manuscript (Unit II). My discussion of Unit XXXIV
led me to mention one page of Unit XXIII. Sellier assigns
to the 'preparatory phase' all of Units XXIII to XXV
(what I called Group E), as well as Units XXXII to XXXIV
(Group D), and also Unit XXXV (C). Sellier does not
include Unit II in the same phase, but I have given my
reasons for dating that manuscript 1656. We must assume
that by virtue of its very individual character, it was
put aside, and did not join the stock of papers until
later, when it went with other 'simple' Units.[25]

I begin by summarizing the apologetic content of Unit
II and Group D (on miracles). As I see it, neither of
these collections of *pensées* was apologetic in origin,
but both open onto themes which are subsequently worked
into the Apologia. Unit II touches upon the reasons for
unbelief - the passions, self-love, custom - and the way
the passions can be tamed; by developing new habits.
Faith is of the heart rather than of reason, and the heart
is thus the seat of the conflict between devotion and
concupiscence. The Christian life is happier than the
life of the *honnête homme*. There are reasons for accepting

Christianity, to be found in Scripture, and its credentials include the fact that it alone teaches that man is
born in sin, and that it alone has been prepared from the
beginning of time.

The theme of perpetuity comes again in the thoughts on
miracles (Units XXXIII and XXXIV). These discuss further
the reasons for unbelief, define the action of grace on
the heart, taming self-love, and adumbrate the notion of
the hidden God and of 'figures.' Two papers from Unit
XXXIV, to which we allied one sheet from Unit XXIII (515-
24), offer a number of thoughts which point to the conclusion that man is incapable of knowing unambiguously truth,
justice, or *le bien*. Pyrrhonism is the authority for the
first of these claims, and observations of man's propen-
sity to distraction lead Pascal to the third one.

We thus find, in a series of notes made in all probability during the winter 1656-7, some of the essential ideas
of the Apologia: aspects of man's *misère*, reasons for
belief and unbelief, together with suggestions of a method
for substantiating Christianity's claims. We shall find
this pattern repeated with Units XXIII to XXV (Group E):
specific preoccupations of the winter of 1656-7 took on
an increasingly apologetic colour, and Pascal found himself noting down at the same time other ideas, often with
potential for apologetic use.

Unit XXXV. Before we turn to Group E, we must consider
Unit XXXV, which comes first on Copy 12449, immediately
following the twenty-eight *liasses à titres*, and immediately
preceding the group on miracles.[26] It accumulates documentation with which to refute the argument that if (as was
believed) the Pentateuch was burned during the exile and
restored by Esdras, this weakened the authority of Scripture. Pascal argues characteristically in two ways – that
the fable is false; and that if it were true it could not
be used to attack the authority of Scripture, because both
the Pentateuch and the story of Esdras come to us with
the same credentials.

Although Unit XXXV is the first of the seven 'early'
Units in the order of the Second Copy, it does not follow
that it was actually the first to be written. Indeed, it
is most unlikely that Pascal made these notes on Esdras
before being taken up by the subject of miracles. Jean
Mesnard holds that they are 'contemporains des pensées sur
les miracles ou, plus probablement, un peu postérieurs.'[27]

He bases this statement on the position the Unit occupies
on the Second Copy, and also on a paragraph in Gilberte
Périer's *Vie de Pascal*. Gilberte has been talking about
the miracle of the Holy Thorn and Pascal's reflections.

> On ne pouvait nier la vérité de ces miracles, ni les
> conséquences qu'il en tirait pour la preuve de Dieu et
> du Messie, sans choquer les principes les plus communs
> sur lesquels on assure toutes les choses qui passent
> pour indubitables. On a recueilli quelque chose de ses
> pensées là-dessus, mais c'est peu, et je croirais être
> obligée de m'étendre davantage pour y donner plus de
> jour, selon tout ce que nous lui en avons ouï dire, si
> un de ses amis ne nous avait donné une dissertation
> sur les livres de Moïse, où tout cela est admirablement
> bien démêlé et d'une manière qui ne serait pas indigne
> de mon frère. Je vous renvoie donc à cet ouvrage...[28]

The allusion is manifestly to Filleau de la Chaise, *Discours sur les Preuves des Livres de Moïse*, published in
1672 but evidently known in Pascalian circles before that
date. A perusal of Filleau's text does not help resolve
the chronological problem, however, as there is no reason
to suppose that Filleau was transcribing an argument
Pascal propounded in 1657. Furthermore, there is no
reference in Filleau to the Book of Esdras and the re-
constitution of the Pentateuch, although the matter is
germane to the argument, in which Filleau answers three
objections to the claims made for Moses. The discussion
is set in a framework provided by Pascal's views on the
role of reason in evaluating the facts on which Christianity is in large measure based, and by a development on
the vital necessity for each one of us to examine the
facts and decide. The search for truth needs to be initiated by the will, to override the strong impulse coming from the passions to do nothing about it. Other
proofs than the ones here described can be found, says
Filleau, which have the great value of making the truth
attractive to the heart. The Pascalian origin of these
ideas will be obvious, but whereas the introduction calls
upon *liasse* 13° (probably early, as we saw in chapter
30), the conclusion draws on the expansion to section
12° (427, etc.) which one cannot believe to be of such
an early date. I therefore incline not to associate the
Esdras fragments with the papers on miracles, but there

is no reason seriously to doubt that the Esdras fragments are relatively early.[29]

Units XXIII-XXV. One can follow the evolution of the apologetic project more clearly in the other Units of this preparatory phase. Units XXIII-XXV (Group E) contain many traces of the winter 1656-7. In Unit XXIII (comprising nos 515-91), no. 524 echoes fragment 840 from Unit XXXIII, while nos 516-17 (written on the same page as 524) have to do with the dissension within the Church. Fragments 515-24 were discussed in chapter 30. No. 543 appears to be a jotting for the sixth *Provinciale*, which makes it very early (April 1656). The same sheet gives us 541-3, crossed out, and 536-40, which appear on the verso side and are probably later. Lafuma noted that no. 550 is taken up in the *Abrégé de la Vie de Jésus-Christ*, which he attributed to the years 1655-6, although this has been contested.[30] No. 553 echoes no. 886 (XXIV), and no. 563 echoes no. 859. Nos 567-9 (on a single sheet) deal with the Pope, with one sentence on miracles; there are various geometrical designs on the verso. No. 573 also echoes no. 859, and no. 574 answers those who say they would believe if only they could be shown a miracle.

Unit XXIV (592 to 634) - of which Jean Mesnard says that 'formé de notes très elliptiques et de citations, [il] touche autant à la polémique qu'à l'apologétique'[31] - contains no. 602 on Church discipline (probably a note for the tenth *Provinciale*), 604 on the Pope (akin to no. 567 in Unit XXIII) and 610, which must be a note for the eleventh *Provinciale*. Between fragments 601 and 602 is a small piece of paper, which is the bottom of the page which recorded no. 923, with 924 on the reverse side. No. 924 was evidently removed by Pascal's heirs who, ever scrupulous, allowed the rest of the sheet (containing the last lines of no. 923) to remain in place.[32] No. 924 is a personal text, akin to letters to Mlle Roannez written in the latter part of 1656; no. 923, 'sur les confessions et absolutions sans marques de regret,' ties in with the tenth *Provinciale* (2 August 1656).

In Unit XXV (635 to 729) there are three fragments which have to do with miracles,[33] four which have to do with the Pope,[34] and a much larger number containing notes on themes treated in the *Provinciales*.[35]

These three Units contain more than these notes on the early stages of the Jesuit-Jansenist controversy, however.

In the first place, the controversy broke out afresh at
the end of 1657, with the publication of a Jesuit *Apologie
pour les Casuistes*. The reaction of the Paris clergy was
violent. Several factums were published, and Pascal collaborated on several of them.[36] Some of the fragments in
the Units of Group E are related to these writings, and
while it is possible that Pascal was using material already collected,[37] it is simpler to assume that the notes
in question do date from the first months of 1658. Thus,
when Pascal refers to the Jesuits being invited back to
Venice after fifty years (704/XXV), something which happened in 1657, his source is probably the *Apologie pour
les Casuistes*.[38] The official reply to the *Apologie* –
the *Premier Ecrit des Curés de Paris* of January 1658 –
was almost certainly written by Pascal, and fragment 679
(XXV) is probably a note taken in preparation for it.[39]
The second *Ecrit* (April 1658) echoes no. 598 (XXIV),[40]
while the so-called *Projet de mandement contre l'Apologie
pour les Casuistes* of a couple of months later contains
one phrase which recalls no. 599.[41]

In the second place, there are many precise links
between fragments in these Units, and fragments incorporated in the twenty-eight *liasses à titres*. These links
are of two kinds. First, there are material indications
that fragments in Group E were originally written on the
same sheets as fragments now in Group B (the *liasses*).
Tourneur showed that nos 635-6 (XXV) were originally
separated from 637-9 by no. 153, and that nos 333-4 followed no. 639 on the same page.[42] Recently Pol Ernst has
examined the material evidence very thoroughly and suggested that several pages can be wholly or partially reconstructed. At least five of these reconstructed pages
contain fragments now in the *liasses à titre* as well as
fragments from Unit XXIII.[43] Two fragments in Unit XXIV
(nos 620 and 624) are on the same ruled paper as several
fragments in Unit I and in the *liasses à titres*. As this
paper is invariably found at the top of the *liasses* in
question, it looks as if Pascal continued with Unit XXIV
after he had stopped work on the *liasses*.[44] One cannot
push this observation too far, however, as the earliest
fragments found in Unit XXIV (the ones connected with the
Jesuits) are above the ones using ruled paper. Probably
we ought simply to call Unit XXIV a collection of papers
Pascal did not get round to sorting out. We may wish to
believe that it was finally put together a little later

than Units XXIII and XXV, and that it contains fragments
generally later than those in the other two Units under
discussion.[45] More evidence will be forthcoming on this.

The second kind of link between these Units and the
liasses is of content. A few phrases reappear in the
liasses, and several ideas are taken up in the Apologia.
Exact verbal parallels are rare. No. 634 in Unit XXIV is
close to no. 35. In Unit XXV, no. 695 is like the last
part of no. 131, and no. 723 is the exact double of no.
41. Very occasionally we can say that a certain formulation must antedate the precise plan of the twenty-eight
dossiers, and that another must have been written when
the plan was firm. Thus no. 577 (XXIII) straddles sections
5° and 12° in a way one fancies Pascal would have avoided
after those different parts of the argument were allocated
a specific place; conversely, the stepwise argument of
no. 613 (XXIV) implies that sections 5° and 6° are already
set up. Once again we are led to suspect that Unit XXIV
is rather later in date (generally speaking) than Unit
XXIII. The titles suggest the same thing: none of the
titles of the *liasses* appear in Unit XXIII and only one
(ordre, three times) in XXV, whereas several are recorded
in Unit XXIV.[46]

This impression is strengthened further when we look
at the different thoughts contained in these Units: Unit
XXIV seems much closer to the classified fragments than
do the other two Units, although there is no absolute
distinction to be drawn, obviously. The subject-matter
covered in these three Units is diverse. The first fragment
we come across in Unit XXIII is entitled 'Misc[ellenea],'
a description Jean Mesnard applies to the whole *liasse*.[47]
The subject-matter can be divided broadly into two categories: reflections on man, and reflections on theological or biblical matters. (There are also notes on style
and organization.)

The paper in Unit XXIII which contains nos 515-24 records, besides reflections on the Church and on style,
a series of different thoughts on man's changeability.
We cannot think of more than one thing at a time (523),
so we can distract ourselves from grief (522). Our nature
is only 'un continuel changement' (520). Pascal gives the
example of his own changing views on justice; he now
believes that man cannot be expected to discover justice
for himself. In no. 518, entitled 'Pyrrh,' he opines that
man's place is in the middle; any extreme is likely to be

an impoverishment (cf. no. 519). The same idea is echoed
at the end of the *pensée* on distraction (522): 'Il n'est
ni ange, ni bête, mais homme.'

Some of these ideas recur. The phrase just cited is
repeated and elaborated in no. 678 (Unit XXV). Mediocrity
recurs in nos 681 and 723 (XXV), change in 672 and 673.
The ideas are recognizable also in no. 558 on the diversity of phenomena. Nature never repeats herself, and
neither do we in our judgments. It is very difficult to
find the spot from which to judge a thing objectively.
This is not dissimilar to the analogy of a boat and the
port to indicate the need for a 'point fixe' in deciding
moral questions (697, 699/XXV). On custom we have no. 634
(XXIV): custom often dictates our choice of trade.

The theme of justice is taken up in no. 525, which looks
forward to the argument of section 5°. Customs are rarely
reasonable or just, but they are followed because they
are commonly believed to be reasonable or just. It is
right to follow them, but on different grounds, which
most people simply would not appreciate. Montaigne is specifically criticized, as he is in no. 577 ('il n'a pas vu
la raison de cet effet,' another anticipation of section
5°). There are several references to Montaigne in Unit
XXV also.[48] Another fragment there says that 'justice'
is 'ce qui est établi' (645).

The counterbalancing theme of section 5° (force) is
present in no. 554 ('La force est la reine du monde et
non pas l'opinion') an idea which corrects and refines
no. 665 (XXV): 'L'opinion est comme la reine du monde
mais la force en est le tyran.' The opinion which pre-
vails is the one backed by strength (711).

The key notion of section 5°, the 'renversement continuel du pour au contre,' is found in no. 613 (XXIV), entitled 'Grandeur, Misère.' The comments of philosophers
surprise ordinary men, and the philosophers are in their
turn surprised by Christians.

There are references to the Christian perspective on
515-24 too. Though there is no certain human justice,
'il y en a selon que Dieu nous l'a voulu révéler' (520);
it is good that we can distract ourselves - 'selon le
monde non selon Dieu' (523). The same contrast is made
in relation to styles of living in no. 693 (XXV).

Fragments in Unit XXIV which see man as unable to find
rest lead into the overtly apologetic fragments. Distraction stops man from thinking 'comme il faut' (620). No.

621 presents man as always at the centre of a conflict
between passion and reason. (This idea reappears in Unit
I, more polished, as no. 410.) No. 622, connected with
the notion of *divertissement*, paints man's despair when
he cannot escape thinking about himself. Pascal added
the title 'Ennui,' possibly when he considered creating
a separate *liasse* for the topic.

The theme of the self-loving self prompts a number of
reflections, to the extent that we can term this an
apologetic nucleus in Pascal's writing of this date. No.
597, addressed to Miton, denounces the ethic of *honnêteté*
which disguises but does not alter the unjust nature of
the self (mentioned also in no. 668/XXV). In no. 642
(XXV), likewise addressed to Miton, Pascal says that
Miton is unable to understand why *honnêteté* goes against
man's natural impulse. We hide from ourselves the truth
- our duplicity and contradictory nature (665/XXV).
Pascal says he was surprised to find there were even
fewer experts in 'l'étude de l'homme' than in the study
of the abstract sciences (687/XXV).

The beginning of wisdom is to hate one's amour-propre
(617/XXIV). Yet no (other) religion has made resistance
to amour-propre a cardinal tenet. Knowing our nature,
we necessarily wish to be liberated from it. This predisposes us in favour of Christianity, which addresses
itself to this very point (595/XXIV). We must hate our
concupiscence and seek 'un être véritablement aimable'
(564/XXIII). Secular systems look for *le vrai bien* in
divertissement. Philosophers show this is vain, but have
nothing better to replace it (626/XXIV). We are impelled
to seek for *le vrai* and *le bien*, even if we find only
false objects masquerading as True and Good (661/XXV).
We can only love something which is within us. The kingdom of God is of this sort (564/XXIII, 616/XXIV). Finally,
worn out by the search, we will embrace Christ the liberator (631). Then we shall find the antidote to concupiscence, charity, implanted by God (536/XXIII). It is the
same with our search for truth. Christ has revealed where
we are strong, where we are weak; before him, there was
only the uncertainty of Pyrrhonism (691/XXV, 600/XXIV).

There are also a couple of fragments on the psychological basis of belief. The will plays an important part as
it determines the perspective we adopt (539/XXIII). Faith
is a gift of God which cannot be obtained by reasoning
alone - another point where Christianity corresponds to

human experience more surely than do other religions
(588/XXIII, cf. 703/XXV). Consequently reason has finally
to yield to feeling - but feeling is virtually indistinguishable from fancy, and reason cannot really help to
make the distinction (530/XXIII; on the curious interplay
of reason and feeling cf. no. 646, from Unit XXV). In
another important fragment (695/XXV), Pascal says that
the doctrine of original sin is admittedly a 'folly,'
something reason would never have found unaided, and
which it will always reject. Yet without that doctrine,
man cannot be explained. This fragment is addressed
directly to the unbeliever.

Other apologetic themes are touched on by *pensées* in
these three Units. The observer notes how we diminish
the role of religion in our lives. Imagination, which
magnifies little things (cf. 531), grievously reduces
the stature of God (551). Man is insensitive to the important things, and over-sensitive to small things (632).
Religion is neglected - men will risk their lives to
defend 'le bien public' but not to defend religion (540).
We do things whose outcome is uncertain, while we neglect
to do things for religion on the grounds that it is not
certain (577; Pascal argues ingeniously that religion is
more 'certainly possible' than is the likelihood that we
shall live to see tomorrow).

Our sensitivity to big issues is a sign, Pascal says,
of 'un étrange renversement' (632), our failure to seek
the truth about ourselves, the sign of 'un aveuglement
surnaturel' (623). In no. 633 he says that we have an
instinct which propels us upwards, despite our wretched
condition which binds us to earth. Religious convictions,
finally, are essential to our thinking on basic questions.
Our morality depends on our opinion on whether the soul
is mortal or immortal (612).

The most striking thing about these thoughts on the
human condition is that they are so closely related to
the apologetic enterprise.[49] When we read part one of
the Apologia in the *liasses à titres* we notice just the
opposite: that Pascal soft-pedals his own Christian interpretation in order better to win the opponent over.
The transitional phase, which caused Pascal some difficulty, will have to review the evidence in a different
light. Material for this review is contained in abundance
in the Units under discussion. We can therefore easily
understand why it was not incorporated in the first ten

liasses, and we are free to believe that Pascal could
have made use of it when he amplified his transition
section. At the same time, we are also free to believe
that Pascal wrote these notes before making the important
decision to exclude the Christian perspective from the
first part of his Apologia. Nearly everything he says
has its roots in the ideas analysed at the start of this
section.

If these Units contain a large amount of material relevant to part one of the Apologia, part two is less well
represented. Here the distinction between Units XXIII
and XXV on the one hand, and Unit XXIV on the other, is
clear. In Unit XXIII there are a number of personal
reflections on the New and Old Testaments. Some of the
ideas can be put to apologetic use later, but for the
moment that is not Pascal's primary concern. Germs of
apologetic themes can be found in no. 544 on the universality of redemption, and in no. 545, a meditation on
the first epistle of John, based on Saint Augustine, which
mentions 'le souvenir de leur chère patrie de la Jérusalem
céleste.' Pascal several times opposes 'les élus' and
'les réprouvés' (546, 562, 566). Even the 'obscurités de
l'écriture' help to separate one group from the other
(566). But Pascal does not in this collection wonder
about reaching the *réprouvés*; his remarks on conversion
are all made in the context of the uncertainty of the
believer who searches the Scriptures for reassurance
(548, 549). In the note used in the *Abrégé* (550) Pascal
observes how as a result of apparent chance, a predicted
mystery is accomplished.[50] Three fragments offer figurative interpretations of details in the Old Testament
(570, a much amplified version of a note in 26°, fragment
350; 573, developing an idea added to no. 859 in Unit
XXXIV; 590, possibly connected with no. 283 in 22°).

In no. 576 we see one of Pascal's fundamental principles
(that of the half-truth) which needs to be tested), suggested it seems by reflecting on heresy:

> Les deux raisons contraires. Il faut commencer par là.
> Sans cela on n'entend rien, et tout est hérétique. Et
> même à la fin de chaque vérité il faut ajouter qu'on
> se souvient de la vérité opposée.

(In Unit XXIV, no. 619, this principle is applied to
human systems.) Only once in Unit XXIII does Pascal seem

to be defining faith with the outsider in mind. This is
fragment 588, which echoes no. 424 in Unit II;

> La foi est un don de Dieu. Ne croyez pas que nous
> disions que c'est un don de raisonnement. Les autres
> religions ne disent pas cela de leur foi. Elles ne
> donnaient que le raisonnement pour y arriver, qui n'y
> mène pas néanmoins.

In Unit XXV there are two theological notes (662 and 690);
neither is apologetic.[51]

In Unit XXIV, by contrast, there is only one non-
apologetic religious reflection (618), while there is a
group of a dozen or so important observations on prophecies and on the role of the Jews. On the witness made by
the Jewish nation, no. 592 says that if all the Jews had
been converted there would be only suspect witnesses;
had they all disappeared, there would have been no witnesses at all. There is more on the Jewish witness in
nos 614 and 615. In no. 593, Pascal argues that the re-
fusal of Jesus by the carnal Jews shows up the mediocrity
of their expectations. 'Ils sont des témoins sans reproche,
et qui plus est par là ils accomplissent les prophéties.'
Thus, prophecies are 'les seuls miracles subsistants,'
but they can be disputed. The idea is further developed
in no. 594. There have been a series of miracles and
particular prophecies. But the prophecy of the Messiah,
and its fulfilment, make a 'miracle subsistant.' Once
the divine nature of the prophecy is acknowledged, the
rest can be believed. And Pascal added: 'Dieu voulant
aveugler et éclairer,' as he is evidently very conscious
of the fact that nothing is universally accepted. Specific prophecies about the Messiah and the Jewish nation
are detailed in nos 607-9, and in the brief no. 624. All
these fragments can be linked with a moment in the evolution of the plan analysed in the previous chapter. We
saw there that after Pascal had opened a dossier entitled
'Fondements,' he saw the need to create new dossiers for
the separate grounds he had discerned, in the first instance the allied themes of 'Prophéties' and 'Figures.'

As well as *pensées* about religion and the human condition, Units XXIII and XXV (not XXIV) contain a large
number of reflections on style. Their presence suggests
that Pascal is already conscious of the problem inherent
in the task of presenting the Christian faith to a non-

believer. Many of them simply note matters of vocabulary
or conventional 'poetic' beauty. Pascal is very suspicious
of eloquence, and seeks as natural a style as possible.
Other fragments show his concern about persuasion. We
must always respect the feelings of the person we wish
to persuade, and acknowledge his instinct to resist us
(528-9, 710), trying to understand his point of view and
to meet his objections (669, 701). He evidently conceives
of a 'conversation' with an atheist who comes out with
'big words' like 'I deny religion' (658).

Other fragments are specifically related to the organization of his thoughts. In no. 532 he still believes that
he must note his thoughts down pell-mell, as they come,
as 'disorder' is the only appropriate order for his subject. In nos 683-4 he notes the difficulties in systematically subdividing, which betrays the real order (694).
At the same time he can take pride in the originality of
the 'disposition des matières' (the phrase replaces the
word 'ordre') he has found. Clearly we are here at the
borderline between a preparatory collecting of thoughts,
and the careful ordering of the thoughts into a convincing
structure.

Unit XX. One other Unit should perhaps be associated
with Units XXIII to XXV, and that is Unit XX. It comprises
reflections on the importance of reason, rather than
authority or majority opinion, in the natural sphere,
followed by notes taken from Montaigne on the unreliabi-
lity of other men's judgment. The connection with Pascal's
earlier discussion of authority and judgment is clear.
The phrase 'vous avez beau faire, si faut-il ou croire,
ou nier, ou douter' (505) is echoed in the classified
fragments (nos 170 and 44), the search for a rule in Unit
XXV (697, 699). One of the quotations is used in no. 60.
These notes almost certainly belong to the preparatory
phase.

In this part of the chapter I have been discussing those
Units which are known to have been extant at the end of
1658.[52] They do not necessarily exhaust the stock of
pensées composed at that time. The Units still to be discussed, whose date is disputed, undoubtedly contain many
fragments written during the same period. It has, however,
seemed preferable to discuss these disputed cases in section (b) rather than here. Surveying the material discussed

in this section, what conclusions can we draw? In particular, can we answer the first of the questions raised
at the beginning of the chapter, which was whether the
material in these Units elucidates further the genesis
of the Apologia?

To answer that question satisfactorily, we would have
to know why the fragments in these Units were not classified. We cannot say that it was because none of them
was relevant. Some are not, but many are. Nor can we say
that Pascal never got round to these particular sheets
of paper. We have seen that some of them were originally
written on sheets which Pascal cut up, and that other
parts of the page are in the *liasses*. The fragments we
are considering here were therefore excluded deliberately.
We are therefore thrown back onto two theories: either
Pascal rejected them because he did not think they would
fit, or else he put them aside because he wished to consider them further. Given that so many fragments illuminate, rather than obscure, his grand design, the theory
of wholesale rejection is not very plausible, and it must
be confessed that one cannot see, in the case of each and
every fragment relevant to the Apologia, why Pascal would
even have wished to reconsider them. But there are a
number of instances where this theory does make sense.
There are first of all the fragments on the Old Testament
which join together ideas which Pascal wished to keep
separate. There are also many observations on man which
adopt an explicitly Christian perspective. The plan that
we know avoids these hints of Christian doctrine. As we
were able to infer from the composition of the *liasses*
themselves several indications of changes of this kind
in the initial plan, I incline to believe that the evidence of these Units (notably XXIII to XXV) should be
interpreted in the same way.

Certainly we are safe in saying that Pascal had written
more in 1658 than just the classified *pensées*, and that
many of these unclassed fragments could have been incorporated in his plan. One is perpetually astounded at the
richness of the ideas that were pouring from Pascal's
pen. Even when his attention was fixed on his Apologia,
he did not hammer it out systematically; the thoughts
continued to spurt forth sponteneously, leaping from one
subject to another. It looks as if Pascal continued until
he had solved the one major problem posed by his expanding design - the new transition phase studied in the

previous chapter - and that once he had seen a solution he tied up his *liasses* (twenty-seven of them at least) and put other active material (Units I, XXIII, XXIV, XXV) to one side. As far as I can tell, he never returned to these. Other material which he laid aside, however, he did return to, as it is located with other fragments which external evidence obliges us to consider late. The Units which scholars have believed late are examined in the next section.

(b) choses qui doivent arriver dans la suite des temps (485/XI)

I have already dispatched what I am calling Group D (in chapter 30), Groups A and B (in chapter 31), and Groups C, E, and H (in the first part of this chapter). All the material in these groups was written, I believe, before the beginning of 1659, when Pascal fell ill. In this new section I shall deal with Groups F, G, and J. These Groups are generally held to be late, because some of the material they contain was (either certainly or probably) written late. I shall argue that the amount of material which is certainly late is quite limited, that much of the material which is said to be 'probably' late can with equal plausibility be assigned to 1658, and that other material in these Groups belongs to 1658 also.[53]

Units XXI, XXII, and XXVI-XXXI. Units XXVI-XXXI (Group F) are in sequence on both Copies, and can be taken together. Four of them contain material we can be fairly sure was written in 1660 (or later). Two papers in Unit XXVI cannot have been written before mid-1660. One, containing fragments 749-52, refers to the death of Cromwell in 1658, and the re-establishment of the English monarchy in May 1660. Another, fragment 735, is on the back of a draft of a letter which is dated 19 February 1660. This last is in Gilberte's hand. Other pages are written by Gilberte: another six in Unit XXVI, one in XXVII, and one in XXVIII.[54] We know that Pascal was staying with her from May to September 1660 and we can assume that it was during this period that Pascal dictated some thoughts to her. She visited him late in 1661, but the earlier visit is the more likely occasion.[55]

Another reason for assigning a late date is that two fragments appear to refer to books published in 1659. In the case of no. 798, entitled 'Epigrammes de Martial,' the source is beyond dispute: it is a collection of Epigrams published by Port-Royal with a preface by Nicole.[56] The parallel case is not quite so clear-cut. No. 822 (in Unit XXX) is entitled 'Histoire de Chine,' and is believed to have been inspired by Fr Martin's *Sinicae Historiae*. This is certainly possible, maybe probable, but we shall see later that a question mark remains.[57]

We can agree, then, that three Units certainly, four probably, all six possibly, were constituted in 1660 at the earliest. We can go one step further, and agree that other fragments in these Units were probably written at the same time as the ones we have been able to date. Immediately above fragment 798 we find notes for a projected *Discours sur la condition des Grands* (published after Pascal's death by Nicole), numbered 797 by Lafuma.[58] No. 796 is also a note for the *Discours sur la Condition des Grands*.

The reference to the English monarchy (750) has similar implications. Immediately beneath it, Pascal noted a reflection about the different attitudes of those who judge by intuition, and those who reason things out. All he says here is that they are two different kinds of people, who do not understand each other. The idea is fully developed in a famous page on the 'Différence entre l'esprit de géométrie et l'esprit de finesse' (512), which together with 513-14 constitute Unit XXII. It is usually bracketed with Unit XXI (one page, fragments 509-11), although there the distinction drawn is not quite the same.[59] Whatever one thinks of no. 511, it would seem reasonable to associate no. 512 with no. 751, and also with an addition made to no. 821 in Unit XXX. There may also be a link, more tenuous, with no. 765 (XXVI), written by Gilberte. Certainly it makes more sense to ally no. 512 with no. 751 than with the much earlier opuscule *De l'esprit géométrique*.[60]

The fragments written by Gilberte also have their parallels elsewhere. One pattern which recurs is that of an objection which Pascal answers by turning it to advantage. We find it in nos 734 and 735 (on the existence of false miracles which, far from invalidating true miracles, indicates that we do not rule true miracles out), no. 747 on the similar argument about false and true religions, and no. 746 on the silence of Tacitus and Josephus. This same pattern is found on other papers in Unit XXVI which

were not written by Gilberte: no. 760, on the 'uninspired'
portions of Scripture, and no. 748, which voices the objection that the Christian who has the hope of salvation
has also the fear of hell. On the same page as no. 760
is no. 763, about the prophecies reported in the New
Testament which, Pascal says paradoxically, are there to
make it more difficult to believe. We are back here with
the obscurity/clarity opposition, and that is the subject
of no. 758 also. Do we say that these different fragments
are grouped together because they belong to the same
period, or has Pascal simply put together thoughts belonging to different times, which are aimilar in content?
They can certainly be paralleled by earlier fragments.
Clarity vs obscurity is a theme of *liasse* 19° and the
objection of no. 748 is exactly the argument treated in
section 12°. The pattern objection/response is not unknown to the *liasses*.[61] Already then the argument from
internal evidence is proving ambivalent, as it can be
used to 'prove' an earlier date as plausibly as to prove
a later.

In other cases, the parallel works in one direction
only – towards 1658, either to classified fragments or
to fragments I have assigned to the same period. When
there is no indication that a given fragment might be
late (other than that of being housed in the same Unit
as pages known to be from 1660), I hesitate to rule out
the earlier date. The same Unit XXVI which contains so
much evidence of Gilberte's collaboration houses fragment
731-2, which doubles fragment 610-11 in Unit XXIV, and
no. 733 on the 'erreurs contraries,' which is a development of no. 576 in Unit XXIII. Some of the ideas touched
upon in no. 733 are found in the first of the *Ecrits sur
la Grâce*;[62] they are used also (in a different context)
in the fifth *Ecrit des Curés de Paris* of May 1658. No.
756 and no. 759 would be at home in *liasse* 6°, no. 767
in 5°, no. 768 in 2° or 5° (cf. no. 99) or 6°. Even more
significant, a note classified in *liasse* 24° (320) clearly
refers to the fuller text, found here as no. 753.

The argument for an earlier date is stronger in the
case of some of the other Units in this group, especially
with the next two, Units XXVII (770-91) and XXVIII (792-8).
Both contain one paper in Gilberte's hand, but both contain material one would wish to date earlier.

Three fragments in Unit XXVII are close to ideas found
in no. 136, the long development on *Divertissement*, to be

found in *liasse* 8°. No. 771 combines briefly two motifs
from that essay: that kings need distraction, and that
it is one of nature's laws that we need to have a change.
This will remind us of no. 520 (XXIII, and certainly
early). The same paper has a couple of observations on
style - another link with the early fragments I have discussed - and a remark on nature ('elle passe et revient')
which may be behind no. 27 in *liasse* 2°. No. 773 elaborates on the text 'Rien ne nous plaît que le combat mais
non pas la victoire.' In no. 136 we read: 'ce n'est que
la chasse et non la prise qu'ils recherchent.' No. 779
starts from the observation of children who 's'effrayent
du visage qu'ils ont barbouillé'; the self-same words
come in no. 136. I cannot believe that these separate
notes were made two years or more later than the longer
essay.

Nos 780 and 781 are the draft prefaces for parts one
and two. Here again, it would seem more likely that they
belonged to the period when the Apologia was beginning
to fall into place, than later on.[63] The first preface
ties in nicely with nos 683-4 and 694 (XXV), and the
second with no. 190 (classed in *liasse* 15°). The bottom
page contains a lot of separate notes. One of them (no.
791) reappears in the first fragment of the third of the
Ecrits sur la Grâce, which were certainly written before
Pascal's illness, possibly as early as 1655.[64] (If one
could prove the earlier dating, all of fragments 782-91
would have to be examined in the way we examined the
bottom papers in Unit XXXIII and the top pages in Unit
XXIII, in chapter 30.)[65]

No. 775 is echoed in the questionnaire Pascal submitted
to Barcos in 1657 (no. 831), though there may be no connection. No. 774 itself, though undoubtedly written and
corrected by Gilberte, expands on a fragment from Unit
XXIV (623); it does not seem destined for the Apologia
so much as for the misguided semi-faithful. In this it
is different from fragment 623.

In the case of Unit XXVIII, one's doubts concern the
first fragment only, numbered 792-3. Although it is
located in a Unit believed to have been constituted late,
there is evidence, both external and internal, for believing no. 793 itself to have been early. The tone of
the last paragraph captures the emotional urgency of the
Memorial. And there is a sequel, which the family considered too personal for the profane eyes of the copyists.

It is known through the Recueil Original, and Lafuma
gives it the number 931. A marginal jotting (932) probably
refers to the Passion. Such texts are usually ascribed
to the period following Pascal's second 'conversion.'

Whatever the precise date, the ideas expressed link it
closely to the phase in the growth of the Apologia discussed in the previous chapter. The first three sentences
set it firmly in the context of sections 17° and 19° and
of the fourth page of no. 149:

> Dès[66] là je refuse toutes les autres religions.
>   Par là je trouve réponse à toutes les objections.
> Deus absconditus.
>   Il est juste qu'un Dieu si pur ne se découvre qu'à
> ceux dont le coeur est purifié.

Pascal continues by listing reasons for believing the
claims of Christianity: perpetuity of the doctrine of
the fall and the redemption, the Redeemer prophesied by
diverse holy men. In the first draft, he continued with
a personal profession of faith: 'Ainsi je tends les bras
au Libérateur.' (The same phrase is used in no. 631/XXIV,
one of those which short-circuit the fuller arguments:
'Il est bon d'être lassé et fatigué par l'inutile recherche du vrai bien, afin de tendre les bras au Libérateur.') Subsequently, no. 793 was considerably revised
and more involved reasons given: the whole sequence of
what preceded and what followed the coming of the Messiah;
the synagogue which prefigured the Church; the dispersed
Jews, witnesses to the truth of the prophecies. Pascal
then sums up and concludes:

> Je trouve cet enchaînement,[67] cette religion toute
> divine dans son autorité, dans sa durée, dans sa per-
> pétuité, dans sa morale, dans sa conduite, dans sa
> doctrine, dans ses effets et // ainsi je tends les
> bras, etc.

It is thus a personal affirmation, which by a series of
additions and expansions to the first part is made more
suited to an Apologia. One of the changes suggests that
Pascal had its precise location in mind, following sections 17° and 18° ('Religion aimable'): he deleted the
words 'Deus absconditus' and added after the third sentence:

Dès là cette religion m'est aimable et je la trouve
déjà assez autorisée par une si divine morale, mais
j'y trouve de plus...

If 'Perpétuité' has its own dossier, the other themes
given by no. 793 seem to have gone together, at least to
begin with, into a single chapter entitled 'Preuves de
Jésus-Christ.' I would therefore associate the elaboration of this fragment, like ones to be found in Unit XXIV,
with a precise moment in the expansion of the second part
of the Apologia. It is most improbable that Pascal would
have formulated his thoughts in this way once the strands
of the argument had been separated out. If it was put
aside (so that it found its way into a Unit constituted
in 1660 or later) rather than going into Unit XXIV, or
into *liasse* 19°, that might be because Pascal envisaged
working on it further.

The three Units XXIX to XXXI contain only one fragment
to which a late date has been assigned. That is no. 822
in Unit XXX, and as I have said, it is not absolutely certain that Martin's book on Chinese history is the source.
Internal evidence for the other fragments in Unit XXX, as
well as for those in the adjoining Units, is inconclusive.

Three strands are easily discernible in Unit XXIX
(798-820): man, the Bible, and the apologetic argument.
Several of the reflections on the Bible could be mirrored
by classified *pensées*, without there being any parallels
close enough for us to talk of textual variants. Nos
816-17 have the same dialectical pattern found in Unit
XXVI, of taking an objection and parrying it, but this
could equally well be paralleled from the *liasses*, as we
saw. The apologetic fragments in this Unit include no.
800, which discerns a pattern in Scripture and in nature
that counteracts our tendency to self-elevation or self-
abasement, and no. 808, which is a key *pensée* on the
'Trois moyens de croire.' These notions are central to
the Apologia. No. 809 counters the objection that some
doctrines are incomprehensible by saying that the opposite is just as incomprehensible. This idea reappears
as a note in no. 149, which in turn reappears in 19° as
no. 230. Lafuma even notes a parallel between no. 813
and the fifteenth *Provinciale*, which would push nos
811-14 (on the same sheet) back to November 1656.

In Unit XXX (821-5) an addition to no. 821 shows that
Pascal is familiar with the distinction between reason

and intuition we noted in a late fragment of XXVI. The
main text of no. 821, however, is on the importance of
habit in human behaviour, and when Pascal says that habit
dictates the choice of trade, we are put in mind of no.
634 (XXIV) and behind that of no. 37 in *liasse* 2°. The
general argument ties in with section 12° also, as, in
a different way, does no. 823. This Unit also contains
a page which seems to belong with no. 432 in Unit IV,
still be to be discussed.[68] Arguments for and against a
late date seem to be evenly balanced.[69]

Unit XXXI, finally, comprises a double sheet, divided
into two (826-7, 828-9). One is reluctant to believe it
late, as no. 826 is briefly summarized in no. 247 (20°)
and no. 828 (on the other side of the page) is on the
creation of society by force, and it gives an example
which is found in one of the first fragments filed in
liasse 2°, no. 50. Beneath it, no. 829 seems to refer
to the Stoics. As the sheet is written on both sides,
Pascal could not have filed these fragments in his usual
way. In Jean Mesnard's view, the sheet is found here because it is not exclusively apologetic in intent.

I conclude, therefore, that while there is clear evidence that these six Units were not formed before 1660,
and that some fragments could not have been written before that date, it would be imprudent to augment their
number, as other fragments found here could well have
been written – and in some instances certainly were written – before the end of 1658.

Units II to XIX (Group J). The remaining Group comprises
eighteen Units, II to XIX. I have already dealt with Unit
II. The others fall naturally into two parts: Units III
to V, similar in the topics covered and in being known
only by the Copies, and VI to XIX, which document the
role of the Jews. Unit XI is an odd man out and can conveniently be studied in connection with Units III to V.
Objective clues as to the date of composition of these
papers are very limited. No. 453 (VIII) has on it a manuscript note which points to the last period of Pascal's
life. Two references to China may indicate a date later
than 1659, although this reading can be questioned. And
that is all. It has not prevented scholars from claiming
confidently that all these papers are late.[70] I prefer
to approach them with an open mind, and I shall show that
with the first three Units at least, internal evidence
points as much to 1658 as it does to 1660.

Units III, IV, V. These three Units[71] show Pascal res-
ponding to an imagined objection, that if Christians are
right, God's existence would not be open to doubt. No.
429 treats this as a genuine difficulty experienced by
a serious seeker, who is bewildered. Pascal's answer, of
course, is that Christianity does not teach that God is
everywhere manifest to the naked eye. He is usually 'hidden.' But he has occasionally revealed himself, and one
such revelation is enough to assure us that he is hidden,
not absent (440, 448). Even hidden, God instructs us (a
sign of his mercy, and a pointer to what we may expect
from a total revelation later, 438). The truth, then, is
not that everything reveals God, but that everything can,
properly understood, instruct man of his true condition,
which is double. God can be found only if he is diligently
sought; he hides himself because we are, in our fallen
state, unworthy of him. This is appropriate to our essential spiritual needs (444, 445, 446, 449, 450). Only
Christianity understands man in his fullness, and explains
the contradictions (430).

If some of the developments recorded here answer the
objection in a fairly neutral manner,[72] others imagine
the objection put by an adversary, and the reply in these
cases is more vehement. This is so in the case of the
two longest and most important statements here, nos 427
and 449. With no. 427 we must ally nos 428 (an alternative
version of one part of 427), 432 (a series of notes taken
up in 427), and no. 821bis in Unit XXX (which seems to
be a complementary portion of 432).[73] The answer is the
same: God is hidden, and Christianity has never claimed
anything different. He is known only to the man who seeks
him. This leads Pascal to chastise the person who does
not seek. Given that mortality is the one inescapable
fact about human existence, such indifference is unnatural,
supernatural, 'marque d'un étrange renversement.'[74] One
could fit in here no. 434, describing men as criminals
condemned to death.

Christianity teaches two things about man, says Pascal.
One is that human nature is corrupt, fallen from its original state of grace, and the other that it has been
redeemed, by the blood of Christ. There is a nice paradox
here: the enemies of Christianity, proclaiming that God
is not manifest, and displaying their own indifference
to the last things, are in fact presenting a witness for
Christianity, first because the obscurity of God is just
what we would expect, second because their supernatural

indifference is a sign of man's corruption (439). What
the impious say, therefore, is strength to the cause (441).

Pascal has no sooner reached this conclusion than he
sees a parallel argument to be made. If the impious are
unwitting witnesses to man's corruption, then another
group of enemies of Christianity are unwitting witnesses
to redemption: the Jews. The Jews are bracketed with the
pagans in nos 442 and 431, and more is said about them
in nos 433, 435, and 436. The last-named leads us out of
this subsection, to no. 481 in Unit XI. Before we follow,
let us ask when the cluster of thoughts we have been discussing is most likely to have been written.

In the absence of a manuscript, internal evidence is
all we have.[75] The close interrelatedness of these fragments, the fact that many of them are longer than the
average, and, one is tempted to add, the fact the manuscripts have all disappeared, all suggests we should look
upon them as a unified group, witnessing to an attempt
by Pascal to work out carefully one sequence of his
Apologia.[76] Second, one notices that the two most significant developments speak as if they belong to a preface.
'J'espère montrer ici' 'Qu'ils donnent à cette lecture'
'preuves que j'ai ramassées ici' (427) 'Je n'entreprendrai
pas ici' (449).[77] Third, we can notice textual parallels
with fragments in the *liasses à titres* or in Units believed to be early. I have quoted no. 632 (XXIV), and
mentioned no. 432/821bis (XXX).[78] No. 427 also absorbs
no. 596 (XXIV, crossed out).[79] No. 429, which which I
started this discussion, is surely an expansion of no. 2,
in *liasse* 1°, and it recalls no. 623 from Unit XXIV. The
words of no. 6 are frequently echoed in no. 427 and elsewhere. The close relationship of no. 427 with *liasse* 12°,
and of no. 449 with *liasse* 15°, has been fully demonstrated
earlier in this study.[80] In addition, the fragments on
how Christianity understands and satisfies man's deepest
needs chime in with *liasse* 17°, especially nos 214, 215,
216, and 220.

Can these observations be correlated with the argument
of the previous chapter, making this set of *pensées* a
part of the 1658 expansion of the design? Surely it corresponds remarkably closely with the hypothesis offered
there (in sections a and d) about a first preface. In the
absence of any clear evidence to the contrary, I incline,
therefore, to think of the papers of Group J, preserved
by the Copies, as having been written in 1658.[81] Their

absence from the *liasses* proves neither that they did not
exist nor that they were considered unsuitable. The only
difficulty with this reading concerns fragment 436, discussed below.

   Unit XI.[82] If we read Unit XI (458-82) immediately after
Units III to V, we are immediately struck with the high
number of similarities. The last paragraph of no. 430
echoes no. 477, while no. 468 echoes no. 442 (and also,
again, no. 6). Elements of no. 449 can be recognized in
nos 460, 461, 464. The main themes of no. 427 reappear.
The idea that God can be proved from nature is said to
be unbiblical in nos 463 and 466, the latter adding that
what the Bible teaches is man's contradictory nature.
There is evidence in plenty of corruption (471). It is
right that only those who seek should find God (472).
No. 482, entitled 'Preuves,' may perhaps be the missing
conclusion to no. 427.[83] And once again we find diverse
thoughts on the Jews: 469, 474, 476. Links between Jews
and Christians are made in 462 (on prophecy), 475, and
480 (on sincerity). All of these thoughts could be slotted
quite easily into the relevant *liasses.*[84] Some fragments
are on man: 465 on children (probably of Port-Royal, cf.
no. 63), no. 470 on 'la recherche de la gloire,' 478 on
'le divertissement,' 479 on 'les philosophes,' evidently
a jotting intended for *liasse* 9°. No. 477 is in part an
echo of no. 71 in *liasse* 3°. One particularly interesting
fragment is no. 467, which notes a possible transition
from the theme of corruption to the theme of redemption
and which is entitled 'Ordre,' thus bringing it into the
orbit of *liasse* 1°, whose connection with a preface has
already been emphasized.

   Problems nevertheless remain. The three quotations
which make up fragment 459 seem to have strayed from
fragment 489, which is Unit XVII and quite distinct.[85]
A special difficulty is created by no. 481, which impli-
cates also no. 436 in Unit V. No. 481 is entitled 'Contre
l'histoire de la Chine'; it mentions only 'les historiens
de Mexico,' and adds 'Différence d'un livre reçu d'un
peuple ou qui forme un peuple.' The reference to Mexico
is to be explained by a passage in Montaigne's essay
'Des Coches' (III.6); it does not recur. The last sentence
can be understood by reference to no. 436. In no. 436,
which bears the title 'Antiquité des Juifs,' Pascal argues
that the Greeks, the Egyptians, and the Chines have written their own histories after the event, and so they

cannot be trusted. 'Toute histoire qui n'est pas contem-
poraine est suspecte.' The only example he develops is
that of Homer's *Iliad*. He concludes: 'Il y a bien de la
différence entre un livre que fait un particulier, et
qu'il jette dans le peuple, et un livre qui fait lui-
même un peuple.' Now in no. 481, as we have seen, this
argument is seen specifically as being directed 'contre
l'histoire de la Chine,' as if this is a particular issue
or objection. Furthermore, fragment 822 in Unit XXX is
entitled 'Histoire de la Chine' and asks the question:
which is more credible, Moses or China (ie, the Old Testament record of history or the Chinese record)? This title
is normally understood to refer to a book by Fr Martin,
Sinicae Historiae, which appeared in December 1658.[86] If
we wish to maintain that fragment 436 (or any of the
others) is earlier, we must look for another source. Two
are possible, but less likely than Martin. Montaigne
mentions China in the same essay as Mexico, but not in
a way which would account for Pascal choosing the phrase
'Histoire de la Chine' twice as a title.[87] And the argument that Adam was not the first man of all was advanced
in 1655 by Isaac de La Peyrère in a book called *Praeadamitae*.[88] Pascal refers to the Preadamites in fragment
575 (XXIII). Of course, one must not be so naive as to
assume that Pascal knew nothing of Chinese national history before 1659; but the title, and the threefold recurrence of the same point does seem to indicate a specific
source, with Martin's book as the most likely candidate.
Mesnard and Sellier both make the point that none of the
classified *pensées* refer to the Chinese question.[89] Does
this invalidate my hypothesis concerning Units V and XI
(and hence Units III-IV also)? Can we clutch at the straw
offered by Philippe Sellier, who believes that nos 436
and 437 were placed in the wrong dossier?[90] I shall
shortly be quoting another reference to China (454/IX)
which is just as ambivalent.

Units VI to X, XII to XIX. The Units still be to discussed are all concerned with the Jewish nation, and can
be associated with fragment 8: 'Voir ce qu'il y a de clair
dans tout l'état des Juifs, et d'incontestable.' They
are of two kinds - developed thoughts (VI, VII, IX, X,
XIII, and XIX) and documentation (VIII, XI, XII, XIV, XV,
XVI, XVII). Unit XVIII contains a number of short notes
which fall into both categories. We shall take it as our
starting-point.

Units XVIII and VII. Looking first at the notes which
were clearly to have been expanded, one is struck by the
fact that many of the expansions come in the *liasses à
titres*, Group B.[91] Thus, the first note, 'Nous n'avons
point de roi que César' (490), is quoted in Latin in
liasse 25° (no. 340), with a short comment. No. 491, the
only fragment in these fourteen Units which does not relate to the Jews, is entitled 'Nature corrompue,' which
refers either to *liasse* 16° or (more likely in view of
the line that follows) to a time when 'Nature corrompue'
was a general heading for anything which would illustrate
the first tenet of Christian teaching.[92] In no. 492,
entitled 'La sincérité des Juifs,' the first two jottings
recur as no. 384 in Unit I, and the first appears also
in two fragments filed early in *liasse* 23°: 297 and 294.
The fourth jotting is incorporated in no. 272 (20°). The
title of no. 492 is explained by a sentence which reads
'Sincères contre leur honneur et mourant pour cela. Cela
n'a point d'exemple dans le monde ni sa racine dans la
nature.' The title reappears on no. 452, sole occupant
of Unit VII. Pascal comments there on the fact that the
Jews have been faithful guardians of a book which witnesses against them. This idea leads Pascal to the notion
of the 'témoins non suspects,' discussed in the next
paragraph. No. 494, a marginal jotting with the heading
'Juifs témoins de Dieu,' gives a reference to Isaiah
(the borderline between thought and reference is not
always clearly drawn), and it is expanded on the right-
hand side of the page (no. 495). The idea and the reference recur in *liasse* 17°, no. 204. The theme of the Jewish
witness is found elsewhere - in *liasse* 25° (331) and on
two papers in Unit XXIV (592-3, 615). Finally, the theme
of the *éclat* and the ignominy of Jesus whom Gentile and
Jew alike 'regardent comme leur centre' (499, cf. 388 in
Unit I) is touched upon, although in different terms,
in nos 270 (20°) and 308 (24°).

Unit XIX. The impression that there is a close link
between the thoughts recorded here and certain chapters
in the second part of the Apologia is maintained when
we look at the rather longer developments in the other
Units of this Group. We can start with Unit XIX, containing the four fragments numbered 500-3. No. 500,
scribbled at the top of the page, reappears in *liasse*
24° (no. 317). The subject of the main text is Figures,
and the ideas are developed separately on fragments filed
in *liasse* 20°. There is no need to repeat the analysis

given in chapter 20.[93] No. 501 sets out to prove that the
Old Testament is a figurative text, by looking at the
promises of wealth and noting contradictions. Pascal
wrote 'La 3 [preuve] est que pour accorder le sens d'un
auteur,' then broke off. He changed this later to 'Or
pour entendre le sens d'un auteur.' The sequel is found
on a different sheet, no. 257, where the first paragraph
ends: 'pour entendre le sens d'un auteur il faut accorder
tous les passages contraires.' No. 502 gives a reasoned
justification for the Old Testament's being a figurative
text. Jesus came in fulfilment of the prophecies; it was
therefore necessary that the prophecies should be zeal-
ously preserved by witnesses who were not suspect.[94] By
having the prophecies couched in ambiguous terms, so that
those who were blinded by concupiscence would understand
the promises as applying to material goods, the two conditions could be met.[95] The rejection, by carnal Jews,
of the true, spiritual, meaning, is symbolized by their
rejection of Jesus. At the same time, by rejecting him
they completed the fulfilment of prophecy and added the
final proof (cf. 262 and 273 and also 237 which alludes,
as does the text of 502, to Jesus as a 'scandal'). Fragment 502 is continued as no. 503.[96] Before moving to a
broad conclusion, Pascal mentions a few other related
ideas - the visiable as a sign of the invisible, with
the specific example of the crossing of the Red Sea as
a sign of Redemption (this recurs in no. 275; cf. also
no. 238), and the revelation by Jesus himself that there
was a 'true' meaning different from the obvious one
(also found in no. 253, which gives the same examples).[97]
Thus, there are several parallels with nos 502-3 among
the classified *pensées*, particularly *liasse* 20°, and in
the Units I am associating with the preparatory stages.
Even if the full explanation, as it is given in 502-3,
is not spelled out in the *liasses*, it complements and
illumines what is written there, and is surely implied
by many developments.

  Unit X. Unit X is short - a brief paragraph followed
by some jottings (456) plus some additional jottings,
in part overlapping with these, written sideways in the
bottom right-hand corner (457). The basic point is that
one nation has existed for 4000 years, and they claim
that their ancestors taught that man was corrupt, alienated from God, but had the promise of redemption. The
first part of this was expanded, and the notes which

follow clarified slightly. Pascal mentions the time of
the prophets, who prophesied both the manner and the time
of the coming of Jesus; the 400 years of dispersal, when
the Jews had to carry their message to pagan nations.
They were then under a curse, but they survived. No. 457
repeats the figures (1600 + 400), brings a new precision
to the two-pronged prophecies ('le temps clairement, la
manière obscurément') and in addition notes '5 preuves
des figuratifs' and 'Hypothèse des apôtres fourbes.' The
basic ideas here take us to Units VI and IX, while the
others lead directly to the *liasses à titres*. The 'hypothèse des apôtres fourbes' is no. 310 in *liasse* 24°; cf.
318, 322 and the end of 236 (19°, in place before later
sections had evolved). The five proofs may connect with
no. 501 (which only got as far as three, but was incomplete). The 1600 + 400 years are mentioned in no. 335
(25°) and in no. 793, which we associated with the development of the *liasses*. The distinction between the two
kinds of prophecy is mentioned in the *liasses*, notably
in nos 270, 332, and 255, and in Unit I (390, 392). The
figure 4000 also comes in 332 and in 793. The rudimentary
character of these references, and their reappearance in
fragments either classified or (in my opinion) early,
oblige me to assign nos 456-7 to a relatively early date.
No. 332 could well be the first expansion of no. 456, and
no. 270 the first attempt at an explanation.[98]

Units VI and IX. The other two Units of this sub-group
(VI and IX) are much more developed and are less easy to
date with assurance. Fragment 451, which constitutes Unit
VI, is entitled 'Avantages du peuple juif' and it summarizes Pascal's views. The advantages are that the Jewish
nation is one family, claiming a single ancestor, that
it is of great antiquity, that God's revelations to man
can be studied in the history of this one people, and
that it has lasted all these years, despite enormous obstacles. Further, it has a law which is very old (enshrined in a book older than Homer and Hesiod), astonish-
ingly perfect, and this law has been preserved unchanged,
despite its severity which must have tempted people to
modify it.

Similar to this is fragment 454 (Unit IX). Other nations
and religions have nothing in their moral code or the
proofs they put forward to command their allegiance. The
Jewish nation, on the other hand, has credentials which
are quite extraordinary. Pascal mentions their independence,

their antiquity, that they are one family, that their
religion is monotheistic, that they have a law given by
God which is admirable, which precedes all other laws,
and which has been copied by other nations. And they have
a religious doctrine more impressive than any others.
They teach that man is corrupt, but will be redeemed,
and they saw it as their mission to convert nations to
their belief.

Precise links with the *liasses* are few. A note (crossed
out) in the margin of 454 (no. 455) is found in *liasse*
25° as no. 348 (the first fragment filed). Nos 280 and
281 carry a distant echo of nos 451 and 454. There is a
vague parallel with no. 793 also, and I have argued that
that fragment is quite early. No. 454 repoens the question of Chinese references in Pascal.

> Je vois donc des faiseurs de religions en plusieurs
> endroits du monde et dans tous les temps, mais ils
> n'ont ni la morale qui peut me plaire, ni les preuves
> qui peuvent m'arrêter, et qu'ainsi j'aurais refusé
> également, et la religion de Mahomet et celle de la
> Chine et celle des anciens Romains et celle des
> Egyptiens...

Does the reference to China force us to believe that no.
454 was written after Pascal's illness? No. 436, another
fragment which presented the same ambivalence as to date,
mentioned Egyptian and Chinese histories, and the *Iliad*.
(No. 451 also mentions Homer.) The title of no. 436,
similar to the title of nos 451, 452, 454, and 492, was
'Antiquité des Juifs.' On the other hand, Greece, Rome,
and Egypt (not China!) are mentioned in no. 281, and
the reference to Mahomet in no. 454, as well as the first
sentence of the passage quoted, do seem to bring it into
the orbit of *liasse* 17°.

Units VIII, XII-XVII. One group of notes on the piece
of paper which constitutes Unit XVIII has not yet been
mentioned. Fragments 493, 497, and 498 are all entitled
'Prophétie(s)' and give a number of biblical references.
In this they are not very different from fragments 490,
492, and 494. Many of these references reappear elsewhere,
notably on the long fragment no. 453 (Unit VIII). There
is an argument in no. 453, but most of the space is occupied with documentation to support the argument, and it
was obviously composed before an open Bible. The object

is to show that 'les vrais juifs et les vrais chrétiens
n'ont qu'une même religion,' and Pascal argues that although the Jewish religion appears to attach great importance to race, to certain rituals, or to sacred objects,
those things are important only as signs. The essence of
Jewry is love of God and obedience, and if that is lacking, God will not be obliged to honour his promises, but
will repudiate the Jews and work his redemption among
Gentiles. Although they are abandoned, the Jews will keep
together as a nation.

Before we attempt to assign a date to this important
fragment, it should be noted that it is part of a group
of papers which document this and related matters.[99] Some
of these have headings, some do not; some give brief
references, some longer quotations. Brief notes on prophecies make up no. 487 (Unit XVI). The second half of
this page is quite close to the last part of no. 453. One
paragraph, encircled and given a separate number by Lafuma
(488), completes the argument of no. 453 by referring to
the rejection of Jesus as the final proof of his claims;
the Jews are 'témoins irréprochables.' I have already
discussed the ramifications of this idea.

Similar to no. 453 is no. 489 (XVII). Covering ten
pages, it is punctuated by headings, and is largely a
reading of Isaiah. The most significant ideas are that
the Jews will have their understanding obscured, and will
reject the true Messiah; and that the Jews will be re-
proved and the Gentiles converted. The last page extends
this, noting that the temple will be no guarantee of God's
continued blessing. Here the source is Jeremiah. No. 489
uses much of the same material as no. 486 (XV), a long
list of quotations in Latin. Two marginal additions to
502 (one dictated) incorporate material from 489 into
that fragment. There is also some confusion as to the
connection of no. 459 (Unit XI) with the end of 489.[100]

The other three Units (XII to XIV) are not markedly
similar in their argument to the ones we have been analy-
sing, but they have much the same aspect. No. 483, entitled 'Prophéties,' takes off from the *Pugio Fidei*, with
long quotations from Isaiah 49-51, and then passes to
other Old Testament texts. No. 484 comes from another
source: Jean Boucher's *Triomphes de la religion chrétienne*,
and no. 485 is a translation of parts of the Book of
Daniel (in part dictated), with annotations in the margin.
All have to do with prophecy.

Can we date these different papers? A single clue points
to a later date, but internal evidence, once again, points
overwhelmingly to an earlier. One phrase from no. 453, on
the theme of circumcision, recurs almost exactly in *liasse*
22° (288); the idea is mentioned also in no. 279, and in
liasse 20°, nos 268 and 270. The continuing existence of
the Jews is a familiar theme; there are several echoes
of no. 453 in nos 258 and 259 (also 20°). No. 259 mentions
the sceptre of Judah, another motif which occurs often;
it is the last quotation recorded in no. 483. In fragment 339 the sceptre is mentioned in the same breath as
the seventy weeks of Daniel. This too is a familiar motif.
In the classified *pensées* it is used to illustrate broader
themes; there is no hint of this perspective in the arithmetical comments of no. 485. The connected motif of the
fourth monarchy appears in nos 338 and 317. No. 484 is
entitled 'Prédictions des choses particulières'; *liasse*
26°, it will be recalled, has the title 'Figures particulières.' A brief note recorded in *liasse* 26° (350) is
almost identical with part of no. 484 and one reference
on the last page of 487 is given also in no. 258. No.
334, though brief, is cast in the same mould as the longer
collections of prophetic references. The only question
here is whether Pascal had time to document himself systematically in 1658. At least we know that he did something along these lines before abandoning the *liasses*,
because we have the notes on the Rabbinical tradition in
Bundle 21°. And many of the precise references to the Old
Testament attest to some research, even if Pascal relied
on a handful of easily accessible source books.

The external clue is a note, in two different versions,
which can be read on two pages of no. 453, which Lafuma
believes an indication of the life of self-abnegation
Pascal led during the last year or two before his death.[101]
If this documentation really is late - and the late dating
would implicate other fragments too - then we must conclude
that Pascal was taking systematic notes in order to amplify what he had already noted in the classified papers.
It is, however, more plausible to think that the classified fragments, which reflect the same concerns, were
roughly contemporary.

It is obvious that I have been able to establish very
little in this part of the chapter. All I have done is
to challenge the reasoning of those who have assumed that

because a handful of fragments can be assigned, with some
degree of plausibility, to 1660, many more, which were
grouped with them at Pascal's death, must be of the same
vintage. I have argued that the number of fragments that
can be dated with certainty is very small, and that
against the argument from physical proximity must be set
the argument from verbal similarity. This last argument
is, however, surprisingly double-edged, as fragments can
be found which are closely parallel both to fragments
known to be late, and also to fragments classified in the
twenty-eight *liasses* or else in Units which it is reasonable to assume were contemporary with the *liasses*.

To the second of the three questions posed earlier –
concerning the later evolution of Pascal's thought – it
is therefore not possible to give a satisfactory answer.
The only point that might be made (but it is not firmly
grounded) is that the fragments whose late date can hardly
be challenged (the ones written by Gilberte, and the page
on the English monarchy) do perhaps have a slightly different feeling from the general run of *pensées*. If the
pensées we have been discussing in these last pages are
indeed late, then we can say that Pascal was continuing
to document himself, and occasionally to include thoughts
triggered off by recent books in his argument. If, on the
other hand, most of these so-called late fragments in
fact antedate the illness, then the story of the evolution
of the Apologia in 1658 – our first question – could be
described in richer detail. The growth of part two from
something relatively simple to something more complex
would be due in part to a period of careful study of the
Old Testament, particularly the prophecies. And if Units
III to V are, as I incline to believe, earlier than 1659,
I would have to argue that much of the material was collected when Pascal thought of part one as illustrating
the first article of faith (the corruption of man), and
that the decision to present this first part as pure
secular observation, free from a theological framework,
was crucial. There is no real difficulty in accepting this
view of what happened. As well as accounting for a lot of
the problematic details, it makes good sense psychologically. The exposition of part one becomes a strategy,
planned by a man whose perception of life was profoundly
theological. All of this is, however, in the present
state of our knowledge, speculative.

If the second question cannot be answered with any
degree of reliability, it would seem as if the third
question (does the evolution of Pascal's thought show
the plan of 1658 to have become inadequate?) would have
to be shelved. That is fortunately not the case, however.
The reason why we cannot be sure that more than a handful
of fragments were written after 1659 is that the internal
evidence (which is all we have in most cases) is quite
inconclusive. There seems to be no distinction we can
draw on textual grounds between pre-1659 and post-1659.
If this is so, then it follows that the answer to the
question on inadequacy is quite unambiguous: there is no
inadequacy, the later fragments are indistinguishable
from the 1658 fragments and could easily have been written
before Pascal became seriously ill. I conclude therefore
that whatever be the true story of the evolution of
Pascal's Apologia, there is no reason whatsoever to en-
tertain any doubt about the validity of the plan which a
patient study of the *liasses* reveals.[102]

CONCLUSION

'Comment lire les *Pensées*
peut sembler une question superflue.
Bien sûr qu'il faut les lire
dans l'ordre de la *Copie*'
(Annie Barnes, 'Comment lire les *Pensées*,'
CPR 20-1, 1972, p. 9).

Conclusion

My primary task in this book has been to show that Lafuma
was right when he argued that the Copies of the *Pensées*
housed in the Bibliothèque Nationale shed light on
Pascal's plan. Lafuma asked us to believe that the plan
of the Apologia - what Pascal called the 'disposition
des matières' - was not, as had always been assumed, lost
forever but that the skeleton outline was discernible in
the order preserved by the two seventeenth-century Copies
of the BN manuscript collection. In particular, he claimed
that the first part of the Copies recorded faithfully the
content of twenty-eight bundles ('*liasses*') which were to
have been the basis of the twenty-eight chapters of the
Apologia. This view has on the whole prevailed, although
in some circles its importance has been minimized.

I have wished to test Lafuma's theory, not so much by
re-examining the material evidence, well sifted by this
time, but by examining systematically the order of the
Copies themselves. Much of the scepticism that was expressed at the time of Lafuma's first publications was
based on the idea that the order of the Copies is uncon-
vincing, and that therefore, even if it did record
Pascal's attempts to classify his material, it was without significance, or at least of no great use to us in
our search for greater understanding of Pascal's writings.
I believe that I have shown that the incoherence of the
Copies is merely superficial. It is possible, by careful
analysis, to discover the guiding principle behind the
details of Pascal's classification, and to present the
fragments, whose position in each *liasse* owes more to
chance than to logic, in such a way that the inner coherence becomes manifest. The first twenty-eight chapters,
which discussed the twenty-eight *liasses* in order, tackled
this question. The result, summarized in chapter 29, seems
to me to dispel all reasonable doubt.

The material lay-out of the Copies was the subject of a second part of the book, prefaced by an account of preparations for the Apologia in Pascal's earlier work (chapter 30). I was able to show that the apparent anomalies in the classification could best be explained by supposing that the plan was being refined as the *liasses* grew in size, and that the apparently random order of fragments often pointed to a precise pattern in the growth of the concept which the *liasse* in question was to illustrate (chapter 31). The thirty-five 'Units,' which contain the *pensées* that remained outside the twenty-eight *liasses*, are more difficult to account for. But the hypothesis that they show that Pascal abandoned his work of classifying – because it dissatisfied him, moreover – is gratuitous, and there is indeed a lot of evidence which should make us chary of embracing it. The unclassified fragments show the same preoccupations, by and large, as the classified ones, and are often couched in similar language. Many of them – perhaps the majority – seem to have been written during the same period as the classified ones. The simplest hypothesis – that Pascal stopped classifying because of ill health – still seems the best. I should, however, add to that the rider that some fragments were probably excluded from the *liasses* not because the plan was inadequate, but because the plan had shown Pascal the wisdom of a tactic (to keep theological considerations out of part one) with which some of the fragments already written conflicted. They could have been revised without much difficulty. That was the argument of chapter 32.

If it can be agreed that Pascal's plan can be known, and that Pascal did not come to consider it inadequate, we have to go on to ask if this knowledge affects our understanding of Pascal to any significant degree. By way of conclusion, I should like to suggest various ways in which the continuing study of Pascal might take note of the results I have affirmed.

First I should like to see an end of the unproductive scepticism which says, every time the question of the plan arises, that we cannot know and therefore should not bother.[1] In fact it is difficult to talk for long about Pascal without making statements which imply some conception of the plan, and these statements might as well be as accurate as we can make them. It is not correct, for example, to say that for Pascal Christianity

is true because it fits.[2] Nor is it correct to say that
in the last analysis faith is a wager; the wager is a
digression in Pascal's main argument, and is addressed
to one kind of opponent, as a debating tactic.[3] The objection R.E. Lacombe made concerning fragment 199 - that
the location of other fragments on man's inability to
attain truth makes it unworkable to assume, as fragment
199 does, the existence of God - is partly met when one
realizes that fragment 199 does not belong with the other
pensées on that subject.[4]

  Some of these questionable inferences are made because
the writer is subconsciously influenced by the order of
the edition he or she is using. So, second, I would like
to be assured that editions which incorporate Lafuma's
findings have indeed superseded older editions which ignored the order of the Copy. The prestige of the Brunschvicg
edition - justified by its great importance in making
Pascal accessible to countless thousands of readers for
three-quarters of a century, and by the quality of the
critical apparatus - has made it surprisingly resilient,
and books and articles are still appearing which refer
to the Brunschvicg number only.[5] One can readily understand the attraction of the Brunschvicg edition, because
Brunschvicg did take care to group fragments according
to rational principles, and the reader has an impression
of coherence which he does not find in the Lafuma-type
edition. The latter is based on fidelity to one or other
of the Copies, and for contingent reasons, the fragments
contained in each group (*liasse* or Unit) follow each other
in a disconcertingly random way. The superiority of the
Lafuma-type edition emerges only when we try to relate
group to group. Brunschvicg is much less convincing in
his overall pattern than he is inside each small section;
even if he were more convincing, his plan would still
bear only the most generalized resemblance to Pascal's
own.[6] Lafuma, on the other hand, does present us with the
evidence that can lead us to recover Pascal's plan, and
for that reason must be accounted the safer guide. It is
a pity that we do not have a readable edition based on
the evidence of the Copy, and I acknowledge that in speaking of 'Lafuma,' I am really thinking of the gloss on
Lafuma which is enshrined in the first part of this book.
Nevertheless, one can legitimately argue than an edition
which contains none of the vital evidence for Pascal's plan
is ultimately a blunt tool compared with one which does.

I naturally do not wish to imply that nothing good has come out of the Brunschvicg years – nor that work based on the Copy has been seriously hampered by the absence of this book. There are enough good books on Pascal in existence to make either claim absurd.[7] (I justify the present book more by the detail of the application than by the guiding idea itself.) A scholar who scrutinizes every fragment will be led to make his own groupings, and he might free himself from whatever is misleading in Brunschvicg. Admitting this, we can still say that for the vast majority of readers – men and women who will read the *Pensées* seriously, but not subject them to the kind of exhaustive analysis required of a specialist – the Brunschvicg order will plant certain suggestions in the mind; and that conversely, the plan, once grasped, has its own fruitful suggestions to make which are not likely to come from another source. There is, moreover, a dynamism in Pascal's thinking which is very much underplayed in Brunschvicg's arrangement.

The most clear-cut example of Brunschvicg's order distorting the subtlety of Pascal's thinking would be the historical proofs, which he places at the end, after he has given the *pensées* on the psychological reasons for accepting Christianity. By putting the historical proofs into what is effectively an appendix, Brunschvicg both minimizes and maximizes their importance, for a reader must assume one of two things: either that they are of little importance, as the main work has been completed, or else that they are the corner-stone on which Christianity either stands or falls.[8] Pascal's scheme, on the other hand, integrates them perfectly into the psychological pilgrimage of the unbeliever. Pascal does not claim that they bring conviction, merely that they show that belief does not go against reason, and that a good case can be made, which it is unreasonable not to accept. When the demonstration is over, the interlocutor will be, one hopes, better disposed, but that is not, and cannot be, the last word. Contained within a framework, they form part of an overall scheme which is remarkable for its inner coherence.

And so my third plea must be that the coherence of the *Pensées* should never be lost from view. When the plan does not guide us, it is easy to miss it, or to see it fitfully. But once the plan is known, and it is possible to relate the details to the larger whole, then the

coherence is not in doubt. It is important that we should
see the details in perspective, because whether one views
Pascal essentially as an apologist, or as an imaginative
writer with a vision to convey, the relation between the
various elements of the mosiac is clearly crucial. In any
complex entity, the overt meaning of a given statement
has to be complemented by the implied meanings which come
from its relation to other statements inside the same work,
and with something as externally fragmented as the *Pensées*
the need for vigilance in this respect is even greater
than it is elsewhere.

The coherence of the *Pensées* viewed as an apologia rests
on Pascal's conception of reason and faith. Reason and
faith co-exist in a delicate balance which can easily be
upset if, by redistributing the portions of his argument,
editors make Pascal appear to give too much weight to
proof. Pascal's case thrives on the exposure of contradiction, and if too much is proved too soon, or if (on the
other hand) contradictions are left unreseloved, distortion results. The deepest of all the contradictions is
that the goal of the enterprise - bringing the opponent
to accept a religion which rests on a personal act of
faith - is by definition beyond the power of men to attain
by human means. The gift of grace, necessary for conversion, is not automatic. What then does Pascal hope to
achieve? The structure of the Apologia makes it clear
that he is not in contradiction with himself. To Pascal
the interesting question is not why some men believe, but
why some do not. His diagnosis is that in the war between
grace and concupiscence, concupiscence has been able to
erect a number of barriers. If grace attacks these barriers from without, it should be possible to co-operate
with grace by attacking them from within, by destroying
some of the grounds concupiscence gives for confidence,
and by questioning some of the assumptions concupiscence
has wished upon us. Thus he can point to the unsatisfying
nature of the choices self-love gives us, to the logical
dilemmas it poses, and he can question the view of Christianity as joyless and unreasonable. Many of the 'reasons'
against Christianity he sees as rationalizations, and he
believes that once the underlying fear has been removed,
the need for the rationalization will be less, and the
unbeliever will be more open to the reasons Christians
can give for their faith. But these reasons cannot produce
faith. Pascal insists that there are three 'moyens de

croire' (808), and the one means which cannot be side-
stepped is 'l'inspiration,' or grace. The other means
('la raison, la coutume') are not self-sufficient, but
they work with grace, because we belong to three orders
of being: body, mind, and spirit.

The complication here is that the printed word is mediated through the mind, even if it may reach the spirit,
and even if the mind may then make decisions which affect
the body. It is reason which has to judge the point at
which it will submit (174). In reading the Apologia, we
are constantly called upon to exercise our judgment. And
one of the most important ways in which we can do this
is by resisting the temptation to isolate the part from
the whole. Hugh Davidson, who has written most illumin-
atingly about the 'trois moyens de croire,' makes this
point with particular force:

> We gravitate according to temperament and interest
> toward one or the other of these two poles [Nature/
> Scripture] in our interpretation of Pascal. Some want
> to track down and clarify the biblical (and related)
> quotations or allusions. Some want to understand and
> develop Pascal's acute view of human existence. *To the
> extent that either of these tendencies becomes exclu-
> sive, the sense and rhythm of Pascal's thought is lost.*[9]

This is the self-same error as the one Pascal taxed
philosophers with. We owe it to Pascal to see him whole.

It has never been too difficult to see the Apologia in
general terms. Once the ghost of the Port-Royal edition
was laid, the two inescapable divisions of the Apologia,
as outlined in fragment 6, gave us the essential novelty
of Pascal's approach, psychological rather than rational.
What emerges more and more as one studies the plan, and
tries to relate all the fragments to the overall scheme,
is the degree to which that is so. The Apologia does not
comprise a psychological part and a rational part; it is
all conceived as an argument *ad hominem*, and the true
function of the rational proofs cannot be understood if
they are studied in isolation.

The *Pensées* should always be seen as part of a rhetorical strategy.[10] The unstated premiss to any argument is
in the mind of the imagined opponent, and the sequence
is dictated more by psychological than by purely logical
considerations. That is true right from the outset. The

unsympathetic charge that in part one Pascal was simply
copying Montaigne and that the abiding interest of that
part is attributable as much to Montaigne as to Pascal
is seen to be unfair.[11] It is of course true that many
of the piquant details do come from Montaigne, and that
if Pascal had not drawn on Montaigne, it would have been
much less telling. But it is 'telling' in a very specific
way. Pascal's alleged plagiarism is seen as a deliberate
strategy: Montaigne is so much admired that the opponent
will be bound to accept all the details laid out for him
in these pages. If Pascal can build up a case with elements the opponent (generally hostile at this stage of
the dialogue) cannot refute, his first battle will be
more easy to win. Pascal's portrait of man may be Jansen-
istic in its emphasis on corruption,[12] but the examples
are taken from an unimpeachable source. The unstated premiss here is: 'Montaigne says, and you accept him as a
guide.'

Pascal draws upon Montaigne, but even when he is close
enough to Montaigne to use his vocabulary, the syntax is
his own, and the cumulative effect quite unlike Montaigne.
The altered syntax gives a note of tension absent from
the sixteenth-century writer. This tragic note, to which
so many readers have responded, is also part of the strategy,[13] and should not be used to yield conclusions about
Pascal's spiritual drama (although it does reveal something of his temperament). It has been projected by some
readers and commentators onto the whole enterprise, whereas it should be obvious that the overall pattern can provoke feelings of tragedy only if one adopts a point of
view radically different from Pascal's own.[14] However, as
an attempt to induce or to represent such feelings in the
interlocutor at one moment in his journey from indifference to concern, it is very appropriate. Once the attack
on the opponent's nerves is deemed to have produced its
effect, that tragic tone disappears.

The effect of part one differs from Montaigne also by
virtue of the fact that Pascal has selected and arranged
according to his own pattern. This is done not only to
demonstrate a thesis, but to produce a particular effect
on the mind of the opponent.[15] Janet Morgan has compared
this interestingly to the effect grace is known to have:
Pascal wishes to change the opponent's perspective on
things.[16] With a changed outlook, he will be more receptive to grace, should the call ultimately come.

The picture of the human condition, based upon Montaigne, is only one phase in a long and intricate duel. The portrayal of contradictory man is intended to leave the reader with the need to enquire further. Enquiries lead to philosophers and to religions. As soon as the enquiry reaches Christianity, the opponent is ready with objections, all of which Pascal skilfully meets.

One such objection concerns the validity of using reason at all. Quoted out of context, this argument has proved a persistent stumbling-block to Pascal's critics. Pascal's best argument, we are told, is that Christianity is a good bet, and that is a very feeble argument. In context, the 'wager' can be seen as part of a lively debate. Pascal had said in part one that faith is of the heart (7, 110), and that the sceptic position is very strong (131). One must imagine the opponent seizing on these, and saying that it is surely impossible after that to continue with the attempt to put the Christian case. To which Pascal characteristically has two counters. The first is to say: radical scepticism is your position, not mine. But even if we accept it, all it means is that the argument must be conducted on other lines altogether, for example self-interest, and out of self-interest it is more prudent to opt for Christianity than to choose against it (418). The second counter, which is double-barrelled, is to say that although faith is of the heart, the mind and the body are implicated too, and in the same essay, Pascal talks of the role of self-discipline, implying that there is some connection between that and our readiness to believe or disbelieve.[17] The role of the mind is important and complex, and will be developed at length in future sections.

Pascal foresees other objections, and is ready with his counter-arguments. Sometimes the charge of inconsistency can be met if we restore the implied remark which provoked Pascal's observation. For example, the opponent imagines that Christianity teaches that God is visible in his creation (427), and Pascal says that that is not so. After hearing what Pascal has to say, the opponent is evidently convinced, for in no. 244 he objects that we have no light. This extreme also has to be moderated. Pascal's position on so many issues is that two contradictory perceptions contain half the truth, and must somehow be reconciled. On those occasions when he himself appears to be adopting an exclusive stance, restoration of the debating context

can make the exclusiveness seem temporary, part of a tactic. Another reason for apparent inconsistency is that
the common ground between apologist and his opponent
changes in the course of the discussion, and assumptions
can be made at one stage which would not have been possible earlier.[18] It is possible that an objection of Roger
Lacombe could be met, at least in part, by this approach.[19]
He finds Pascal's argument concerning God's justice inconsistent with his earlier scepticism. The unbeliever's
view is that it is unjust that a person should be punished
without a cause, and so the notion of the transmission
of original sin offends our idea of justice. In the early
part of the Apologia, Pascal's answer has to be by way of
an attack on the opponent's confidence, and he implies
that he has no right to talk as if he knows what justice
is ('notre misérable justice,' 131). Later, having moved
beyond this sceptical position, he can arrange the elements differently, and say that it is not just to punish
for no cause; we are punished, God is just, therefore
there must be a cause (205). It may not be a very good
argument, but in the light of the shifts in the debate,
it is not wholly inconsistent.

I am arguing that every part of Pascal's presentation
must be understood in relation to the whole if we are to
avoid either giving it too much emphasis, or interpreting
the words too literally. This is so with part one, and
with the argumentative central portion of the Apologia;
it is also true of the chapters which give the historical
or rational proofs.[20]

In the overall strategy of the Apologia, the rational
proofs occupy a very special place. It is here that the
paradox of the enterprise - using reason to achieve a
goal that reason cannot reach - is at its most acute.
One would think that Pascal's oft-repeated warning against
an over-reliance on reason would make critics wary of
seeing the historical sections as constituting the key
proof for Christianity, and discussing them in isolation.
Seen in isolation, they appear arid, and to a modern reader not very convincing, and if it is believed that they
bear the onus of Pascal's whole case, an unsympathetic
response can be damaging. To a certain degree, of course,
they do have to be examined critically on their own merits,[21]
but they also have to been in relation to the whole.

When we see them in their correct context, the historical
proofs become much less problematical, for three reasons.

In the first place, we understand better the frame of mind Pascal expects of his reader. At this stage, he is committed to searching, and has been shown that most searches end up in blind alleys. Reason can take us part of the way, but it cannot in abstraction prove the specifics of Christianity. The reader has therefore been enlightened as to the true nature of Christian doctrine, quite distinct from a belief merely theistic, and he can see the immediate advantages of the theological account of man which Christianity gives. In talking of man's corruption, Christianity fits the facts of the portrait already drawn, which thus becomes part of the evidence, as well as a psychological tactic. In talking of a state of grace before the fall, it offers at least in theory an explanation of man's dissatisfaction. And in talking of a redeemer, it offers a way out. The issue hinges therefore on the legitimacy of the teaching concerning the claim of Jesus to be the Messiah. Reason can be used to examine the evidence for this claim.[22]

Second, the examination which then follows is directed less at the question 'Is it true?' as at the question 'How could it be true?'[23] It is almost a digression – though a rich and an important one – aimed to quieten doubts which reason has to voice, and to show that Christianity is not unreasonable.[24] Pascal has not forgotten how much he has granted to the sceptics, nor that he has said that reason has to work from premises it cannot prove. In this light, the essay on the 'disproportion de l'homme' (199) takes on a new importance. Pascal shows there that we can never know the whole, only the part, yet the part is imperfectly known if we do not know the whole. This thinking underlies part two. The whole, like infinity, can be known only as a hypothesis. But hypotheses can be tested, by reason. That is how Pascal tackles the phenomenon of the prophecies, and Jesus as fulfilling the prophecies. It is significant that his approach to the historical proofs makes use once again of the notion that only a hypothesis can bring the pieces into a meaningful relationship. In essence he is saying: 'I can show you a way in which the contradictory fragments appear to fit together.' One such commanding hypothesis is the notion of the hidden God. As a hypothesis, it has the very great advantage of fitting the facts, and of making sense. Pascal treats it seriously as a meaningful decision taken by God, not as a facile way of dodging difficulties.

Fallen human nature necessitates it, and the range of
matters which can then be explained by it makes it seem
very plausible. What began as a way of meeting an objection has become a positive principle of interpretation.
A second basic assumption is the notion, of which part
one has already convinced us, that many a truth turns
out to be a half-truth, and must be tested. Even where
details of Pascal's demonstration can be shown to be wrong,
and hence to need correction, the principle of his method
stands, and our attention should be held by that.

When he has heard the arguments from history, the interlocutor admits that Christianity could be true, even that
it very likely is true, but that is not the end of the
road. The third way in which the plan sets the historical
proofs into perspective is by showing how the discussion
continues. The next question is: 'What can I then expect
of Christianity, if I accept it?,' and that is answered
in section 27°. Once that is done, the apologist's task
is accomplished. Reason is satisfied, advice has been
given about preparing the body and the will, and the heart
must now await the coming of grace.

I have argued that the debate between the apologist
and his adversary lends a dimension to the Apologia which
affects our understanding of each part. Even the rational
proofs are not offered as the ultimate argument, for which
the opponent is at last prepared, but as the discourse
which the opponent needs at this stage of his journey.
The plausibility of Pascal's case is further strengthened
by another aspect of the unity of the presentation: the
high degree of correspondence between the two parts. The
Christian view of truth, felicity, and justice picks up
in a positive way negative points made earlier. The concrete examples with which both parts are studded often
link up, so that in reading part two we are conscious of
outstanding questions being implicitly resolved. Even the
three orders, used by Pascal to explain the nature of the
kingship of Christ, were prefigured by a reflection on
tyranny (58).[25]

Our assessment of Pascal's Apologia must take into account all the factors I have been discussing. It would
be foolish to judge it solely by the number of converts
it produces, even if the result of that enquiry were not
as totally negative as has sometimes been suggested.[26]
The modern unbeliever's reaction to Pascal's arguments
has been thoroughly explored by Roger Lacombe. His

conclusion is that provided the reader is temperamentally receptive, Pascal's portrayal of the human condition can bring him to the point where he is prepared to make the leap of faith, but he rejects Pascal's assumption that from that point on the reader can be led to accept the validity of Christianity on rational grounds. The fact that Pascal's first part uses authorities which no longer have any hold over us - Epicureans and Stoics, sceptics à la Montaigne - is no real obstacle, for we could easily replace them with our modern authorities: Freud for his revelation of unconscious motivation, Marx for his faith in man's ability to create a Utopian society.[27] Updating the second part is more difficult, for biblical scholarship since Pascal's day has left very few of Pascal's assumptions standing.[28] Pascal's example might, however, predispose us to thinking that if he was able to make out a good case in the light of what was believed in his time, we can at least allow the possibility of our modern knowledge being used in a similar way.

Whether we read books of popular apologetics, or theological explorations of the problems inherent in the whole subject, we are constantly reminded of Pascal. The same rationalists who ridicule Pascal's arguments from Scripture are frequently disturbed by the anti-rationalism of his pronouncements on faith as preceding reason.[29] This is, however, a position which has won widespread acceptance in our own times.[30] Twentieth-century science has confirmed Pascal's position concerning the real but limited role of reason in a universe which defies rational comprehension, and recent theology is very much concerned to emphasize the primacy of faith. It is said that the true Christian tradition is that which maintains that faith precedes reason and is sufficient.[31] In two recent articles, Jean Mesnard has shown how in all essential matters Pascal is very modern.[32] Only in his insistence on the gulf between man and God does he appear out of sympathy with modern thought. Modern theology emphasizes also the radical distinction between 'general revelation' and the specifically Christian revelation.[33] Christ is known in a personal encounter,[34] and the apologist is essentially a witness.[35] In urging the unbeliever to start seeking, Pascal is an apologist for our time.[36] 'Les Pensées occupent aujourd'hui une place éminente dans ce qui s'est substitué à l'apologétique, la théologie fondamentale.'[37] It is not surprising that Marcel Guersant wrote, in 1954: 'il n'y a pas

d'autre apologétique possible que celle qui s'inspire des
méthodes et qui suive les voies positives indiquées par
Pascal.'[38] It is not surprising either that books meant
for the honest unbeliever of today often make statements,
and even adopt strategies, which recall Pascal.[39]

Yet Pascal's name is rarely evoked. When he is quoted,
it is usually because of two or three well-worn phrases.
This suggests that there is no direct influence of Pascal
on modern apologetics. The lack of influence is not surprising: as long as Pascal is presented in a fragmentary
way, it could hardly be otherwise.

Pascal's claim that it was on the 'disposition des
matières' that his reputation would rest thus comes to
appear sound. When his *Pensées* are read as fragments,
their impact is dulled. Piece by piece, they reflect much
that was current in seventeenth-century Christian apologetic writing.[40] But previous apologists had not joined the
pieces together in the way Pascal did, and the whole nature of his Apology is different from theirs.[41]

As soon as the full context of Pascal's apologetic arguments are restored, it becomes clear that the questions
we should be asking have to do more with rhetoric than
with straightforward apologetics.[42] Are the problems
raised answered, and if so, are they answered in a consistent manner? Can they reasonably be expected to have the
specific effect Pascal wants at that moment in the evolution of his opponent's attitude?

It is a short step from this to other questions, of a
purely literary kind. Pascal's *Pensées* have to be studied,
like any other literary work, for intrinsic qualities of
style and structure. Once again, it is vital to have the
overall shape in mind. Once we have grown accustomed to
seeing all Pascal's thoughts as part of a single whole,
with nothing relegated to the humble status of an appendix, then we are more ready to recognize the imaginative
coherence of the *Pensées*. With Pascal we can experience
that pleasure which is the sign of an authentic artistic
masterpiece, of discovering that all the parts echo and
reflect other parts, and that the meaning resides in, or
emerges from this formal patterning. Motives balance, or
are replaced by others. Dialectical patterns (*grandeur/
misère*, the three orders) recur in new contexts. Hidden
connections bind part two to part one.[43]

As we study the Apologia as an imaginative structure,
we discover that Pascal gives us, on the level of our

imagination, the experience of fragmentation followed by integration and resolution, which is what he hopes our ultimate spiritual experience will be.

Much attention has been paid recently to Pascal's language.[44] I believe that further research will show that in the fields of imagery and sentence structure (to take the most obvious) there is an evolution in Pascal's use of language which corresponds to the evolution of the overall plan. For this purpose we can make a threefold division somewhat different from the one proposed hitherto. First, Pascal arranges quotations which show the *misère* of man. Second, these come to form a pattern characterized by *contrariété*. Third, Christianity is proposed as a way of solving and therefore resolving the contradictions.

The 'tragic' style of Pascal clearly belongs to the first of these stages. Pascal's sentences have an impact all their own, cutting out all unnecessary words. His sentence 'Plaisante raison qu'un vent manie à tous sens' (44) is very different from the fuller statement of Montaigne: 'Vraiment il y a bien de quoi faire si grande fête de la fermeté de cette belle pièce qui se laisse manier et changer au branle et accidents d'un si léger vent!' A few lines before that is a superb example of Pascal riding roughshod over normal syntax, producing an effect much more imaginative than intellectual:

> Le plus grand philosophe du monde sur une planche plus large qu'il ne faut, s'il y a au-dessous un précipice, quoique sa raison le convainque de sa sûreté, son imagination prévaudra.

He will force the reader to participate, by questions and imperatives, and by a dramatic narrative style, as in the paragraph on the magistrate and the preacher immediately preceding the last quotation. Images, dramatic, dynamic, startling, are fairly frequent in this part of the Apologia.[45] He is not above using personal examples to stimulate a reaction. We may certainly talk of imaginative power, but we cannot yet speak of imaginative coherence.

Imaginative coherence begins at the point where the argument begins to advance through awareness of paradox.

```
Que l'homme maintenant s'estime son prix.
Qu'il s'aime
    car il y a en lui une nature capable de bien
        mais qu'il n'aime pas pour cela
            les bassesses qui y sont
Qu'il se méprise
    parce que cette capacité est vide;
        mais qu'il ne méprise pas pour cela
            cette capacité naturelle.
Qu'il se haïsse, qu'il s'aime
                il a en lui la capacité
                    de connaître la vérité
                et d'être heureux;
        mais il n'a point de vérité, ou constante
                        ou satisfaisante (119).[46]
```

Man falls apart, in two pieces, but language (in particular, the resources of syntax) bridges the gulf by an
imaginative resolution. The two parts are made to correspond exactly. Time after time what we experience is fragmentation by reason together with unification by language.[47]
What to reason is negative, is to the imagination positive.
It is not merely contradiction; the two halves are made
as parallel as is possible.[48] Allied to this syntactical
device are the frequent plays on words. These forge a
link where none appears to exist:

```
Par l'espace l'univers me comprend...
Par la pensée je le comprends (113).
```

```
C'est le coeur qui sent Dieu et non la raison.
Voila ce que c'est que la foi. Dieu sensible au coeur,
    non à la raison.
```

```
Le coeur a ses raisons que la raison ne connaît point
                                        (424, 423).
```

If custom can be called 'second nature,' nature can be
called a 'first custom' (126). There is no question here
of a tragic tone; Pascal is exulting in a new truth, in
the possibility of reconciling the terms of a dilemma.
Reason meets paradox, incompatibles, half-truths which
only imagination can fit together.

The third stage comes when reason finds that there is an explanation. The half-truths are reconciled now in Christianity, which goes deeper than the rational explanations. Christianity shows the same superiority over the philosophers as imagination does over reason. The paradox is carried up into Christianity, with the doctrine of the two natures of man, and of the two natures of Christ. 'Les Juifs en éprouvant s'il était Dieu, ont montré qu'il était homme' (306). The duality enables Pascal to continue to write double-barrelled, balancing sentences, but there is no longer the tension between the explicit meanings.

> Elle nous apprend que par un homme tout a été perdu
> et la liaison rompue
> entre Dieu et nous
> et que par un homme la liaison est réparée (205).

Adam and Jesus are both identified as 'un homme.' The change of tense removes the incompatibility, the still portrait of opposites becomes the dynamic vision of history. What was no longer is. With man now seen to be partaking of the divine, man's qualities can be attributed to God within him, and the contradiction of no. 119 resolved in the statement of no. 373: 'Il faut n'aimer que Dieu et ne haïr que soi.' The paradox is removed[49] (or, in some cases, immediately explained), and the style is now quiet and confident.[50]

This imaginative experience is not irrelevant to Pascal's avowed aim as an apologist. In the first place, it prefigures the activity of grace. Conversion becomes an imaginative, if not a lived experience, and part of the reader's affective being. Second, it increases the degree to which Christianity is attractive to us. Pascal's purpose was to make Christianity more attractive and less unreasonable than it had appeared to be at the outset. Valid points have been made. But perhaps the most attractive feature of all in Pascal's version of Christianity is the pattern which he draws out of the complex issues involved. Whether we find the reasoning true or false, Pascal's arguments in part two are still able to produce the desired effect - that of making us ready to receive God's grace - because to anyone responsive to that kind of unity which we seek in works of art, the coherence of Pascal's vision is itself impressive and telling. As we grow more familiar with the motifs and patterns that recur, we find them more and more plausible. Pascal's words become our words, his systems become our systems. For such a reader, Pascal does not need to be adapted, any more than we need to rewrite *Phèdre* or *King Lear*. Once all the parts of a man's vision have been integrated into a single unified whole, we tamper with it at our peril.

The coherence I claim to have found in the way the fragments were sorted by Pascal is thus no sleight-of-hand, no clever trick to attempt to fabricate unity where none existed. We have to dig into the *liasses* to find their coherence, but the coherence is reflected, nearer the surface, in all other aspects of the *Pensées*. The plan - imperfectly realized, but clearly visualized - is one of the major expressive elements in Pascal's writing, and we should let it guide us as we seek to penetrate more deeply into the inner workings of one of the most powerful minds our civilization has known.

APPENDICES

APPENDIX A
Suggestions for reading the *Pensées*

One obvious practical use to which this research could be put would be to suggest to a new reader of Pascal an intelligible order which he could follow; see introduction, p. 25. This appendix is designed for such a person, and I have thought it less confusing to use Lafuma's numbering of the *liasses* rather than my revised numbering.

The thousand fragments known as the *Pensées* have the appearance of pieces of a vast jig-saw puzzle, and we know that Pascal had an overall design. Indeed, he began to sort the fragments into dossiers, each to be the basis of a separate chapter. But he sorted only half of them, and his arrangement does not make the new reader much wiser. It is, however, possible to use this arrangement, and other clues, to arrive at a very plausible notion of Pascal's ground-plan, and hence to read the fragments in an order which gives a fair idea of his argument. Not all the thousand are equally interesting, naturally. We offer here a suggestions for a reading of selected *Pensées* which (despite the drawback of having to hop backwards and forwards) makes as much sense as any other, and much more sense than the order in which the fragments are printed. I use the numbering of L. Lafuma's Luxembourg edition of 1951, which is followed in the various editions put out since 1958 by the Editions du Seuil. It is also used in the English translation by A.J. Krailsheimer (Penguin Classics, 1966). It has the merit of recording objectively the order in which the fragments were copied at Pascal's death, and is the basis of all attempts to solve the puzzle.

In this account, I reverse the order of chapters 14° and 15°, and restore an empty dossier, which Lafuma numbered 15bis. Roman numerals refer to the *Pensées inédites* published in 1962 and numbered thus by Lafuma (Seuil, 1963): they do not appear in all editions or translations.

Pascal's chapter-titles are preserved. This guide can be supplemented by the summary given in chapter 29. In that chapter, and throughout the whole book, except for this appendix, I have renumbered the chapters from 14 on, to conform to my presentation of them.

Preliminary to Part One

1° *Ordre*
   Basic aim and framework: *12*, *6*
   First part prepares unbeliever to desire to seek:
   4, 5, 11, 7
   (Difficulty of ordering first part in 780, 683, 694,
   532, 696)

Part One, *'Misère de l'homme sans Dieu' (6): 403*, *75*, 656

2° *Vanité*
   Chapters 2° and 3° are ordered around a number of loosely related themes: the division into Vanité and Misère is not at all rigorous. It is only in 5° that the dynamics of the argument and the intricate relationships become apparent.
   Vanity = false importance: cf. 93, first sentence.
      Vanity of the world: 16, 46 = 413, 40
      Twin desire, for truth and felicity: *28*, 697, 23
      Truth eludes us: *44*, 45, 48, XI, 33, 52, 412
      Motivated not by reason, but by amour-propre: 31, VIII,
                                   628, 685, 806, 37, 35,
      Happiness eludes us too: 24, 27, 771, 36, 39, 43, 47
3° *Misère*
   Last point of 2° continued: 73, 56, 70
   Other points of 2°: 63, 72
   Concupiscence and society: 74, 421a, 668, 978, 597, 642,
   Justice eludes us: 64, 58, *60*, 66
   Ultimate mystery: 68
4° *Ennui*
   An abortive chapter, continuing themes of 2° and 3°: 77, 78
                                                 79, *62*.
5° *Raisons des effets*
   'Vain opinions are really sane: *101*, 80
   Reason: only force is incontestable: 97, 577b, 98, 99a
      reality of physical danger: 87, 89
      force is the basis of justice: *103*, 81, 85, 86, 645, 71

to question justice is to fall in the rule of force
once more: 94
One is obliged therefore to take up a third position,
seeing the strengths and weaknesses in popular opinion: 93, 91, 92, 90
6° *Grandeur*
All is not loss
Social order: 118, 106
'Wretchedness' implies a high calling: 633, 437, 116, 117
Thought: 759, 620, 111
superior level to corporeal: 113
not inconsistent with wretchedness: 114, cf. end of 122
not inconsistent with earlier criticisms: 756
we cannot disregard opinions of others: 470, 411, IX
scepticism cannot be total: *109*, 112 = 406, *110*
7° *Contrariétés*
Man is therefore contradictory: 124, 123
'Truths' are often half-truths: 576, *122*, 613
Moral consequences of man's duality: *121*, *119*, 130, 450
Philosophers tend to take sides: 127
Doubts cannot be resolved by natural reason, but
Christian revelation claims to have an answer: *131*
8° *Divertissement*
Human condition leads us to despair: 135, 134, 133
So we distract ourselves: *136*
glossed in 478, 522, 773, 137, 132, 139, 415
Conclusion: 414
9° *Philosophes*
Stoics: 626, 142, 144, 829, 141, 143, 140, XII, 145
Stoics and Epicureans, each give half the picture:
407, 410, 678, 443, 399, 398, 430, 400
10° *Le Souverain Bien*
148 is the beginning of a discourse into which 8° and
9° would fit
Dispute over the sovereign good: 147, 479, 76
Fruitlessness of the search: 397, 661, 401
Consequence, a readiness to turn to Christianity: 631

Preliminaries to Part Two: (1) the human initiative

11° *A P.R.*
149 probably notes used for a lecture delivered 'à
Port-Royal'; a transition from part one to part two
greatly amplified in the following chapters.

12° *Commencement*
Addresses unbelievers: 405, 160, 162, 156, 161, 150
The discourse: *427*, glossed in 612; 153, 165-6; 434, 428
                               823, 632, 383, 164, 163,
                               596; 157
If reason cannot attain truth, at least it can be used
in the search for the sovereign good; it can recognize
the superiority of Christianity, and take steps to
embrace it: 418
13° *Soumission et usage de la raison*
The correct use of reason: 167, 170, 183, 179, 173, 174
The limits of reason: 182, 188, 175, 185
Authority of Scripture; the miracles: 820, *180*, 169, 184
15° *Transition de la connaissance de l'homme à Dieu*
Awareness of limitations (a recapitulation of previous
themes) leads to a consciousness of God the Creator,
and a desire to explore further.
     198, 201, 194 (cf. 68), *199*, 200 (cf. 113), 193, 202

Preliminaries: (2) the divine initiative

14° *Excellence de cette manière de prouver Dieu*
Jesus Christ, the only proof of the living God:
   189, *449*, 190, 191, 192
Universe demonstrates one or other of the Christian
truths: 442, 468
Nature proves not God, but man's corruption: 781, 466,
                                     463, (3)
15°bis *La nature est corrompue*
(It is now assumed that this dossier, known only by
the chapter-heading on Pascal's table of contents,
was not empty, but misplaced, being nos 416 and 417.)
The Christian doctrine of redemption underscores
man's present corruption: 417, 416

Part Two, 'Qu'il y a un Rédempteur' (6)

16° *Fausseté des autres religions* (cf. 149, first part)
Christianity has true understanding of man's need:
   393, 215, 205, 210, 211, *208*, 212, 219, 595, 600
Claim of Mahomet is by comparison very weak:
   203, 204, (1), 209, 218
17° *Rendre la religion aimable*
On the issue of whether redemption is universal.
Balances 15°bis and 16° (a).
467, 221, 222, 911, 912

18° *Fondements de la religion et réponse aux objections*
Basis of Christianity surer than Mahomet: 243.
(Balances 16° (b))
Objections answered (see end of 149): 226, 241, 809,
230, 231, 239
Specific notion of the 'hidden God': 244, 440, 448,
444-6, XIV, 439, 242, 234, 236, 394, 461, 232, 235,
233, 237
19° *La loi figurative*
O.T. to be read as a figure: 274, *501*, 257, 276, 259,
260, 272, (cf. 279)
Key to cipher given by Jesus: 253, 268, 267, 269, 475,
271; 264, 256, 275
Reason for ambiguity: 270, 255
The Jewish witness to Christ: *502-3*, 496, 614, 469,
273, 262, 593, 495, 391, 488
20° *Rabbinage*
Rabbinical authority for figurative interpretation
Rabbinical tradition on original sin: 278
21° *Perpétuité*
Preliminary distinction between carnal and spiritual
readings: (cf. 243), 287, 286, 289, 480
Messianic promise: 454, 451, 456, 452
Continuity: 284, 425, 421b, *281*, 390, 282, 394, 392
Church: 285, 776
22° *Preuves de Moïse*
Authoritative record: 436, 292, 290, II, 296, 474, 435
Second phase, zeal: 294, 297
23° *Preuves de J.C.*
Prophecies of J: 388, 608, 487, 315, 319, 317, 305,
314, 311
Gospel portrait: 318, 316, 322, 310, 812; 321; 303,
309, 307
Obscurity of J: 300, 499, *308*, *298*
24° *Prophéties*
Strongest argument: 326, 385, 335, 344, *332*, 456 (end)
Conditions concerning the time: 333, 336, 339, 329
All fulfilled: 338, 324, 325, 327, 346, 447, 331;
594, XV, 793
25° *Figures particulières*
Specific details: (349, 350), 484, 570
26° *Morale chrétienne*
(cf. 6 'Félicité de l'homme avec Dieu')
Happiness and virtue: 357, 426, 460, 373a, 376, 618,
365, 355
Limbs of a Body: 368, *360*, 370, 374, 372, 373b, 359

Grace and the law: 824, 367, 366, 364, 944
Morally appropriate: *351*, 358, 353, 354, 352, 800, 545
27° *Conclusion*
Conversion: 482 (end), *835*, 379, 574, 378, 874, 842
Faith: 588, (7), 380, 381, 382
Discipline: 377, 975, *821*, 808

APPENDIX B
The place of 'Transition de la connaissance de l'homme à Dieu'

The authenticity of the *table des titres* has been a basic
assumption of this book, yet I have presumed to invert
the order of Pascal's fourteenth and fifteenth titles
('Excellence de cette manière de prouver Dieu'/'Transition
de la connaissance de l'homme à Dieu'), to which I have
given the numbers 14° and 15° respectively. The chief
reason for this liberty is that when the switch has been
made, the resulting shape makes much better sense than
does the alternative, of leaving them in the order of the
Copies.

I shall first summarize the argument, omitting section
14° ('Transition'). Then I shall summarize section 14°
and ask where it best fits. We shall see how other commentators have coped with the difficulty, and then ask
how the mistake, if that is what it is, could have arisen.

In section 12° (no. 427), Pascal attacks those unbelievers who, despite the overwhelming evidence of *misère*,
persist in their attitude of aggressive indifference to
Christianity, which they say cannot be proved. There are
two essential articles in the Christian faith, says
Pascal: the corruption and the redemption of man. The
man who will not seek God illustrates the corruption of
man. If reason has no way to decide, the choice must be
made on the basis of self-interest, and self-interest
dictates that we do take the claims of Christianity very
seriously.

Nevertheless, the difficulties facing anyone who wants
to prove the validity of Christianity are real. One must
realize that reason does have a role to play, albeit a
limited one. Reason, for example, can legitimately examine
the historical claims of Jesus, which rest on his miracles
and fulfilment of prophecy. Such is the drift of section
13°.

In section 15° ('Excellence,' the fourteenth title on
the table; La. 189-92), Pascal states that God can be
known only through Jesus, who can be proved by the prophecies. Through Jesus we can be sure of God's existence,
know something of his nature and purpose, and because
that purpose involves the redemption of mankind, we can
understand our own situation as both corrupt and redeemed.
One fragment in this *liasse* is entitled 'Préface' and is
echoed in an unclassed fragment headed 'Préface de la
seconde partie.'

Section 16° ('Nature corrompue,' nos 416-17) appears
to follow on from this. Not only does Jesus provide the
only means for knowing God, he provides the only way to
know ourselves, and the only possibility of virtue and
felicity. Christianity, Pascal goes on in section 17°,
explains man's predicament, offers the remedy, and gives
man a full understanding of himself.

The bundle 'Transition' (193-4, 198-202) may be summarized thus: if the world without God is composed of
misère with no hope of anything better, and if the world
offers no guarantee of meaning, the natural reaction is
to despair. Blasé indifference is impossible; a man must
examine the credentials of the various religions which
claim to offer an explanation. And in Christianity he is
impressed by the prophecies and their fulfilment in
Jesus (no. 198). Although the world does not tell us anything of the nature of God, it does teach us what is our
own situation in the universe, and it suggests the power
of the creator. Reason therefore does have a role to
play, and can be applied to the question of God as Creator,
and man's relation to him as a creature (no. 199). Reason
therefore has a double function: to recognize our limitations in the vast universe created by God, and to examine
the historical evidence for man's religions.

It is clear that the title of this collection of fragments, 'Transition,' has a precise meaning; Pascal is
moving from an enquiry centred on man and his human experience to an enquiry directed to God and what can be
known of him. It fits perfectly between what I am calling
the thirteenth and the fifteenth sections. It picks up
the first part of section 12°, considers as does section
13° the legitimate use of reason, shows how far reason
can go in search for the true religion, and arrives at
the same point as section 13°: among the world's religions,
we find the religion of Jesus, and the fact of the

prophecies. And in section 15° (my numbering) we read
that we have to get beyond metaphysical proofs of God
the Creator, that only Jesus can show us that God is a
God of love, and reveal to us our own destiny. If we insert section 14° ('Transition') at this point, we are
blurring the movement of the argument, and we thereby
separate 15° from 16°, which clearly belongs with it.
Fragment 417, indeed, summarizes the ground covered in
nos 189, 192, and 449.

My argument might be countered with the objection that
by giving my own summary of each section, I am slanting
it in the direction I wish it to go. I can only refer
readers to the detailed discussion of the content of the
liasses in question, and affirm that my summaries are
based on a reading of all the evidence which seems relevant. Admittedly, other commentators have summarized the
argument in such a way that the original order is not
dislocated. But a close scrutiny of these versions generally shows a slight hiatus in the argument, or a suppression of some of the fragments which should be taken into
account.

Thus, J. Mantoy,[1] after presenting section 13° briefly
(p 80), remarks that Pascal rarely attempts to prove God
(p 82); he mocks the claims of the deists because our
approach to God must be supernatural, by Jesus (15°).
In section 14°, Pascal criticizes our reason (p 83). In
this scheme, section 15° becomes a kind of digression.
And fragment 198 is not mentioned. The summary on page
20 handles the two *liasses* more skilfully: 'La preuve de
Dieu par Jésus-Christ nous met seule en communication
avec Dieu' (15°), 'L'homme désire cette communication
et en est incapable par lui-même' (14°). Mantoy relegates
sections 17° and 18° to a footnote (p 94) and picks up
the argument with the scriptural proofs of section 19°.

Pol Ernst's presentation[2] pinpoints well the incoherence of the order preserved by the table and the Copies
at this point. While he calls sections 13°, 14°, and 15°
a 'groupe homogène' (p 278), he is forced to present
Pascal coming back on his tracks to the theme of reason.
'Excellence' shows us that reason is useless in the
search for God. 'Mais si Jésus-Christ constitue à lui seul
la preuve par 'excellence' de Dieu, est-ce à dire que la
raison n'a absolument aucun role à jouer dans la recherche?'
(p 256). Section 14° shows reason's incapacity, while saying
that it can be used to discern the true religion.

Michel and Marie-Rose le Guern[3] attempt to justify the
given order by saying that 15°, like 13°, has to do with
Pascal's method, refusing metaphysical proofs in favour
of mediation of God to man through the person of Jesus
(p 147). Section 14° is then called 'une dernière mise
en condition de son lecteur' (p 150), without it being
related in any way to section 15°. The problem of the
sixteenth title is not solved, and the discussion turns
immediately after section 14° to a new division, 'Les
preuves de la religion chrétienne' (p 168).

Writing in 1951, Jean Mesnard presented the three
chapters with his customary elegance.[4] Man must use his
reason properly (13°), and a proper use does not mean
elaborating a rational proof of God. God can be proved
by the mediator, and we do have a way to prove Jesus'
claims (15°). What will be the relation of man to God,
of a finite being to infinity? The gulf can be bridged
by the initiative of God, by grace, merited by Jesus
(14°). As an equally elegant account could be given with
sections 14° and 15° in the order I am proposing, this
version does not, I believe, silence doubts. And the
discussion in Mesnard's later book on the *Pensées* is
rather different, and tends to confirm my stand.[5] After
he has analysed section 15°, Mesnard passes immediately
to section 16°. Then he writes: 'Entre les deux chapitres
dont on a vu l'étroite correspondance se développe l'un
des plus importants de *l'Apologie* dont le sujet semble
au premier abord tout différent.' He justifies its place
in this group of *liasses* by saying that Pascal is tackling
the problem of 'la fin de l'homme.' But he does not answer
his own implicit question, as to why it should come
between 15° and 16°. His general justification would be
equally valid were 'Transition' to be placed before
'Excellence'; and as I have already said, its links with
13° cease to present any difficulty if it does go in
that position.

Finally, A.J. Krailsheimer, in the chapter of his book
which outlines the first part of the Apologia, passes
straight from 13° to 14°, and then writes: 'Here at the
mid-point (chapter 14 out of 28), the analysis of man's
state gives way to a discussion of the remedies proposed
by other religions, and, finally, by Christianity.'[6]
His summary does not mention 15°, but resumes (p 61)
with a discussion of the proofs from Scripture. But it
is clear that the *liasse* on 'Excellence' is part of what

Krailsheimer regards as the second half, which is the position I take.

There remains the question: why should there be an error in the list of titles? Our knowledge of the precise circumstances in which the fragments were classified, and then abandoned, make it impossible to be at all dogmatic. Assuming that the list of titles was compiled mechanically from the dossiers lying on Pascal's table, the real question is: why should two of the *liasses* be out of place? It would be imprudent to speculate; it could easily be purely accidental.[7] All we have to say is that he inserted one at not quite the right place, and did not notice his mistake when he made the list of titles.

APPENDIX C
The editions of Brunschvicg, Stewart, and Chevalier

In my conclusion I touched upon the dangers of knowing Pascal only in the Brunschvicg arrangement.[2] This is not the place to give a detailed critique of Brunschvicg's choices. Four further observations can, however, be made. (a) Brunschvicg places all the psychologial *pensées* in the first half of his exposition, relegating to the second half such matters as the superiority of Christianity, the Jewish religion, Figures, prophecies, the Jewish witness, Jesus, miracles, and the Church (including recent controversy). This means that the second part is no longer within any dramatic frame, and Béguin was probably right when he said that as a result half of the readers of Brunschvicg's Pascal gave up before the end. How much more telling is Pascal's own scheme, where the historical proofs are followed by a chapter on felicity and a final chapter on conversion, and where even the historical proofs are given added interest by the pattern of enigma and resolution through the theory of the hidden God.

(2) In Brunschvicg's first part the dynamic thrust is muffled. Section II on 'Misère' (with nothing to indicate a parallelism between the goals of 'le vrai' and 'le bien') is followed immediately by sections on the need to search, and on the difficulty of finding God in nature, and the three ways of believing. We then return abruptly (section V) to considerations of injustice, and of the inadequacy of reason and the will (VI). This sixth section corresponds roughly to Pascal's 6° and 7°, with the conclusion that man is contradictory, and motivating in this way a desire to find a solution.

(3) The motif of man's greatness is split into two parts in this sixth section: it is stated at the beginning, where the evidence is that man has the faculties of thought and reason. The claims of reason are then attacked, leading to a position of total pyrrhonism, at which low

point Brunschvicg introduces the fragments which argue
that we find irreducible elements of Greatness even in
Wretchedness. In a general way, this is not too remote
from Pascal's order (especially if we remove Brunschvicg's
sections III and IV), but the absence of nos 110 (in IV)
and 131 (in VII) robs it of the dynamic upward thrust
which Pascal's conception manifests so strongly.
(4) After section VI, Brunschvicg turns to the religious
quest, beginning naturally with a group of *pensées* which
argue that only Christianity satisfies man's longing for
the Sovereign Good. Brunschvig's order contrasts the
reality of original sin from which we cannot escape with
the Christian ideal of loving God and serving each other
as members of a body. Christian attitudes are the sole
guarantee of felicity. He even includes the 'Mystère de
Jesus' at this point (Br. 553). A new section (VIII)
talks of Christian doctrine and the concept of 'le Dieu
caché,' plus one or two other related explanations, such
as 'raisons pourquoi figures' (502), concluding that
Christianity is 'sage et folle.' Were it not for this
conclusion, one would be tempted to see this section as
a prelude to the historical proofs which follow. Without
getting lost in examples of the illogicality of some of
Brunschvicg's specific decisions, I can only reaffirm
that though Brunschvicg's order seems fairly plausible
as we move from page to page, we have no sense of a
magisterial tapestry, in which the motifs left behind
will recur in their appointed place. What is often called
'l'ordre du coeur' is not absent from the Brunschvicg
edition (eg, the recurrence of fragments on man's wretchedness in section VII), but the final effect is fragmentary – a Suite rather than a Symphony.
    No other pre-Lafuma edition enjoys the same prestige
as Brunschvicg. But two other editions should be mentioned
here, both claiming to be guided by the *Discours* of
Filleau de la Chaise. H.F. Stewart was the first to propose such an edition, and in 1921 he gave a detailed account of what the edition could have been. He did not
himself produce such an edition for another twenty years,
and in the interim Jacques Chevalier had followed Stewart's
lead, and devised his own edition, along similar lines.[3]
    H.F. Stewart's edition (different in detail but not in
its structure from the 1921 project) is a remarkably
faithful realization of the scheme outlined by Filleau
de la Chaise in his *Discours*. Naturally it is open to

the same criticism as was Filleau's account. In addition,
one suspects that in two cases, Stewart has included more
fragments than Filleau's text implied. When Filleau talks
of the search for meaning being undertaken by a study of
the philosophers, he seems to have in mind the philosopher's understanding of the Sovereign Good. Stewart, however, includes a consideration of scepticism at this
point. When Filleau mentions the free-thinker's objection
that the doctrine of original sin is unjust, he says that
we cannot judge divine justice: 'les idées que nous avons
de ce qui est juste ou injuste sont étrangement bornés,
puisqu'enfin il ne s'agit entre nous que d'une justice
d'homme à homme.' Stewart inserts here Pascal's thoughts
on human justice (5°). It is true that in neither case
does Filleau's text offer a clear opening for these subjects to be treated earlier on, but the superiority of
Pascal's own scheme, where these considerations have
been already settled in a non-religious context, is evident.[4] Also, Stewart has a short section separating the
first look at the Jews from the section on the Bible,
comprising an objection to the doctrine of the Fall, duly
answered by Pascal. I see no justification for this in
Filleau; nor are the *pensées* purportedly formulating the
objection very convincing. They are all more plausible
in the mouth of the Christian than the agnostic. Generally,
however, Stewart's presentation is to be preferred to
Brunschvicg, because it does convey something of the
dynamism of Pascal's argument. If it is still not the
ideal format, the is because Filleau's *Discours* does not
have the authority of the Copies, and can only be second-
best.

Jacques Chevalier, who also took Filleau de la Chaise
as his starting-point, treated him much more freely.
Part one, for example, begins, as did Brunschvicg, with
reflections on language and 'l'esprit de géométrie,' and
it does not bind itself to Filleau's subdivisions. (Consequently, justice can be dealt with in this section.)
Chevalier's part one takes him through the search (philosophers, other religions, Jews: the beginning of part two
in Stewart), and he concludes with the diagnosis and the
Christian solution, and with a list of the marks of a
true religion. The final *pensée*, somewhat surprisingly,
is no. 131.

Before he comes to the Proofs, which he calls part
three, Chevalier inserts a second part, which he entitled

'le Noeud.' This is concerned with the instruments of
faith - reason, the 'machine,' and the heart. It concludes with no. 149. It is the least satisfactory part
of Chevalier's arrangement, and is clearly not justified
by Filleau's text, which at this point presented the
claims of the Bible. If 'le Noeud' is seen as an expansion of the myriad ideas contained in 'Infini rien,'
however, it could be argued that Chevalier is not far
from Pascal's own thinking. The difference is that Pascal
talked of the role of reason when he had limited himself
to generalities about the Christian diagnosis, and the
search among the world's religions came after these questions had been settled. Pascal is careful to have us see,
first, that the search is one of the legitimate uses of
human reason, and second, that the final handing over of
reason to faith comes at the end, when reason has done
all it can, making the final choice a matter of the will
alone. There is something very awkward about moving back
from the 'trois moyens de croire' (808) to no. 149, which
brings us into the centre of the debate once more.
Pascal's intentions are more faithfully rendered by
Filleau and Stewart. Chevalier was possibly too much
influenced by Brunschvicg's section IV.

A general caution which should be issued against using
editions which replace Pascal's authentic order with
something else is that individual fragments are necessarily coloured by their context, and it requires considerable will-power to resist the subtle suggestiveness
that comes from the links on the printed page. We need
not dwell on this point; here is one example. Fragment
308 on the three orders if placed by Chevalier in his
conclusion, immediately after thoughts on the 'sagesse
et folie' of Christianity, and is meant to underline the
point, made earlier, that the would-be convert must be
prepared to leave 'l'ordre des esprits'[5] for the superior
order, of charity. We know that Pascal's intention was
very different: he evoked the three orders in order to
show that Christ did come as a King, as the prophets had
foretold, but that his kingdom was 'not of this world.'
Stewart's allocation of this *pensée* to a section on the
life of Jesus, pairing it (as did Brunschvicg) with no.
499, is much more satisfactory.

APPENDIX D
Editorial decisions:
fragment 131

I referred in note 75 of the introduction to Lafuma's arbitrary transcription of the second paragraph of fragment 131. From the manuscript, it is clear that Pascal wrote a first version (a) which he revised later. Here is the text:

> Et que comme on rêve souvent qu'on rêve, entassant un songe sur l'autre, [ne se peut-il faire que cette moitié de la] vie n'est elle-meme qu'un songe sur lequel les autres sont entés, dont nous nous éveillons à la mort, pendant laquelle nous avons aussi peu les principes du vrai et du bien que pendant le sommeil naturel, [tout cet écoulement du temps, de la vie, et ces divers corps que nous sentons,] ces différentes pensées qui nous y agitent n'étant peut-être que des illusions pareilles à l'écoulement du temps et aux vains fantômes de nos songes?

(The passages in brackets were later struck out.)
When he revised it, he added in the margin two passages (b and c) which were to go immediately before the one just quoted:

> On croit voir les espaces, les figures, les mouvements, on sent couler le temps, on le mesure, et enfin on agit de même qu'éveillé. De sorte que la moitié de la vie se passant en sommeil, par notre propre aveu, où, quoi qu'il nous en paraisse, nous n'avons aucune idée du vrai, tous nos sentiments étant alors des illusions, qui sait si cette autre moitié de la vie où nous pensons veiller n'est pas un autre sommeil un peu différent du premier, dont nous nous éveillons quand nous pensons dormir?

Et qui doute que si on rêvait en compagnie et que par
hasard les songes s'accordassent, ce qui est assez
ordinaire, et qu'on veillât en solitude, on ne crût
les choses renversées?

At the end of 'c' he wrote 'Enfin,' and he changed the
first two words of 'a' to 'Enfin.' He had second thoughts
about this, however, and immediately deleted 'c' and the
word 'Enfin' as well as the parts in 'a' which I put in
square brackets. The copyists saw what Pascal meant; the
second sentence of 'b' should read as follows: 'De sorte
que la moitié de la vie se passant en sommeil [etc.] ...
qui sait si cette autre moitié de la vie ... n'est pas
un autre sommeil ... dont nous nous éveillons quand nous
pensons dormir, comme on rêve souvent qu'on rêve entas-
sant un songe sur l'autre? [La] vie n'est elle-même qu'un
songe...' Later in the paragraph he also crossed out a
phrase of fifteen words, but probably because he sensed
there was too much repetition, he then put a vertical
stroke through the whole of 'a.' Clearly, then, the only
passage we are obliged to retain is 'b.' Editors have
generally included 'c' and 'a' too, putting them in
square brackets to show that they were deleted by Pascal.[1]
This practice is defensible, but it is a pity not to
mention that 'a' was written before 'b,' as implying the
opposite gives a distorted picture of the process of rewriting.

In the Delmas editions, Lafuma also follows the usual
custom, except that he omits from 'a' the words struck
out by Pascal, simply restoring the article before 'vie.'
(He prints it in italics and encloses it in square brackets. One naturally assumes the square bracket and the
italic to signify an editorial addition, necessary to
complete the sense of the sentence. But Lafuma nowhere
explains his use of italics, and says on page 26 that
square brackets indicate words crossed out on the manuscript!) The trouble with that is that he is really mix-
ing two states of the text without giving the reader the
means to make his own judgment.

The missing phrases are restored in the Luxembourg
edition, but 'b' is mangled. This time, the order is a,
b, c, but the only part he marks as having been suppressed
by Pascal is 'c' plus the last clause of 'b'! The last
clause of 'b' was actually what we might call an instant

afterthought. On the manuscript, sentence 'b' ends at
the words 'un autre sommeil un peu différent du premier,'
and Pascal wrote immediately the first three words of
sentence 'c': 'Et qui doute.' He scratched them, and
added a clause to 'b': 'sur lequel nos songes sont entés
comme notre sommeil paraît.' This was immediately dis-
carded in favour of the definitive version ('dont nous
nous éveillons quand nous pensons dormir'), and sentence
'c' follows.

The clearest way to transcribe this would surely be
as follows, with square brackets indicating passages that
were crossed out:

> du premier[. Et qui doute] [sur lequel nos songes sont
> entés comme notre sommeil paraît.] dont nous nous
> éveillons quand nous pensons dormir. Et qui doute...

Lafuma puts the whole lot in brackets and italics (his
sign for deletions), including the phrase 'dont nous
nous éveillons quand nous pensons dormir,' which was not
delted by Pascal; this phrase is also enclosed by Lafuma
in dashes, indicating that it was a later addition.
Nothing separates 'Et qui doute' from 'sur lequel...,'
making that sequence incomprehensible.

Nor is the transcription of the rest of the sentence
satisfactory. I gave earlier a perfectly clear modern
version of the sentence, as it is found in Brunschvicg,
Chevalier, and (with minor differences) Anzieu. The manuscript has a full stop after 'illusions,' which leaves
the first half of the sentence without a verb; clearly,
this has to be corrected in a modern transcription. (The
Copy gives a semicolon.) Lafuma (understandably perhaps
in a critical edition) leaves it in, and he prints 'ou'
for 'où' (which was correct in the Delmas). Surprisingly,
he is followed in both these decisions by Sellier and
Le Guern. Lafuma also introduces a full stop of his own
after 'paraisse,' making the first part of the sentence
even less intelligible.

APPENDIX E
The strata of fragment 418
(Infini rien)

In chapter 12 I remarked that our understanding of fragment 418 has been much aided by the work of scholars who
have patiently laid bare the different strata of the
text, enabling us to distinguish the different phases
of its composition. This has been the approach of two
of the famous fragment's most distinguished commentators,
Georges Brunet and Henri Gouhier.[1] In one important particular, however, Brunet and Gouhier read the evidence
quite differently, and on the main issue involved, it
seems to me that Brunet's reading is by far the more
plausible. As Gouhier's commentary is probably more widely
consulted than Brunet's, and as he does not say that he
is in disagreement with Brunet, the point should be explained in more detail. Other related issues can be discussed along with it.

The 'Infini rien' essay covers three sides of a very
involved manuscript, with one paragraph found on the
fourth side, along with sundry other thoughts that do
not belong directly with the argument of the main essay.
These sheets are pages 3, 4, 7, and 8 of the Recueil
Original. It will, however, be simpler to renumber them
1, 2, 3, 4. Pages 2 and 4 are the verso sides of pages 1
and 3. Page 1 does not come into the present dispute.

If we look at a reproduction of page 2 (both Brunet
and Gouhier reproduce it), we immediately see that there
is what Brunet calls a 'normal part' and a number of additions squeezed into all the available space – a blank on
the right-hand side of the page, written horizontally,
the left-hand margin, for which Pascal has turned his
sheet though 90°, writing towards the edge of the paper,
and the top space, which Pascal has treated similarly,
so that the topmost addition appears to be upside-down
as we look at the page in the normal position.

The first 'normal' text covered about half the page, and beneath it Pascal drew a line. For future reference we shall have to divide it into two – a paragraph of four lines, and the rest. Below the line, Pascal subsequently wrote an unrelated thought of four lines, and again drew a line. Another development (9 lines) was written beneath this line. I shall designate these four passages by the letters 2A, 2B, 2C, and 2D. (They are identified and summarized below.)

The addition in the left-hand margin is arranged in two columns, the first (level with 2A and 2B) of five lines, the second (level with 2C and 2D) of seven lines, with an additional three lines crushed in at the top, level with 2D, which has a wider left-hand margin than 2C. These additions I designate 2LX and 2LY, and the extra addition to 2LY I shall call 2LYY, using the sign '2L' to signify the whole of this passage. The upside-down passage at the top of the page had originally three lines; an addition of three short lines has been squeezed in above it. I call these 2T and 2TT.

There is finally the added material fitted into the blank to the right of the final words of 2B. Pascal managed to get quite a lot down before the presence of 2C obliged him to give up, and start on a new sheet (page 3). This right-hand addition I am calling 2R. Page 3 is written in such a way that the left-hand margin becomes progressively wider, so that by the time he had reached the bottom of the page, he must have turned the sheet round, gradually, by about 45°. The body of the text comprises two paragraphs, which I call 3A and 3B. In the space to the left are eight lines with the title 'Fin de ce discours,' which I call 3F.

The passage on page 4 which interests us was the first one to be written. It consisted of eight lines, perhaps nine; the opening has been much modified, and one sentence added. I call this passage 4A, and the sentence added 4AA.

Before discussing the hypotheses of Brunet and Gouhier, it might be as well to identify and summarize (or quote) the passages I shall be examining.

(2A) 'Parlons maintenant ... aucun rapport à lui.' Having no point of contact with an infinite being, we cannot by natural means resolve the question of his existence or non-existence.

(2B) 'Il est² ou il n'est pas ... Gagez donc qu'il est,
sans hésiter.' Reason cannot decide, so which way will
you place your bet? You have to bet, or choose, one way
or the other. Which way will self-interest gain most?
By accepting God's existence: if you are wrong, you lose
nothing, and if you are right, you gain in all respects.
(2C) This is fragment 422, and lies outside the present
argument.³
(2D) 'Qui blâmera donc les chrétiens ... cela n'excuse
pas ceux qui la reçoivent.' Christians cannot be reproached for not accounting for their faith in rational
terms. All right, replies the interlocutor, but if Christians cannot be taxed with inconsistency, converts who go
over to Christianity when there is no reason are surely
open to criticism.
(2LX) 'Je confesse, je l'avoue ... apprenez de ceux qui
ont été liés comme vous et qui parient.' Continued as
2LY: 'maintenant tout leur bien ... qu'avez-vous à perdre?'
That is convincing, but is it all obscure to reason?
Pascal replies that there is a way of accounting for it,
based upon Scripture. The interlocutor complains that he
is not free to decline. Reply (bottom line of 2LX): learn
from those who have been similarly unfree, and who now
wager all that they have, that the way to induce belief
is to adopt certain patterns of behaviour. The opponent
says he is frightened to do that. But what will you lose?
asks Pascal.
(2LYY) 'ce sont gens ... dont vous voulez guérir.' These
people have gone the same way as you, and known the same
longings as you.
(2T) 'O ce discours me transporte ... avec cette bassesse.'
The interlocutor accepts, and Pascal discloses the source
of his strength.
(2TT) 'mais pour vous montrer ... vos grands obstacles.'
The reason why this method works: it reduces the strength
of the passions, which are the major obstacle to faith.
(2R) 'Cela est admirable ... trois à gagner.' I see I
must wager, but you are asking me to wager too much. Here
begins the argument about probability and the wager.
(3A) 'Il faudrait jouer ... la perte du néant.'
(3B) 'Car il ne sert de rien de dire ... si les hommes
sont capables de quelque vérité, celle-là l'est.' Continuation of the wager argument.
(3F) 'Fin de ce discours.' What harm would it do to opt

for the existence of God? It would improve the quality
of your life, and you would see more and more all the
benefits, as well as the insignificance of what you sac-
rificed.
(4A) 'Il est vrai mais apprenez ... vous en demandez les
remèdes.' Your inability to believe comes from your passions. So work at reducing the passions rather than at
increasing the number of arguments. You want faith and
do not know how to acquire it.
(4AA) 'Et je suis fait ... que je fasse?' I am unable to
believe, so what should I do?

The additions here are clearly of two distinct kinds,
one being mathematical and the other moral. One question
which arises is: which came first? It is also clear that
the moral argument (2L, 2T, 3F, and 4A) was composed in
stages. In what order, precisely? Brunet believes that
the moral argument preceded the mathematical argument,
and that 4A was a later addition to the text of (2L).[4]
Gouhier, on the other hand, believes that the mathematical argument was set down first, and that the whole of
page 4 was covered before Pascal decided to develop 4A,
using the space at the left and at the top of page 2. It
seems to me that Brunet is irrefutably right on this
matter.

The argument hinges as much on the lay-out of the different passages (with the various signs telling us where
to go next) as on the logic of the content. But it will
be clearer if we familiarize ourselves first with the
sequence of ideas.

On Brunet's argument, 2L was a new sequel to the argument which had ended (2B) with the words 'Gagez donc qu'il
est sans hésiter.' The opponent would have said 'That's
fine, but is reason not to be satisfied at all?' - 'Je
le confesse, je l'avoue, mais encore n'y a-t-il point
moyen de voir le dessous du jeu? Oui, l'Ecriture et le
reste, etc.' Rather than elaborate here on the 'etcetera,'
Pascal moved immediately to another fancied objection:
'Oui, mais j'ai les mains liées et la bouche muette, on
me force à parier, et je ne suis pas en liberté, on ne me
relâche pas.' The answers, subsequently modified (I put
the words later deleted in square brackets) read: '[Il
est vrai mais] apprenez de ceux qui ont été liés comme
vous et qui parient / maintenant tout leur bien que la
manière par où ils ont commencé, c'est en faisant tout
comme s'ils croyaient' (etc.). The opponent is won over,

and Pascal very neatly concludes, clinching many of his
points (this is 2T).

Later, Pascal made three additions to the text: 4A,
2LYY, and 2TT. The crucial one is 4A. It is a difficult
passage to transliterate simply as the first clause exists
in two versions, neither syntactically complete. The words
enclosed here in square brackets represent an edited con-
flation of the possibilities open to us:

> Il est vrai, mais apprenez au moins que votre impuissance
> à croire [vient de vos passions, puisque la raison vous
> y porte et que néanmoins vous ne le pouvez.] Travaillez
> donc non pas à vous convaincre par l'augmentation de
> preuves de Dieu, mais par la diminution de vos passions.
> Vous voulez aller à la foi et vous n'en savez pas le
> chemin. Vous voulez vous guérir de l'indifélité et vous
> en demandez les remèdes. Apprenez les (?etc.) de ceux
> q (?etc.).

On Brunet's reading, with which I agree, this opens out
the phrase (2LX) 'Il est vrai mais apprenez de ceux qui
ont été liés comme vous.'

Gouhier's view, I have said, is quite different. He
maintains that Pascal had written 2R and 3, but had not
filled his left-hand margin, when he wrote 4A on the back
of page 3.[5] This raises a number of awkward questions.
First, what could Pascal have had in mind when he wrote
the words 'Il est vrai'? Evidently, the interlocutor must
just have spoken. If it is supposed to have followed the
'demonstration' of the strong mathematical reasons for
accepting, then where is the interlocutor's interpolation?
Pascal did add it, immediately above 'il est vrai' ('Vous
ne pouvez croire' changed into 'Je suis fait d'une telle
sorte que je ne puis croire. Que voulez-vous donc que je
fasse?,' 4AA) but we shall see shortly that that formulation links up with 2LX, not with 3B.

A second question which arises concerns the end of 4A,
the words 'apprenez les de ceux.' Whether the next mark
is the q of 'qui' or 'etc.', the phrase clearly joins
onto something already in existence, and the obvious,
indeed the only candidate is the bottom line of 2LX,
'apprenez de ceux qui ont été liés.' The third difficulty
comes from the way 2LX is written. If Gouhier is right,
the first part would have been written to introduce 4A,
and the rest to follow on from it.[6] Yet is it clear that

2LX was originally a single sequence: 'on ne me relâche pas. [Il est vrai mais] apprenez de ceux qui ont été liés' (etc). Later, the words in brackets were deleted - manifestly at the time when the text was opened up to admit 4A, which opens and closes with the identical words. Two other textual details seem to us to be relevant. After he had scratched 'Il est vrai mais,' Pascal added above the words 'mais apprenez,' then crossed them out. On the next line of 4A, he wrote 'apprenez-les de ceux.' One can assume that he thought this join - a repeated word, such as we find frequently in Pascal - was more appropriate on page 4 than on page 2, where the word 'apprenez' would have appeared twice in succession. The other textual detail concerns the same sentence. The first version had the following syntax: 'Apprenez de ceux qui ont été liés ... que la manière par où ils ont commencé, c'est en faisant' (etc.). In the revised version, the syntax is changed, by pausing before the word 'que,' and starting a new sentence: 'Suivez la manière.' It is very likely that this revision was made when Pascal was reading his new text (Tourneur's reading): 'Apprenez-les (i.e. les remèdes) de ceux'; it is no longer possible to continue with a noun clause. Furthermore, when Pascal added a sentence at the beginning of 4A, he actually wrote not quite what I printed in the previous paragraph, but this: 'pas. Et vous ne pouvez croire.' That proves that the added sentence (4AA) was expressly conceived as following the penultimate line of 2LX, and not as following 3B. One question might be raised: that the 'Il est vrai' of 2LX does not make a great deal of sense. That, however, is not strictly relevant to the debate, and the answer is simply that, as we know from the previous sentence of 2LX, Pascal was moving quickly. That is why he had to elaborate later; the transitions were too abrupt. A final argument may be introduced here. The argument of the passage I have quoted (4A) is continued in the next addition (2LYY), and it is reasonable to assume that they were written at the same time. Passage 4A, in summary, is one of three additions made to 2L and 2T.

That is not the end of our problems. Given that 4A was written after 2L and 2T, where in the sequence do we place the mathematical argument of 2R and page 3? And what about the 'Fin de ce discours' (3F)? Before tackling this question, let us settle an apparently simpler matter: the lowest fragment on page 2. I called this 2D, but it must

have been conceived all along as an addition to 2A, to be
placed between 2A and 2B. Not only does it address itself
to the question of 2A, expressing a misgiving at the dogmatic way in which reason has been shelved, the link which
Pascal wrote in at the end connects it very precisely to
the opening of 2B. Pascal wrote: 'Examinons donc ce point,
et disons Dieu est ou.' Now, 2B began 'Il est ou il n'est
pas,' and Pascal changed the 'Il' to 'Dieu.' There is one
indication, however, that Pascal did not actually mark on
his sheet that 2D was to go in higher up the page until a
little later. I shall return to this. It involves consideration of Pascal's 'signes de renvoi,' as does the
rest of this discussion.

I believe that there is clear external evidence that
the moral development was written before the mathematical
development. When Pascal began 2L, he had already written
2D (otherwise the new passage would have gone in the space
2D now occupies). 2L is preceded by a clear mark - a triangle with two lines at the bottom. This sign was also
written in after the words 'sans hésiter' (2B), and later
deleted. It appears no fewer than five times on pages 2
and 3; all but two of these have been scratched out.
Pascal must have crossed it out at the end of 2B when he
decided that instead of adding the moral argument at that
point, he would expand on the mathematics of the wager.
This addition (2R) starts immediately to the right of the
deleted sign. It spills over, as we know, onto a new
sheet. Would Pascal have taken a new sheet if there was
still space on page 2? Gouhier thinks he did, and that
he only filled the space of 2L and 2T because there was
not a millimetre to spare on pages 3 and 4 when he wrote
that development.[7] If my reading of the function of 4A
has been accepted, however, that argument does not hold
water. Pascal therefore wrote his mathematical page, to
go between 'sans hésiter' and the moral argument (beginning
'Je le confesse' and marked by a triangle). The triangle
appears again half-way down page 3, at the end of what we
called 3A. I take this to mean that the mathematical argument once stopped there. But Pascal found he had to go on
further, so he deleted the triangle for the second time,
and he will remember to add it at the bottom of the page,
where it sends the reader back from the mathematical argument ('celle-là l'est') to the other.

What of the fifth use of the triangle? This occurs at
the end of 2A. I fancy that when Pascal noticed that he

had not indicated where 2D was to go, he put his favourite
sign, then immediately realizing he had already used that
sign on this page, he crossed it out, and substituted a
different sign (a line with three vertical bars). This
new sign is put in place also at the beginning of 2D, as
we should expect.

   This explanation seems to make sense of the five appearances of the triangle. Brunet and Gouhier both find the
triangle a stumbling-block. Brunet suggests that the two
scored out triangles on page 2 indicate Pascal's hesitation about the correct place for 2D (although the triangle
never adorned 2D): 'deux signes de renvoi identiques ...
ont été placés d'abord à la fin des [2A] et [2B], puis
raturés tous deux et transformés en pâtés, sans doute
parce que la position du second etait défectueuse.'[8] He
tries to explain the presence of the triangle at the end
of 3A by saying that when Pascal completed the mathematical passage (2R, 3A, 3B), 2L was without a house; that he
wanted to reintroduce the dialogue element into the text,
and that he then 'remembered' the passage on the previous
page, and that before finding its proper location, he had
toyed with the idea of putting 2L, etc. between the two
halves of page 3.[9] This seems highly improbable. Gouhier
even suggests that when Pascal put his sign at the end of
3B, he placed the corresponding sign 'par erreur' at the
end of 2B; 'il l'a, bien entendu, annulé.'[10]

   Finally, there is the unattached passage entitled 'Fin
de ce discours' (3F). As Pascal wrote no sign joining it
to the rest of his text, we must assume that there was
no reason to do so – it was to follow on from 3B, and the
reader's eye would be caught by the title, and would turn
to it as a matter of course.[11] Nevertheless, as we know,
there is a sign at the end of 3B which sends us back to
page 2. The obvious way to react to this is to regard 2L
and 2T as an insertion, after which we are to read 3F.
That is the way the passage is recorded on the Copies,
followed by Tourneur, Anzieu, and Sellier. Some editors
have introduced a modification to this scheme, which is
not justified by Pascal's marking, but which is more logical, and that is to put 3F before 2T. That was Brunschvicg'
solution, followed not only by Chevalier, but by Lafuma and
Le Guern, despite their nominal fidelity to the first Copy.

   Brunet and Gouhier both have observations on this matter.
Gouhier, who as we have seen believes that Pascal wrote
4A immediately after page 3, and that 2L, etc. was a later
expansion of 4A, would have us read 3F immediately after

3B, 3B being the 'discours' to which 3F is the 'fin.' He
is then obliged to say that the triangle at the end of 3B
is there to indicate not that 2L, etc. follow 3B directly,
but that when we come to turn the page (after reading 3F),
we should take 2LX first.[12] This is open to the obvious
objection that if that were Pascal's intent, he would
surely have put his sign either at the end of 3F, or at
the beginning of 4A.

Brunet, whose comments seem much more pertinent, is disturbed by the difficulty of putting the pieces of the text
in a logical sequence.[13] He does not accept, as we have
done hitherto, that 2T was written immediately after 2LY.
The first idea, then, would have been to insert 2L (only)
between 3B and 3F. The question 'Quel mal vous arrivera-t-
il?' (3F) would follow the question 'Qu'avez-vous à perdre?'
(2LY). The logic of this reading is probably what has made
editors switch 2T and 3F. We are to imagine, then, that
Pascal completed 3B, wrote his sign (because he knew that
2L must follow), and then wrote, in the space on page 3,
the paragraph which would serve as conclusion. The terms
he uses in 3F show that the wager argument was still vib-
rating in his mind.

At a later stage - perhaps when he corrected 2L and made
the two additions, 4A and 2LYY - Pascal, forgetting (?)
3F, wrote another conclusion, 2T. Brunet and Gouhier have
both pointed out that 2T does not follow very smoothly
onto the end of 2LY: 'O ce discours me transporte,' etc.
is a strange response to the question 'Qu'avez-vous à
perdre?'[14] Brunet thinks it reads better as a sequel to
3B.[15] The 'discours' in question is thus the mathematical
argument, as in the 'Fin de ce discours' on page 3. Also,
the movement from the end of 3B ('si les hommes sont capables de quelque vérité, celle-là l'est') to the new text
is exactly the same as the movement from 3B to 2LX, which
began 'Je le confesse, je l'avoue.' If that is so, then
2T becomes not the sequel to 2L, but an alternative to it;
at the same time, by its content, it reads like a variant
of 3F.

Gouhier thinks that the difficulty of the hiatus between
2LY and 2T was resolved when Pascal added three lines (2TT),[16]
but Brunet is not of this opinion. The phrase 'pour vous y
montrer que cela y mène' (2TT), he says, refers to the
'chemin de la foi' of ... 3F![17] There is no need to go this
far. I see no difficulty in taking the word 'y' to refer to
the penultimate sentence of 2LY, 'cela vous fera croire.'
Grammatical transitions are not handled with any care in

these pages. 2TT would indeed be better placed if it followed the penultimate sentence of 2LY directly.

Despite the challenging nature of Brunet's observations,
the resulting picture is even more tortuous than usual. It
is not easy to see just when Pascal could have written 2T.
Along with 3F? Why then is there no connecting mark? When
he revised 2L? Why then does it not follow more smoothly?
Brunet seems to attach insufficient importance to the marks
by which Pascal indicated clearly the sequence he wished
his readers to follow. But it is evident that the text
needed further revision, if the jumps and the overlappings
were to have been ironed out.

One final question: can we be sure that the expansion
of 2L (4A) was made after the mathematical development of
page 3? J. Orcibal believed that the opposite was true,
and M. Horino says that the question cannot be decided.[18]
It is, however, unlikely that Pascal would have started
his mathematical passage in the right-hand margin of page
2 if he had already written page 4, with the verso still
empty. I therefore incline to believe that page 3 did
precede page 4.

We conclude that the different parts of fragment 418
(pages 2 and 3) were written in this order:

(a) the basic text of page 2 (2A, 2B)

(b) the additions (422, 2D). 2D was to have been inserted
between 2A and 2B, though no indication was written
into the ms.

(c) the 'moral' addition (2LX and 2LY, and possibly 2T
also), to follow 2B.

(d) the 'mathematical' addition: 2R and 3A, to be placed
between 2B and 2L.

(e) a further extension to this (3B)

(f) the 'mathematical' addition would precede the 'moral'
addition, as the sign of the triangle made clear. The
moral addition would then be followed by a paragraph
entitled 'Fin de ce discours' (3F). 2T may have been
added at this time, or a little later.

(g) Revisions were made to 2L, resulting in three new
passages: 4A, 2LYY, and 2TT.

(h) While revising page 2, Pascal added a sign to indicate
the place for 2D, between 2A and 2B.

(i) 4A was given a new first sentence, making the link
with 2LX clearer (4AA).

This scheme should make it easier to distinguish the technical from the creative aspects of revision, and to distinguish more clearly the 'moral' and the 'mathematical' passages, while seeing how they belong together (cf. 3F).[19]

Notes

Introduction

1 Blaise Pascal, *Pensées sur la religion et sur quelques autres sujets*, ed. L. Lafuma (Paris: Editions du Luxembourg 1951, second edition 1952), t.I, *Textes*, fragment 696, p 397. All references, normally indicated by the fragment number only, are to this edition. For a minor qualification to this statement, see n74.

  This edition should not be confused with another edition of the *Pensées* prepared by Lafuma but on different lines, and published by Delmas in 1948 (second edition 1952). The principles behind both editions are discussed below, section (c).

2 E. Morot-Sir asks us to avoid the word apologia in writing of Pascal, because it implicitly puts Pascal into the same category as traditional apologists ('Du nouveau sur Pascal?' *RN* 18 [1977] 278). But I cannot see that there is anything amiss in the statement that Pascal was planning an apologia (of a new kind) and as a consequence, his projected work can perfectly well be called his Apologia.

3 Etienne Périer's account of the composition and editing of the *Pensées* formed the preface of the Port-Royal edition of 1670 (*Pensées de M. Pascal sur la religion et sur quelques autres sujets* [Paris: Deprez, 'second' edition 1670]). It has been frequently reprinted by subsequent editors, eg, L. Brunschvicg (ed.), Pascal, *Pensées et Opuscules* (1897) 303-16; ibid., *Oeuvres de Blaise Pascal XII: Pensées I* (Paris: Hachette, Les Grands Ecrivains de la France 1904) clxxx-cxcix; L. Lafuma (ed.), *Pensées* (Paris: Editions du Luxembourg 1951), t.III, *Documents* 133-45; ibid., *Oeuvres complètes* (Paris: Aux Editions du Seuil 1963) 494-501; G. Couton and J. Jehasse (eds), reproduction of 1670 edition (Saint-Etienne: Centre Interuniversitaire 1971) 37-97.

E. Périer underlines the 'confusion' of the papers:
'On les trouva tous ensemble enfilés en diverses
liasses, mais sans aucun ordre et sans aucune suite ...
La première chose que l'on fit fut de les faire copier
tels qu'ils étaient, et dans la même confusion qu'on
les avait trouvés ... Il y avait tout sujet de croire
que ... l'on ne considérerait ce volume ... que comme
un amas confus, sans ordre, sans suite...'
   In the five editions mentioned above, the crucial
passage comes respectively on pp 310-11, cxc-cxci,
139-40, 498, 68-71. It forms the thirty-second to
thirty-fifth paragraphs of the preface. The Luxembourg
edition prints 'considérait' in error.

4 This use of Copy 9203 was in accordance with the wishes
of Dom Jean Guerrier, who gave it to Saint Germain-des-
Près 'pour faciliter la lecture de l'Original' (quoted
by L. Lafuma, 'La Copie 9203 et le classement de Pascal'
in *Ecrits sur Pascal* [Paris: Editions du Luxembourg
1959] 189-90).

5 Victor Cousin, 'Rapport à l'Académie française sur la
nécessité d'une nouvelle édition des *Pensées* de Pascal,'
Journal des Savants Apr.-Nov. 1842. On the exaggerated
claims of Cousin to be blazing a totally new trail,
see J.J. Desmorest, 'Victor Cousin et le manuscrit des
Pensées de Pascal,' *MLN* 66 (1951) 255-9. D. Anzieu has
noted that for all his boasting, Cousin really used
the BN Copy 9203 (which is easy to read) rather than
the manuscript (which is not). See 'Pascal mystifié,'
Annales de l'Université de Paris 37 (1967) 192.

6 The Port-Royal edition can be studied in a modern reproduction, with the Brunschvicg numbering added:
*Pensées de M. Pascal sur la religion et sur quelques
autres sujets*, ed. G. Couton and J. Jehasse (Saint-
Etienne: Centre Interuniversitaire 1971). There is a
thorough bibliographical study by Thérèse Goyet: 'Le
visage de 1670' in *Les Pensées de Pascal ont 300 ans*
(Clermont-Ferrand: Bussac 1971) 31-78. We need not
here discuss the changes of substance introduced by
the first editors. For further information on the Port-
Royal edition, see L. Lafuma, 'Observations sur les
premières éditions des *Pensées* de Pascal' in *Controverses pascaliennes* (Paris: Editions du Luxembourg
1952) 121-43, and 'La mise au point de l'édition de
Port-Royal (1663-1669)' in *Histoire des Pensées de
Pascal* (Paris: Editions du Luxembourg 1954) 29-38;

C.H. Boudhours, 'Le duc de Roannez et l'édition des
Pensées,' in *Ecrits sur Pascal* (1959) 61-79; J. Mesnard,
Pascal et les Roannez (Paris: Desclée de Brouwer 1965)
881-9; D.A. Askew, 'Pascal's *Pari* in the Port-Royal
Edition,' *AJFS* 5 (1968) 155-82; J. Mesnard, 'Les Edi-
tions de Port-Royal,' *CPR* 20-1 (1972) 66-82; Maria
Vamos, 'Pascal's *Pensées* and the Enlightenment,'
Studies in Voltaire and the Eighteenth Century 97 (1972)
1-145.

7 Jean Mesnard has argued that the modifications made
by Pascal's friends can sometimes bring us closer to
Pascal's intentions (*CPR* 20-1 [1972] 76-81). The fact
remains that the architecture of the book is quite unlike what Pascal might have had in mind. Cf. M. Guersant,
introduction to his edition of the *Pensées* (Paris:
Club français du livre 1954) x: 'Le moins que l'on
puisse dire est que l'on aperçoit mal le mouvement
ascendant de la dialectique pascalienne et le resserre-
ment progressif de la persuasion dans le coeur et
l'esprit de l'athée ... D'une apologie de combat, Port-
Royal avait fait un livre d'édification pieuse.' The
Port-Royal order is studied by P. Ernst, *Approches
pascaliennes* (Gembloux: Duculot 1970) 532-40; his table
makes it quite clear that the Port-Royal editors did
not respect Pascal's classification.

8 Filleau's *Discours* was published by Desprez in 1672
with an essay on the Pentateuch: *Discours sur les
Pensées de M. Pascal, où l'on essaie de faire voir
quel était son dessein. Avec un autre discours sur
les Preuves des Livres de Moyse*. It has been reprinted
by many editors of the *Pensées*, and can be consulted
in the third volume (*Documents*) of Lafuma's Luxembourg
edition, pp 85-116. In 1922 V. Giraud published three
Pascalian discourses of Filleau, the third being 'un
traité où l'on montre qu'il y a des Démonstrations
d'une autre espèce, et aussi certaines que celles de
la Géométrie, et qu'on en peut donner de telles pour
la Religion chrétienne' (Paris: Bossard, Collection
des Chefs d'oeuvre méconnus). I discuss the *Discours*
in the last section of chapter 31.

9 Nicole's *Traité de l'Education d'un Prince*, 1670,
explicitly uses Pascal's argument to impress on the
prince the claims of Christianity (Part II, paras
XLI-XLIII, 66-73). The relevant passage is quoted,
with italics added and with its tail chopped off, in

the Grands Ecrivains de la France edition of Pascal
(*Pensées* I [1904] ccxxxix-ccxli). See R.E. Lacombe,
L'Apologétique de Pascal (Paris: PUF 1958) 33.

Gilberte Périer, Pascal's sister, included a para-
graph on the 'dessein' of the Apologia in her *Vie de
Monsieur Pascal*, first published in 1684. R. Francis
(*Les Pensées de Pascal en France de 1842 à 1942* [Paris:
Nizet 1959] 113) thinks Gilberte's paragraph wihout
significance as a statement of Pascal's plan. This was
E. Janssens' conclusion also (*RNP* 12 [1905] 425-8, and
La philosophie et l'apologétique de Pascal [1906] 72-6;
see below, n18), quoted with approval by R.E. Lacombe,
L'Apologétique de Pascal (1958) 34 n77. P. Ernst, 'Le
témoignage de 'Gilberte Pascal' sur l'Apologie,' *DSS*
75 (1967) 23-47, argues that the second version of the
Vie was intended to replace Filleau, and that as an
indication of the general thrust of Pascal's argument
it is very (even suspiciously) perceptive. Ernst believes, in fact, that these paragraphs were not written
by Gilberte. In any case, they reveal not the plan but
the spirit of the Apologia (p 44). Gilberte Périer's
text can most profitably be studied in the critical
edition of J. Mesnard (Blaise Pascal, *Oeuvres complètes*
[Desclée de Brouwer 1964] I, 539-642). See J. Pommier,
'La *Vie* de Pascal par Gilberte Périer,' *ALM* 57 (1964).
See also P. Polman, 'La biographie de Blaise Pascal
par Gilberte Préier,' *Revue d'Histoire ecclésiastique*
45 (1950) 95-135, L. Marin, 'A propos d'une *Vie de
Pascal*: texte, récit, livre,' *MLN* 90 (1975) 475-96.

10 On the history of the *Pensées*, see especially R. Francis
Les Pensées de Pascal en France de 1842 à 1942 (Paris:
Nizet 1959), and L. Lafuma, *Histoire des Pensées de
Pascal (1656-1952)* (Paris: Editions du Luxembourg
1954). The eighteenth century exception is Ducreux
(1780) mentioned by R. Francis, p 40, L. Lafuma, pp
50-1; and cf. Patricia Topliss, *The Rhetoric of Pascal*
(Leicester: University Press 1966) 155.

11 Patricia Topliss devotes eight pages of her book to
the question under the heading 'An Enigma for Editors'
(*The Rhetoric of Pascal* [1966] 152-9). Cf. Morris
Bishop, *Pascal, the Life of Genius* (New York: Reynal
and Hitchcock 1936) 264: 'The reconstruction of Pascal's
Apology from his *pensées* is an exercise which has fas-
cinated a long line of literary paleontologists.'

12 As an illustration one could quote Faugère, introduction to *Pensées* (Paris: Andrieux 1844) lxxi: 'sans prétendre avoir retrouvé l'ordonnance rigoureuse du monument que Pascal se proposait d'élever, nous avons cherché à nous en approcher le plus possible.' Nineteenth-century views for and against the possibility of reconstituting the plan are usefully listed at the beginning of Janssen's study (see n18, below) 418-21 (pp 61-5). See also R.E. Lacombe, *L'Apologétique de Pascal* (1958) 11 n1.

13 See R. Francis, *Les Pensées de Pascal en France* 113-14, and 34: 'Il était plus d'un accommodement avec le texte des Pensées.' Francis remarks that editors have different philosophical aims, and that Filleau's account is sufficiently general to allow great diversity in the detailed application of the *Discours* to the fragments.

14 *Pascal: Pensées et Opuscules* (Paris: Hachette 1897) 268-9. *Pensées*, I (Paris: Hachette, Les Grands Ecrivains de la France 1904) li-lxv. This replaced a two-volume edition in the same collection done by Faugère (1886-95).

15 Already in 1898 V. Giraud was asking: 'Est-ce à dire qu'il faille absolument renoncer à se figurer le dessein de Pascal? Non: mais à condition de parler de *dessein*, et non de *plan*, de consentir à ne pas trop préciser dans le détail, et de ne pas prétendre retrouver l'ordre rigoureux qu'aurait suivi la dialectique de Pascal' (*Pascal, l'homme, l'oeuvre, l'influence* [Fribourg 1898] 88); cf. E. Boutroux: 'Il ne peut être question de tracer un plan des *Pensées*, ni même de l'ouvrage en vue duquel elles ont été jetées sur le papier' (*Pascal* [Paris: Hachette 1900] 158); J. Chevalier: 'Il est donc vain de chercher à restituer le plan de l'*Apologie*' (*Pascal* [Paris: Plon 1922] 171); A. Valensin: 'Renoncer à la prétention de découvrir le plan définitif, qui n'a jamais existé' (*Balthazar* [Paris: Aubier 1934] 121); H. Lefebvre: 'le plan d'ensemble que les exégètes s'acharnent vainement à retrouver ... il n'y a pas et il ne peut y avoir de plan des *Pensées* (*Pascal* II [Paris: Nagel 1954] 89, 102). Changing the terms, E.B.O. Borgerhoff wrote in 1957: 'These indications [of a general plan] do not provide us with a clue to the correct *sequence* of the fragments: this aspect of the Pensées must forever

remain a matter of arbitrary decision' ('The Reality of Pascal: The *Pensées* as Rhetoric,' *Sewanee Review* 65 [1957] 16-17).

Editors have continued to evolve their own personal solution to the 'enigma' with no hope of hitting on Pascal's own plan. Jean Hytier, unable to complete an 'édition psychologique ... selon l'ordre complexe d'un réseau d'intentions,' settled for an 'édition esthétique' with the fragments grouped according to their form (*Ouevres de Blaise Pascal*, IV [Paris: Piazza 1929] iv-v). The same year Henri Massis proposed, in the absence of any likelihood of agreement about Pascal's own plan, to arrange the fragments in a way which would at least help the reader (a reasonable ambition, which begs several questions - *Les Pensées de Blaise Pascal* [Paris: A la cité des livres 1929] xxiii-xxv). In 1963, E. Jacques wrote: 'Le problème de l'ordre des *Pensées* n'a pu trouver, jusqu'à ce jour, de solution vraiment cohérente. C'est un chaos traversé d'eclairs' (*Le troisième centenaire de la mort de Blaise Pascal* [Brussels 1963] 6). Sixty years before, Janssens had concluded his long examination of the problem see n18) with the same metaphor, but with the terms reversed: 'Les clartés que l'on peut découvrir sur ces deux questions nous semblent posséder un certain éclat. N'aurait-on pas grand tort de les mépriser pour ce motif que certaines ombres les entourent?' It is more than the age-old and insoluble dispute between optimists and pessimists; despite the dates of the last two quotations it is the optimists who have finally seen their faith rewarded, as modern scholarship has patiently pieced together the evidence.

16 See H. Gouhier, *Blaise Pascal: Commentaires* (Paris: Vrin 1966) 175 n96; R.E. Lacombe, *L'Apologétique de Pascal* 38 n86; R. Francis, *Les Pensées de Pascal en France* 109.

17 Sainte-Beuve acknowledges his debt to Frantin (*Port-Royal* III, 21 [1848 ed.] 337 n1; Pléiade edition [1954] II, 376n.) An honourable mention is accorded to Frantin by M. Guersant (introduction to Pascal, *Pensées* [1954] xiii) and others, but Francis is sceptical; he thinks Frantin is just a convenient stick to beat Cousin with (p 15, cf. pp. 39-41).

18 E. Janssens, 'Un problème "pascalien": le plan de l'Apologie,' *RNP* 12 (1905) 418-53, 13 (1906) 5-17;

'Le problème du plan' in *La philosophie et l'apologétique de Pascal* (Paris: Alcan 1906) 61-135.
19 R.E. Lacombe (*L'Apologétique de Pascal* 38 n86) lists
a number of commentators who have used Filleau to
guide their own exposition: Boutroux, Lanson, Petitot,
Hetzfeld, Laporte.
20 H.F. Stewart, 'Vers une nouvelle édition de l'Apologie
de Pascal,' *French Quarterly* 3 (1921) 132-51. This
article concludes with a detailed plan for an edition,
fitting in all the relevant fragments. Stewart produced
an edition realizing these ideas (though with many differences of detail) in 1942 (*Pascal's Apology for
Religion* [Cambridge: University Press]) and again in
1950 (*Pascal's Pensées with an English translation*
[London: Routledge and Kegan Paul]).
21 *Pascal: Pensées*, ed. J. Chevalier (Paris: Gabalda 1925)
viii: 'Pour le plan général, nous l'avons emprunté,
comme l'a judicieusement conseillé de son côté H.F.
Stewart, au discours de Filleau de la Chaise ... Nous
ne prétendons point que ce dût être le plan définitif
de Pascal: mais c'est celui qu'un jour il exposa lui-
même dans ses grandes lignes, et c'est, de tous, celui
qui s'approche sans doute le plus de sa pensée.' Other
editions of Chevalier followed, all on the same plan,
though with some textual emendations. More details
will be found in n3 of Appendix C.
22 'Without prejudice' here means, in effect, without
being too bothered by the judgment of E. Périer. Among
those who have found Périer's description ('sans aucun
ordre et sans aucune suite') an obstacle may be cited
R.E. Lacombe, *L'Apologétique de Pascal* 24-5, and nn 51
and 52; and P. Topliss *The Rhetoric of Pascal* 162.
Against that can be set the trenchant views of Michel
and Marie-Rose Le Guern (*Les Pensées de Pascal* [Paris:
Larousse 1972] 9): '"Sans aucun ordre et sans aucune
suite," ce n'est que l'opinion d'Etienne Périer,' and
we should remember the full quotation: 'enfilés en
diverses liasses, mais sans aucun ordre...' As we
shall see, the crux of the question is the nature of
the *liasses*, which may furnish a clue as to the 'order'
desired, even if they do not have the appearance of
order.
    L. Lafuma lost no opportunity to denounce Etienne
Périer's testimony (*Recherches pascaliennes* [Paris:
Editions du Luxembourg 1949] 55-6, 70-2, etc.).

M. Guersant defended Périer vigorously in the introduction to his edition of the *Pensées* (Paris: Club
français du livre 1954) xxxvii-xlii.

23 On the history of the 'Recueil Original' see L. Lafuma,
Recherches pascaliennes 30-45.

24 *Les Pensées de Pascal disposées suivant l'ordre du
cahier autographe* ... par G. Michaut (Fribourg 1896).

25 'Mais c'est précisément ce qui en fait la supériorité'
says Michaut in his introduction, p lxxxi. He goes as
far as to say (p lxxxii) that this is 'le désordre où
[Pascal] les a laissées.'

26 *Original des Pensées de Pascal*, notes par L. Brunschvicg
(Paris: Hachette 1905).

27 G. Michaut, introduction to *Les Pensées de Pascal*...
lxxxiii.

28 L. Brunschvicg, introduction to the Grands Ecrivains
edition of the *Pensées* I (1904) iii-v.

29 L. Lafuma proved the extreme fragility of Brunschvicg's
hypothesis, but that was forty-five years later. See
Mercure de France 301 (1 Dec. 1947) 664-7, *Recherches
pascaliennes* 24-6, also *Histoire des Pensées de Pascal*
31-2.

30 J. Dedieu (ed.), Pascal: *Les Pensées et oeuvres
choisies* (Paris: L'Ecole 1937) 43.

31 Ibid. 43, 59.

32 Z. Tourneur (ed.), Blaise Pascal: *Pensées* (Paris:
Cluny 1938), especially xxxiii-xxxv.

33 P.L. Couchoud, 'Un manuscrit reconstitué de Pascal:
Les "Liasses enfilées" de Pascal et les feuillets
dispersés d'un "Discours",' *La Nef* 37 (Dec. 1947)
44-79. Fuller exposition of the same argument is in
Discours de la condition de l'homme (Paris: Albin
Michel 1948). The conclusions Couchoud drew from the
evidence he presented won little support, and as a
result the evidence itself tended to be overlooked.
He later retracted a little, and a subsequent article
is more useful: 'La crise des *Pensées* de Pascal,'
Le Flambeau 38 (1955) 160-85.

On the number of sections contained in the copy,
assessments have varied. Dedieu, Tourneur, and (for
a while) Lafuma distinguished only 26 sections in the
first part of the Copy, all failing to separate 12°
('Commencement') from 11° ('A P.R.'). This is understandable: on Copy 12449 the section is not marked
off as a new chapter, and on both Copies the title is

placed towards the left-hand margin, unlike most other
titles. See below, n46. On Lafuma's change of mind,
compare the second (1952) edition and the original
(1948) edition published by Delmas, as well as the
two verions of the paper mentioned in the next note:
Mercure de France (1 Jan. 1948) 82, and *Recherches
pascaliennes* (1949) 47; and see his *Controverses pascaliennes* (1952) 24 n1.

Lafuma at first counted only 33 sections in the
second part. It is possible to argue that there should
be 28 + 36 sections (see below, pp 10 and 493 n74, and
p 573 n1).

34 L. Lafuma insisted that he had been able to prove what
Tourneur had merely presumed to be so (*Recherches
pascaliennes* [Paris: Delmas 1949] 137 n2). R. Francis
did not think the claim justified (*Les Pensées de
Pascal en France*, 131). Lafuma's first major article
on this topic appeared in the *Mercure de France* 301
(1 Dec. 1947) 663-73, and 302 (1 Jan. 1948) 72-84,
under the title 'Rémontrances et suggestions aux éditeurs des *Pensées* de Pascal.' It was reprinted with
some corrections of detail, as 'Ce que nous apprennent
les manuscrits des *Pensées*' in his *Recherches pascaliennes* 21-53. Lafuma explored and refined his insights
in a number of articles, many of which will be quoted
in the following pages, but he never gave the complete
and definitive statement we were hoping for. As well as
the *Recherches pascaliennes*, Lafuma published another
volume of separate studies, which he called *Controverses
pascaliennes* (Paris: Editions du Luxembourg 1952).
See also the first chapter ('La rédaction des *Pensées*
[1656-1662]') in his *Histoire des Pensées de Pascal*
(1954) 11-28, and the introduction to *Le manuscrit des
Pensées de Pascal 1662* (Paris: Les Libraires associés
1962).

35 Commentators had always accepted Etienne Périer's
statement that Pascal 'prenait le premier morceau de
papier qu'il trouvait sous sa main' (*Préface de
l'édition de Port-Royal*, paragraph 29). Lafuma attributed E. Périer's mistake to the fact that some of
Pascal's papers had been cut into smaller sizes before
his friends came across them (*Histoire des Pensées
de Pascal* 32). On the matter of the large sheets, see
L. Lafuma, *Recherches pascaliennes* 57, 72, etc., *Controverses pascaliennes* 45, *Histoire des Pensées* 22.

36 Lafuma was well aware of what Couchoud had written
   (see *Controverses pascaliennes* 24 n2, 76-9 and 87 n1),
   but thought Couchoud was mistaken. J. Mesnard has reproached Lafuma with not paying enough attention to
   Couchoud ('Aux origines de l'édition des Pensées: les
   deux copies' in *Les Pensées de Pascal ont 300 ans*
   [Clermont-Ferrand: Bussac 1971] 4).
37 R.E. Lacombe, *L'Apologétique de Pascal* 26 n53; L.
   Lafuma, 'La Copie 9203 et le classement de Pascal' in
   Ecrits sur Pascal (1959) 195-200. Lafuma says that if
   someone other than Pascal did the sorting, one would
   have to explain (a) why some papers were already cut
   and put in bundles (Périer dixit); (b) how such work
   could have been done on a manuscript notoriously difficult to decipher (Périer is categoric: 'La première
   chose que l'on fit fut de les faire copier tels qu'ils
   étaient...,' preface to Port-Royal edition, paragraph
   33); (c) why none of the papers we can safely date
   1659 or later was affected; (d) how anyone could have
   constituted the dossier on Miracles, from which the
   irrelevant notes have *not* been removed; (e) what the
   'original copy' referred to by E. Périer could have
   been.
   The suggestion for this article may have come from
   a letter Roger Pons wrote to Lafuma, following discussion with him, in September 1958. It was published
   after Pons's death ('Entretien sur les manuscrits de
   Pascal,' *CUC* [Nov.-Dec. 1962] 84-9). Pons pointed out
   that Lafuma's earlier refutation of Brunschvicg (see
   n29) did not prove that the classifying was not the
   work of, say, the Duc de Roannez, subsequently abandoned because it was too difficult. Pons mentions two
   arguments which Lafuma did not take up: that nobody
   would have been allowed to cut the papers, and that
   the copyists would not have been asked later carefully
   to copy the remains of an embryonic arrangement which
   had been abandoned. As Jean Mesnard has said (*Les
   Pensées de Pascal* [Paris: SEDES 1976] 24), diverse
   fragments which are still together on one sheet are
   always together on the Copy also. Mesnard is speaking
   of Copy 9203, but the same is true of Copy 12449.
   Lafuma's third argument had been first put forward
   by Marcel Guersant in the introduction to his edition
   of the *Pensées* ([1954] xix).

38 Generally it was the early *liasses* which came under
   fire. Z. Tourneur in his edition of 1938 removed fragment 1 from the first bundle. Antoine Adam ('Sur les
   Pensées de Pascal' *IL* 9 [1957] 6) queried three fragments from *liasse* 2°: no. 15 (akin to no. 117 in section 6°), no. 22 (not separable from no. 48 in 3°),
   and no. 30 (close to a preoccupation of section 5°).
   Roger Lacombe (*L'Apologétique de Pascal* [1958] 27 n53)
   believed nos 3, 7, and 10, as well as no. 1, to be
   misplaced in the first bundle, and found the distribution among the next three dossiers arbitrary, citing
   no. 24, and nos 51 and 60, which he said should not
   be separated. In the introduction to his edition (p
   xxvi), Marcel Guersant opined that no. 110 was 'classé
   sans aucune justification possible dans la liasse
   Grandeur.'

39 In his *Recherches pascaliennes* 58-9, L. Lafuma says
   he can find only one fragment (out of 365) attached
   to the wrong bundle, no. 293. But he is talking only
   of papers containing more than one fragment, and his
   main point is that when Pascal classified papers of
   that kind, he always (with that one exception) scored
   out the other fragments if they did not belong to the
   same section. He does not commit himself on the single
   fragment papers. So his example is one case out of 14,
   not one out of 365.
       There is incidentally a mathematical flaw in Lafuma's
   presentation which has not, I believe, been pointed
   out (though Lafuma silently corrected it in his *Histoire des Pensées* [1954] 32). He makes (p 58) the
   curious statement: 'Pour 365 fragments ... il y a 351
   papiers; 324 de ces papiers retiennent chacun 1 fragment, 12 de ces papiers retiennent chacun 2 fragments,
   1 de ces papiers retient 3 fragments.' There are thus
   324 + 12 + 1 = 337 papers and 337 + 12 + 2 = 351 fragments, and not 351 papers and 365 fragments. In order
   to write '365 fragments,' Lafuma must have added 12 +
   2 again, to 351. These statistics are in any case
   questionable, as editorial decisions as to whether a
   given paper contains one or more fragments are fairly
   arbitrary and do not always correlate with the existence or otherwise of a dividing mark on the manuscript.

40 When is a plan not a plan? When it is a *classement* -
   such apparently is the view of A. Béguin, 'Les editions

et l'ordre des *Pensées*,' *Critique* 4 (1948) 885:
'[Tourneur et Lafuma] nous livrent ce qui peut être
encore discerné, non pas du plan de Pascal, mais,
chose très différente, du *classement* provisoire de
ses notes.' Cf. H. Gouhier, *Blaise Pascal: Commentaires* (1966) 183: 'Ainsi, grâce aux éditions de Tourneur et de Lafuma, nous avons l'espoir de travailler
en disposant de ce qui était pour Pascal l'équivalent
de nos dossiers. Mais il paraît prudent de ne pas y
chercher les lignes d'un plan, fût-il provisoire.'
Also M. Autrand, introduction to *Pascal: Pensées*
(Paris: Bordas 1966) 20: 'un classement de commodité
qui facilitait le travail de l'auteur.' For a different
view of the relation of *plan* and *classement*, see n103.

41 The facts were marshalled by Annie Barnes, 'La table
des titres de la Copie des *Pensées* est-elle de Pascal?'
FS 7 (1953) 140-6. See also L. Lafuma, 'La Copie 9203
et le classement de Pascal,' in *Ecrits sur Pascal*
(1959) 187-205, and J. Mesnard, 'Aux origines de l'édition des *Pensées*: les deux Copies,' in *Les Pensées de
Pascal ont 300 ans* (1971) 8-9, 25.

42 Henri Gouhier finds the absence of manuscript suspicious
in itself, but it is not the only important manuscript
to disappear, as Lafuma remarked (see *Blaise Pascal,
l'homme et l'oeuvre*, published as *Cahiers de Royaumont*
1 [Paris: les éditions de Minuit 1956] 94). Cf. also
P. Ernst, *Approches pascaliennes* (1970) 659.

43 R.E. Lacombe, *L'Apologétique de Pascal* (1958) 28 n54;
H. Gouhier, *Blaise Pascal, Commentaires* (1966) 181.
Marcel Guersant also believed that the titles were
not Pascal's (introduction to his edition of the
Pensées [1954] xxiii).

44 Often added later, as if the section titles were already set down (J. Mesnard, *Les Pensées de Pascal* 24).

45 See L. Lafuma, *Histoire des Pensées de Pascal* 105;
also J.J. Demorest, 'Pascal et l'édition des Pensées'
MLN 71 (1956) 103-4. Some of these cross-references
indicate changes to be made in the allocation. As
Lafuma remarked ('La Copie 9203 et le classement de
Pascal' in *Ecrits sur Pascal* [1959] 191), had the idea
been the copyist's, he would have implemented it, not
noted and solemnly copied it.

46 Lafuma's numbering gives to some of these titles (but
not all) the status of *pensées*. Only one presents no
problems at all: 'Que la loi était figurative,' no.

245. No. 167 originally read: 'Soumission et usage de
la raison' and Pascal added 'en quoi consiste le vrai
christianisme.' The copyist clearly understood this
as the title of the chapter. The title of 19° ('Fondements de la Religion et Réponse aux Objections')
exists as a separate flyer (R.O. 43). The last bundle
of all is entitled 'Conclusion,' but the top paper
might be an alternative title: 'Qu'il y a loin de la
connaissance de Dieu à l'aimer' (377). The title of
11° ('A P.R.') is added at the top of no. 149. The
title of 12°, 'Commencement,' is not found in the
manuscript, but it exists in the Copy. The fact that
a cross marked the beginning of no. 150 implies that
the title existed independently, and that it is the
title of more than no. 150 alone. Tourneur noted the
fact (edition [1938] 98 n1) but did not draw the expected conclusion, and hence failed to separate 12°
from 11° (149). See n33. Anzieu corrected this in his
1960 revision of Tourneur (see below, n86).

There are many other title-like fragments in Pascal's
manuscript; they are brought together by Lafuma in an
appendix to the Luxembourg edition (I, 550), and on
p 341 of his *Manuscrit des Pensées de Pascal* (1962).
To them could be added 'Les combinaisons des miracles,'
R.O. 41.

47 'Ennui et qualités essentielles à l'homme' (copy) becomes 'Ennui' (table), 'Excellence de cette manière
de prouver Dieu' becomes 'Excellence,' 'Transition de
la connaissance de l'homme à Dieu' becomes 'Transition,'
'Rendre la religion aimable' is reduced to 'Religion
aimable,' 'Fondements de la religion et réponse aux
objections' to 'Fondement,' 'Que la loi était figurative' to 'Loi figurative,' and 'Figures particulières'
to 'Figures.'

48 A. Blanchet ('Le plan des *Pensées* de Pascal est-il
vraiment retrouvé?' *Etudes* 274 [1952] 242 n2) holds
that the 'papillons' are authentic *pensées*, reduced
in size by the compiler's scissors. Lafuma perhaps
implies the same when he says that nine titles are
preserved on small papers, 'petits parce que rognés'
(*Histoire des Pensées* 105).

49 L. Lafuma, *Recherches pascaliennes* 56. Lafuma retracted
later, as he admitted in a paper read in 1954 ('Les
manuscrits des *Pensées*: ce qu'ils nous apprennent' in
Cahiers de Royaumont 1 [1956] 84); his change of mind

is reflected in the revised text (1952) of his Delmas
edition of the *Pensées* 23 n25. The original (1948)
version of this note read: 'L'ordre des chapitres
suivi par le copiste ne préjuge en rien de celui qu'aurait suivi Pascal'; it became in 1952: 'L'ordre des
chapitres ... est sans doute celui qu'aurait suivi
Pascal.' See also *Histoire des Pensées* 85 and 105-6.

50 Why should the first ten titles be distinguished from
the last eighteen? I suggest an answer to this question in chapter 31, end of sections (a) and (d).

51 This is unambiguously the case for both tables on Copy
9203. On Copy 12449 the second title has been added
later, but as the first title is scored out, as on
Copy 9203, one assumes that the omission was an oversight. Jean Mesnard (*Les Pensées de Pascal* 28) observes
that the fifth *liasse* itself has only one title; the
table must therefore have been drawn up before the
title-flyers were added to the bundles - another reason for refusing to attribute it to a copyist.

52 On this point, H. Gouhier (*Blaise Pascal: Commentaires*
181) is ambivalent: 'Si l'on voyait cette table écrite
de la main de Pascal, il n'y aurait évidemment plus de
question. Mais, en l'absence d'un tel document, il
faut bien attacher une certaine importance à la diffi-
culté de mettre les 27 liasses sous les 28 titres.
Admettons qu'un titre de la table renvoie à un casier
vide: ceci explique l'écart entre les 28 titres et les
27 liasses.' But although that seems to resolve the
difficulty, in a note (17), Gouhier admits that he
hesitates to attribute the table to Pascal. It is
curious that P.L. Couchoud, who was one of the first
to argue that Pascal was the author of the table
(*Discours de la condition de l'homme* [1948] 10) does
not mention the problem of the extra title.

53 J. Mesnard, 'Aux origines de l'édition des *Pensées*:
les deux *Copies*,' in *Les Pensées de Pascal ont 300
ans* (1971) 26, 29. See chapter 16, below, and 31,
page 376.

54 J. Mesnard (*Les Pensées de Pascal* [1976] 35) has a
different explanation. He holds that the Second Copy
opens with 'Series I' because that unit began with
the table, and a table will naturally come at the
beginning of the work; the compilers of the First Copy
preferred to give pride of place to the ordered sequence of chapters. But this implies that the Copies

were organized simultaneously, whereas we know that
the different books of the First Copy were separate,
available to whoever was working on a particular section.

55 That was the view of Antoine Adam in his review of
Lafuma's Delmas edition, *RSH* 57-8 (1950) 134, and in
his article 'Sur les *Pensées* de Pascal,' *IL* 9 (1957)
6: 'Les dossiers de Pascal étaient constitués autour
d'un certain nombre de rubriques, mais ces rubriques
représentaient le groupement de ses réflexions et des
matériaux accumulés, et non pas le plan définitivement
adopté ... Le 'niveau' que les travaux de M. Lafuma
nous ont permis d'atteindre, ce n'est donc pas l'ordre
des *Pensées*, mais l'état des papiers de leur auteur.'
R.E. Lacombe's remarks imply a similar scepticism
(*L'Apologétique de Pascal* 25-7).

56 In this paragraph I give the numbers for the separate
liasses which are familiar from Lafuma. In order to
accommodate 'La nature est corrompue' as an independent
member of the series, however, Lafuma's 16°-27° should
become 17°-28°, and that is the numbering I shall be
using throughout the rest of this book.

57 H. Gouhier, *Blaise Pascal: Commentaires* (1966) 181-2.

58 M. Guersant (ed.), *Les Pensées de Blaise Pascal* (1954)
xxxiv.

59 A. Barnes, 'La conférence à Port-Royal et les liasses
de Pascal,' *FS* 10 (1956) 239, reprinted in *Ecrits sur
Pascal* (1959) 98.

60 L. Marin (ed.), *Blaise Pascal: Pensées* (Didier 1969).

61 P. Topliss, *The Rhetoric of Pascal* 163. Cf. pp 169-70.

62 On this, see chapter 12, section (a) and also n3.

63 P. Topliss, *The Rhetoric of Pascal* 178-9 and 184.

64 P. Ernst, *Approches pascaliennes* 651-60. His own re-
numbering of the *pensées*, however, leaves them where
they are.

65 Patricia Topliss, for all her criticisms, admits that
'although the evidence the Copy affords of Pascal's
intentions is incomplete and not wholly unquestionable,
it is definitely the best we possess' (*The Rhetoric of
Pascal* 164).

66 A. Béguin, 'Les éditions et l'ordre des *Pensées*,' 880,
886, held that the chapters were an 'étape,' and in-
ferior as evidence to the *Discours* of Filleau de la
Chaise (but is not the lecture reported by Filleau an
'étape' also?). Many other critics have insisted that

the outline of the Apologia was never finally fixed,
eg, V.L. Saulnier, 'Le problème des papiers de Pascal,'
Le Bulletin des Lettres 10 (1948) 318; J. Mantoy, *Des
"Pensées" de Pascal à l'"Apologie"* (Paris: L'Ecole
1955) 21; G. Coulet, 'Pascal écrivant,' *Annales de la
Faculté des Lettres et Sciences humaines d'Aix* 37 (1963)
157; P. Sellier edition of the *Pensées* (Paris: Mercure
de France 1976) 18.

67 M. Guersant, introduction to his edition of the
Pensées xlv-xlvi.

68 L. Goldmann and J. Chevalier, 'Echange de vues au
sujet du 'Plan' des *Pensées* de Pascal,' *DSS* 23 (1954)
597-604. L. Goldmann, intervention (1954) at Royaumont
(*Cahiers de Royaumont* 1 [1956] 104-10). Ibid., *Le Dieu
caché* (Paris: Gallimard 1955) 220-7.

69 As well as removing fragment no. 1 (see n38), Tourneur
put no. 208 after no. 131, and inserted no. 403 as a
gloss on no. 74b, which he kept separate from 74a.

70 The distinction goes back to Cousin and Faugère (J.
Mesnard, *Les Pensées de Pascal* 18). In 1942, Tourneur
produced an 'édition paléographique' of all the fragments of which the Recueil Original preserved the manuscript. The order is not quite the same as that followed
in 1938 - for example, the titled sections come between
the two categories of unsorted material, whereas in
1938 they had come at the beginning. This paleographic
edition enabled editors to improve greatly the accuracy
of the text itself, but as all signposts have been
removed - the fragments are neither numbered nor even
clearly distinguished - all but the most intrepid
scholars are virtually denied access (Z. Tourneur,
Pensées de Blaise Pascal, édition paléographique
[Paris: Vrin 1942]).

71 See n1. The second edition (1952) incorporates both
categories into a single volume, and numbers all the
fragments consecutively.

72 L. Lafuma gives no explanation of the asterisks in
the edition itself. Chapter 18° (19°) contains two
sets of asterisks as there are in that chapter two
sets of assigned unclassed fragments. English translations that follow Delmas numbering (John Warrington
[London: Dent 1961]; Martin Turnell [London: Harvill
Press 1962]) are even more obscure on this point. The
former makes no visible distinction, while in the latter,
the asterisks are replaced by single-line spaces.

73 See n1. The three volumes contain respectively Text,
Notes, and Documents. Lafuma defended his Delmas ar-
rangement in his *Histoire des Pensées de Pascal* 84.
However, he admitted at Royaumont the same year that
the Luxembourg system was the only really valid one
(*Cahiers de Royaumont* 93).

74 Pascal *Oeuvres complètes* (Paris: Aux editions du Seuil,
Collection L'Intégrale 1963). Lafuma also followed the
order of the Copy in an edition of the *Pensées* produced
by the Club du Meilleur Livre (director: Samuel de Sacy)
in 1958, and by the Editions du Seuil in 1962 (Livre de
vie, préface d'André Dodin).

In these later editions two minor modifications were
made to the numbering, both hinted at in the 1952
Luxembourg edition (I, 20, 437), but not incorporated
then. Lafuma now agrees with Couchoud that there were
34 'series,' not 33, and so XXX (821-9) is split into
two (821-5, 826-9), and renumbered accordingly. Second,
Lafuma now follows the Second Copy in grouping three
fragments on Esdras, not recorded by Copy 9203. These
constitute virtually a thirty-fifth 'series.' In 1952
they were distributed among a number of fragments derived from the Recueil Original and numbered 953, 949,
968. From 1958 they become 970-2, and fragments 950-72
are renumbered accordingly. I shall use the later numbering for both series and fragments. The Seuil presentation was used for the translation A.J. Krailsheimer
did for Penguin Classics, Harmondsworth, 1966. (For
recent thinking on the number of Units, see chapter 32,
n1.)

In 1962, Jean Mesnard published some newly discovered
fragments in a slim volume entitled *Textes inédits*
(Desclée de Brouwer, Bibliothèque Européenne). They are
not numbered. Lafuma was able to incorporate them in
his 1963 edition, pp 639-40, and he numbered them I-XV.
I propose to refer to them by the numerals 1101-15.

75 One cannot deny that the Luxembourg edition has a number of unsatisfactory features, and anyone who has
worked with it over a period becomes acutely conscious
of them. Despite its originality, many editorial decisions are surprisingly conventional:

(a) Decisions as to what constitutes a separate
fragment, in those cases where Pascal put a dividing
line but did not cut along it, can always be challenged.
Does one allocate a fresh number or not? Lafuma is

sometimes the victim of his own Delmas edition. R.O.
12 records seven sentences, of which the first, second,
and sixth were crossed out, and the seventh was written
in to the right of the fourth. Lafuma wished to classify
the fourth, fifth, and seventh as notes for the *Provinciales* and the others as 'Notes diverses.' This obliged
him to give two numbers (610 = Del. 799 and 611 = Del.
986), which look very odd on the page. It is, moreover,
not clear why he chose the numbers 610 and 611 for
fragments which follow his no. 606. Elsewhere Lafuma
feels obliged to give two numbers to a single fragment
because Brunschwicg did. See n11 to chapter 20. A different system altogether would have been advisable,
giving the number of the section or unit, the place of
the paper in the unit, and the place of the fragment
in the paper. In his 1962 edition (Seuil, Livre de Vie,
26), Lafuma explained quite clearly that a double space
dividing two fragments means that the fragments were
on separate sheets; a single space means that the fragments were on the same sheet, but were clearly marked
to be divided; no space at all between two fragments
implies that the editor is responsible for distinguishing them. In the examples he gives of the latter, the
second fragment actually starts a new page, and so the
typographical subtlety is lost on the reader. In 1958
no explanation was offered.

Deleted fragments also constitute a special case.

(b) The transcription of ms. variants is not always
clear, and seems at times to be based slavishly on
Tourneur (see n70). Lafuma's explanations of his typographical signs (p 28) are quite inadequate. As one
example of unclear transcription among many, one could
cite the second paragraph of no. 131. The manuscript
of this passage is a kind of cryptogram, which an
editor should either reproduce scrupulously, or interpret correctly. Lafuma tries to do a bit of both, and
the result is wholly confusing; moreover he prints as
if deleted, a passage which is not deleted, and vice
versa. See Appendix D.

(c) Lafuma's notes are disappointing, skating over
several difficulties, and neglecting certain post-
Brunschvicg discoveries which would have made his information more generally reliable. Particularly unfor-
tunate is Lafuma's evident ignorance of A.M. Dubarle,
'Quelques allusions scripturaires des *Pensées* de

Pascal,' *SPT* (1941-2) 84-95, which corrected many
traditional identifications of biblical quotations.
Naturally too, there has been much more work done on
the elucidation of textual enigmas since 1951.

Criticisms (a) and (c) are met by Philippe Sellier
in an edition published by Mercure de France in 1976
(see n86 below), and by Michel Le Guern in an edition
prepared for the Gallimard Folio series (1977), but
neither is a critical edition.

76 *Le manuscrit des Pensées de Pascal 1662* (Paris:
Libraires associés 1962). Unsupported references in
my text to the state of the manuscript – corrections,
marginal additions, etc. – can be quickly verified by
recourse to this publication.

77 J. Mantoy, *Des "Pensées" de Pascal à l'"Apologie"*
(1955) 17. J. Steinmann (ed.), Pascal, *Pensées* (Monaco:
Editions du Rocher 1961). Cf also J.J. Demorest, review
of Lafuma's Luxembourg edition, *RR* 44 (1953) 145.

78 Steinmann is not consistent; in his first chapter, he
puts the twelve fragments in a different order, and he
also begins his second chapter not with no. 52 but with
nos 46 and 44-5. And unfortunately he did not exclude
the title-flyers from his reorganization, so that in
some cases the titles come at the end in his presentation.

79 L. Lafuma, *Controverses pascaliennes* 87 n1. It is difficult to see how the word 'series' avoids the difficulty; one sheet is no more a series than it is a
bundle. Cf *Recherches pascaliennes* 65, and *Histoire
de Penseés* 31. H.T. Barnwell (introduction to a new
edition of John Warrington's English translation
[London: Dent 1973] viii) calls them 'sets.' Jean
Mesnard in his recent book on the *Pensées* (*Les Pensées
de Pascal* [1976] 24-5 and 33 n1) employes the word
'units,' and this is the term I shall adopt.

80 L. Lafuma, 'Le puzzle des *Pensées*' RSH 59 (1950) 171,
and *Controverses pascaliennes* 49-50.

81 R. Francis, *Les Pensées de Pascal en France* 131-2.

82 J. Mesnard, 'Aux origines de l'édition des *Pensées*: les
deux Copies' in *Les Pensées de Pascal ont 300 ans* 4, 9-10.

83 Roger Pons had actually raised this question back in
the early fifties: 'La présentation authentique des
Pensées de Pascal,' *IL* 3 (1951) 172 n6.

84 L. Lafuma, *Recherches pascaliennes* 77 (article entitled
'Les deux "copies des *Pensées*"' 77-81).

85 Lafuma, *Recherches pascaliennes* 78.
86 Pascal, *Pensées, nouvelle édition établie pour la
   première fois d'après la copie de référence de Gilberte
   Pascal*. Ed. P. Sellier (Paris: Mercure de France 1976).
   Though not a critical edition in the sense of providing
   all the documentation available concerning variants,
   this edition is rich in perceptive observations, and
   the annotation is both helpful and well-informed. I
   have, however, not adopted his numbering for the book,
   as the Lafuma ordering is clearly much more widely
   known, and the material is laid out there in such a
   way that it is possible to adapt it to recent developments, and still find it a useful working tool. Sellier's
   conclusions concerning the chronology are also too
   wholesale, as I shall argue in chapter 32.
      Sellier's edition - not to be confused with the edi-
   tion the same scholar did for the Collection Théma/
   anthologie in 1972 - is the only one since 1951 to have
   made a significant contribution to the purely editorial
   problem. Even in 1972, the Brunschvicg order was being
   followed, in an edition by J. Haumont which was published by J. De Bonnot. The text was 'corrected' in
   the wake of Hytier, Tourneur, and Lafuma (p 215). In
   1953 F. Duviard produced an edition on similar lines
   to Chevalier's, asserting that Tourneur and Lafuma had
   committed a grave error (Classiques Hatier 1953; see
   p 17). Chevalier was also the basis of the translation
   published by Penguin Books in 1961. Tourneur's 1938
   edition was revised by D. Anzieu (Colin 1960), who
   modified Tourneur's numbering, and incorporated some
   of the results of Lafuma's work, but otherwise remained
   faithful to Tourneur's principles. Anzieu had been responsible for the text of an edition published by La
   bonne Compagnie in 1947, with annotations by Geneviève
   Lewis (cf p xxii). This edition followed the Brunschvicg
   order and numbering, and was used as the basis for subsequent editions put out by Hachette in 1948 (? - this
   is the date of printing: The Bibliographie de la France
   of 7 May 1948 gives the date as 1946, and the 'dépôt
   légal' is November 1946, which would give it priority
   over La bonne Compagnie, dated 1947, registered 23 Jan.
   1948), 1949 (*Pensées et Opuscules*), 1950 (Collection du
   Flambeau with introduction by R. Garric), 1972 (Livre
   de poche), and 1973 (Les chefs d'oeuvre des Lettres and
   Le Livre de Paris). The responsibility of Geneviève Lewis

and Anzieu (especially the latter) is rarely acknowledged as clearly as one would like. The Classiques
Garnier, meanwhile, have gone on reprinting an extremely mediocre edition of 1925 (C. des Granges,
Brunschvicg numbering).

The Garnier-Flammarion edition of 1973 (ed. D.
Descotes) followed the Delmas ordering. An interesting
attempt to do a different Delmas-style edition was
made in 1954 by Marcel Guersant: *Les Pensées de
Blaise Pascal* (Paris: Club français du livre 1954).
But though the introduction - which I have cited frequently already - is masterly, the classification of
Pascal is handled with too much freedom, and the result
is disappointing. A. Wautier's attempt to redo Guersant's
edition (Paris: Laffont 1960) is no improvement. Pol
Ernst has no hesitation in joining together the names
of Havet, Brunschvicg, Chevalier, Dedieu, Guersant,
and Wautier as editors who have 'dismembered' the
Apologia (*Approches pascaliennes* [1970] 543. See the
detailed tables, pp 544-613).

87 J. Mesnard, *Les Pensées de Pascal* 29. In his article
on the Copies (in *Les Pensées de Pascal ont 300 ans*
28) Mesnard said that the ideal order would be chronological, but he did not find that order in either Copy
(ibid 16). He is of the opinion that the *liasses* were
found, and copied, in an arbitrary order, and that the
inheritors of the papers postponed until later the task
of putting the *liasses* into sequence. But that does not
explain why one Copy (12449) was made in a way which
ruled out any possibility of rearranging the pieces
later.

It should be added that J. Mesnard has subjected
both Copies to a minute examination, and his conclusion is that neither Copy is the first one made. Both
were, however, done with the minimum delay - the work
on Copy 9203 probably overlapped with the work on the
true first copy - and their authenticity is in no way
diminished by this demonstration. ('Aux origines de
l'édition des *Pensées*' in *Les Pensées de Pascal ont
300 ans* 1-30).

88 Jean Mesnard's judgment of the question is unambiguous:
'Ces vingt-huit chapitres fournissent une ébauche sub-
stantielle et ordonnée de *l'Apologie de la religion
chretiénne* demeurée à l'état de fragments ... Il va de
soi que Pascal n'est pas mort au moment précis où ses

papiers se trouvaient dans un ordre parfaitement har-
monieux. Mais cette imperfection est le reflet de la
vie; elle n'empêche pas qu'une grande part d'harmonie
subsiste' ('A l'origine de l'édition des *Pensées*' in
Les Pensées de Pascal ont 300 ans 27, 29). Such a
judicious assessment of the situation takes the edge
off statements like the one by Ernest Mortimer (*Blaise
Pascal: The Life and Work of a Realist* [London: Methuen
1959] 188): 'We ourselves venture the view that the
book of the *Pensées* with all its great evangelistic
and apologetic force can never recreate the book of
the Apology.' True, but it can give us a very good
idea of the 'book of the Apology' Pascal had in mind.

I in no way dissent from the paragraph in which Louis
Marin speaks of the 'symbolic' acts, first of cutting
up the fragments, thus creating between them a space
which only the reader can fill, and then of pasting
the fragments onto larger sheets, symbolizing the
reader's attempt to restore a relation between one
fragment and another (*La Critique du discours* [Paris:
Editions de minuit 1975] 23-4). Of course there are
spaces to fill, and as many ways to fill them as there
are readers prepared to do so. My attention has been
held rather by another 'act': that of grouping and
filing certain fragments (with the spaces, inevitably)
according, I believe, to certain principles which
should guide the reader as he attempts to find appropriate matter with which to make the spaces manageable.

89 Lafuma (Delmas), Guersant, Wautier, Anzieu, etc., not
to mention the associations made by Brunschvicg, Stewart,
Chevalier, and the rest.

90 Jean Mesnard, writing early in the Lafuma era, was very
sensible on this: 'Gardons cependant présents à l'esprit
les textes non classés, de façon à éclairer, le cas
échéant, les textes classés.' (*Pascal* [Paris: Hatier
Boivin 1951] 139). Same approach twenty-five years
later: 'Le commentaire des fragments rangés dans les
28 liasses invite à de fréquents rapprochements avec
les autres' (*Les Pensées de Pascal* 50).

91 Even Lafuma - indeed, particularly Lafuma. J.L. Couchoud,
not without reason, calls Lafuma's redistribution 'un
tri aussi arbitraire et moins fin que celui de Brunschvicg' ('La crise des *Pensées* de Pascal,' *Le Flambeau*
38 [1955] 173). Cf. M. Guersant, introduction to Pascal:
Pensées (1954) xxviii. Lafuma himself would have been

surprised at the criticisms: 'il est évident,' he wrote
in 1949, 'que pour tel ou tel fragment on pourra
hésiter sur le choix du chapitre qui lui convient le
mieux: mais ce ne seront là que des cas exceptionnels'
(*Recherches pascaliennes* 47-8). He is more modest in
1954 (*Histoire des Pensées de Pascal* 84).

Let one example suffice. Lafuma allocates six fragments to the thirteenth chapter ('Soumission et usage
de la raison'), evidently because they all have to do
with reason. Only one of the six (820, on rival claims
of reason and authority) would seem to belong to the
specific argument of this *liasse*. No. 505, which seems
similar, has to do more with the difficulty, in a humanist system, of finding criteria, a problem raised by
no. 21 (2°). No. 539, in which the will is said to
interfere with reason, appears to go with no. 12 (1°)
on the obstacles in the way of belief. In no. 768 reason's power and prestige is indicated by our strong
dislike of being thought stupid, and the classified
fragments attach this notion to bundle 5° (98-100 on
'l'esprit boiteux'). No. 425 is echoed very closely by
no. 284 in 'Perpétuité,' and no. 588, which opposes
reason and faith, clearly belongs to the concluding
section. Anzieu, in his revision of Tourneur (1960)
puts both the last-named into 1°, and assigns only
fragment 695 ('Le péché originel est folie devant les
hommes') to 13°. Lafuma places no. 695 in 11°, and
there is undoubtedly an affinity with no. 149; however,
the classified fragment which comes closest to no. 695
is no. 131 in section 7°.

Anyone interested in seeing how the fragments have
been distributed by Lafuma and Anzieu can consult the
useful table in P. Ernst, *Approches pascaliennes* 625-41.
On pp 614-25, Ernst subjects the proposals for the first
liasse to a detailed scrutiny.

92 New Haven: Yale University Press.
93 J. Mesnard, *Pascal* (1951) 139-40. Consciously or not,
Roger Pons speaks in similar terms. 'Le plan de Pascal
n'était pas linéaire, ni géométrique, mais convergent
... Cet ordre ... est fait d'allées et venues, d'amorces
et de reprises, de subtiles enlacements ... L'examen
des liasses et de leur contenu permet de mieux saisir
cet ordre à la fois insinuant et autoritaire. La pensée
progresse en fourmillant; elle ne s'interdit pas les
va-et-vient, les retours et les reculs. Une dialectique

serrée se cache pourtant sous l'efflorescence, le libre enchevêtrement des thèmes' ('La présentation authentique des *Pensées* de Pascal,' *IL* 3 (1951) 177). The twenty-seven bundles were used as the basis of an analysis of the Apologia by J. Mantoy, *Des 'Pensées' de Pascal à l''Apologie'* and by Michel and Marie-Rose Le Guern, *Les Pensées de Pascal,* who also echo Jean Mesnard: 'Il ne faut pas y voir des cadres de pensée posés au départ de la construction d'un système philosophique qui serait le développement des conséquences de ces principes. Il s'agit au contraire de thèmes dynamiques qui évoluent, se modifiant à mesure que progresse la démarche de Pascal' (p 211).

94 E. Morot-Sir, *Pascal* (Paris: PUF 1973) 49.

95 I thus take a completely different view from J. Mantoy (*Des 'Pensées' de Pascal à l''Apologie'* [1955] 18): 'Toutes ces remarques nous invitent à survoler de très haut les *Pensées*, à délaisser les détails, à chercher les ensembles, si nous voulons découvrir l'idée géné-rale qui se dégage des divers fragments classés d'une liasse.'

Marcel Guersant expresses particularly clearly our duty to respect Pascal's classification, even when it baffles us (introduction to Pascal: *Pensées* [1954] xxxiii): 'Il est impérieux d'interpréter le sens d'un fragment d'après l'objet de la liasse dans laquelle Pascal l'a rangé et il est défendu de se porter en faux contre cette affectation sous prétexte que la raison en échappe ou qu'elle contredit un sens que l'on aper-çoit.' Roger Pons had already seen that the result of this disciplined enquiry would be extremely fruitful: 'Le Pascal des vingt-sept liasses nous instruit plus encore quant il déconcerte nos provisions que quand il se coule dans nos hypothèses' ('La présentation authen-tique des *Pensées* de Pascal,' *IL* 3 [1951] 177). These words were echoed by H. Coulet in a different context. 'N'hésitons pas à mettre en question les suites de pages même les plus cohérentes en apparence, et ne nous étonnons pas si ce génie dont la pensée multiple avait le don de la simultanéité déroute souvent notre faible logique' ('Pascal écrivant,' *Annales de la Faculté des Lettres d'Aix* 37 [1963] 158).

96 P. Ernst, *Approches pascaliennes* 3.

97 Marcel Guersant had already said that if an editor were to elucidate the sense of each *liasse* - an essentia

condition for a sensible distribution of the unsorted
fragments - he would be obliged to reshuffle the classified *pensées*, and he reproached Lafuma for apparently
neglecting to do this (introduction to his edition
[1954] xxvii; cf. p xxiii: 'une *ventilation* pour établir
l'*ordre* dialectique des matières, non un classement de
détail pour établir la *suite* l'un par rapport à l'autre
des fragments'). For some reason, editors have been
more willing to change the order of the fragments in
the first *liasse* than in the other *liasses*. Thus
Tourneur removed fragment 1, and placed the important
fragments 6 and 12 at the beginning. In his revision
of Tourneur, Anzieu restored no. 1 (putting it last),
and rearranged nos 7-11 in the order 11, 7, 9, 10, 8.
Lafuma tried a different order in the first Delmas
edition (an experiment he wisely did not repeat): 5,
1, 2, 3, 4, 7, 9, 6, 11, 8, 10, 12. Steinmann, whom
one would have expected simply to reverse the order of
the Copy and run from 12 down to 1 (see page 14),
chose to rearrange them thus: 12, 5, 11, 7, 6, 2-4
(rightly undivided), 9, 10, 8, 1.

The reversed order (12 to 1) was adopted by S. Wada
in a thesis (in Japanese): 'Une étude de l'Apologie
de la Religion chrétienne de Pascal d'après l'édition
intégrale Lafuma,' *Memoirs of the Faculty of Letters,
Osaka University* 10 (1963) 253-441, although for most
of the other chapters the ordering is individual. He
reverses the order of the Copies for sections 7°, 10°,
14°, and 15° also.

No two commentators, it is clear, see the first
liasse in the same way. Ernst proposes to make sense
of it by reading the fragments in the order: 2-5, 7,
11; 12, 6, 9, 10, 8, 1. For my part, I would recommend:
12, 6, 8, 1, 9, 10; 4, 2-3, 5, 11, 7. See chapter 1.

98 Cf. J. Mantoy, *Des 'Pensées' de Pascal à l''Apologie'*
17: 'Pour avoir l'intelligence du plan de l'*Apologie*,
nous pourrions donc nous borner à scruter les fragments
classés.' Roger Barrault, who edited a selection of
Pensées for the Nouveaux Classiques Larousse collection
(1965), also made sparing use of what he called the
'PNC' ('papiers non classés'). Ernst defends his decision with passion on pp 614-15.

99 Such as a rhetoric which prefers questions to clear
statements and which enunciates each point three times
over ('What I tell you three times is true' said Lewis

Carrol's Bellman), and a dogged insistence on pursuing lines of enquiry which can manifestly lead nowhere, as is evidenced by the first pages of each of his twenty-seven chapters.

100 The only problems I have encountered have been with nos 82 and 96 in section 5°, with nos 291 and 293 in section 23° (Lafuma XXII).

101 'Tous ceux qui ont écrit à partir de notes qu'ils avaient prises savent combien le classement, qui n'est jamais que provisoire, de celles-ci subit de modifications pendant la création,' A. Wautier (ed.) ([Paris: Laffont 1960] 19).

102 Préface à l'édition de Port-Royal (see n3), para. 4.

103 One is happy to find support for this view coming from Jean Mesnard ('A l'origine de l'édition des *Pensées*' in *Les Pensées de Pascal ont 300 ans* [1971] 6). Mesnard says that a 'classement' represents a more advanced conception than a 'plan,' in contrast to those critics quoted in n40.

104 L. Lafuma, *Histoire des Pensées de Pascal* 25, is unequivocal on this: 'une fois les grandes lignes de son ouvrage arrêtés ... il ne les a plus modifiés.' Lafuma bases this dogmatic judgment on the similarities between what we find in the *Pensées* and fragments 780-1 and 6, but there are other and better reasons. On the fragility of the reason Lafuma gives, see chapter 32, n64.

105 Adapting Jean Mesnard's system, I include in the text, where appropriate, the number of the Series or Unit where the fragment is found in Copy 9203, eg, 383, 386 (I) indicates that fragments 383 and 386 come from Unit I. I also note, when it is known, if any fragments come from the year 1656-7 (before the Apologia had come into focus), or if any come from the years 1660-1. The great majority of fragments were probably written in 1657 and 1658, as I shall argue in chapter 32.

106 The titles for these subdivisions are taken from appropriate *pensées*.

107 In the Luxembourg edition, the sections are not numbered, although an initial list (p 29) and the table of contents (p 555), both of which reproduce the abbreviated titles of Pascal's table (though without saying so) supply numbers (absent from the original table), from 1° to 27°. The Seuil edition also includes the 'blank' title 'La nature est corrompue,' to which

Lafuma allotted the number 15bis (p 528). I have had
to number my chapters differently, first because I
have inverted bundle 14° and 15° and second because
there is no longer any reason to withhold a proper
number from the sixteenth title. Lafuma's sections
16°-27° therefore become chapters 17-28.

108 This is not quite the same as the lecture Pascal is
said to have given in 1658, as several fragments used
in my summary may have been written later. See chapter
31, section (e).

109 Cf. J.L. Couchoud, 'La crise des *Pensées* de Pascal,'
Le Flambeau 38 (1955) 181, in connection with fragments
694-6: 'Qu'on est loin du désordre qui, l'année dernière, était le propre de toute étude de l'homme.'

110 The *Pensées* will form Vol. V of the *Oeuvres complètes*
in course of publication by Desclée de Brouwer. At
present only two volumes of the set have appeared
(1964, 1970).

111 Albert Béguin had asked for such an edition in an eloquent page in his review article, 'Les éditions et
l'ordre des *Pensées*' 888: 'Que faut-il demander à une
édition de Pascal? Qu'elle intéresse la curiosité des
spécialistes, au prix d'une longue et laborieuse initia-
tion? ou bien qu'elle mette à la disposition de quiconque s'interroge sur l'homme et sur Dieu la réponse,
aussi accessible qu'il se peut, d'un des esprits les
plus fermes qu'il y ait jamais eu? La réponse à ces
questions ne me paraît pas discutable.' Béguin picks
up the argument in the preface he wrote for L. Lafuma's
Recherches pascaliennes 12-14. Lafuma answered Béguin
in a chapter of his *Recherches pascaliennes*: 'Observations en marge d'un article de *Critique*' 135-47, but
the case for editorial responsibility (pp 145-7) is
not well argued. H. Gouhier made the same point as
Béguin in his preface to the selection of *Pensées*
edited by L. Marin (Paris: Didier 1969) 4: 'Or, "la
suite" des "pensées" selon l'érudition n'est pas celle
qui fait immédiatement comprendre la pensée de Pascal.
L'ordre à suivre, en pareil cas, doit être établi en
tenant compte de ce que le lecteur attend de sa lecture.'
Even L. Lafuma begrudingly admitted that he would not
deny the interest in 'popularizing' Pascal, but rightly
refused to countenance any open betrayal of Pascal's
intentions (*Ecrits sur Pascal* 205).

In 1950 Roger Pons declared: 'Je refuse le dilemme

suivant: un Pascal vrai et illisible - ou un Pascal
lisible et arbitraire' ('Les manuscrits de Pascal,'
CUC [Mar. 1950] 54) and Jean Mesnard has expressed a
similar belief: 'Il reste à concilier les exigences
de l'objectivité avec celles de l'agrément ... Nous
nous refusons à établir une contradiction entre ces
deux exigences; l'édition la plus érudite peut et doit
être en même temps la plus parfaitement élégante'
(*Pascal* 138-9). The fact remains, however, that an
objective presentation of the uncompleted Apologia
presents the reader with problems with which the
honnête homme, of whatever century, is impatient.

112 I had proposed such an edition to the University of
London Press in the sixties, and the proposal was
provisionally accepted. The acceptance was later withdrawn, very graciously, when the series (Textes français
classiques et modernes)was discontinued. I see now that
it would have been open to the very criticism that was
made earlier of Lafuma and others: preparing an edition
before undertaking the research enshrined in the present
book would have been putting the cart before the horse.

CHAPTER 1

1 'Excellence de cette manière de prouver Dieu,' XIV in
Lafuma's numbering, 15° in mine.
2 J. Mantoy, *Des 'Pensées de Pascal à l''Apologie'* (1955)
20: 'Nous laissons de côté la première liasse: Ordre,
dans laquelle ont été classées toutes les ébauches du
plan.' Antoine Adam, 'Sur les *Pensées* de Pascal' *IL* 9
(1957) 6: 'Pascal y a tout simplement groupé les différents projets qui lui venaient à l'esprit, aussi
bien sur les modes de présentation ... que sur la ligne
générale de l'argumentation.' H. Gouhier, *Blaise Pascal:
Commentaires* (1966) 181: 'des notes de travail, hors
séries, et non celles d'une introduction ou d'un premier chapitre.' P. Sellier, edition (1976) 17: 'où il
consigne son programme à court terme,' and p 40 n1:
'rassemble des notes où Pascal, lors de l'agencement
des vingt-sept rubriques provisoires de l'Apologie
[2°-28°], a indiqué les projets nouveaux qui germaient
en lui.' M. Guersant, edition (1954) xxiv and xxxiii:
'aide-mémoire ou canevas,' 'des fragments dont la
signification apologétique et la cohérence sont nulles.'
On fragment 1, Tourneur commented: 'Le premier texte

rangé sous le titre géneral d'*Ordre* ne s'y rapporte
pas du tout, alors qu'il se rapporte, par l'identité
du filigrane et l'analyse du sujet, aux articles 2 et
3 de la seconde partie, placés avant un article intitulé Ordre' (édition [1938] xxxiv; the 'articles' in
question are nos 385 and 386 in Unit I).Tourneur's
observation is not at all clear; if the subject-matter
of no. 1 recalls no. 385 (not 386), the paper on which
it is written is identical with no. 386 - but not 385.
Lafuma replied: 'Nous trouvons absolument normal qu'il
ait versé à son dossier *Ordre* un papier destiné à lui
rappeler qu'il avait prévu un chapitre sur la *Fausseté
des autres religions*' (*Recherches pascaliennes* [1949]
139). R.E. Lacombe simply remarks that four of the
twelve fragments of Bundle 1° are 'visibly' out of
place (*L'Apologétique de Pascal* [1958] 27, continuation
of n53).

The fragments contained in the first *liasse* were put
by Faugère (1844) at the very end of the apologetic
fragments, as chapter 10 of part two. Molinier (1877)
put them in the same place, without making it clear
whether they were meant to conclude the apologia, or
to inaugurate a series of appendices (covering miracles,
Jesuits, style, 'pensées diverses,' etc.).

3 P. Ernst, *Approches pascaliennes* (1970) 17-47.
4 Are entitled 'Ordre' fragments 387, 467, 683, 684, 694.
   Fragment 109 ('Contre le pyrrhonisme') originally bore
   the same title. The word 'Ordre' (deleted) is also
   found at the head of no. 594 but there it is the first
   word of the phrase 'Ordre général du monde.' The phrase
   'ordre du monde' comes again lower down, in a paragraph
   Pascal had already written, and in order to avoid the
   repetition, he substituted the word 'conduite' in the
   first line.
5 The Roman numerals indicate the Units or Series in
   Lafuma's numbering. Units I, XXIII, and XXV were probably
   put aside by Pascal when he was setting up his twenty-
   eight dossiers, Units XXVI and XVII were not constituted
   before 1660, which means that the *pensées* they contain
   may be later than 1658. There is no question of the
   late date of fragments 737 and 745 (see below nn 21,
   and 25), but there is room for doubt concerning the
   other fragments quoted here (see n28, and also chapter
   32). Thus all but a handful of the fragments considered
   in this chapter can be assigned to the period 1657-8,

and it may be that some of the doubtful ones date from
that period also.

6 The words 'Une lettre' were added later; the original
heading was 'De la folie, (etc.).'

7 Michel and Marie-Rose Le Guern look on this as a dialogue within a letter, in the manner of the *Provinciales*
(*Les Pensées de Pascal* [1972] 72).

8 P. Ernst (*Approches pascaliennes* 46) appears to limit
the 'Introduction générale' to two letters ('La lettre
qu'on doit chercher Dieu' followed by 'La Lettre d'ôter
les obstacles') plus some explanations of the plan and
the proofs (hypothesis one). On p 18, where he quotes
the five references to letters, he assumes the entire
Apologia will be in epistolary form (hypothesis two).

9 In nos 76 and 45 respectively.

10 Fragment 76 is on the same sheet as fragment 60 and
was scored out when the latter was put into bundle 3°.
Cf. P. Sellier, edition (1976) 68 n25.

11 A.J. Krailsheimer, *Pascal* (Oxford: University Press
1980) 46.

12 Editors have had differing reactions to the manuscript
page which contains nos 2, 3, and 4 (R.O. 29).
Brunschvicg separated the two parts of no. 3 and attached
the first to no. 2 (Br. 227 and 244). P. Ernst also
believes nos 2 and 3 inseparable, and recommends deliberately ignoring Pascal's separation mark (*Approches
pascaliennes* 29). P. Sellier (1976) groups nos 2, 3,
and 4 under a single number (38), but replaces the gap
in no. 3 by a separation line. M. Le Guern (1977) also
groups nos 2-4 together, leaving single line spaces
between 2 and 3, 3a and 3b, and 3 and 4.

13 For a different point of view, see Marie Louise Hubert,
Pascal's Unfinished Apology (1952) 146-8.

14 Though only, I think, in the two prefaces, 780-1. No.
148 ('Seconde partie') constitutes a special case (see
below, chapter 10). It has become a critical commonplace
to divide the Apologia into two parts, but not everyone
can agree where the division comes, and this hesitation
seems significant. See chapter 31.

15 Jean Mesnard (*Les Pensées de Pascal* [1976] 179-80)
links no. 12 specifically with the second part of the
Apologia (beginning with section 11°).

16 L. Brunschvicg, note to La. 387, Br. 241. H. Gouhier
commends Brunschvicg's note for its great clarity
(*Claise Pascal: Commentaires* [1966] 171 n88).

17 P. Ernst *Approches pascaliennes* 44. But on p 28, Ernst
   had accepted the other interpretation: 'Que lui répond
   Pascal? Nous ne le saurons jamais. Tout au plus pouvons-
   nous affirmer qu'il est sur le point d'affirmer quelque
   chose, et que de cette réponse, l'on possède au moins
   le début.'
18 See chapter 31, first part of section (a) and also n41.
19 It is not the only objection to Ernst's hypothesis,
   which appears characteristically to be based upon his
   own summaries and paraphrases rather than on Pascal's
   actual text. It is inconceivable that a preface could
   start with the question (first sentence of no. 2):
   'Que dois-je faire?' which must be a response to the
   'lettre qu'on doit chercher Dieu.' Cf. no. 5: 'Une
   lettre d'exhortation à un ami pour le porter à chercher.
   Et il répondra: mais à quoi me servira de chercher,
   rien ne paraît'; no. 2: 'Que dois-je faire? Je ne vois
   partout qu'obscurité.' Nor is the link between the
   two parts clear in Ernst's scheme.
20 This is not to say that there are no vestiges of what
   might have been at one stage conceived as a general
   preface. This possibility is discussed in chapters 31
   and 32.
21 In fragment 745 (XXVI), the 'admirable manière d'écrire
   de Salomon de Tultie' (alias Pascal) is compared to
   Montaigne and Epictetus. This note is a gloss on the
   verso of fr. 744 (XXVI), which I am associating with
   2°. Both fragments are in Gilberte Périer's hand, and
   the obvious immodesty led J. Bédier to suppose the
   gloss to have been Gilberte's own (J. Bédier, 'Pascal
   et Salomon de Tultie' in *Mélanges offerts à M. Gustave
   Lanson* [1922] 178-82). B. Croquette (*Pascal et Montaigne*
   [Geneva: Droz 1974] 154) accepts Bédier's position,
   but neither P. Sellier nor M. Le Guern in their recent
   editions even mention it. It cannot be said that
   Bédier's arguments are conclusive: would Gilberte have
   been so ready to cite Montaigne and Epictetus? And the
   final 'etc.' followed by an afterthought is one of the
   hallmarks of Pascal's own style (cf. fragments 258,
   620, 794, 809, 971). The immodesty is softened by the
   ironic pseudonym. See the very interesting discussion
   by L. Marin, '"Pascal": text, author, discourse' in
   YFS 52 (1975) 143 and n24.
22 There is no manuscript extant of no. 694, a particularly
   important *pensée* for the present enquiry. It very likely

was written on the same sheet as 693 and 695, also
missing from the R.O.

23 Michel Le Guern proposes a totally different interpre-
tation. He reads the title 'Prin[cipes]' and believes
the fragment is a reflection on the preface to Descartes'
Principes de la Philosophie (*Pascal et Descartes* [Paris:
Nizet 1971] 48; edition [1977] II, 302, n1 to LG 472).
The manuscript appears, however, to give, quite clearly,
'Pyrr.' J.L. Couchoud takes 'mon sujet' to mean man
(*Discours de la condition de l'homme* [1948] 25).

24 B. Croquette, *Pascal et Montaigne* 111-12, makes the
interesting observation that Pascal's borrowings from
Montaigne draw not on the self-portraiture but on the
evidence of *misère* and folly which Montaigne gathered
together. Elements of a critique of Montaigne can be
found in fragments 89, 525, 577, 649, 680, 689, 780,
872, as well as 745 (see n20).

25 No. 737 probably dates from 1660 and has been seen as
one of a series of thoughts triggered off by reading
Descartes (Michel and Marie-Rose Le Guern, *Les Pensées
de Pascal* 16, following Michel Le Guern, *Pascal et
Descartes* [1971] 50).

26 One can understand how no. 109, now 'Contre le pyrrhonisme,' but originally entitled 'Ordre,' could fit
into this plan ('le faire chercher chez les philosophes,
pyrrhoniens et dogmatistes' 4). But it evidently seemed
too important to be thrown away in an initial survey.

27 P.L. Couchoud explains 'd'ordre' as 'dans un ordre'
(*Discours de la condition de l'homme* 31 n3, cf. also
p 7). Cf. no. 298.

28 Fragments 780-1 belong to Unit XXVII, which was probably
constituted around 1660. It is not impossible that
nos 780-1 were actually written earlier. It would
certainly make sense if they had been set down in 1658.
The idea of 780 tallies closely with the fragments in
Unit XXIII on 'Ordre,' and no. 781 is like no. 190,
assigned in 1658 to *liasse* 15°. Whatever the facts of
the matter, it is clear that a 'discourse' was conceived, sketched, and abandoned, and that vestiges of
the unwritten portions were filed in the first bundle.

29 Port-Royal edition of 1678, no other source known.

CHAPTER 2

1 In chapter 31 I argue that he had probably filed about
fifteen papers in Bundle 3° before opening Bundle 2°.

2 Fragment 76 is on the verso of fr. 60, and is crossed
  out. Likewise fragment 197, on the verso of fr. 194.
  Both are therefore very early. See chapter 31, n2.
3 1104, 1106, 1107, 1108, and 1111 are the fourth, sixth,
  seventh, eighth, and eleventh *pensées* presented by J.
  Mesnard in his *Textes inédits* of 1962, pp 30-2 (reprinted by Lafuma [Seuil] 639). Fragment 196, like 197,
  is found on the verso of no. 194, and is crossed out.
  Only the fragments listed here as being in Unit XXVI
  are known for certain to be late.
4 Fragment 197 could not be used, as it was written,
  along with no. 195 and 196 on the verso of the sheet
  containing fr. 194, and Pascal wanted no. 194 for his
  chapter 'Transition' (14°, Lafuma XV). It reads:

> Rien ne montre mieux la vanité des hommes que de
> considérer quelle cause et quels effets de l'amour,
> car tout l'univers en est changé. Le nez de Cléopâtre.

This in turn reads like a reference to something known
already - no. 413:

> Qui voudra connaître à plein la vanité de l'homme
> n'a qu'à considérer les causes et les effets de
> l'amour. La cause en est un je ne sais quoi. Corneille.
> Et les effets en sont effroyables. Ce je ne sais quoi,
> si peu de chose qu'on ne peut le reconnaître, remue
> toute la terre, les princes, les armées, le monde
> entier.
>   Le nez de Cléopâtre, s'il eût été plus court, toute
> la face de la terre aurait changé.

5 My italics. For 'vain' and 'vanité' in this sense, see
  60, 73, 95, 131, 136, 144, 149, 199; 403, 427, 626, 628,
  896.
6 Cf. fragment 208, where 'vanité' replaces 'orgueil,'
  to describe the danger avoided by one school of philosophers. The current sense is found also in fr. 77,
  315, 351, 627, 919, 920.
7 On this *pensée*, see the article by C. Gandelman, 'La
  Dé-Iconisation janséniste de l'art: Pascal, Philippe
  de Champaigne' in *Hebrew University Studies in Literature* 5 (1977) 213-47.
8 P. Ernst, *Approches pascaliennes* (1970) 78.
9 Lafuma numbers this final section 45.
10 Ernst, *Approches pascaliennes* 77-8.
11 L.M. Heller ('Note on a *pensée*: Pascal and Montaigne,'

29 [1974] 216-20) believes that fr. 552 is a personal note, not intended for publication. Lafuma too, in the Delmas edition, classified it among the 'Notes personnelles' (Del. 753).

CHAPTER 3

1 Fragment 76 is on the same double sheet as no. 60, and does not really belong to this section. I presented it in chapter 2 (section c).
2 J. Mesnard, *Pascal* (1951) 141.
3 No. 978 is known to us through the Périer manuscript. Only one of these fragments can be assigned definitely to Pascal's last years, no. 749. Units II and XXXIV are relatively early.
4 The word was added to 414, and struck from 136, which now bears the title 'Divertissement.' On the ms., no. 136 was entitled 'Misère de l'homme' (R.O. 139).
5 Fragment 625 uses it in the same limited way.
6 See below, chapter 12 (c).
7 For other examples where Pascal's thinking comes close to La Rochefoucauld's, cf. nos. 526, 535 (XXIII), 671, 674, 724 (XXV). Pascal discusses *honnêteté* in other fragments from a different point of view. Much better, he says, that a man should be looked on as an *honnête homme*, with all that implies of wide culture and 'universality,' than that he should be labelled mathematician, preacher, etc. (647, XXV). This fragment is echoed by 587 (XXIII), 605 and 611 (XXIV) and 195 (on back of 194), while nos 715 (XXV) and 732 (XXVI) are probably jottings for it. In fr. 778 (XXVII) Pascal comments that men take pride in the one thing they cannot be taught: in having the qualities of an *honnête homme*. No. 792 (XXVIII) contrasts the show men give of friendship with the kind of remarks they make about 'friends' who are not present.
8 G. Chinard, *En lisant Pascal* (Geneva: Droz 1948) 85-6.
9 J. Mesnard, *Les Pensées de Pascal* (1976) 188 n1.
10 Ernst, *Approches pascaliennes* 93, 94.
11 Mesnard, *Les Pensées de Pascal* 186-90.
12 See chapter 31, section (a).

CHAPTER 4

1 *Ennui* was also the theme of two unclassified fragments brought into the previous chapters, 414 and 771. See chapters 2 (d) and 3 (a).

2 Fragment 622 belongs to Unit XXIV, and there is evidence
  to suggest that Pascal gave up his detailed sorting at
  about the time he came across no. 622 and others on
  similar paper. See chapter 32 (a). J. Mesnard also uses
  no. 622 to explain the fourth *liasse* (*Pascal* [1951]
  142; *Les Pensées de Pascal* [1976] 191), as does R.
  Barrault in the Nouveaux Classiques Larousse presentation ([1965] 66). It impinges also on section 8°,
  'Divertissement' (see chapter 8).
3 D. Westgate, 'The Augustinian Concept of Amour-Propre
  and Pascal's *Pensées*,' *NFS* 10 (1971) 11-12.
4 J. Mesnard, *Les Pensées de Pascal* (1976) 191.
5 J. Mesnard, *Pascal* (1951) 142. Borrowed without
  acknowledgment by P. Ernst, *Approches pascaliennes*
  (1970) 100, and amplified by the words 'sans cesse.'
  J. Orcibal borrowed it too, but more discreetly (*SAPR*
  2 [1951] 36).
6 Ernst, *Approches pascaliennes* 103.

CHAPTER 5
1 See introduction, n51.
2 Fr. 84 is on the verso of fr. 83, and is scored out.
  I mention it in chapter 14. P. Ernst considers it 'sans
  rapport avec l'objet même de la liasse' (*Approches
  pascaliennes* [1970] n1 on p 687), and M. Sato ignores
  it also ('Sur la "Raison des effets" de Pascal,' *ELFF*
  16 [1970] 20-6). T.W. Harrington, on the other hand,
  does use it in his discussion of section 5° (*Vérité
  et méthode dans les 'Pensées' de Pascal* [Paris: Vrin
  1972] 52). L. Marin, who uses fr. 84 as a key text,
  finds it significant that the fragment 'belongs' to
  the *liasse* 'Raisons des effets'; 'La raison (ou les
  raisons) des effets naturels comme signes ... ne peut
  être trouvée dans la trop courte axiomatique de la
  physique cartésienne' (*La Critique du discours* [Paris:
  Minuit 1975] 104).
     Fr. 102 comes at the end of para. 3 of fr. 101; it
  was crossed out and the fourth paragraph added. P.
  Ernst (loc. cit.) does not allow that it is an independent fragment, and T.M. Harrington (pp 35-6) agrees
  with him. Brunschvicg separated them (Br. 324-759);
  Anzieu, following Tourneur, does as Ernst wishes (A.
  100); Sellier, faithful to the Second Copy, omits fr.
  102. Sato does not mention it in his article.
3 Fr. 797 was written in 1660, and nos 767 and 769 may
  be late also. All the rest can be dated 1657 or 1658.

4 Fragment 94 is expanded in fr. 977, but this latter fragment is not authentic. See L. Lafuma, 'Une pensée inédite,' in *Controverses pascaliennes* (1952) 173-85.

5 P. Sellier (ed. 1976, no. 130) emends it thus, without comment: '...comme de savoir bien jouer du luth. [Ne point jouer du luth] n'est un mal...' Cf. Brunschvicg ed. no. 329 and note.

6 T.W. Harrington (*Vérité et méthode dans les 'Pensées' de Pascal* [1972] 52) would add the name of Descartes, as he does not exclude fr. 84 from this section.

7 J. Mesnard, *Les Pensées de Pascal* (1976) 194. Also his article 'Pascal et la contestation,' *Revue d'Auvergne* 85 (1971) 185-97.

8 Brunschvicg acted as if Pascal had placed the sign marking the separation between the two at the wrong point on the paper. Br. 80 = La. 98 and 99a, run on without even a new paragraph; Br. 536 = La. 99b. The manuscript does not separate 99a from 99b, but 99b has a smaller left-hand margin than the rest. Tourneur and Anzieu join 98 and 99 together as if they are a single *pensée* (T. 94, A. 98).

9 P. Ernst, *Approches pascaliennes* 111-12. The same connection seems to be implied by Jean Mesnard, *Les Pensées de Pascal* 198. In the manuscript, no. 82 is apparently not separated from no. 81. But that is because the line at the end of no. 81 was crossed out when Pascal added the last three sentences of no. 81.

10 T.W. Harrington, *Vérité et méthode dans les Pensées de Pascal* 24-58. Harrington also presents the material in four groups plus a conclusion: conflicting apprehensions of truth (my section c and part of section a), different apprehensions of justice (roughly my sections b and d), concrete manifestations of this difference (the rest of a), similarity of two distinct things (a category limited to the brief fragment 97 on force and concupiscence). No. 82 and 84 become a conclusion plus epilogue. This scheme seems to me to take section 5° out of its context, and hence make abstract what was basically dynamic. It is unsatisfactory, also, to have to invent separate categories for individual fragments (97, 82, 84).

Harrington does not mention an article by M. Sato which appeared in 1970, the same year as Ernst's book (see n2). He would surely agree with Sato's conclusion, that 'le sens qui accorde tous les fragments classés

dans la liasse 5°, c'est la dialectique pascalienne.'
Sato divides his discussion into two: 'Economy' (my
section d), and 'Opinion.' He makes an interesting link
with the theme of the three Orders, elaborated later
in the Apologia.

   J. Mesnard's treatment of this chapter is close to
my own, although he proceeds in the order badc (*Les
Pensées de Pascal* 192-9).

11 As A. Brimo remarked in a Toulouse thesis now forty
years old, Pascal's position is sharply distinct from
that of the idealists and that of the realists (*Pascal
et le Droit* [Paris: Sirey 1942]).

12 See chapter 31, section (c)

CHAPTER 6

1 406, 411 (I); 437 (V); 470, 472 (XI); 491 (XVIII);
620, 633 (XXIV); 738, 741, 756, 759 (XXVI). No. 1109
is the ninth *penSee* included in Jean Mesnard's *Textes
inédits* of 1962 (p 32; Seuil 639). Unit XXVI is known
to have been set up later, but only 738 and 741 can
be assigned with certainty to the years 1660-1.

2 The two late examples here (738, 741) are connected,
not surprisingly, with Pascal's reading of Descartes
(M. Le Guern, *Pascal et Descartes* [1971] 50-4).

3 The question mark is quite unambiguous in the manuscript, although an exclamation mark would seem more
appropriate.

4 The title of this fragment is 'Nature corrompue,'
which might point to section 16° as its home. But we
know from no. 6 that 'nature corrompue' is also one
way of describing the whole of part one.

5 J. Mesnard, *Les Pensées de Pascal* (1976) 200.

6 Ernst takes it that way (*Approches pascaliennes* [1970]
130). See the discussion in R.E. Lacombe, *L'Apologétique de Pascal* (1958) 18 n32.

CHAPTER 7

1 See chapter 28, section (a).

2 Fr. 886 is in the same Unit (XXXIV) as no. 905, entitled 'Pyrrhonisme,' which I quote a little further
on. Both are early (1656-7).

3 The turn of the Stoics and atheists will come in due
course (in sections 9° and 12°).

4 Cf. no. 406, quoted in the previous chapter, section
(e).
5 J. Chevalier suggests a different interpretation, which
seems to me to strain the word *vrai* somewhat. The search
for truth, he says, keeps man from usurping the place
of God. To the seeker, Jesus will say 'You would not
seek me if you had not already found me' ('Echange de
vues' with L. Goldmann, *DSS* 23 [1954] 602–3).
6 There is reason to believe that the contradictions
mentioned in no. 404 include more than those which
form the subject of *liasse* 7°; its position in Unit I
brings it into the orbit of chapters 9°, 10°, and 11°
(see chapter 31, end of section a and n35). This squares
with the fact that the parallels in no. 131 were crossed
out - they will reappear later. But as I have discussed
the whole of no. 131 here, and as no. 404 uses the word
'contrariétés' it has seemed advisable to mention no.
404 in the present chapter. I shall mention it also
in chapters 9 (see n5) and 11 (p 138).

CHAPTER 8

1 On this question, see chapter 31, section (a).
2 M. Le Guern, 'Pascal au travail: la composition du
fragment sur le divertissement,' *RUO* 36 (1966) 209–31.
For fr. 39, see p 219. See also chapter 31, n32.
3 I believe all these fragments to date from 1657 (522–3)
or 1658. There is some dispute about nos 478 and 773,
which I shall consider in chapter 32.
4 No. 134 was in fact a marginal gloss on no. 133.
5 Our understanding of fragment 136 is greatly increased
if we can read the different versions the passage went
through, but only part of the rejected material is
reproduced by Lafuma. It can be studied in the photostat and paleographic editions, in the Tourneur-Anzieu
edition of 1960, pp 90–103 (A. 134), and in M. Le
Guern's article (see n2). Lafuma follows Brunschvicg
(Br. 139), but Brunschvicg at least explained what he
was doing. Lafuma's use of a dash to indicate additions,
in both the Luxembourg and the Seuil editions, is difficult to handle with confidence. Sellier's presentation
is at times perplexing. Le Guern is the most consistent,
but the scope of his edition means that many variants
go unrecorded.

6 Although the first sentence, beginning 'Et ainsi le conseil qu'on donnait à Pyrrhus' was not crossed out, the position of Pascal's cross-reference sign (at the beginning, not the end, of the sentence) and the fact that Pascal replaces the word 'Car' with 'Et ainsi' at the beginning of the passage immediately following the deletion, indicate that it should be included in the cut. Sellier pops it in in another place, and gives no explanation (S. 168).

7 This passage, later replaced by the last four lines of page 94 in the Luxembourg edition, can be found on p 96 (last two paragraphs, beginning 'Car pour parler selon la vérité des diverses conditions des hommes, ceux que nous appelons de grande qualité, comme un surintendant, un chancelier, etc.').

8 'Ainsi l'homme est si malheureux, etc.' (top of p 95).

9 The text of the first two paragraphs ('Car pour parler selon la vérité ... comme un surintendant, etc.' and 'Le divertissement est une chose') can be read on p 96; the third is 'Ainsi l'homme est si malheureux' (p 95).

10 I read the evidence differently from M. Le Guern ('Pascal au travail' 224): 'En relisant sa dernière phrase, Pascal y retrouve celle qu'il vient d'écrire au bas de la page precédente, avec exactement les mêmes images. Il barre alors le B écrit en tête de cette page-ci et le met au début du dernier paragraphe. Etonnant procédé de composition!' It is simpler to believe, in the presence of two almost identical passages, that one is a conscious reworking of the other.

11 The original text (after 'suffisent pour le divertir' 95) read: 'Car quel objet a celui-ci qui se tue aujourd'hui à la chasse, sinon celui de se vanter demain entre ses amis de ce sanglier qu'il aura pris, etc.'

12 P 96: the beginning of the sentence is changed to suit the changed circumstances ('Prenez-y garde, etc.'), and it is preceded by a new sentence ('Sans divertissement ... en cet état').

13 Fragment 523 is written on the same page as 522, cited in the course of my discussion of no. 136. It is almost certainly an early example, written in the first months of 1657.

14 No. 779 is also a development of a remark in no. 136, about our fearing objects of our own creation, but the idea is closer to the general theme of *liasse* 2° than *liasse* 8°.

CHAPTER 9

1 Fragment 933 is known only from the Recueil Original,
  and fragment 988 only from the Deuxième Recueil
  Guerrier. Fragment 1112 is the second of the *pensées*
  published by Jean Mesnard in 1962 (*Textes inédits*
  32-3; Seuil, 640). All six probably date from 1658.
2 Units I, XXIV, and XXV were put together in late 1658;
  on the date of the others there is room for doubt.
3 No. 545 will be discussed in chapter 27.
4 Mentioned in chapters 6 and 2 respectively.
5 No. 404, quoted in chapter 7, could as easily fit in
  here.

CHAPTER 10

1 Unit XI contains one fragment which is usually dated
  1659, but I would be surprised if no. 479 itself was
  as late as that. All the others belong to the year
  1658, except perhaps no. 805.
2 At best, the location of the Sovereign Good in God,
  who must be known by faith, could coincide with the
  first definition of no. 6. But it does not tally with
  the second definition. That is why, of the two explanations suggested by Jean Mesnard (*Les Pensées de Pascal*
  [1976] 224 n1) I prefer the first, elaborated in the
  following paragraph.
3 No. 76 is physically inseparable from no. 60, so
  Pascal had to sacrifice one or the other when he
  classified his fragments. Naturally he chose to keep
  no. 60, which is more developed. No. 76 is consequently found, crossed out, in dossier 3°, and bears
  a number which at first glance implies that it belongs
  there as of right. I cited it in chapter 2.
    No. 479 ('Pour les philosophes, 280 souverains
  biens') implies an intention to develop the idea in
  section 9° rather than here, but as we shall see, the
  material of section 9° could be assimilated in no.
  148 around this point. The figure 280, instead of
  288, is taken as indication that Pascal used the 1652
  edition of Montaigne's essays, which contains this
  misprint (A. Uhlír, 'Montaigne et Pascal,' *RHLF* 14
  [1907] 442-54, especially pp 452-3). The BN catalogue
  contains three entries for 1652. Two of them appear

to be identical in all respects except the publishers'
names on the title-page (A. Courbé or P. Rocolet). The
third (Rés. Z. 360) is actually an edition of 1635.
4 Fr. 148 occupies two sides of a single sheet. There is
no punctuation after the last word.
5 See chapter 30, p 313, and chapter 31, p 354. Cf.
P.L. Couchoud, *Discours de la condition de l'homme*
(1948) 12.

CHAPTER 11

1 Pol Ernst, 'La trajectoire pascalienne de l'Apologie,'
ALM 84 (1967) 8-11. In that study, he preferred to
interpret the initials as meaning 'Apologie à Port-
Royal,' but in his later *Approches pascaliennes* he
reverts to the traditional explanation. See chapter
31, n79. The argument put forward in the present chapter is in any case unaffected by my interpretation of
the enigmatic title.
2 H. Gouhier, *Blaise Pascal: Commentaires* (1966) 181,
Ernst, *Approches pascaliennes* (1970) 196. These texts
will be quoted and answered below, section (d).
3 Fr. 1113 is the thirteenth *pensée* in the *Textes inédits*
edited in 1962 by J. Mesnard (p 33; Seuil, 640).
4 This implies, of course, that the order in which we
read the various parts of no. 149 does not correspond
to the order in which they were written. We shall be
examining fr. 149 from that point of view later, in
chapters 30 (c) and 31 (b).
5 Jean Mesnard, in his presentation of the *Textes inédits* which include *pensée* no. 1113, assumes the 'roman'
mentioned there to refer to the historical proofs, but
he gives no reason for this interpretation, which I
hesitate to accept.
6 Despite the title ('Grandeur'), no. 472 is obviously
more relevant to this eleventh section than to the
sixth.
7 Gouhier, *Blaise Pascal: Commentaires* 181.
8 Ernst, *Approches pascaliennes* 196.
9 Gouhier, *Blaise Pascal: Commentaires* 180; Ernst,
Approches pascaliennes 185-6. Michel Le Guern (edition,
1977, no. 139 and n1, 287-8) rearranges the text
slightly, beginning with page 2 and its sequel on page
3. 'L'incompréhensibilité' of the title thus refers to

the paragraph on the idea 'Incroyable que Dieu s'unisse
à nous' (pp 2-3). The disadvantage of this presentation
is that it breaks up the natural sequence of ideas from
page 1 onto page 2 of the ms.
10 The Copies, in fact, do not clearly distinguish 11°
and 12°. See introduction, n33.

CHAPTER 12

1 *Blaise Pascal: Commentaires* (1966) 181, 304.
2 Cf. Patricia Topliss, *The Rhetoric of Pascal* (1966)
181, Pol Ernst, *Approches pascaliennes* (1970) 654,
Michel and Marie-Rose Le Guern, *Les Pensées de Pascal*
(1972) 134-40, P. Sellier, edition (1976) 360 nl. Jean
Mesnard, on the other hand, does not make any explicit
connection between *liasse* 12° and fr. 427, which he
sees as a development of the theme of 16°, 'La nature
est corrompue' ('Les éditions de Port-Royal,' *CPR* 20-1
[1972] 75-6).
3 The temptation to make fragment 427 into an introduction goes back to 1670, and has been yielded to by
many editors and commentators since, including Faugère,
Louandre, Molinier, Janssens, Brunet, Lacombe, Barrault,
Couchoud, Gouhier, Topliss, Marin, Le Guern. 'A cet
égard, le classement de 1670 ne me paraît pas avoir
exercé une influence heureuse,' comments Jean Mesnard
('Les éditions de Port-Royal,' *CPR* 20-1 [1972] 76).
It was Lafuma's solution in the Delmas edition. Lafuma
repented of his decision, but evidently not in time to
change the Delmas text for the second edition in 1952.
In *Controverses pascaliennes* ([1952] 86) he described
fr. 427 as 'quelques pages ... qui paraissent destinées
à l'introduction de la seconde partie.' Cf. *Histoire
des Pensées de Pascal* (1954) 25. In chapter 32 (b),
I shall suggest that no. 427 may indeed have been intended originally to fill the role of general introduction. But the place of the twelfth *liasse* in the
scheme shows that Pascal wished the ideas to be developed at a much later stage of his book.
4 Patricia Topliss, too much influenced by the Delmas
arrangement (*The Rhetoric of Pascal* [1966] 181).
5 Ernst, *Approches pascaliennes* 654. See introduction,
p 12 and n64.
6 L. Lafuma, Luxembourg ed. (1951) I, 115 ('le commencement de la seconde partie de l'ouvrage'), *Recherches*

pascaliennes (1949) 145 ('c'est à dire commencement de
la seconde partie de l'ouvrage projeté par Pascal').
Cf. *Controverses pascaliennes* 24 n1.

   Other eminent Pascal scholars have interpreted the
title 'Commencement' to mean that the second part begins
at section 12°: J. Mesnard (*Pascal* 146: 'La seconde
partie commence, à notre avis, au chapitre XII - intitulé
d'ailleurs *Commencement*'), Michel and Marie-Rose Le
Guern (*Les Pensées de Pascal* [1972] 130: 'Si la douzième
liasse dans les papiers classés porte le titre 'Commencement,' c'est qu'elle marque le début de la partie
proprement théologique de l'apologie'), P. Sellier
(edition [1976] 111 n1: 'Il s'agit bien d'un "Commencement," car la liasse "A.P.R." est une plaque tournante
dans le projet d'*Apologie*: concluant la réflexion
anthopologique des liasses [2° à 10°], elle annonce une
recherche plus proprement religieuse'). For my own view
of where the second part begins, see chapter 15.

7 It would be interesting to know if the word 'Commencement' is a later addition, but the manuscript of fr.
164 does not preserve it. We know it only from the
Copies.

8 Michel and Marie-Rose Le Guern question this assimilation of the 'règle des partis' with 'Infini rien' (*Les
Pensées de Pascal* 132): 'Le point d'application n'est
nullement identique. Ce n'est pas de l'existence de
Dieu qu'il est question ici, mais d'un problème beaucoup plus limité: celui du temps que l'homme a à passer
sur terre.' They believe that any suggestion as to the
place of the Wager is purely gratuitous (ibid. 54).

   Their argument has, however, not received support
from other commentators. Philippe Sellier (ed. 1976,
353 n2) calls 418, like 427, 'une dilatation interne
de la liasse "Commencement"' - which assumes without
justification that Unit II is later than 1658; however,
it is the logical connection which interests us here.
Pol Ernst and Henri Gouhier also associate no. 418
with section 12°, but as we have seen, neither is convinced that section 12° should come twelfth in the
series. They see it as an introductory chapter (*Approches
pascaliennes* 692 n6, *Blaise Pascal: Commentaires* 304).
Patricia Topliss joins no. 418 and 427, with the same
result (*The Rhetoric of Pascal* 180 n4).

9 Both these possibilities are suggested by P. Ernst,
Approches pascaliennes 217-18.

10 I would not follow those who have explained the word
   'commencement' by reference to no. 162: 'Commencer par
   plaindre les incrédules'; Pascal seems to me to be
   thinking in fr. 162 of a particular development, not
   of a significant phase in the overall apologetic design.
   Cf. P. Ernst, *Approches pascaliennes* 217-18, P. Sellier,
   edition 111 n1.

11 The manuscript of Units III and IV being lost, there
   is unfortunately no sure way to date them. They are
   usually thought to belong to Pascal's final years, but
   in chapter 32 I challenge this assumption.

12 The doubts expressed in the previous note extend to
   Units V and XI also. Units II and XXXIV and also 924
   I date 1656-7, XXIII and XXV 1657-8, XXIV 1658. The two
   fragments from Units XXIX and XXX are possibly of the
   same date; no. 748 is from 1660. For fr. 821bis see n16.

13 Or 'il y a.' Pascal wrote originally 'Il n'y a que
   deux' then crossed out 'a que deux' and substituted
   'trois.' It looks as if he meant to delete 'n' and
   'que deux.'

14 The final sentence of no. 434 ('C'est l'image de la
   condition des hommes') is not authentic. It is omitted
   by Sellier (S. 686) and Le Guern (LG 405). Cf. J.
   Mesnard, *Les Pensées de Pascal* 320 n1, and Le Guern's
   note (edition, II, 281).

15 The reference to no. 680 seems clear. I therefore disagree with Michel and Marie-Rose La Guern, who write:
   'Ce n'est pas à Montaigne qu'il pense, mais à ces
   libertins qu'il a pu recontrer dans les milieux scien-
   tifiques, dans les salons, ou dans l'entourage du duc
   de Roannez,' (*Les Pensées de Pascal* 138). The sentiment
   may indeed apply to Pascal's contemporaries, but the
   word itself comes from Montaigne (III.9). For fr. 680,
   see B. Croquette, *Pascal et Montaigne* (1974) 66 and
   p 150 nn 55-6. Croquette implies (p 150) that there
   is a connection between frags. 427 and 680, but he
   does not explicitly quote Montaigne as a source for
   the 'mollement' of fr. 427.

16 I use Lafuma's paragraph numbers (I, 439-41) although
   they are bizarre. For example, he puts para. 14 between
   15 and 16 and he gives no number to the sentence following para. 18, although it is separated from it. He
   places the marginalia along with the text, often at
   an arbitrary place. Sellier (S. 662) makes a few changes,
   but is hardly more satisfactory. Lafuma's presentation

of this fragment is, however, a great improvement on that of Brunschvicg, who rearranged the paragraphs in the Grands Ecrivains edition (Br. 194bis), having omitted the fragment entirely from his *Pensées et Opuscules*, apart from recording certain portions in footnotes as variants of the text of 427 (Br. 194).

Lafuma could have easily clarified the situation by a brief note indicating that the basic text, dictated, is formed by paras 2-4, 6-9, 13, 15, and 16. Pascal added paragraph 1 at the top, 18-20 at the bottom, and 21 in the left-hand margin level with para. 20. Para. 5 is written into the space between paras 4 and 6. Paras 11, 12, and 14 are in the left-hand margin opposite 9 and 13; para. 10 is crushed in between 9 and 13, and para. 17 between 16 and 18. The second sentence of para. 7 (numbered 22 by Lafuma, but printed along with 7!) is found in the left-hand margin level with 18; there is no sign linking them. It is impossible to guess why the paragraph numbered 15 precedes the one numbered 14 in Lafuma's edition (in fact that particular paragraph should follow para. 12), nor why in para. 15, the word 'tout puissant' has been reduced to 'puissant.'

The ms. is found in Unit XXX, following no. 821, and it would have been less confusing if Lafuma had given it a number appropriate to that position. The reason for the bizarre number 432 is that Unit IV records, after no. 431, a series of seven jottings evidently closely related to the twenty-one short paragraphs we have been considering. Lafuma takes them to be the sequel and numbers them 23 to 29; Brunschvicg (Grands Ecrivains) prints them as Br. 194ter. Sellier wisely numbers the two pages separately (S. 662, 684) defining them simply as 'deux ensembles de notes' established for fr. 427 (ed. 1976, p 370 n10). Sellier inserts the marginal additions differently from Lafuma, and runs paras 19-21 together. Brunschvicg runs 19 and 20 together.

17 See chapter 31, section (c), and 32 (n83).
18 The words 'comme qu'il y a' are wrongly indicated by Lafuma as having been struck out by Pascal.
19 G. Brunet, *Le Pari de Pascal* (Paris: Desclée de Brouwer 1956); H. Gouhier, *Blaise Pascal: Commentaires* (1966) chap. 5. In one important matter, Gouhier reads the evidence quite differently from Brunet. See Appendix E.

20 No. 422 is a personal note; the explanation of G. Brunet
(*Le Pari de Pascal* [1956] 69-71) seems to me more convincing than those of H. Gouhier (*Blaise Pascal: Commentaires* 255-6) and L.M. Heller ('La correction fraternelle' *DSS* 83 [1969] 17-24). Ideas sprout in all
directions; for this reason, Unit II is interesting
for a study of the genesis of the Apologia (see chapter
30, d). In at least one instance, we leave the preoccupations of section 12° far behind: no. 425, suggested
by the last sentence of no. 421, I use for section 22°.
21 Fr. 663 is simply a reflection suggested by reading
Descartes (M. Le Guern, *Pascal et Descartes* [1971] 61-3).
22 No. 924, known through the Recueil Original, is very
close to letters written to Mlle de Roannez in September
and December 1656, and is certainly quite independent
of the Apologia. See chapter 30, n59.
23 The title of no. 908, 'Superstition [et] concupiscence,'
links up also with no. 366 in section 27°.

CHAPTER 13

1 Cor. 1:18, 'For the preaching of the cross is to them
that perish foolishness.'
2 See chapter 30, section (f).
3 The idea comes from Grotius on Mohammed (Sister Marie
Louise Hubert, *Pascal's Unfinished Apologia* [1952] 81).
L.M. Heller's attempt to play down Grotius as a precise
source of Pascal's *pensées* on Mohammed does not invalidate Sister Hubert's observations concerning this fragment, or fr. 453 (which she discussed on pp 79-80) and
fr. 498, which names Grotius (p 80). See L.M. Heller,
'Anti-Islamic Polemic in Pascal's *Pensées*,' *Neophilologus*
55 (1971) 246-60.
4 P. Ernst, *Approches pascaliennes* (1970) 237.
5 This is another Pascalian paradox, once more inter-
weaving 'grandeur' and 'misère.' See Brigitte Wanner,
'Connaissance: conscience de l'ignorance,' *Archiv für
das Studium der neueren Sprachen und Literaturen* 213
(1976) 125-7: 'La grandeur de l'homme est la conscience
de son ignorance.'

CHAPTER 14

1 I naturally do not think the allocation of some of
these doubles to bundle 14° was made for no better

reason than that Pascal happened to be struck by a
different aspect of the thought than on the day he
filed the originals in earlier dossiers (J. Mantoy,
Des "Pensées" de Pascal à l'"Apologie" [1955] 18).

2 The words 'où il est' were crossed out by Pascal along
with the original version of the following phrase, I
assume in error. Brunschvicg made the same assumption
(Br. 693), as does Le Guern (LG 184).

3 Thus in the manuscript. Could it be a slip of the pen
for 'dans'?

4 Thus in the manuscript and most editions. Lafuma
prints 'et.'

5 The old view was to see in fr. 201 the expression of
Pascal's own anguish, what E.B.O. Borgerhoff called the
'rallying cry for the neuro-pathological interpretation
of the *Pensées*' (*Sewanee Review* 65 [1957] 23). Jeanne
Russier (*La foi selon Pascal* [1949] 8) quotes Havet
(ed., 1887, p xxx; the passage is taken over from the
1852 edition, p xxxix), Brunschvicg (note to Br. 206),
Valéry ('Variation sur une pensée,' *Revue hebdomadaire*
(14 July 1923) 161-70, and *Variétés* [1924] 137-53) and
E. Baudin, *La Philosophie de Pascal* (*Cahiers de philosophie, Etre et penser* 16 [June 1946] 51). The list is
far from exhaustive. (Cf. for example G. Duhamel, *Les
Confessions sans pénitence* [Paris: Plon 1941] 142-3.)
Mlle Russier herself doubted that the voice of fr. 201
was Pascal's own, and quoted parallel phrases in nos
427, 194, 68, and 429 which were manifestly part of a
dialogue (*La foi* 8-10). This point of view had already
been suggested by Geneviève Lewis (ed., La bonne compagnie [1947] xviii n4), following a hint of Z. Tourneur
(*Une Vie avec Blaise Pascal* [1943] 20) - she saw fr.
201 as an objection to be refuted - and by G. Chinard,
En lisant Pascal (1948) 49-53.

Since the publication of Jeanne Russier's book, it
has become commonplace to see fr. 201 as part of the
dialectic, to be attributed to the agnostic opponent.
Thus L. Lafuma (note in Luxembourg edition of 1951,
II, 41, referring to a sentence of fr. 199 which
does not appear to be very relevant), R. Pons ('La
publication authentique des *Pensées* de Pascal,' *IL* 3
[1951] 177), Marie Louise Hubert, *Pascal's Unfinished
Apology* (1952) 143, J. Mesnard, *Pascal* (1951) 169,
also *Cahiers de Royaumont* 1 (1956) 381, discussing a
paper by M. de Gandillac on 'Pascal et le silence du

monde' (see pp 348-50). Valéry's argument was answered by A. Béguin in his *Pascal par lui-même* [1952] 47-8), J. Mesnard ('Le drame de la foi chez Pascal,' *CUC* [March 1958] 313-14), J.J. Demorest, 'Pascal's Sophistry and the Sin of Poesy' in *Studies in Seventeenth-Century French Literature Presented to Morris Bishop*, ed. J.J. Demorest (Ithaca: Cornell University Press 1962) 132-52, especially 142-3, and more recently by P. Ernst (*Approches pascaliennes* [1970] 261-2), who coins the phrase 'effroi méthodique.' And so in the same year, 1970, Annie Barnes could say: 'Je croyais ... que nous étions d'accord que ce n'est pas Pascal, mais le libertin qui parle' (paper published in *CPR* 20-1 [1972] 13). Nevertheless, P. Sellier in his edition of the *Pensées* published in 1976 (p 134 n19) finds in fr. 201 an echo of feelings expressed directly in fr. 199. That the 'old' view is still current among non-specialist readers is hardly doubtful. In his book on Berlioz, Jacques Barzun speaks of the 'cry of a soul as desolate as Pascal's in the face of the infinite spaces' (*Berlioz and the Romantic Century* [Boston: Little, Brown and Co. 1950], unchanged in the 1969 edition [New York: Columbia University Press] 489). One recent example was R. Gullon's article 'On Space in the Novel' (*Critical Inquiry* 2 [1975] 17-18). As will be seen from the text, my own view is that Pascal is attributing to the atheist an anguish born of his own imagination; that is, the view which has prevailed for the last thirty years is formally correct, but partisans of the older view of the matter do have an intuition which it would be misleading to discount completely. E.B.O. Borgerhoff's commentary is particularly apt ('The reality of Pascal: The *Pensées* as Rhetoric,' *Sewanee Review* 65 [1957] 23-6).

6 Although Pol Ernst does evoke no. 68, rather unwillingly he does not exploit it sufficiently and instead of associating no. 194 with no. 198, he prefers to join it to nos 200 and 201 (*Approches pascaliennes* 262-3). He sees 194 and 201 as indicating the 'despair of the atheist,' to which the other five fragments give a reply: use your reason well (200), do not expect too much of it (199) as man is blind (198) and too much the slave of habit (193). God will provide (202). This framework seems to me seriously to undervalue no. 198, as well as to ignore obvious connections and create other more

doubtful ones. M. Guersant (edition [1954] lx-lxi)
attempts to distinguish no. 68 and no. 194 - and thereby justify Pascal's separate location of the two fragments. He says that in no. 68 Pascal wished to use
contingence to establish the fragility of human life;
in no. 194 he asks the bigger question: why is there
contingence?

7 I cannot accept the theory of J.P. Mayer that the two
halves of fr. 199 should be reversed ('Pascal relu:
un nouvel arrangement de la Pensée sur la "Disproportion de l'Homme"') *FS* 29 [1975] 257-65). No argument
of any weight is produced to support this strange contention, so clearly at odds with the plain meaning of
the text which, as we have said, is not at all difficult to summarize. See my answer to Mayer in *FS* 31
(1977) 277-80: '"La Disproportion de l'Homme:" Pascal's
Editors Defended'; and the continuation of the debate
in *FS* 32 (1978) 145-6 and 275-7. There is nothing to
add, except that I now agree that there should be a
full stop after 'considérations.' Even if it is not
wholly certain, the rest of the line is blank, implying
the end of a paragraph.

8 *Pensée* 199 was probably originally planned for an
earlier stage in the Apologia. The first title read
'Incapacité,' not 'Disproportion,' and the final sentence, characteristically incomplete, read: 'Enfin
pour consommer la preuve de notre faiblesse je finirai
par ces deux considérations.' This sentence should
probably have been deleted when the essay was moved
to its present position. The essay certainly fits better
here than it would have done in an earlier section. As
Roger Lacombe observed (*L'Apologétique de Pascal* [1958]
13-14), Pascal's aim here is not to show man as contradictory, but to stop him from studying nature. Or
rather, from studying nature for its own sake, and
exclusively. Lacombe finds it odd that Pascal should
refer to God before he has proved God. But surely Pascal
is saying that study of nature does lead man to understand that there must be a Creator. Such a conclusion
would have been premature in an earlier section, but
it is very appropriate at the stage we have now reached.

9 Scientific observations similar to those mentioned in
no. 199 are used in no. 782 (Unit XXVII) to reach conclusions about man's presumption and the need to think
differently from the majority. Two well-known notes on

Descartes echo the remarks about scientists and philosophers in no. 199: no. 84 (on back of no. 83, hence
found in the fifth *liasse*) and no. 553 (XXIII). No.
84 absorbs the dictated note 887 (XXXIV, 1656). Cf.
also 518-19 (XXIII) and in a different sphere, 681
(XXV).

10 It is not clear why Lafuma uses the title for no. 41
also, as neither Pascal's manuscript (R.O. 23) nor
the Copies justify it. Lafuma's table on p 385 implies
that there is no manuscript extant for no. 723, but it
is in fact on p 439 of the R.O.

CHAPTER 15

1 R.E. Lacombe, *L'Apologétique de Pascal* (1958), last
sentence of n54 on p 28. The Port-Royal edition combined no. 449 with nos 781, 189, 190, 192, and also
416 (see next chapter) to make up its twentieth chapter.

2 R.E. Lacombe joins 427 and 499, but sees both as a
preface (*L'Apologétique de Pascal* 35 and n80; see also
206 n10). A similar suggestion is made by Patricia
Topliss (*The Rhetoric of Pascal* [1966] 178). No. 449
is used to explain section 15° by Michel and Marie-Rose
Le Guern, *Les Pensées de Pascal* (1972) 148.

3 The Unit numbers are: 429 (III), 442, 449 (V), 463,
466, 468 (XI), 623 (XXIV), 781 (XXVII). I suspect that
they all antedate Pascal's illness, though only no.
623 is clearly in that category. See chapter 32, section (b).

4 See section 25°. The prophecies were mentioned also
in no. 180 (13°).

5 The Mémorial, Pascal's record of the experience which
led to his definitive conversion in 1654, is traditionally counted among the *Pensées* (La. 913), although it
is clearly not a public document, but rather the most
intensely personal of all the thoughts Pascal committed
to paper.

CHAPTER 16

1 H. Gouhier, *Blaise Pascal: Commentaires* (1966) 181 and
n17.

2 Cf. his introduction to his edition of *Le manuscrit
des Pensées 1662* (1962) 23: 'Pascal n'avait encore
rien classé dans une liasse prévue avec le titre "La
nature est corrompue".'

3 R. Barrault (ed.), Pascal, *Pensées*, *extraits* (Larousse
  1965) 119. Fragment 491 is also mentioned in connection
  with bundle 16° by Annie Barnes ('La table des titres
  de la Copie des *Pensées* est-elle de Pascal?,' *FS* 7
  [1953] 145), but only to make the point that anyone
  who holds Arnauld or Nicole responsible for the chapter
  title 'La nature est corrompue' has to explain why they
  should give such importance to the title of such a very
  modest fragment.
4 J. Mesnard, 'Aux origines de l'édition des *Pensées*:
  les deux Copies' in *Les Pensées de Pascal ont 300 ans*
  (1971) 29; further developed in *Les Pensées de Pascal*
  (1976) 42-3.
    P. Sellier in his edition ([1976] 30 n2, 135, 137 n6,
  372 n1) very curiously ignores Mesnard's suggestion,
  although he refers to the 1971 article in another connection (p 9). His solution of the enigma is to regard
  'La nature est corrompue' and 'Fausseté des autres
  religions' as a double title for a single section, and
  his principal candidate among the unclassed papers is
  the block formed by fragments 438-50 from Unit V, which
  he argues should not be split up and given thirteen
  numbers. No. 449 thus appears in Sellier's theory as
  part of section 16°/17°. He notes a parallel with fr.
  205 (17°). If we are right in reversing 14° and 15°,
  this reading is not markedly different from our own.
  But we have obviously kept fragments 438-50 distinct,
  and we have assigned several of them to section 19°.
  Sellier also refers us to no. 471. M. Le Guern also
  ignores Mesnard's research (edition, 1977, I,162).
5 I discuss other explanations in chapter 31, beginning
  of section (a).
6 Consequently, I repeat, all my numbers from 14° to the
  end differ from Lafuma's, usually by being one unit
  higher, but in one case (14° = Laf. XV) being one unit
  lower.
7 Fr. 1110 comes tenth in J. Mesnard's edition of *Textes
  inédits* (1962) 32; Seuil 639.
8 Cf. no. 6, in which the first part of the Apologia was
  summed up in the words 'Que la nature est corrompue.'
  The implications of this broader interpretation of the
  title of *liasse* 16° will be explored in chapter 31.

CHAPTER 17

1 P. Ernst, *Approches pascaliennes* (1970) 290.

2 Brackets added to clarify the thought.
3 No. 565 was written below the separation-line at the
  end of no. 564, on the left-hand side. Presumably there
  was once another text alongside it, but Pascal's scissors have kept no. 565 with no. 564. It is a diagram,
  unexplained, which few editions reproduce accurately.
  (Two recent exceptions: P. Sellier, ed. 1976, p 257,
  M. Le Guern, ed. 1977, II, 104.) L.M. Heller ('Anti-
  Islamic Polemic in Pascal's *Pensées*,' *Neophilologus*
  55 [1971] 248) explains it thus: 'a curious doodle ...
  depicting Pagans and Mohammed as having partially
  emerged from the uncharted wastes of Ignorance of God,
  while Christ towers above and between both, in perfect
  knowledge of God.'
4 There is no final *s* on 'misérables' in Pascal's manuscript, but the sense clearly is: in contrast to Mahomet
  who is alone, Jesus has the witness of the Jews, 'subsistants et vagabonds' (cf. 608), and 'misérables' (cf.
  311 and 793, where they are called 'd'admirables témoins').

CHAPTER 18

1 Br. 781. The same page also includes fragments 903-9.
  It is the last paper in Unit XXXIV, and grows out of
  the dispute with the Jesuits in 1656-7. See chapter
  30, n83.

CHAPTER 19

1 Fragment 921 is known to us through the Recueil Original
  and fragments 1114-15 are taken from the *Textes inédits*
  of Mesnard, 33 (Seuil, 640, nos XIV and XV). Units
  XXXIII and XXXIV go back to the preoccupation with
  miracles. Nos 734 and 735 are much later (1660).
2 Cf. no. 2 (1°): 'Je ne vois partout qu'obscurités.'
3 Fragment 781 is the 'Préface de la seconde partie,'
  and as such belongs to section 15°.
4 This helps to answer the question left hanging in the
  air by the final sentence of Henri Gouhier's chapter
  on 'Le Dieu qui se cache' (*Blaise Pascal: Commentaires*
  [1966] 243): 'Tout apparaîtrait raisonnable sauf ce
  qui rend raison de tout: qu'y a-t-il de divin, en
  effet, dans la volonté de se cacher?'
5 Gouhier, *Blaise Pascal: Commentaires* 238.

6 P. Ernst, *Approches pascaliennes* (1970) 335.
7 L. Lafuma, edition, II, 45.
8 Cf. J. Dedieu, 'Survivances et influences de l'apologétique traditionnelle dans les *Pensées*,' *RHLF* 38
  (1931) 39 n2. 'A mon sens il l'en a séparée [la théorie
  du dogme] nettement.'
9 The words *aveugler/éclaircir* are also used in no. 822
  to refer to the fact that the obscurities of the Old
  Testament are offset by passages which illuminate us.
10 It was probably in place before *liasse* 20° was devised.
  See chapter 31, section (c).
11 This phrase has given much trouble to editors. I give
  the reading of Brunschvicg, Tourneur, and Sellier. Le
  Guern gives 'J'admire (etc.).' Lafuma reads 'J'admire
  une première et auguste religion.'
12 The reading proposed by Tourneur, Sellier, and Le
  Guern seems to me to be borne out by the manuscript.
  The word is different from the 'Par' of the next sentence, and yet it is not 'De' (the traditional reading)
  either. The same comment applies to the fourth sentence,
  quoted below.

CHAPTER 20

1 A.M. Dubarle ('Pascal et l'interprétation de l'Ecriture,'
  SPT 2 [1941-2] 350) says Pascal deleted the sixth proof
  because it would interest a Christian, but not the agnostic for whom the Apologia was intended, but this
  seems to me to overlook the reappearance of the same
  idea in the title; besides, Pascal is not really addressing an agnostic any longer. J. Mesnard ('La
  théorie des figuratifs dans les *Pensées* de Pascal,'
  RHPC 35 [1943] 243 n136) actually remarks that 'il y
  a cercle vicieux à vouloir prouver par Jésus-Christ
  et les apôtres "que l'Ecriture a deux sens que Jésus-
  Christ et les apôtres ont donnés".' But there is no
  vicious circle, if the phrase were simply transferred
  from its original position as sixth proof to the title-
  line. In his recent study of the *Pensées* (p 255),
  Mesnard's argument is closer to Dubarle's: 'il a ensuite rayé ce paragraphe, sans doute parce qu'il
  n'avait pas sa place dans un raisonnement dirigé contre
  les Juifs.' Sellier omits the sentence (S. 305), but
  refers to it in n1 of p 388 in a gloss on La. 457.
2 The manuscript reads 'données,' 'corrected' to 'donné,'

but it was dictated by Pascal, and 'donnés' (as in Lafuma's edition for Seuil, Anzieu's revision of Tourneur, Sellier, and Le Guern) is plainly correct.

3 Reference is also made to nos 492 (XVIII) and 835 (XXXIII). Fr. 502-3 is one fragment, not two. See n11.

4 More exactly, Boucher's gloss on Augustine. See Le Guern's note (LG 235, I, 309), and J. Mesnard, 232, n70 of the article cited in n1 above.

5 The pronoun 'elle' in the first sentence refers to 'la loi,' and the pronoun 'ils' in the second sentence to 'la loi et les sacrifices.' Probably 'ils' should be understood in both sentences.

6 The notion contained in the heading 'Figures' was originally quite general. See the discussion in chapter 31, section (c).

7 The basic text of no. 260 consisted of two pairs of paragraphs separated by a line. No. 265 comprises two sentences, also separated by a line. The first sentence of 265 reappears, slightly amplified, at the top of no. 260, above the title, on the left-hand side of the page. The second, also amplified, reappears as the third paragraph of 260. Between the third and fourth paragraphs of no. 260 one sentence was added, before Pascal had properly embarked on his fourth paragraph. Alongside this, and the first lines of the fourth paragraph, is an additional sentence ('Les prophètes ont dit...'), usually printed just before the fourth paragraph, although in fact it is an addition to the second paragraph, making the transition between the two halves of the fragment.

8 Pascal is following the lead of Fontaine in the Royaumont Bible for no. 246 if not for no. 248 (J. Mesnard, 'La théorie des figuratifs,' *RHPC* 35 [1943] 233).

9 A note in the nineteenth bundle (223, akin to no. 389) implies that no. 255 should be moved to that dossier.

10 Le Guern's edition (II, 70) does include it. Jean Mesnard ('La théorie des figuratifs dans les *Pensées* de Pascal' 35 [1943] 243) has this to say on the title: 'Nulle part Pascal ne l'a développé; peut-être voulait-il reprendre simplement les arguments du *Pugio fidei*; peut-être a-t-il compris que cette preuve pouvait convaincre seulement des Juifs; peut-être surtout le sens spirituel atteint de cette façon lui semblait-il beaucoup trop vague; or il vise un sens très précis. Cependant, en montrant le témoignage involontaire des Juifs

en faveur des Chrétiens, Pascal aurait pu impressionner
l'incrédule.' In the following paragraph, however, I
record other observations of Pascal to which the phrase
'Preuves par les Juifs' could apply. Cf. no. 8 (1°):
'Voir ce qu'il y a de clair dans tout l'état des Juifs
et d'incontestable.'
11 The fragment entitled 'Raisons pourquoi figures' (La.
502-3) was dispersed on the Recueil Original (pp 394,
419-20, 145), and Brunschvicg, who reunited the first
three sheets (Br. 571), still kept the last separate
(Br. 675). The suspension marks with which Brunschvicg
introduced Br. 675 in the *Pensées et Opuscules* (they
do not figure in the Grands Ecrivains edition) in fact
replace the word 'trébucheront,' which was the last
word of Br. 571, and which Pascal repeated at the top
of Br. 675. Tourneur (II, 316 n4) suggests that the O
we can read (?) at the bottom of Br. 571 was probably
repeated at the beginning of Br. 675, but disappeared
when the edges were trimmed for the Recueil Original.
Lafuma, like Tourneur and Anzieu, has the second fragment follow the first directly, but he still gives the
last page a separate number (503). He repeats the word
'trébucheront' in conformity with the manuscript, yet
keeps Brunschvicg's suspension marks.
12 Probably because the last part of the Apologia had
not taken shape at the time he filed it. See chapter
31 (c).
13 Sister Marie Louise Hubert, *Pascal's Unfinished Apology*
(1952) 79-80.

CHAPTER 21

1 See Sister Marie Louise Hubert, *Pascal's Unfinished
Apology* (1952) 83.
2 It is not clear from the manuscript whether the word
'Rabins' (*sic*) refers to the sentences quoted or to
one added later: 'Où est Dieu? où vous n'êtes pas et
le royaume de Dieu est dans vous.' Sellier and Le
Guern both put it after the third sentence. Placed
where it is, however, the addition must be understood
as an illustration of the principal idea, so my gloss
is not substantially affected.
3 There are references to rabbinical teaching on the
coming of the Messiah in nos 338 (25°) and 483 (XII,
which I associated with section 25°).

CHAPTER 22

1 Unit XXXIV, early.
2 Frag. 390 comes from Unit I; the other three, though
  they belong technically to different Units (VI, IX, X)
  are all part of the expansion created by the need to
  document his ideas.
3 A marginal addition to no. 273 (made at the same time
  as the text, to judge by the writing) comes straight
  from no. 391, invoked in chapter 20.
4 I agree with H. Gouhier (*Blaise Pascal: Commentaries* [1966
  234 n41) that this word is 'pour,' not 'par.' Sellier
  (313) gives 'pour,' but Le Guern (264) maintains 'par.'
5 There are also three early notes directed against the
  Jesuits, condemning them for turning their back on
  tradition, and the word used is 'Perpétuité' (707,
  Unit XXV; 866, 871/894, Unit XXXIV). We have come
  full circle, with this reference, to the 'carnal'
  Christians, by whom true Christianity should not be
  judged. See chapter 30, end of section (e).

CHAPTER 23

1 The reference has been elucidated by B. Croquette,
  Pascal et Montaigne (1974) 43.
2 No. 1102 is the second *pensée* in the *Textes inédits*
  edited by J. Mesnard in 1962, pp 29-30. It is reproduced
  on p 639 of the Seuil edition. See P. Ernst, *Approches
  pascaliennes* (1970) 417n, and the reproduction of no.
  1102 on the facing page.
3 The first copyist read 'que,' but this was changed to
  'qui,' which is how the second copy records it (Sellier
  ed. 373 n4). 'Qui' is maintained by Sellier (688) and
  Le Guern (407), while Lafuma preferred 'que.' Cf. 481,
  quoted immediately below ('qui forme un peuple'). The
  manuscript of La. 436 is not extant.
4 *Recherches pascaliennes* (1949) 59. Cf. Luxembourg edition, II, p. 56
5 Ernst, *Approches pascaliennes* 422-5.

CHAPTER 24

1 Units XXXIII and XXXIV are early. No. 933 is known
  only through the Recueil Original. Nos 907-2 are the
  Esdras fragments, or Unit XXXV. This Unit is not recorded by Copy 9203, and hence the three fragments are
  not grouped in the Luxembourg edition, where they are
  numbered 953, 949, and 968. The Seuil edition in this
  instance follows Copy 12449. See chapter 32, n26.

2 No. 488 was originally part of no. 487, and Pascal
  moved it to the end of the fragment for reasons of
  logic. Editors have given it a separate number. I used
  it in chapter 20. See below, n10.
3 P. Ernst, *Approches pascaliennes* (1970) 436-7.
4 See chapter 31, section (c).
5 Ernst, *Approches pascaliennes* 437. For '230' read '320.'
6 The three fragments on Esdras have a similar function.
7 See chapter 30, section (e).
8 Cf. also no. 835 (XXXIII). On no. 454, see chapter 22,
  pp 229-30.
9 *Recherches pascaliennes* (1949) 48-9.
10 As well as proving him mortal and human, his death
   fulfils the prophecies - and confounds the Jews, as
   we know from chapter 20, section (c). Cf. no. 488.
11 On the lower orders (body and mind) cf. nos 58 (3°),
   698 (XXV). There is an interesting parallel in no.
   1112, where Pascal talks of 'un homme véritablement
   vertueux mais sans éclat' in connection with the
   philosophers' limited view of history.
12 Among the commentators who have used this fragment to
   characterize Pascal's own method, are L. Brunschvicg
   (Grands Ecrivains ed. of *Pensées* I, pp lvi-lvii), F.
   Strowski, *Les Pensées de Pascal* (Paris: Mellottée 1930)
   95, J. Chevalier, *Pascal* (1922) 172, J. Orcibal, 'Vers
   le Pascal de l'histoire,' *SAPR* 2 (1951) 36, H. Lefebvre,
   Pascal, II (1954) 97, R.E. Lacombe, *L'Apologétique de
   Pascal* (1958) 39 n87, H. Gouhier, *Blaise Pascal: Commentaires* (1966) 184, J. Mesnard, *Pascal* (1951) 140
   and *Les Pensées de Pascal* (1976) 168, 343, P. Sellier,
   edition of the *Pensées* (1976) 370 n9 and 377 n10. H.
   Davidson (*The Origins of Certainty* [Chicago: University
   of Chicago Press 1979] 51-2) writes: 'he adopts the
   order of the heart, but he adds a new dimension by
   intellectualizing it.' Jeanne Russier, however, found
   this assimilation of apologetic method and 'l'ordre du
   coeur' unacceptable (*La foi selon Pascal* [1949] 180),
   and L. Lafuma agreed with her ('L'ordre de l'esprit et
   l'ordre du coeur selon Pascal,' *Recherches de science
   religieuse* 46 [1958] 416-20). Lafuma believed his argument strengthened by the new reading he proposed:
   'rabaisser' for 'échauffer' in the second paragraph.
   'Le but de l'Apologie aurait été d'instruire le lecteur,
   croyant ou incroyant; Pascal ne pouvait avoir la prétention de le "rabaisser".' But Pascal is persistently
   attacking presumption, notably the presumption of the

rationalist, and I do not see why he should be disso-
ciated from the 'order' he here describes. Cf. no. 234
(18°): 'Dieu veut plus disposer la volonté que l'esprit.
la clarté parfaite servirait à l'esprit et nuirait à
la volonté. Abaisser la superbe.' Recently, J. Mesnard,
P. Sellier, and M. Le Guern have restored the word
'échauffer,' without comment (*Les Pensées de Pascal*
336; S. 329, LG 280). H. Davidson uses that form also
(p 42). For a gloss on the word 'échauffer,' see
Lacombe's note (87).

CHAPTER 25

1 The date of many of these fragments is debatable. No.
840 is definitely early (1656-7).
2 It would be relevant to quote here no. 718 ('Les
prophéties étaient équivoques; elles ne le sont plus')
if we could be sure that that reading, which comes
from the Copies, is authentic. There is another fragment, no. 880, which the Copies record as 'Les 5 propositions étaient équivoques; elles ne le sont plus,'
and the manuscript is on p 439 of the R.O. Pol Ernst
suggests that as the manuscript sentence traditionally
assigned to no. 880 originally adjoined no. 719, it
is probably the original of no. 718, wrongly deciphered
by the copyist ('Pascal au Travail' in *Méthodes chez
Pascal* 145). Where, one wonders, did the copyists find
the source of no. 880? Why should Pascal want to use
it twice? Although these questions appear to be unanswerable, Ernst's point is well taken, and Sellier
adopts the reading '5 propositions' in his edition
(S. 596).
3 This fragment is probably a draft for part of the
Abrégé de la Vie de Jésus-Christ (L. Lafuma, 'Notes
pascaliennes,' *DSS* 7-8 [1950] 208-10).
4 The rest of no. 326 - two sentences - links up with
theme of the necessity to believe, which Pascal insisted upon in his twelfth section. Cf. no. 386 and
no. 159, and see chapter 31, section (c).
5 'Tout cela' is the reading of Tourneur (T. 463),
Gouhier (*Blaise Pascal: Commentaires* [1966] 218),
Le Guern (LG 364). Lafuma and Sellier (S. 4) give
'l'avènement.' The manuscript is practically unread-
able.
6 The third sentence of fragment 385, which looks from
the manuscript as if it was an afterthought, is on the

Jews as witnesses and unwilling instruments, and was
absorbed by no. 391, cited in chapter 20, section (c)
and also in chapter 22, n3.

7 Later amplified: 'des gens qu'ils ont crus prophètes.'
8 The phrase 'les Juifs subsisteront toujours' recurs
in a marginal note made higher up the page - 'Ce qui
a précédé, ce qui a suivi, tous les juifs subsistants
et vagabonds' (La. 608) - itself echoing no. 793, in
which we can also read 'les ténèbres des juifs effroy-
ables et prédites.' Cf. chapter 19 (a). The dispersal
of the Jews was mentioned in chapter 24.
9 Cf. no. 495.

CHAPTER 26

1 The very paucity of examples provided has its advantages. Before the riches of the Copy were revealed,
Jean Mesnard could write that the 'figures particulières' are meant to indicate 'la légitimité des figures
messaniques,' citing as an example of 'figures particulières' no. 248, which shows, he said, 'par des
exemples concrets que les prophètes ne s'arrêtaient
pas à la teneur matérielle de leurs actes' ('La théorie
des figuratifs dans les *Pensées* de Pascal,' *RHPC* 35
(1943) 249 n165). We are now obliged to say that the
'figures particulières' are specific anticipations of
the life and work of Jesus.
2 P. Ernst, *Approches pascaliennes* (1970) 481. Also J.
Mesnard, *Les Pensées de Pascal* (1976) 269.

CHAPTER 27

1 The last four are known only from the Recueil Original.
Unit XXXIV is early, Units II, XXIII, XXIV, and XXV
were all extant in 1658.
2 A.M. Dubarle, 'Quelques allusions scripturaires des
Pensées de Pascal,' *SPT* 1 (1941-2) 85-7.
3 The last words supplied by Pascal's editors.
4 No. 912 was quoted in chapter 18.
5 No. 918 comes directly from St Augustine (P. Sellier,
Pascal et Saint Augustin [Paris: Colin 1970] 462-3.

CHAPTER 28

1 Fr. 975 is known only from the Port-Royal edition. The
fragments from Units XXXIII and XXXIV are early (1656-7),

those from XXIII and XXV were probably written at about
the same time.

2 For this reference, see T. Shiokawa, *Pascal et les
miracles* (Paris: Nizet 1977) 174-5.

3 Lafuma's note (II, 69) prints 883 instead of 846; 883
is the Delmas number.

4 Pascal subsequently added 'Par la Machine' to the
first line, and he interrupted his sentences at the
words 'qui fait' in order to note: 'dont la preuve est
souvent l'instrument, *fides ex auditu*, mais cette foi
est dans le coeur.'

5 Joel 2:28. Cf. fragments 301 ('effundam spiritum meum')
328 ('vos fils prophétiseront'), 498 ('Vocation des
gentils. Joel 2.28').

6 Chevalier, Tourneur (1938), Anzieu, Lafuma (Delmas),
Guersant. It is there in J. Mesnard's *Les Pensées de
Pascal* (1976) 296, but in spite of Mesnard's claim to
be presenting an authentic text ('Dans nos citations,
nous opérerons toujours automatiquement [sic] les corrections nécessaires' 7), there is definitely no exclamation mark in the manuscript, and it should be suppressed. Brunschvicg got it right, as do Sellier and
Le Guern and as did Tourneur in 1942 and Lafuma in the
Luxembourg edition; could Mesnard be relying too much
upon Anzieu?

CHAPTER 29

1 In most cases our summary is sufficiently close to our
exposition for it to be a simple matter to expand or
to verify this account by referring to the relevant
chapter. There are three exceptions which our earlier
discussion will be found to justify: (1) sections 2°,
3°, and 4° are conflated, beginning with 2°b, inserting 2°a and 2°c between 3°a and 3°b, and inserting
2°d between 3°c and 4°; (2) section 10° is inserted
between 9°a and 9°b; (3) 17°b and 19°a are placed
between 19°b and 19°c.

CHAPTER 30

1 *Préface sur le Traité du Vide*, in Pascal, *Oeuvres
complètes* ed J. Mesnard, Desclée de Brouwer, II (1970)
780. Henceforth this edition will be referred to as
O.C.

2 *O.C.* II, 555 (letter of 26 Jan. 1648).

3 J. Miel, *Pascal and Theology* (Baltimore: The Johns Hopkins Press 1969) 197.

4 H. Gouhier, *Blaise Pascal: Commentaires* (1966) 116-25.

5 Letter to Gilberte, 1 Apr. 1648. *O.C.* II, 582. On the interpretation of this letter, see T. Shiokawa, *Pascal et les Miracles* (Paris: Nizet 1977) 68-73.

6 *O.C.* II, 851-63.

7 J. Mesnard, presentation of the letter in *O.C.* II, 850.

8 Ibid. 858.

9 Ibid. 777.

10 Ibid. 923-6.

11 Pascal's correspondence with Fermat is in *O.C.* II, 1132-65, and the *Traité du Triangle arithmétique* follows, 1166-1332. On the publication, see *O.C.* I, 33-7.

12 *Entretien avec M. de Sacy*, Seuil, 296. See below, 15.

13 La. 913. The Memorial is traditionally included among the *Pensées*.

14 The famous meditation on 'Le mystère de Jésus' (La. 919) was probably written shortly after this experience. Marcel Raymond makes the interesting observation that henceforth Pascal will not allow other men to 'sleep' ('La conversion de Pascal,' *Revue de Théologie et de Philosophie* 13 [1963] 34).

15 The *Entretien avec M. de Sacy*, published by Desmolets in 1728, was recorded by Fontaine in his Mémoires (c1697, publ. 1736), and it has exercised the talents of several excellent scholars. For my part, I accept Jean Mesnard's brilliantly argued theory that the text which Fontaine put into his *Mémoires* was a written script of Pascal's which Sacy had glossed. See *O.C.* I (1964) 236-50. Two critical editions have been published: by P. Courcelle (Paris: Vrin 1960) and by A. Gounelle (Paris: PUF 1966). On the first of these one should consult the review by René Pintard, *Revue des Etudes anciennes*, 63 (1961) 541-8. Lafuma reprints the *Entretien* in the Seuil edition, 292-7. On the uneasy truce between Pascal and Port-Royal, see J. Malet 'Remarques à partir de *L'Entretien*,' *Revue du Pacifique* 1 (1975) 74-82.

16 J. Mesnard, *O.C.* I, 249: 'On a peut-être souligné trop exclusivement le rapport de *l'Entretien* avec l'apologétique pascalienne. Le problème soulevé dans cet écrit relève au fond de la pédagogie.' H. Gouhier has written well of the 'fin apologétique précise'

which he detects in the *Entretien* (*Blaise Pascal: Commentaires* [1966] 87, cf. pp 93-8).

17 Pascal might be in this category himself. Cf. fr. 520 (XXIII), written late 1656 or early 1657.

18 H. Gouhier, *Blaise Pascal: Commentaires* [1966] 97.

19 Gouhier (*Blaise Pascal: Commentaires* 167) goes so far as to say that Pascal used his notes for Sacy as an 'instrument de travail.' Some of the parallels will be mentioned below. I do not, however, mention all the parallels suggested by Gounelle in his commentary, as many of them strike me as forced.

20 See P. Courcelle, *'L'Entretien' de Pascal et Sacy: Ses sources et ses énigmes* (1960) 129-39. On no. 131, see also Y. Maeda 'L'Entretien avec M. de Sacy' in *Ecrits sur Pascal* (1959) 16-17. M. Maeda used the similarity of the *Entretien* with the opening of no. 131 to prove the authenticity of the text of the *Entretien*. He made the nice point that the text of the *Entretien* is closer to the manuscript of no. 131, which Fontaine could not have known, than to the Port-Royal edition of the *Pensées*. Courcelle was able to make the same point with regard to nos 149 and 208.

21 *O.D.* I, 70-2. The text is given in the Seuil edition of *Oeuvres complètes* 348-59, under the title of *Réflexions sur la Géométrie en général*. For the date, I follow J. Mesnard (*Les Pensées de Pascal* [1976] 355). Cf. J. Miel, *Pascal and Theology* (1969) 153 n11. The traditional date assigned was 1658-9 (G.E. IX, 231-4); Lafuma gives 1657-8 (Seuil, 348). It is interesting to find the famous denigration of geometry (G.E. X, 4-5) strikingly foreshadowed here: 'Sur quoi on peut apprendre à s'estimer à son juste prix, et former des réflexions qui valent mieux que tout le reste de la géométrie' (Seuil, 355).

22 Seuil edition of *Oeuvres complètes* 348-55.

23 'Et puisque nous ne savons ce que c'est qu'âme, corps, temps, espace, mouvement, vérité, bien ni même être...' and 'Enfin il examine si profondément les sciences, et la géométrie, dont il montra l'incertitude dans les axiomes et dans les termes qu'elle ne définit point, de centre, de mouvement, etc.' (Seuil, 294, with the 1728 text restored. Lafuma, following Bédier, gives 'comme d'étendue' for 'de centre.' See Courcelle's edition, pp 8 and 33.)

24 How do we define *être* without the word *c'est*? Cf.

Entretien, Seuil, 294 and *De l'esprit géométrique*, Seuil, 350.

25 Seuil, 355-9.

26 By the time Pascal was meditating on the problems of presenting an apologia, he was less ready to say that geometric order was 'le plus parfait entre les hommes.' 'Ordre ... Je sais un peu ce que c'est, et combien peu de gens l'entendent. Nulle science humaine ne le peut garder. Saint Thomas ne l'a pas gardé. La mathématique le garde, mais elle est inutile en sa profondeur' (694/XXV).

27 Fragments 110 and 131 were written before the *liasses* were constituted in 1658, though as the handwriting is quite dissimilar, we must not imply that they were written together. Geometrical designs in the margin of no. 110 bring it into the orbit of the work on the cycloid, which suggested to Tourneur that it was written after June 1658 – but it could be that Pascal used the first page to hand, and he was then in the process of filing no. 110. Cf. Z. Tourneur, édition paléographique (1942) 196 n2, also P.L. Couchoud, *Discours de la condition de l'homme* (1948) 25. On the date of nos 418-26, see below, n82.

28 The identification of no. 76 with the 'lettre de la folie de la science humaine et de la philosophie' of no. 408 is suggested by the two brief quotations given in no. 408, as they are repeated in full in no. 76. On the question which came first, see chapter 31, n30. Fr. 60 can be identified with another 'letter,' on similar grounds: the 'lettre de l'injustice,' no. 9.

29 It is not wholly evident which part of no. 76 came first – the full page or the half page. Most editors put the full page first, and it certainly makes much more sense like that. Philippe Sellier, however (edition [1976] 68 n25), has argued for the other reading. If, as seems plausible, the two sheets, now separate (R.O. 69-70, 365-6), were originally a single large sheet, and Pascal had covered pages 1, 3, and part of 4 with no. 60, Sellier's interpretation would mean that he completed p 4 first, and then went back to p 2. I adopt the usual reading.

30 When Pascal came to file his *pensées*, he chose to preserve no. 60 (in *liasse* 3°) and delete no. 76. Before he did that, however, he wished the two to be run together in some way. In the margin, adjoining the second

half of page 2 (the paragraph on the incomprehensibility of the soul), Pascal wrote 'transposer après les
lois article suivant.' P.L. Couchoud (*Discours de la
condition de l'homme* 16) takes the 'titre (*sic*) suivant'
to mean the whole of that 'Seconde partie' noted by no.
148: 'Que l'homme sans la foi ne peut connaître le vrai
bien, ni la justice.' It is certainly striking that the
Sovereign Good and Justice are joined both on the paper
60-76 and in no. 148, but Couchoud's theory does not
work out happily in practice. Most editors and scholars
agree that 'les lois' is a reference to no. 60, but
they have interpreted the instruction in a variety of
ways. The obvious meaning is: to take out the paragraph
in question and put it immediately after no. 60, which
is to follow no. 76. That is B. Croquette's interpretation (*Pascal et Montaigne* [1974] 98). Editors have,
however, been reluctant to follow Pascal, and they extend the instruction to cover the whole of no. 76.
Tourneur put the first part (only) of no. 76 immediately
before no. 60 (T. 56-7) and added a characteristically
unclear note (p 36, end of n2 of p 35); Anzieu, more
faithful to Pascal's words, put all of no. 76 immediately after no. 60 (A. 59-60). Le Guern follows Tourneur (LG 56, and 262 n1).

As Pascal deleted no. 76, there is much to be said
for following the Copies, as Lafuma and Sellier do,
and relegating no. 76 to the end of the section. (In
his reproduction of the manuscript, published in 1962,
Lafuma was unable to do this satisfactorily, and the
half-page had to stay with no. 60.)

B. Croquette makes the interesting observation (p 98,
cf. pp 15 and 20) that both sides of the first sheet,
ie, the first part of both fragments 60 and 76, are
based on the same passage from the *Apologie de Raymond
Sebond*.

31 Ed. Anzieu, 40 n1.
32 The whole passage is modelled on Montaigne, *L'Apologie
de Raymond Sebond*, supplemented by the essay 'De juger
de la mort d'autrui' (III.13). One quotation Pascal
knew through Montaigne's essay 'De l'utile et de l'honnête' (III.1); he had noted it among the jottings preserved in Unit XX (507).
33 Couchoud believes this subject to be the 'deux infinis'
(no. 199) which in the hypothetical Discourse would
precede no. 76 (*Discours de la condition de l'homme* 16).

34 Cf. *De l'esprit géométrique* 350: 'La géométrie ... ne
définit aucune de ces choses, espace, temps, mouvement,
nombre, égalité, ni les semblables qui sont en grand
nombre, parce que ces termes-là désignent si naturellement les choses qu'ils signifient, à ceux qui entendent
la langue, que l'éclaircissement qu'on en voudrait
faire apporterait plus d'obscurité que d'instruction.'
Along with the opening sentence of no. 109, Pascal
deleted the title 'Ordre' and substituted 'Contre le
pyrrhonisme.' P.L. Couchoud (*Discours de la condition
de l'homme* 21) reads the new title as 'Contre le pyrrhonisme 2' but the hieroglyphic he, like Tourneur (1938
edition, 52 nl), interprets as '2' (and which Lafuma
omits, as does Tourneur in his paleographic edition)
is not aligned with the new title and could just as
well be the bottom portion of a squiggle removed by
the scissors. Or it could be part of the original title
('Ordre'): it is on the same line, and is written in
the same ink. And is it relevant to mention that on
the other side of the sheet we can read '1 La Raison'?

35 Cf. *L'Entretien* 294: 'Et puisque nous ne savons ce que
c'est qu'âme, corps, temps, espace, mouvement, vérité,
bien, ni même être, ni expliquer l'idée que nous nous
en formons, comment nous assurons-nous qu'elle est la
même dans tous les hommes, vu que nous n'en avons
d'autre marque que l'uniformité des conséquences, qui
n'est pas toujours un signe de celle des principes?
car ils peuvent bien être différents et conduire néanmoins aux même conclusions, chacun sachant que le vrai
se conclut souvent du faux.'

36 'le raisonnement bien conduit portait à les croire,
quoi-qu'il les faille croire sans l'aide du raisonnement' *O.C.* II, 555.

37 *De l'esprit géométrique*, Seuil, 351.

38 *Entretien*, Seuil, 296.

39 Ibid.

40 Tourneur actually moved no. 208, which Pascal filed
in *liasse* 17°, to make it follow no. 131 (T. 125bis,
I, 67). Both fragments are on paper with the same
watermark. The sentence quoted was crossed out.

41 H. Coulet argues plausibly from the variants of a
phrase found three times in the manuscript ('l'homme
passe l'homme,' 'concevons donc que l'homme passe
infiniment l'homme,' [sachez] apprenez que l'homme
passe infiniment l'homme') that the page of 131

described above was corrected after the sequel had been written and revised ('Pascal écrivant,' *Annales de la Faculté des Lettres d'Aix* 37 [1963] 157).

42 H. Coulet (pp 156-7) suggests that the most logical solution would be to remove the recto side only of the last page, so that fr. 208 still follows fr. 131, but with the 'Car enfin' passage as its sequel. It is, however, unsatisfactory to have the verso ('D'où il paraît...') follow anything but the paragraph on the inconceivable mystery of original sin. Maybe it was for that reason that Pascal struck out the whole of the verso side.

43 Cf. *Entretien* 'l'état de l'homme à présent diffère de celui de sa création' (p 296). See chapter 31, n39.

44 P.L. Couchoud, *Discours de la condition de l'homme.*

45 See A. Béguin, 'Etudes pascaliennes' in *Critique* 4 (1948) 881-4, L. Lafuma, *Controverses pascaliennes* (1952) 76-9, R. Pons, 'Les manuscrits de Pascal,' *CUC* (Mar. 1950) 54-6, D. Anzieu, 'Pascal mystifié,' *Annales de l'Université de Paris* 37 (1967) 196.

46 Both sheets of fr. 199 are marked with the letter H and also with the number 9, encircled. Couchoud saw them as linked, and interpreted them, quite instinctively, as 'Discours sur l'Homme, chapter 9.' He overlooked two similar indications, where the letter and the number are joined: 'H.3.' and 'H.5' (nos 200 and 198). It is, frankly, difficult to fit no. 198 and the sequel it implies into the early stages of a Discourse on Man. Curiously, although Couchoud's hypothesis is discounted, at least in the precise form he gave it, his implied explanation of the letter H seems to have stuck (see, for example, the editions of P. Sellier, 1976, p 125 n5, and M. Le Guern, 1977, I, 297, n1 to LG 184). In this respect one might note also that towards the bottom right-hand side of the verso of no. 109 is the note 'l la Raison,' encircled in exactly the same way as the 9 of no. 199, and that the figure 13 found three times on no. 76 is decorated similarly.

47 This evidently follows something on the inadequacy of reason as an instrument for understanding the natural world, cf. 76. Couchoud allocates no. 76 to a later chapter in the *Discourse*, and nos 109 and 110, which would seem to be connected, to a much later stage still.

48 'C'est ce qui nous rend incapables de savoir certainement et d'ignorer absolument.' Cf. 131: 'Incapables

d'ignorer absolument et de savoir certainement.' The idea goes back to the *Entretien* (Seuil, 293).

49 On the manuscript is a figure 13 (similar to the 9 of H9 [no. 199]) written over the figure 12.

50 No. 47 is a secular parallel to a paragraph in a letter Pascal wrote to Mlle Roannez, Seuil, 270, letter VIII (? January 1657). No. 47 is clearly the later version.

51 Note the reference (no. 45) to a 'chapitre des puissances trompeuses.'

52 'Ils se soutiennent tous entre le néant et l'infini, étant toujours infiniment éloignés de ces extrêmes' (Seuil, 352).

53 Here again, cf. the second page of no. 149: 'Tout ce qui est incompréhensible ne laisse pas d'être. Le nombre infini.'

54 This theme comes in the sequel to the page of no. 149 discussed above.

55 The phrase is incomplete, but Pascal's thought is clear.

56 See letter 4: 'Faut-il recourir à l'Ecriture pour montrer une chose si claire? Ce n'est pas ici un point de foi, ni même de raisonnement. C'est une chose de fait. Nous le voyons, nous le savons, nous le sentons' (ed. L. Cognet [Paris: Garnier 1965] 63). The phrase 'ni même de raisonnement' put us in mind also of *De l'esprit géométrique*, as does the first paragraph of the same letter 4, with its careful distinction between a definition and a description. 'Oui, dit le Père, c'est à dire que vous voulez que je substitue la définition à la place au défini; cela ne change jamais le sens du discours, je le veux bien' (ed. L. Cognet, 55, cf. *Esp. Géom.*, Seuil, 349). There is a nice irony here, Pascal attributing to a fictitious Jesuit a rational attitude which he had found wanting in a Jesuit eight years before (Lettre au très révérend Père Noël, 29 Oct. 1647, *O.C. II*, 518-27).

57 In Letter 4, Pascal wonders what effect certain aspects of Jesuit teaching will have on 'ces libertins qui ne cherchent qu'à douter de la religion' (ed. L. Cognet, 61).

58 On the period of the miracles, see H. Gouhier, *Blaise Pascal: Commentaires* 131-67, and T. Shiokawa, *Pascal et les Miracles* (Paris: Nizet 1977), an essential work. If I go over the same ground again, it is because I

have a slightly different view of the evolution which
took Pascal from a project on miracles to the Apologia
itself.

59 This reaction is referred to in the *Rabat-Joie des
Jansénistes* 5 (see next note). See Mère Angélique's
letter to the Queen of Poland of 5 May 1656 (G.E. IV,
348-50), and T. Shiokawa, *Pascal et les Miracles* 97,
99-100.

There is a paper of which only a short extract is
recorded by the copies - the rest is known through the
Recueil Original (10 K) - which is headed 'Sur le
miracle.' Although I am associating it with the Port-
Royalists' first reactions, it may have been provoked
by the official confirmation of the miracle late in
October (Shiokawa, 135). It contains the following
moving wish: 'Comme Dieu n'a pas rendu de famille plus
heureuse, qu'il fasse aussi qu'il n'en trouve point de
plus reconnaissante.' Lafuma gives that sentence the
number 922. Below it comes 923, accusing the Jesuits
of avoiding the judgment of both God and the Church
by deviousness. On the verso, no. 924, very different,
concerns the difficulty of the devout life. Letters
written to Mlle de Roannez on 24 Sept. and 24 Dec.
echo this paragraph. This intimate text was kept to
one side by Pascal's heirs, and hence never reached
the yes of the copyists. They did, however, allow the
bottom of the page (blank on the side where 924 is
written, but containing on the other side the last
lines of 923) to remain in place, and the Copies record
it between fragments 601 and 602 in Unit XXIV. Editors
have reacted differently to this confusing situation.
Lafuma, in his note to no. 923 says the text is known
in part by the Copy, but gave no further explanation.
Sellier follows the second Copy faithfully, and trans-
cribes the last lines of 923 after no. 601 as S.499.
Curiously, there is no note, and no Lafuma number in
the Concordance. The note to fr. 923 (S. 753) gives
the desired information. Le Guern (LG 514) puts all of
922-4 into Unit XXIV. Really only 922-3 belong there,
as we have seen. Le Guern also inverts the words 'impies' and 'indignes' in no. 923.

60 On these pamphlets and their attribution, see H.
Gouhier *Blaise Pascal: Commentaires* 151-61, nn9, 10,
20, 24, 32; T. Shiokawa, *Pascal et les Miracles* 103-16,
and nn106, 114, 131; and A. Arnauld, *Oeuvres* XXIII

(1779) vii-viii. The brief titles are: *Le Rabat-joie
des jansénistes*, *Réponse à un écrit publie sur le
sujet des miracles*, the Jesuit *Défense de la Vérité
catholique*, and Arnauld's *De l'autorité des miracles*
(XXIII, 33-82).

61 C. de Lingendes, *Concionum in Quadragesinam* (1661)
II, 1-55, *Sermons sur tous les Evangiles du Carême*
(1666) I, 156-78. On Lingendes it is essential to
consult Shiokawa, who has discovered that the Latin
text of his sermons is considerably more apposite than
the abridged French version published in 1666 (*Pascal
et les Miracles* 113-15, 136-52). Cf. H. Gouhier, *Blaise
Pascal: Commentaires* 159 nn39-40.

62 It comes towards the end of the sixteenth letter: 'Vous
calomniez celles qui n'ont point d'oreilles pour vous
ouïr, ni de bouche pour vous répondre. Mais Jésus-
Christ, en qui elles sont cachées pour ne paraître
qu'un jour avec lui, vous écoute et répond pour elles.
On l'entend aujourd'hui, cette voix sainte et terrible,
qui étonne la nature et qui console l'Eglise. Et je
crains, mes Pères, que ceux qui endurcissent leurs
coeurs, et qui refusent avec opiniâtreté de l'ouïr quand
il parle en Dieu, ne soient forcés de l'ouïr avec
effroi quand il leur parlera en Juge' (p 322). There
is a sketch for part of this paragraph in fr. 902. It
is sometimes assumed that Pascal toyed with the idea
of writing a *Provinciale* about miracles (H. Gouhier,
Blaise Pascal: Commentaires 161, also J. Orcibal,
'Vers le Pascal de l'histoire,' *Société des Amis de
Port-Royal* 2 [1951] 34-5 and P.L. Couchoud, 'La crise
des *Pensées* de Pascal,' *Le Flambeau* 38 [1955] 179).
But the only reason for thinking that Pascal would
have inserted his opuscule on miracles into the series
of *Provinciales* is that a phrase of 859 is addressed
to 'Mes Révérends Pères,' like Letters 11 to 16, and
that no. 840 is addressed to 'Mon père.' It seems
stretching the evidence too far to assume, with Lafuma
(*Histoire des Pensées* [1954] 91) that the singular
('Mon Père') brings fr. 840 into the same orbit as the
seventeenth and eighteenth *Provinciales* (early 1657),
which were both addressed to le Père Annat. These two
letters are a direct reply to *La Bonne foi des Jansénistes* whereas the context of fr. 840 is quite different.
In his note to fr. 840 (Luxembourg II, 157), Lafuma
identifies the Jesuit father again as Annat, but

specifically in his role of author of *Le Rabat-joie des Jansénistes*. *Le Rabat-Joie* preceded *La Bonne Foi* by four months, and the *Provinciales* of that period steer clear of the subject of miracles. In short the two vocatives of Unit XXXIII hardly constitute evidence of an embryonic *Provinciale*. In both cases the vocative could simply be a natural form to use when one is writing in the midst of a war of pamphlets. It must be admitted, however, that Lafuma's associations do fit with what we can deduce about the dating of the fragments in question, fr. 859 being probably written in 1658, and 840 in 1657.

63 There is no serious reason to believe that Pascal collaborated on the *Réponse*. For the sources of this and other attributions, see H. Gouhier, *Blaise Pascal: Commentaires* 152 n10. L. Cognet was sceptical (ed. of *Les Provinciales* [1965] liii). T. Shiokawa remarks that the most reliable witnesses point to Antoine Le Maître as the author (*Pascal et les Miracles* 106 n114).

64 Units XXXIII and XXXIV (Seuil numbering; in the Luxembourg edition they appear as XXXII and XXXIII) are actually *liasses* complete with pin-holes, often in the bottom quarter of the page. Only seven of the twenty-eight pages bear no apparent traces of pin-holes: those containing fragments 834, 835-6, 850, 851, 855, 856, and 880.

The papers which make up these two Units – sixteen in Unit XXXIII, twelve in Unit XXXIV – all contain thoughts on miracles. Many contain thoughts on other subjects too – notes for the *Provinciales*, which set them in their context, or notes on other topics, which show how the reflection on miracles led Pascal to move in other directions.

Brunschvicg naturally divided them up and redistributed them, each separation necessitating a distinct number. Lafuma brought them together again, but gave them as many numbers as they had with Brunschvicg. More consistently, Sellier and Le Guern give the same number to all the fragments which were written down on the same page, though Sellier distinguishes material on the recto and verso of a single sheet.

65 There are some *pensées* on miracles in Units XXIII and XXV, and a few of these can be safely attributed to the same period as Units XXXIII and XXXIV: see below, n69.

66 The dating of the papers on miracles poses an apparently
   insoluble problem. Between the autumn of 1656 and the
   following Easter, a fairly intense debate went on between the Jesuits and the Jansenists on the subject of
   the correct interpretation of the Port-Royal miracle.
   Pascal's thoughts on the subject are contained for the
   most part in two dossiers (Units XXXIII and XXXIV):
   twenty-six sheets recording eighty-one fragments in
   Lafuma's numbering. Some of the sheets can be dated
   to within a month or so by reference to the *Provinciales*.
   One such is the bottom sheet of all, nos 903-12. No.
   903, a series of jottings encircling no. 904, and probably written about the same time, contains the germ
   of many characteristic ideas on miracles. These are
   often developed elsewhere. In some instances, Pascal's
   further development touches on ideas which surfaced
   in the public debate in 1657. This first discrepancy
   in the dates can easily be resolved if we say that
   Pascal did not need the stimulus of Arnauld to arrive
   at similar conclusions himself. Among the *pensées*
   which could have flowed naturally out of no. 903 is
   another seminal one, no. 840. Unfortunately, this
   theory does not account for everything. The last stage
   in the public debate was the sermon of Lingendes, and
   Pascal refers to Lingendes (who is now known to have
   intervened before this) both in a doctrinal questionnaire he submitted to Barcos (830-1, Unit XXXII) and
   in no. 878 (on the back of 877). The words of the
   questionnaire are echoed in no. 891, on a sheet which
   contains ten fragments (882-91), and includes one note
   (884) on the persecution of the nuns, a motif usually
   associated with the 1656 fragments. What is disturbing
   is that nos 877-8 contain so many parallels with the
   fragments I have assigned to 1656, that I am bound to
   say that had Pascal not mentioned Lingendes, I would
   have confidently included this page with the others.
   Should I therefore revise my dating of the other sheets?
   This would be unwise, as several of them do link up
   with themes I cannot avoid allocating to 1656. Fortunately, as I have said, our lack of precision, while
   it is regrettable, does not affect our understanding
   of the genesis of the Apologia to any significant extent.
67 Cf. fr. 834 'Fondement de la religion. C'est les miracles,' and fr. 872 'L'Eglise est sans preuve s'ils
   ont raison.'

68 Although not for St Paul, who dwells on the miracle of his own conversion (903b).
69 Cf. Jean Mesnard, 'A l'origine des *Pensées*: les deux Copies' in *Les Pensées de Pascal ont 300 ans* (1979) 28, and *Les Pensées de Pascal* (1976) 39-40, 49-50. Roger Pons remarked in 1950 that in the 'Series' the notes on miracles 'sont les seules à être restées groupées. Pascal a donc dépassé, puis rejeté son point de départ' ('Les manuscrits de Pascal' *CUC* [Mar. 1950] 54). L. Lafuma believed that Pascal would have returned to the subject, treating it in a non-polemical way (*Recherches pascaliennes* [1949] 49).

It is clear that miracles do have their appointed place in Pascal's overall scheme, and that the general observations of 1656 bore fruit. There is, however, no evidence of a continuous development. Only three fragments of the first thirty-one Units look as if they belong to the period that we have been discussing: 568 (XXIII) 'Il n'est pas possible de croire raisonnablement contre les miracles' surrounded by thoughts on the authority of the pope (567, 569); 726 (XXV) which is close to 567b: 'L'unité et la multitude, *duo aut tres in norum*, erreur à exclure l'un des deux...': 'Papes. Dieu ne fait point de miracles dans la conduite ordinaire de son Eglise. C'en serait un étrange si l'infaillibilité était dans un, mais d'être dans la multitude cela paraît si naturel, que la conduite de Dieu est cachée sous la nature, comme en tous ses autres ouvrages'; 648 (XXV) entitled 'Miracles' in which Pascal says it is nver pleasant to be out of step, and exceptions have to be scrutinized very carefully - but fairly. No. 574 (which I shall be quoting shortly) answers those who say they would believe if they could be shown a miracle. It is located close to no. 568 in Unit XXIII. Miracles are mentioned on other occasions, but the theme is not treated with any fullness. Pascal talks of belief in miracles in fragment 734 (XXVI), but that was written much later (see chapter 32, page 406 and n54).
70 Cf. also no. 425 in Unit II: 'la seule qui ait toujours subsisté parmi les hommes.' Also 421, last sentence.
71 On no. 960 (Lux. 962), notes which were partly used for the twelfth *Provinciale* (9 Sept. 1656), Pascal wrote: 'il y a quelque chose de surnaturel en un tel aveuglement.'

72 Cf. 841: 'Ainsi ceux qui refusent de croire les miracles d'aujourd'hui pour une prétendue contradiction
chimérique ne sont pas excusés.'

73 'Tout se passe alors comme si la question des miracles
s'élevait au-dessus du contexte d'une polémique occa-
sionnelle pour se situer dans le contexte d'une apologétique générale, et ceci simplement parce que Pascal
traite de la signification des miracles en tant qu'elle
concerne un des fondements de la foi' (H. Gouhier,
Blaise Pascal: Commentaires 166).

74 Cf. no. 131 (deleted): 'Qu'on accorde donc aux pyrrhoniens que la vérité n'est pas de notre portée, ni
de notre gibier, qu'elle ne demeure pas en terre...'

75 The Sentence was dated 22 Oct., and Pascal wrote to
Mlle de Roannez as soon as he had seen the text, probably on the evening of Thursday the 26th (see also
next note). This is the date proposed by P. Sellier;
J. Mesnard had proposed Sunday the 29th. (J. Mesnard
Pascal et les Roannez [1965] 471-2, and for a commentary on the paragraph which concerns us, pp 542-3;
P. Sellier, *Pascal et la Liturgie* [Paris: PUF 1966]
68-70). For the letter in question, see Seuil, 267,
where it is numbered IV.

76 The phrase 'deus absconditus,' quoted (in French) in
the letter to Mlle de Roannez, is found on another
fragment: 'Toute condition et même les martyrs ont à
craindre par l'Ecriture. La peine du purgatoire la
plus grande est l'incertitude du jugement. Deus absconditus.' That this fragment (921) dates from the
same period is suggested by the words 'Mes pères,'
which are written on the verso (Z. Tourneur, ed.
paléographique [1942] 26 n2). Although the expression
'Deus absconditus' is biblical (Is. 45:15), P. Sellier
suggests that the precise source is the hymn 'Adoro
te devote, latens Deitas' from the liturgy of the Holy
Sacrament, celebrated on Thursday, 26 Oct. (*Pascal et
la Liturgie* 69).

77 L. Cognet (ed. p 314 n3) thought the attribution of
the quotation was a mistake. H.F. Stewart in his edition of the *Provinciales* ([Manchester 1919] 320, note
p 201) gave the source as *Liber formularum spiritualis
intelligentiae* (Migne, *Patrologiae, cursus completus,
patres latini* 50 [1846] col. 746). But the reference
is wrong, and with a work of about 300,000 columns, a
wrong reference is virtually lost for ever. T. Shiokawa

has however solved the mystery (*Pascal et les miracles*
170 n164): it is a false attribution due to Du Perron
(*Traité du Saint Sacrement de l'Eucharistie* [1622] 5;
cf. p 423), whom Pascal is summarizing at this point.
The real author is Saint Bruno, *Homilia* XXXIV (Migne,
165 [1854] col. 790-1).

78 The allusion is expanded slightly in no. 563 (XXIII)
entitled 'Hérétiques.' Sellier refers us to Ezekiel
ch. 22, but there is nothing there, or indeed elsewhere in the Old Testament, which brings the ideas
together in the way Pascal describes.

79 This develops an idea found in one of the separate
fragments of no. 903, and it will reappear in no. 573
(XXIII). Before making this addition, Pascal had written that miracles are a sign of our need to involve
the body as well as the mind, and he added: 'figure
des sacrements.'

80 On the epistemology of the eighteenth Letter, see E.
Bloomberg, 'Les sens, la raison et la foi dans le 18^e
Provinciale,' *Orbis Litterarum* 30 (1975) 40-50. The
view that the ideas expressed in the eighteenth *Provinciale* are to be identified with what is called a doctrine of the three orders has been seriously challenged
by Janet Morgan, 'Pascal's Three Orders,' *MLR* 73 (1978)
755-66.

81 I have already quoted no. 960; 'il y a quelque chose
de surnaturel dans un tel aveuglement.' Fr. 964 (Lux.
966) also notes 'aveuglement surnaturel.' The idea
goes back at least as far as 1 Apr. 1648, when Pascal
wrote to Gilberte of 'cet aveuglement charnel et judaïque qui fait prendre la figure pour la réalité'
(*O.C.* II, 583). It may have been brought into prominence by meditating on the healing of the man who was
born blind (John 9, cf. 840, 903), which story may have
seemed particularly significant by virtue of Marguerite
miraculous cure. The word 'aveuglement' reappears with
the same implication in 893, and the verb in 841 and
892 as well as 893.

82 Many different dates have been proposed for the 'Infini
rien' essay, ranging from 1654 to 1658 or even later.
See H. Gouhier, *Blaise Pascal: Commentaires* 249-50 and
notes. Since Gouhier's book, Michel and Marie-Rose Le
Guern have opted for 1655 (*Les Pensées de Pascal* 34),
and Sellier, holding that Copy 12449 respects the
chronology of composition, feels obliged to include

it among the 'développements de 1659-1662' (ed. pp
351-60). I agree with Gouhier (p 251) that some importance should be attached to Brunet's observation (see
n92) that other papers with the same watermark as Unit
II are clearly relevant to the work of late 1656. I
shall return to this group of papers in section (g).
Here I content myself with observing that it includes
nos 903-12 (Unit XXXIV) and also no. 960 (Lux. 962),
which records Pascal's reaction to Jesuit accusations
of imposture, answered publicly in the twelfth *Provinciale* on 9 Sept., and which contains many notes used
in subsequent *Provinciales*. L. Cognet (ed. *Provinciales* [1965] xlviii) has suggested that the last sentence of 418 is very likely a rejoinder to an accusation made in a Jesuit pamphlet of May 1656. Nor does
the mathematical bias of the long development given
to the text of 418 oblige us to abandon the date of
1656. See the Grands Ecrivains edition (V, 415-21)
for evidence that Pascal's interest in these questions
was still alive at that time. It is not likely to be
later than 1658, because several of the ideas contained
in the satellites are developed in the classified fragments. In one instance Pascal copied a *pensée*, improv-
ing the text as he did so (425 = 284).

83 This aspect also can be traced back to August 1656 and
the *Rabat-Joie*. Port-Royal was accused of denying that
Jesus died for all men, which was the Calvinist reading of the five condemned propositions which Port-Royal
always maintained were not meant to be taken in that
sense. Pascal defines his position on the universality
of redemption in nos 910-12, on a paper which includes
ideas used in twelfth and thirteenth *Provinciales*.

84 Fr. 842 reappears as no. 291 (23°) with one antithesis
reserved for the Conclusion: 'les miracles ne servent
pas à convertir mais à condamner' (379). Fr. 835 has
a clear echo in no. 236 (19°).

85 Cf. the end of the twelfth *Provinciale*: 'C'est une
étrange et longue guerre que celle où la violence
essaye d'opprimer la vérité' (ed. Cognet, 234).

86 In the tenth *Provinciale* (2 Aug. 1656), the Jesuit is
made to say: 'C'est ainsi que nos Pères ont déchargé
les hommes de l'obligation *pénible* d'aimer Dieu actuel-
lement ... Cette dispense de l'obligation *fâcheuse*
d'aimer Dieu est le privilège de la loi evangélique
par dessus la judaïque' (pp 189-90). To which the

writer comments: 'C'est le comble de l'impiété' (p 191) Cf. letter 17: 'Je vous dis que vous anéantissez la Morale Chrétienne en la séparant de l'amour de Dieu dont vous dispensez les hommes' (p 331).

87 Holy fear arises when one believes in God; it is tempered by hope. Unholy fear is experienced by a man who doubts the existence of God, yet lives in fear that he may be wrong.

88 T. Shiokawa, *Pascal et les Miracles* chap. 5, especially pp 204-6.

89 Thus, Henri Gouhier deals with this stage in the development of the Apologia under the title 'Les deux apologétiques' (*Blaise Pascal: Commentaires* 163-73). P.L. Couchoud had spoken of 'deux courants de pensée destinés à s'amplifier et à se réunir' ('La crise des *Pensées* de Pascal,' *Le Flambeau* 38 [1955] 178).

90 A fragment in the other dossier (847) distinguishes our experience of falsehood from our experience of injustice in a more nuanced way, and looks forward to the opening chapters of the Apologia.

91 But see the observations of P. Ernst, 'Pascal au travail,' in *Méthodes chez Pascal* (1979) 149-50.

92 See the paleographic edition of Z. Tourneur (1942) 162 n9, and G. Brunet, *Le Pari de Pascal* (1956) 48-51. Brunet does not mention all the fragments with this watermark, as he did not see that nos 903-12 (R.O. 343-4) and no. 960 (Lux. 962, R.O. 397-8, Tourneur, p 41 n7) belong in the same category.

93 Tourneur, édition paléographique, 66 n2.

94 'Que vous êtes aise de savoir les règles générales pensant par là jeter le trouble et rendre tout inutile. On vous en empêchera, mon Père, la vérité est une et ferme.'

95 516: One would like to think the pope infallible for doctrine, and 'les docteurs graves' for judgments on behaviour. (The 'docteurs graves' are familiar to readers of the *Provinciales*, especially letter 6, but also letters 5, 13, 14, 17.) 517: St Augustine came at the right time, as today he would get nowhere.

96 No. 524 alludes to an Essay by Montaigne (I.31).

97 Tourneur, édition paléographique, 233 n9 and 301 n2.

98 Cf. the definition of conversion (378) quoted at the end of the previous section.

99 The tracking down of watermarks produces one other group. Most of the papers on miracles (832-4, 835-6,

837-9, 840, 841, 842-5, 846, 851, 854, 855, 857-8,
881, 901-2) have the mark BC/DV. So does 604 (XXIV)
entitled 'Eglise, pape' ('Il n'y a presque plus que
la France où il soit permis de dire que le concile
est au-dessus du pape') and 52 (2°) on Pyrrhonism.
It is not difficult to believe that these thoughts
date from the same period. But when the same watermark
leads to 205, 257-9, 372, 486, 500-1, and 502 (first
page), I feel we must be prudent.

100 Fr. 885, in the same writing as 891, and manifestly
the first fragment on the page (Pascal's cross is
visible just before it), remarks on the flagrant injustice of the Molinists. On the verso, scribbled
sideways, is an observation on the nuns, whose piety
is further indicated by being persecuted (884). Clearly
we are still in familiar territory.

   Fr. 886 and 887 follow fr. 885. They were dictated,
and grossly misspelled. Pascal crossed them out and
rewrote them to the right.

101 It is tempting to link the first (886) with 896: 'Pyrrhonisme est le remède à ce mal et rabattra cette vanité,'
the *mal* in question being apparently the accusations
of Calvinism levelled against the Port-Royalists. The
one on Descartes (887) would seem to be directed more
against the *honnête homme* who trusts him. It has been
suggested that from the context, the reference to
Descartes would appear to be to his ideas on grace and
the Eucharist, but this is not self-evident (F. Strowski,
Les Pensées de Pascal [1930] 70-1). M. Le Guern says
simply that 'il est impossible de rattacher [le fragment 887] à une idée particulière ou à une oeuvre précise' (*Pascal et Descartes* 42).

102 The quotation is from Ecclesiastes as modified by the
text of the Liturgy for the Feast of the Assumption
(P. Sellier, *Pascal et la Liturgie* 29).

103 This date for the start of serious work on the Apologia
is attested by Gilberte (*Vie de Monsieur Pascal*, O.C.
I, 622): 'il avait environ trente-quatre ans quand il
commença de s'y appliquer. Il employa un an entier à
s'y préparer en la manière que ses autres occupations
lui permettaient, qui était de recueillir les différentes pensées qui lui venaient là-dessus; et à la fin
de l'année, c'est à dire la trente-cinquième, qui était
la cinquième de sa retraite, il retomba dans ses incommodités d'une manière si accablante qu'il ne put

plus rien faire les quatre années qu'il vécut encore.'
Pascal's thirty-fourth birthday fell on 19 June 1657.
Lafuma comments: 'Si elle écrit "environ trente-quatre
ans," c'est que vraisemblablement c'est seulement à
cette date que cet ouvrage devint sa préoccupation
principale, aussitôt après l'arrêt brusque des *Provinciales* (avril 1657)' (*Histoire des Pensées de Pascal*
22).

Gilberte's account of what happened twelve months
later is less trustworthy. See chapter 31, n88.

CHAPTER 31

1 The title of an important article of Hugh Davidson on
this matter: *Romanic Review* 49 (1958) 12-24.

2 A few *pensées* are written on both sides of the sheet
(44, 131, 148, 149, 199, 208, 418-26) and others have
different thoughts recorded on the back (60/76, 194/
195-7). Such examples are, however, exceptional, and
probably early, as Pascal must have seen the disadvantage of that method as soon as he realized that his
thoughts would have to be regrouped.

3 Even there, we have to tread warily. Editors have
generally repeated that by its subject-matter no. 62
could not be later than 1656, which is very early for
an isolated fragment of this kind. M. Le Guern, however, is able to assign it to 1657 (note to LG 58).

4 Tourneur was a pioneer in this kind of enquiry, and
recently Pol Ernst has been attempting (with, it seems,
remarkable results) to reconstruct Pascal's original
sheets, basing his argument on watermarks, and also
on signs of adjoining fragments left by careless cutting. See his article 'Pascal au travail' in *Méthodes
chez Pascal* (Paris: PUF 1979) 141-53. I use his results
when I can, but in his paper he was only offering examples, and clearly the full publication of his research will be of the greatest importance. Meanwhile
I am left only with the impression that Tourneur's
indications need to be carefully checked, a task impossible without the equipment Ernst has been able to
use.

5 The order of filing is obviously not to be confused
with the order of composition. Too many factors play
a part for us to believe that as he filed his fragments, these were coming to hand in the sequence in

which they were written. Even the order of filing is
suggestive rather than conclusive. The sum total of
these suggestions is, however, remarkably consistent.
6 J. Mesnard, 'Aux origines de l'édition: les deux Copies'
in *Les Pensées de Pascal ont 300 ans* (1971) 26, 29;
Les Pensées de Pascal (1976) 43.
7 On the evidence of the watermark, we can assume that
190 is quite early; it is written on the same paper
as 'Infini rien' (418-26). See chapter 30, section (g),
and also n82 of that chapter.
8 The point was made well by R.E. Lacombe, *L'Apologétique
de Pascal* (1958) 35. He quotes in support sentences
from nos 427 and 449. 'Ainsi, loin que la première
partie ait simplement un rôle de préparation, elle
constituerait déjà une partie de la preuve proprement
dite: chacune des deux parties de l'Apologie aurait
pour objet de démontrer l'une des deux vérités fonda-
mentales du christianisme.' J. Mesnard quotes the same
texts, specifically in relation to nos 416-17 (*Les
Pensées de Pascal ont 300 ans* 29). See also H. Gouhier,
Blaise Pascal: Commentaires (1966) 168, and P. Topliss,
The Rhetoric of Pascal (1966) 183.
  P. Ernst also notes the appositeness of the title
'La nature est corrompue' to the first part of the
Apology. But his conclusion was radically different
from ours. Noting that titles 1°-10° come in a separate
column from 11°-28°, he proposed to insert them bodily
in the place indicated by the unclaimed title, which
then becomes a general title for part one (*Approches
pascaliennes* [1970] 651-60). In my view, this transposition raises too many problems to be wholly satisfactory, though it has its seductive side.
9 There is no need to believe that the title is late.
It certainly belongs to the original text of no. 12,
and it recurs in other fragments. No. 109, which I
interpreted in chapter 30 as part of the post-Sacy
Discourse, was for a while given the title 'Ordre.'
10 It is not difficult to connect the contents with a
particular moment in the working out of the plan. See
below, n43.
11 I can well believe that no. 6 is relatively early, as
it echoes the *Entretien avec M. de Sacy*: 'l'un ...
ignorant sa *corruption*, a traité la *nature* comme saine
et sans besoin de *réparateur* ... l'autre, éprouvant la
misère présente ... traite la *nature* comme nécessairement

infirme et *irréparable*' (Seuil, 296). The word *félicité*
comes in the passage on Epictetus (p 293), and the words
sans Dieu have their equivalent in the stipulation 'sans
la lumière de la foi' in the passage on reason (ibid.).

12 See below, pp 376 and 416.

13 Nos 66-7 are on paper which turns up again, notably
in Unit XXV and once in Unit XXXIV (877-9). Fragment
33 in *liasse* 2° is on the same paper. See n19.

14 The position of no. 403 in Unit I challenges my hypothesis, as it is found at the end, not at the beginning,
of a sequence of *pensées* corresponding to part one.

15 Cf. chapter 30 (c), p 313.

16 Z. Tourneur, édition paléographique [1942] 182 n1.

17 No. 412 is on man's inevitable folly.

18 Tourneur, éd. paléographique, 170 n5. He does not reproduce it, and I have not been able to read it myself.
It comprises the end of three lines which have been
crossed out, and the end of five lines which were left
intact.

19 No. 33 is on the same paper ('filigraine au huchet')
as nos 66-7, and was dictated to the same person
(Tourneur, éd. paléographique, 172 n1 and p 186 n4).

20 Fragment 23 is entitled 'Vanité des sciences.' Nos 16
and 32 are entitled 'Vanité.' All three titles appear
to have been added, evidently after the appropriate
location was found. The case of no. 46, also entitled
'Vanité,' is different. There the title was written
with the *pensée* which is simply a reminder to include
something developed elsewhere. Cf. chapter 2 (a).

21 Another indication: fragments 27 and 86 were originally
together (P. Ernst, 'Pascal au travail au jour le jour'
in *Méthodes chez Pascal* [1979] 145; Ernst prints '66'
in error), so bundle 5° was under way by the time Pascal
filed no. 27, and he had not yet come across no. 80.
Another indication, however, this time furnished by
Tourneur in his 1938 edition (p xxxv), warns us to be
cautious. Apparently nos 69 and 82 were once together.
(As Tourneur's descriptions are anything but clear, it
might be added that his other examples of fragments
which once belonged together are 14-15 and 212-13. The
reference to article 270 should read 270-1.)

22 Noted in chapter 5 (a).

23 Seuil, 296.

24 According to a recent PhD thesis (Judith Cochran,
   Dissertation Abstracts International 35 [1975] 5393-A),
   Pascal's ideas on Epictetus came to him via Montaigne.

25 As Tourneur indicated (édition paléographique, 196 n6),
   no. 115 was written immediately after no. 116, but was
   separated from it and filed on top of it. The subject
   is different, though equally relevant to the topic
   'Grandeur.'

26 This is slightly out of order, as I have not yet had
   cause to cite fragments 410-407 from Unit I. See below.

27 He also expanded it somewhat, and the polished version
   goes into Unit I as no. 413, following the one on *le
   divertissement* which was at that time assigned to the
   dossier on *Misère* (414).

28 The fact that a note on philosophers 'qui ne discutaient
   pas l'immortalité de l'âme' is found at this point in
   Unit I (no. 409), might mean that Pascal had not yet
   seen that that particular thought is more important
   for the theme of immortality (cf. 12°) than for what
   it says about philosophers. Generalized, it gives fr.
   164 (12°). No. 409 is akin to no. 612 in Unit XXIV.
   See also below, n64.

29 Unless, of course, Couchoud is right and this is a
   vestige of a Discourse on man. This reading is perfectly
   plausible. As no. 148 is written on both sides of the
   paper, it must be quite an early piece, very likely
   antedating the plan by several months, maybe a couple
   of years. See chapter 30, p 313.

30 Brief quotations noted on fr. 408 are given in full on
   no. 76. See chapter 30, n28. Is no. 408 a preliminary
   note or a later reminder to use the material, lost
   when no. 60 was filed and no. 76 crossed out? The remark 'cette lettre avant le divertissement' would point
   to the later date, for I shall argue shortly that the
   liasse 'Divertissement' was not constituted immediately.
   It is nevertheless surprising that Pascal should still
   be talking of a 'letter,' and also that he chooses the
   two quotations as a way to remind himself of no. 76.
   He added '280 sortes de souverain bien dans Montaigne,'
   another quotation from the same source, which is not
   quoted in no. 76, though it is very relevant. If no.

408 had come first, we might have expected to find this example used. The most sensible solution is to see fr. 408 as an indication that the ideas of fr. 76 were to be reworked.

The note '280 sortes de souverain bien dans Montaigne' reappears as fr. 479 (XI), where it bears the indication 'Pour les philosophes.' In fact, the dispute goes into section 10° ('Le souverain bien'); the words 'souverain bien' are not used in any of the fragments filed in 'Philosophes' (9°). See chapter 10, n3.

31 All the fragments in *liasse* 8° except no. 135 (untitled) have the title 'Divertissement.' No. 135 originally followed no. 137; both were dictated (Tourneur, édition paléographique, 213 n1).

32 There is an indication that *liasse* 2° was still open as Pascal compiled *liasse* 8°. Two notes on the page containing nos 133-4 are crossed out and filed in 2° (nos 19-20). It is possible that the explanation of an observation made by M. Le Guern in his study of no. 136 is similar (*RUO* 36 [1966] 219). Noting that the first page of no. 136 had its margins removed, while the other sheets have separate brief thoughts on *Divertissement* in the margin, Le Guern writes: 'Pascal aurait découpé lui-même la marge au moment où il établissait le classement de ses notes ... sans doute afin d'insérer dans une autre liasse des éléments dont la place ne se justifiait plus dans le dossier sur le *Divertissement*. Il est très vraisemblable que le fragment 39 ... provient de cette page.' But this hypothesis does not really square with what I have proposed, at least at first blush. Apart from the implications of 'ne se justifiait plus,' at odds with what I see as the likely sequence of events, it is hard to see why 39 should be detached from 136 and put in a totally different place. If, however, Pascal put no. 136 aside in order to work on it further, it becomes quite plausible. I am forced to admit, none the less, that the physical aspect of the manuscript itself does not make me any more ready to accept Le Guern's theory.

33 That point was made clearly in no. 414 (I).

34 No. 410 expands a note in Unit XXIV (621).

35 I mentioned no. 404 in chapter 7, partly because of the word 'contrariétés' and partly because it is echoed in the final portion of no. 131, filed in *liasse* 7°. However, that part of no. 131 was deleted, and in a

way no. 404 belongs more appositely to the transition
from the real end of part one to the next phase of the
argument. Hence, I mentioned it again in the last paragraph of chapter 9 (n5).

36 The *table de titres*, left-hand column. See below, end
of section (d).

37 In no. 380, and also in no. 821, Pascal quotes Psalm
119: 36: 'Inclina cor meum deus.' This is the translation used in the office of Terce, not the Vulgate, and
it prompted Annie Barnes to say that the biblical insight into conversion, familiar to Pascal through regular meditation on the Liturgy, was a vital source of
his apologetic writing ('Littérature et liturgie au 17e
siècle,' *FS* 20 [1966] 16-21). Philippe Sellier's book
on Pascal and the Liturgy appeared the same year; he
discusses nos 380 and 821 on p 30.

38 This motif is first found as a sequel to the important
fragment no. 832 on miracles; Lafuma gives it a separate
number (833): 'Toute religion est fausse qui dans sa
foi n'adore pas un Dieu comme principe de toutes choses
et qui dans sa morale n'aime pas un seul Dieu comme
objet de toutes choses.' The emphasis in chapter 17°
is rather different.

39 This is the principal reason for my saying that p 1
was written later than p 2. P 2 is full of crossings
out and it disintegrates half way through the verso
side into notes. It contains several phrases which reappear, properly articulated, in the text of p 1, and
also in the concluding part of no. 131.

One of the phrases amplified on p 1 is 'Vous n'êtes
pas dans l'état de votre création,' which is used in
the form 'Vous n'êtes plus maintenant en l'état où je
vous ai formés.' In the first version it is like a
sentence on the deleted last page of no. 131, where
Pascal defines one of the two basic tenets of Christianity: 'L'homme dans l'état de la création [replacing
'dans la création'] ... est élevé au-dessus de toute
la nature.' The idea goes back to the *Entretien* (see
chapter 30, n43). On the problems of fr. 149, see also
below, nn58, 59.

40 Tourneur's opinion that nos 356-9 were written on the
same sheet is plausible, though no more (édition paléographique, 291 n7).

41 Fragments 2 and 3 in the first *liasse* show Pascal
sketching a transition between parts one and two in

the form of questions from his interlocutor, and the
first of these is close to no. 244. The other questions
are: what can he understand of man, presented both as
a god and as completely feeble? Is there any stability?
Does not Christianity teach that God is manifest in
the world?

42 Editors, including Lafuma and Sellier, present the two
parts of this page (the first written by Pascal, the
second dictated), as two separate fragments. Le Guern,
faithful to the manuscript, leaves them together (LG
227).

43 It would appear that *liasse* 1° ('Ordre') records this
stage in Pascal's thinking. As well as several fragments on faith and reason, and on self-discipline,
there is one on obscurity (2-3; see n4), one on Mahomet's
witnesses (1), and a note to examine the 'état des
juifs' (8).

44 No. 396 is a personal reflection. No. 395 links the
need to search for God with the theme of distraction.
No. 394 will be mentioned in the next paragraph.

45 'Morale' and 'doctrine' are joined in no. 189 (15°);
Jesus teaches both.

46 I believe no. 793 to be intimately connected with this
stage in the expansion of the plan, but as it belongs
to a Unit which contains late fragments, I cannot use
it here. See chapter 32, pp 409-11.

47 Cf. 503 (XIX), 793 (XXVIII), 892 (XXXIV).

48 No. 288 is different, and is expanded in the last fragment filed, no. 279.

49 No. 222 was dictated, and Pascal added the words 'Voyez
Perpétuité' on the back.

50 See n46.

51 Edition paléographique [1942] 276 n4. Both quote Joel
2:28.

52 Pascal would have found no. 349 (26°) when he filed no.
305 in Bundle 23°. See P. Ernst, 'Pascal au travail au
jour le jour,' *Méthodes chez Pascal* (1979) 145. According to Ernst, these two fragments were written on the
same sheet as no. 390.

53 Cf. no. 384 in Unit I. No. 384 was not detached from
no. 383, and hence is out of place. See below, n64.

54 One of these is fr. 292, and the same sheet records a
very different thought, which Lafuma numbers 293. It
reappears in *liasse* 12° as no. 159. See below, n55 on
fr. 326.

55 This idea links up also with no. 293 and no. 159 (see
   above, n54). No. 153, filed, like no. 159, in *liasse*
   12°, is similar. Nos 153, 386, and also nos 324-31
   (originally one sheet) are all on ruled paper, as are
   other fragments in Unit I. See chapter 32, n44. On no.
   387, see below, section (d), p   .
56 Fragment 391 in Unit I is absorbed by a long essay entitled 'Raisons pourquoi figures' (502-3) and this
   would have found its most appropriate home in *liasse*
   20°.
57 See section (f).
58 M. Le Guern in his edition (LG 139) starts with p 2,
   and prints p 1 immediately after what I have called
   the first development. However one looks at it, the
   existence of p 1 presents a problem. P. Ernst has suggested that it might be more sensible to give p 1 a
   different number from the rest ('Pascal au travail au
   jour le jour' in *Méthodes chez Pascal* [1979] 149);
   however, p 1 was intended to be the prelude to p 2.
59 Three sheets were used for no. 149. 'Page 1' (R.O.
   317-18) corresponds to a half sheet. 'Pages 2 and 3'
   (R.P. 321-2, 325-6) are the two halves of a sheet which
   at some point was cut in two. The sheet from which
   'page 4' (R.O. 57) was extracted was identical in format and watermark to the second sheet. At the time
   Pascal classified his papers, the first half dozen
   lines were removed and placed in *liasse* 19°. (See P.
   Ernst, 'Pascal au travail au jour le jour' in *Méthodes
   chez Pascal*, Plate XIX). Ernst has reconstructed the
   original page, and he reports that the sequel comprised
   at least four fragments, also separated by Pascal's
   scissors: 411 (I), 631 (XXIV), 138 (8°), and 626 (XXIV).
   (He also believes that the other half of the sheet is
   the one containing 796 and 797-8, on the grounds that
   it has the corresponding watermark, upside-down like
   the watermark of 626.)
      This list is revealing. Evidently Pascal had not got
   far into Unit I and *liasse* 8° when 'page 4' was filed.
   And the location of the two fragments which went into
   Unit XXIV shows that papers were not placed immediately
   in the position they came to occupy. We must therefore
   be prudent in our deductions.
60 P. Ernst ('Pascal au travail au jour le jour' in
   Méthodes chez Pascal 146) indicates that no. 231, not
   crossed out in the Copies, was written on the same

page as nos 133-4 - short jottings which include two
ideas taken up in no. 60. It has every appearance of
being quite early.

61 The initials AR which Tourneur discerned on the manuscript of no. 234 bring it into line with the last two
pages of no. 149 and with no. 244, as well as with no.
353 in *liasse* 27°, which glosses the notion (mentioned
in 234) of 'abaissement' (édition paléographique, 222
n5, 224 n13, 252 n3, 255 n3, 290 n4).

62 Cf. no. 12: 'faire souhaiter aux bons qu'elle fût vraie.
The word is used in the same way in no. 255 (20°).

63 No. 164 echoes no. 612, from Unit XXIV, and is probably
relatively early. Cf. above, n2.

64 Fragments 383 and 384 were not separated by Pascal's
scissors, though they are independent of each other.
Both fit in with my reading of Unit I. For no. 384, see
note 53. A less clumsy version of no. 383 comes in
Unit XXIV, no. 632. It is the same theme as in no. 409
(see n28), but generalized now.

65 See introduction, nn33, 46.

66 See above, p 366 and n49.

67 J. Mesnard, *Les Pensées de Pascal* 34; P. Sellier, edition (1976) 30 n1.

68 Mesnard, *Les Pensées de Pascal* 35. Cf. P.L. Couchoud,
'gestation du projet d'Apologie' (*Discours de la condition de l'homme* [1948] p 11).

69 P. Sellier, edition (1976) 31 and 56 n29. Cf. 31 n3:
'une table de matières plus étoffée.' In the discussion
at Clermont (*Méthodes chez Pascal* 167-8) Sellier explained that in his opinion Unit I and *liasse* 1° both
represent a 'bilan' made after *liasses* 2° to 28° were
in place.

70 J. Mesnard, *Pascal* (1951) 112. Mesnard's arguments make
it difficult to go along with those who conclude, on
the basis of Gilberte's *Life*, that the illness struck
Pascal in the early summer of 1658 (see notably, R.
Francis, *Les Pensées de Pascal en France* [1959] 134).
Gilberte says no more than that the troubles began with
an attack of toothache which seems to have been at the
origin of the competition to solve the problem of the
cycloid or *roulette*, in May 1658 (*O.C.* I, 585-6; see
J. Mesnard, *Pascal et les Roannez* 646-9). Pascal was
able to see the cycloid affair through to its conclusion at the end of the year, and the work and the disputes involved provoked the reaction of extreme fatigue.

See also L. Lafuma, *Controverses pascaliennes* (1952)
40. Gilberte tends to round figures off, and her testimony - that Pascal languished for four years - should
not be pressed too literally. Couchoud's suggestion
that Pascal classed his papers late in 1659 has never
looked convincing. See next note.

71 The only attempt to assign a late date to a classified
fragment was made by Couchoud, who believed that no.
53 refers to a book published in 1659, *Discours de la
condition de l'homme* 28. Lafuma exploded this theory
(*Recherches pascaliennes* [1949] 87 n3. Cf. *Histoire
des Pensées de Pascal* [1954] 128). And although Lafuma,
following Brunschvicg, says that no. 59 refers to the
'bataille des Dunes' of 14 June 1658, J. Mesnard has
expressed doubts on this (*Cahiers de Royaumont* 1 [1956]
103). The date of 1658 for the *terminus ad quem* has won
almost universal acceptance. Cf. J. Mesnard, *Pascal*
(1951) 137, D. Anzieu, edition (1960) lxiii, Michel
and Marie-Rose Le Guern, *Les Pensées de Pascal* (1972)
10 and M. Le Guern, edition (1977) 15, P. Sellier, edition (1976) 17. L. Lafuma made the interesting observation that none of the papers that can be firmly assigned to 1660 was cut up, implying that Pascal was
no longer interested in distributing his *pensées* into
separate dossiers ('Les manuscrits des *Pensées*: ce
qu'ils nous apprennent,' in *Cahiers de Royaumont* 85;
'L'histoire des manuscrits des *Pensées* et le problème
de leur édition,' *Table Ronde* 171 [1962] 43. Cf. 'Le
puzzle des *Pensées*,' *RSH* 59 [1950] 172 n3, reprinted
in *Controverses pascaliennes* [1952] 51 n1). In 1976,
during the meetings at Clermont Ferrand recorded in
Méthodes chez Pascal, J. Mesnard said: 'Je dois dire
que cette date, mise à l'épreuve de toutes sortes
d'objections, résiste bien' (p 163). Apart from Couchoud, only Antoine Adam, in his review of Lafuma's
Recherches pascaliennes, has expressed the opposite
view. 'On n'a pas le droit de s'appuyer sur la phrase
de Gilberte Périer. On n'a pas le droit de placer
avant 1659 la formation des liasses et par conséquent
toutes les *Pensées* classées' (*RSH* 57-8 [1950] 135).
I have lingering doubts. See chapter 32, n102.

72 See volumes VIII and IX of the Grands Ecrivains edition.

73 The state of the Units, which frequently blur the distinction between pre-1659 and post-1659, made J. Mesnard
write that 'l'idée d'un classement interrompu par le

fait des circonstances extérieures est indéfendable'
(*Les Pensées de Pascal* 29) but I cannot see that the
interesting evidence he produces weakens the standard
explanation. The Units are discussed in the next chapter.

74 These texts have been reprinted a number of times.
Both are found in vol. III of the Luxembourg edition
of the *Pensées* (1951) 89-116, 133-45. The paragraphs
of the preface which summarize Pascal's talk run from
p 133 to p 138. On Filleau de la Chaise, and the edition of three of his Discours by Victor Giraud in
1922, see n8 of my introduction.

75 Pascal, *Pensées* (Luxembourg 1951) III, 91.

76 Ibid. 134. One notes Etienne Périer's insistence that
the talk was more or less improvised.

77 J. Mesnard has remarked that if a lecture did take
place 'at Port-Royal,' it would have been the Paris
Port-Royal ('Les séjours de Pascal à Port-Royal des
Champs,' *SAPR* 2 [1951] 25). More recently, P. Magnard
has written of the lecture as if it spread over two
days, 'A P.R.' and 'A P.R. pour demain'! (*Nature en
histoire dans l'Apologétique de Pascal* [Paris: Les
Belles Lettres 1975] 396).

78 P. Ernst, 'La trajectoire pascalienne de *l'Apologie*,'
ALM 84 (1967) 6-7. I do not agree about the full stop
on the ms of no. 122 (there is a faint mark, which
might be a full stop), but it is very probable for
no. 149 page 4 (R.O. 57). Ernst remarks that both
copies record the full stop each time the initials
appear. Does this mean that the copyists knew that
it was an abbreviation?

79 J. Mesnard (*Cahiers de Royaumont* 1 [1956] 100), admitted with engaging candour that he had often tried,
but without success, to find a different explanation.
P. Ernst ('La trajectoire pascalienne de *l'Apologie*,'
ALM 84 [1967] 8-11) made four suggestions: 'Apologie:
Preuves de la Religion,' 'Apologie: Prosopopée de la
Religion.' He subsequently disowned this study (*Approches pascaliennes* 691 nn1, 3), and in his book returns to the traditional reading, p 185.

80 Philippe Sellier in his edition ([1976] 17-18), while
acknowledging that the lecture - read: 'talk' - probably did take place, refuses to go any further. 'De-
mandée à brûle-pourpoint à l'apologiste, elle n'a pas
pu laisser de traces dans les écrits pascaliens. Les

fragments intitulés A.P.R. ne sauraient donc être des
notes préparatoires à ce discours ... Enfin, placer
ce discours à Port-Royal demeure une pure hypothèse.'
P.L. Couchoud kept the lecture and the talk distinct,
arguing that on the first occasion (the lecture at
Port-Royal) Pascal presented an argument based on
probability only, and that it was the criticisms of
his listeners (Arnauld, Nicole, Sacy perhaps) which
gave Pascal the idea of writing on the authentic proof
of Christianity (*Discours de la condition de l'homme*
[1948] 26-7). For this 'gratuitous' assumption, Couchoud
was much criticized.

81 L. Lafuma, *Controverses pascaliennes* 43, *Histoire des
Pensées de Pascal* 22. The remark he made at Royaumont
(*Cahiers de Royaumont* 1 [1956] 99) is more nuanced:
'Il a dû utiliser ces papiers pour la conférence; il
n'a pas dû les emporter tous: il les a classés comme
ça pour avoir une idée générale, et les papiers APR,
il a dû les emporter.' In his *Recherches pascaliennes*,
however, Lafuma had said that the classifying was
undertaken 'en vue de la préparation de son ouvrage sur
la Religion' (p 58) which is more plausible, even if
the date assigned (second half of 1658) is arbitrary.
    Annie Barnes also seems to believe that 'Pascal com-
mence son classement en vue de la conférence' (*FS* 10
[1956] 238, reprinted in *Ecrits sur Pascal* [1959] 96).
Likewise Roger Pons ('Entretien sur les manuscrits de
Pascal,' *CUC* [Nov.-Dec. 1962] 86). On the other side,
Philippe Sellier (edition [1976] 18) is quite firm:
'Rien n'indique le moindre rapport de causalité entre
le travail réfléchi de classement opéré par Pascal
vers mai 1658 et ce discours improvisé.'

82 *Controverses pascaliennes* 43.

83 See the discussion between J. Mesnard and L. Cognet,
Cahiers de Royaumont 1 (1956) 99.

84 Roger Pons' suggestion that the letters A.P.R. at the
top of the second column of the table of titles apply
to the whole of 11°-28°, implying that the lecture
covered all these chapters, is difficult to defend
(*CUC* [Nov.-Dec. 1962] 87).

85 This is the position of L. Lafuma, *Recherches pascaliennes* 84, 90 ('l'auditeur qu'il a imaginé n'est qu'une
figure de rhétorique; sa documentation orale est in-
existante (ou du moins nous ne l'avons pas découverte)'),
Histoire des Pensées de Pascal 23, 33, *DSS* 7-8 (1950)

20. P. Ernst also called the existence of the witness into question, but only as a self-styled devil's advocate (*ALM* 84 [1967] 28-36). Jean Mesnard is more circumspect (discussion of a paper by Lafuma in *Cahiers de Royaumont* 1 [1956] 100). Cf. also R. Francis, *Les Pensées de Pascal en France* (1959) 133.

It is difficult to see what is proved by the absence of oral documentation, or even what the phrase really means. The fact that neither Gilberte nor anyone else mentions the talk is much less damaging than the silence which envelops the lecture at Port-Royal; Filleau mentions it, and if he enjoyed the confidence of a survivor of the original audience, his witness should be welcomed, not rejected out of hand.

86 On the reasons for replacing Filleau's text by another, the essential documents are Gilberte Périer's letter to Dr Vallant of 1 Apr. 1670, in vol. III of the Luxembourg edition of the *Pensées* 147-8, and the *Avertissement* to the *Discours* written in 1670 or 1671 (ibid. 88). There is a mysterious hint that all was not well in a letter of Arnauld to Périer dated simply 11 Aug. (1668?), ibid. 119. Cf. also p 124 (Brienne to Gilberte, 7 Dec. 1668). The fact that Filleau's text was rejected by no means makes it without any validity. Cf. M. Guersant's edition of the *Pensées* (1954) xlv-xlix, and my introduction, n9. On the ambivalence and inconsistency of Gilberte, see Guersant, xl-xlii, and Marie Louise Hubert, *Pascal's Unfinished Apology* (1952) 140.

87 A. Béguin, preface to Lafuma's *Recherches pascaliennes* 11-12, R.E. Lacombe, *L'Apologétique de Pascal* 31 n68, H. Gouhier, *Blaise Pascal: Commentaires* 175-6 and n97.

88 Jean Mesnard, *Pascal et les Roannez* 648. Mesnard accepts the view that it was indeed the Duc de Roannez who remembered the occasion of the lecture, and on these grounds, maintains the date of May-June. But he gives no proof, and his statement is quite tentative in expression. 'Nous aurons à nous demander si le duc ne fut pas le témoin ... Si l'on répond à cette question d'une manière affirmative, etc.' (ibid. 649).

If we could be sure that the talk did take place in May or June, we could accept Mesnard's hypothesis as at least very plausible. But there is only one reference which relates the talk to other events in Pascal's life, and that comes in Etienne Périer's preface (Lux.

III, 138), where we are told that 'peu de temps après il tomba malade d'une maladie de langueur et de faiblesse.' Taken at face value, that seems unambiguous: Pascal fell ill early in 1659, so the talk must have been given towards the end of 1658. This is Lafuma's position (*Recherches pascaliennes* 91-2, cf. *Histoire des Pensées* 23, discussion at Royaumont in *Cahiers de Royaumont* 102). If he is right, the witness cannot be the Duc de Roannez. In his *Recherches* (p 85) he suggested that the link figures were Arnauld and Nicole. The following year, however, in the first of four 'Notes pascaliennes' (*DSS* 7-8 [1950] 205-7), he showed that that hypothesis did not hold water. He did not have another name to put forward. In his view there was in any case no need of one, as Filleau was basing his discourse entirely on the Copy. M. Guersant (edition [1954] xlix-liii) argued for Philippe Goibaud Du Bois, but Goibaud was no more a companion of the Duc de Roannez and Pascal in 1658 than was Filleau (*Pascal et les Roannez* 654, 656-7).

There is, however, another way of interpreting Etienne Périer's remark. He may have been confusing the illness proper with the first symptoms (toothache) which attacked Pascal in the previous May or June. This reading fits in perfectly with Mesnard's view of what happened, and it becomes suddenly more plausible when we look at Gilberte's *Vie de Monsieur Pascal*. This is what Gilberte says (second version, *O.C.* I, 622): 'Il avait environ trente-quatre ans quand il commença de s'y appliquer. Il employa un an entier à s'y préparer ... et à la fin de l'année, c'est-à-dire la trente-cinquième qui était la cinquième de sa retraite, il retomba dans ses incommodités d'une manière si accablante qu'il ne put plus rien faire...' Now, although the sentence ends by evoking Pascal's incapacity (Jan. 1659), and although the phrase 'à la fin de l'année' would normally mean the end of the calendar year (ie, Dec. 1658), the curious phrase 'c'est-à-dire la trente-cinquième' makes it possible that the 'year' in question was 'Pascal's thirty-fifth year,' which ended in June 1658. But Gilberte uses figures very imprecisely; the expression 'la cinquième de sa retraite' is a case in point. I cannot follow M. Guersant who wishes to make 'la fin de l'année' refer to 1657, the end of the calendar year which fell during Pascal's thirty-fifth year (edition

[1954] xli–xlii). As the date Dec. 1657 is quite implausible, Guersant concludes that Gilberte is an unreliable witness. But there are better arguments to
support this conclusion, arguments which Guersant
marshals with skill.

More to the point is the fact that two paragraphs
later (*O.C.* I, 623), Gilberte speaks of the attack of
toothache as the beginning of Pascal's malady. It is
clear from Gilberte's own account, as well as from external evidence, that it was some months before Pascal
was obliged to stop working. But Etienne Périer, who
does not enter into these details, could have evoked
the illness at a point where it would have been more
appropriate to mention the toothache and Lafuma seems
to have taken Périer too literally. See n70.

It is amusing to find Lafuma placing such trust in
Etienne Périer, whom he generally lost no opportunity
to denounce. Similarly, it is surprising that he should
lean so heavily on Gilberte despite her obvious shortcomings. Guersant's pages (xxxvii–xlii) are concerned
as much with vindicating the son as they are with dis-
crediting the mother. On Gilberte, see R. Polman, 'La
biographie de Blaise Pascal par Gilberte Périer,' *Revue
d'Histoire écclésiastique* 45 (1950), esp. 113–18. He
points out that Gilberte consistently underplays Pascal's
scientific activity.

89 See H. Gouhier's note in *Blaise Pascal: Commentaires*
175 n96. He cites Sainte-Beuve, Vinet, Janssens, Stewart,
Chevalier, and Hubert. To these names we can add that
of Duviard (see introduction, n86). Cf. A. Béguin,
Critique 4 (1948) 886: '[le] seul texte qui autorise
une hypothèse vraisemblable sur le plan arrèté par
Pascal.' V. Giraud, who edited the *Discours* in 1922,
called it 'un document capital, et celui peut-être qui
nous offre la restitution la plus précise, la plus
intelligente et la plus complète du dessein qu'avait
conçu l'auteur des *Provinciales* quand il eut l'idée
d'écrire une Apologie de la religion chretienne' (p 11).

90 L. Lafuma, 'La source du *Discours sur les Pensées* de
Filleau de la Chaise,' *Recherches pascaliennes* 83–92.

91 Henri Gouhier puts the matter very well (*Blaise Pascal:
Commentaires* 178): 'Sans aller jusqu'à déclarer, avec
Louis Lafuma, que ... le témoin invoqué par [Filleau]
est une fiction littéraire, en admettant que Filleau
et Périer aient recueilli les souvenirs d'un auditeur,

il reste permis de se demander dans quelle mesure ils
ont interprété ce qu'ils ont entendu en complétant avec
ce qu'ils ont lu: et comment savoir si le plan de la
conférence reconstruite dans leurs textes vient de ce
qu'ils ont entendu ou de ce qu'ils ont lu?' Lafuma's
contention that a remark of Etienne Périer implies that
he scorned Filleau's 'witness' smacks of special plead-
ing (*Recherches pascaliennes* 83 n1, *Histoire des
Pensées de Pascal* 23).

92 L. Lafuma (*Recherches pascaliennes* 86-7) gives two examples (454 and 451), but in neither case is the late
date he proposes entirely beyond question, as we shall
see in chapter 32, section (b). No. 454 is mentioned
also by R.E. Lacombe (*L'Apologétique de Pascal* 29 n59).
Lacombe also lists nos 292, 296, and 421 as evidently
having inspired Filleau.

93 Because the example is the Great Fire of London of
1666, Filleau has been denounced as patently unreliable,
notably by G. Chinard (*En lisant Pascal* [1948] 27).
But whatever Chinard says, Filleau does not in fact
give the example as being Pascal's. He introduces it
with the words 'Et en effet,' implying a personal intervention. Marie Louise Hubert made the same observation (*Pascal's Unfinished Apology* 140-1). Chinard took
the example, and some of his other arguments, from
Jean Laporte, 'Le coeur et la raison selon Pascal,'
Revue philosophique 103 (1927) 439-47. Laporte's article was reprinted in book form in 1950. See p 151,
and also p 154 for a possible source for the example
of the Great Fire of London.

94 Another example, from later on in the *Discours* (p 101):
'C'est ce que M. Pascal aurait fait voir clairement,
soit qu'il la considérât du côté du fait, ou qu'il en
examinât le fond et les beautés. Et chacun en pourra
juger par un petit article qu'on a liassé exprès dans
ces fragments, et qui n'est qu'une espèce de table des
chapitres qu'il avait dessein de traiter, et de chacun
desquels il toucha quelque chose en passant dans le
discours dont j'ai parlé.' The reference would appear
to be either to no. 482 or to no. 402, though neither
was included in the 1670 edition.

95 Cf. Annie Barnes, in *Cahiers de Royaumont* 101-2.

96 Cf. no. 427.

97 Filleau's infidelity to Pascal resides principally in
the way he has glossed Pascal's argument, obscuring

the distinction which Pascal thought essential, between
conviction and certainty. See J. Laporte, 'Le coeur et
la raison selon Pascal,' *Revue philosophique* 103 (1927)
439-47 (the article, which covered 100 pages, was reprinted in book from in 1950, and there the passage
in question is on pp 147-58); G. Chinard, *En lisant
Pascal*, ch. 2; Jeanne Russier, *La foi selon Pascal*
(1949) 319-27; J. Mesnard, intervention at Royaumont
(*Cahiers de Royaumont* 101); R.E. Lacombe (*L'Apologétique de Pascal* 29 n60 and also p 45).

98 A. Barnes, 'La conférence à Port-Royal et les liasses
de Pascal,' *FS* 10 (1956) 231-40, reprinted in *Ecrits
de Pascal* (1959) 83-98, with a reply from Lafuma, pp
99-115. Patricia Topliss agreed (*The Rhetoric of
Pascal* 167). Lafuma's intransigence was also commented
on pertinently by A. Béguin in the preface he wrote
for Lafuma's *Recherches pascaliennes* 11-12. R.E.
Lacombe agreed with Béguin (*L'Apologétique de Pascal*
31 n68). R. Francis, *Les Pensées de Pascal en France*
133, accuses Lafuma of contradicting himself because
he said elsewhere (*Recherches pascaliennes* 56) that
the order of the Copies was established by Nicole and
Arnauld, on the basis of what they remembered of the
lecture. See n88, p 565.

99 We shall see in the next chapter that Pascal possibly
documented himself more fully on Old Testament matters
after his illness, when Filleau would have been one of
his companions. Hence his greater familiarity with
this aspect of Pascal's thought. Cf. J. Mesnard, *Pascal
et les Roannez* 655, 659, 686. See, however, pp 417-22.

100 *FS* 10 (1956) 232, *Ecrits de Pascal* 86. The similarity
between no. 149 and Filleau's 'plan' has been noted
by P. Ernst (*ALM* 84, p 47). Cf. also A. Béguin in
Critique 4 (1948) 886, J. Chevalier, Pléiade edition
(1936) 821; revised edition (1962) 1086, also edition
of the *Pensées* (Gallimard 1937) 13, R.E. Lacombe,
L'Apologétique de Pascal 30. Lacombe rightly pointed
out, against Béguin, that no. 149 is far from accounting for everything on Filleau (ibid. n64).

101 In 1672, the *Discours sur les Pensées* was followed by
a shorter *Discours sur les Preuves des Livres de Moise*
(reprinted in Giraud's edition [1922] 103-45). The
main argument there is that it is inconceivable that
the Pentateuch should be in any way a deception, whether
of the Jews by Moses, or of other nations by the Jews.

The framework, once again, is a consideration of the reasons for unbelief, and is no less reminiscent of Pascal than the parallel passages in the first Discours. Gilberte Périer, indeed, implies that Pascal's views are 'admirably well' represented by Filleau in this Discourse (*O.C.* I, 618; see also below, p 397). For the date of this *Discours*, see J. Mesnard, *O.C.* I, 560. On the burning importance of the question of the Pentateuch once the *Tractatus theologico-politicus* had burst upon Europe, in the same year as the Port-Royal edition of the *Pensées*, see J. Orcibal, 'Les jansenistes face à Spinoza,' *RLC* 23 (1949) 441-9.

102 See nn74 and 86.

103 As, for instance, Roger Pons: 'Sa préface confirme pour l'essentiel les conceptions ou les déductions de Filleau. Il n'y a rien à conclure de cette resemblance. Etienne Périer travailla d'après Filleau, comme Filleau avait travaillé d'après la copie' ('La présentation authentique des Pensées de Pascal,' *IL* 3 [1951] 174).

104 P. Ernst, *ALM* 84 (1967) 38-9.

105 A. Barnes, in *FS* 10 (1956) 233, *Ecrits sur Pascal* 87-8.

106 See H.F. Stewart, *Pascal's Apology for Religion* 203-31, L. Lafuma, *Recherches pascaliennes* 89-90, *Ecrits sur Pascal* 107-9, A. Barnes, ibid. 87, and *FS* 10 (1956) 233. One example will have to suffice. Filleau, para. 67, p 111: 'Je n'entreprendrai pas d'entrer plus avant dans ce qu'on peut dire pour *la vérité de l'histoire evangélique*, sur laquelle M. Pascal nous a liassé de si *belles remarques*, mais qui ne sont presque rien au prix de ce qu'il eût fait, s'il eût vécu. Il avait tant de pénétration pour ces choses-là, et c'est une source si inépuisable, qu'il n'aurait jamais cessé d'y faire de nouvelles découvertes. Que n'eût-il point dit du *style des Evangélistes*, et de *leurs personnes*; des *Apôtres en particulier*, et de *leurs écrits*; des *voies par* où cette *religion s'est établie*, et de l'état où elle est; de cette étrange quantité *de miracles*, de *martyrs* et de *saints*; et enfin de tant de choses qui marquent qu'il est *impossible* que *les hommes* seuls s'en soient mêlés. Quand je serais aussi capable que je le suis peu de suppléer à son défaut, ce n'en est pas ici le lieu. Ce serait achever son ouvrage dont je n'ai voulu que montrer le plan. Mais *quoique* je m'en sois mal acquitté, et quelque imparfait que nous l'ayons, c'est toujours *assez pour* faire voir quel il eût été...'

Here is Etienne Périer's version (p 137): 'Enfin il n'oublia rien de tout ce qui pouvait servir à *la vérité de l'histoire évangélique,* faisant de très *belles remarques* sur l'Evangile même, sur *le style des évangelistes,* et sur *leurs personnes*; sur *les apôtres en particulier,* et sur *leurs écrits*; sur le nombre prodigieux *de miracles,* sur les *martyrs*; sur les *saints*; en un mot, sur toutes *les voies par* lesquelles la *religion* chrétienne *s'est* entièrement établie. Et *quoiqu'*il n'eût pas le loisir, dans un simple discours, de traiter au long une si vaste matière, comme il avait dessein de faire dans son ouvrage, il en dit néanmoins *assez pour* convaincre que tout cela ne *pouvait être* l'ouvrage *des hommes...*'

107 A. Barnes, *FS* 10, pp 233, 238, *Ecrits sur Pascal* 88, 95-6. P. Ernst, *ALM* 84, pp 42-3.

108 L. Lafuma, *Ecrits sur Pascal* 107-8.

109 Annie Barnes, *FS* 10, pp 237-8, *Ecrits sur Pascal* 93-5. P. Ernst,s table of parallels (*ALM* 84, p 39) is misleading on this.

110 G. Chinard, *En lisant Pascal* esp. 21-9.

111 Eg, Chinard, *En lisant Pascal* 33, A. Barnes, *FS* 10, p 231, *Ecrits sur Pascal* 84, P. Topliss, *The Rhetoric of Pascal* 168, H. Gouhier, *Blaise Pascal: Commentaires* 177 and n5, P. Ernst, *ALM* 84 (1967) 36. For a different assessment, A. Adam, *Histoire de la Littérature française au XVIIe siècle* (Paris: Domat 1951) II, 266 n1: 'Les différences sont sensibles, mais tiennent au faible génie d'Etienne Périer.' E. Janssens, *RNP* 12 (1905) 437, and *La philosophie et l'apologétique de Pascal* (1906) 91, believed that Etienne Périer's version is merely a 'schéma logique,' while Filleau gives us the words and the spontaneous examples of Pascal himself. The most reasoned defence of Filleau as opposed to Etienne Périer is the one made by Sister Marie Louise Hubert, *Pascal's Unfinished Apology* 128-42, esp. 131-3, 134-5.

112 Annie Barnes says of this character: 'Filleau l'introduit bien aussi, mais indirectement, confusément ... *après* avoir donné en détail la peinture de l'homme, et sans jamais l'appeler indifférent.' (*FS* 10, p 234, *Ecrits sur Pascal* 89). This is unfair, because Etienne Périer does the same: 'Il commença d'abord par une peinture de l'homme ... Il supposa ensuite...' (p 134).

CHAPTER 32

1 I should explain again that in the Seuil edition,
   Lafuma's presentation of what he called the 'Séries,'
   is different from what he had proposed in the Luxembourg edition. There, there were only 33 Units. A note
   at the head of Unit XXX indicated that there was a
   line on the Copy separating no. 825 from no. 826, and
   that Unit XXX should perhaps be regarded as two units
   (I, 437). In his *Histoire des Pensées* ([1954] 31)
   Lafuma expressed the opinion that the signs separating
   the transcript of one Unit from the next were unreliable. Nevertheless, in 1958 he retracted and nos 826-9
   became Unit XXXI, with a consequent change in the numbering of Lux. XXXI-XXXIII.
     At the same time, he grouped three fragments which
   Copy 9203 does not record, but which are grouped on
   Copy 12449. See below, n26, and introduction, n74.
   This makes for a total of 35. J. Mesnard considers
   that the table of chapter-headings should count as another Unit, which would make 36 (*Les Pensées de Pascal
   ont 300 ans* [1971] 10). Since cresting at that figure,
   the tide has receded a little, as Philippe Sellier has
   told us that Units III and IV should not have been
   divided. See n71. I nevertheless maintain the now traditional Seuil numbering.
2 Roger Pons, 'La présentation authentique des *Pensées*
   de Pascal,' *IL* 3 (1951) 173.
3 *Recherches pascaliennes* (1949) 66.
4 Anzieu, edition (1960) lxiii-lxiv.
5 Eg, by J. Steinmann and by A.J. Krailsheimer in their
   editions.
6 Sellier's description of Unit I. I expressed reservations about the description in chapter 31 (see p 377).
7 P. Sellier, edition, 12-13.
8 See below, n26.
9 I assign each group a letter for future reference. 'A'
   indicates Unit I, and 'B' the 28 *liasses à titres*.
10 The date of May 1658 implies a connection between the
   classifying of existing fragments and the lecture. I
   argued against this assumption in chapter 31 (see
   n88). I would prefer the date 'fin 1658' in this title.
11 P. Sellier, edition, 542. The chronological order proposed is not markedly different from that of P.L.

Couchoud (*Discours de la condition de l'homme* [1948]
11), but Couchoud put the integration of the two halves
of the Apologia back to 1659. In view of Pascal's ill
health, this date is implausible.

12 See chapter 30, n82.

13 J. Mesnard, *Les Pensées de Pascal* (1976) 32-7.

14 While admitting that 'l'ordre idéal, le seul qui per-
mette d'échapper à l'arbitraire, serait, à notre avis,
un ordre chronologique' ('Aux origines des *Pensées*
de Pascal' in *Les Pensées de Pascal ont 300 ans* 28),
Mesnard does not think that ideal order is guaranteed
by the Second Copy. 'C^1 et C^2 fournissent deux ordres
possibles; on ne peut rien dire de plus' (ibid. 16).

15 P. Sellier sees in the 'simplicity' a sign that Pascal
'sait désormais où il va' (edition, 13).

16 When Lafuma writes that Units I, IX, and XIX contain
papers cut up ready for filing, 'IX' is a misprint for
'XI' (*Recherches pascaliennes* 65).

17 The same reasoning explains why Unit XXXII (the Barcos
questionnaire, 'simple') has been put with Units XXXIII-
XXXIV ('complex'). All three Units deal with miracles.

18 'Si aucun rapport logique n'apparaît entre des pensées
portées par un même feuillet, du moins ont-elles toutes
chances d'être unies par un rapport chronologique:
elles sont contemporaines.' J. Mesnard in *Les Pensées
de Pascal ont 300 ans* 28).

19 Noting that some fragments are written by Gilberte,
who was Pascal's host in the summer of 1660, Mesnard
says that this indication as to the date 'doit évidemment s'étendre à *toutes les unités* qui contiennent des
fragments de la main de Gilberte ... Voilà donc *trois
liasses successives* qui sont à peu près contemporaines
et non antérieures à 1660' (*Les Pensées de Pascal* 45,
my italics). That is strictly true only of the constituted *liasses*, not of the constituent elements.

20 Roger Pons was one of those who believed that Pascal
did little work on the Apologia after 1658 ('La présentation authentique des *Pensées* de Pascal, *IL* 3
[1951] 172). The opposite view was held by R. Francis
(*Les Pensées de Pascal en France* [1959] 133-4). See
also A. Adam's review of Lafuma's *Recherches pascaliennes* in *RSH* 57-8 (1950) 135.

21 The evidence is marshalled by L. Lafuma in his *Histoire
des Pensées de Pascal* (1954) 23-4. Etienne Périer tells
us of Pascal's prolonged illness (preface to the Port-

Royal edition, Seuil, 497, also 500-1) which is confirmed by a letter from Carcavi to Huyghens of 14 Aug.
1659. He travelled with difficulty to Bienassis in
May 1660, and there stayed with his sister and brother-
in-law. A letter to Fermat, 10 Aug. 1660 (G.E. X, 4-6)
implies that he is in quite a pitiful state; Lafuma's
interpretation of this letter as indicating an improvement in his health seems to me unwarranted. He returned
to Paris on Oct., and was reasonably active, though
still not well (G.E. X, 16 n1 and 47). Cf. G.E. X, 37
n1, J. Mesnard, *Les Pensées de Pascal* 359.

22 As did J. Mesnard in his *Pascal* of 1951, 112-13.

23 I believe to be late nos 734-47, 749-52, 765-6, and
probably 748, 760-3 in Unit XXVI; 774 in Unit XXVII;
794 and 796-8 in Unit XXVIII; probably Unit XXII and
possibly XXI. Of 822 (XXX) I am less sure. On the other
hand nos 731-3 and 753 (XXVI) are probably early, as
are 771, 773, 779-81 in XXVII, 792-3 in XVIII, and
Unit XXXI.

24 Also XXX.

25 At some stage these pages were folded and kept in his
pocket. See G. Brunet, *Le Pari de Pascal* (1956) 27.

26 'Unit XXXV' indicates the Esdras fragments (Lafuma,
Seuil 970-2). In the Seuil edition Lafuma prints the
three fragments together in the second part of his
appendix, 'Fragments non enregistrés par la copie.'
The first part of the appendix gives the many fragments
known from the Recueil Original but not recorded by
Copy 9203. The source for the Esdras fragments, on the
other hand, is given as 'la second copie.' The distinction is misleading because although the Esdras fragments
are, exceptionally, recorded by Copy 12449, the manuscripts of all of them do exist, in three different
places in the Recueil Original. That is why the Luxembourg edition recorded them as part of the R.O. material,
with the numbers 953, 949, and 968 (respectively).

The presentation of this Unit in different editions
is somewhat confusing. Most editors discern three
fragments, but Sellier divides the longest (La. 970)
into two separate ones, starting afresh with the paragraph on Tertullian (which, unlike the rest, was dictated). Tourneur (1938 edition) gave no. 970b in a footnote, with the Latin and Greek quotations translated.
The order of the fragments in Sellier's edition (faithful to Copy 12449) is different from what we find in

Lafuma (and Anzieu): 971 and 972 precede the two halves of 970 (S. 415-18). To confuse matters still further, Le Guern follows the order 972, 971, 970 (LG 708-10).

27 J. Mesnard, *Les Pensées de Pascal* 39.

28 *O.C.* I, 618.

29 P. Ernst has stated that one of the Esdras fragments (no. 972, Lux. 968) was originally on the same page as nos 206, 316, 566, and 570-1 ('Pascal au travail au jour le jour' in *Méthodes chez Pascal* [1979] 144). This lends support to my position. Two of the *pensées* written with no. 972 went into the *liasses*, and the rest into Unit XXIII. We shall see very shortly that Unit XXIII contains several fragments that mirror the preoccupations of 1656-7, and that nothing in that Unit causes me to doubt that it was constituted by 1658. Fragments 566 and 570-1 are, however, not among the fragments we can ascribe with confidence to 1656-7, and they are probably somewhat later. We should note also that Copy 12449 records the Esdras fragments *before* the fragments on miracles, but as we shall see, Sellier's theory that Copy 12449 is faithful to the chronology of the Units is not to be pushed very far.

30 P. Sellier, *Pascal et la Liturgie* (1966) 79, thinks that the number of liturgical echoes in the Prelude and Epilogue point to a later date, and he suggests 1658-9. The argument is not conclusive, and it could in any case be that the frame was written some time after the compilation of the 500 or so items of the *Life* itself. J. Mesnard also gives the later date (*Les Pensées de Pascal* 359).

The watermark and the ink traces on nos 550-2 suggest that this page is contemporary with nos 585-6 (Z. Tourneur, édition paléographique, 74 n5). Tourneur studied nos 585-6 at great length in his *Beauté poétique* (Paris: Vrin 1933), without clarifying the question satisfactorily. He showed that a lot of Pascal's ideas on eloquence are worked by Nicole into his *Dissertatio de vera pulchritudine et adumbrata* (1659), but that does not oblige us to believe that Pascal wrote them in 1658 or 1659. On the contrary, many examples cited by Tourneur go back to the year of the *Provinciales*. In the case of nos 585-6, M. Le Guern believes Pascal to be influenced by a letter of Descartes to Balzac, which was published in 1657 (*Pascal et Descartes* [Paris: Nizet 1971] 83-4, and edition

[1977] 308-9). Lafuma cites 585-6 among the late fragments, but offers no justification (*Recherches pascaliennes* 116, *Histoire des Pensées de Pascal* 24).

31 *Les Pensées de Pascal* 34.
32 See chapter 30, n59.
33 648, 726, 728. On 728 see T. Shiokawa, *Pascal et les
Miracles* (1977) 174 n177.
34 677, 708, 714, 726 again.
35 644 (implying 640-3 also), 653, 654, 659, 666-7 (implying 668 also), 676, 692, 700, ?706, 707 (perpetuity),
718 (cf. 880, XXXIII, and see chapter 25, n2), 721-2,
725 (cf. 864, XXXIV), 727, 729.
36 The texts are all given in L. Cognet's edition of *Les
Provinciales* (Paris: Garnier 1965), and Cognet discusses the question of Pascal's contribution in his
introduction and in the notes.
37 L. Cognet (ed.), *Les Provinciales* lxii-lxiii.
38 M. Le Guern (edition, 1977), note to LG 597.
39 The relevant passage is quoted in part by Lafuma.
(Lux. II, 125), more extensively by Le Guern (note to
LG 573). On the Copies, fr. 679 is entitled 'Prov,'
but that might refer not to a letter still in the
planning stage, but to the condemnation of the *Provinciales* (6 Sept. 1657), known in Paris on 18 Oct.
40 Ed. Cognet, 426, Seuil, 479, giving the same examples,
of Athanasius and Elias. The relevance of Elias is
clearer in the *Ecrit*.
41 Ed. Cognet, 465, Seuil, 486: 'toute la société des
casuistes ne saurait assurer la conscience contre la
vérité éternelle.'
42 Z. Tourneur, édition paléographique, 95 nn3, 5, 172 n1,
225 n11.
43 P. Ernst, 'Pascal au travail au jour le jour' in
Méthodes chez Pascal (1979) 141-53. He cites the page
containing nos 536-40 (536-43), from which no. 354 was
extracted, and 544-9, from which no. 140 was taken.
No. 160 belonged with no. 562, and no. 294 with no.
589. No. 566 was originally on the same page as nos
570-1, and that page contained nos 206 and 316 as well
as no. 972 (Lux. 968). See pp 143-5 and Plate XVIII.
There is one error on p 143: the space which once
housed no. 354 comes before, not after, no. 538.
44 The location of the ruled paper presents a very real
problem. It is striking that the fragments on this
paper in the twenty-eight *liasses* are in every case

except perhaps one of the last to be filed. (1° 1, 3°
53, 6° 105, 21° 279, 24° 324-31. There is no manuscript
extant for no. 323.) Why then is the paper found in
the middle of Unit XXIV and distributed throughout
Unit I? Because, says Mesnard, Pascal continued to
constitute these Units after he had stopped adding to
the *liasses à titre*, and Mesnard therefore does not
bracket XXIV ('éléments postérieurs à la constitution
des 28 liasses') with XXIII ('éléments contemporains').
See *Les Pensées de Pascal* (1976) 42, 45 and cf. p 26,
and L. Lafuma, 'Le puzzle des *Pensées*,' RSH 59 (1950)
170-2, reprinted in *Controverses pascaliennes* (1952)
45-52. This solution, on the face of it very plausible,
does not square with my reading of Unit I as witnessing
to a stage Pascal went beyond in the way he actually
constituted the twenty-eight *liasses*. And on what conscious principle is Unit XXIV constituted? It is also
noteworthy that while the Units contain relatively few
papers with pin-holes, most of them are in Units I,
XXIV, XXXII, and XXXIII.

Tourneur and Lafuma, who draw attention to the ruled
paper, are not wholly accurate in the indications they
give. Tourneur does not mention 330, 404, and 624:
Lafuma (Lux. edition, I, 371) puts his note beside 622
and 625 instead of 620 and 624. In *liasse* 25° Lafuma
wrongly continues noting 'papier réglé' as far as no.
332 instead of stopping at 330 or 331 (ibid. 199. The
paper recording no. 331 is not as obviously ruled as
are the others, but as Copy 9203 gives all of no. 323-
31 under one number, we can assume that they all belonged together).

45 J. Mesnard's (separate) comments on Units XXIII and
XXIV say this, essentially (*Les Pensées de Pascal* 42).
At least one fragment in Unit XXIV is later than a
corresponding fragment in Unit XXV: cf. nos 630 and 664.
Units XXIII and XXV, on the other hand, overlap, and
when we find corresponding fragments, the earlier one
is sometimes in Unit XXIII (522/678), sometimes in XXV
(665/554).

46 Ennui (622), Recherche du vrai bien (626, cf. 'Le
Souverain bien'), Prophéties (609, 624), Figuratif (cf.
'La loi figurative': 607, 614, 615).

47 J. Mesnard, in *Les Pensées de Pascal ont 300 ans* 27;
Les Pensées de Pascal 6, 8, 36, 42. Lafuma, on the
other hand, saw it as the title of 515 only (*Controverse*

pascaliennes 25 n1, answering Couchoud). P. Ernst, who
reconstructs a page which contained two fragments Pascal
put into *liasses* (206, 316), one Esdras fragment and
two pieces which went into Unit XXIII (566, 570-1)
concludes that the title Miscellenea must refer to
the 'textes non retenus' which it comprises ('Pascal
au travail,' commentary to Plate XVIII). J. Mantoy
('Des "Pensées" de Pascal à l'"Apologie"' [1955] 158
n48) even suggested that Pascal intended to publish
'un recueil de maximes diverses.' For my part, I would
note that the title comes three times in Unit XXIII,
with fragments 515, 559, 572, all of which deal with
language. Is that therefore what Pascal had in mind
when he joined separate fragments by the common title
'Miscellenea'? One other piece of evidence must be
given. Fragment 170, now in *liasse* 13° and bearing the
title 'Soumission,' was originally entitled 'Miscell.'
This fragment has nothing to do with language, and the
first title may well mean that before Pascal had a
framework he had thought of some of his notes as
'miscellaneous reflections.' I have already argued
that the fragments in *liasse* 13° go back to the period
of the miracles.
48 643, 649, 680, 689. Montaigne is quoted in nos 518,
520, 522, 524, 525, 526, 530, 533, 540, 552, 555, 558,
574, 576, 577; 627, 628, 629, 634; 638, 643, 649, 655,
656, 661, 668, 672, 678, 680, 681, 683, 688, 689, 705,
724 (B. Croquette, *Pascal et Montaigne* [1974] 51-68).
On the possible links between quotations taken from
the same page, which connect several fragments in these
Units to other fragments in the *liasse* see ibid. 91-9.
49 This is, deliberately, a generalization. But it applies
to nos 595, 596, 600, 612, 613, 617, 618, 620, 623,
626, 629, 631, 632, 633, and by extension it could
apply to 597, 619, 622, 634.
50 I quoted no. 550 in chapter 25 (a).
51 No. 662 is an observation of the co-presence of grace
and nature, no. 690 on the imputation of sin.
52 I do not see any reason to believe that the Units I
have been discussing contain any material written after
1658, despite Lafuma's unsubstantiated remark that
there are 'only three' fragments in Unit XXIII which
were definitely written after 1659 (*Recherches pascaliennes* 66).
    The only other suggestion that one of these papers

might be later than 1658 comes from Michel Le Guern's
explanation of fragments 660-3 (*Pascal et Descartes*
58-63). His explanation implies that Pascal knew
Descartes' letter of 1641 to 'Hyperaspistes.' The
correspondence in question was not published before
the end of May 1659. But as Le Guern says (p 63), there
is no proof that Pascal did not see the correspondence
earlier, in manuscript form. No. 663 is a note on infinity in the natural realm, a theme I have associated
with the year 1656. See also above, n30 on fr. 585.

53 The presence of fragments dating from 1660 in Units
XXVI, XXVII, and XXVIII makes it certain that those
Units, at least, were constituted in 1660 or 1661. I
would assign Unit XXII, and perhaps XXI, to the same
period. In the case of all the other Units in these
Groups there is room for doubt, to a lesser or greater
degree.

54 The manuscript of the following fragments are in
Gilberte's hand: 734, 735, 736-43, 744-5, 746, 747,
765-6 (XXVI); 774 (XXVII); 794 (XXVIII).

55 The period May-Sept. 1660 is proposed by J. Mesnard
in his book on the *Pensées* (p 45). Previously, he had
assumed that Gilberte's handwriting pointed to the
time when she was with Pascal in Paris, at the end of
1661 (*Cahiers de Royaumont* I [1959] 66). Michel Le
Guern accepted the later date in his *L'Image dans
l'oeuvre de Pascal* (Paris: A. Colin 1969) 51 n6. Lafuma
does not seem to have asked himself when Gilberte was
with Pascal, as he talks of Pascal dictating 'quelques
notes' to her 'au cours de cette période douloureuse,'
that is, before May 1660; but he adds 'à moins qu'elles
ne soient seulement de 1661' (*Histoire des Pensées de
Pascal* 24).

56 *Epigrammatum delectus* (printing date 20 Aug. 1659).
P. Ernst remarks that it is conceivable that Pascal
saw a proof copy some time before the date of publication ('Pascal au travail au jour le jour' in *Méthodes
chez Pascal* 150 n9).

57 The Chinese question is complex, and it affects several
Units besides XXX: V (no. 436), IX (454), and XI (481),
and others by association with the *pensées* cited. See
below, discussion of nos 481 and 454, pp 415-16 and 420

58 For the dating proposed for no. 797, see Lafuma's note
(II, 147-8). He mentions, among other reasons, that
the paper on which frs 797-8 were written was made

in the region where Pascal sojourned in the summer of
1660. Unfortunately, however, the same paper is also
used for a classified fragment, no. 338/25° (Tourneur
[1942 edition] 287 n5. The watermark B Rodier is very
distinct). Pol Ernst, who demolishes Lafuma's argument
in the note cited above, n56, believes the page recording 797-8 (and 796 also, although 797 cannot have
followed 796 directly) to be the other half of the
page which started with no. 241bis, though he hesitates
to conclude that they were written at the same time
(commentary to Plate XIX).

59 See M. Le Guern (edition [1977] note 1 to LG 466) and
J. Mesnard, *Les Pensées de Pascal* 90-1. The question
is lucidly treated by Elizabeth Moles, 'Three Categories
of Intelligence in Pascal,' *AJFS* 8 (1971) 259-68.

60 As does Lafuma (Lux. edition, II, 97). J.L. Couchoud
saw Units XXI and XXII as annexes to XXV ('La crise
des *Pensées* de Pascal,' *Le Flambeau* 38 [1955] 180 and
n2.

61 Eg, nos 2-3 and 5 (1°), 150, 158 (12°), 228, 244 (19°),
273 (20°), 298 (24°), 382 (28°), and also no. 391 (and
by extension 389) in Unit I.

62 The thinking behind fr. 733 (which comprises a number
of short developments on the theme of 'les erreurs
contraires') is recognizably that of the first *Ecrit
sur la Grâce* (Seuil, 311-14). In no. 733 Pascal notes
that when contrary errors co-exist, they destroy each
other. That of the two errors he has in mind (presumably Calvinist and Molinist, although the Molinists
are not named) the Calvinist is the more terrible as
the Calvinists are in schism. That the true faith contains what is true in all positions. That error is
possible because of the double nature of Christ. That
as men are fallen and redeemed, they can often be
described by oxymoron. That heretics assume that the
acceptance of one truth implies the rejection of its
literal opposite, whereas the relation of form and
content in a verbal utterance is not so exact, and
what looks like a formal denial can express a complementary truth. Examples are given, notably of the dual
nature of Christ.
    The first (so-called) of the *Ecrits sur la Grâce* –
it begins with a summary of the second one, and so
cannot be first in time – tackles the question 'does
salvation depend on the will of man or of God?' Pascal

argues that two different levels are involved, and that
the mutually contradictory views put forward by Calvinists and Molinists fail to make the necessary distinctions. The Augustinians have the full Catholic doctrine.

An epilogue to this exposition echoes fr. 733. The
Church is torn by 'des erreurs contraires' (those of
the Calvinists being the more terrible because they
are schismatic), but is not inconsolable because the
co-existence of errors leads to the establishment of
the truth. Pascal then adds another thought (also echoing 733): there are other instances of partial truths
leading to heresy, such as the doctrine of the nature
of Christ who was both man and God.

The last sentence of no. 733 takes us to the second
part of the first *Ecrit*, published only in 1947 (Seuil,
314-17, cf. L. Lafuma, *Deux pièces imparfaites sur la
Grâce et le Concile de Trente* [Paris: Vrin 1947] 34-46).

To date fr. 733, therefore, it would seem that all
that is necessary is to put a date to the first *Ecrit
sur la Grâce*. That is less easy than it sounds. Jan
Miel, who challenged many assumptions about the *Ecrits*
in his book *Pascal and Theology* (Baltimore: The Johns
Hopkins Press 1969) argues that Pascal's interest in
these questions antedates the *Provinciales*, even suggesting 1647 as a possible date for the short *Second
Ecrit*. But on the *Premier Ecrit* he concludes rather
lamely that the method used 'could suggest a rapproche-
ment' with something Nicole reported Pascal saying
'presumably around 1656-58' (p 199). And he mentions
parallels that have been noted with the *Cinquième
Ecrit des Curés de Paris* of May 1658.

These parallels are two. There is a link of the idea
of counter-errors destroying each other (Seuil, 481).
A little later, Pascal says that the Calvinists and
Jesuits are not equally at fault as the latter are
not in schism (pp 483-4). These parallels are, however,
not conclusive as to the date of fr. 733 (except in so
far as they render it most unlikely that fr. 733 was
written later than April 1658), because the context of
the *Cinquième Ecrit des Curés de Paris* is quite different from that of the *Premier Ecrit sur la Grâce*, and
Pascal appears simply to be borrowing ideas he had
developed for a different purpose. In the *Cinquième
Ecrit* Pascal is reacting to the Calvinists, who are
using Jesuit notions on casuistry as a stick with
which to beat the entire Catholic Church.

To confuse the matter even further, one is obliged
to note that the terms which Nicole uses to report
what Pascal said about writing a dissertation on grace
do not rule out a later date still. 'Il m'a même dit
quelquefois, que s'il eût disposé de son esprit, et
que ses maladies continuelles ne lui en eussent pas
ravi l'usage, il n'aurait pu s'empêcher de s'y appliquer' (quoted in the Seuil edition, 311).
There is an echo of no. 733 in no. 241 (*liasse* 19°).
The dual nature of Christ is there said to be the
'source des contrariétés.'

63 L. Lafuma used fragments 780-1 to prove that Pascal
did not modify the outline of his Apologia after 1658
(*Histoire des Pensées de Pascal* 25). I agree with his
conclusion, but hesitate to base it on this piece of
'evidence' as I feel happier with an earlier dating
for nos 780-1.

64 The so-called *Troisième Ecrit* is in the form of a letter
written to someone who is distrubed by the statement
made by the Council of Trent, 'que les commandements
ne sont pas impossibles aux justes.' The parallel with
fr. 791 comes towards the end of the first fragment of
the *Troisième Ecrit* (Seuil, 323). J. Mesnard believes
the correspondent to be the Duc de Roannez (*Pascal et
les Roannez* 515 nl). Jan Miel (*Pascal and Theology*
199-201) argues convincingly that the letter should
be dated 1655, that is before the first *Provincial*.

If Miel's argument is accepted, then the *Troisième
Ecrit* and the *Premier Ecrit*, quoted in n62, are independent. However, the paper containing no. 791 also
records ideas which seem relevant to the *Premier Ecrit*
and fr. 733: on words and meaning (784, 789), on contradictory formulations in the Bible (785), on the two
opposites (786, but the opposition here is Jesuits/
Jansenists), on the two states of man (788). On no.
786, see J. Miel, p 185 and n101.

65 The first fragments on the page (782-3) are in the
same general area as the long essay on the two infinites
(199).

66 For this reading of the text, see chapter 19, n12.

67 See chapter 19, n11.

68 Lafuma actually numbers it 432, which is very disconcerting. (I shall renumber it 821[bis].) Le Guern moves
it into Unit IV (LG 403); Sellier, more logically,
keeps it in Unit XXX, and gives it its own number
(S. 662). He does not call it a part of 432, but

describes both as notes for 427. See chapter 12, n16.

69 Ernst's researches offer a clue, but it turns out to be no less double-edged than the others. He believes that the paper containing no. 822 also contains no. 385 (I) and nos 593, 594-5 (XXIV). (See P. Ernst, 'Pascal au travail au jour le jour,' *Méthodes chez Pascal* [1979] Plate XVII, for a reconstruction of this page.) He deduces from this that Units I and XXIV remained 'open' after 1659. This appears to confirm J. Mesnard's view of these two Units (*Les Pensées de Pascal* 42, 43, 45). Yet my reading of the evidence, while allowing this possibility for Unit XXIV, makes it difficult to believe that Unit I was constituted late. See chapter 31, section (a), and also above, n44. No. 385 is used in part in fr. 326. The writing of no. 823 resembles that of no. 822.

70 See particularly J. Mesnard, *Les Pensées de Pascal* 43-5; P. Sellier (edition, 1976) 18.

71 Although the first Copy records Units III (427-31) and IV (432-5) separately, a note implies that they are in fact one Unit. See P. Sellier, edition, p 370 n10, and J. Mesnard, 'Aux origines de l'édition des *Pensées*: les deux Copies' in *Les Pensées de Pascal ont 300 ans* 24.

72 I noted earlier the presence in Unit XXIII of fragments addressed to the seeker rather than the unbeliever.

73 See above, n68.

74 No. 632 (XXIV), taken up into 427. Cf. 383 (I).

75 L. Lafuma frequently said that fr. 427 was written in 1661-2 (*Recherches pascaliennes* 66, Lux. edition, II, 76, *Controverses pascaliennes* 86, *Histoire des Pensées de Pascal* 25). In the last-named he justified the statement by saying: 'il commence même à rédiger, comme le rapporte le Père Beurrier, quelques pages qui semblent destinées à l'introduction de la seconde partie de son ouvrage, c'est à dire le très beau fragment sur l'immortalité de l'âme.' The note in the Luxembourg edition quotes the remark of Beurrier which is behind this allegation: 'il me dit que, depuis deux ans, il avait commencé à mettre par écrit ses pensées pour combattre toutes sortes d'impies et pour montrer clairement la vérité de la religion catholique, apostolique et romaine, pour les étendre au long dans le livre qu'il avait dessein de composer, si Dieu lui rendait la santé' (cf. *O.C.* I, 869). Why Lafuma took this

general statement to refer to no. 427 is a mystery.
Lafuma leaves without a comment the phrase 'depuis
deux ans' which, if true, would mean that the *Pensées*
were written after the eighteen-month illness. As J.
Mesnard says in his presentation of Beurrier's chapter
(ibid. 865), Beurrier is a very unreliable witness.

76 P. Sellier reads the evidence as meaning that fragments
438-50 were not divided on the manuscript (edition
[1976] 372 n1).

77 No. 428, however, reads more like a preface to part
two than a general preface. 'Avant que d'entrer dans
les preuves de la religion chrétienne, je trouve nécessaire de représenter...'

78 The date of XXX is more problematic than that of Unit
XXIV. In Unit XXX, no. 823 is another note on the
theme of indifference.

79 No. 731, which might look as if it reflects the thinking of no. 427 ('Ces gens manquent de coeur. On n'en
ferait pas son ami') is actually about something different, as one can see from fr. 610. Brunschvicg missed this (Br. 30, 194, 196 = La. 610, 427, 731).

80 P. Sellier identifies fr. 427 with the 'Lettre pour
porter à rechercher Dieu' of fragments 4, 5 and 11
(edition, 360).

81 A.J. Krailsheimer says that fr. 427 is 'probably con-
temporaneous with the Wager' (*Pascal* 63), but while
this is a refreshing change from the normal way of
dating it, I cannot think of it as being as early as
the date I have proposed for Unit II.

82 Most of the originals of Unit XI are lost. Only three
papers remain: 468-9 (in Pascal's hand), 464-6, and
467 (both dictated, to the same scribe). Sellier interprets 458 as the title of 459 (S. 697). On the
second copy, no. 459 is followed by La. 973 (inserted
on the verso of the previous page), on the Jesuits.
If Lafuma is right in saying that Pascal did not cut
up his papers after 1659 (see chapter 31, n71), then
Unit XI would have to be pre-1659, as would other related Units which Lafuma believed late.

83 No. 482 must be earlier than no. 402 in Unit I, which
is closer to the final selection of proofs.

84 Some, indeed, do reappear in the *liasses*. Fr. 474 is
allied to fr. 1102, and hence to no. 296. Fr. 476 is
taken up in no. 272.

85 The second Copy adds a fourth quotation, which is

also the last quotation of fr. 489. See below, n100.

86 Munich. An Amsterdam edition is dated 1659. Martini was a Jesuit missionary. M. Hay (*The Prejudices of Pascal* [London: Neville Spearman 1962] 22) thinks that was enough to make Pascal wish to refute him, which he did in a hasty, unthinking way.

87 B. Croquette does not even mention the reference to China in his list of borrowings from Montaigne (*Pascal et Montaigne* 48).

88 La Peyrère's book is a commentary on the theological implications of Romans 5:12-14. He mentions Chaldeans, Egyptians, Scythians, Chinese, Mexicans (ch. 8). In another work of the same year (*Systema theologicum ex Praeadamitarum*), La Peyrère refers to Scaliger's work *Opus de emendatione temporum* (1583), which evidently claimed that the history of such peoples as the Chaldeans, Egyptians, Gauls, and American Indians implied that the world was in its 'octingenties octagies (*sic*) millesimus septuagesimus tertius' - ie, 880,073rd - year (III.7). The number was translated by La Peyrère's English translator (p 177) as '808 score thousand and 73,' whatever that means. I have been unable to locate this quotation.

89 J. Mesnard, *Les Pensées de Pascal* 44 and discussion of P. Ernst's paper in *Méthodes chez Pascal* 163-4; P. Sellier (edition, 1976) 341 n4. Cf. ibid. 390 n6.

90 P. Sellier (edition) 372 n1.

91 This reading differs from that of J. Mesnard, *Les Pensées de Pascal* 43. It is strengthened by P. Ernst's contention that the page that contained nos 490-9 originally contained no. 252 also. I might add that the order in which Lafuma records the ten fragments of R.O. 277 is as inexplicable as the order adopted by the authors of the Copies. The most reasonable order would seem to be
(a) top line, 491 with 494 (left) and 490 (top right)
(b) centre left, 493, 496, 497
(c) centre right, 495, 492
(d) bottom, 499, 498
The Copy keeps the groups, but shuffles the order round: 491, 490, 494; 495, 493, 497, 496, 492; 498, 499. Le Guern (LG 454) is on the right track, but places 494 after 493 and 497, and places 496 after 495 and 492. Sellier (S. 736) follows the Copy, except that for the second group he chooses the order: 495, 496, 492, 497, 493. (497 is omitted from the concordance, p 515.)

92 Jewish teaching also (see below). That explains its appearance on this sheet. A change to the text of no. 491 shows Pascal modifying a doctrinaire statement to make it more appropriate to the neutral theology he adopted for part one: 'L'homme n'agit plus par la raison qui fait son être' becomes 'L'homme n'agit point...'

93 See chapter 20, section (c), pp 211-12.

94 Cf. 494 and 495 in Unit XIX, 592, 593, and 615 in Unit XXIV, and also 488 in Unit XVI. The word 'témoins' with this precise meaning comes only once in the *liasses* (331), although in a more general sense it comes also in 204 and 291.

   The theme of the 'témoins suspects' goes back, however, to the time of the *Provinciales*: 'Comme les Juifs qui portent les livres, qui ne sont point suspects aux gentils, ils nous portent leurs Constitutions' (964, Lux. 966). One note on the same page ('Notre religion qui est toute divine') seems to look forward to no. 243. The Jesuit Constitutions are mentioned on no. 877 (Unit XXXIII) and also on nos 920 and 952 (Lux. 954).

95 Cf. no. 614 (XXIV), 496 (XIX), and 469 in Unit XI.

96 See chapter 20, n11.

97 They were noted on one of the developments on miracles (835).

98 Cf. my comment in chapter 20, pp 219-20.

99 Units VI to XVII are all written and laid out in a similar way, with the striking exception of Units X (456-7) and of course XI.

100 See Lafuma's note to no. 459. M. Le Guern (note to LG 427) tells us that Copy 9203 includes the last quotation of no. 489 among the quotations of no. 459. This indication should read: Copy 12449. It appears in both places in Sellier's edition (S. 697 and 735).

101 Lux. II, 83, and 'Notes pascaliennes,' *DSS* 7-8 (1950) 207-8.

102 I have accepted in this chapter the usual view, that Pascal did indeed classify his *pensées* before being overtaken by illness early in 1659. If, however, we abandon that hypothesis, many of the problems raised by this chapter disappear. A. Adam in his review of Lafuma's *Recherches pascaliennes* (RSH 57-8 [1950] 135) was of that opinion (see chapter 31, n71) and he cited evidence that Pascal had resumed work in 1660. But although it has its attractions, such a radical theory does present disadvantages. As I said earlier (p 339),

Pascal must have been writing at the same time as he was sorting, as the act of classifying inspired fresh ideas. This makes me reluctant to propose a late date for Pascal's work on the *liasses*. Once again I have to conclude that I cannot be sure. There is certainly much more to be discovered about the composition of the Apologia.

CONCLUSION

1 For example, J. Terrasse, at the end of his chapter 'Pascal et l'ironie: *Les Pensées*' in *Rhétorique de l'essai littéraire* (Montreal: Presses de l'Université du Québec [1978] 42) directs this shaft at Patricia Topliss: 'Que vaut une étude de l'art de persuader dans les *Pensées*, dans l'ignorance de ce qu'eût été l'ordre des arguments dans la version définitive?' Terrasse would have us believe that we should abandon any attempt to read the *Pensées* as a rhetorical strategy, and instead study them as expression. 'La figure renvoie au public auquel l'oeuvre s'adresse, et pourtant, si le paradoxisme est l'expression d'une vision du monde, la référence à l'auditoire est superflue' (p 30). This is another case of fighting a half-truth with a half-truth. Both readings are possible, and they are complementary.

2 B. Norman, 'Logic and Anti-Rhetoric in Pascal's *Pensées*,' *FF* 2 (1977) 24.

3 The obvious example of a critic exaggerating and distorting the importance of the wager is L. Goldmann in *Le Dieu caché*, 1955. This has been commented on many times. See, for example, A. Blanchet, 'Pascal est-il le précurseur de Karl Marx?,' *Etudes* 292 (1957) 321–37; J. Mesnard, 'Le drame de la foi chez Pascal,' *CUC* (Mar. 1958) 311–13, 315; and *Les Pensées de Pascal* (1976) 314–17.

4 R.E. Lacombe, *L'Apologétique de Pascal* (Paris: PUF 1958) 13–14. He dismisses the evidence of the Copy in a footnote (19).

5 The most disconcerting example of Brunschvicg being chosen in preference to Lafuma is the Saint-Etienne reproduction (1971) of the Port-Royal edition, where it would clearly have been so useful to have seen how the first editors used their own copy. It is regrettable too to find a student guide using Brunschvicg (C. Genet

in the Hatier 'Profil d'une oeuvre' series, 1973).
Among other critics in the seventies to have given
Brunschvicg references only are: Ian Alexander. A.
Badawi, Edward Bloomberg (though not in his *Romantic
Review* article), A. Glauser, R. Ledent, L.M. Heller
(though Delmas is used in his article in *Dix-septième
siècle*), Kathleen Jamieson, L. Marin (in *La Critique
du Discours*), J.L. Marion, M. Scholtens (who consistently spells the name of his chosen editor with a q),
P. Secretan, E. Tassing (who also facours icq), H. Van
Lier. Two articles in *Yale French Studies* no. 49 give
Brunschvicg, but that might be a decision of the review,
not the authors (Buford Norman and Virginia Howe). In
YFS no. 52, however, Louis Marin gives both Brunschvicg
and Delmas, as he does elsewhere. Brunschvicg and Delmas
are also both given by Maria Vamos. Sara Melzer, like
several others, gives both Brunschvicg and Lafuma, but
(unlike others) gives Brunschvicg first. On editions
which perpetuate Brunschvicg, see introduction, n86.

   Apart from Brunschvicg, Lafuma has few rivals. In
his book on *Science and the Human Comedy* (Toronto 1976),
Harcourt Brown uses Anzieu, while M. Tetel (article in
Saggi e Ricerche in 1974) and J. Terrasse (*Rhétorique
de l'essai littéraire*, Montreal 1978) use Chevalier.
The Delmas numbering is rarely used nowadays (two exceptions from 1973: C.S. MacKenzie and Pierrette
Fourcade-Guillaume). The vast majority of writers on
Pascal do appear to have adopted Lafuma's 'objective'
scheme, especially since the publication of the Intégrale edition in 1963.
6 'Il n'y a pas de contexte dans l'édition de Brunschvicg,'
   said L. Lafuma in a review of L. Goldmann's *Dieu caché*
   in *Etudes franciscanes* 7 (1956) 177. He taxed Goldmann
   with inconsistency in using the Brunschvicg edition
   while insisting that nothing should be studied out of
   context. Cf. J. Mesnard, 'Le drame de la foi chez
   Pascal,' *CUC* (Mar. 1958) 313, 315.
7 One has only to read the critical study of Roger Lacombe
   to see that a highly intelligent and scrupulous reader,
   using the Brunschvicg edition and indeed explicitly
   rejecting Lafuma's claims (see pp 23-8) can bring out
   the strands of Pascal's thought in a wholly acceptable
   way. Cf. below, n30, on R. Amadou.
8 Brunschvicg could point to fr. 12 for justification
   ('et puis montrer qu'elle est vraie'), but the evidence

of the Copies enables us to be more nuanced. The historical proofs occupy the last six of Brunschvicg's fourteen sections, beginning with Br. 589. For a more ample discussion of Brunschvicg and other editions, see Appendix C.

9 H.M. Davidson, *The Origins of Certainty: Means and Meanings in Pascal's 'Pensées'* (Chicago: University of Chicago Press 1979) 144 n4.

10 'The Pensées ... should ... be read ... as tactical projects and sketches' (J.J. Demorest, 'Pascal's Sophistry and the Sin of Poesy,' in *Studies in Seventeenth-Century French Literature Presented to Morris Bishop* [1962] 143).

11 See the conclusion of F.M. Chambers, 'Pascal's Montaign *PMLA* 65 (1950) 790-804.

12 R.E. Lacombe, *L'Apologétique de Pascal* (1958) 313. Note, however, J. Dedieu's insistence that Pascal is Augustinian, rather than specifically Jansenist ('Survivances et influences de l'apologétique traditionnelle dans les *Pensées*,' *RHLF* 37 (1930) 481-513, and 38 (1931) 1-39). Dedieu returned to the point in his review of Jeanne Russier's *La foi de Pascal*, *DSS* 9-10 (1951) 35-49, and thereby stirred up a veritable hornet's nest (see *DSS* 17-18 [1953] 59-77). Pascal's relation to Augustinian apologetics is discussed by Julien-Eymard d'Angers, 'Les *Pensées* de Pascal à la lumière des apologétiques de son temps,' in *Textes du Tricentenaire* (Paris: Fayard 1963) 167-94. That Pascal was permeated by St Augustine is demonstrated by Philippe Sellier's study (1970), and that the distinction between Augustinianism and Jansenism is often difficult to draw is obvious as soon as one tries to do so. The difference - essential - is more one of historical context than of doctrine.

13 D.C. Potts ('Pascal's Contemporaries and "le divertissement",' *MLR* 57 [1962] 31-40) has shown that the *honnête homme* whom Pascal regarded as his adversary made an analysis of *le divertissement* very similar to Pascal's. But the *honnête homme* felt no anxiety, and that is what Pascal had to awaken (p 39).

14 On the proper perspective for viewing the 'tragic' Pascal, see the remarks of P.H. Simon, 'Pascal, l'histoire et la Justice' in *Le Jardin et la Ville* (Paris: Seuil 1962) 46-58, esp. 50-3. Simon rightly sees the negative aspects of certain *pensées* as moments in a

rhetorical strategy ('renversement du pour au contre'), Pascal's own vantage-point being significantly different from the one provisionally adopted by his persona. Cf. J. Mesnard, 'Le drame de la foi chez Pascal,' *CUC* (Mar. 1958) 314-15, an article which treats the whole question most authoritatively: 'Si la pensée de Pascal passe par un moment de tension, elle s'achève dans l'apaisement.' Simon nevertheless finds, both in the emotional charge of the writing and in the clear implications of some of Pascal's statements, an exaggerated pessimism which must be attributed to 'une théologie de la corruption irrémédiable' (p 57). Cf. above, chapter 14, n5.

15 E.D. James notes that whereas 'the ultimate aim of Pyrrhonism ... was to achieve *ataraxia* or unperturbedness,' for Pascal 'Pyrrhonism was to be a means of perturbing the unperturbed' ('Scepticism and Religious Belief: Pascal, Bayle, Hume' in *Classical Influences on Western Thought, A.D. 1650-1870* [Cambridge: University Press 1979] 93).

16 Janet Morgan, 'Pascal, Concupiscence and "La Machine",' *MLR* 71 (1976) 272-81.

17 Writers have pointed out that 'custom' does not apply only to the body. Janet Morgan, art. cit., 279, H.M. Davidson, *The Origins of Certainty* 84-90.

18 See the excellent (Brunschvicg-based) article by R. Amadou, 'Remarques sur la dialectique des *Pensées* de Pascal,' *Age nouveau* 66 (1951) 85-93. 'Les textes contradictoires des *Pensées* sont des moments de la dialectique pascalienne' (p 86). Amadou sees three stages in the argument. The first chapters are addressed to the *libertin*, not even interested in seeking, and are aimed to awaken that desire. The next chapters are addressed to the seeker, and encourage the use of reason - up to a certain point. The final stage suggests the adventure of faith that lies beyond the limits of reason. Amadou argues that for fallen man, whose faculties are double-edged, Pascal's apologetic method is the only valid one.

19 *L'Apologétique de Pascal* 146.

20 Even if one is temperamentally more drawn to part one (cf. the Davidson quotation earlier), part two cannot be left to the specialists (R.E. Lacombe, *L'Apologétique de Pascal* 312).

21 As was done by R.E. Lacombe, in his *L'Apologétique de*

Pascal in 1959. See also M. Hay, *The Prejudices of Pascal* (London: Neville Spearman 1962) and E. Eydoux, *Dialogue avec Blaise Pascal* (Marseille: Eydoux 1968).

22 In his article 'Théologie de la foi et méthode apologétique dans les *Pensées*' (*Méthodes chez Pascal* [1979] 53-61), P. Golliet argues from an examination of fr. 149 that it is not a matter in the Apologia of disputing questions of dogma but of revealing the authority of God, making Jesus recognizable.

23 Kathleen Jamieson ('Pascal vs Descartes: A Clash over Rhetoric in the Seventeenth Century,' *Communication Monographs* 43 [1976] 44-50) makes the simple point that Pascal rejected Descartes' certainty-based method for a probability-based rhetoric.

24 In Jean Mesnard's words, religion is presented as reasonable, not rational (*Les Pensées de Pascal* 179 n1).

25 See, however, Janet Morgan, 'Pascal's Three Orders,' *MLR* 73 (1978) 757-8.

26 'Je ne crois pas que les *Pensées* aient converti un seul homme au christianisme,' Elie Faure, *Montaigne et ses trois premiers nés* (Paris: Crès 1926) 227, part of a passage recently reprinted as the presentation of the Pascal number of *Europe* (597-8, Jan.-Feb. 1979; see p 5). Annie Barnes has reminded me that Méré died a Christian.

27 See J.E. d'Angers' conclusion to his paper published in *Pascal: Textes du Tricentenaire* 194.

28 On Pascal's ambivalent attitude to biblical criticism, see R.E. Lacombe, *L'Apologétique de Pascal* 210-13. Lacombe commends Pascal for seeing the need for a critical reading of the Bible, but points out that by relying for guidance on the theologians of Port-Royal, Pascal was fatally unaware of the direction which biblical criticism was moving around 1660, and his remarks do nothing to ward off the attacks which were to come with increasing vehemence. J. Orcibal has argued that Pascal's Apologia would have survived Spinoza. 'Pascal n'a jamais dit en effet qu'ombres et lumières fussent à chaque moment placées aux mêmes points, ni même que la proportion d'ombre et de lumière restât constante. Pour que son Apologie fût, d'après ses propr principes, ruinée, il faudrait que l'histoire n'offrît plus au surnaturel aucun point d'insertion, que la loi fût, non plus "au-dessus de" la raison, mais "contre" elle, que Mahomet eût autant de droits à notre amour

que le Christ' ('Vers le Pascal de l'histoire,' *SAPR*
2 [1951] 41-2).

If from one point of view, Pascal's treatment of
biblical evidence seems almost laughably inadequate,
from another, theologians have been quick to salute
the validity of his insights. The well-known study of
M.J. Lagrange is a case in point ('Pascal et les
prophéties messianiques,' *Revue biblique* 3 [1906]
533-66). See also H. Morikawa, 'Sur la théologie biblique dans *les Pensées* de Pascal,' *Kwansei Gakuin
University Annual Studies* 17 (1968) 39-51. P. Golliet,
'Théologie de la foi et méthode apologétique dans les
Pensées' says that if we follow Pascal literally, his
argument is unacceptable. 'Mais dans l'ensembble,
s'est-il tellement trompé? Les progrès récents de
l'exégèse rendent plus difficile que jamais de l'affirmer' (p 61).

29 This accusation was first made by a reader of the very
first edition: L'abbé Villars in the fifth dialogue of
his book *De la délicatesse*, published by Barbin in the
last third of 1671.

30 In his book *Questions of Religious Truth* (London:
Gollancz 1967), W. Cantwell Smith said that the debate
is between a faith in reason and a faith in God (p 25).
A. Dulles ('Justifier la foi chrétienne,' *Communio* 3
[July 1978] 41-53) says it is recognized that reason
cannot constitute a completely coherent system. 'La
raison n'est plus apte, désormais, à fournir un ensemble complet et cohérent dont la vérité serait certaine.' Most of the articles in that number of *Communio*
(on 'la cause de Dieu') are pertinent to the present
discussion. On the role of faith and reason in Pascal's
Apologia, see I.W. Alexander, 'Raison, existence, être
selon les notions de Pascal,' in *Mouvements premiers*
(1973) 51-63, and T. Shiokawa, 'La connaissance par
l'autorité selon Pascal,' *ELLF* 30 (1978) 1-14.

31 J.H. Walgrave, 'Le grand malentendu théologique,'
Communio 3 (July 1978) 6-16.

32 J. Mesnard, 'Un penseur moderne: Pascal?,' *Nouvelles
de l'Institut catholique de Paris* (June 1978) 15-25;
'Dieu par Jésus-Christ,' *Communio* 3 (July 1978) 27-40.

33 Cf. Alan Richardson, *Christian Apologetics* (London:
SCM 1947), esp. ch. 5. Cf. also the article of J.L.
Marion quoted in note 35 below, p 17 n1. Modern think-
ing is less dismissive of 'le Dieu des philosophes'

than was Pascal. Cf. W.C. Smith, *Questions of Religious Truth* 85, Hans Küng, *On Being a Christian* (New York: Doubleday 1976), esp. the section on 'The Challenge of the World Religions' 89-116. On Pascal's attitude, see H. Gouhier, 'Le refus de la philosophie dans la nouvelle apologétique de Pascal,' *CPR* 20-1 (1972) 19-37.

34 The motif of encounter is a commonplace of contemporary theology. Cf. among others, W.C. Smith *Questions of Religious Belief* 122, and A. Dulles, 'Justifier la foi chrétienne' (*Communio* 3, July 1978, 41-53).

35 J.L. Marion, in an article with a Pascalian title: 'De connaître à l'aimer: l'éblouissement' (*Communio* 3 [July 1978] 17-28).

36 A point well made by M. Guersant in the introduction to his edition (1954) lxxxi.

37 P. Sellier, *Pascal et Saint Augustin* 517.

38 M. Guersant, edition (1954) lxxxviii.

39 Many years ago, H.F. Stewart remarked that Matthew Arnold's *Literature and Dogma* (1873) 'constantly echoes the argument and the very expressions of the Apology' (*Pascal's Apology for Religion* [1942] xviii, note). A recent book of this kind, *Reasons for Faith* by O.R. Barclay (London: Inter-Varsity Press 1974), while it is concerned, as its title indicates, only with the rational case for Christianity, begins with preliminary cautions about the nature of faith and the nature of Christianity, of which Pascal would certainly have approved. Barclay's remark about 'wishful thinking and wishful unthinking' (p 18) implies a very Pascalian attitude to unbelief.

40 See J. Dedieu, 'Survivances et influences de l'apologétique traditionnelle dans les Pensées,' *RHLF* 37 (1930) 481-513 and 38 (1931) 1-39. On Pascal's originality, in particular his reasons for rejecting the traditional arguments from nature, see also J. Dagens, 'Tradition et innovation dans les *Pensées* de Pascal,' *Rivista di letterature moderne* 4 (1953) 23-32.

41 J. Dedieu insists that Pascal is original neither in presenting a picture of the *misère* of the human condition, nor in dwelling on man's aspiration for happiness, but he is very original in combining these two motifs ('Survivances et influences de l'apologétique traditionnelle dans les *Pensées*' 513). Original too, I would add, in adopting a style familiar to the *honnête homme*.

42 The case for considering the *Pensées* in this way was
   forcibly put by E.B. Borgerhoff in an important article
   entitled 'The Reality of Pascal: The *Pensées* as rhetoric,'
   Sewanee Review 65 (1957) 15-33.
43 Cf. Jean Mesnard, 'La théorie des figuratifs dans les
   Pensées de Pascal,' *RHPC* 35 (1943) 244: 'Dans la seconde
   partie des "Pensées" Pascal soumet donc l'Ancien Testament à la même analyse que l'homme dans la première
   partie. L'un et l'autre sont réduits à l'état de tissu
   de contradictions, de chiffre. L'analogie va plus loin:
   la solution de l'un et l'autre chiffre se trouve en
   Jesus Christ en qui "toutes les contradictions sont
   accordées".' (The reference is to no. 257.) In an article which first appeared in Japanese in 1970, M.
   Hirota showed how the notion of 'figure' illuminates
   the whole of Pascal's thinking (see the *Hitotsubashi
   Journal of Arts and Sciences* 17 [1976] 18-27).
44 Two articles in *YFS* 49 (1973): Virginia K. Howe, '*Les
   Pensées*, Paradox and Signification' 120-31, B. Norman,
   'Thought and Language in Pascal' 110-19. E. Morot-Sir,
   Le metaphysique de Pascal (Paris: PUF 1973), and
   'Pascal versus Wittgenstein, with Samuel Beckett as
   the Anti-Witness,' *RN* 15 (1974) 201-16. L. Marin,
   '"Pascal": Text, Author, Discourse...' *YFS* 52 (1975)
   129-51, and *La critique du discours* (Paris: Editions
   de Minuit 1975). B. Norman, 'Logic and Anti-Rhetoric
   in Pascal's *Pensées*' 22-33. Sara E. Melzer, 'Codes of
   Space in the *Pensées*,' *FR* 51 (1978) 816-23 and 'Pascal's
   Pensées: The Rhetoric of *invraisemblance*,' *PFSL* 8 (1977-8)
   51-64, reworked as 'Invraisemblance in Pascal's *Pensées*:
   The Anti-Rhetoric' *RR* 73 (1982) 33-44.
45 See M. Le Guern, *L'Image dans l'Oeuvre de Pascal* (Paris:
   A. Colin 1969) 224-47, 252-4. Cf. also F. Germain, 'Imagination et vertige dans les deux infinis,' *RSH* 97 (1960) 31-
   40, in which the author argues that Pascal puts persuasion
   above rigour of thought. On this point, see Le Guern 220-3.
46 E.B.O. Borgerhoff, 'The Reality of Pascal: The *Pensées*
   as Rhetoric' (pp 29-30) treats no. 121 similarly.
47 Recent writing on language (see n33) tends to stress
   discontinuity, with resolution taking place on a different level. See E. Morot-Sir's comments on divine
   language (*RN* 15 [1974] 210-14), L. Marin's remarks on
   the 'discourse of love' realized only in Jesus (*YFS* 52
   [1975] 151 and *La critique du discours* 417).
48 This is apparent from the two fragments in the first

liasse which give a bird's-eye view of the whole strategy. No. 12 shows Pascal concerned with uncovering
the psychological mechanism which lies behind belief
and unbelief. Even there the syntax makes parallels
between the stages he envisages. No. 6 simply states
the two main concerns of the enterprise in two different ways, and the connection is left to the syntax.
Both formulations suggest that there will be a discernible parallelism between the two halves. Gérard Antoine
in an article on 'le langage de Pascal' (*Table Ronde*
171 [Apr. 1962] 56-71) talks of the antitheses being
crowned (p 57) but unfortunately he does not develop
the point. B. Norman, 'Logic and Anti-Rhetoric in
Pascal's *Pensées*' 27-8, quotes two 'parallel structures'
(frs 784 and 388), insisting that Pascal explains nothing. Insofar as this leads Norman to conclude that the
reader is stimulated to provide his own connections
(pp 30-2), this is a valid comment on Pascal's rhetorical strategy, but it seems to me to play down the
positive implications of the formal associations.

49 For a discussion, often difficult, but stimulating,
of the way paradox is 'tenuously resolved by a figure,'
see the article by Joseph Weber, 'Person as Figure of
Ambiguity and Resolution in Pascal,' *PMLA* 84 (1969)
312-20.

50 L.M. Heller has noted that in the second half of the
Apologia, Pascal no longer has recourse to his own
personal experience. In the first half he used this
device to provoke a response from the reader. ('Autobiographical Allusions in Pascal's Apology,' *RUO* 43
[1973] 602-13.) Similarly, the frequence of images
declines dramatically. Although M. Le Guern in his
book on Pascal's imagery (*L'Image dans l'Oeuvre de
Pascal*) does not consider the images from this point
of view, a glance at the index will quickly show how
infrequent images are after the mid-point (14°) of the
Apologia. Take away the observations on the Bible as
a figurative text and one is left with very few examples. For a different perspective, see P. Sellier,
'L'ascension et la chute,' *CPR* 20-1 (1972) 116-26.

APPENDIX B

1 J. Mantoy, *Des "Pensées" de Pascal à l'"Apologie"*
(1954).

2 P. Ernst, *Approches pascaliennes* (1970).
3 M. and M.-R. Le Guern, *Les Pensées de Pascal* (1972).
4 J. Mesnard, *Pascal* (1951) 148-9.
5 J. Mesnard, *Les Pensées de Pascal* (1976) 228.
6 A.J. Krailsheimer, *Pascal* (Oxford 1980) 56.
7 See chapter 31, pp 374-5.

APPENDIX C

1 Sister Marie Louise Hubert has interesting comments
  on Brunschvicg, Stewart, and Chevalier in her *Pascal's
  Unfinished Apology* ([1952] 9-18). Patricia Topliss's
  observations merely summarize Hubert, without acknowledgment (*The Rhetoric of Pascal* [1966] 155). See also
  A. Béguin, 'Les éditions et l'ordre des *Pensées*,'
  Critique 4 (1948) 887.
2 *Pensées et Opuscules* (Paris: Hachette 1897). *Pensées*,
  ibid., Les Grands Ecrivains de la France, three volumes,
  1904. Also as vols XII-XIV of *Oeuvres complètes*, ibid.
  1914.
3 H.F. Stewart, 'Vers une nouvelle édition de *l'Apologie*
  de Pascal,' *French Quarterly* 3 (1921) 132-51. (Ed.),
  Pascal's Apology for Religion (Cambridge: University
  Press 1942). Also *Pascal's Pensées with an English
  Translation* (London: Routledge and Kegan Paul 1950).
    The bibliography of Chevalier's editions is a little
  complicated. The Gabalda edition (*Pensées sur la vérité
  de la religion chrétienne*, 1925) was the first, and
  it was reissued in 1927. In 1936 the Bibliothèque de
  la Pléiade brought out a complete Pascal, edited by
  Chevalier, and the same company (Gallimard) published
  the *Pensées* alone the following year. In one detail
  at least the 1936 text differs from that of 1925: in
  fr. 44 (Chevalier 102) the word 'troupes' ('Ces troupes
  armées') replaced 'trognes' with a note to say that
  'certains des éditeurs ont lu, à tort ce semble: trognes.' 'Trognes' is actually the copyists' reading, and
  has recently been vigorously defended by Le Guern (see
  note 12 to LG 41). Cf. Tourneur (1938 edition, 18 n2).
    The 1936 edition was reprinted in 1950, unchanged.
  In 1949, however, Chevalier had revised the text
  (Boivin, an edition not listed in R. Francis *Les
  Pensées en France* [1958] 378). This revised version
  was then used for the new Pléiade edition, which came
  out in 1962, although the date of the copyright is

1954. The preface, moreover, was dated 1953 and yet
it refers to articles published in 1955 and 1956. See
n1 to p xviii on p 1363 – where the reference is wrongly
given as p xvi! The 1962 edition was reprinted in 1976.
The revised version is used also in the edition put
out by the Biblioâtres de Paris in 1960, and in the
Livre de Poche edition of 1962, prefaced by J. Guitton.

A brief digression on two further changes to the
text of no. 44 might be welcome. From 1949 Chevalier
accepts the reading Lafuma (following Couchoud) proposed in his first Delmas text: 'ils se font accompagner' for 'ils se sont accompagnés.' (Geneviève Lewis
makes the same choice in the deluxe edition of 1950.)
Jean Pommier informed us in his review of the Delmas
edition (*RHLF* 49 [1949] 181) that Lafuma had wisely
gone back to the traditional reading, which he did in
the second Delmas and in the Luxembourg, but from 1958,
'font accompagner' is back.

Another new change made in 1949 was to replace 'halle-
bardes' by 'arbalétriers' (in the same paragraph). In
the first Delmas, Lafuma has proposed 'balestriers'
which he then changed to 'balafrés (?).' Le Guern has
a different suggestion: 'balourds.'

4 E. Janssens, another staunch supporter of Filleau de
la Chaise, also implies that justice comes in only
when the interlocutor raises an objection (*RNP* 12
[1905] 449, *La philosophie et l'apologétique de Pascal*
[1906] 109.)

5 Chevalier's word. It is not the word Pascal uses for
the highest order, as Annie Barnes reminded us ('Comment lire les *Pensées*,' *CPR* 20-1 [1972] 10).

APPENDIX D

1 Guersant and Steinmann also print them, without any
indication that they were later deleted.

APPENDIX E

1 G. Brunet, *Le Pari de Pascal* (Paris: Desclée de Brouwer
1956). H. Gouhier, *Blaise Pascal: Commentaires* (Paris:
Vrin 1966), ch. 5. G. Coulet commented on Brunet's
book: 'Il est impossible de ne pas être frappé par le
caractère nouveau que prend ainsi le texte' ('Pascal
écrivant,' *Annales de la Faculté des Lettres et Sciences*

humaines d'Aix 37 [1963] 149). The question is partly treated by M. Horino, 'Sur le processus du "Pari" de Pascal,' *ELLF* 34 (1979) 19-44, to which the reader is referred for a fuller survey of critical opinion than given here. There are, however, many problems which M. Horino does not mention, and his principal argument (see below, n12) is not strong enough to bear the weight he places upon it. His distinction between a 'first version' based on Charron with reminiscences of others (my pp 1, 2A, and 2B) and a double development, both very original, is well taken.

2 This became 'Dieu est' when it was amplified later.
3 Brunet and Gouhier have conflicting views on the significance of this sentence. I find Brunet's explanation (pp 69-71) more plausible than that of Gouhier (pp 255-6). Gouhier's reading was adopted also by L.M. Heller, 'La Correction fraternelle,' *DSS* 83 (1969) 17-24. Horino's treatment of no. 422 is inadequate (art. cit., 20-22). See n19 below.
4 Brunet, 75, and 95.
5 Gouhier, 265.
6 Gouhier, 271.
7 Gouhier, 266. In his article (p 30) M. Horino arrives at the same conclusion by a different route. He believes that Pascal would not have written his moral addition on p 2 if p 3 had been available. If it was not available, that was not, he argues, because it was already filed (Gouhier's supposition) but because Pascal simply did not have any spare paper to hand. One cannot be dogmatic about this. Evidently, the blank sheet was available when Pascal wrote 2R in the only space left on p2, and p 3-4 is evidently the other half of the large sheet Pascal had folded and cut. Hirota's argument is therefore not wholly convincing. But certainly the way the words are crammed onto p 2 does indicate an initial reluctance on Pascal's part to start a new sheet.
8 Brunet, 72.
9 Ibid. 90.
10 Gouhier, 270 n34.
11 Ibid. 270.
12 Ibid. 270.
13 Brunet, 91.
14 Gouhier, 273.
15 Brunet 91.

16 Gouhier, 273.

17 Brunet, 93.

18 J. Orcibal, 'Le fragment infini-rien et ses sources,'
   Cahiers de Royaumont 1 (1956) 176 n5. M. Horino, art.
   cit., 26, 43 n7.

19 The wickedly and wittily entitled study of P. Lønning
   (*Cet effrayant Pari* [Paris: Vrin 1980]) arrived long
   after the above was in the hands of the editor.
   Lønning treats the difficulties of the manuscript in
   his third chapter. We agree on the primacy of the
   moral argument over the mathematical, and on the interpretation of the triangles (though Lønning does
   not mention the scored-out triangle following 2A).
   Lønning's treatment of the intricacies of additions
   within additions is, however, inadequate. Some of his
   incidental insights are helpful, such as that Pascal
   began the mathematical addition (2R) on p 2 in order
   to give himself a 'flying start' (Lønning uses the
   English expression), that La. 422 is quite irrelevant
   to the argument of the rest, and that many of the additions were very likely triggered off by discussion
   with acquaintances to whom Pascal showed the first
   sheet.
        In chapter 4 (106-8) Lønning has interesting obser-
   vations on 2T. He explains the apparent hiatus by
   imagining 2T as an independent record of the reaction
   of Pascal's interlocutor. Further, he argues that 2T
   must have been written before 3F, because had the new
   sheet been available, Pascal would not have crushed
   his addition into such a constricted space. He explains
   3F as an elaboration of the cryptic 'etc.' of 2TT,
   made, necessarily, after the mathematical development
   of 2R, 3A, and 3B. This last point does not wholly
   convince me, but I think that Lønning's argument does
   tip the balance in favour of the earlier dating for
   2T.

Bibliography

This bibliography lists every item mentioned in the course of the book. Items not asterisked are of minimal interest, at least for the purposes of this study. A double asterisk designates an item particularly relevant to the subject of the present enquiry.

I. *Editions of Pascal*

Complete editions (listed alphabetically according to editor's name)

**Oeuvres de Blaise Pascal*, Paris: Hachette, Les Grands Ecrivains de la France, 14 vols. Première série, *Oeuvres jusqu'au Mémorial de 1643*, ed. L. Brunschvicg and P. Boutroux, 3 vols, 1908. Deuxième série, *Oeuvres depuis le Mémorial de 1654*, ed. L. Brunschvicg, P. Boutroux, F. Gazier, 8 vols (numbered IV-XI), 1914. Troisième série, *Pensées*, ed. L. Brunschvicg, 3 vols (numbered XII-XIV in 1914), 1904

L'oeuvre de Pascal, ed. J. Chevalier, Paris: Gallimard, Bibliothèque de la Pléiade 1936. Reprinted 1950

Ibid., revised edition 1962. Reprinted 1976

Oeuvres de Blaise Pascal, ed. P. Faugère, Paris: Hachette, Les Grands Ecrivains de la France, 2 vols, 1886, 1895

Oeuvres de Blaise Pascal, ed. J. Hytier, Paris: Piazza, 6 vols, 1929. (*Pensées* are vols IV-V)

**Oeuvres complètes*, ed. L. Lafuma. Paris: Aux Editions au Seuil, Collection L'Intégrale 1963

**Oeuvres complètes*, ed. J. Mesnard, Paris: Desclée de
Brouwer, five volumes announced, two volumes published
to date: 1964, 1970

Pensées, manuscript material

**[Recueil] *Original des Pensees de Pascal 1711*, BN,
manuscrits, fonds français, no. 9202

**Ibid. *Original des Pensees de Pascal*, facsimile du
manuscrit 9202 (fonds français) de la Bibliothéque
Nationale, ed. L. Brunschvicg, Paris: Hachette 1905

**Ibid. *Le manuscrit des Pensées de Pascal 1662* ed. L.
Lafuma, Paris: Les Libraires associés 1962

**'Copie des Pen[séés] de Pasc[al]' BN manuscripts,
fonds français no. 9203

**'Receuil' (including a second copy of the *Pensées*),
ibid., no. 12449

Pensées, including *Pensées* with selected other works, and
including extracts (arranged in alphabetical order according to editor's name)

**Pensées*, ed. D. Anzieu, Paris: Colin, Bibliothéque de
Cluny, 2 vols, 1960

  Pensées, ed. M. Autrand, Paris: Bordas 1966

 **Pensées* (extraits), ed. R. Barrault, Paris: Larousse,
Collection Nouveaux Classiques Larousse 1965

**Pensées*, ed. L. Brunschvicg, Paris: Hachette, Les Grands
Ecrivains de la France, 3 vols, 1904, Reprinted in 1914
as vols XI-XIV of *Oeuvres complètes*

**Pensées et Opuscules*, ed. L. Brunschvicg, Paris: Hachette
1897

  Pensées et Opuscules, Paris: Hachette 1948 (Dépot légal,
Nov. 1946)

  Pensées et Opuscules, Paris: Hachette 1949

Pensées, Introduction by R. Garric, Paris: Hachette, Collection du Flambeau 1950 (Reproduces Brunschvicg)

Pensées, Paris: Hachette, Livre de Poche 1972 (Reproduces Brunschvicg)

Pensées, Paris: Hachette, Collection Les chefs d'oeuvre des lettres 1973 (Reproduces Brunschvicg)

Ibid., Collection Le Livre de Paris 1973 (identical to previous item)

Pensées sur la vérité de la religion chretienne, ed. J. Chevalier, Paris: Gabalda, 2 vols, 1925

Pensées, ed. J. Chevalier, Paris: Gallimard 1937

Pensées sur la vérité de la religion chrétienne, ed. J. Chevalier, Paris: Boivin 1949

Pensées, ed. J. Chevalier, Paris: Les Biblioâtres de France 1960

Pensées, text as in Chevalier 1949, preface by J. Guitton. Paris: Librairie Générale française, Collection Livre de Poche 1962

**Les Pensées et oeuvres choisies*, ed. J. Dedieu, Paris: L'Ecole 1937

Pensées, ed. D. Descotes, Paris: Garnier-Flammarion 1973

Pensées, ed. C. des Granges, Paris: Garnier 1925

Pensées et Opuscules (textes choisis), ed. F. Duviard, Paris: Hytier 1953

Pensées, fragments et lettres, ed. P. Faugère, Paris: Andrieux 1844. Second edition, Leroux 1897

**Les Pensées de Blaise Pascal*, ed. M. Guersant, Paris: Le Club français du livre 1954

Pensées, ed. J. Haumont, Paris: J. de Bonnot 1972

Pensées, ed. E. Havet. Paris: Dezobry and Magdeleine 1852

**Pensées sur la religion et sur quelques autres sujets*, ed. L. Lafuma, Paris: Delmas, 2 vols, 1948

Revised edition of the above, one volume, 1952

**Pensées sur la religion et sur quelques autres sujets*, ed. L. Lafuma. Paris: Editions du Luxembourg, 3 vols, 1951. Second edition 1952

Pensées, ed. L. Lafuma, Paris: Club du meilleur livre, 2 vols, 1958

**Pensées*, ed. L. Lafuma, Paris: Aux Editions du Seuil, Collection Livre de vie, 2 vols, 1962

**Pensées*, ed. M. Le Guern, Paris: Gallimard, Collection Folio, 2 vols, 1977

Pensées, précédées des principaux Opuscules, ed. G. Lewis, Paris: La bonne compagnie 1947

Pensées sur l'homme et Dieu. Choix et classement de Geneviève Lewis, gravures originales d'Albert Gleizès, Casablanca: Editions de la Cicogne 1950

Pensées, ed. C. Louandre, Paris: Charpentier 1854

Pensées (choix), ed. L. Marin, Paris: Didier 1969

Pensées, ed. H. Massic, Paris: A la cité des livres 1929. Revised edition, Grasset 1935

***Textes inédits*, ed. J. Mesnard, Paris: Desclée de Brouwer 1962

**Les Pensées de Pascal disposées suivant l'ordre du cahier autographe*, ed. G. Michaut, Fribourg: Apud Bibliopolam Universitatis 1896

Pensées, ed. A. Molinier, Paris: Lemerre 1877

*[Port-Royal edition] *Pensées de M. Pascal sur la religion et sur quelques autres sujets*, Paris: Desprez, second edition 1670

*Reproduction of above, ed. G. Couton and J. Jehasse, Saint-Etienne: Centre interuniversitaire 1971

Revised edition, Amsterdam: Wolfgang 1684

Ibid. Paris: Desprez 1686

Pensées, ed. P. Sellier, Paris: Hatier, Collection Thema/*anthologie* 1972

***Pensées: nouvelle édition établie pour la première fois d'après la copie de référence de Gilberte Pascal*, ed. P. Sellier, Paris: Mercure de France 1976

*Pensées sur la religion et sur quelques autres sujets, ed. J. Steinmann, Monaco: Editions du Rocher 1961

*Pascal's Apology for Religion, ed. H.F. Stewart, Cambridge: University Press 1942

**Pensées, ed. Z. Tourneur, Paris: Cluny 1938

**Pensées, édition paléographique, ed. Z. Tourneur, Paris: Vrin 1942

Pensées, ed. A. Wautier, Paris: Laffont, 1960.

English translations (arranged chronologically)

The Thoughts of Blaise Pascal, trans. W.F. Trotter. London: Dent, The Temple Classics 1904. Republished in Everyman's Library 1931

*Pascal's Pensées with an English translation, ed. H.F. Stewart, London: Routledge and Kegan Paul 1950

Pensées, trans. J. Warrington, London: Dent 1960

*Revised edition of the above with introduction and notes by H.T. Barnwell, London: Dent 1973

The Pensées, trans. J.M. Cohen, Harmondsworth: Penguin Books 1961

*Pensées, trans. A.J. Krailsheimer, Harmondsworth: Penguin Books 1966

Editions of the Provinciales

*Les Provinciales, ed. H.F. Stewart, Manchester: University Press 1920

**Les Provinciales, ed. L. Cognet, Paris: Garnier 1965

II. Critical and other studies of Pascal

Composite volumes

*Blaise Pascal, l'homme et l'oeuvre, Paris: Les éditions
de minuit, Cahiers de Royaumont Philosophie I, 1956.
Abbreviated to Cahiers de Royaumont I

*Ecrits sur Pascal, Paris: Editions du Luxembourg 1959

*Pascal. Textes du Tricentenaire. Paris: Fayard 1963

*Les Pensées de Pascal ont trois cents ans, Clermont-
Ferrand: Bussac 1971

*Méthodes chez Pascal, Paris: PUF 1979

Individual studies

*Adam, A. Review of L. Lafuma: edition (Delmas 1948),
Recherches pascaliennes and other works, RSH 57-8
(1950) 133-6

*--. Histoire de la Littérature française au XVIIe siècle
t. II: L'epoque de Pascal, Paris: Domat 1951

*--. 'Sur les Pensées de Pascal,' IL 9 (1957) 6-8

*Alexander, I.W. 'Raison, existence, être selon les
notions de Pascal' in Mouvements premiers (Etudes
offertes à Georges Poulet) Paris: Corti 1973, 51-63

*Amadou, R. 'Remarques sur la dialectique des Pensées
de Pascal,' Age nouveau 66 (1951) 85-93

Angers, J.E.d'. 'A propos d'une thèse marxiste sur les
Pensées de Pascal,' Etudes franciscanes 7 (1956) 178-88

*--. 'Les Pensées de Pascal à la lumière des apologétiques
son temps' in Pascal: Textes du Tricentenaire, 1963, 167-

Antoine, G. 'Le langage de Pascal,' Table Ronde 171
(April 1962) 56-71

*Anzieu, D. 'Pascal mystifié,' Annales de l'Université
de Paris 37 (1967) 177-97

*Askew, D.A. 'Pascal's pari in the Port Royal edition,'
AJFS 5 (1968) 155-82

Badawi, A. 'Influences islamiques sur la littérature française à l'époque classique,' *Studia Islamica* 45 (1977) 5-25 (15-24)

**Barnes, Annie. 'La table des titres de la Copie des *Penséss* est-elle de Pascal?' *FS* 7 (1953) 140-6

**--. 'La conférence à Port-Royal et les liasses de Pascal,' *FS* 10 (1956) 231-40. Reprinted in *Ecrits sur Pascal*, 1959, 83-98

--. 'Littérature et liturgie au 17e siècle,' *FS* 20 (1966) 15-24

--. 'Comment lire les *Pensées*,' *CPR* 20-1 (1972) 9-14

Baudin, E. *Etudes historiques et critiques sur la Philosophie de Pascal*, in *Etre et penser, cahiers de Philosophie* 16-19 (1946-7)

Bédier, J. 'Pascal et Solomon de Tultie' in *Mélanges offerts à M. Gustave Lanson*. Paris: Hachette 1922 178-82

**Béguin, A. 'Les édition et l'ordre des *Pensées*,' *Critique* 4 (1948) 875-88

*--. *Pascal par lui-même*, Paris: Seuil 1952

**--. See Lafuma, L. *Recherches pascaliennes*

Bishop, Morris. *Pascal, the Life of Genius*, New York: Reynal and Hitchcock 1936

**Blanchet, A. 'Le plan des *Pensées* de Pascal est-il vraiment retrouvé?,' *Etudes* 274 (1952) 237-45

--. 'Pascal est-il le précurseur de Karl Marx?,' *Etudes* 292 (1957) 321-37

*Bloomberg, E. *Les raisons de Pascal*, Paris: Les nouvelles éditions Debresse [1973]

--. 'Les sens, la raison et la foi dans la 18e *Provinciale*,' *Orbis Litterarum* 30 (1975) 40-50

**Borgerhoff, E.B.O. 'The Reality of Pascal: The *Pensées* as Rhetoric,' *Sewanee Review* 65 (1957) 15-33

*Boudhours, C.H. 'Le duc de Roannex et l'édition des *Pensées*' in *Ecrits sur Pascal*, 1959, 61-79

Boutroux, E. *Pascal*, Paris: Hachette 1900

Brimo, A. *Pascal et le Droit*, Paris: Sirey 1942

Brown, H. 'Science and the *Pensées* of Pascal,' in his *Science and the Human Comedy*, Toronto: University Press 1976, 45-74

**Brunet, G. *Le Pari de Pascal*, Paris: Desclée de Brouwer 1956

Chambers, F.M. 'Pascal's Montaigne,' *PMLA* 65 (1950) 790-804

*Chevalier, J. *Pascal*, Paris: Plon 1922

*Chinard, G. *En lisant Pascal*, Geneva: Droz 1948

Cochran, Judith. *Entretien de Pascal et Sacy sur Epictèt et Montaigne: Montaigne's influence on the Pascal of 1655*. PhD thesis, Duke University, *DAI* 35 (1975) 5393-A

*Couchoud, P.L. 'Un manuscrit reconstitué de Pascal: Les "Liasses en filées" de Pascal et les feuillets dispersés d'un "Discours",' *La Nef* 37 (Dec. 1947) 44-79

**--. *Discours de la condition de l'homme*, Paris: Albin Michel 1948

**--. 'La crise des *Pensées* de Pascal,' *Le Flambeau* 38 (1955) 160-85

*Coulet, G. 'Pascal écrivant' *Annales de la Faculté des Lettres et Sciences humaines d'Aix* 37 (1963) 149-58

*Courcelle, P. *L'Entretien de Pascal et Sacy: Ses sources et ses énigmes*. Paris: Vrin 1960

Cousin, V. 'Rapport à l'Académie française sur la nécessité d'une nouvelle édition des *Pensées* de Pascal, *Journal des Savants* 1842, 243-52, 333-58, 406-26, 490-505, 532-53, 608-25, 678-91

*Croquette, B. *Pascal et Montaigne*, Geneva: Droz 1974

Dagens, J. 'Tradition et innovation des les *Pensées* de Pascal,' *Rivista di letterature moderne* 4 (1953) 23-32

*Davidson, H. 'Conflict and Reolution in Pascal's *Pensées* *RR* 49 (1958) 12-24

*Davidson, H.M. *The Origins of Certainty: Means and Meanings in Pascal's 'Pensées.'* Chicago: University of Chicago Press 1979

*-- and P.H. Dubé. *A Concordance to Pascal's Pensées*. Ithaca: Cornell University Press 1975

*Dedieu, J. 'Survivances et influences de l'apologétique traditionnelle dans les *Pensées*,' *RHLF* 37 (1930) 481-513 and 38 (1931) 1-39

--. 'Le sens de l'apologie de Pascal,' review of J. Russier, *La Foi de Pascal*, *DSS* 9-10 (1951) 35-49. See also *DSS* 17-18 (1953) 59-77

**Demorest, J.J. 'Victor Cousin et le manuscrit des *Pensées* de Pascal,' *MLN* 66 (1951) 255-9

*--. Review of Pascal, *Pensées*, ed. L. Lafuma (Editions du Luxembourg, 1951), *RR* 44 (1953) 145-6

**--. 'Pascal et l'édition des *Pensées*,' *MLN* 71 (1956) 103-4

*--. 'Pascal's Sophistry and the Sin of Poesy,' in *Studies in Seventeenth-Century French Literature Presented to Morris Bishop*. ed. J.J. Demorest, Ithaca: Cornell University Press 1962, 132-52

*Dubarle, A.M. 'Quelques allusions scripturaires des *Pensées* de Pascal,' *SPT* 1 (1941-2) 84-95

*--. 'Pascal et l'interprétation de l'Ecriture,' *SPT* 2 (1941-2) pp 346-79. [Despite the date, a note on p 379 indicates that the proofs were corrected in July 1943!]

Duhamel, G. 'L'homme qui cherche en gémissant' in *Les Confessions sans pénitence*, Paris: Plon 1941, 139-82

**Ernst, P. 'La trajectoire pascalienne de *l'Apologie*,' *ALM* 84 (1967)

**--. 'Le tmoignage de "Gilberte Périer" sur l'Apologie,' *DSS* 75 (1967) 23-47

**--. *Approches pascaliennes*, Gembloux: Duculot 1970

**--. 'Pascal au travail au jour le jour,' in *Méthodes chez Pascal*, Paris: PUF 1979, 141-53

Eydoux, E. *Dialogue avec Blaise Pascal*, Marseille: Emmanuel Eydoux 1968

Faure, E. *Montaigne et ses trois premiers nés*, Paris: Crès 1926

**Filleau de la Chaise. *Discours sur les Pensées de M. Pascal, ou l'on essaie de faire voir quel était son dessein. Avec un autre discours sur les Preuves des Livres de Moïse*. Paris: Deprez 1672

**--. *Discours sur les Pensées de M. Pascal, suivi du Discours sur Moïse et du traité: 'Qu'il y a des demonstrations...'* ed. V. Giraud. Paris: Boussard 1922

Fourcade-Guillaume, Pierrette. 'Quelques aspects du baroque dans les fragments pour l'apologie de Pascal,' *Baroque* 6 (1973) 121-31

**Francis, R. *Les Pensées de Pascal en France de 1842 à 1942*, Paris: Nizet 1959

Gandelman, C. 'La Dé-Iconisation janséniste de l'art: Pascal, Phillippe de Champaigne,' *Hebrew University Studies in Literature* 5 (1977) 213-47

*Gandillac, M. de.'Pascal et le silence du monde,' in *Cahiers de Royaumont* 1 (1956) 342-65

Genet, C. *Pensées* (Pascal), Paris: Hatier, Collection Profil d'une oeuvre 1973

*Germain, F. 'Imagination et vertige dans les deux infinis de Pascal,' *RSH* 97 (1960) 31-40

Giraud, V. *Pascal, l'homme, l'oeuvre, l'influence*, Fribourg: Imprimerie-librairie catholique suisse 1898

Glauser, A. 'Montaigne et le "roseau pensant" de Pascal,' *RR* 66 (1975) 263-8

*Goldmann, L. *Le Dieu caché*, Paris: Gallimard 1955

**-- and J. Chevalier. 'Echange de vues au sujet du "Plan" des *Pensées* de Pascal,' *DSS* 23 (1954) 597-604

Golliet, P. 'Théologie de la foi et méthode apologétique dans les *Pensées*,' in *Méthodes chez Pascal*, Paris: PUF 1979, 53-61

**Gouhier, H. *Blaise Pascal: Commentaires*, Paris: Vrin 1966. Revised edition 1971

--. 'Le refus de la philosophie dans la nouvelle apologétique de Pascal,' *CPR* 20-1 (1972) 19-37

Gounelle, A. *L'Entretien de Pascal avec M. de Sacy: Etude et commentaire*. Paris: PUF 1966

*Goyet, Thérèse. 'Le visage de 1670,' in *Les Pensées de Pascal ont trois cents ans*, Clermont-Ferrand: Bussac 1971, 31-78

*Harrington, T.W. *Vérité et methode dans les 'Pensées' de Pascal*, Paris: Vrin 1972

Hay, Malcolm. *The prejudices of Pascal*, London: Neville
Spearman 1962

Heller, L.M. 'La correction fraternelle,' *DSS* 83 (1969)
17-24

--. 'Anti-Islamic Polemic in Pascal's *Pensées*,' *Neophilologus* 55 (1971) 246-60

--. 'Autobiographical Allusions in Pascal's Apology,'
RUO 43 (1973) 602-13

--. 'Note on a *pensée*: Pascal and Montaigne,' *Orbis
Litterarum* 29 (1974) 216-20

Hirota, M. 'Figure et vérité: Une notule sur les *Pensées*
de Pascal,' *Hototsubashi Journal of Arts and Sciences*
17 (1976) 18-27

*Howe, Virginia. '*Les Pensées*: Paradox and Signification,'
YFS 49 (1973) 120-31

**Hubert, Sister Marie Louise. *Pascal's Unfinished Apology:
A Study of His Plan*, New Haven: Yale University Press
1952

Hurino, M. 'Sur le processus du "Pari" de Pascal,'
ELLF 34 (1979) 19-44

Jacques, E. *Le troisième centenaire de la mort de
Blaise Pascal* Brussels: chez l'auteur 1963

James, E.D. 'Scepticism and Religious Belief: Pascal,
Bayle, Hume,' in *Classical Influences on Western Thought
A.D. 1650-1870*, ed. R.R. Bolgar, Cambridge: University
Press 1979, 93-104

Jamieson, Kathleen. 'Pascal vs Descartes: A Clash over
Rhetoric in the Seventeenth Century,' *Communication
Monographs* 43 (1976) 44-50

*Janssens, E. 'Un problème "pascalien": le plan de l'Apo-
logie,' *RNP* 12 (1905) 418-53 and 13 (1906) 5-17. Reprinted as 'Le problème du plan' in his *La philosophie
et l'apologétique de Pascal*, Paris: Alcan 1906, 61-135

*Krailsheimer, A.J. *Pascal*, Oxford: University Press 1980

**Lacombe, R.E. *L'Apologétique de Pascal: Etude critique*,
Paris: PUF 1958

**Lafuma, L. 'Rémontrances et suggestions aux éditeurs
des *Pensées* de Pascal' *Mercure de France* 301 ([1 Dec.]

1947) 663-73, and 302 ([1 Jan.] 1948) 72-84. Reprinted in his *Recherches pascaliennes* 1949, 21-53 under the title 'Ce que nous apprennent les manuscrits des *Pensées*'

**--. *Recherches pascaliennes*, Paris: Delmas 1949. Préface d'Albert Béguin

*--. 'Notes pascaliennes,' *DSS* 7-8 (1950) 205-10

**--. 'Le puzzle des *Pensées*,' *RSH* 59 (1950) 170-2

**--. *Controverses pascaliennes*, Paris: Editions du Luxembourg 1952 1 (1956) 78-91

**--. *Histoire des Pensées de Pascal*, Paris: Editions du Luxembourg 1954 (n.d. in later impressions)

**--. 'Les manuscrits des *Pensées*: ce qu'ils nous apprennent' in *Cahiers de Royaumont* 1 (1956) 78-91

--. 'A propos d'une thèse marxiste sur les *Pensées* de Pascal,' *Etudes franciscanes* 7 (1956) 172-8

--. 'L'ordre de l'esprit et l'ordre du coeur selon Pascal,' *Recherches de science religieuse* 46 (1958) 416-20

**--. 'La Copie 9203 et le classement de Pascal,' in *Ecrits sur Pascal*, Paris: Editions du Luxembourg 1959, 187-205

--. 'L'Histoire des manuscrits des *Pensées* et le problème de leur édition,' *Table Ronde* 171 (April 1962) 38-4

Lagrange, M.J. 'Pascal et les prophéties messianiques,' *Revue biblique* 3 (1906) 533-60

*Laporte, J. 'Le coeur et la raison selon Pascal,' *Revue philosophique* 103 (1927) 93-118, 255-99, 421-51. Reprinted in book form, Paris: Elzévir 1950

Ledent, R. *Ce que Pascal a vraiment dit*. Verviers: Marabout 1975

Lefebvre, H. *Pascal*, Paris: Nagel, 2 vols, 1949 and 1954

**Le Guern, M. 'Pascal au travail: La composition du fragment sur le Divertissement,' *RUO* 36 (1966) 209-31

*--. *L'Image dans l'oeuvre de Pascal*. Paris: A Colin 1969

*--. *Pascal et Descartes*, Paris: Nizet 1971

*-- and Marie-Rose Le Guern. *Les Pensées de Pascal, de l'anthropologie à la théologie*, Paris: Larousse 1972

MacKenzie, C.S. *Pascal's Anguish and Joy*, New York: Philosophical Library 1973

Magnard, P. *Nature et histoire dans l'Apologétique de Pascal* Paris: Les Belles Lettres 1975 (Publications de l'Université de Dijon 48)

**Maeda, Y. 'L'Entretien avec M. de Sacy,' in *Ecrits sur Pascal* 1959, 9-19

Malet, J. 'Remarques à partir de *L'Entretien*,' *Revue du Pacifique* 1 (1975) 74-82

**Mantoy, J. *Des "Pensées" de Pascal a l'"Apologie*," Paris: L'Ecole 1955

*Marin, L. '"Pascal": Text, Author, Discourse,' *YFS* 52 (1975) 129-51

--. 'A propos d'une *Vie de Pascal*: texte, récit, livre,' *MLN* 90 (1975) 475-96

*--. *La Critique au discours: sur la "Logique de Port-Royal" et les "Pensées" de Pascal*, Paris: Editions de Minuit 1975

Martin, P. 'Etude d'un texte français: Pascal, "Vanité",' *IL* 28 (1976) 41-53

Mayer, J.P. 'Pascal relu: un nouvel arrangement de la Pensée sur la "Disproportion de l'Homme",' *FS* 29 (1975) 257-65. See Pugh, A.R. --. "La Disproportion de l'Homme": A Reply' *FS* 32 (1978) 145-6.

*Melzer, Sara E. 'Pascal's *Pensées*: The Rhetoric of *invraisemblance*,' *PFSCL* 8 (1977-8) 51-64

*--. '*Invraisemblance* in Pascal's *Pensées*: The Anti-Rhetoric' *RR* 73 (1982) 33-44

*--. 'Codes of Space in the Pensées,' *FR* 51 (1978) 816-23

*Mesnard, J. 'La théorie des figuratifs dans les *Pensées* de Pascal,' *RHPC* 35 (1943) 219-53

**--. *Pascal*, Paris: Hatier Boivin 1951

--. 'Les séjours de Pascal à Port-Royal des Champs,' *SAPR* 2 (1951) 15-23

*--. 'Le drame de la foi chez Pascal,' *CUC* (March 1958) 310-24

*--. *Pascal et les Roannez*, Paris: Desclée de Brouwer, 2 vols 1965

**--. 'Aux origines de l'édition des *Pensées*: les deux

copies,' in *Les Pensées de Pascal ont trois cents ans*, 1971, 1-30

*--. 'Pascal et la contestation,' *Revue d'Auvergne* 85 (1971) 185-97

**--. 'Les Editions de Port-Royal,' *CPR* 20-1 (1972) 66-82

**--. *Les Pensées de Pascal*, Paris: SEDES 1976

--. 'Un penseur moderne: Pascal?' *Nouvelles de l'Institu catholique de Paris*, June 1978, 15-25

--. 'Dieu par Jésus-Christ,' *Communio* 3 (July 1978) 29-40

*Miel, J. *Pascal and Theology*, Baltimore: The Johns Hopkins Press 1969

*Moles, Elizabeth. 'Three Categories of Intelligence in Pascal,' *AJFS* 8 (1971) 259-68

**Morgan, Janet. 'Pascal, Concupiscence and "La Machine",' *MLR* 71 (1976) 272-81

*--. 'Pascal's Three Orders,' *MLR* 13 (1978) 755-66

Morikawa, H. 'Sur la théologie biblique dans les *Pensées* de Pascal,' *Kwansei Gakuin University Annual Studies* 17 (1968) 39-51

*Morot-Sir, E. *La métaphysique de Pascal*, Paris: PUF 1973

--. *Pascal*, Paris: PUF 1973

**--. 'Pascal Versus Wittgenstein, with Samuel Beckett as the Anti-Witness,' *RN* 15 (1974) 201-16

*--. 'Du nouveau sur Pascal?' *RN* 18 (1977) 272-9

Mortimer, E. *Blaise Pascal, the Life and Work of a Realist*, London: Methuen 1959

Nicole, P. *Traité de l'éducation d'un Prince*, Paris: Savreux 1670

*Norman, G.B. 'Thought and Language in Pascal,' *YFS* 49 (1973) 110-19

*--. 'Logic and Anti-Rhetoric in Pascal's *Pensées*,' *FF* 2 (1977) 22-33

Orcibal, J. 'Les jansénistes face à Spinoza,' *RLC* 23 (1949) 441-68

**--. 'Vers le Pascal de l'histoire,' *SAPR* 2 (1951) 29-42

--. 'Le fragment infini-rien et ses sources,' *Cahiérs de Royaumont* 1 (1956) 159-86

*Périer, Gilberte. *La Vie de M. Pascal*, in *Pensées de Pascal sur la religion, etc.*, Amsterdam: Wolfgang 1684. Ibid., Paris: Desprez 1686

*Pintard, R. Review of Courcelle, *L'Entretien de Pascal et Sacy*, *Revue des Etudes anciennes* 63 (1961) 541-8

*Polman, P. 'La biographie de Blaise Pascal par Gilberte Périer,' *Revue d'Histoire ecclésiastique* 45 (1950) 95-135

*Pommier, J. 'La *Vie* de Pascal par Gilberte Périer' *ALM* 57 (1964)

**Pons, R. 'Les manuscrits de Pascal: à la source d'un Pascal nouveau,' *CUC* (March 1950) 48-58

**--. 'La présentation authentique des *Pensées* de Pascal,' *IL* 3 (1951) 169-77

**--. 'Entretien sur les manuscrits de Pascal,' *CUC* (Nov.-Dec. 1962) 84-9

Potts, D.C. 'Pascal's Contemporaries and "le divertissement",' *MLR* 57 (1962) 31-40

Pugh, A.R. '"La Disproportion de l'Homme": Pascal's Editors Defended,' *FS* 31 (1977) 277-80. See Mayer, J.P.
--. '"Disproportion de l'Homme": A Rejoinder' *FS* 32 (1978) 275-7.

*Raymond, M. 'La conversion de Pascal,' *Revue de Théologie et de Philosophie* 13 (1963) 24-40

*Russier, Jeanne. *La foi selon Pascal*, Paris: PUF, 2 vols. 1949

*Sainte-Beuve, C.A. *Port-Royal*, Paris: Hachette, 5 vols. Vol. 3, 1848

--. Ibid. Paris: Gallimard, Bibliothèque de la Pléiade 1954

**Sato, M. 'Sur la "Raison des effets" de Pascal,' *ELLF* 16 (1970) 20-6

**Saulnier, V.L. 'Le problème des papiers de Pascal,' *Le Bulletin des Lettres* 10 (1948) 317-19

Scholtens, M. *Le mysticisme de Pascal*, Assen: Van Gorcum 1974

Secretan, P. '"Pensées" politiques de Pascal, rapportées à la théorie des ordres,' *Freiburger Zeitschrift für Philosophie und Theologie*, 25 (1978) 142-60

*Sellier, P. *Pascal et la Liturgie*, Paris: PUF 1966

*--. *Pascal et Saint Augustin*, Paris: A. Colin 1970

*--. 'L'ascension et la chute,' *CPR* 20-1 (1972) 116-26

**Shiokawa, T. *Pascal et les miracles*, Paris: Nizet 1977

--. 'La connaissance par l'autorité selon Pascal,' *ELLF* 30 (1978) 1-14

*Simon, P.H. 'Pascal, l'histoire et la Justice,' in his *Le Jardin et la Ville*, Paris: Seuil 1962, 46-58

**Stewart, H.F. 'Vers une nouvelle édition de *l'Apologie de Pascal*,' *French Quarterly* 3 (1921) 132-51

Strowski, F. *Les Pensées de Pascal: Etude et analyse*, Paris: Mellottée 1930

Tassing, E. 'Le nihilisme dans les *Pensées* de Pascal,' *Studia Neophilologa* 47 (1975) 70-87

Terrasse, J. 'Pascal et l'ironie: *les Pensées*,' in his *Rhétorique de l'essai littéraire*, Montreal, Presses de l'Université du Québec 1978, 27-42

Tetel, M. 'Conscience chez Montaigne et Pascal,' *Saggi e Ricerche di letteratura francese* 14 (1975) 9-35

*Topliss, Patricia. *The Rhetoric of Pascal*, Leicester: University Press 1966

Tourneur, Z. *Beauté poétique*, Melun: Rozelle 1933

--. *Une Vie avec Blaise Pascal*, Paris: Vrin 1943

*Uhlíř, A. 'Montaigne et Pascal,' *RHLF* 14 (1907) 442-54

Valensin, A. *Balthazar*, Paris: Aubier 1934

Valéry, P. 'Variation sur une pensée,' *Revue hebdomadaire* 14 July 1923, 161-70. Reprinted in *Variétés*, Paris: Gallimard, I, 1924, 137-53. Also in *Oeuvres*, Paris: Gallimard, Bibliothèque de la Pléiade, I, 1957, 458-73

Vamos, Maria. 'Pascal's *Pensées* and the Enlightenment,'

Studies in Voltaire and the Eighteenth Century 97 (1972)
1-145

*Van Lier, H. 'Pascal, *Pensées*, section V, fragment 298,'
Le Langage et l'Homme 31 (May 1976) 35-44

Villars, l'abbé. *De la délicatesse*, Paris: Barbin 1671

Wada, S. 'Une étude de l'Apologie de la Religion chrétienne de Pascal d'après l'édition intégrale Lafuma,'
Memoirs of the Faculty of Letters, Osaka University 10
(1963) 253-441

Wanner, Brigitte. 'Connaissance: conscience de l'ignorance,' *Archiv für das Studium der neueren Sprachen und
Literaturen* 213 (1976) 125-7

*Weber, J. 'Person as Figure of Ambiguity and Resolution
in Pascal,' *PMLA* 84 (1969) 312-20

*Westgate, D. 'The Augustinian Concept of Amour-Propre
and Pascal's *Pensées*,' *NFS* 10 (1971) 10-20

III. *Other works referred to*

[Annat, R.P.] *Rabat-Joie des Jansénistes ou Observations
nécessaires sur ce qu'on dit être arrivé au Port-Royal,
au sujet de la sainte Epine*. Par un Docteur de l'Eglise
Catholique, [n.p., n.d.] [1656]

Arnauld, A. *Oeuvres*, Paris: d'Arnay, t. XXIII 1779

Arnold, M. *Literature and Dogma*, London: Smith, Elder
and Co. 1873

Barclay, O.R. *Reasons for Faith*, London: Inter-Varsity
Press 1974

Barzun, J. *Berlioz and the Romantic Century*, Boston:
Little, Brown and Co., 2 vols, 1950. Revised edition,
New York: Columbia University Press 1969

Dulles, A. 'Justifier la foi chrétienne,' *Communio* 3
(July 1978) 41-53

Du Perron, J.D. *Traité du Saint Sacrement de l'Eucharistie*, Paris: Etienne 1622

Gullon, R. 'On Space in the Novel.' *Critical Inquiry* 2
(1975) 11-28

Huygens, C. *Oeuvres complètes*, La Haye: M. Nijhoff 1889, t. II, Correspondance

Küng, H. *On Being a Christian*, trans. E. Quinn, New York: Doubleday 1976

La Peyrère, I. de *Praeadamitae* and *Systema theologicum ex Praeadamitarum* (bound together), [n.p., n.d.] [1655]. Four different editions are listed in the BN catalogue.

Lingendes, C. de *Concionum in Quadragesimam*, Paris: Muguet, 3 vols, 1661

--. *Sermons sur tous les Evangiles du Carême*, Paris: Muguet, 2 vols, 1666

Marion, J.L. 'De connaître à l'aimer: l'éblouissement,' *Communio* 3 (July 1978) 17-28

Martini, M. *Sinicae Historiae*, Munich: Straubius 1658

--. Ibid. Amsterdam: Blaev 1659

Migne, J.P. *Patrologiae, cursus completus, patres latini*, Paris: Migne, 221 vols, 1844-64

Montaigne, M. de *Essais*, Paris: A. Combé 1652. Also P. Rocolet, same date

--. Ibid. In *Oeuvres complètes*, Paris: Gallimard, Bibliothèque de la Pléiade 1933

Richardson, A. *Christian Apologetics*, London: SCM 1947

Smith, W. Cantwell *Questions of Religious Belief*, London: Gollancz 1967

Walgrave, J.H. 'Le grand malentendu théologique,' *Communio* 3 (July 1978) 7-16

Index to *Pensées*

This index limits itself to identifying the pages or chapters where a given fragment is discussed specifically; passing references are not included. The *liasses* and the Units are listed too, and supplementary information on the individual fragments can sometimes be obtained by following up the references to the *liasse* or Unit in which a particular fragment is lodged. Occasionally a group of fragments within a *liasse* or Unit is discussed as a group, and here too, the reference is not repeated for each individual fragment (see 324-31, 515-24, 536-43, 734-47, 784-9, 882-91, 903-12).

46-62, 347-8
13: 55
14: 50, 55, 557 n21
15: 56, 487 n38, 557 n21
16: 49, 50, 56, 58, 556 n20
17: 55, 58, 74
18: 51
19: 54, 81
20: 54, 69
21: 51, 55, 59, 66, 130, 261
22: 22, 55, 487 n38
23: 49, 51, 52, 58, 71, 556 n20
24: 58, 61, 487 n38
25: 54, 160
26: 54, 55, 80, 348, 556 n18
27: 58, 112, 556 n21
28: 51, 53, 54, 55, 57, 66, 69, 88, 120-1, 134, 334
29: 56
30: 55, 81, 487 n38
31: 50, 56
32: 49, 50, 58, 82, 349, 355, 556 n20
33: 53, 56-7, 69, 107, 134, 333, 556 n19
34: 57
35: 56, 71, 103, 173, 351, 353
36: 50, 51, 58, 66, 74, 111, 117, 348, 355, 414
37: 56, 80, 103, 414
38: 55
39: 57, 80, 111, 113, 355, 514 n2, 558 n32
40: 50, 55
41: 55, 172, 400, 526 n10
42: 56, 71
43: 58
44: 51, 52-4, 56, 61, 68, 69, 80, 82, 88, 89, 90, 107, 121, 130, 134, 313, 406, 442, 554 n2, 597-8 n3

45: 53, 55, 313, 509 n9, 543 n45
46: 50, 55, 58, 556 n20
47: 57, 111, 313, 543 n50
48: 55
49: 55, 56
50: 55
51: 54, 69, 70, 487 n38
52: 57, 553 n99
Liasse 3°, Misère (nos 53-75): 63-73, 345-7, 348
53: 70, 563 n71, 578 n44
54: 65, 66, 74
55: 65, 74
56: 66, 70
57: 70
58: 69, 70, 88, 91, 439, 533 n17
59: 70, 563 n71
60: 55, 68, 69, 76, 89, 134, 302, 305, 306, 307, 313, 348, 406, 487 n38, 539 nn28, 30, 540 n32, 554 n2, 562 n60
61: 69
62: 71, 554 n3
63: 71
64: 69, 70
65: 66
66: 69, 91, 134, 345, 348, 556 n19
67: 69, 91, 345, 348, 556 n19
68: 71, 171, 353
69: 47, 64, 556 n21
70: 65, 111, 334
71: 71, 72, 73, 98, 126, 351
72: 71, 72, 130
73: 65, 74
74: 64, 67, 68, 88, 96, 345, 492 n69
75: 47-8, 66, 72, 108, 114, 130, 345
76: 32, 56, 62, 66, 132, 302, 305, 306, 307, 313, 506

226: 143, 197
227: 195
228: 206, 245, 581 n61
229: 202
230: 192, 198, 413
231: 198, 561 n60
232: 203
233: 206
234: 201, 263, 534 n12, 562
    n61
235: 204
236: 201, 202, 203, 204,
    206, 240, 267, 421,
    551 n84
237: 206, 420
238: 205, 420, 529 n10, 531
    n12
239: 198
240: 196, 364
241: 197, 583 n62
241bis: 198, 201, 371-2,
    581 n58, 585 n82
242: 199, 560 n42
243: 195, 226, 227, 228,
    243, 321, 362-3, 560
    n42, 587 n94
244: 198, 436, 560 n41, 562
    n61, 581 n61
Liasse 20°, Loi figurative
    (nos 245-76): 209-22,
    369, 373-4
245: 211, 488 n46
246: 217, 530 n8
247: 215, 414
248: 217, 530 n8, 535 ch26
    n1
249: 215
250: 217, 424
251: 224, 251, 530 n4
252: 218, 586 n91
253: 215, 217, 420
254: 218, 224
255: 205, 219, 220, 421, 530
    n9
256: 217, 225
257: 212, 213, 420, 595 n43

258: 213, 424
259: 213, 217, 424, 530 n5
260: 213-15, 217, 218, 220,
    530 nn6, 7
261: 220
262: 221, 420
263: 213
264: 219, 321
265: 213, 530 n7
266: 213
267: 212, 213, 215-16
268: 215, 424
269: 216, 269
270: 216, 219, 220, 224,
    419, 421, 424
271: 216
272: 214, 217, 218, 419,
    585 n84
273: 221, 420, 532 ch22
    n3, 581 n61
274: 210, 211, 223, 225,
    529 nn1, 2
275: 217, 222, 420
276: 212
Liasse 21°, Rabbinage (nos
    277-8): 223-5, 369
277: 223
278: 223-4, 228
Liasse 22°, Perpétuité (nos
    279-89): 195, 226-33,
    365-6, 372
279: 214, 227-8, 424, 560
    n48, 578 n44
280: 232, 422
281: 227, 230, 231, 232-3,
    234, 333, 422, 532
    ch22 n4
282: 231-2, 234, 243, 321
283: 227, 404
284: 230, 499 n91, 551 n82
285: 233
286: 166, 229, 261, 329-30
287: 228
288: 228, 424, 560 n48
289: 191, 229
Liasse 23°, Preuves de Moïse

359: 261, 559 n40
360: 260
361: 259
362: 259
363: 262
364: 262
365: 259
366: 261, 330, 366, 522 n23
367: 261
368: 260
369: 259
370: 260
371: 260
372: 260
373: 259, 260, 444
374: 260
375: 261
376: 259
Liasse 28°, Conclusion (nos
    377-82): 265-72, 328,
    352-3, 367, 372-3
377: 270, 373, 489 n46, 536
    n6
378: 267, 331, 552 n98
379: 267, 536 n2
380: 269, 271, 358, 559 n37
381: 269-70, 358, 359
382: 270, 354, 581 n61
Unit I (nos 383-417): 343,
    377
383: 156, 375, 560 n53, 562
    n64, 584 n74
384: 236, 419, 560 n53, 562
    n64
385: 249, 365, 368, 505 n2,
    534 nn5, 6, 584 n69
386: 162, 237, 368, 375, 505
    n2, 534 n4, 561 n55
387: 37, 43, 162, 375, 505
    n4
388: 240, 366, 419, 596 n48
389: 205, 365, 367, 530 n9,
    581 n61
390: 231, 234, 333, 365,
    421, 560 n52

391: 221, 364, 532 ch22 n3,
    535 n6, 561 n56, 581
    n61
392: 222, 232, 234, 364,
    365, 421
393: 185, 363
394: 202, 364, 560 n44
395: 560 n44
396: 131, 560 n44
397: 134, 363
398: 125, 127, 138, 143, 363
399: 125, 363
400: 126, 363
401: 126, 140, 141, 363
402: 158, 328, 344, 357,
    363-4, 376, 569 n94,
    585 n83
403: 47, 63, 64-6, 346, 357,
    492 n69, 556 n14
404: 106, 110, 138, 184,
    356, 512 n6, 516 n5,
    558 n35
405: 152, 355, 356, 375
406: 100, 351, 355, 514 ch7
    n4
407: 124, 355, 356
408: 32, 132, 306, 313,
    355, 506 n6, 539 n28,
    557 n30
409: 155, 557 n28, 562 n64
410: 124, 125, 126, 356,
    402, 548 n41
411: 99, 561 n59
412: 62, 268, 556 n17
413: 50, 347, 509 n4, 557
    n27
414: 66, 112, 120, 356, 510
    ch4 n1, 558 n33
415: 120
416: 180-2, 343, 376, 555
    n8
417: 180-2, 343, 376, 555
    n8
Unit II (nos 418-26): 305,
    314, 315-17, 328, 330,

UNIVERSITY OF TORONTO ROMANCE SERIES